Praise for *Hello, Startup*

There is a huge gap between a good CS education and what is considered "common knowledge" in start-up engineering teams. Most of us had to learn this stuff through blogs, co-workers, and, of course, the school of hard knocks. But *Hello, Startup* finally collects a lot of this wisdom into one place. I wish I'd had a book like this when I was getting my start in the industry.

—*Jay Kreps, CEO of Confluent Inc.*

As a startup founder, you are expected to learn an unbelievable amount of knowledge from an incredibly diverse set of disciplines in a very short period of time. While I treasure the experience of beating my head against the wall and eventually figuring things out, I wish I had this guide when I first got started.

—*Bowei Gai, Co-Founder and CEO of CardMunch*

Jim will give you a guided and well-informed look at what it takes to build a software startup. There is no jargon or fluff—just practical, simple, and proven advice, presented in an easily readable book. If you've ever wondered, "How do I come up with startup ideas?" or "What technology should I use for this project?" or "How do I get awesome startups to hire me?" then *Hello, Startup* is for you.

—*Eugene Mirkin, Entrepreneur in Residence at Array Ventures*

D1211385

Like Jim, I started my career working for big, established companies. I'm now the co-founder of my own company, prismic.io, and this experience is teaching me a lot every single day. This book captures a lot of these learnings and explains not only how, but also why a startup can be a great way to unleash your true potential.

—*Sadek Drobi, Co-Founder of prismic.io*

If every computer science department gave out this book as a graduation gift, two good things would happen across the tech industry: the worst tech companies would go out of business, and the good ones would become dramatically more productive.

—*Brent Vincent, Founder of Adacio*

With the exploding interest in technology startups, *Hello, Startup* is a uniquely practical and entertaining book on how to develop startups. I wish I had this resource at the start of my entrepreneurial journey.

—*Sean Ammirati, Partner at Birchmere Ventures*

Hello, Startup

A programmer's guide to building products, technologies, and teams

Yevgeniy Brikman

Beijing · Boston · Farnham · Sebastopol · Tokyo

Hello, Startup

by Yevgeniy Brikman

Copyright © 2016 Yevgeniy Brikman. All rights reserved.

Printed in the United States of America.

Published by O'Reilly Media, Inc., 1005 Gravenstein Highway North, Sebastopol, CA 95472.

O'Reilly books may be purchased for educational, business, or sales promotional use. Online editions are also available for most titles (*http://safaribooksonline.com*). For more information, contact our corporate/institutional sales department: 800-998-9938 or *corporate@oreilly.com*.

Editor: Angela Rufino
Acquisitions Editor: Mary Treseler
Production Editor: Nicole Shelby
Copyeditor: Gillian McGarvey
Proofreader: Jasmine Kwityn

Indexer: Judy McConville
Interior Designer: Monica Kamsvaag
Cover Designers: Edie Freeman and Ellie Volckhausen
Illustrator: Rebecca Demarest

October 2015: First Edition

Revision History for the First Edition
2015-10-15: First Release

See *http://oreilly.com/catalog/errata.csp?isbn=9781491909904* for release details.

978-1-491-90990-4

[LSI]

To Mom, Dad, Lyalya, and Molly

Contents

Preface

```
main( ) {
  printf("hello, world");
}
```

When you learn a new programming language, the traditional first step is to go through a "Hello, World" tutorial that teaches you everything you need to know to get a basic program working, such as one that prints the text "Hello, World" to the screen. This book is the "Hello, World" tutorial for building products, technologies, and teams in a startup environment.

I wish I had a book like this when I was in college. By the time I graduated, I had a BS, a master's, a bunch of internships—and absolutely no idea what I was doing.

One of the first big projects I built by myself was a desktop application for performance testing at Thomson Financial. I had no idea how to create a user interface, so I randomly sprinkled text fields, menus, and buttons across the screen. I had no idea how to reason about performance, so I randomly sprinkled caches and thread pools across the code. And I had no idea how to think about code maintenance, so I didn't bother with tests or documentation, but I did manage to cram several thousand lines of code into one gigantic file.

My first project at TripAdvisor was to add new sort options to the web page that listed all the hotels in a city. It was a quick task—just enough to become familiar with the codebase—and I was able to get it done and pushed to production in my first week. Shortly thereafter, I was in my manager's office for our first one-on-one meeting, and I watched as he clicked on the hotel listings for Paris, selected the new sort option, and waited. And waited. And waited. It took nearly two hours for the page to load. Well, it was probably closer to two minutes, but I'm pretty sure there is a law of special relativity that causes time to dilate when you're sweating profusely and hoping you can melt through the floor and disappear. Later that night—much later—I figured out that my fancy new code was making two database calls every time it compared hotels during the sorting process. It takes on the order of $n \log n$ comparisons to sort n items, so for Paris, which has roughly 2,000 hotels, that works out to roughly 40,000 database calls for a single page load. I might not have melted that day, but our database server nearly did.

I remember lots of other nasty bugs, ugly code, uglier user interfaces, site outages, and late nights. But mostly, I remember having tons of questions and no easy way to find an answer. What technologies should I learn and use? Why should I bother with automated tests? How do I build a product that doesn't look terrible? How do I get people to use my product? How do I negotiate a job offer? Should I negotiate for more salary or more equity? What is equity, anyway? Should I work at a large company or join a startup?

I learned the answers to these questions and many others the hard way. I tried to capture what I learned—much of it the result of painful trial and error—in blog posts and talks (*http://www.ybrikman.com*). But after realizing that thousands of other developers were going through the same trial-and-error process, making the same mistakes, and still having nowhere to turn with the same questions, I decided it was time to do something more substantial. This book is the result. Of course, some lessons you can only learn by making your own mistakes, but for the rest, I hope *Hello, Startup* will save you a lot of pain by letting you learn from the mistakes of others.

One of my biggest mistakes was not paying enough attention to the startup world early in my career. My first few jobs were all at big, established institutions (Cisco Systems, Thomson Financial, Cornell University), and it was only later and somewhat accidentally that I made the jump into the startup world (LinkedIn, TripAdvisor). What I saw there astonished me. I learned more in my first few months at a startup than I had in all the years of work, internships, and schooling before that.

A startup is not just a smaller version of a larger company [Blank and Dorf 2012, xvii], much like quantum mechanics is not just a smaller version of classical mechanics. Classical mechanics describes the behavior of large objects (e.g., a baseball or planet) moving at relatively slow speeds with rules that are predictable and deterministic. Similarly, large companies tend to move slowly and live in a world with predictable rules because the customers and products are all known. Quantum mechanics describes the behavior of tiny objects (e.g., photons and electrons) moving at extremely high speeds with rules based on uncertainty, probability, and non-determinism. Similarly, startups tend to move at a hectic pace to survive in an unpredictable world where nothing is known. While many people are familiar with classical mechanics and large companies, you won't have a complete picture of the world unless you also understand quantum mechanics and startups, and that means you'll need new ways of thinking and new ways of working.

In many ways, the way you work is the way you live, as you will spend half of your waking hours at work. Wouldn't you prefer to spend those hours doing something that makes you happy? I used to think that all software jobs involved endless cubicle farms, pointy-haired bosses, TPS reports, and enterprise code. Fortunately, there is an alternative, which I hope to show you in this book by introducing you to the way work gets done at some of the best startups in the world. The ideas from these companies will be useful even if you never join a startup, and will grow even more useful as startups become more and more ubiquitous.[1]

This book is based on my own experiences plus a considerable amount of research, including a series of interviews with programmers from some of the most successful startups of the last decade, such as Google, Facebook, Twitter, GitHub, Stripe, Instagram, Coursera, Foursquare, Pinterest, and Typesafe (the full list of interviewees is in "Interviews" on page 20). You'll find their stories and thoughts throughout the book. They offer a raw glimpse into startup life, with no marketing or PR spin—just programmers sharing their successes, mistakes, and advice.

What will you find in this book?

My goal with *Hello, Startup* was to create a practical, actionable, how-to guide to startups. The book consists of three parts: Products, Technologies, and Teams. In the following sections, I've listed the chapters you'll find in each part, and for each chapter, I've outlined the concrete techniques, tools, and skills you will learn from reading it.

---

1 In the United States alone, nearly 500,000 small businesses are created per month [Kauffman Index of Entrepreneurial Activity Interactive 2014] and they account for more than 66% of new jobs [Small Business Trends 2014].

PART I: PRODUCTS

Chapter 1, Why Startups

> Why today, more than any other time in history, startups are your best opportunity to build products that touch millions of lives; what is a startup; why you should work at a startup; why you shouldn't work at a startup.

Chapter 2, Startup Ideas

> How to come up with startup ideas; idea journals, constraints, and pain points; ideas versus execution; Boyd's Law; how to use the customer development process to quickly and cheaply validate your ideas.

Chapter 3, Product Design

> Design skills everyone should learn; how to design a user interface that doesn't make users feel stupid; principles of user-centered design, including personas, emotional design, simplicity, and usability testing; principles of visual design, including copywriting, reuse, layout, typography, contrast and repetition, and colors; how to design a minimum viable product (MVP).

Chapter 4, Data and Distribution

> Metrics every startup should measure; data-driven product development; A/B testing; why the best product doesn't always win; marketing, viral growth, and sales strategies for startups.

PART II: TECHNOLOGIES

Chapter 5, Picking a Tech Stack

> How to decide whether to build software in-house, buy a commercial product, or use open source; how to choose the initial tech stack; how to evolve a tech stack and rewrites; how to evaluate programming languages, frameworks, and databases.

Chapter 6, Clean Code

> Why a programmer's job is not to write code but to understand it; how code layout, naming, error handling, Don't Repeat Yourself (DRY), the Single Responsibility Principle (SRP), loose coupling, and high cohesion lead to code that's easier to understand; why functional programming leads to code that's easier to reuse; why refactoring is the essence of writing code well.

Chapter 7, Scalability

> How to scale a startup to more users and more developers; how to make changes to your code without being afraid; how Test-Driven Development (TDD) leads to better code; how to introduce design reviews, pair coding, and code reviews at your startup; why the readme is the most important file in your codebase; if you can't measure it, you can't fix it; how to do back-of-the-envelope calculations to reason about performance.

Chapter 8, Software Delivery

> What happens to the code after you write it; why you should use source control, an open source build system, and continuous integration; how to set up configuration management, automated deployment, and continuous delivery; how to instrument your code with logging, monitoring, and alerting.

PART III: TEAMS

Chapter 9, Startup Culture

> Why you should define your company's mission and values; trade-offs between a management-driven hierarchy and a flat organization; the role of culture in hiring, promotions, and motivation; how to design the ideal office for programmers; trade-offs with working remotely; communication policies and process at a startup.

Chapter 10, Getting a Job at a Startup

> How to find a startup job using your network; how to get your résumé noticed; how to get good at interviews, whiteboard coding, and asking good questions; how to think about salary and equity; how to negotiate a job offer.

Chapter 11, Hiring for Your Startup

> Why people are the most important part of a startup; who to hire, including co-founders, early hires, generalists, and specialists; how to find great candidates (and how to perfect your company branding so that they can find you); why whiteboard coding is a terrible interview process (and the alternatives you should use instead); how to make an offer they can't refuse.

Chapter 12, Learning

> The most interesting software developer in the world; why you should write blog posts, articles, papers, and books; why you should talk at meetup

groups, tech talks, and conferences; why you should open source almost all of your code; why you should share almost everything you know.

Key ideas

In addition to the concrete techniques, tools, and skills just listed, three key ideas that are essential for startup success are repeated again and again throughout the book: startups are about people, great companies are the result of evolution, and speed wins.

STARTUPS ARE ABOUT PEOPLE

The major problems of our work are not so much technological as socio-logical in nature.

—[DEMARCO AND LISTER 1999, 4], TOM DEMARCO AND TIMOTHY LISTER, *PEOPLEWARE*

Most of what you learn in classes and books on startups—such as marketing plans, product design, system design, testing strategy, hiring plans, and organizational design—are just the outputs of a startup. You cannot fully understand startups solely by studying the outputs, just as the prisoners chained up in Plato's Cave cannot fully understand the outside world solely by studying the shadows it casts on the wall in front of them [Plato 2008, Book VII].

This book will try to get you to step out of the cave and look not only at the outputs but the people who create them. You'll not only learn how to come up with great product designs but also how to design products for people. You'll see not only how to write effective automated tests but also why automated tests are essential for allowing people to change code without fear. And you'll learn not only how great companies are organized but also why the most important part of building a great company is knowing how to find and motivate the right people.

GREAT COMPANIES ARE THE RESULT OF EVOLUTION

A complex system that works is invariably found to have evolved from a simple system that worked.

—[BOOCH 1991, 11], JOHN GALL

When you see the neck of a giraffe, you have to realize that it isn't long because of some plan put together by a divine being at the beginning of time. The neck started out small and grew longer over thousands of generations as the result of random mutations that happened to increase the giraffe's odds of survival in a particular environment. Likewise, when you see a successful company, you have to realize that it didn't succeed because of some plan the founders put together when they created the company. Most startups change and grow over the course of thousands of experiments, some of which happen to increase the company's odds of survival in a particular market, and the result usually looks little like what the founders originally envisioned.

Instead of worrying about how to come up with a perfect plan (think *Waterfall development*), this book will focus on how to build a startup using incremental and iterative development (think *Agile* and *Lean*). Whether you're building products, technologies, or teams, you'll see that the best way to start is by building the smallest thing that can possibly work—a *minimum viable product* (MVP)—and then gradually evolving it into something bigger based on feedback from your customers (for products), code reviews and tests (for technology), and employees (for teams).

SPEED WINS

The world is changing very fast. Big will not beat small anymore. It will be the fast beating the slow.

—RUPERT MURDOCH

If great companies are the result of evolution and iterative development, then the company that can iterate the fastest will win. Many of the ideas in this book are about how to iterate faster—how to shorten the feedback loop so you can speed up your learning, and ultimately, your evolution. Customer development helps you find product/market fit faster. Clean code and automated tests let you build technology faster. A strong culture helps you build a team more quickly. And somewhat counterintuitively, you will see later in this book that building things faster will also allow you to build things that are higher quality. Speed wins.

This book covers a lot of ground

Entire books, even multiple books, have been written about each of the topics and themes in *Hello, Startup*, so this book focuses on the most fundamental ideas to get you started—a "Hello, World" tutorial, so to speak—and refers you to additional resources for when you're ready to learn more. It's also worth mentioning the topics this book does *not* cover: namely, the legal and financial aspects of a startup. If you're interested in the details of writing business plans, raising money from investors, or filing for an IPO, you'll want to read some of the books listed in "Recommended reading" on page 529.

Of course, reading a book on startups, by itself, can no more make you a great developer or founder than reading a book on exercise can make you a great weightlifter. An exercise book can teach you specific routines and exercises, but the first time you step up to a barbell, you'll still be a weakling. It's only after spending thousands of hours in a gym practicing, sweating, and applying what you read that you'll be able to move some serious weight. Likewise, the goal of this book is to teach you the tools and techniques you'll need in a startup, but you'll need to invest a lot of time practicing these techniques before you get them right.

That said, it's not really about right or wrong. All models are wrong, but some are useful [Box and Draper 1987, 424]. The tools and techniques in this book have proven useful for startups in the past and I hope you will find them useful in the future. Think of them not as canned solutions, but as a way to build a vocabulary for thinking about certain types of problems and coming up with your own solutions.

Who should read this book?

If you work in a startup or are considering joining the startup world, or you work in a large company and want to run it like a startup, you should read this book. It will introduce you to all the basic ideas you need to build a successful company—and a successful career—in the world of rapidly changing, uncertain tech ventures. Although at its core this is a book for programmers, by programmers, only Part II, Technologies, is significantly technical. Part I, Products, and Part III, Teams, should be accessible to technical and non-technical audiences alike.

If you're a programmer at the start of your career, this book is for you. *Hello, Startup* is a collection of everything I wish I knew when I was in college—all the advice, tips, and tricks I wish someone had told me when I was starting my career. As a young programmer, you probably know a couple of programming languages; perhaps you've mastered a few libraries and frameworks; maybe you've built some small apps as part of schoolwork. Suddenly, someone is offering you money for your skills, and you will soon find out if what you learned in school holds up in the real world. Let me save you the suspense: it doesn't. You can find that out the hard way and repeat the mistakes that thousands of other programmers have made before you, or you can read through this book and get your career moving in the right direction from day one.

If you're an experienced developer, this book will force you to take a more systematic look at the work you've been doing every day. Are you still forcing interview candidates to traverse binary trees on a whiteboard? Did you select the technology for your latest project based on a gut feeling or the latest hot trend online? Do you have a TODO somewhere that says "write documentation"? Do you feel like your company has gotten too big, too slow, and is no longer innovating? Then you'll find yourself nodding and smiling when you read the stories in this book. You'll be able to apply the advice to your existing job, or perhaps you'll figure out that it's time for a change.

If you are a manager, executive, or investor involved with high-tech companies, this book will help you understand why time estimates are off by an order of magnitude, or why your best developer just jumped ship to another company, or why the latest AgileExtremeScrumPairProgrammingDevOps™ process is not making your team any faster. Much of your success depends on understanding how programmers think, what they actually do all day, and how to motivate them. The stories in this book are the kind of honesty you won't get in a one-on-one with your direct reports.

If you're not already involved with but are interested in startups, this book is an insider's look at how the sausage is really made. Trying to understand a successful startup by studying only the end product (e.g., the website, the mobile app, the cool gizmo) is like trying to understand someone's college experience by studying only the diploma; it's an impressive looking piece of paper, sure, but it doesn't capture the years of classes, study sessions, exams, and homework—or the success and failures—that were necessary to get it. Companies like LinkedIn or Facebook might look simple from the outside, but they are not—and this book will reveal all the creativity, problem solving, and sleepless nights that occur within such companies to make that possible. In short, if you have any interest in startups, this book is for you.

Conventions used in this book

The following typographical conventions are used in this book:

Italic

> Indicates new terms, URLs, email addresses, filenames, and file extensions.

Constant width

> Used for program listings, as well as within paragraphs to refer to program elements such as variable or function names, databases, data types, environment variables, statements, and keywords.

Constant width bold

> Shows commands or other text that should be typed literally by the user.

Constant width italic

> Shows text that should be replaced with user-supplied values or by values determined by context.

Safari® Books Online

 *Safari Books Online* is an on-demand digital library that delivers expert *content* in both book and video form from the world's leading authors in technology and business.

Technology professionals, software developers, web designers, and business and creative professionals use Safari Books Online as their primary resource for research, problem solving, learning, and certification training.

Safari Books Online offers a range of plans and pricing for enterprise, government, education, and individuals.

Members have access to thousands of books, training videos, and prepublication manuscripts in one fully searchable database from publishers like O'Reilly Media, Prentice Hall Professional, Addison-Wesley Professional, Microsoft Press, Sams, Que, Peachpit Press, Focal Press, Cisco Press, John Wiley & Sons, Syngress, Morgan Kaufmann, IBM Redbooks, Packt, Adobe Press, FT Press, Apress, Manning, New Riders, McGraw-Hill, Jones & Bartlett, Course Technology, and hundreds more. For more information about Safari Books Online, please visit us online.

How to contact us

Please address comments and questions concerning this book to the publisher:

O'Reilly Media, Inc.
1005 Gravenstein Highway North
Sebastopol, CA 95472
800-998-9938 (in the United States or Canada)
707-829-0515 (international or local)
707-829-0104 (fax)

We have a web page for this book, where we list errata, examples, and any additional information. You can access this page at *http://bit.ly/Hello_Startup*.

To comment or ask technical questions about this book, send email to *book-questions@oreilly.com*.

For more information about our books, courses, conferences, and news, see our website at *http://www.oreilly.com*.

Find us on Facebook: *http://facebook.com/oreilly*

Follow us on Twitter: *http://twitter.com/oreillymedia*

Watch us on YouTube: *http://www.youtube.com/oreillymedia*

Acknowledgments

This book could not have happened without the help of a huge number of people. I decided to write a book in the first place thanks to the advice and help of Joe Adler, Adam Trachtenberg, Joshua Suereth, and Nilanjan Raychaudhuri. My fellow hackers, Florina Xhabija Grosskurth, Matthew Shoup, Prachi Gupta, and Bowei Gai, helped me at every step of the way with ideas and feedback. The folks at O'Reilly (and beyond), especially Angela Rufino, Mary Treseler, Nicole Shelby, Gillian McGarvey, and Mike Loukides, helped this newbie writer create something that was worth publishing. And I had lots of help with intros from Peter Skomoroch, Sid Viswanathan, and Jiong Wang, and with legal questions from James Yeagle.

A number of brave volunteers read the early release of this book and fought through the content before it was fully polished and ready: Alistair Sloley, Joseph Born, Clarke Ching, Jay Kreps, Ara Matevossian, Prachi Gupta, Matthew Shoup, Martin Kleppmann, Dmitriy Yefremov, David J. Groom, Molly Pucci, Steve Pucci, Alla Brikman, and Mikhail Brikman. I'm grateful for you taking the time to review my work and for all the feedback and help you offered.

A huge thank you to the amazing programmers I interviewed: Brian, Daniel, Dean, Flo, Gayle, Jonas, Jorge, Julia, Kevin, Martin, Mat, Matthew, Nick, Philip, Steve, Tracy, Vikram, and Zach (see the following section). Without your stories, advice, and feedback, this would have been a much more limited, boring, and incomplete book.

Finally, I owe most of the good things in my life to my family. Mom, Dad, Lyalya, and Molly—this book is for you.

Interviews

As part of the research for *Hello, Startup*, I interviewed programmers from some of the most successful startups of the last decade. From these discussions, I learned which problems come up again and again at almost every startup; I got a broader perspective on how different companies think about these problems and the most common patterns and practices for solving them; and I was inspired to learn what it takes to become a great developer. I've worked all of these ideas into the book and have included direct quotes throughout the text from the following interviewees:

Brian Larson (https://twitter.com/larsonite)
Staff Software Engineer at Google, Principle Software Engineer at Twitter

Daniel Kim (https://www.linkedin.com/pub/daniel-kim/1/333/592)
Software Engineer at Facebook, Engineering Manager at Instagram

Dean Thompson (https://www.linkedin.com/in/deansthompson)
Co-Founder of Transarc Corporation, Co-Founder and CTO of Premier Health Exchange, Co-Founder and CTO of Peak Strategy, Co-Founder and CTO of mSpoke, Director of Engineering at LinkedIn, CTO of NoWait

Florina Xhabija Grosskurth (https://www.linkedin.com/in/florina)
Web Developer, Product Specialist, and Manager at LinkedIn, Director of People Operations at Wealthfront

Gayle Laakmann McDowell (https://www.linkedin.com/in/gaylemcd)
Founder and CEO of CareerCup, Founder and Co-President of Seattle Anti-Freeze, VP of Engineering at KeenScreen Inc., Software Engineer at Google

Jonas Bonér (http://jonasboner.com/)
> Co-founder and CTO of Triental AB, Founder and CEO of Scalable Solutions AB, Co-founder and CTO of Typesafe

Jorge Ortiz (https://www.linkedin.com/in/jorgeo)
> Founder at Joberator, Software Engineer at LinkedIn, Server Engineer at Foursquare, Hacker at Stripe

Julia Grace (http://juliahgrace.com/)
> Co-Founder and CTO at WeddingLovely, CTO at Tindie

Kevin Scott (https://www.linkedin.com/in/jkevinscott)
> SVP Engineering and Operations at LinkedIn, VP Engineering/Operations at AdMob, Senior Engineering Director at Google

Martin Kleppmann (http://martin.kleppmann.com/)
> Co-founder of Go Test It and Rapportive, Senior Software Engineer at LinkedIn

Mat Clayton (https://twitter.com/matclayton)
> Co-founder and CTO of Mixcloud

Matthew Shoup (https://www.linkedin.com/in/matthewshoup)
> Web Developer at Indiaplaza.com, E*Business Manager at VNUS Medical Technologies, Senior Hacker in Residence at LinkedIn, Principal Nerd at NerdWallet

Nick Dellamaggiore (https://www.linkedin.com/in/nick)
> Principal Staff Engineer at LinkedIn, Infrastructure Lead at Coursera

Philip Jacob (https://www.linkedin.com/in/whirlycott)
> Founder and CTO StyleFeeder, Engineering at Stackdriver, Staff Software Engineer and TLM at Google

Steven Conine (https://www.linkedin.com/pub/steven-conine/0/8/474)
> CTO and Co-founder at Spinners, Founder of Wayfair

Tracy Chou (https://www.linkedin.com/in/triketora)
> Software Engineer at Quora, Software Engineer at Pinterest

Vikram Rangnekar (https://www.linkedin.com/in/vikramr)
    Co-founder at Voiceroute, Co-founder at Socialwok, Senior Software Engineer at LinkedIn

Zach Holman (http://zachholman.com/)
    One of the first engineering hires at GitHub

PART I

Products

Why Startups

The age of the tech startup

About 540M years ago something amazing happened on planet Earth: life forms began to multiply, leading to what is known as the "Cambrian explosion". Until then sponges and other simple creatures had the planet largely to themselves, but within a few million years the animal kingdom became much more varied. ... Something similar is now happening in the virtual realm: an entrepreneurial explosion. Digital startups are bubbling up in an astonishing variety of services and products, penetrating every nook and cranny of the economy. They are reshaping entire industries and even changing the very notion of the firm.

—[A CAMBRIAN MOMENT 2014], *THE ECONOMIST*

At this very moment, somewhere in the world, two programmers are sitting in a garage and creating our future, one line of code at a time. We are in the era of the high-tech startup. Silicon Valley is leading the way, but every major city, from Boulder to London to Tel Aviv to Singapore, is trying to build its own startup hub. In the United States alone, there are more than 1,000 venture capital firms and two million angel investors who collectively invest around $50 billion in young businesses every year [Hollas 2011]. In 2010, US entrepreneurs founded more than 30,000 new high-tech and communications technology companies [Hathaway 2013, 7], or nearly four new tech startups every hour of the day.

The startup revolution is here, and in this chapter, I'll explain why that's something you'll want to pay attention to (reading this book is a good start!). I'll talk about some of the things that make startups great and why you should consider joining one or even starting your own. To keep the discussion honest, I'll also confess to the things that make startups terrible and why they are not for everyone. But first, I'll define what I mean by *tech startup* in this book, as the phrase can mean different things to different people.

What is a tech startup?

This book is primarily focused on tech startups. The *tech* part is easy to explain. If your company's business primarily depends on *building* technology—whether that technology is the actual product you sell or if the technology is used to sell some other product—you're a tech company. If you primarily *use* technologies that already exist, then you're not. For example, GitHub is a tech company because they build and sell technology that makes it easier for programmers to collaborate. Likewise, TripAdvisor is a tech company: they sell travel products (e.g. hotel rooms, vacation packages, flights), but to make that possible, most of the work is building technology such as hotel pages, user accounts, review storage, photo storage, and search features. A local restaurant is not a tech company, even if that restaurant has a fancy website and even if that website is written in Flash and auto-plays music. That's because the restaurant's primary activity as a business is to create food and a great atmosphere for diners, and not technology.

So that takes care of the word *tech*, but what about the word *startup*? The prototypical startup is a week-old company with two developers in a garage. But the word *startup* is sometimes also used to describe much bigger and older companies. For example, the *Wall Street Journal* [Phillips 2014b] uses *startup* to refer to:

- Snapchat: $10 billion valuation, 2 years old, 20+ employees
- Uber: $42 billion valuation, 5 years old, 550+ employees
- SpaceX: $4.8 billion valuation, 12 years old, 3,000+ employees

So it doesn't seem like a startup is defined by how much it's worth (from $0 to $42 billion), how old it is (from 1 week old to 12 years old), or how many employees it has (from 3 to 3,000). So what is a startup? To answer this question, let's look at a few definitions from well-known entrepreneurs. We'll start with Eric Ries:

A startup is a human institution designed to create a new product or service under conditions of extreme uncertainty.

—[RIES 2011A, 27], ERIC RIES, *THE LEAN STARTUP*

Creating products and services makes sense, and startups definitely face lots of uncertainty, but so do most local restaurants, which face failure rates similar to most startups [Miller 2007]. You generally wouldn't call the local pizzeria a startup, so we need more. Let's see what Paul Graham has to say:

> A startup is a company designed to grow fast. Being newly founded does not in itself make a company a startup. Nor is it necessary for a startup to work on technology, or take venture funding, or have some sort of "exit." The only essential thing is growth. Everything else we associate with start-ups follows from growth.
>
> **—[GRAHAM 2012B], PAUL GRAHAM, CO-FOUNDER OF Y COMBINATOR**

In addition to uncertainty, you now have another essential ingredient for a startup: massive growth. The goal of a local pizzeria usually isn't massive growth; it's to attract enough customers every night for the owner to make a reasonable income. On the other hand, although the food delivery company SpoonRocket has been profitable since 2013 [Sciacca 2013], it was designed for growth and continues to raise more money, spread to new cities, and get new customers. So SpoonRocket is a startup, but will it be a startup forever or does it become an "established company" at some point? To answer that question, let's turn to Steve Blank and Bob Dorf:

> A startup is a temporary organization designed to search for a repeatable and scalable business model. Within this definition, a startup can be a new venture or it can be a new division or business unit in an existing company.
>
> **—[BLANK AND DORF 2012, XVII], STEVE BLANK AND BOB DORF,**
> **THE STARTUP OWNER'S MANUAL**

An established business has a product that has been proven to work in the market, so the focus is on scaling, optimizing, and efficient execution. A startup has no idea what product will work in the market, so the company is primarily focused on experimentation and trial and error—on searching for a repeatable and scalable business model. In other words, the final ingredient of startups is that they run in *search mode*. Now that we have all the ingredients, let's put them together. A tech startup is an organization with the following characteristics:

- Product: technology

- Environment: extremely uncertain

- Goal: massive growth

- Mode of operation: search

For the purposes of this book, I'm not concerned with the age of the organization, how many employees it has, what industry it's in, or how much money it makes. The material in this book will apply to a brand-new three-person company or a new venture within an established 3,000-person company as long as you're building technology, your environment is constantly changing, your primary goal is growth, and you're running in search mode. This might not be the way most people think of the word *startup*, but I'm not aware of any other word or phrase that captures these ideas better. I briefly considered calling the book *Hello, Organization Designed for Massive Growth That is Searching for a Repeatable Business Model and Building Technology in an Extremely Uncertain Environment*— but *Hello, Startup* sounded a bit sexier, so I'll stick with *startup*.

Why you should work at a startup

So now that you know what a tech startup is, why all the fuss? What makes them so great? There are three main reasons you should consider working at, or even starting, a tech startup: more opportunity, more ownership, and more fun.

MORE OPPORTUNITY

Here's a fun fact: you are a cyborg. Over time, your mind and body have been enhanced with artificial components and technology. It happened so gradually that you probably didn't even notice, but if you and all of your augmentations were sent a few thousand years back in time, you would have superpowers compared to the purely organic beings back then. There are the obvious physical enhancements that are possible due to modern medicine such as glasses, contact lenses, hearing aids, fillings, braces, dentures, cardiac pacemakers, heart valve replacements, hip replacements, artificial hearts, 3D-printed ears, hair implants, breast implants, skin grafts, titanium bones, and prosthetic limbs. But all of that barely scratches the surface of how intertwined you are with technology.

For example, this book, and more generally, writing, are technologies that augment the abilities of your mind. You can extend your memory by "storing" words on paper. You can extend your computational abilities by working through math problems step by step on a whiteboard. You can extend your ability to communicate by sending someone a letter, email, or text message. And every time you draw a diagram, chart, table, timeline, or blueprint, you are literally using writing to enhance your ability to think [Victor 2014].

These days, you do much of your thinking in a digital medium. You might be reading a digital version of this book on a tablet or an e-reader and you probably purchased it in an online bookstore (e.g., O'Reilly, Amazon, iTunes). You might get your news from Twitter and Reddit, put your résumé on LinkedIn, file your taxes using TurboTax, get your entertainment from YouTube and Netflix, and stay in touch with your friends and family via Gmail and Facebook. Nearby, in your pocket, purse, or on a desk, you probably have a smartphone. You use it to enhance your communication (e.g., phone calls, text messages), your memory (e.g., calendar reminders, alarms, photos), your sense of direction (e.g., GPS, Google Maps), your entertainment (e.g., music, videos), and to help gain knowledge (e.g., Google, Siri, Yelp, Stocks, Weather). The phone is a part of you. You carry it with you wherever you go, you sleep next to it, you check it dozens of times per day, and you rely on it constantly. In fact, you probably feel lost and nervous without it.

Now head outside. Did you walk past a car, bus, or train? These marvels of technology, which are designed on computers and built in factories full of robots, enhance your ability to travel vast distances in a short amount of time. Now look up. Somewhere above you an airplane might pass by, powering its way across the sky using jet engines, radio, and autopilot. Somewhere above that, satellites and space stations are orbiting the earth, taking pictures, measuring the weather, and routing phone calls.

But this is only the beginning. Soon you'll be wearing technology (e.g., Apple Watch, Google Glass, Jawbone Up), locking your doors with your phone (e.g., August Smart Lock, Lockitron, Goji), using your phone to monitor and diagnose diseases (e.g., spot heart attacks early by tracking blood pressure and performing an electrocardiogram straight from your phone [Topol 2015, 6]), relying on robots instead of people for a wide variety of tasks (e.g., replacing cleaning staff with the Roomba vacuum robot, replacing FedEx with Amazon's Drone Delivery), using "replicators" to create physical objects (e.g., printing DNA at home [Lee 2014] or emailing a wrench to outer space [LeTrent 2014]), traveling in robot-controlled vehicles (e.g., a self-driving car from Google or Tesla), and traveling to outer space (e.g., via Virgin Galactic or SpaceX).

What do all of these technologies have in common? They all rely on software. In other words, as Marc Andreessen predicted in 2011, "software is eating the world" [Andreessen 2011]. As technology becomes more and more ubiquitous, software companies will take over more and more industries. For example, Amazon dominates the book industry, controlling 41% of all new book purchases and 65% of all online book purchases [Milliot 2014]. In the US entertainment industry, 50% of households now use Netflix, Hulu, or Amazon Prime [Leichtman Research Group 2014] and YouTube reaches more 18– to 34–year-olds than any cable network [YouTube Statistics 2014]. In the travel space, Airbnb has more than 1 million homes listed and is adding 20,000 more per week. Compare that to the InterContinental Hotels Group, which is one of the largest hotel companies in the world (they own the Holiday Inn and InterContinental chains) and has just 700,000 rooms [Griswold 2014]. In the communications industry, WhatsApp users send 7.2 trillion messages per year, compared to 7.5 trillion text messages per year across the entire global telecommunications industry [Evans 2014]; and Skype users make over 200 billion minutes of international calls per year, which is already 40% the size of, and growing 50% faster than, the global telecommunications industry [Gara 2014]. Software companies are becoming dominant in many other industries as well, such as LinkedIn in the recruiting industry; Paypal, Square, and Stripe in payments; Uber and Lyft in transportation; Spotify and Pandora in music; and so on.

The biggest change of all is coming from mobile. The smartphone takes all the software that changes how you live and puts it into a package that includes a fast CPU, lots of memory and storage, unparalleled connectivity (3G, LTE, WiFi, Bluetooth, NFC, GPS), a plethora of built-in technologies (microphone, camera, accelerometer, fingerprint recognition, gyroscope, barometer, proximity sensors), a touchscreen, and speakers. And this package is so small and useful that you have it with you at all times and in all places. As a result, mobile has become one of the fastest-growing technologies in human history (see Figure 1-1).

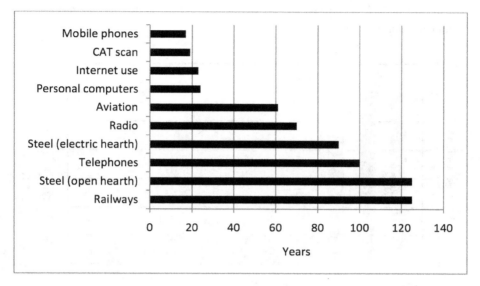

Figure 1-1. Number of years to reach 80% coverage for select technology (chart courtesy of Wiliam Jack and Tavneet Suri, based on data from the World Bank [Jack and Suri 2010])

The numbers around mobile are staggering. As shown in Figure 1-2, far more people on earth have access to mobile phones than TVs, bank accounts, and even safe drinking water and toothbrushes [Hall 2011]. By 2020, 80% of the adults on earth will have access to a smartphone. In other words, mobile is eating the world [Evans 2014].

Tech startups are at the head of a great deal of the software and mobile revolution. This is because a revolution means an enormous amount of change, and change is something startups are better equipped to handle (and initiate) than big companies. Some tech giants are responding by trying to run parts of their organization like a startup,[1] but many will be unable to keep up and startups will displace them. In fact, every generation of startups is growing faster than than the one before it, as shown in Figure 1-3. Companies like Facebook, Google, Groupon, and Zynga grew faster in a decade than most corporations grew in the entire 20th century [Blank and Dorf 2012, xxviii]. In 1958, the average tenure for

---

1 For example, Google X is a semisecret branch of Google that is in permanent search mode, exploring projects such as wearable technology, self-driving cars, high-altitude WiFi balloons, and glucose-monitoring contact lenses [Gertner 2014].

a firm on the S&P 500 index was 61 years. Today, that number is down to just 18 years [Innosight 2012].

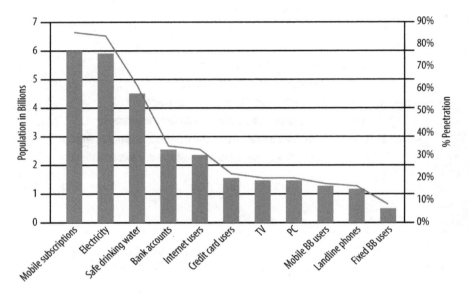

Figure 1-2. Putting global mobile in context (chart courtesy of Chetan Sharma [Sharma 2012])

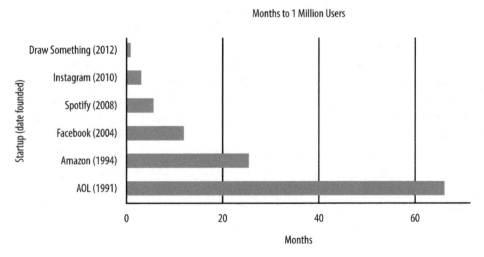

Figure 1-3. Months to one million users, based on data from [Fralic 2012]

Startups are reaching billion-dollar valuations twice as fast as they did back in 2000 [Van Grove 2014], not because of a bubble, but because it is easier to build and grow a company than ever before. Here are some of the things that have lowered the barrier to entry for startups:[2]

Open source

Instead of having to write everything from scratch, a modern startup can leverage the code in over 10 million open source repositories [Doll 2013]. Many of these repositories are developed, tested, and documented by a large community of developers, which means you not only save time by using open source but you also get access to projects that are larger and higher quality than anything you would be able to build in-house. See Chapter 5 for more information on open source and choosing a tech stack.

Services

Startups can also leverage hundreds of services that make it dramatically easier and faster to get up and running. For example, instead of building your own data center, you can use AWS, DigitalOcean, or Rackspace. Instead of building your own monitoring software, you can use New Relic, KISSMetrics, or MixPanel. Instead of building your own email service, you can use Amazon SES, MailChimp, or SendGrid. If you need a logo, you can use DesignCrowd; if you need legal services, you can use RocketLawyer; if you need to accept payments, you can use Stripe; if you need to manage customer data, you can use Salesforce; and if you need to provide customer support, you can use Zendesk.

Distribution

Distribution is easier than ever before, both in terms of marketing your product and in terms of being able to run a distributed company with employees all over the world. For marketing, due to the ubiquity of technology, the Internet, and mobile phones, you have instant access to more people than ever before through search engines, mobile app stores, advertising, email, and social media channels like Twitter, Facebook, LinkedIn, Reddit, Hacker News, and YouTube (see "Distribution" on page 159 for more details). For building a distributed company, you have access

---

2 See *http://www.hello-startup.net/resources/* for a comprehensive list of service providers, tools, and products for startups.

to a plethora of collaboration tools such as GitHub, Skype, Google Hangouts, JIRA, Slack, HipChat, Basecamp, Asana, Trello, and many others.

Information

These days, there is a lot more information available on how to build a successful startup. This includes books (such as this one!), courses (the free online Stanford course, How to Start a Startup 2014, makes an excellent complement to this book), blogs (especially Paul Graham's essays), meetup groups, conferences, accelerators, and incubators.

Money

Thanks to open source, services, easier distribution, and more information, startups need less money than ever before. And when you do need money, you have plenty of options, including not only traditional venture capital firms, but also angel investors (e.g., AngelList), crowdfunding (e.g., KickStart, Indiegogo, Lending Club, Kabbage), and government funding and incentives for startups (e.g., Startup-Up NY 2014 and Singapore Startups Government Funding and Assistance Schemes).

All of this means that we are at a remarkable time in history. Software is taking over every industry, smartphones are changing how we live our lives, and startups are able to reach more people in less time than ever before. In other words, software is eating the world, mobile is eating the world, and as a result, startups are eating the world. As a programmer, you have the unprecedented opportunity to join this feast and touch millions of lives by joining a startup and writing some code.

MORE OWNERSHIP

So why not write code at a big, established company? What advantages does working at a startup offer over tech giants such as Microsoft, Cisco, or IBM? Isn't it better to work for a more "stable" company that has thousands of employees, has been around for years, and provides job security?

Well, let's talk about job security. Perhaps your parents or grandparents worked at the same company for 50 years, climbed the career ladder, and retired with a golden watch. You won't have that luxury because those types of jobs are long gone. In the United States, the average person born in the early 1960s held 11.3 jobs between the ages of 18 and 46 [BLS 2012] and this number might be on the way up, as the average person born in the early 1980s has had an average of 6.2 jobs by age 26 [BLS 2014]. That means that the average job tenure is under three years. And big companies don't seem any safer than little ones. For example, in 2014 alone, Cisco laid off 6,000 employees, IBM laid off 13,000 employees, Microsoft laid off 18,000 employees, and HP laid off 27,000 employees [Tolentino 2014]. Job security is dead.

> One piece of advice I got when I was deciding where to go after university was that you should think of Silicon Valley as one big company, with a Facebook department, a Google department, and a bunch of small startup departments. Sometimes departments get re-orged and don't exist independently anymore, but all the people just join other groups. I think this is a pretty good analogy. People move around quite frequently between different companies here.
>
> If you're even a semi-competent software engineer, you don't really have to worry about the risk of joining a startup. You're probably getting paid a reasonable salary, perhaps not as much as at the biggest companies, but it's going to be enough for you to pay your bills and loans, and to get by. If that startup flops, you just go find another job, so it's not really risky.
>
> **—[CHOU 2014], TRACY CHOU, SOFTWARE ENGINEER AT QUORA AND PINTEREST**

The real risk is not losing your job because you joined a tiny startup—after all, there is no guarantee you won't lose your job at a big company—but the risk of losing an opportunity. When you choose to work at one company, you're implicitly choosing not to work at many others. In that respect, the death of job security might not be such a bad thing. If you stay at the same job for a long time, you are probably missing out on better opportunities elsewhere.

At big companies, stagnation is a common problem. You end up doing the same tasks over and over again, so you no longer feel challenged, you stop learning, and you get bored. Moreover, you have little say in what you work on, and your contributions usually feel small and unimportant. Working for a large company is a bit like being one of the thousands of oarsmen on a large galley ship. You're doing repetitive, back-breaking work, but your contribution is completely lost in the wake of everyone else's rowing. If anyone gets any credit, it's the person at the helm, even if they seem to do little more than wear an impressive hat.

And although you've got little say in where the ship goes, when you do make an effort to make a difference, you find that it's incredibly hard to turn a big ship.[3]

> In my experience, at larger companies, your success or failure is often based around what group you end up in, if upper management feels that the work being done in that group is strategic, aligns with the business, will matter when earnings come around, that sort of thing. While that's important, I prefer environments where you have more of a say in your fate and your success or failure is based around your ability to execute and build something that the market wants.

—[GRACE 2014], JULIA GRACE, CO-FOUNDER OF WEDDINGLOVELY, CTO AT TINDIE

At a small company, you usually have more *autonomy*. You have more say in what you work on, when you'll work on it, and how you will do it. You also have less red tape, bureaucracy, and politics. Most importantly, as a founder or early employee of a startup, you get to define the company culture (see Chapter 9). For example, what is the company's mission and what are its values? Will you be transparent or secretive with your communication? Will you have an open floor plan or private offices? Will employees be able to work from home? Will you organize the company using a management hierarchy or keep the company flat? Will you track hours and vacation time or just focus on results? At a large company, most of these decisions have already been made, and you have to live with them. At a startup, many of these decisions will be up to you.

Each decision you make at a small startup has a big impact on the company. Moreover, you'll see your impact sooner because small companies usually have a faster feedback loop than large companies. Every line of code you write and every feature you build will make a visible difference. You're no longer just a small cog in a big machine, but a significant influence on the entire organization. The result is that you will feel more connected to the company's mission and feel a heightened sense of *purpose*. It's hard to care about increasing the profit margin of a huge company, but at a small startup where you are responsible for its very survival, it's easy to feel inspired and connected.

Startups also give you more opportunities for *mastery*. You'll be faced with a huge variety of tasks and you'll constantly have to learn new things as you go.

---

3 Apparently, if you're on a fully loaded supertanker traveling at normal speed and you can see an iceberg in your path, it's already too late [Vella 2013].

You might be writing database queries one day, designing a user interface the next day, answering customer service emails the day after that, and putting together an investor pitch deck in between. You'll develop skills that will be useful for the rest of your career and you'll learn to deal with pressure, stress, and risk. You'll be pushed beyond your comfort zone, which is where learning really happens. This is why many people learn more in three months at a startup than three years at a big company.

> *[At previous companies,] I felt like there was all of this architectural cruft that had carried on over the years that would take a massive amount of effort to change, and I was in no position to even start arguing with people what to do about it. So I felt very beholden to decisions of people that came before and what they thought was the right way to do things.*
>
> *At Foursquare, there was only a handful of engineers, most of the decisions had not been made yet, and I would get to make the decisions and it would be much better. And that panned out. I did get to make a lot of decisions. They weren't necessarily good ones. Three-and-a-half years later, I was like, I'm so sorry, I'm so sorry, don't quit because of this terrible choice I made three years ago. But it was a great learning experience. I definitely learned a lot.*
>
> **—[ORTIZ 2014], JORGE ORTIZ, SOFTWARE ENGINEER AT LINKEDIN, FOURSQUARE, AND STRIPE**

Together, autonomy, mastery, and purpose are three of the most powerful human motivators (see "Motivation" on page 403). If you've found a job that offers all three, then you've found a job that you will love and a place where you can do work you're proud of.

MORE FUN

Startups can be more fun. In a big company, you have a product that already works in the market, so your primary task is to optimize it. In a startup, all you have is a bunch of guesses about what might work in the market, and the focus is on search. It turns out that searching is a lot more fun.

A search can feel like a battle of you against the world. Fighting to stay alive creates stronger bonds than trying to increase profit margins by 2%; struggling to bring something new into the world is more exciting than optimizing something already there; celebrating your first public launch, becoming profitable, or an IPO is far more memorable than the annual Christmas party or the latest performance review cycle.

> *The coolest day in my life, to be very honest—I mean, Silicon Valley pays well and all that—but the greatest joy I ever got was this call in the middle of the night from one of my co-founders, who said, "someone is paying us 50 bucks!" That was how much we were charging for our software through PayPal and the money had just landed in our account. All I could think was that we made this software, this thing we put online, and now someone is giving us **real** money for it. I was afraid to withdraw the money because, well, I was worried our software was going to crash and the customer would come back and ask for the 50 bucks back, and I don't even know if I have 50 bucks, so let's not touch it.*

**—[RANGNEKAR 2014], VIKRAM RANGNEKAR,
CO-FOUNDER OF VOICEROUTE AND SOCIALWOK**

Even the "crappy" days at a startup can be fun. The ghetto office, the need to scrape by on a budget, the constant sense that you have no idea what you're doing can all be terrifying, but also exciting. They teach you to appreciate the small victories in life rather than becoming obsessed with promotions or politics.

> *Some of my favorite memories at LinkedIn are from when I first joined, for the first two years at the East Embarcadero office. There were pretty much no benefits and we still loved working there. Lunch was typically frozen burritos or perhaps a random food truck that might or might not show up that day. It was quite a contrast to the lavish treatment of engineers at Valley startups these days. That said, we were still treated really well. One of my favorite memories was when Reid Hoffman personally paid for an ice cream truck to stop by the office one summer day to treat the company.*
>
> *It was a crazy office. It was situated between the dump, an airport, a golf course, and East Palo Alto. The bathrooms were flooding all the time. We had multiple break-ins. But it was super fun. We had scooter races around the office, Guitar Hero competitions, and epic Nerf wars. Ian McNish had this giant toy bazooka and he would tag you in the back of the head with it. It was almost concussion-inducing.*

One thing I really liked was our weekly product all-hands meeting, where all the product managers and engineers would get in the room and just go over the numbers. We launched the recruiter product in around Fall '05, and we were like, wait, we are making money? People actually want to pay for this? Then we started making a million dollars, and we were like, oh my God, we're making a lot of money!

—[DELLAMAGGIORE 2014], NICK DELLAMAGGIORE,
SOFTWARE ENGINEER AT LINKEDIN AND COURSERA

Startups are inherently about change, and are thus more open to doing things differently, which is why the most fun company cultures are found at startups and not huge corporations. You've probably heard of the basics available at most tech companies, such as a casual dress code and free snacks, drinks, and meals, but it goes beyond that. For example, HubSpot regularly hosts talks from thought leaders, reimburses an unlimited number of books for employees, does a semi-random "seat shuffle" every three months, and has an unlimited vacation policy [Hubspot 2013]. Evernote also has an unlimited vacation policy, but they go a step further by offering employees a $1,000 bonus for actually taking a vacation [Bryant 2012]. At Asana, employees get $10,000 to customize their office setup, as well as access to in-house yoga, massage, and a full-time on-site chef who cooks customized meals for the employees [Drell 2011] (check out Chapter 9 for more startup culture hacks).

Some of these might sound like silly perks, but they have a way of changing what you do from being "just another job" to something more. If you're lucky enough to catch a ride on a *rocketship*—that is, a highly successful, hypergrowth startup—it can be life changing. For me, LinkedIn was a blur of incredible moments: scaling the site to handle hundreds of millions of members; hackday competitions in Mountain View, New York, Berlin, Amsterdam, and Toronto; the InDay Speaker Series, with talks from Sheryl Sandberg, Marc Andreessen, Arianna Huffington, Thomas Friedman, Cory Booker, Bryan Stevenson, and even President Barack Obama; the IPO in New York; holiday parties in the Ferry Building, Club Auto Sport, and Giants Stadium; T-shirts to commemorate every product launch and celebration (*http://bit.ly/yb-shirts*);[4] and much more. At times, it was hard to believe that someone was paying me for all of this.

The fact that startups have the courage to stray from the safe path in an attempt to do something new is what makes them an amazing place to work. And, as shown in Figure 1-4, having the courage to stray from the safe path is also the key to living a remarkable life [Newport 2012, chap. 6].

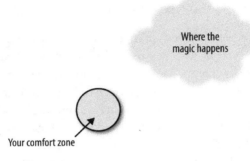

Figure 1-4. Where the magic happens

Why you shouldn't work at a startup

So far, this chapter has made it sound like startups are better than established companies in every way. They aren't. Startups have problems of their own, some of them far worse than big companies. In fact, startups are all about extremes: the highs are much higher and the lows are much lower.

Joining a startup is not for everyone. Founding a startup is for even fewer people. In this section, I'll present some of the drawbacks to the startup world: it's not glamorous, you'll have to sacrifice a lot, and you probably won't get rich. I'll also discuss some of the trade-offs between joining someone else's startup and founding your own.

IT'S NOT GLAMOROUS

Steve Jobs has been on the cover of *Time*, Elon Musk has appeared on the cover of *Fortune*, Twitter is constantly referenced on TV, and there is a movie about Facebook. Tech entrepreneurs have become the new rock stars and some pro-

---

4 Another alternative title I considered for the book was *How to Never Pay for a T-Shirt Again* (*http://bit.ly/shirts-matter*).

grammers even have agents [Widdicombe 2014]. For the most part, that's great. Anything that gets kids excited about technology is a good thing, and an entrepreneur or programmer is arguably a better role model than a rock star or an athlete. But, as is often the case with the media, it creates a distorted image of what the startup world is really like.

Seeing entrepreneurs on the cover of every magazine creates the myth of an entrepreneur-hero who single-handedly comes up with a brilliant strategy, surmounts all obstacles, defeats all competitors, changes the world, and becomes rich in the process. Movies like *The Social Network* portray startup life as an endless series of parties and successes. In reality, no entrepreneur and no startup is actually like that. For one thing, the vast majority of startups fail. And of the few startups that do succeed, it's not because they had a single hero with a eureka moment but because there was a team of people grinding it out day after day, constantly iterating and evolving the product and the company. The true story behind every startup includes a huge number of missteps, failures, pivots, arguments, and fights. Sometimes there are betrayals or fallouts. There is always fear, stress, and pain. And in the end, the winner is usually not a brilliant strategist who came up with the perfect plan ahead of time, but a scrappy team that survived even when things did not go according to plan.

In other words, a startup is 99.9% hard, unglamorous work. At 11 p.m. on a Thursday, while your loved ones are at home, relaxing in front of the TV, you'll be deploying new code. And at 2 a.m. on a Friday night, while your friends are all out partying, you'll be furiously coding away to fix a bug in the release from the night before. And all day Saturday and Sunday, while people with normal jobs take the time to get away from their work by going on hikes and road trips, you'll be afraid to be more than five feet from your computer, because a website needs to run 24/7 and you're on call this week.

Large companies have the luxury of hiring specialists dedicated to some of these tasks, but in a tiny startup, just about everyone has to be a generalist, and you'll have to do a little bit of everything. You might have to set up cubicles, estimate how much toilet paper to get for the bathroom, learn how to hire a VP of sales, set up payroll, fill out all sorts of legal and tax forms, create pitch decks for investors, design a logo, and a whole lot more. Some programmers love this because they get to learn lots of new skills, but other programmers would much rather be coding.

*There's a big difference between building a business and solving interesting engineering problems. There **are** interesting engineering problems in* *startups, but very frequently, your business will not succeed or fail based on how well you solve those engineering problems. The exception to this is startups focused on hard scientific problems. For example, I have a friend who has a battery company and his business will succeed or fail based on the scientific breakthroughs they make, as well as how well they run the business. This hard science component is not applicable to 99% of web startups; most web startups succeed or fail based almost entirely on execution, meaning marketing, sales, product, and engineering. We think as engineers that if we can write great code and build something that can scale to a million people that we will be successful and lauded in the community and people will say, "Oh, you're so amazing," and they'll want to acqui-hire us for millions of dollars. That's what we read in TechCrunch and that's what we hear about at meetups, but it is very very far from reality.*

—[GRACE 2014], JULIA GRACE, CO-FOUNDER OF WEDDINGLOVELY, CTO AT TINDIE

For developers who have spent their careers at big companies, it often comes as a surprise that much of the work you do at a startup has nothing to do with engineering. Big companies have their own distractions to take you away from coding, such as useless meetings or heavy processes and methodologies (see "Process" on page 432), but at a startup, the non-engineering tasks are often an essential part of the job. This work is worth doing to build a company, but it can be mundane. Despite the reputation startups have for being "sexy" places to work, a lot of the time is actually filled with drudge work and tasks that are decidedly not sexy. And the higher up you go in the organization, the less time you'll spend on the engineering tasks you love.

I love getting in the zone, banging out code, realizing it's midnight, and holy crap, you have this cool thing you've just built. As you scale up a business, as the leader of it, you realize you can't do that as much anymore. It happens gradually. You don't really notice it.

When it's just five people, you're spending very little of your time talking to people about career development, thinking about their promotion cycles, the pay rates. As you get to where you have 50 people, all of a sudden, you find you're doing it 10% of your time. You get to 100 people and now you have four or five people that are reporting to you that each have 20 people, and now it takes up 50%–75% of your time. And then you get bigger, and all of a sudden, you're starting to be the public face of the business. And that crushes the last little bit of coding time you have. If you have to be on the road, talking to investors, doing presentations, and going to talks, the rest of your time gets sucked up. Your schedule becomes so variable that it's hard to get blocks of solid time where you can do honest engineering work. The evolution happens slowly enough over time that one day you wake up and you realize, "Oh wow, I haven't coded in four months."

—[CONINE 2014], STEVEN CONINE, FOUNDER OF WAYFAIR

Many developers have trouble transitioning from a coding role to a leadership role such as CEO, CTO, or VP. If you've never had such a role, you might expect that being part of the executive team will make you feel important, respected, and powerful. You imagine yourself spending all your time drawing up strategies, giving orders, and moving chess pieces around a board, like a five-star general. In reality, you'll be more of a salesperson crossed with a psychiatrist. You'll spend a lot of time trying to get someone, anyone, anywhere, to care about your company. You'll also spend lots of time listening to your employees, trying to figure out their needs, dealing with their complaints, and figuring out how to motivate them. You will get to make decisions, but many of them will be painful, risky, and unpopular. And no matter how much you try, you'll get some of these decisions wrong. Some people thrive in this sort of environment, but if you're not one of them, a leadership role might not be for you.

People have this vision of being the CEO of a company they started and being on top of the pyramid. Some people are motivated by that, but that's not at all what it's like. What it's really like: everyone else is your boss—all of your employees, customers, partners, users, media are your boss. I've never had more bosses and needed to account for more people today. The life of most CEOs is reporting to everyone else—at least that's what it feels like to me and most CEOs I know. If you want to exercise power and authority over people, join the military or go into politics. Don't be an entrepreneur.

—[LIBIN 2012], PHIL LIBIN, CEO OF EVERNOTE

IT'S A SACRIFICE

Building a successful startup is incredibly hard. It's hard to hire great people when competing against big companies. It's hard when great people you've managed to hire decide to leave. It's hard to fire people who turned out to not be great. It's hard to motivate people. It's hard to motivate yourself when nothing is working and you're running out of money. It's hard to raise money. It's hard to keep investors from derailing your business after they've given you money. It's hard to focus on the long-term direction of the company when you have to worry about short-term survival. It's hard to bring a new product into a constantly changing market. It's hard to spend so much time working on something—building it, selling it, marketing it—and still no one seems to take notice. It's hard to fend off the competition when they suddenly do take notice. It's hard to make dozens of decisions every single day with not nearly enough information and with each one putting a lot of time and money, and many careers, at risk. And it's hard when you make mistakes—and you will make many mistakes—because you have no one to blame but yourself.

All of this means that working at a startup involves a lot of sacrifice. Some people manage it better than others, but working at a young startup often means you won't get to see your friends and family as much as you like; in addition, your health might even suffer. Startups have ruined marriages, caused mental and physical health problems, and worst of all, even driven some founders to suicide [Feld 2014]. It rarely gets that bad, but long hours and too much stress are common problems.

I was 26 and ended up in the doctor's office. I was experiencing short-term memory issues. He did some blood tests and he said, "You have the numbers of a 60-year-old, so we have a problem." I realized I didn't want to be on that path, so later I told my boss, "Look, I'm leaving. I'm not enjoying myself, I'm working 90 hours a week, and I've been doing it for eight or nine months." And he said, "Yeah, I'm at the doctor with heart troubles myself, so I'm going to probably leave, too." I learned that you have to pace yourself at a startup. You have to work hard, but you also have to find a way to do this on a sustainable basis.

**—[JACOB 2014], PHILIP JACOB, FOUNDER OF STYLEFEEDER,
SOFTWARE ENGINEER AT STACKDRIVER AND GOOGLE**

A startup is an emotional roller coaster. There are extreme highs and extreme lows. For some people, this is part of the charm. For others, it's more stress than they can handle. It's particularly stressful for founders. If you're an *employee* of a startup that has failed, it's disappointing, but you shake it off and move on to your next job. But if you're the *founder* of a startup that has failed, it will feel like you've let everyone down. Your employees gave you years of their lives, your customers gave you their money and trust, your investors funded you, your family supported you, and in the end, you did not deliver. Your dream is dead, and that can be devastating.

YOU PROBABLY WON'T GET RICH

Most startups fail. The numbers vary depending on what you define as a "startup" and as "failure," but the typical failure rate is somewhere around 75% [Gage 2012]. Three out of four times, despite all the pain and sacrifice, the startup goes nowhere. And if you're one of the lucky few that does succeed, you're still unlikely to get rich. That's because in the startup world, returns are distributed according to a power law distribution, where a tiny number of winners get the vast majority of the money. In an analysis of more than 600,000 startups since 2000, just 34 companies—well-known giants such as Facebook, Twitter, LinkedIn, and Uber—accounted for 76% of the total market cap [Van Grove 2014]. If you're at one of these giants you might get rich, but your odds of ending up at such a company are fairly low. If instead you ended up at one of the other startups, even if it were successful, the returns would be small and would mostly go to the investors (see "Equity" on page 451 for more information).

You also shouldn't expect to get rich from your salary. Most early startups pay a lower salary than the market, so if anything, you actually run the risk of making less money by joining a startup. If the company is successful and grows, your salary usually will, too, but rarely enough to make up for several years of being paid less. And don't assume you'll be able to make up for it by getting promoted into senior roles (e.g., CTO, VP) just because you were an early hire. This is because in the early days, you'll be faced with long hours, rapidly changing requirements, and tight deadlines, all of which make it nearly impossible to produce high-quality software. As the company grows, the ad hoc, hacky, legacy system you built will begin to buckle under its own weight, and more "experienced" hires will be brought in to "clean it up." Although it took a heroic effort to build that system and it's the reason those new hires have a job in the first place, it doesn't make a strong case for a high-level position [Church 2012].

In short, joining a startup to get rich is a bad idea. It's not only unlikely to happen, but also a weak motivation. The desire for money will not be enough to get you through the brutally hard work of building a company. If anything, it can actually reduce motivation, as I'll discuss in "Motivation" on page 403.

> *I want to remind you that financial success is not the only goal or the only measure of success. It's easy to get caught up in the heady buzz of making money. You should regard money as fuel for what you really want to do, not as a goal in and of itself. Money is like gas in the car—you need to pay attention or you'll end up on the side of the road—but a well-lived life is not a tour of gas stations!*

—[O'REILLY 2009], TIM O'REILLY, FOUNDER OF O'REILLY MEDIA

JOINING VERSUS FOUNDING A STARTUP

As I've mentioned a few times in this chapter, your startup experience will be different as a founder than as an early employee of a startup. Here's the basic trade-off: as a founder, you will have to make ten times the sacrifice in exchange for a chance at ten times the reward. By sacrifice, I mean you will be faced with an order-of-magnitude more stress, risk, and long hours, and by reward, I mean that in exchange for this pain, you could earn an order-of-magnitude more money and reputation if you succeed. Founding a company is a high-risk, high-reward game, and as most people are not equipped to handle that much risk and the stress that goes with it, most people should not be entrepreneurs, no matter what great ideas they have.

Even if you can handle the stress, there is another factor to consider. I came across it while writing this book and it completely changed the way I thought about founding a company. As a founder, if you get lucky enough to build a successful startup (remember, the odds are roughly one in four), it will take you on average seven to eight years to reach a successful exit (i.e., an acquisition or IPO) [Lennon 2013].[5] Of course, it's really only an "exit" for the investors—the

---

5 For example, consider the age of some of the most successful startups of the last decade at the time of their IPOs or acquisitions: Facebook was 8 [Facebook 2014], Google was 6 [Google 2014], Twitter was 7 [Twitter 2014], LinkedIn was 8 [LinkedIn 2014], WhatsApp was 5 [Hoff 2014], and Zappos was 10 [Zappos 2014].

founders will usually stay on at least a couple years more.[6] So here's the rule of thumb to take away from this: only start a company if you're willing to spend the next decade of your life working on it.

If you're 20 years old, you'll be working on the company until you're 30. If you're 30, you'll do little else until you're in your 40s. When I heard this statistic, I went back to my list of startup ideas and threw half of them away. I realized that many of them were just "get rich quick" schemes at their core, and there was no way I'd be able to spend the next decade toiling away at them.

A successful exit isn't the only reason to found a company—as I've mentioned before, it's one of the worst reasons to do anything related to startups—but so many people see startups as a "get rich quick" scheme that if you take away nothing else from this chapter, remember this: building a startup probably won't make you rich, and if it does, it won't be quick. Success is rare, and when it happens, it takes on the order of a decade.

During that decade, you're going to have to work very hard. Harder than you've worked at anything else in your life. It might be easier than ever to start a company, but making it successful is just as hard as ever. Any founder will tell you that bringing a new product into the market, changing user habits, and hiring the right people all while making ends meet is one of the hardest things you will do in your life.

> *I think the hardest thing is that the success function is very discontinuous. For example, you're trying for months to figure out how to accelerate user growth. You try to introduce some features which you think will help make the metrics go "up and to the right," but nothing really works. For ages, nothing happens. And then, suddenly, some massively successful thing happens totally unexpectedly.*
>
> *Since you have no idea in advance where these discontinuities are going to be, it seems then that the only reasonable behavior is to work really hard. You have a finite length of runway, so if you can maximize the amount of stuff you can get done, that maximizes the chance that you're going to hit that next discontinuity before you die. And if you die before*

---

6 In fact, if a founder tries to leave immediately after an IPO, it will hurt the founder's reputation, the company, and the stock price, so most founders stick around for at least a few more years. As for acquisitions, most of the contracts involve a *cliff* or *vesting period* of one to two years to help transition the company over. The founders only get the financial rewards of the acquisition after this period, so this sort of contract is usually referred to as the *golden handcuffs*.

you get to that next discontinuity, you know that you worked so hard that you couldn't have possibly done anything else to get there faster.

—[KLEPPMANN 2014], MARTIN KLEPPMANN,
CO-FOUNDER OF GO TEST IT AND RAPPORTIVE

Because the success function is very discontinuous, working at a startup, especially as a founder, is a bit like running a marathon with a blindfold on. You know it's a long race, but you can't see the mile markers or a clock, so you have no sense of how far you've gone and you're not even sure if you're running in the right direction—but you can't slow down and take a break—or someone will surely pass you. So you keep chugging along as fast as you can, chasing after that next discontinuity.

For most programmers, joining someone else's startup gets you enough of the benefit with far fewer drawbacks. In fact, rolling the dice on several startups is one of the best ways to have a fun and successful career as a programmer. If you start a company, the odds that it'll be the next Google or Facebook are very low, but as a founder, you're committed, and you'll have to stick with it for 5–10 years to find out. During that same time period, as an employee, you could join three or four different startups for a few years each and significantly increase your chances of finding a successful one.

The 100th engineer at Facebook made far more money than 99% of Silicon Valley entrepreneurs. Small slices of gigantic pies are still themselves gigantic.

—[MOSKOVITZ 2013], DUSTIN MOSKOVITZ, CO-FOUNDER OF FACEBOOK AND ASANA

Just as there are lawyers who chase ambulances, there are engineers in Silicon Valley who chase IPOs and acquisitions. This isn't a bad thing. These engineers hop from pre-IPO company to pre-IPO company and contribute value to each one by building products and helping to scale the organization. In return, they get to develop a wide variety of skills, enjoy the unique culture at each company, accumulate some stock options, and after a few years, they walk away with lots of fun experiences under their belts, and in many cases, a fair bit of money in their pockets.

If you knew which engineers to pay attention to, you could probably get pretty good at predicting which companies will soon have a massive IPO or acquisition. For example, in the last few years, I've watched several friends of mine rotate through LinkedIn, Facebook, and Twitter, joining each company a few years before it had an IPO. How did they know? There are three primary signs. First, look for products you and most people you know are already using. Most developers are *early adopters*, so if a lot of them are flocking to a particular technology, there's a good chance the rest of the world will soon follow. Second, look for companies that have raised a lot of money through multiple rounds of financing. The more money invested, the more the investors will want to see big returns, and the most common way to make that happen is for the company to go public or get acquired. Third, look for companies that are growing at an incredible pace and will need more money to sustain that growth until they become profitable.[7]

If you're more likely to get rich and have fun by joining someone else's startup, is it ever a good idea to start your own? Yes: when you simply can't *not* do it [Moskovtiz 2014]. That is, the best reason to start a startup is because you are so passionate about an idea that you must bring it into the world. You're doing it not for fame or fortune but because it's important enough to you that you are willing to go through all of the pain, risk, and sacrifice to make it happen.

Just make sure not to confuse the dream of accomplishing a specific mission with the dream of building a startup. Sometimes a startup is the best way to accomplish your dream, but in many cases you'd be better off starting a lifestyle business (e.g., a work-from-home consultant), joining someone else's company, or doing research at a university. A startup is just a means to an end [Payne 2013b].

Recap

Do you know the best thing about startups? ... You only ever experience two emotions: euphoria and terror. And I find that lack of sleep enhances them both.

—[HOROWITZ 2014, 21], MARC ANDREESSEN,

CO-FOUNDER OF NETSCAPE, LOUDCLOUD, OPSWARE, AND NING

You've now seen both the light and dark sides of startup life. Startups can be more fun, but they can also be more stressful. You get more autonomy, but you

---

7 A few companies to watch in 2015 and 2016, at least based on their fundraising, growth, and recent developer migration patterns, are Uber, Airbnb, Square, Stripe, Dropbox, Pinterest, PagerDuty, Slack, Zenefits, and GitHub.

also get more drudge work. You could make a huge impact on your career and the world, but you are also very likely to fail. The question is, is a startup right for you?

There is only one way to answer this question: try it. That doesn't mean everyone should go out and start a company, but at least once in your life, just about everyone should work at a startup. And for that matter, everyone should also work at one big, established company. Startups aren't for everyone and big companies aren't for everyone, so it's a good idea to try both to see which one fits you.

> I've worked in large companies and I've worked in small companies. I think it's valuable to go between the two because there are different skills that you have to rely on. In startups, there's this sense of energy, you're doing new things that are resonating with people, changing how they communicate, or travel, or whatever it happens to be. When you're working at larger companies, you need the ability to communicate and think about the perspectives that other people have. But I think sometimes, when you just want to get something done, it's nice to have a bank account with three million dollars and nobody in your way.

—[JACOB 2014], PHILIP JACOB, FOUNDER OF STYLEFEEDER,
SOFTWARE ENGINEER AT STACKDRIVER AND GOOGLE

Perhaps after trying it out, you'll find that startup life is for you. Maybe you'll even be inspired to become an entrepreneur. In some sense, everyone is already an entrepreneur. Adam Smith wrote that every person "becomes in some measure a merchant" [Smith 2003, chap. IV]. You sell your time, knowledge, and resources to others, either to someone else's company or to customers of your own company. The days of working at the same job and climbing a career ladder for many years are over. Self-employment is at record levels [Monaghan 2014] and the peer-to-peer economy is on the rise, powered by startups such as Uber, Sidecar, Lyft, Airbnb, TaskRabbit, Homejoy, and Etsy.

Of course, renting out a room in your house or doing consulting work is not the same as creating a startup, but as self-employment becomes more ubiquitous, it will hopefully make people more accepting of startups and less attached to the false sense of job security of larger companies. You may even realize that the modern notion of a "job" as some entity that floats around and to which you're entitled after college makes no sense. There are no jobs. There are just things you can do that someone else—an employer or a customer—finds valuable enough that they'll pay you for it.

> When you grow up you tend to get told the world is the way it is [...] Try not to bash into the walls too much. Try to have a nice family, have fun, save a little money.
>
> That's a very limited life. Life can be much broader once you discover one simple fact: Everything around you that you call life was made up by people that were no smarter than you and you can change it, you can influence it, you can build your own things that other people can use.
>
> Once you learn that, you'll never be the same again.
>
> —[JOBS 2011], STEVE JOBS

Startup Ideas

Every startup begins with an idea. Google started with the idea that the hyperlinks between web pages are similar to citations between academic papers, and can be ranked the same way. LinkedIn started with the idea that the best way for professionals to find other professionals on the Internet was through a network of people they trust. DropBox started with the idea that there had to be a better way to share files across computers than carrying around a USB memory stick.

When I was getting ready to write this book, I asked a number of friends what startup topics they wanted to know more about. One of the most common questions I got was, "How do entrepreneurs come up with brilliant startup ideas?" Many people think of Steve Jobs, Reid Hoffman, Henry Ford, and Larry Page as possessing a creativity superpower. And like most superpowers, they see creativity as a binary property: either you have it, or you don't.

In this chapter, I hope to convince you that creativity is a skill that can be learned. Like any skill, some people will be better at it than others, but just about anyone can come up with good ideas. To see how, in the first half of this chapter, I'll explore where ideas come from. In the second half of the chapter, I'll describe how to validate that an idea is worth turning into a product.

Where ideas come from

One of the biggest misconceptions about ideas is that they spontaneously pop into your mind, fully formed, as if from thin air. When you think of the process of coming up with great ideas, you might think of a light bulb turning on for the first time in Thomas Edison's workshop, or an apple falling on Isaac Newton's head, or Archimedes yelling "Eureka!" as he lowers himself into a bathtub. While a single eureka moment is a convenient and memorable way to tell a story, it's not how most ideas actually come into the world.

In fact, Archimedes himself never mentions the word "eureka" in his writings—that story comes from Vitruvius, a Roman author who lived nearly 200 years after Archimedes, and most scientists suspect Vitruvius largely made up the whole story [Biello 2006]. Similarly, an apple never actually struck Newton in the head, and he didn't discover the principles of gravity in a single moment but over 20 years of research [Berkun 2010, chap. 1]. And Thomas Edison didn't invent the light bulb (light bulbs had been around for more than 70 years when Edison started working on them) but a filament that made the light bulb commercially viable, and he did it not in a single moment of insight but after more than 6,000 experiments with different filament materials [Alfred 2009].

Ideas don't just magically appear. They grow and evolve, a theme that you will see often throughout this book. And ideas don't grow and evolve from nothing. Just as there is a law of conservation of energy in physics, which states that energy is never created or destroyed but just repurposed into different forms, there is also a law of conservation with ideas: all new ideas are just the result of combining existing ideas. You can think of the information inside of your head as a number of discrete data points. An idea is just the connection between these data points. To create a new idea, you aren't generating new data points out of thin air but just connecting data points that were already there. Instead of thinking of a new idea as a light bulb that pops up above your head, a better metaphor is to think of a new idea as turning on a light bulb to illuminate something that was already there.

Every single new, creative thing that you've ever seen is just a mashup of ideas that came before it. This is beautifully captured in a video series called *Everything is a Remix* by Kirby Ferguson [Ferguson 2010]. For example, Microsoft Windows copied many of its features from the Apple Macintosh, which in turn copied most of its early ideas from the Alto computer at Xerox PARC, which itself was mostly inspired by the NLS computer at the Stanford Research Institute. Almost all the hit songs from the past 40 years—everything from "Let it Be" by The Beatles, to "Don't Stop Believing" by Journey, to "No Woman No Cry" by Bob Marley, to "Under the Bridge" by The Red Hot Chili Peppers, to "Poker Face" by Lady Gaga—are based on the exact same four chords (if you don't believe me, check out "The 4 Chords Song" by the Axis of Awesome (*http://bit.ly/ 4-chord*) for a highly entertaining and eye-opening demonstration). Seventy-four of the top 100 movies of the last decade were sequels, remakes, or adaptations of books, cartoons, or comic books. There are now 11 *Star Trek* movies, 12 *Friday the 13th* movies, and 23 *James Bond* movies. There are even movies like *Transformers:*

Dark Moon, which is the second sequel to a movie based on a cartoon based on a Hasbro toy line based on Japanese toy line. Still with me?

All the great startup ideas mentioned at the beginning of this chapter are also remixes. Google was not the first search engine (there were at least 10 before it, such as Yahoo!, Excite, and AltaVista) and its most important idea, the PageRank algorithm, was based on citation analysis and the field of bibliometrics, both of which had been around since at least the early 60s. LinkedIn was not the first social network (it was heavily inspired by SixDegrees.com and even acquired the Six Degrees Patent [Six Degrees Patent 2013]), nor the first online network for professionals (Ryze, Xing, and Spoke were all founded in the early 2000s), nor the first online job board (Monster and HotJobs were founded in the late 90s), and not even Reid Hoffman's first attempt in the social space (he founded a social network for dating called SocialNet in 1997).

Even the book you're reading now is just a remix of the hundreds of sources in the references and the interviews I had with other startup programmers. This section in particular is a remix, as a lot of it is borrowed from the *Everything is a Remix* video series and the book *Steal Like an Artist*. It's like a self-referential, meta-mashup of a remix.

All of this mixing and copying might seem like a bad thing, but it's not. Modern society has tried to demonize copying by calling it plagiarism, fraud, and counterfeiting, and by discouraging it through things like patents and copyrights, but the truth is that "we are all building with the same materials" [Ferguson 2010] and mash-ups and remixes are the normal way of developing new ideas.[1] That's because creativity boils down to three stages that are all various forms of remixing [Ferguson 2010]:

1. Copy

2. Transform

3. Combine

Copying is always the first thing you do when you're learning a new creative endeavor. Babies learn by imitating adults, artists learn by imitating the masters,

---

1 Actually, patents and copyrights were originally created to *encourage* the spreading of new ideas, but patent law and copyright law have mutated beyond recognition into "intellectual property" laws, which are now doing more to stifle innovation than to help it. See [Ferguson 2010] for more information.

and programmers learn by copying and pasting. Transforming is like copying, but you make some improvements to the original idea, much like Thomas Edison did when he developed a new filament for the light bulb. Combining means taking several existing ideas and putting them together into a whole that is greater than its parts. For example, Gutenberg did not invent the screw press, movable type, ink, or paper, but he was able to put them together into a printing press, which was quite different from the parts that made it up.

Copy, transform, and combine is built deeply into every organism. In fact, that's how you become an organism: your cells copy themselves (mitosis), transform (due to random mutations), and combine (when you reproduce). In a very real sense, you are a mash-up of your mother and your father and all of your ancestors. This doesn't mean that you should try to come up with new ideas by just blindly stealing the work of others, but that the best way to do creative work is to study, credit, remix, mash up, and transform [Kleon 2012, chap. 1].

So if you want to have good startup ideas, you need a whole bunch of ingredients that you can study, credit, remix, mash up, and transform—that is, you need a lot of knowledge.

KNOWLEDGE

The best thing you can do to come up with a lot of new ideas is to learn a lot of old ideas. Because new ideas are just connections between old ideas, the more ideas you have in your head, the more connections you'll be able to create between them.

> *Knowledge and productivity are like compound interest. Given two people of approximately the same ability and one person who works ten percent more than the other, the latter will more than twice outproduce the former.*
>
> **—[HAMMING 1995], RICHARD HAMMING, "YOU AND YOUR RESEARCH"**

If knowledge is like compound interest, then the sooner you invest, the better. Do anything you can to start learning today (reading this book is a good start!), even just a little bit, and it will grow into something bigger than you'd expect. But what should you invest your time in learning? One of the most effective strategies is to try to become a *T-shaped person*:

People who are both generalists (highly skilled at a broad set of valuable things—the top of the T) and also experts (among the best in their field within a narrow discipline—the vertical leg of the T).

—VALVE HANDBOOK FOR NEW EMPLOYEES, 46

Let's look at these in reverse order, first considering experts, and then generalists.

Experts

To become an expert, you have to be intensely, almost obsessively curious about a specific topic. That topic doesn't need to have anything to do with startups or making money—in fact, it's probably better if it doesn't—but just something that fascinates you for its own inherent qualities. The topic should be specific, probably more specific than your major in college. For example, if you studied computer science, you could become an expert in machine learning, distributed systems, or computer graphics, or even fields outside of your major, such as genetics, cognitive psychology, or user interface design. Of course, you don't have to study the topic in college, as you can develop expertise on the side (e.g., become an expert in robotics by building drones as a hobby) or on the job (e.g., become an expert in payment systems by working at a bank).

You need to develop enough expertise to get to the cutting edge of your chosen discipline. This allows you to come up with startup ideas by trying to push on that edge, such as Larry Page building up enough expertise in graph theory, bibliometrics, and the web to be able to push the cutting edge of search technology. Reid Hoffman was able to create LinkedIn because, as an entrepreneur and investor, he had to become an expert in networking, and along the way, he realized that there was an opportunity to enable professional networking on the Internet.

To build expertise, you'll need to do a lot of research, including reading all the top books and papers in your field, studying all of the top companies and products in related industries, subscribing to relevant magazines, blogs, and publications, going to conferences and meetups, and connecting with the experts in the field (or, at the very least, following them on Twitter). You'll also need to do a lot of hands-on practice. This happens naturally if your area of expertise is part of your full-time job, and it's one of the reasons it's a good idea to work for someone else's company before starting your own. If it's not part of your day job, then you'll need to spend some time on side projects, 20% projects, and hackathons (see "Autonomy" on page 406 for more information).

Generalists

Some of the most valuable startups in the world are the result of combining knowledge across several disciplines. For example, by combining an understanding of the human body with an expertise in technology, you get one of the hottest industries today: biotech. For example, several dozen companies are building medical sensors that you can mount on your smartphone, such as AliveCor's electrocardiogram reader, IBGStar's blood glucose meter, and FotoFinder's dermatoscope for skin cancer screening.

To be a generalist, you have to regularly seek out new ideas. Some people are naturally curious about everything and find this easy. If you're not one of them, you might have to make a deliberate effort to get out of your comfort zone and experience a wide variety of literature, movies, travel, and activities. One way to do this is to come up with *top five* lists. For example, you could make a list of all literary genres (e.g., history, psychology, science fiction, math, computer science, biology, etc.) and try to read the five most famous books from each one, or make a list of all school subjects (e.g., math, physics, history, biology, English, etc.) and either try to take a class on the top five topics from each one, or for the ones you don't have time to take, try to read the best textbook on the topic instead.[2] for a list of resources that help you get started with "top five" lists.]

This is a fun approach to expose yourself to a broad range of new ideas. Every time I've done something like this, I've always been struck by how much overlap there is between seemingly unrelated areas of human knowledge. I found the writing advice in *On Writing Well* to be remarkably similar to the clean code advice in *Code Complete*. I learned as much valuable information on how to price products from a psychology book like *Thinking, Fast and Slow* as from any business or economics book I've ever read. I even found my girlfriend's dissertation research on the rise of Communism in 1940s Eastern Europe to be remarkably insightful when trying to understand how startups grow in modern-day Silicon Valley.

The reason for all of this overlap is because most books, movies, and classes are actually about people. Programming books are not about code but about how to write code that people can understand. Psychology books are not about the

---

2 See *http://www.hello-startup.net/resources/startup-ideas*.

brain but about how people think. And sci-fi, fantasy, and horror movies are not about technology or aliens or monsters but about what people may have to do to survive when faced with unusual circumstances. And because all of this knowledge is fundamentally about people, the same core principles come up again and again in many different forms, and therefore, those principles are useful in almost any discipline. It's similar to how almost all athletes practice not only their sport but also strength training and conditioning at the gym, as that develops a broad physical fitness that is useful in any sport. Likewise, by studying not only your own discipline but also a variety of other disciplines, you develop a broad mental fitness that will help you develop a deeper understanding of any area of expertise. The goal, as Steve Jobs said, is to try to "expose yourself to the best things that humans have done" [Denning 2011]. See Chapter 12 for more information on learning.

Once you have a good combination of deep and broad knowledge, you have to turn it into ideas.

GENERATING IDEAS

The words or the language, as they are written or spoken, do not seem to play any role in my mechanism of thought.

—[HADAMARD 2007, APPENDIX II], ALBERT EINSTEIN

Have you ever thought about *how* you generate ideas? This is actually hard to do because creativity just seems to happen. New ideas appear in your consciousness as if by magic, as if there was someone else handing them to you from behind the curtain of your subconscious, and as if this was the one part of your thought process that you had no control over. But it turns out this isn't entirely accurate. In reality, you don't control the vast majority of your thought process.

In his book *The User Illusion*, Tor Nørretranders shows that most of human thought happens at a subconscious level. Obviously, you have no conscious control over many of your basic body functions, such as heart rate, digestion, and hormone levels, but the role of the subconscious goes far beyond that. Many studies have attempted to measure the "bandwidth" of consciousness (i.e., how much information you can process) and the results are typically in the range of 10 to 40 bits per second. By contrast, other studies have measured that the subconscious receives on the order of 11 million bits per second from your sensory organs. In other words, "only one millionth of what our eyes see, our ears hear, and our other senses inform us about appears in our consciousness" [Norretranders 1999, 126]. Because your subconscious decides what information to discard and what to present to your consciousness, that implies that "consciousness cannot initiate an action, but it can decide that it should be carried out" [Norretranders 1999, 243]. In other words, you can't force your mind to have creative thoughts, though you can evaluate those thoughts when you happen to have one. Does that mean you have no influence over creativity?

Not quite. You can't force your subconscious, but you can train and direct it. This might sound strange, but you do it all the time. Every time you learn something new, it starts off as a conscious activity, and after enough practice, it becomes a subconscious activity. For example, when you first learned to drive, it probably took every ounce of your concentration for you to keep the car on the road, to drive within the speed limit, and to remember to use the turn signals. After a few years of practice, all of these actions become automatic, and you're able to drive with ease, listen to the radio, and hold a conversation all at the same time. The same is true of learning to ride a bike, or learning basic arithmetic, or learning to read. By deliberately focusing your consciousness on a particular task, you gradually train your subconscious to do it, and eventually, the subconscious can take over completely. In fact, you've trained your subconscious to read so well that you can't *not* do it. As soon as you look at the words on this page, your subconscious automatically processes them and you hear them in your conscious mind.

Clearly you can teach your subconscious to ride a bike or read text, but how can you teach it to come up with new ideas? To do that, you have to put your subconscious in the right environment for creativity.

ENVIRONMENT FOR CREATIVITY

Throughout history, there have been many instances of *multiple discovery*, when two or more scientists or inventors independently come up with the same idea at roughly the same time, such as Isaac Newton and Gottfried Wilhelm Leibniz publishing the first papers on calculus in the 17th century, Charles Darwin and Alfred Russel Wallace both advancing the theory of evolution in the 19th century, and Elisha Gray and Alexander Graham Bell both filing a patent for the discovery of the telephone on the same day [List of Multiple Discoveries 2015]. These are not coincidences, but an indication that the environment has a massive influence on the emergence of new ideas.

I invented nothing new. I simply assembled the discoveries of other men behind whom were centuries of work. Had I worked fifty or ten or even five

*years before, I would have failed. So it is with every new thing. Progress
happens when all the factors that make for it are ready, and then it is
inevitable. To teach that a comparatively few men are responsible for the
greatest forward steps of mankind is the worst sort of nonsense.*

—HENRY FORD

So what kind of environment encourages new ideas? It varies from person to
person, but here are the most common ingredients:

- Give yourself plenty of time.
- Keep an idea journal.
- Work on the problem.
- Get away from work.
- Add constraints.
- Look for pain points.
- Talk to others.

Give yourself plenty of time

One of the biggest factors in creativity is time. You saw earlier that rather than
instantaneous eureka moments, ideas grow and evolve, sometimes over a long
period of time—such as Newton's ideas on gravity, which took 20 years to
develop. You cannot force creativity and you cannot rush it. If you try, perhaps by
offering external pressure or rewards, you'll actually reduce creativity (see "Motivation" on page 403).

Therefore, above all else, remember to give yourself plenty of time. Incuba-
tion is an essential ingredient in problem solving, so when planning any activity
that involves creativity, make sure to factor in lots of time for letting your subconscious work on problems [Adams 2001, 50].

Keep an idea journal

One of the most ubiquitous techniques used by almost all creative people, from
Leonardo da Vinci to Marie Curie to Thomas Edison to Richard Branson, is to
write down your thoughts in an *idea journal* [Bianchi 2013]. An idea journal is not
the same as a diary. It's not for writing down what you did once per day, but for

jotting down notes, goals, opinions, thoughts, questions, sketches, and observations any time you have them throughout the day. You can use a small notebook and a pen (e.g., a Moleskine), the voice recorder on a smartphone (this is especially effective if your phone has voice control, as you can push one button and say something along the lines of "Siri, take note..."), a mobile note-taking application (e.g., Evernote, Google Docs), email (e.g., send an email to yourself with #thoughts in the subject and add a filter to automatically move emails with that hashtag to a specific folder), or any other mechanism that you always have at hand and is very low friction.

Low friction is probably the most important point. Your goal is to write down just about everything that strikes you as interesting. Anything that makes this harder (e.g., having to go to your office and turn on the computer) will make the idea journal much less effective.

Perhaps the biggest source of friction is your own judgment. Do not judge your ideas at this stage. It doesn't matter if they seem silly, incomplete, or embarrassing—write them down anyway. You're not committing to doing anything about these ideas and you don't have to show them to anyone, so you have nothing to lose by writing them down. But you do have a lot to gain because writing down an idea is a bit like planting a seed. Slowly, over time and with a little bit of luck, it might grow into something bigger. Or maybe it won't, in which case it stays in your idea journal and doesn't bother anyone.

One of the most important factors in having good ideas is having a lot of ideas. The implication here, of course, is that to have more good ideas, you also need to have more bad ideas. This is backed by research, including studies at MIT [Girotra, Terwiesch, and Ulrich 2009] and Carnegie Melon [Chan et al. 2011] that found that the best way to generate exceptional ideas was not to increase the *average* quality of the ideas but to increase the *variance*. That is, you need to generate really wild ideas, including some that are incredibly bad, but also some that are incredibly good. In fact, a UC Davis study [Simonton 2003] found that eminent achievers in science and other disciplines didn't produce higher quality work, on average, but simply more work [Chan 2012].

That's why it's so essential to write down every idea and not judge too early—you want to get comfortable with producing as many ideas as possible, especially those that are wild and unexpected, and not stunt your progress by doubting yourself or discarding ideas.

Someone asked me where I get all my good ideas, explaining that it takes him a month or two to come up with one and I seem to have more than that. I asked him how many bad ideas he has every month. He paused and said, "None."

And there, you see, is the problem.

—SETH GODIN, FOUNDER OF SQUIDOO.COM, AUTHOR [GODIN 2009]

Turning a half-formed thought bouncing around in your head into concrete words on paper will make the thought clearer, and will often lead to new thoughts that you should write down as well. Also, the mere act of writing the idea down will help you remember it better—I've lost many ideas because I was sure that I'd remember them, and a few minutes later they were gone.

Every now and then, go back and review your idea journal. Some of the ideas will seem silly—no big deal, just skip them and keep reading. Some of the ideas will feel foreign, almost as if someone else had written them in your journal and you're seeing them for the first time. But a few will almost always trigger some new thoughts, or remind you of some new information you came across recently, or you'll realize you can combine them with a different idea in your journal. In this way, ideas slowly grow and evolve. If writing down ideas is like planting a seed, then reviewing and updating ideas is a bit like watering or even cross-pollinating the plants. Every time I go back to my idea journal, I'm amazed to see how things have changed—or, I suppose, how *I* have changed—and I always walk away with something new.

Work on the problem

Because ideas come from the subconscious, you need to get your unconscious mind to think about the topic you're interested in. And the best way to do that is spend a lot of time thinking about that topic with your conscious mind:

If you are deeply immersed and committed to a topic, day after day after day, your subconscious has nothing to do but work on your problem. And so you wake up one morning, or on some afternoon, and there's the answer. For those who don't get committed to their current problem, the subconscious goofs off on other things and doesn't produce the big result. So the way to manage yourself is that when you have a real important problem you don't let anything else get the center of your attention—you keep your thoughts on the problem. Keep your subconscious starved so it *has to work on **your** problem, so you can sleep peacefully and get the answer in the morning, free.*

—[HAMMING 1995], RICHARD HAMMING, "YOU AND YOUR RESEARCH"

Work on the problem, learn as much about it as you can, and then give your subconscious mind a chance to do its thing by getting away from work.

Get away from work

One of the things you should write down in your idea journal is not only the idea, but also where you were when you got the idea, and what you were doing. Once you start doing this, you may notice that you don't get your best ideas while at your desk, working. A study at McGill University found that molecular biologists have most of their best ideas when they are away from the lab [Johnson 2011, chap. 2]; Albert Einstein made some of his greatest discoveries during his violin breaks [Suzuki and Suzuki 1993, 90]; many people have their best ideas while in the shower; I do my best thinking while out on a walk.[3]

It seems that the best way to have great ideas is to work on something intensely for a period of time and then to get away from work and let your subconscious work on the problem while you do something fairly relaxing. There are a few reasons why this might be the case. One is that taking regular breaks helps you break your fixation on a single path of thinking and allows you to step back and see the bigger picture [Ariga and Lleras 2011]. Another factor is that the deep concentration and focus you need in order to do work is counterproductive to coming up with new ideas. The brain is most creative when it is relaxed and the frontal lobe, the part you use for analytical thinking and decision making, is largely inactive [Liu et al. 2012].

Make a habit every day of spending at least 20 minutes doing something that relaxes you and lets you listen to your own thoughts. That can be a walk, a long shower, a meditation session, lying in a hammock, writing in a diary, drawing, sculpting, woodworking, or playing music. Whatever it is, have your idea journal handy, and get ready to jot down some notes.

---

3 Studies show that taking a brief walk can significantly improve creativity [Oppezzo and Schwartz 2014].

Add constraints

Try this fun exercise from the book *Made to Stick* [Heath Heath 2007, 119-120]: set a timer for 15 seconds and write down as many things that are white in color as you can think of. Do this exercise before reading any further. I'll wait.

How many did you get?

Now, let's move on to the second part of the exercise. Reset your timer for 15 more seconds, but this time, write down as many white things in your refrigerator as you can think of.

How many did you get this time?

Most people find that they get as many (or more) items in the second part of the exercise as the first. Clearly the number of white things in a refrigerator is a tiny subset of the number of white things in the entire universe, but you probably found the refrigerator exercise easier. This is because constraints breed creativity.

Another great example of this is the book *Not Quite What I Was Planning: Six-Word Memoirs by Writers Famous and Obscure*. The book starts with a tale about Ernest Hemingway and how he was challenged to write a story in just six words. The result:

For sale: baby shoes, never worn.

—ERNEST HEMINGWAY

The book is full of other wonderful stories, in the form of memoirs, that show the remarkable creativity that is possible with just six words:

- *"Born in the desert, still thirsty." —Georgene Nunn*

- *"Cursed with cancer. Blessed with friends." —Nine-year-old cancer survivor*

- *"Well, I thought it was funny." — Stephen Colbert*

—[FERSHLEISER AND SMITH 2008], *NOT QUITE WHAT I WAS PLANNING: SIX-WORD MEMOIRS BY WRITERS FAMOUS AND OBSCURE*

It may seem counterintuitive that reducing your options would increase your ability to come up with creative solutions, but it makes sense when you realize that working memory is much smaller than long-term memory. You might have many thousands of ideas and concepts in your head, but you can only consider a small fraction of them at a time. It's a bit like juggling. A system with no constraints is like trying to keep 100 balls in the air: you can't keep track of them all, you're constantly dropping them, and you spend most of your time picking them up and starting over.

Constraints are especially helpful if you're having trouble coming up with any ideas at all, or if it feels like you're staring at a blank sheet of paper and having trouble getting the first word onto the page. One way to add constraints is to "live in the future, and then build what's missing" [Graham 2012c]. In a talk called "The Future Doesn't Have to Be Incremental" [Kay 2012], Alan Kay described how they "lived in the future" at Xerox PARC, the company that pioneered technologies such as the modern personal computer, the graphical user interface (GUI), ethernet, laser printing, and object-oriented programming. At PARC, the researchers played a game that later became known as the *Wayne Gretzky Game*, named after the greatest hockey player of all time, who attributed much of his success to a simple strategy: "skate to where the puck is going, not where it's been."

The idea behind the *Wayne Gretzky Game* is similar: you want to put the puck way out there, perhaps 30 years or more, so far out that you don't have to worry about how you will get there. You ask yourself a question along the lines of "wouldn't it be ridiculous if, in 30 years, we didn't have...?" For example, when Alan Kay played this game in 1968, he thought it would be ridiculous if people didn't have laptop and tablet computers by the mid-90s. This seemed like a crazy idea in the 60s, when most computers were large boxes with switches (no screens at all, let alone touchscreens, and no keyboards or mice), but the point of the game is you don't have to worry about the implementation details. It's just a way to get big ideas to come into your head. Once you find an idea you like, you can work backward to see what it would take to bring it into the world.

Another way to add constraints is to go in the other direction: look for new enabling technologies that are just starting to appear on the market and try to find a gap between how things *have* been done and how they *can* be done now that these technologies are available [Levie 2014b]. Or, to borrow Reid Hoffman's formulation, you ask yourself, "Is this how the world should be?" [Hoffman 2014]. A great example is the company Plangrid. They noticed that many construction companies were still using paper blueprints, which were expensive to create, print, share, and update. With the emergence of enabling technologies such as tablet computers and wireless Internet, Plangrid realized this isn't how the world should be, and created software to manage blueprints digitally on mobile devices.

Perhaps the easiest way to add constraints is to look for something wrong or painful. Looking for pain points is such a powerful technique that it merits a more detailed look.

Look for pain points

One of the best ways to use your idea journal is not just to take notes when you come up with an idea, but also to jot down anything that irks you, causes pain or unnecessary friction, or just feels wrong. Any time you hear yourself saying the phrase "this is stupid, there has to be a better way" [Al-Qudsi 2011], write it down. In other words, use your idea journal not only for remembering solutions, but also for remembering problems. Any problem that is particularly painful, or frequent, or affects a lot of people is a potential startup idea. Where there is pain, there is opportunity.

The important thing is to write down the problem even if you don't know how to solve it yet. If you see the problem again and again, perhaps in slightly different contexts, and you jot down your thoughts about it each time, your understanding will slowly grow. Eventually, you might get to the heart of the issue and a solution will become obvious. Or, you may accidentally stumble across a solution later on, sometimes much later, and sometimes in totally unrelated circumstances, but you won't be aware it's a solution unless you remember that you had the problem in the first place. Charles Kettering, famed inventor and former head of research at GM, once said that "a problem well stated is a problem half solved."

Learning to identify and fix particularly nasty problems is a valuable skill. In one of Paul Graham's essays, he explains that "schlep"—a Yiddish word for tasks that are particularly tedious and unpleasant—is all around us, but people dislike it so much that they often choose to be totally blind to it. As a result, if you're willing to spot schlep and roll up your sleeves to fix it for everyone else, you can build some very valuable products:

The most striking example I know of schlep blindness is Stripe, or rather Stripe's idea. For over a decade, every hacker who'd ever had to process payments online knew how painful the experience was. Thousands of peo-

ple must have known about this problem. And yet when they started start-ups, they decided to build recipe sites or aggregators for local events. Why? Why work on problems few care much about and no one will pay for when you could fix one of the most important components of the world's infrastructure? Because schlep blindness prevented people from even considering the idea of fixing payments.

—[GRAHAM 2012A], PAUL GRAHAM, CO-FOUNDER OF Y COMBINATOR

Talk to others

Talking about your ideas, questions, or pain points with other people is a powerful tool for creativity. Much like writing your thoughts down, presenting them verbally so another person can understand them helps you understand them better yourself, and sometimes leads to new ideas. I've even found that you don't always need another person there. Sometimes I'll go for a walk and talk to myself, out loud, or even pretend to give a talk to an imaginary audience, and while it makes me look mildly insane, it's also a remarkably effective tactic for generating lots of new ideas (which I furiously scribble in my idea journal mid-stride). In programming, there is even a name for this technique: *rubber duck debugging*. When struggling with a tricky bug, you describe it in full detail to a rubber duck or any other inanimate object. By the time you're done talking, you often know the solution.

If you do have another person there, you benefit from their feedback, questions, corrections, and more generally the fact that no two people have the same information in their heads. One person might know A and B, and another might know C and D, and by combining A and C, or B and D, or A-B-C-D, or some other permutation, a new idea may emerge [Asimov 2014].

With a science like molecular biology, we inevitably have an image in our heads of the scientist alone in the lab, hunched over a microscope, and stumbling across a major new finding. But [Professor Kevin] Dunbar's study showed that those isolated eureka moments were rarities. Instead, most important ideas emerged during regular lab meetings, where a dozen or so researchers would gather and informally present and discuss their latest work. If you looked at a map of idea formation that Dunbar cre-

ated, the ground zero of innovation was not the microscope. It was the conference table.

—[JOHNSON 2011, 224] STEVEN JOHNSON, *WHERE GOOD IDEAS COME FROM*

Even if the other person is not an expert in the topic you're discussing, you can still get just as much value. While I was working on this book about startups, my girlfriend was working on her PhD in Eastern European history. There is little obvious overlap between the topics, but we found remarkable connections between our writing, and found it helpful to regularly discuss our ideas and struggles with each other. Because my girlfriend is not an expert on startups, every time I had to explain my thoughts to her, I found myself using lots of metaphors and analogies, which unlocked lots of creative thoughts in my head. And because historians and programmers think about problems in very different ways, her responses often revealed new perspectives I hadn't considered.

You can discuss your ideas with others over a cup of coffee, by the water cooler, during lunch, while out on a walk, during a meeting, or as part of an official brainstorming session. Try out a few techniques and you'll quickly know which one works best for you, especially if you keep track in your idea journal not only of what ideas you have but also where you got them. You can even share and discuss your ideas with strangers on the Internet. You can post your ideas in blogs, on social media (Twitter, Facebook, LinkedIn), and discussion boards like Reddit and Hacker News. This may even put your ideas in front of potential customers, something we'll discuss more as part of "Validation" on page 48.

But before we get to that, let's discuss the most common objection to discussing your ideas with others: stealth mode.

STEALTH MODE

Before launch, some startups try to run in *stealth mode*, keeping all of their ideas and products completely hidden from the outside world. There are two primary reasons why you might keep your thoughts secret:

- You're afraid other people will laugh at your ideas.
- You're afraid other people will steal your ideas.

The first objection is a fear of criticism. Most of us are taught in school that you need to get the "right" answer on every test, and if you don't, you are punished with bad grades. This teaches most people to be afraid of making any mistakes, to be afraid of sharing any work until it's perfect, and to be afraid of failure. In the startup world, this is the opposite of the mentality you need. As Steve Blank wrote, "If you're afraid to fail in a startup, you're destined to do so" [Blank and Dorf 2012, 33]. Making mistakes is a natural way to learn—in some cases, the only way to learn—and getting feedback is without a doubt the best way to improve your work.

The most successful people I know make a deliberate effort to regularly seek out feedback. They send all of their work in an early and unfinished form to a trusted group of friends. They take each bit of feedback and fold it into the project, making it better, bit by bit. The end result is the collective work of many minds and far better than what any one person could accomplish. To do this, you have to see criticism not as an attack on your character, but as someone taking time to help you improve. You have to learn to not misinterpret "this is stupid" as "you are stupid." And you have to realize that every great essay starts with a rough draft, every great book needs an editor, and every great athlete needs a coach.

> *The trouble with keeping your thoughts secret, though, is that you lose the advantages of discussion. Talking about an idea leads to more ideas. So the optimal plan, if you can manage it, is to have a few trusted friends you can speak openly to. This is not just a way to develop ideas; it's also a good rule of thumb for choosing friends. The people you can say heretical things to without getting jumped on are also the most interesting to know.*
>
> **—[GRAHAM 2004A, 46], PAUL GRAHAM, CO-FOUNDER OF Y COMBINATOR**

The second objection, that someone might steal your ideas, is usually not a legitimate concern. Most people just aren't interested in stealing startup ideas, running off with them, and turning them into companies. They are too lazy, too busy, and most importantly, they just aren't as impressed with or as passionate about the idea as you are. As Howard H. Aiken said, "Don't worry about people stealing your ideas. If your ideas are any good, you'll have to ram them down people's throats." If you don't believe me, then head over to *http://www.hello-startup.net/resources/startup-ideas* to see a list of other people's startup ideas. There are some great ideas there, but browse through them and see how many of them you want to "steal" and turn into a company.

In reality, what attracts competitors is not an idea but *traction* around an idea. It's only after you launch a product and it starts to show success that everyone will try to copy you, so don't worry about discussing your ideas early on. Moreover, if you're worried that someone is going to steal your idea and beat you just from overhearing your idea, then that idea probably wasn't defensible to begin with. By *defensible*, I mean that a good business idea should include some sort of *differentiators* that put a huge distance between you and the competition (see "Focus on the differentiators" on page 133 for more info). For example, compare "I have an idea for a new photo sharing app" to "I have an idea for a low-cost way to launch objects into space" [Srinivasan 2013]. If your idea is not inherently defensible, then even if you're able to keep it a secret until launch, a competitor will still find it easy to copy the idea after your launch and will probably beat you anyway. And no, there's really no such thing as a "first mover advantage" in most industries. The phrase was first popularized in a 1988 paper called "First-Mover Advantages" [Lieberman and Montgomery 1988], but 10 years later, the same authors published another paper called "First-Mover (Dis)advantages" [Lieberman and Montgomery 1998], in which they backed off many of their claims. Moreover, a 1993 study of 500 brands in 50 product categories found that almost half of market pioneers fail and that the mean market share of those that survive is much lower than that found in other studies [Tellis and Golder 1993].

It's also important to understand that a business doesn't consist of just ideas. It consists of ideas and execution. Perhaps someone can steal your idea, but it's a lot harder to steal execution. Let's look into ideas and execution a bit more closely.

IDEA VERSUS EXECUTION

A popular meme in Silicon Valley is that ideas are worthless and execution is everything. This is a false dichotomy. A startup isn't just one idea followed by some completely mindless, repetitive process known as "execution." A startup consists of thousands of repetitions of finding problems, coming up with ideas to solve them, and then executing those ideas:

---

1. Problem: we need an office.

2. Idea: let's rent some office space in Mountain View.

3. Execution: search Google for available office space.

---

1. Problem: office space in Mountain View is crazy expensive.

2. Idea: let's raise some money from investors.

3. Execution: search through LinkedIn contacts for investors.

---

1. Problem: I don't know any investors.

2. Idea: let's find someone who can introduce us.

3. Execution: search for contacts on LinkedIn who know investors.

The "ideas are worthless" meme probably originated as a response to the "business guru" who shows up with a vague idea and believes that alone is a ticket to vast riches. But just as ideas aren't the result of a single eureka moment, startups aren't the result of a single idea, nor a single bit of execution. To be successful, you need a sustained stream of good ideas and efficient execution, and it's pointless to discuss them as separate entities.

It's not an idea, but an idea maze: a thousand decisions along the way, some of which lead to death, some do not. The final product is one successful path through the maze, but doesn't show all the potential failures.

—[SRINIVASAN 2013], BALAJI S. SRINIVASAN, STANFORD STARTUP ENGINEERING CLASS

After you come up with an idea, one of the first steps through the "idea maze" is to try to check if the market thinks your idea is as valuable as you do. This is known as validation.

Validation

One of the fun things about living in Silicon Valley is that someone, somewhere is always testing their ideas on you. When a startup launches its food delivery service, San Francisco is usually the first city with access. When Google tries out its self-driving cars, it launches them in Mountain View. And when I ride on a BART train, total strangers pitch their startup ideas to me. Aaron Levie said it best:

By living in the Bay Area you are basically agreeing to be a beta tester for all the crazy ways we'll live in the future.

—[LEVIE 2014A], AARON LEVIE, CEO AT BOX

All of these folks are trying to do the same thing: *validate* their ideas in the market. That is, they are trying to test that their idea works, that they've identified a real problem, and that they can build a valuable business on top of it. Regardless of how good you think your idea is, how much thought you put into it, and how smart you are, no one can predict if an idea will succeed or not. Venture capitalists, whose entire job is to select the winners, dedicate enormous resources to validating ideas (e.g., hiring experienced entrepreneurs as partners, vetting founders through an extensive referral network, performing due diligence checks) and they still lose money on more than 60% of their investments.[4] If they can't tell which ideas will work and which won't, it's safe to say no one can.

The surprising fact is that companies large and small, established corporate giants as well as brand new startups, fail in 9 out of 10 attempts to launch their new products.

—[BLANK 2013, VII], STEVE BLANK, *THE FOUR STEPS TO THE EPIPHANY*

The road to startup success is paved with failure. Actually, failure isn't the right word. The right way to look at startups and products is as *experiments*. The goal of an experiment is to support or disprove a hypothesis. As a scientist, you cannot fail at an experiment—you can only learn. As Thomas Edison famously said after unsuccessfully testing out thousands of materials as light bulb filaments, "I have not failed. I've just found 10,000 ways that won't work."

Some of the most valuable learning is often from experiments that don't go as planned, such as when Dr. Spencer Silver tried to develop a super-strong adhesive, but instead got one that was fairly weak, though reusable. Instead of seeing it as a failure, Dr. Silver persisted, and a few years later turned it into a product

---

4 Fred Wilson wrote, "Early stage VC is a lot like baseball, if you get a hit one out of every three times, you are headed to the hall of fame." [Wilson 2013]

that would become one of his company's most famous: the 3M Post-it note [About Post-it Brand 2015].

All successful companies leave behind a trail of unsuccessful experiments:

- Google: Wave, Buzz, Labs, Health, Video, Answers, Notebook, Audio Ads
- Facebook: Beacon, Places, Credits, Deals, Questions, Gifts, Lite, Email
- LinkedIn: Answers, Events, Twitter and GitHub integration, Signal
- Virgin: Cola, Clothes, Vodka, Brides, Vie, Cars, Pulse, Wine, Jeans
- Apple: Apple III, Lisa, Macintosh Portable, Newton, eMate, G4 Cube, Ping

Sometimes when a product doesn't work out, the entire company has to change direction, which is known as a *pivot*:

- Instagram started as Burbn, a location-sharing mobile app similar to Four-Square. Photo sharing was just one of the features of the app, but when photos grew in popularity, the company pivoted and launched a new mobile app called Instagram. A few years later, they were acquired by Facebook for $1 billion [Markowitz 2015].
- Groupon was originally a website for political action called The Point. Struggling to make ends meet, CEO Andrew Mason launched Groupon as a side project, and then pivoted the whole company to focus on Groupon when it started to take off. A few years later, Groupon was valued at $12 billion and went public [Penenberg 2012].
- Twitter was originally a podcasting platform called Odeo. The company was struggling and decided to pivot to microblogging. Twitter went public in 2013 at a valuation of around $18 billion [MacMillan Levy 2013].

The unsuccessful products and the pivots are not failures. They are like rough drafts of an essay. It always takes a few revisions until you have something workable, not just with writing but with any non-trivial task in life. There simply is no shortcut that will get you to a good idea without first stumbling over a large number of bad ideas. Of course, in the startup world, you have a limited amount of time and money—typically referred to as the startup's *runway*—so to ultimately be successful, you need to be able to identify bad ideas as quickly as possible. This idea is often called *fail fast*, but as mentioned earlier, I think "fail" is the wrong word, as it makes it seem like failure is the goal and that it's OK to be reckless and sloppy. In reality, learning as quickly as possible is the goal, so I prefer *speed wins*.

SPEED WINS

On one of my very first days working at TripAdvisor, I was running late. I was supposed to meet with the CEO, Stephen Kaufer, for the new hire lunch. I was rushing around and managed to miss his office several times. Finally, a secretary pointed me in the right direction: "Look for the door with a single sheet of paper hanging on it." I ran off in the direction she suggested and eventually saw it. The door to his office had a single A4 sheet of paper with two words scribbled on it. As I got closer, I was able to read it:

Speed Wins.

This was TripAdvisor's mantra, and Kaufer would explain it at lunch that day and at many company all-hands meetings afterward. Startup success, at every level, comes down to speed. You have to build products faster, you have to write code faster, you have to hire faster, and most importantly, you have to learn faster.

Why the massive hurry? Isn't it a better idea to take your time and "do it right"? To answer this question, consider Figure 2-1. In the ideal world, you start with an idea, invest some effort to build a proof of concept, show it to users, find out they love it, invest some more effort to scale out the proof of concept, and eventually you have a stable, successful product.

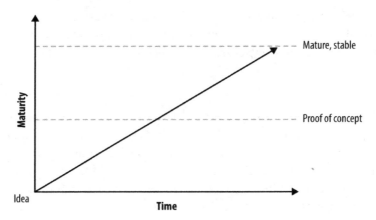

Figure 2-1. Product development (ideal)

Anyone who has ever built a product knows that reality never works out that way. As shown in Figure 2-2, in the real world, you start with an idea, invest some time to build a proof of concept, show it to users, and find out it doesn't work. Now you go back to the drawing board, come up with another idea, build another proof of concept, show it to users, and once again, it doesn't work. You repeat this over and over again, until eventually, if you're lucky, you finally find a product that can actually be successful and is worth scaling.

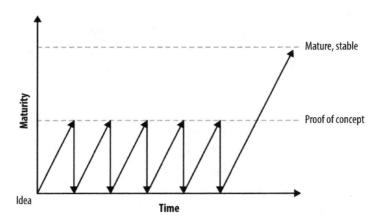

Figure 2-2. Product development (reality)

This means that you spend the vast majority of your time in a trial-and-error phase, as shown in Figure 2-3. In a trial-and-error world, the one who gets to errors the fastest will win.

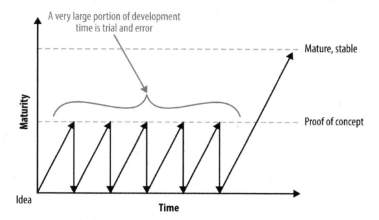

Figure 2-3. Product development (trial and error)

As an example, consider Figure 2-4, which shows hypothetical development timelines for the same project built using a Waterfall methodology versus a Lean or Agile methodology.

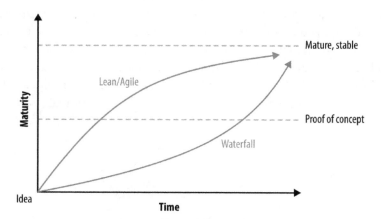

Figure 2-4. Agile/Lean versus Waterfall product development (ideal)

One of the central tenets of the *Lean* and *Agile* methodologies is to get a working product in front of users as quickly as possible, even if the product is far from complete. The *Waterfall* methodology, on the other hand, tries to build a complete solution before it reaches users. In an ideal world, over the long term, the two methodologies would probably take roughly the same amount of time to build a fully scaled, mature product. But in the real world, most projects hit a wall at the "proof of concept" stage, as shown in Figure 2-5.

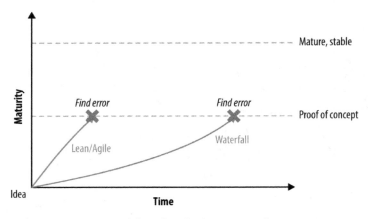

Figure 2-5. Agile/Lean versus Waterfall product development (reality)

Notice that the Agile and Lean methods find errors much earlier in the process, whereas in the Waterfall process, you will have built a much more complete product before realizing it was the wrong thing. This costs a lot of time and money and once you've invested heavily in a product and written a lot of code, it's harder and more demoralizing to throw it away. But you have to throw it away and go back to the drawing board. And not just once, but over and over again, as shown in Figure 2-6. The difference between how long each methodology takes to reach an error—or, more generally, to get feedback from real users—is what speed wins is all about.

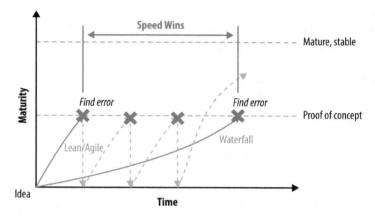

Figure 2-6. Agile/Lean versus Waterfall product development (speed wins)

Although I like to use the phrase *speed wins* because it's short and memorable, it's probably more accurate to say that *frequency wins*. It's not about one person magically doing the same amount of work in half the time. It's about organizing the work so that you can get feedback sooner. This is because systems with shorter feedback loops almost always beat systems with longer ones. For example, faster feedback loops improve your value curve: many customers will be willing to pay more for a product you can deliver in a month than one you deliver to them in a year (a dollar today is worth more than a dollar tomorrow). Faster feedback loops improve your risk curve: it's easier to get people to buy into a project where you will turn the unknowns into knowns a month from now than a project where you will have to keep pumping money into it for five years before you have any idea if it will work. And faster feedback loops improve your code: it's cheaper and easier to fix a bug you introduced five minutes ago and found immediately through an automated test (see "Automated Tests" on page 296) than a bug you introduced five months ago and found because a customer complained about it.

The benefits of faster feedback loops show up outside of software as well. For example, US Air Force Colonel John Boyd identified the same principle in dog fights between the Russian MiG-15 and the American F-86 fighter planes. Although the MiG-15 was a better aircraft (it could climb faster, turn faster, and had better distance visibility), the F-86 could beat it 9 times out of 10. The reason was that the F-86 had a hydraulic flight stick, whereas the MiG-15 had a manual flight stick, so it took slightly more energy to control the MiG-15 than the F-86. In a dog fight, both pilots are constantly going through a sequence called OOPA (observe, orient, plan, act), and the hydraulic controls of the F-86 lets its pilot go through OOPA just a little bit faster.

> Boyd decided that the primary determinant to winning dogfights was not observing, orienting, planning, or acting better. The primary determinant to winning dogfights was observing, orienting, planning, and acting faster. Speed of iteration, Boyd suggested, beats quality of iteration.

—[SESSIONS 2006], ROGER SESSIONS

That last sentence is *Boyd's Law*: speed of iteration beats quality of iteration. It's a surprising law, but it makes sense when you're dealing with complicated, unpredictable, and often chaotic systems. It's a bit like investing: your odds of success are higher with a diversified portfolio in which you make many small bets across a variety of stocks than if you put all your eggs in one basket by betting all your money on a single stock.

Here's the fundamental idea behind Boyd's Law, speed wins, Agile, and Lean: some of your assumptions are wrong. The problem is, you don't know which ones.[5] You might be building the wrong thing, marketing it to the wrong audience, or have the wrong business model. To build a successful product, you have to identify where you're wrong and fix it. And because everything changes rapidly in the startup world, you have to repeat the identify-and-fix process continuously.

> You know that old saw about a plane flying from California to Hawaii being off course 99% of the time—but constantly correcting? The same is true of successful startups—except they may start out heading toward Alaska.

—[WILLIAMS 2005], EVAN WILLIAMS, FOUNDER OF BLOGGER, TWITTER, AND MEDIUM

If you had infinite time and budget, you could build a product in any order and at any rate. But startups in the real world have a limited runway so it becomes a game of trying to test the riskiest, most fundamental assumptions as quickly and as cheaply as possible. Do not misinterpret this as an excuse for cutting corners, cowboy coding, ignoring all best practices, shipping mediocre

---

5 John Wanamaker, known as the father of modern advertising, once said: "I know that half of my advertising dollars are wasted. I just don't know which half."

products, or building hacks on top of kludges on top of jury-rigged masses of duct tape and gum. There are times when you'll need to take shortcuts, but the shortcuts are not the goal. The goal is to identify experiments that give you the most learning for the least cost.

For some products, the minimum experiment will require a fairly polished experience. For others, something bare-bones may suffice. And in some cases, you don't need to build a product at all, as we'll discuss in "The MVP" on page 125. As a general rule, err on the side of "done is better than perfect." Or, as Reid Hoffman put it, "if you're not embarrassed by your first release, you've launched too late." That said, there are a few places where speed does not win. Any time you're dealing with legal concerns, security, privacy, or money, take your time and err on the side of "measure twice, cut once."

So here's what we've learned so far: most of your ideas won't work, most of your assumptions are wrong, you're in a constant race against time, and 9 out of 10 products fail. The odds are stacked against you, but there is something you can do to improve your chances: customer development.

CUSTOMER DEVELOPMENT

The classic way to develop products is to lock your developers, product managers, and designers in a building, give them a year to work, and when they are done, try to sell the product to customers. The problem, as you saw earlier, is that many of your assumptions are wrong, so the end result of such a product development process is unlikely to be successful. And the assumption that is wrong most often is usually not about how to build the product or what technology to use, but that there are customers who want the product in the first place. A study by CB Insights of over 100 startup postmortems showed that the number-one reason for startup failure, by a large margin, was "no market need" [The Top 20 Reasons Startups Fail 2014].

In *Four Steps to the Epiphany*, Steve Blank describes a process called *customer development* that you should run in parallel with the product development process. Instead of waiting until the product is done to see if there are any customers for it, you involve customers in the development process from day one. This way, you can continuously test your assumptions and get rapid feedback on each stage of development. Although it's tempting to spend all your time on product and technology, especially if you're a programmer, the only way to be sure that your efforts are not in vain is to spend some time with customers.

In a startup no facts exist inside the building, only opinions.

—[BLANK 2013, 9], STEVE BLANK, *THE FOUR STEPS TO THE EPIPHANY*

Customer validation is about recognizing that your product ideas are just unproven hypotheses that need to be tested as quickly and cheaply as possible with real customers. The sooner you start validating your ideas with people who are not your coworkers, the better your chances of success. How you find customers and how you talk to them can be broken down into three sequential stages:[6]

Step 1: Validate the problem
> Make sure you've identified a problem that customers actually have and that the problem is painful enough that they are willing to pay to solve it.

Step 2: Validate the MVP
> Build a minimum viable product (MVP) of a potential solution and validate it by getting a small number of customers to buy it.

Step 3: Validate the product
> Grow the MVP into a full product and validate that you have a scalable business by getting a much larger number of customers to buy it.

Note that you might have to repeat each of these steps multiple times or even go back to previous steps. For example, it might take you many tries to find a real problem. Once you've found one, it might take you many more tries to build a prototype that customers are willing to buy. Sometimes none of the prototypes will work and you'll have to find a new problem to solve. Similarly, you might have to try many things to scale your prototype into a product, and occasionally you'll find that your prototype works but the business model doesn't scale, and you'll have to go back to a previous step.

For the rest of this chapter, I'll dive a little deeper into how you can validate the problem. In Chapter 3, I'll talk about how you design an MVP around your idea. Finally, in Chapter 4, I will talk about using data and distribution to scale the MVP into a full product.

---

6 This is a simplified version of the customer development process Steve Blank describes in his book *The Four Steps to the Epiphany.*

VALIDATE THE PROBLEM

A remarkable number of products turn out to be solutions in search of a problem. The Segway and Google Wave are two famous examples, but a more subtle one comes from a startup called Patient Communicator, which created an online portal where patients could get in touch with doctors and doctors could manage patient information. If you've ever waited in line for a long time to see a doctor, especially if all you had was a trivial question, this feels like a real problem. We might phrase the problem as "doctors don't have an efficient way to manage patient communication and information." However, the founder of Patient Communicator, Jeff Novich, learned the hard way that this wasn't a real problem:

> The sum total of our efforts—which included hundreds of cold calls, tens of thousands of emails (I was invited to a "top 20 customers" dinner with TK from Tout), seminars, an appearance on FOX News Live, ads, reaching out to our personal networks as well as the Blueprint Health mentor network—was one paying doctor (who later went out of business) and a handshake deal to partner with a small 20-year-old EMR.

—[NOVICH 2013], JEFF NOVICH, FOUNDER OF PATIENT COMMUNICATOR

Novich lists several reasons the company failed, including one I found particularly revealing: "doctors want more patients, not an efficient office" [Novich 2013]. This seems like a subtle difference, as a more efficient office could lead to more patients, but focusing on the wrong problem leads the entire company astray.

For example, consider the dental industry. For years, it focused on products and marketing about "fighting gum disease" and "preventing tooth decay," until some marketing genius realized that the problem customers actually cared about was *how to get white teeth and fresh breath*. Sure, fighting off gum disease and tooth decay could lead to white teeth and fresh breath, but focusing on the wrong problem means all the products, marketing strategies, and sales materials are wrong. If you focus on tooth decay, you probably don't come up with profitable product ideas like tooth whitening strips, breath mints, mouthwash, and 3D whitening toothpaste (whatever that is). This is why you need to validate that you've identified the right problem before running off and solving it. As Harvard Business School marketing professor Theodore Levitt put it, "People don't want to buy a quarter-inch drill. They want a quarter-inch hole!" [Christensen, Cook, and Hall 2006].

It's also important to validate that the problem you've identified is big enough to warrant building a startup around it. There are three aspects to consider when thinking about the size of a problem: frequency, density, and pain.

Frequency: Does the problem you're solving occur often?
Density: Do a lot of people face this problem?
Pain: Is the problem just an annoyance, or something you absolutely must resolve?

—[KUMAR 2015], MANU KUMAR, K9 VENTURES

For example, consider Facebook and LinkedIn. Facebook scores very high for frequency (you might use it multiple times per day to communicate with friends and family) and density (just about everyone with an Internet connection uses it), but a lot lower on pain (there are many other ways to communicate with friends and family, such as in person, via a phone call, text message, IM, blog post, Skype, Twitter, Snapchat, etc.). On the other hand, LinkedIn scores low for frequency (you don't need to update your profile, look for a job, or network that often), medium for density (all professionals can use it), and high for pain (there aren't too many better ways to find a job, find a candidate, or get in touch with a colleague).

Not all products are as obvious as Facebook and LinkedIn, and to be fair, the potential size of these social networks was not obvious in their early days either, so you'll have to do some market sizing to estimate the size of a problem.

Market sizing

The size of the market determines how much money you can make—and therefore how much money you can raise, how big your company can get, what kind of products you can build, what kind of strategies you can use for sales and marketing, and a number of other factors. A good way to think about market size is to consider the different ways you could build a company that makes $1 billion in revenue:

- *Sell product at $1 to 1 billion: Coca-Cola (cans of soda)*

- *$10 to 100 million: Johnson & Johnson (household products)*

- *$100 to 10 million: Blizzard (World of Warcraft)*

- *$1,000 to 1 million: Lenovo (laptops)*

- *$10,000 to 100,000: Toyota (cars)*

- *$100,000 to 10,000: Oracle (enterprise software)*

- *$1,000,000 to 1,000: Countrywide (high-end mortgages)*

—[SRINIVASAN 2013], BALAJI S. SRINIVASAN, STANFORD STARTUP ENGINEERING CLASS

For example, if you have an idea for a product that costs around $10, then to build a startup around it that can scale to $1 billion in revenue, you need a market that has at least 100 million people in it (or more, as you'll probably share the market with competitors), and a lot of capital up front (because you make relatively little money per sale and it takes a long time for a product to reach an audience of millions); in addition, you need to devise a marketing strategy that can reach this huge audience, such as advertising. On the other hand, if you have an idea for a product that costs $100,000, then you're looking for a market of at least 10,000 customers; you might be able to bootstrap the business off of a small number of early customers, and instead of advertising, you might need to focus much more on building a massive sales team.

The following list summarizes different ways to estimate the size of the market (the full list of market-sizing resources can be found at *http://www.hello-startup.net/resources/idea-validation/*):

Advertising

Many advertising companies offer ad-targeting tools that you can use to research the market without actually paying for any ads (although buying ads can be a good way to test your MVP, which we discuss in "The MVP" on page 125). For example, you can use the Google AdWords Keyword Planner to research how many searches there are per month for specific terms. When doing research for hello-startup.net, I looked up about 50 relevant keyword groups (e.g., "startup ideas," "code review tools," "equity calculator") and found that they averaged more than 12 million searches per month. This gave me confidence that "how do I build a startup?" is a real problem. It also helped me hone the language on the resource pages. For instance, I found that "business ideas" was a common synonym people used for "startup ideas." I also used the ad tools from several other companies and found that there are roughly 16 million people interested in startups on Facebook, 2 million people interested in startups on Twitter, and 13 million people who list entrepreneurship as their industry on LinkedIn.

Competition

If there are already companies solving this problem, it's not necessarily a bad thing. If anything, the fact that your idea isn't unique is validation that you've found a real problem. To find a list of competitors, use the advertising tools just described to find the right keywords and try to search Google and the mobile app stores to track them down (it shouldn't be too hard, or their customers won't be able to find them either, in which case, you don't have to worry about them). To see how a specific competitor is doing, you can try website analytics tools (e.g., comScore, Quantcast) and mobile analytics tools (e.g., App Annie, Xyo) to estimate their traffic. You can also see how much funding the competitors have and what investors are backing them using websites like CrunchBase and AngelList.

For example, when I was considering turning hello-startup.net into a mobile app, I did some research on competitors. Through Google, I found several other apps that contained startup resources, such as Elevatr, Tech Startup Genius, and Crazy About Startups. From Xyo, it looked like none of these apps had much traction, with Elevatr in the lead at around 17,000 installs. I also searched for other companion apps for books and found several with more traction, such as an app for George R.R. Martin's *A World of Ice and Fire* (free; 420,000 installs) and an app for Mark Bittman's *How to Cook Everything* ($5; 230,000 installs). This information gave me a ballpark range for how many installs this sort of app could get (from the low thousands up to several hundred thousand) and even different pricing models (free or $5).

Community

Another good way to validate problems is to see if there is already a community of people talking about them. You can search for meetups, conferences, user groups, and online forums to estimate how many people this problem affects. For example, while researching hello-startup.net, I looked on Meetup.com and found 15,000 entrepreneurship groups (4 million members), 3,000 tech startup groups (1 million members), and 2,200 Lean startup groups (650,000 members). On Lanyrd, I found 119 startup conferences and submitted proposals to a few so I could actually talk with the people in these communities. I also found the startups subreddit (roughly 74,000 members), startup and entrepreneurship groups on LinkedIn (roughly 150,000 members), startup topics on Quora (roughly 800,000 followers), and, of course, there's Hacker News (at least 120,000 unique users per day reading about startups).

Market research and reports

Some good old-fashioned research is always worth the effort. Search online for newspapers, books, journals, classes, podcasts, and blogs that discuss your topic. When relevant, you can also look up SEC filings and government reports (e.g., from the US Small Business Administration). During my hello-startup.net research, I found hundreds of blogs that focus on startups (e.g., Paul Graham's Essays, TechCrunch, OnStartups), dozens of books (e.g., *Founders at Work*, *The Lean Startup*, *The Startup Owner's Manual*), and several courses (e.g., Stanford's *How to Start a Startup* and Coursera's *Startup Engineering*).

There are also a number of companies that specialize in gathering data and publishing reports on specific industry topics. Some of the data is free, such as the World Bank Data. For the rest, you can pay a company such as Nielsen Media Research to do market research for you or a company like AYTM to send out surveys to targeted audiences on your behalf.

Product data

If your product is already live, there are many metrics you can gather and analyze to estimate the impact of a new feature. See Chapter 4 for more info.

This list is not comprehensive, but it should be enough to get you started so that you can do some back-of-the-envelope calculations to estimate the size of the market. Once you've identified a problem of a reasonable size, the next step in the validation process is to identify a small number of customers who have that problem and talk to them in person.

Talking to real customers

When you talk to customers, your goal is to learn everything you can about their day-to-day lives and determine the following:

- Is this a real problem for the customer?

- What possible solutions are there to the problem?

- How much is the customer willing to pay to solve the problem?

To answer these questions, you have to "get out of the building" and talk to real customers. However, there's a catch: it's not always effective to directly ask customers what they want. Some customers have no idea what they want. Some customers know what they want, but they tell you they want X even though they actually want Y. Sometimes this is because customers don't want to hurt your feelings, so they tell you they like your product even though they know they'd never actually buy it. Sometimes it's because the customers have an incentive not to tell you the truth, such as not telling you how much money they are willing to pay for a product. Sometimes it's because customers aren't even aware of their own preferences.

> *If I asked all of you, for example, in this room, what you want in a coffee, you know what you'd say? Every one of you would say, "I want a dark, rich, hearty roast." It's what people always say when you ask them what they want in a coffee. What do you like? Dark, rich, hearty roast! What percentage of you actually like a dark, rich, hearty roast? According to [Howard Moskowitz's research], somewhere between 25 and 27 percent of you. Most of you like milky, weak coffee. But you will never, ever say to someone who asks you what you want that "I want a milky, weak coffee."*

—[GLADWELL 2004], MALCOM GLADWELL, *CHOICE, HAPPINESS AND SPAGHETTI SAUCE*

Even if the customer is fully aware of their own needs and even if they are willing to be honest with you, most of the time they still won't be able to help you find a good solution, as customers usually only think in terms of 10% better, faster, and cheaper [Kawasaki 2011]. Many customers will ask you for specific features, but your goal is not to walk away with a long feature list. Small incremental improvements and slightly better features rarely make for good startup ideas, as we'll discuss in "Focus on the differentiators" on page 133, so your real goal is to get a deep understanding of the underlying problem.

If I had asked people what they wanted, they would have said faster horses.

—HENRY FORD

To get to the underlying problem, you'll have to do a lot more listening and observing instead of talking. Don't push your ideas on the customer or try to convince them. Instead, try to get them to do as much of the talking as possible. A classic technique you can use, pioneered by Toyota founder Sakichi Toyoda, is the *five whys*. This technique is best illustrated with an example. Imagine you're the owner of a trucking company and one of your employees, Bob, tells you that his truck won't start. Instead of jumping straight to a solution, you repeatedly ask "why" to get to the root cause:

Bob: The truck won't start.

You: Why?

Bob: The battery died.

You: Why?

Bob: (Investigates) Looks like the alternator isn't working.

You: Why?

Bob: (Investigates) The alternator belt broke.

You: Why?

Bob: (Investigates) The alternator belt is really old and should have been replaced a long time ago.

You: Why?

Bob: I guess we haven't been maintaining the vehicle according to the proper maintenance schedule.

If you solved the first problem you heard, that the truck won't start, your solution would've probably been to replace the truck or the battery, which would only be treating a symptom. By asking the five whys, you're able to uncover the underlying problem: lack of a proper maintenance schedule for the trucks in your fleet. It doesn't always take exactly five whys to get to the root cause, but you should almost always ask why at least once to make sure you're identifying the real problem.

After a number of customer conversations, you should have a better understanding of what the real problems are. Before jumping in and building a solution, there is one final quality you must check for: feasibility.

Feasibility

There are two facets to whether a problem is feasible:

- The problem can be solved.
- The problem can be solved by you.

The first question is about market realities. It combines the market sizing and problem validation from earlier in this chapter with a reality check of whether the technologies you need to solve this problem exist and if the economics of the solution work to create a profitable business. The partners at Sequoia Capital, one of the most successful venture capital firms in the world, ask founders the following question: "Why now?" [Calacanis 2013]. What has changed in the world that now is the perfect time to build this company? What do you know that other people don't? Why didn't somebody build this company two years ago and why will building it two years from now be too late?

For example, Webvan was an online grocery store that became one of the most famous dot-com flops when it went bankrupt in 2001, after having burned through more than $800 million by building warehouses and buying its own fleet of delivery trucks. Today, many new grocery delivery startups are appearing, such as Instacart and Postmates, and they seem to be doing better than Webvan. Their "why now?" story includes the fact that consumers are far more accustomed to ordering things online today than 15 years ago, and the recent advent of smartphones, wireless data, and GPS connectivity makes it possible to build a delivery fleet on top of drivers using their personal vehicles and to build an inventory on top of existing grocery suppliers.

If the problem can be solved, the next feasibility check is if you are the right person to solve it. Part of this has to do with your personal assets, including not only financial resources (e.g., cash and property), but also your skills, knowledge, and connections. This is yet another reason why domain expertise is so essential. Another important aspect is whether this is an idea you really care about. As I mentioned in Chapter 1, building a successful startup will take on the order of 10 years, and requires an enormous amount of hard work and sacrifice, so you not only need to find a problem you can solve but also one you're willing to spend the next decade of your life solving.

Recap

On May 24, 2000, Timothy Gowers gave a talk called "The Importance of Mathematics" at the Millennium Meeting of the Clay Mathematics Institute. Gowers described the famous Cambridge mathematician G. H. Hardy, who was "perfectly content, indeed almost proud, that his chosen field, number theory, had no applications, either then or in the foreseeable future—for him, the main criterion of mathematical worth was beauty" [Gowers 2000]. Many mathematicians prefer to study problems for their inherent beauty rather than any practical benefit they may have. Despite that, mathematics has been the basis for countless discoveries of immense practical value: physicists, chemists, engineers, programmers, and countless others use math on a daily basis to build all the tools and technology of modern society. Often, the more beautiful the math, the more useful it turns out to be in the real world. Even number theory, which seems purely like math for the sake of math, turns out to have many practical applications, including RSA encryption, which is the reason you can exchange information such as passwords and credit cards securely on the Internet. G.H. Hardy would've been disappointed.

All the concepts of mathematics are deeply interconnected, often in unpredictable ways. Gowers argued that there is simply no way to know which parts of math will turn out to be useful in the real world and which ones won't, as shown in Figure 2-7. Therefore, the best we can do is to encourage studying any and all math, even if (or especially if) the initial motivation is the pursuit of beauty rather than practicality.

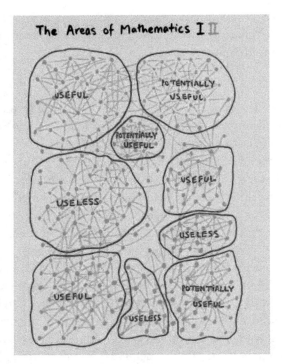

Figure 2-7. Gower's diagram of mathematical knowledge [Gowers 2000]; there is no way to separate the "useful" and the "useless"

The world of ideas is similar: there is simply no way to predict what knowledge will lead to useful ideas and what won't. The best you can do is to learn as much as you can, especially about topics you find beautiful. In other words, "the way to get startup ideas is not to try to think of startup ideas" [Graham 2014], but to turn yourself into a person who has startup ideas. Find a topic you find fascinating and spend a lot of time thinking about it. Write down your thoughts in an idea journal and share them with others. Use constraints, look for pain points, go on lots of walks, and give your subconscious plenty of time to work on what you've learned. Eventually, an idea will sprout.

At this stage, the idea is still fragile. Be careful not to squash it by judging the idea too quickly. Just as you can't predict which mathematical ideas will be important, you also can't predict which of your ideas will grow into something bigger in the future. Larry Page didn't know how big of an idea he had with Google, as back in 1997 he tried to sell the company to Excite for $1.6 million (today, Google is worth around $400 billion) [Carlson 2014]. None of the programmers I interviewed for this book had any idea of how big their startups would become. Neither did any of the founders Jessica Livingston interviewed for the book *Founders at Work*, including Max Levchin (Paypal), Caterina Fake (Flickr), Craig Newmark (Craigslist), and Steve Wozniak (Apple):

> *What surprised me most was how unsure the founders seemed to be that they were actually onto something big. Some of these companies got started almost by accident. The world thinks of startup founders as having some kind of superhuman confidence, but a lot of them were uncertain at first about starting a company. What they weren't uncertain about was making something good—or trying to fix something broken.*
>
> **—[LIVINGSTON 2009, XVII], JESSICA LIVINGSTON, *FOUNDERS AT WORK***

When one of your ideas finally grows into something exciting, validate it before jumping in and building it. Use market research tools to estimate the size of the market. If it looks promising, get out of the building, talk to real customers, and find at least 10 people who will buy your product. It may seem like a silly exercise, especially if you have an idea for a product that will reach millions of customers, but if you can't get those first 10 people to say they'll buy it, your idea is bullshit [Cohen 2010]. If you find your first 10 customers and you've validated that your idea is feasible (Why now? Why you?), then it's time to turn it into a product, which is the topic of Chapter 3.

> *Creativity is not a talent. It is a way of operating.*
>
> **—[CLEESE 1991], JOHN CLEESE**

Product Design

In the previous chapter, you saw how to come up with startup ideas. In this chapter, I'm going to discuss how to design a product around those ideas. In the first half, I'll explain why design is an essential skill for any profession and introduce a number of tools and techniques that everyone should know. In the second half of the chapter, I'll focus on the product design process at a startup, which is all about building a minimum viable product (MVP).

Design

As far as the customer is concerned, the interface is the product.

—[RASKIN 2000, 5], JEFF RASKIN, *THE HUMANE INTERFACE*

For someone browsing the web, Google is a text box and a page of results, and not the bots that crawl the web, the algorithm to rank pages, or the hundreds of thousands of servers in multiple data centers around the world. For someone who needs a ride, Uber is a button on their phone they can push to order a car, and not the real-time dispatch system, the payment processing systems, or all the effort that goes into recruiting drivers and fighting with regulators. And for someone using a smartphone, the iPhone consists of the parts they can see (e.g., the screen), hear (e.g., a caller's voice), and touch (e.g., a button), and not the GSM, WiFi, and GPS radios, the multi-core CPU, the operating system, the supply chain that provides the parts, or the factories in China that assemble them. To a customer, the design of the product is all that matters.

Joel Spolsky called this *The Iceberg Secret*. Just as the part of the iceberg that you can see above the water represents only 10% of its total size, the part of a product that you can see and touch—the user interface—represents only 10% of the work. The secret is that *most people don't understand this* [Spolsky 2002].

When they see a user interface that looks crappy, they assume everything about the product is crappy. If you're doing a demo to a potential customer, above all else you must have a polished presentation. You can't ask them to imagine how it would look and just focus on the "functionality." If the pixels on the screen look terrible, the default assumption is that the product must be terrible, too.

You might think the Iceberg Secret doesn't apply to programmers, but no one is immune. I prefer iPhone to Android, open source projects with beautiful documentation pages to those with plain-text readmes, and blog posts on Medium to those on Blogger. It's almost as if we're all hard wired to judge a book by its cover. But product design isn't just the cover. It's also how it's printed, the title, the praise on the back, the typography, the layout, and even the text itself.

Most people make the mistake of thinking design is what it looks like. People think it's this veneer—that the designers are handed this box and told, **Make it look good!** *That's not what we think design is. It's not just what it looks like and feels like. Design is how it works.*

—[WALKER 2003], STEVE JOBS

Design is how it works. Yes, the iPhone is prettier than most other smartphones, and that counts for something, but it's more than just a question of style. The sharp screen, the fonts, and the layout make it easier to read the text. The buttons are big and easy to use. The touchscreen is precise and the UI is fast and responsive. The phone tries to anticipate your needs, dimming the screen automatically in response to the amount of ambient light, or shutting off the screen entirely when you hold the phone to your ear. You don't have to think about it or fight with it—it "just works." And while other smartphones may have caught up in terms of features and price, they still can't match the experience. This is why Apple invests so heavily in design, and not coincidentally, this is why it's the most valuable company in the world.

Design is a useful skill even if you aren't building a product and even if the word "designer" is not part of your job title. Everybody uses design all the time. You use design every time you create a slide deck for a presentation, format your résumé, build a personal home page, arrange the furniture in your living room, plan out the syllabus for a class, or come up with the architecture for a software system. Design is fundamentally about how to present information so other people can understand it and use it. Given that much of success in life comes down to how well you communicate, it's remarkable just how little design training most people get as part of their education.

Due to my lack of training, I used to think of design and art ability as something you either had or you didn't. My own artistic abilities were limited to drawing stick figures all over my notebooks, so clearly I didn't have that ability. It took me a long time to realize that design and art are both skills that can be learned through an iterative process.

DESIGN IS ITERATIVE

A few years ago, I took an art class with my sister. The art teacher was a family friend, and he would come over to our house and have us paint still lifes and skylines using pencils and water colors. One day, I was working on a fruit still life and struggling to paint an orange. The best I could do was a bland blotch of orange paint in a vaguely circular shape. The teacher noticed I was frustrated and asked me, "What color is an orange?" Not sure if it was a trick question, I replied, "Orange?" The art teacher smiled and said, "What else?" I stared at the piece of fruit for a minute and said, "I guess there's a little white and yellow where the light hits the skin." Still smiling, the art teacher said, "Good. And what else?" I stared at the fruit some more. "And nothing else. It's a goddamn orange. All I see is orange and various shades of orange."

The art teacher leaned over, took the brush from my hands, and began making some changes to my painting. As he worked, he explained what he was doing. "A spherical shape will have a highlight, which we can paint in white and yellow, and some shadows, which can be red, brown, and green. The orange also casts a shadow to the side, so let's use gray and blue for that, and add in some brown and sienna to separate the edge of the orange from the shadow it casts" (see Figure 3-1).

Figure 3-1. How to paint an orange (image courtesy of Charlene McGill (http://www.charmin gart.org/))

I stared back and forth between the canvas and the actual fruit. An orange isn't orange. It's orange, yellow, white, red, brown, sienna, green, and blue. After a little while, I had a few realizations:

- Art involves many concrete tools and techniques that can be learned. The art teacher knew all the ingredients of how to paint something spherical, almost like a recipe: you take several cups of base color, mix in a tablespoon of shadow, add a pinch of highlight, stir, and you have a sphere.

- The representation of an orange in my head is different from what the orange looks like in the real world, but I'm unaware of all the missing details until I try to reproduce the image of an orange on canvas.

- Similarly, the representation of an orange on a canvas is different from what an orange looks like in the real world. This difference is usually intentional because the goal of art is not to create a photocopy of something in the real world but to present it in a specific way that makes you think or feel something.[1]

I'm still not much of an artist, but understanding the mindset of an artist has made me realize that artistic talent is a skill that can be improved by practicing, by training your eye to deliberately observe why something looks the way it does, and by recognizing that the goal of art is to communicate something to the viewer. These same three principles apply to design:

- Design is a skill that can be learned.
- You have to train your eye to consciously recognize why some designs work and others do not.
- The goal of design is to communicate something to the user.

I hope to convince you of all three points in this chapter. The most important thing to keep in mind about the first point is that design is an iterative, incremental process. Your first draft will be awful, but the only way to come up with a good design, and the only way to become a good designer, is to keep iterating. What makes this particularly challenging is that during your life, you've developed a sense of taste from having seen thousands of products created by professional designers, and there is no way your early design work will match up. It's like a music lover who has spent years listening to the beautiful violin concertos of Mozart and Bach, who dreams of playing at Carnegie Hall, and who finally picks up the violin for the first time, excitedly draws the bow across the strings, and is horrified by the screeching sounds that come out. *Everyone* who does creative work goes through a phase where their work does not satisfy their own taste. This is completely normal and the only solution is to do more work. Keep playing the violin. Keep coming up with new designs. Keep iterating and eventually, perhaps after a long time, your skills will catch up to your taste, and you'll finally

---

1 There is a classic story of Pablo Picasso traveling on train when a passenger recognizes him and asks, "Why do you distort reality in your art instead of painting people the way they actually are?" Picasso asks, "What do you mean by the way they actually are?" The passenger pulls out a photo of his wife from his wallet and says, "Well, this is what my wife actually looks like." Picasso looks at the image and says, "She's rather small and flat, isn't she?"

produce work that makes you happy [Glass 2009]. But for now, just remember that done is better than perfect.

The second point is that to get better at design, you need to try to consciously understand why a particular design does or doesn't work for you. Next time you marvel at how simple it is to use an iPad, pause and ask yourself why. What is it about its design that makes it simple enough that almost anyone can use it, from a non-tech-savvy grandparent to a two-year-old? Why is it that these same people can't figure out how to use a desktop computer or a tablet that requires a stylus? We'll discuss what your eye should look for in a design in "Visual Design" on page 97.

Finally, the third point—that the goal of design is to communicate with the user—means that although looking pretty is a valuable aspect of design, it's even more important to recognize that design is about helping people achieve their goals. Therefore, every design needs to start with an understanding of the user, which we'll cover next as part of *user-centered design*.

USER-CENTERED DESIGN

I remember sitting in a conference room at LinkedIn with several co-workers getting ready to kick off our next project. We knew what we wanted to build and we had broken down the work into a list of tasks. All that was left was to record these tasks somewhere so we could track our progress over time. We decided to try out the issue-tracking software that the rest of the company was using. It had all sorts of fancy features, including search, reporting tools, and colorful charts. There was just one problem: we couldn't figure out how to use it.

We had seven professional programmers in that room. We knew what we wanted to do. We thought we knew how to do it, too, as we had all used issue-tracking software many times before, and we had all been using websites—nay, building websites—for several decades. I therefore find it hard to adequately capture just how frustrating it was to to run into an issue-tracking website that utterly stumped everyone in the room. We spent several hours trying to figure out how to define a new project in the issue tracker, how to start a project once we defined it, how to move tickets between projects, how to use the 15 different view modes, why all the charts were empty after we finished a project, and what the 50 different text boxes on the issue-creation screen were for. It was maddening. After lots of frustration, we gave up and ended up using Post-it notes. The issue tracking software was better than Post-it notes in every aspect, except in the one aspect that mattered the most: helping *people* achieve their *goals*.

Notice the emphasis on the words "people" and "goals." Design isn't about buttons, or colorful charts, or features. It's about people and goals. In the story just described, the people were software experts and the issue tracker miserably failed to help us accomplish our goal of tracking the work for our project. Worse yet, it failed at the most important design goal of all:

The number-one goal of all computer users is to not feel stupid.

—[COOPER 2004, 25], ALAN COOPER, *THE INMATES ARE RUNNING THE ASYLUM*

In the past, my process for designing software—if you could really call it a process—consisted of the following steps:

1. Sit down with the team and ask "What features would be cool for version 5.0 of our product?"

2. Come up with a long list of features, argue over prioritization, and set an arbitrary deadline.

3. Work furiously to get as many of the features as possible done before the deadline. Inevitably run out of time and start cutting the features that are taking too long.

4. Cram whatever features were completed on time anywhere they would fit into the user interface.

5. Release version 5.0 to users. Hope and pray that users like it.

6. Repeat.

There are many things wrong with this process, but perhaps the biggest is that at no point do the goals of a real user come into the picture. I built things that were "cool" rather than what users actually needed. I had no idea how to figure out what users actually wanted (something I'll cover as part of "Data" on page 143), but I knew how to add features, so that's exactly what I did. I had a bad case of feature-itis and it took me a long time to find the cure.

The solution is to realize that you can't bolt a "design" onto a product after the engineering and product work. Design *is* the product. It must be part of your process from day one. Here are five principles of user-centered design that you should incorporate into your product development process:

- User stories

- Personas

- Emotional design

- Simplicity

- Usability testing

User stories

Doing design up front does not mean that you need to come up with a detailed 300-page spec, but before you dive into the code, you should be able to define a *user story*. A user story is a short description of what you're building from the perspective of the user. It should answer three questions:

- Who is the user?

- What are they trying to accomplish?

- Why do they need it?

The first question, "Who is the user?", requires you to understand people, which is surprisingly hard. Because you're a person, you probably think you understand why people act the way they do, or at least your own motivations, but as you saw in the previous chapter, the vast majority of your behavior is controlled by the subconscious and you are often completely unaware of it (see "Generating ideas" on page 35).

If you're a programmer, understanding your users is even harder. Every person forms a *conceptual model* in their head of how a product works. While a programmer's model is usually very detailed—often at the level of interfaces, events, messages, APIs, network protocols, and data storage—the typical user's model is usually less detailed, inaccurate, and incomplete (e.g., many users don't differentiate between software and hardware or the monitor and the computer). This mismatch in conceptual models makes it difficult for a programmer to communicate with a user.

And therein is the catch: communication is what design is all about. You're trying to present information to the user, to tell them what can be done, and to show them how to do it. Unfortunately, many programmers don't realize that because they know so much about their software that they think of it in a completely different way than the user. We can't remember what it was like to be a novice. This is called the *curse of knowledge*, a cognitive effect beautifully demonstrated by a Stanford study:

> In 1990, Elizabeth Newton earned a Ph.D. in psychology at Stanford by studying a simple game in which she assigned people to one of two roles: "tappers" or "listeners." Tappers received a list of twenty-five well-known songs, such as "Happy Birthday to You" and "The Star Spangled Banner." Each tapper was asked to pick a song and tap out the rhythm to a listener (by knocking on a table). The listener's job was to guess the song, based on the rhythm being tapped. (By the way, this experiment is fun to try at home if there's a good "listener" candidate nearby.)
>
> The listener's job in this game is quite difficult. Over the course of Newton's experiment, 120 songs were tapped out. Listeners guessed only 2.5 percent of the songs: 3 out of 120.
>
> But here's what made the result worthy of a dissertation in psychology. Before the listeners guessed the name of the song, Newton asked the tappers to predict the odds that the listeners would guess correctly. They predicted that the odds were 50 percent. The tappers got their message across 1 time in 40, but they thought they were getting their message across 1 time in 2. Why?
>
> When a tapper taps, she is hearing the song in her head. Go ahead and try it for yourself—tap out "The Star-Spangled Banner." It's impossible to avoid hearing the tune in your head. Meanwhile, the listeners can't hear that tune—all they can hear is a bunch of disconnected taps, like a kind of bizarre Morse Code.

—[HEATH HEATH 2007, 19], CHIP HEATH AND DAN HEATH, *MADE TO STICK*

As a programmer, when you're designing your software, you're always "hearing the tune in your head." Your user, however, doesn't hear anything. All they have to work with is the user interface (UI) you designed. You can't expect the user to know what you know and you can't rely on filling the gaps with documentation or training—as Steve Krug said, "the main thing you need to know about instructions is that no one is going to read them" [Krug 2014, 51]—so your only option for building a successful product is to get great at design.

This might sound obvious, but it's easy to forget it as a programmer because the tools you use to do your job are the pinnacle of bad design. In part, this is because most software designed for use by programmers is also designed for use by the computer, and the computer doesn't care about usability. All day long, you are dealing with memorizing magical incantations (the old joke goes "I've been using Vim for about two years now, mostly because I can't figure out how to exit it."), learning to parse esoteric formats like logfiles, core dumps, and XML (to be proficient at Java, you must also become fluent in a language called stack trace), and being treated like a worthless criminal by error messages ("illegal start of expression," "invalid syntax," "error code 33733321," "abort, retry, fail"). To be a successful programmer, you have to develop a high tolerance for terrible design, almost to the point where you don't notice it any more. But if you want to build software that normal people can use, you have to have empathy and you have to silence many of your instincts as a programmer.

> *The process of programming subverts the process of making easy-to-use products for the simple reason that the goals of the programmer and the goals of the user are dramatically different. The programmer wants the construction process to be smooth and easy. The user wants the interaction with the program to be smooth and easy. These two objectives almost never result in the same program.*
>
> **—[COOPER 2004, 16], ALAN COOPER, *THE INMATES ARE RUNNING THE ASYLUM***

Even if you get past the hurdle of understanding your users, the second question, "What are they trying to accomplish?", still trips many people up. One of the most common design mistakes is to confuse a user's goals (*what* they want to accomplish) with tasks (*how* they can accomplish it). A classic example comes from the Space Race during the Cold War. NASA scientists realized that a pen could not work in the microgravity of space, so they spent millions of dollars developing a pen with a pressurized ink cartridge that could write in zero gravity, upside down, underwater, and in a huge range of temperatures. The Soviets, meanwhile, used a pencil. This story is an urban legend,[2] but it's a wonderful illustration of what happens when you lose sight of the underlying goal and

---

2 See its Snopes page (*http://bit.ly/nasa-pen*).

become overly focused on a particular way of doing things. As Abraham Maslow said, "I suppose it is tempting, if the only tool you have is a hammer, to treat everything as if it were a nail" [Maslow 1966, 15].

One of the best ways to tell tasks apart from goals is to use the "five whys" technique you saw in the previous chapter (see "Validate the problem" on page 59). The other is to follow Alan Cooper's advice from *The Inmates Are Running the Asylum*:

> There is an easy way to tell the difference between tasks and goals. Tasks change as technology changes, but goals have the pleasant property of remaining very stable. For example, to travel from St. Louis to San Francisco, my goals are speed, comfort, and safety. Heading for the California gold fields in 1850, I would have made the journey in my new, high-tech Conestoga wagon. In the interest of safety, I would have brought my Winchester rifle. Heading from St. Louis to the Silicon Valley in 1999, I would make the journey in a new, high-tech Boeing 777.
>
> **—[COOPER 2004, 150], ALAN COOPER, *THE INMATES ARE RUNNING THE ASYLUM***

The point of the third question, "Why do they need it?", is to force you to justify why you're building what you're building. This is where the customer development process from the previous chapter comes into play (see "Customer development" on page 57). If this product or feature isn't solving an important problem for a real user, you shouldn't be wasting your time building it.

You should always take the time to answer all three user story questions in writing. The act of transforming your product ideas from the ephemeral and fuzzy form of thoughts in your head into concrete words and drawings on paper will reveal gaps in your understanding, and it's cheaper to fix those when they are just a few scribbles on a piece of paper than after you've written thousands of lines of code. A few lines of text and some sketches in a readme, wiki, or Post-it note are enough to force you to walk through the end-to-end experience from the user's perspective and ensure that you know what you're building, who you're doing it for, and why it's worth doing.

Personas

Here's another quick way to significantly improve your design skills: stop designing products for the "average person." The average person has one testicle and one fallopian tube [Burnham 2010], so if you're designing for average, you are designing for no one.

The actual Average User is kept in a hermetically sealed vault at the International Bureau of Standards in Geneva.

—[KRUG 2014, 18], STEVE KRUG, *DON'T MAKE ME THINK*

A better idea is to design for *personas*. A persona is a fictional character that represents a real user of your product who has specific goals, traits, and desires. For example, I designed hello-startup.net for the following personas:

1. Mike: a 19-year-old undergraduate student studying computer science at UMass Amherst. Mike has been obsessed with technology most of his life, started coding in middle school, and spends a lot of his day browsing Reddit and Hacker News. Mike is starting to think about jobs after graduation. He's interested in startups, but his parents are pushing him to join a well-known, established company, and he's not sure what to do.

2. Monica: a 28-year-old Senior Software Engineer working for Oracle. Monica got a computer science degree from MIT and then worked at several big software companies after college, finally landing at Oracle after several years. She is getting bored with the work and is looking for something that will challenge her more and allow her to make a bigger impact in the world. She has a couple of startup ideas, but she's not sure what to do next.

3. Mahesh: a 21-year-old programmer who dropped out of Stanford along with his roommate to start a company. Mahesh and his co-founder have been working on the company for six months, but they are struggling. They are not sure how to design the product, what technologies they should use to build it, how to get customers to use it, or where to find developers to help them.

Each persona should include a name, age, short bio, work history, and a set of skills, beliefs, goals, and any other details relevant to your business.[3] To make it seem even more like a real person, it's a good idea to add a photograph to each persona (preferably a photo you find on a stock photography website and not a photo of anyone you know in real life). Once you have defined personas for your

---

3 See *http://www.ux-lady.com/diy-user-personas/* for a complete guide.

product, never mention the "average user" again, either in user stories or in conversations. Don't let your team argue over whether the "average user" would prefer feature X or Y, as everyone will have a different understanding of what is "average." Instead, only discuss whether your personas would want X or Y. For example, would the "average user" of hello-startup.net want a calculator to help them estimate the value of their stock options? I have no idea. Would Mike, Monica, or Mahesh want such a calculator? I can make an educated guess that Mike and Mahesh would find such a tool useful.

Personas should be based on your market research and customer interviews (see "Validation" on page 48). Your goal is to identify a small number (typically 1–3) of *primary personas* whose goals must be fulfilled or else the entire product is a failure. For example, Mike, Monica, and Mahesh are the primary personas for hello-startup.net, so if they can't find what they need, the product might as well not exist. Your goal is to make these primary personas as happy as possible by figuring out their goals and building a product that is exceptional at helping them achieve those goals, and nothing else (see "Focus on the differentiators" on page 133).

> *The broader a target you aim for, the more certainty you have of missing the bull's-eye. If you want to achieve a product-satisfaction level of 50%, you cannot do it by making a large population 50% happy with your product. You can only accomplish it by singling out 50% of the people and striving to make them 100% happy. It goes further than that. You can create an even bigger success by targeting 10% of your market and working to make them 100% ecstatic. It might seem counterintuitive, but designing for a* **single user** *is the most effective way to satisfy a broad population.*
>
> —[COOPER 2004, 126], ALAN COOPER, *THE INMATES ARE RUNNING THE ASYLUM*

The reason personas are such a powerful design tool is that they force you to think about real people and to take into account their wants, limitations, personalities, and perhaps most importantly, their emotions.

Emotional design

Studies have shown that people interact with computers and software much like they would with another human. Most people act politely toward computers, though occasionally things get hostile; they react differently to computers with female voices than those with male voices; and in the right scenario, people think of computers as team members or even friends [Reeves and Nass 2003]. Have you ever thrown a temper tantrum when your printer refuses to work? Have you ever found a piece of software that you simply love? Have you ever begged and pleaded with your computer that it didn't lose your Word document after a crash? Whether you realize it or not, every piece of software makes you feel something. Most of your emotional reactions are automatic and the parts of the brain that control them have not evolved enough to distinguish between a real person and an inanimate object that acts like a person.

This is why the best designs always have an aspect of humanity and emotion in them. For example, Google has many hidden Easter eggs (e.g., try Googling "recursion," "askew," or "Google in 1998"), April Fools' jokes (e.g., look up PigeonRank and Gmail Paper), an "I'm feeling lucky button," and on many days, they replace their logo with a Google Doodle to commemorate important events. Virgin America replaced the standard, boring flight safety video with an entertaining music video that now has more than 10 million views on YouTube. During the holiday season, Amazon adds a music player to the website which lets you listen to Christmas songs while you shop. On IMDb, the ratings for *This Is Spinal Tap* go up to 11 and they show parodies of famous movie quotes on their error pages, such as "404: Page not found? INCONCEIVABLE. - Vizzini, *The Princess Bride.*" MailChimp includes its mascot, a monkey dressed as a mailman, on almost every page; Tumblr's downtime page used to show magical "tumblebeasts" wreaking havoc in their server room; and Twitter's downtime page shows a "fail whale" (see Figure 3-2).

Freddie

Freddie is our mascot. We don't use him in combination with our logo. Freddie always faces right. Feel free to use winking Freddie for extra personality.

Please don't dress Freddie up (e.g. hats, sweat bands, earrings).

Freddie
Download eps, jpg, or png

Winking Freddie
Download eps, jpg, or png

Bro Freddie
Not cool, bro!

Figure 3-2. MailChimp's Freddie (top), Tumblr's Tumblebeasts (bottom left), and Twitter's fail whale (bottom right)

These might seem like little details, but they are a big deal, as the emotional aspects of a design are as important to users as the functional aspects.[4]

Think of your product as a person. What type of person do you want it to be? Polite? Stern? Forgiving? Strict? Funny? Deadpan? Serious? Loose? Do you want to come off as paranoid or trusting? As a know-it-all? Or modest and likable? Once you decide, always keep those personality traits in mind as the product is built. Use them to guide the copywriting, the interface, and the feature set. Whenever you make a change, ask yourself

---

4 See *http://littlebigdetails.com* for lots of great examples.

if that change fits your app's personality. Your product has a voice—and it's talking to your customers 24 hours a day.

—[FRIED, HANSSON, AND LINDERMAN 2006, 123], JASON FRIED, DAVID HEINEMEIER HANSSON, AND MATTHEW LINDERMAN, *GETTING REAL*

Whatever personality or voice you choose for your product, I recommend that politeness is part of it. If people think of your software as a person, then it's a good idea to teach it some manners. Here are a few examples:

Be considerate

> *The program just doesn't care about me and treats me like a stranger even though I'm the only human it knows.*
>
> **—[COOPER 2004, 163], ALAN COOPER, *THE INMATES ARE RUNNING THE ASYLUM***

Whenever possible, try to design software that acts like a considerate human being who remembers you. Remember the user's preferences, what they were doing the last time they were using your software, and what they've searched for in the past, and try to use this information to predict what they will want to do in the future. For example, most web browsers remember the URLs you've typed in in the past. Google Chrome takes this even further so that as you start to type in "www.goo", it not only completes the URL to "www.google.com" for you, but if this is a URL you've typed in many times before, it will start to fetch the page before you've hit Enter so that it loads faster. Google is also considerate with passwords. If you recently changed your password and you try to log in with the old one by accident, instead of the standard "invalid password" error message, Google shows you a reminder that "your password was changed 12 days ago."

Be responsive

A good design is responsive to the user's needs. For example, Apple laptops detect the amount of ambient light in the room and adjust the screen brightness and the keyboard backlight automatically. Of course, responsiveness doesn't have to be fancy. One of the simplest design elements that is often overlooked is providing basic feedback. Did the user click a button? Show them an indication to confirm the click, such as changing the button appearance or making a sound. Will it take time to process the click? Show an indication that there is work going on in the background, such as a progress bar or an interstitial. Programmers often overlook this because in local testing, the processing happens on their own computer, so it's almost instantaneous. In the real world, the processing may happen on a busy server thousands of miles away, with considerable lag. If the UI doesn't show feedback, the user won't know if the click went through, and will either jam the button down 10 more times or lose confidence and give up entirely.

Be forgiving

Human beings make mistakes. Constantly. Design your software to assume that the user will make a typo, click the wrong button, or forget some critical information. For example, when you try to send an email in Gmail, it scans the text you wrote for the word "attachment," and if you forgot to attach something, it'll pop up a confirmation dialog to check if that was intentional. Also, after you click Send, Gmail gives you several seconds to "undo" the operation, in case you change your mind or forgot some important detail. I wish all software had an Undo button. Sometimes I wish life did, too.

The last point on being forgiving of errors is so important that it's worth discussing it a bit more.

*Eliminate the term **human error**. Instead, talk about communication and interaction: what we call an error is usually bad communication or interaction. When people collaborate with one another, the word error is never used to characterize another person's utterance. That's because each person is trying to understand and respond to the other, and when something is not understood or seems inappropriate, it is questioned, clarified, and the collaboration continues. Why can't the interaction between a person and a machine be thought of as collaboration?*

—[NORMAN 2013, 67], DON NORMAN, *THE DESIGN OF EVERDAY THINGS*

No one likes error messages. No one wants to see "PC Load Letter." And most of all, no one wants to feel like the error is their fault. Online forms are often the worst offenders. You spend a long time filling out dozens of text boxes, click Submit, and when the page reloads, you get an obscure error message at the top of the page. Sometimes it's not clear what you did wrong, and on some particularly rage-inducing websites, all the data you entered is gone. This is an indication that the designer did not think through the *error states* of the application. Here are some rules of thumb to avoid this mistake:

- Instead of error messages, provide help and guidance [Norman 2013, 65]. For example, avoid words like "Error," "Failed," "Problem," "Invalid," and "Wrong." Instead, explain what kind of input you're looking for and how the user's input differs.

- Check the user's input while the user is typing (not after a page submission) and show feedback, both positive and negative, right next to where the user is looking (not at the top of the page).

- Never lose the user's work.

Twitter's sign-up form is a great example. It gives you feedback while you type, either showing a green checkmark if your input is valid or a red X with a brief message explaining what is required instead, as shown in Figure 3-3. For instance, the password field has a small progress bar that fills up as you enter a more secure password; if you enter a username that's already registered, you see suggestions for similar usernames that are available; if you make a typo in your email address, such as *jondoe@gmial.com*, a message shows up that says "Did you mean *jondoe@gmail.com?*" It's a great user experience that makes filling out a form feel less like doing paperwork and more like you're having a conversation with a person who is helpful and politely asks you for clarification when they don't understand you.

In addition to showing helpful messages, you should try to create a design that prevents mistakes in the first place. In Lean manufacturing, this is called a *poka-yoke*, which is a Japanese term for "mistake-proofing." For instance, when you're typing a new question into Stack Overflow, it automatically searches for similar questions to discourage you from submitting duplicates and automatically warns you if your question is likely to be closed for being subjective (e.g., "what is the best X?"), as shown in Figure 3-4.

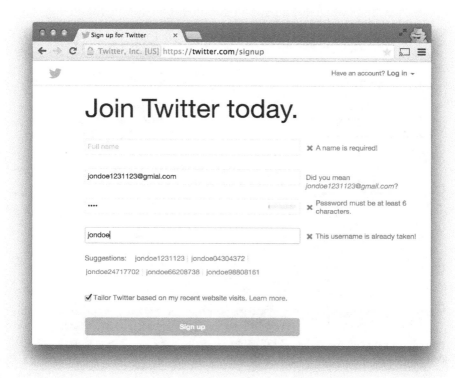

Figure 3-3. Twitter's sign-up page does a great job of showing help and guidance

The gold standard is making errors more or less impossible. For example, PC motherboards are designed so that every component has a different type of connector, as shown in Figure 3-5. This ensures that there is no way to accidentally insert the CPU into a PCI slot or plug an ethernet cable into the VGA slot. Modern ATMs return your ATM card and force you to take it before you can get your cash so that you don't forget your card. It's slightly harder but still possible to do this in software, too. For example, with Microsoft Word, I always dreaded the possibility that my computer would crash before I had a chance to save my work. With Google Docs, this sort of error is effectively impossible because all changes are auto-saved almost instantly. An even simpler version is disabling the Submit button on a form immediately after a user clicks it to make it impossible to submit the form more than once.

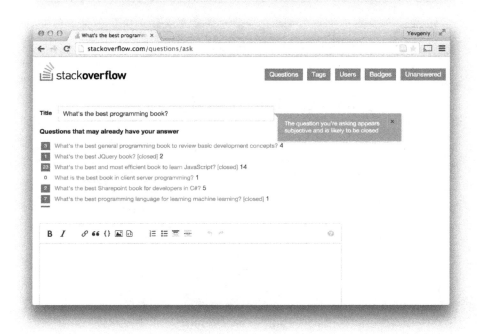

Figure 3-4. Stack Overflow tries to prevent errors

In addition to handling error states, you should also make sure your design handles a *blank state*: that is, what the application looks like the first time a user interacts with it, before she's entered any data [Fried, Hansson, and Linderman 2006, 97]. A design for a new social network might look great when the user has connected with hundreds of friends and can see all of their updates and pictures in the newsfeed, but what does the design look like when the user first signs up? For example, Figure 3-6 shows the blank state Twitter previously used for brand-new users.

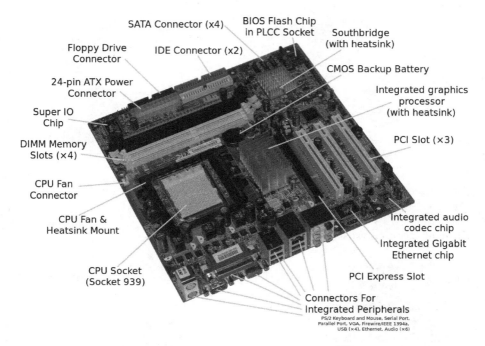

Figure 3-5. Some designs make errors nearly impossible (image from Wikipedia (http://bit.ly/foxconn-mb))

If you show a completely empty newsfeed, your new users will not have a great experience and are not likely to continue using your service. Figure 3-7 shows the new design for Twitter's blank state, which immediately prompts the user to start following popular Twitter accounts.

Figure 3-6. The old design for Twitter's blank state [Elman 2011]

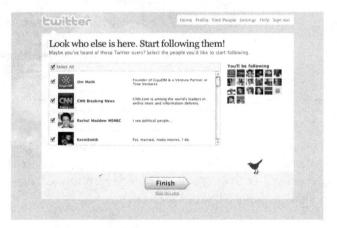

Figure 3-7. The new design for Twitter's blank state [Elman 2011]

Simplicity

Almost every creative discipline shares a single goal: simplicity. Isaac Newton, a mathematician and scientist, said "truth is ever to be found in the simplicity, and not in the multiplicity and confusion of things" [Powell 2003, 29]. Steve McConnell, a programmer, wrote in his book *Code Complete* that "managing complexity is the most important technical topic in software development" [McConnell 2004, 78]. And Jonathan Ive, Apple's chief designer, said that "there is a profound and enduring beauty in simplicity" [Etherington 2013]. Everyone strives for simplicity. The problem is that making things that are simple is not simple.

At first glance, this is unintuitive. We often think of "simple" as minimalistic and as having nothing extra. So if you start with a blank slate and only add a few things here and there, shouldn't you end up with a simple design? If you've ever written an essay or a complicated piece of code, or tried to design a product, you'll know that your first draft is always an overly complicated mess. It takes a tremendous amount of work to whittle that mess down into something simple.

I would have written a shorter letter, but I did not have the time.

—BLAISE PASCAL

A better way to think about it is that projects don't start with a blank slate, but with a vast amount of materials, knowledge, and ideas all mixed together. It's a little bit like sculpting. You start with a huge block of marble and you need to chip away at it, day by day, until you've finally revealed the statue that was within the rock (and within your mind). As Antoine de Saint Exupéry said, "perfection is attained not when there is nothing more to add, but when there is nothing more to remove." You might have to remove extraneous features from a product, redundant words from an essay, or extra code from a piece of software. You keep removing things until all you are left with is the very core of the design, the differentiators, and nothing else (see "Focus on the differentiators" on page 133). That's simplicity.

Simplicity is about saying what is the *one* thing I must get done [Heath Heath 2007, 27]? What is the one thing my product must do? What is the one thing my design must communicate to the user? Ask these questions regularly and after you've come up with an answer, ask them again. Does the product I designed do that one thing? Or did I get lost in the implementation details and end up doing something else?

The opposite question is equally important: what things should my product *not* do? Every extra feature has a significant cost. With physical objects, this cost is relatively obvious. For example, imagine a Swiss Army knife with 10 tools crammed inside: a knife, a screwdriver, a can opener, tweezers, and so on. Now you're considering adding a pair of scissors. Scissors take up a lot of room, so you'll have to make the knife bigger or make all the existing tools more cramped. Either way, it's clear that this will make the knife more unwieldy to use and more expensive to produce. Therefore, you either set the bar very high for adding a new tool, or you remove one of the original 10 tools to make room [Cooper 2004, 27].

The trade-offs in software are identical—every new feature makes the previous features harder to use and makes the software more expensive to produce—but it's not nearly as obvious. In fact, most companies believe that the way to build a better product is to cram more and more features into it, release after release, until it can do everything. Except it can't, because no one can figure out how to use it, as shown in Figure 3-8.

The companies that succeed at designing something simple are the ones that recognize that the number of features you can cram into software isn't constrained by physical limitations, like the amount of space in a knife, but by the mental limitations of a human using it. Design needs to be simple not because simple is prettier, but because human memory can only process a small number of items at a time. If you cram too many things into a design, it will quickly exceed the limits of human memory, and the user will find the product overwhelming and unusable. This is why you have to limit the amount of information in any design (less text, fewer buttons, fewer settings) and the number of features in any product (see "Focus on the differentiators" on page 133).

> *People think focus means saying yes to the thing you've got to focus on. But that's not what it means at all. It means saying no to the hundred other good ideas that there are. You have to pick carefully. I'm actually as proud of the things we haven't done as the things I have done. Innovation is saying no to 1,000 things.*
>
> **—[GALLO 2011], STEVE JOBS**

Most programmers love deleting code, especially as the result of finding a more concise solution to a problem. This usually requires that you understand the problem at a deeper level so that you can come up with an implementation that is more elegant. The same is true of design. You should enjoy the process of removing features and chopping out parts of a design, especially as the result of finding a more elegant solution. As with programming, to come up with a more elegant design, you need to develop a deeper understanding of the problem.

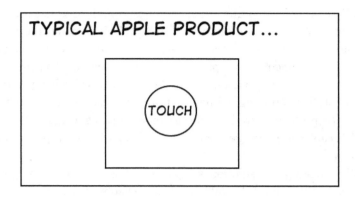

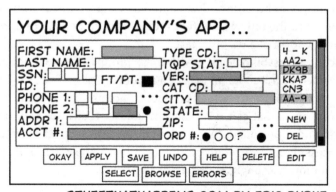

Figure 3-8. Simplicity (image courtesy of Eric Burke (http://stuffthathappens.com/blog/))

Sometimes you develop this understanding through user research, customer development, and techniques like the "five whys". But many interesting problems in the world are *wicked problems*, where you must build the solution *before* you can really understand what problem you were solving. That is, solving the problem gives you a clearer view of the problem, which will allow you to build an even better solution. Building the new solution will lead to an even better understanding of the problem, and the cycle can repeat again and again. Design is iterative, and it can take many iterations to come up with a simple solution for a hard problem.

Actually, making the solution simple isn't the goal. The real goal, in the words of Apple's design chief Johnathan Ive, is to solve problems so that, "you're not aware really of the solution [and] you're not aware of how hard the problem was that was eventually solved" [Richmond 2012]. What matters is not that the solution is simple, but that you make the user's life simple. The iPhone is an incredibly complicated piece of technology, but using it is simple. The only way to find out if you've succeeded at making the user's life simple is to observe them while they are using your product, a process formally known as *usability testing*.

Usability testing

In the previous chapter, I discussed the idea that, no matter how much thinking and validation you do, some of your assumptions will still be wrong. The solution was to test those assumptions by putting the product in front of real customers (see "Customer development" on page 57). The same logic applies to design. No matter how good you become at user-centered design, some of your design ideas will not work, and the only way to figure that out is to put the design in front of real users in the form of a usability test.

Don't confuse usability testing with focus groups. The goal of a focus group is to see how people *feel* about an idea or a product. The goal of usability testing is to see how people *use* your actual product to accomplish specific tasks. While there are companies that can run official usability studies for you, these tend to be expensive and time consuming, and most startups can get by with their own simpler process. Here is a rough outline (see *Don't Make Me Think* [Krug 2014, chap. 9] for a more thorough description):

1. Bring a small number of users (3–5) into your office.

2. Set up recording equipment (e.g., iPhone on a tripod).

3. Record the users while they perform a list of tasks with your product.

4. Have your team watch the recording.

5. Decide what actions to take based on your learnings.

6. Repeat every 3–4 weeks.

If you've never done usability testing before, you'll soon learn that the first time you observe people outside of your company using your product is an eye-opening experience. It takes just a few hours per month, and in return, you will regularly learn things about your product design that you would never have found through any other means. The most important thing to remember is if you're in the room with the users as a facilitator, you are there to observe and not interfere. You can encourage the users and answer logistical questions, but you *cannot help them use the product*, especially if they make a mistake. The user might get frustrated, but the whole point of usability testing is to find these mistakes and frustrations so you can fix them.

In addition to usability testing, there are a few other tools you can use to improve your designs. One option is to build a mechanism directly into your product that makes it easy to send you feedback, such as a feedback form on a web page. Only a small percentage of users will take the time to send feedback, but it's usually valuable content when they do. A second option is to periodically conduct usability surveys. It's a bit like sending a feedback form directly to each user's inbox. There is an art to building usability surveys correctly, so it's a good idea to use a dedicated usability product that will take care of the details for you (e.g., Survey.io).

VISUAL DESIGN

Let's now turn our attention to the visual aspects of design. People have been doing visual design for thousands of years, so it's a deep field. This section will only cover a "Hello, World" tutorial of visual design. When you're getting started with a new programming language, your first goal is always to learn just enough that you can create a program in that language that prints "Hello, World" to the screen, which helps you build confidence by getting something simple working very quickly before you dive deeper and start learning how to build more compli-cated programs. Similarly, in this tutorial, my goal is to introduce you to the basic design skills you need to get something simple working so you can build your confidence before diving deeper and learning how to create more complicated designs.

The basic visual design skills and techniques are:

- Copywriting
- Design reuse
- Layout
- Typography
- Contrast and repetition
- Colors

In this tutorial, I'll primarily focus on two examples: fixing the design of a résumé, which is a design task that almost everyone is familiar with, and designing a website from scratch (specifically this book's companion site, hello-startup.net) which follows a process that is a bit more like what is required for a typical startup. Pay attention not to the specific design decisions I make for the résumé and hello-startup.net, as they won't apply everywhere, but to the thought process behind those decisions.

Copywriting

Although many people think of colors, borders, pictures, and fancy animations as the primary tools of design, the real core of almost all software design is actually text. In fact, you could remove the colors, borders, pictures, and just about everything else from most applications, and as long as you left the text, it would probably still be minimally usable. This is not to say that the other elements don't matter, but most of the information that a user needs in a software product is in the titles, headers, body paragraphs, menus, and links, so even when doing visual design, your first priority should always be copywriting.

> Great interfaces are written. If you think every pixel, every icon, every typeface matters, then you also need to believe every letter matters.
>
> **—[FRIED, HANSSON, AND LINDERMAN 2006, 101], JASON FRIED, DAVID HEINEMEIER HANSSON, AND MATTHEW LINDERMAN, *GETTING REAL***

Take the time to think through what you're going to say to the user and how you're going to say it (see also "Emotional design" on page 83). A good title and headline—the elevator pitch—are especially important, as they are the first thing the user sees when they use your application, or when they see your application in search results, or when you're pitching an idea to an investor. Have you noticed that when you're flipping through a magazine, newspaper, or scientific journal, you only read some of the articles? Have you ever stopped to consider why you read those articles and not the other ones? Your headline must resonate with the personas you're targeting, telling them not only what you do ("Our software can do X"), but also why the user should care ("Our software can do X so you can succeed at Y"). Knowing how to craft a clear message that explains your why—your mission—is one of the keys to success in all aspects of business (see "Branding" on page 176 and "Mission" on page 387).

It's usually a mistake to leave copywriting to the end, or even worse, create a design that only contains placeholder text such as the standard Latin filler text "lorem ipsum." It reduces the most important part of the design, the copywriting, to just the shape of the text so you don't see the variations with real-world data and you don't focus on writing a message that resonates with your audience [Fried, Hansson, and Linderman 2006, 121]. The first thing I did when building hello-startup.net was to write down the information Mike, Monica, and Mahesh (see "Personas" on page 81) would want to see, as shown in Figure 3-9. I started with the outline of the basic sections—information about the book, the author, a way to buy the book, latest news, and startup resources—and then filled in the details. I ended up with a large amount of clean, semantic HTML. It's not particularly attractive, but remember, design is iterative, and this is just the very first draft.

The first draft of the résumé, as shown in Figure 3-10, is loosely based on a style I've seen in hundreds of résumés over the years. It's also a bit ugly, but the copywriting is in place so it's a good starting point.

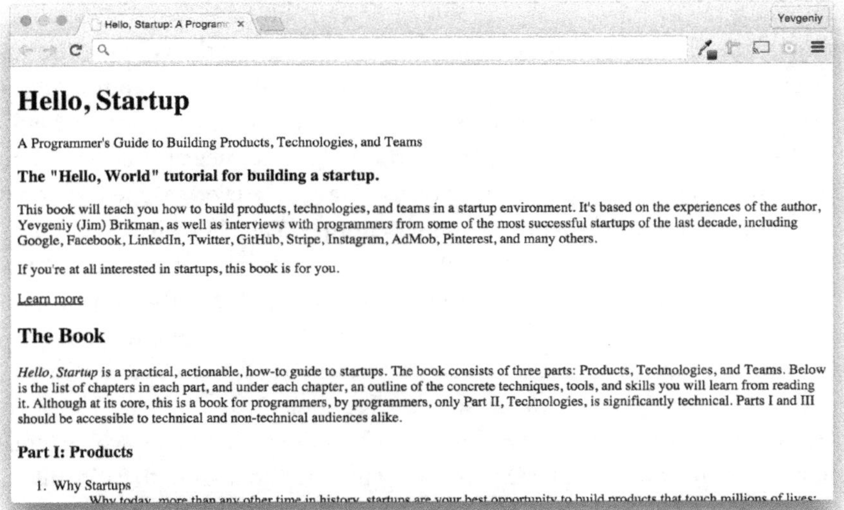

Figure 3-9. Copywriting for hello-startup.net

Design reuse

Good artists copy; great artists steal.

—[SEN 2012], STEVE JOBS

If you're new to design, or almost any discipline, the best way to get started is to copy others. Don't reinvent the wheel, especially if you aren't an expert on wheels. In fact, even if you are an expert on wheels (that is, an experienced designer), you should still reuse existing designs as much as possible (the same logic applies to reusing code, as discussed in "Build in-house, buy commercial, or use open source?" on page 193). When you copy others, you save time, you learn, and you get access to high-quality, battle-tested work. Copy and paste might seem like an unsatisfying way to learn design, but as we discussed in the last chapter, copy, transform, and combine are the basis of all creative work (see "Where ideas come from" on page 29).

Yevgeniy Brikman

ybrikman.com

Summary

Programmer, writer, speaker, traveler.

I love to build beautiful software and products.

Experience

Founder	Atomic Squirrel	2015 - now

Atomic Squirrel specializes in helping startups get off the ground.

Author	O'Reilly Media	2014 - 2015

Wrote the book *Hello, Startup*.

Staff Software Engineer	LinkedIn	2009 - 2014

Led the infrastructure team that brought the Play Framework to LinkedIn. Created and edited the LinkedIn Engineering Blog. Ran the open source program and hackdays.

Software Engineer	TripAdvisor	2008 - 2009

Built core features of the site using Java, Velocity, CSS, and JS.

Software Engineer	Cisco Systems	2006 - 2008

Built VoIP contact center software for the CVP team using Java, Lucene, JSP, Struts, CSS, and JS.

Education

Master of Engineering in CS	Cornell University	2005 - 2006
Bachelor of Sience in CS	Cornell University	2002 - 2005

Figure 3-10. A résumé with many design problems

I start every project by browsing existing designs and seeing what I can reuse or adapt to my own needs. For example, there are thousands of templates for web, mobile, and email that you can use instead of coming up with a design from scratch. One of my favorites is Bootstrap, which is not just a template but an open source, responsive HTML/CSS/JavaScript framework that comes with a default set of styles, behaviors, plug-ins, and reusable components.

If you don't want to jump into code right away, you can use a wireframing or prototyping tool, such as Balsamiq, UXPin, or Justinmind, that lets you put together a design by dragging and dropping from a library of UI elements. There are also hundreds of websites where you can find stock photos, graphics, and fonts, including free options (e.g., Wikimedia Commons, Google Fonts) and paid options (e.g., iStock, Adobe Typekit). Finally, you can also leverage the design community through websites such as Dribbble (a community where designers can share and discuss their work) and DesignCrowd (an online marketplace where you can quickly hire a freelancer to design a logo or a website). See *http:// www.hello-startup.net/resources/design/* and *http://www.hello-startup.net/resources/ images-photos-graphics/* for the full list of design resources.

I loosely based the final design of hello-startup.net on a free Bootstrap template called Agency and the final design of the résumé on a template I found on Hloom.[5] However, to help you train your designer's eye, I won't use these templates right away but instead will build up to them step by step so you can learn to recognize the different aspects of visual design, starting with *layout*.

Layout

A good layout arranges the elements on the screen so that you can infer a lot of information based on their positions relative to one another. One aspect of layout is *proximity*. The proximity between elements indicates if they are logically related or not. Items that are logically connected should be closer together; items that are not connected should be further apart [Williams 2014, chap. 2]. Take a look at Figure 3-11, which shows the original résumé on the left and the exact same résumé, but with slightly better use of proximity, on the right.

---

5 See http://startbootstrap.com/template-overviews/agency/ and *http://www.hloom.com/get/industry +lifer/*.

Figure 3-11. The original résumé on the left, and the same résumé with better use of proximity on the right

I've put two new lines between the different sections (summary, experience, education), but only half a new line between a section header and the contents of that section (e.g., between "Summary" and "Programmer, writer, speaker, traveler"). I've pulled all the information for a single job closer together, but put a new line between different jobs so it's clear where one starts and another one ends. I did a similar fix for the hello-startup.net design, as shown in Figure 3-12.

In the design on the right, it's clearer that "Buy Now," "Latest News," and "Startup Resources" are separate sections because I increased the spacing between them. You can also tell that "Webcast: A Guide to Hiring for your Startup" and the two lines below it are all part of one logical unit because I decreased the spacing between them.

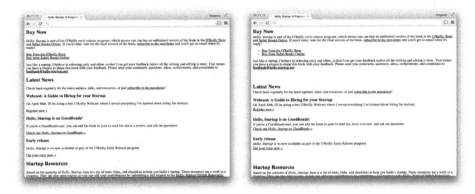

Figure 3-12. The original hello-startup.net design on the left, and the same design, but with better use of proximity on the right

Try to balance the close proximity of related elements with lots of whitespace between unrelated elements. The human mind is limited in how much information it can process at a time, so a key aspect of readability is putting lots of whitespace between elements so that you can focus on just one thing at a time. And I do mean lots of whitespace. Most beginners try to cram everything tightly together, so a good rule of thumb is "double your whitespace": put space between your lines, put space between your elements, and put space between your groups of elements [Kennedy 2014]. Medium, a blogging platform known for its beautiful design, is an inspiring example of just how much you can do with whitespace and typography, as shown in in Figure 3-13.

Another critical aspect of layout is *alignment*. Alignment allows you to communicate that there is a relationship between elements, not by moving them closer together or further apart (as with proximity) but by positioning them along common lines. Here is the golden rule of alignment:

Nothing should be placed on the page arbitrarily. Every element should have some visual connection with another element on the page.

—[WILLIAMS 2014, 13], ROBIN WILLIAMS, *THE NON-DESIGNER'S DESIGN BOOK*

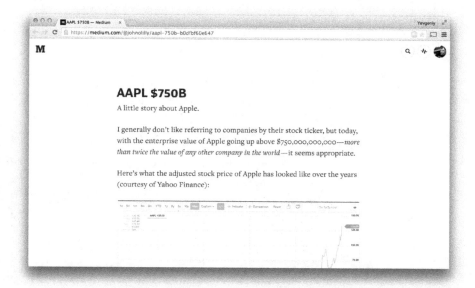

Figure 3-13. A screenshot of Medium showing off their use of whitespace (http://bit.ly/aapl-750b)

Notice how the résumé in Figure 3-11 has many different and seemingly arbitrary alignments: the section headings are center-aligned, the job titles are left-aligned, the company name is center-aligned (but poorly, just using spaces and tabs), the dates are right-aligned (again, poorly), and the job descriptions are center-aligned. Figure 3-14 shows the same résumé, but with a single, stronger alignment.

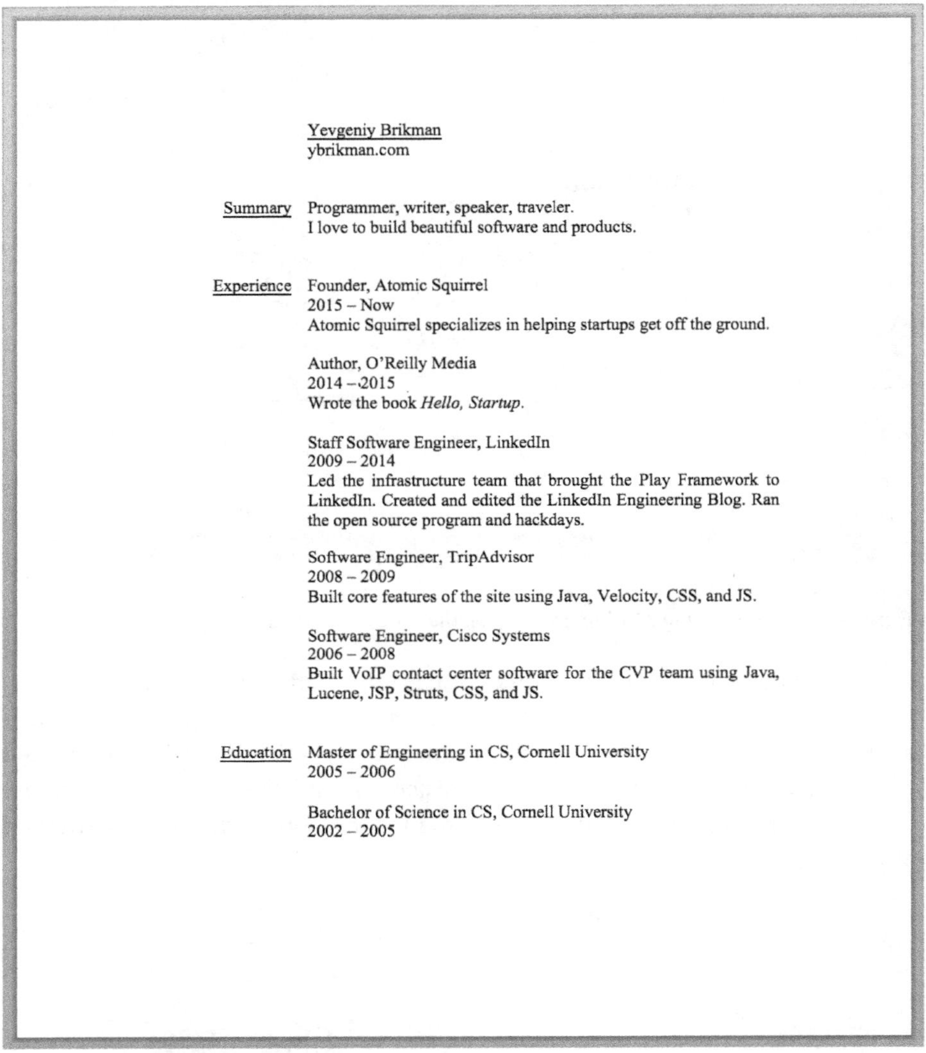

Yevgeniy Brikman
ybrikman.com

Summary   Programmer, writer, speaker, traveler.
I love to build beautiful software and products.

Experience   Founder, Atomic Squirrel
2015 – Now
Atomic Squirrel specializes in helping startups get off the ground.

Author, O'Reilly Media
2014 – 2015
Wrote the book *Hello, Startup*.

Staff Software Engineer, LinkedIn
2009 – 2014
Led the infrastructure team that brought the Play Framework to
LinkedIn. Created and edited the LinkedIn Engineering Blog. Ran
the open source program and hackdays.

Software Engineer, TripAdvisor
2008 – 2009
Built core features of the site using Java, Velocity, CSS, and JS.

Software Engineer, Cisco Systems
2006 – 2008
Built VoIP contact center software for the CVP team using Java,
Lucene, JSP, Struts, CSS, and JS.

Education   Master of Engineering in CS, Cornell University
2005 – 2006

Bachelor of Science in CS, Cornell University
2002 – 2005

Figure 3-14. The same résumé, but with a stronger use of alignment

Notice how this layout is easier to read, as everything is positioned along a strong vertical line between the section headers and the section contents. Of course, there isn't actually a line there, but your mind inserts one, as shown in Figure 3-15.

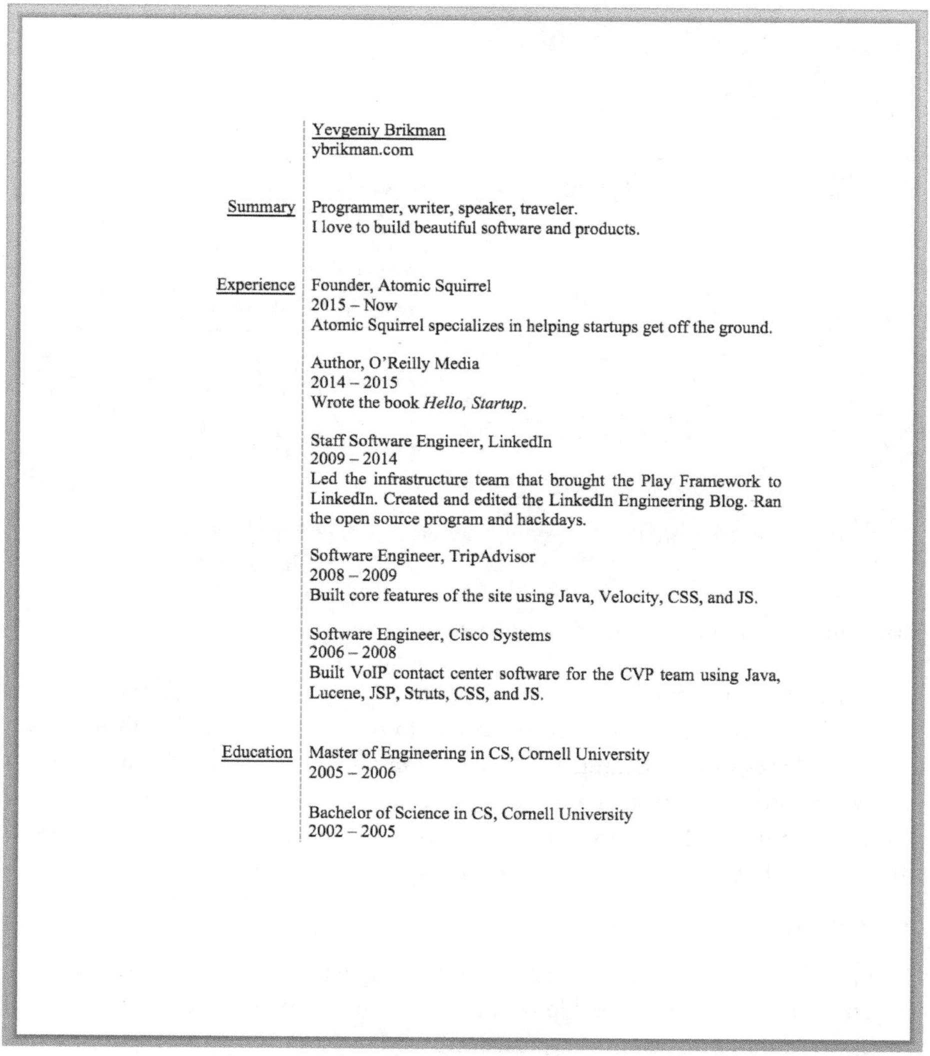

Yevgeniy Brikman
ybrikman.com

Summary | Programmer, writer, speaker, traveler.
I love to build beautiful software and products.

Experience | Founder, Atomic Squirrel
2015 – Now
Atomic Squirrel specializes in helping startups get off the ground.

Author, O'Reilly Media
2014 – 2015
Wrote the book *Hello, Startup*.

Staff Software Engineer, LinkedIn
2009 – 2014
Led the infrastructure team that brought the Play Framework to LinkedIn. Created and edited the LinkedIn Engineering Blog. Ran the open source program and hackdays.

Software Engineer, TripAdvisor
2008 – 2009
Built core features of the site using Java, Velocity, CSS, and JS.

Software Engineer, Cisco Systems
2006 – 2008
Built VoIP contact center software for the CVP team using Java, Lucene, JSP, Struts, CSS, and JS.

Education | Master of Engineering in CS, Cornell University
2005 – 2006

Bachelor of Science in CS, Cornell University
2002 – 2005

Figure 3-15. The mind inserts an imaginary line that helps you make sense of the layout

These sorts of lines show up everywhere in design, so teach yourself to consciously notice them. For example, Figure 3-16 shows hello-startup.net with a better use of alignment. Where is the line in this design?

Figure 3-16. The hello-startup.net design with better use of alignment

As a rule of thumb, try to choose one strong line and and align everything to it. In other words, don't align some things to the left, some things to the right, and some things to the center. Also, use center alignment sparingly, as it doesn't create an obvious strong line for the mind, and results in a design that looks more amateurish. This is just a rule of thumb, so you can certainly break it from time to time but you should do so consciously.

Typography

Typography is the art and science of arranging text so that it is readable and beautiful. In this section, we'll look at just a few of the most important aspects of typography: measure, leading, typeface, and style.

Measure is the length of each line. If lines are too short, the reader will be interrupted too frequently to go to the next line. If lines are too long, the reader will get impatient waiting to reach the end of a line. For example, which version of hello-startup.net is easier to read in Figure 3-17?

Figure 3-17. A comparison of measures on hello-startup.net: 140 characters (top left), 35 characters (top right), 70 characters (bottom left), and 70 characters and justified alignment (bottom right)

Most people find the bottom images easier to read than the top ones, and the bottom-right image to look the best overall for two reasons. First, the justified alignment in the bottom-right image creates strong lines on the sides of each paragraph, which is helpful when reading large amounts of text (this is why this style is used in most books and newspapers). Second, the bottom images use the proper amount of measure, which is around 45–90 characters per line. As a rule of thumb, you want a measure that's just long enough to fit all the letters of the alphabet laid out back to back, 2–3 times [Butterick 2015, sect. line length]:

abcdefghijklmnopqrstuvwxyz abcdefghijklmnopqrstuvwxyz abcdefghijklm

Leading is the amount of vertical space between lines. As with measure, if you have too little or too much leading, the text becomes hard to read. The sweet spot for leading tends to be 120%–145% of the font size [Butterick 2015, sect. line spacing], as shown in the bottom image of Figure 3-18.

Figure 3-18. A comparison of leading on hello-startup.net for a 16px font size: 13px line-height (top), 50px line-height (middle), and 24px line-height (bottom)

The *typeface* is the design of the letters. Every operating system comes with a number of standard, built-in typefaces, such as Arial, Georgia, Times New Roman, and Verdana. Many of these are not particularly good looking, and even those that are tend to be overused and therefore look bland in most designs. One of the simplest things you can do to dramatically improve your designs is to stop using system typefaces. You can get high-quality alternative typefaces from free sites like Google Fonts and paid sites like Adobe Typekit. But how do you know which of the thousands of typefaces you should use?

At a high level, all typefaces can be grouped into five classifications: serif, sans serif, script, decorative, and monospace. The typefaces within a classification vary widely, and some typefaces don't fit neatly within any classification, but here are some rules of thumb that will help you get started.

Serif

Times New Roman, Baskerville, Didot, `Courier`

Figure 3-19. Serif typefaces

Serif typefaces have small lines called serifs at the end of a stroke on each letter or symbol. For example, in Figure 3-19, notice the little lines that jut out to each side from the bottom of the "r" in the word "Serif," almost like the letter is on a pedestal. The stroke used in serif typefaces also tends to vary in thickness at different parts of the letter. For example, in Figure 3-19, the letter "S" in "Serif" is thinner at the top and bottom of the S than in the middle. The serifs and variation in thickness make each letter look more distinct, which helps reading speed, especially for large amounts of text. Therefore, serif typefaces are great for large amounts of body text and print material (most books use serif typefaces for the main body of text). As the oldest style of typeface, dating back not just to the days of the printing press but all the way back to letters carved into stone by the ancient Romans, you can also use serif typefaces in headers when you want a "classical" look.

Sans serif

Helvetica Neue, Arial, Eurostile, Avenir

Figure 3-20. Sans serif typefaces

"Sans" is a French word that means without, so "sans serif" typefaces are those without serifs. Notice how the letter "r" in "serif" in Figure 3-20 does not have any lines jutting out at the bottom. Sans serif typefaces also tend to have a more uniform stroke thickness throughout the letter. For example, in Figure 3-20, the "S" in "Sans" is the same thickness everywhere. Because sans serif typefaces have a simple and uniform appearance, they aren't as good as serif typefaces for large amounts of medium-sized body text, but they are typically better at extreme sizes such as large headers and small helper text. In fact, the tiny details of a serif typeface might look blurry if the letters are too small or you're viewing them on low-resolution screen, so sans serif typefaces are very popular in digital mediums.

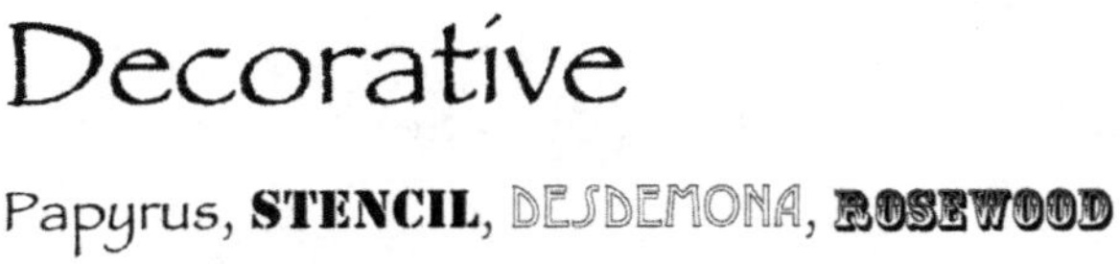

Decorative

Papyrus, **STENCIL**, DESDEMONA, ROSEWOOD

Figure 3-21. Decorative typefaces

As the name implies, decorative typefaces are used as decoration or accents. These typefaces are distinct, fun, and highly varied, which is great when you need some text to really stand out, as you can see in Figure 3-21. However, they tend to be hard to read, so you will typically want to limit their use to a few words in a title or subtitle.

Script

Edwardian Script, Snell roundhand, **Brush script**, Mistral

Figure 3-22. Script typefaces

Script typefaces look like handwriting, cursive, or calligraphy, as shown in Figure 3-22. Similar to decorative typefaces, they are a great way to add an accent to a page, but don't use them for more than a few words or letters because they are hard to read.

Monospace

Andale mono, Courier new, Consolas, PT Mono

Figure 3-23. Monospace typefaces

Each letter in a monospace typeface, as shown in Figure 3-23, takes up the same amount of space, which is typically only useful when displaying snippets of code (that's why all terminals, text editors, and IDEs use monospace typefaces) and text that needs to look like it came from a typewriter.

There are many *styles* that you can apply to a typeface to change how it looks, including text size, text thickness (i.e., bold or thin), text obliqueness (i.e., italics), letter spacing, underline, and capitalization. A particular combination of typeface and style is a *font*. Each font in your design should serve a specific purpose. The résumé violates this rule, as it uses Times New Roman 12pt for all of the text. The only exception is a few underlines for emphasizing the section headings, but the underline is not a good choice. Virtually no book, magazine, or newspaper uses underlines because they make the text harder to read. The only exception is websites, where an underline is used for hyperlinks and therefore should not be used for anything else to avoid confusion. Let's remove the underline and use several different font styles to improve the look of the résumé, as shown in Figure 3-24.

The structure of the résumé is clearer now: all the job and education titles are bold, all the company and school names are bold and italic, all the dates are italic, and all the section headings are in uppercase letters. It's an improvement but it still looks bland because the entire résumé is using just a single typeface, Times New Roman.

It can take a fair bit of experimentation and experience to find typefaces that look good together. If you're new to the whole font business, then you might want to let the professionals handle it. If you Google "font pairings," you will find dozens of websites that give you wonderful, pre-vetted recommendations. For example, the Google Web Fonts Typographic Project (*http://femmebot.github.io/google-type/*) shows dozens of ways to pair fonts available in Google Fonts, Just My Type (*http://justmytype.co/*) does the same thing for Adobe Typekit pairings, and Fonts in Use (*http://fontsinuse.com/*) let's you browse a gallery of beautiful typography from the real world and filter it by industry, format, and typeface. I found lots of great options in Fonts in Use for the résumé, but I chose a conservative set that's likely to work on other people's computers, consisting of Helvetica Neue for headings and titles and Garamond for the body text, as shown in Figure 3-25.

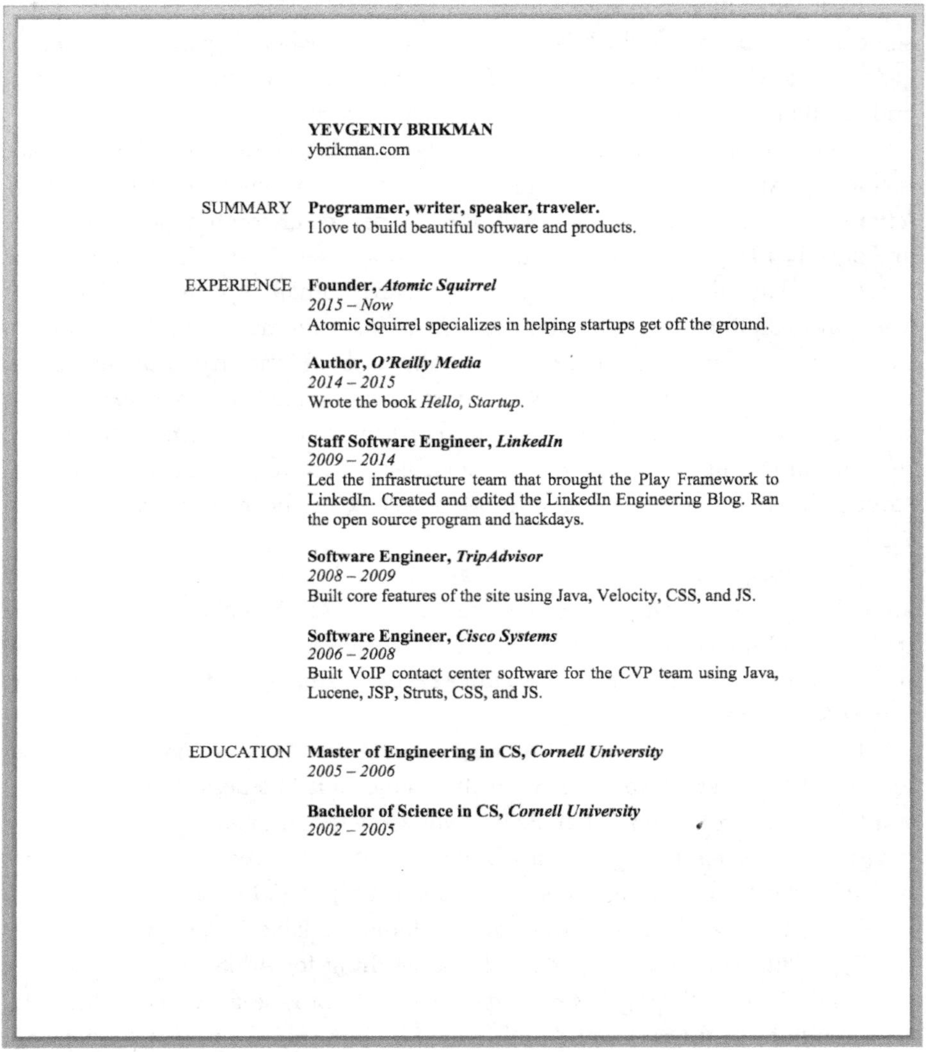

YEVGENIY BRIKMAN
ybrikman.com

SUMMARY **Programmer, writer, speaker, traveler.**
I love to build beautiful software and products.

EXPERIENCE **Founder, *Atomic Squirrel***
2015 – Now
Atomic Squirrel specializes in helping startups get off the ground.

Author, *O'Reilly Media*
2014 – 2015
Wrote the book *Hello, Startup*.

Staff Software Engineer, *LinkedIn*
2009 – 2014
Led the infrastructure team that brought the Play Framework to LinkedIn. Created and edited the LinkedIn Engineering Blog. Ran the open source program and hackdays.

Software Engineer, *TripAdvisor*
2008 – 2009
Built core features of the site using Java, Velocity, CSS, and JS.

Software Engineer, *Cisco Systems*
2006 – 2008
Built VoIP contact center software for the CVP team using Java, Lucene, JSP, Struts, CSS, and JS.

EDUCATION **Master of Engineering in CS, *Cornell University***
2005 – 2006

Bachelor of Science in CS, *Cornell University*
2002 – 2005

Figure 3-24. The résumé with several different font styles

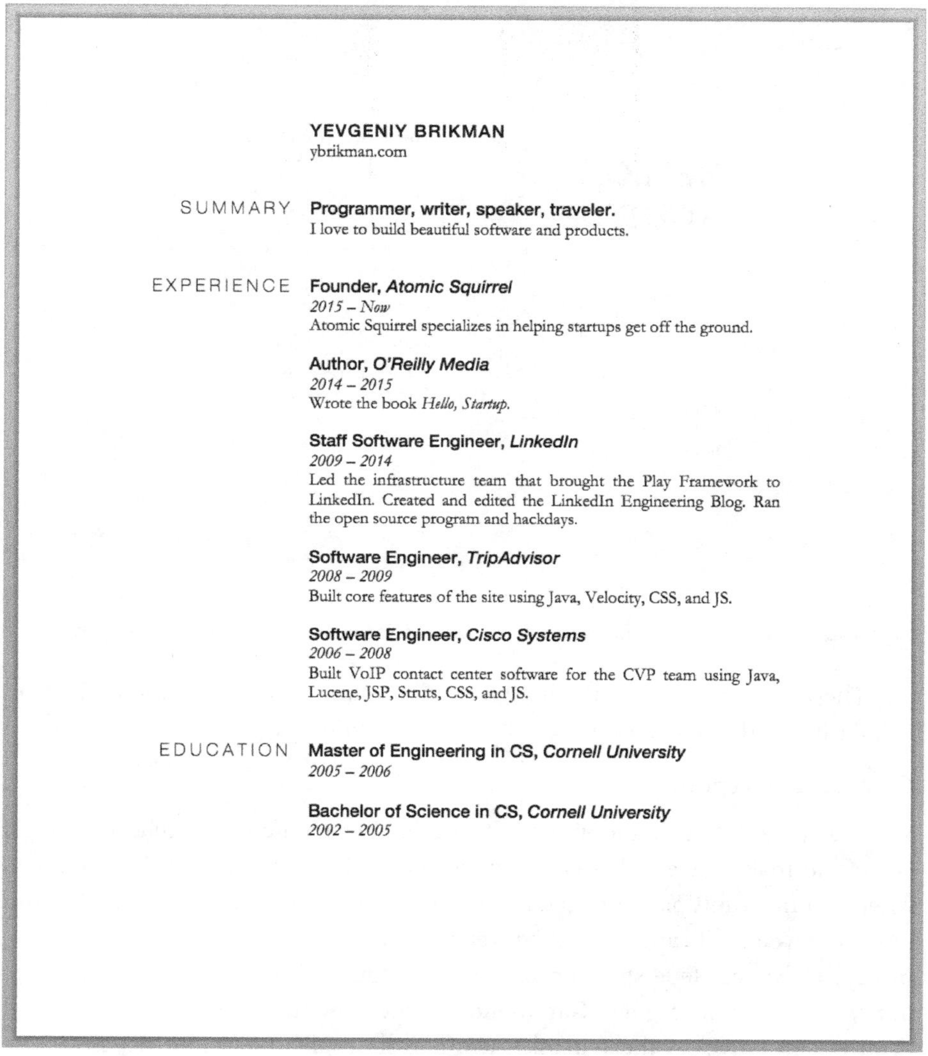

YEVGENIY BRIKMAN
ybrikman.com

SUMMARY   **Programmer, writer, speaker, traveler.**
I love to build beautiful software and products.

EXPERIENCE   **Founder, *Atomic Squirrel***
2015 – Now
Atomic Squirrel specializes in helping startups get off the ground.

Author, *O'Reilly Media*
2014 – 2015
Wrote the book *Hello, Startup*.

Staff Software Engineer, *LinkedIn*
2009 – 2014
Led the infrastructure team that brought the Play Framework to LinkedIn. Created and edited the LinkedIn Engineering Blog. Ran the open source program and hackdays.

Software Engineer, *TripAdvisor*
2008 – 2009
Built core features of the site using Java, Velocity, CSS, and JS.

Software Engineer, *Cisco Systems*
2006 – 2008
Built VoIP contact center software for the CVP team using Java, Lucene, JSP, Struts, CSS, and JS.

EDUCATION   **Master of Engineering in CS, *Cornell University***
2005 – 2006

Bachelor of Science in CS, *Cornell University*
2002 – 2005

Figure 3-25. The résumé with multiple typefaces

For hello-startup.net, I'm using the fonts from the Agency template, which are Montserrat, Droid Serif, and Roboto Slab (all available for free in Google Fonts), as shown in Figure 3-26.

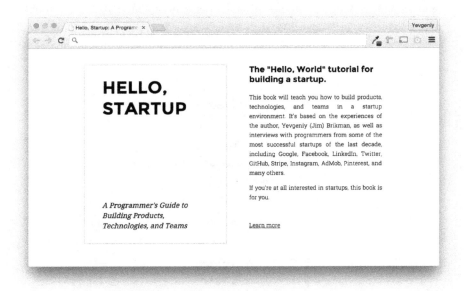

Figure 3-26. The hello-startup.net with the Montserrat, Droid Serif, and Roboto Slab typefaces

These new fonts make the designs look a little cleaner, but overall, they are still fairly bland. We need some contrast to spice things up.

Contrast and repetition

Whereas proximity and alignment tell you that two elements are related, *contrast* is used to make it clear that two parts of the design are different. For example, when you mix multiple fonts, the most important thing to understand is that you need to have significant *contrast* between them. In the résumé, the job titles are in bold Helvetica Neue so you can easily distinguish them from the job descriptions, which are in regular Garamond. Notice how this message is reinforced through *repetition*: all the job titles use one font, all the section headings use another font, and all the body text uses a third font. Once you've defined a purpose for some element in your design—whether that's a font choice or a logo in the corner, or the way elements are aligned—you should repeat it everywhere. This repetition becomes your brand (see "Branding" on page 176 for more information), and if it's distinct enough, the reader will be able to recognize your style anywhere (see Figure 3-27 for an example).

Figure 3-27. Repeating the same style to create your brand (design from GraphicBurger (http:// bit.ly/gb-vol9)).

You can create contrast in your fonts through a combination of varying the style (i.e., text size, thickness, capitalization) and the typeface classification. If you use two fonts that are too similar, such as the same typeface at 12pt and 14pt, or two different fonts that use serif typefaces, then they will be in conflict and the design won't look right. Therefore, each time you introduce a new font, it must be for a specific purpose, and to make that clear, you need to communicate it loudly by having a lot of contrast. For example, in Figure 3-28, I added a lot more contrast to the résumé title by using a big, thin, uppercase font, with lots of letter spacing.

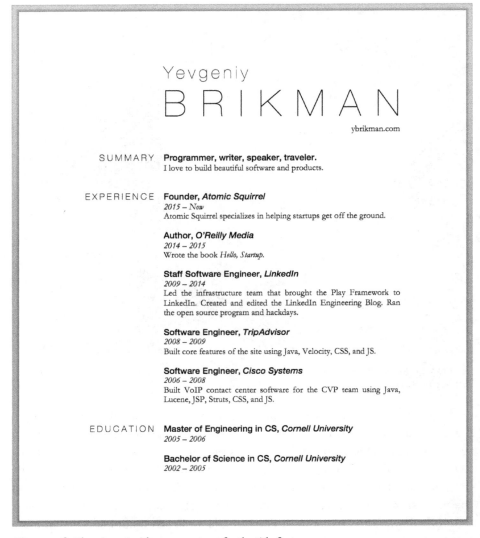

Figure 3-28. The résumé with more contrast for the title font

Another key role of contrast is to focus the user's attention on an important part of the design. While someone reading a book might read every word, users of most products do not:

What [users] actually do most of the time (if we're lucky) is glance at each new page, scan some of the text, and click on the first link that catches their interest or vaguely resembles the thing they're looking for. There are almost always large parts of the page that they don't even look at. We're thinking "great literature" (or at least "product brochure"), while the user's reality is much closer to "billboard going by at 60 miles an hour."

—[KRUG 2014, 21], STEVE KRUG, *DON'T MAKE ME THINK*

Therefore, not only should every font in your design serve a specific purpose, but every screen should have one central thing that it's trying to get the user to do. This is known as the *call to action* (CTA). For example, the main thing I want people to do on hello-startup.net is to learn about the book, so I can add a big Learn More button as a CTA, as shown in Figure 3-29.

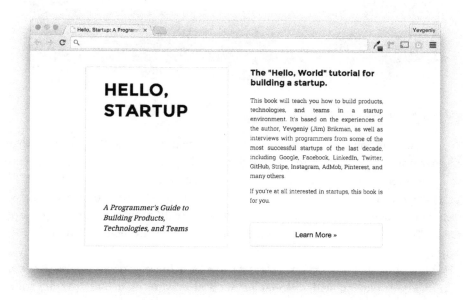

Figure 3-29. The hello-startup.net design with a Learn More button as a CTA

It's a start, but I can make the button jump out more by using colors to increase the contrast.

Colors

OKCupid (*https://www.okcupid.com/*) is a great example of using colors and contrast to make a very noticeable CTA, as shown in Figure 3-30.

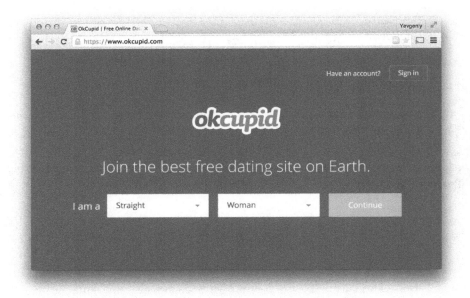

Figure 3-30. OKCupid call to action

As soon as you go to the website, it's clear what the site is (thanks to the clear copywriting) and what you're supposed to do (thanks to the clear CTA). The central placement, the large fonts, and the contrasting colors make it so that the CTA practically jumps out at you. This is the key to using contrast effectively: if two items on a page are not the same, make them very different [Williams 2014, 69]. Or as William Zinsser wrote, "Don't be kind of bold. Be bold." [Zinsser 2006, 70].

How do you know which colors to use to achieve a good contrast? When you're a kid, playing with colored paints and crayons is a blast. As an adult, choosing colors that work well in a design is slightly less fun. Color theory is even more complicated than typography. To do it well, you have to take into account physiology (e.g., putting red text on a blue background can create an effect known as chromostereopsis, which causes the text to be fuzzy, making reading difficult and even painful [Chromostereopsis 2014]), biology (e.g., about 8% of men have color deficiency while 2%–3% of women have extra color sensors and see more colors than average [Roth 2006]), psychology (e.g., each color comes with a number of associations and can have a significant effect on mood), technology (e.g., digital displays use the RGB color model, while most print devices use CMYK), art sensibility (e.g., some colors go together in a harmonious fashion, others do not), and the physics and mechanics of colors (e.g., the color wheel, primary, secondary, and tertiary colors, color mixing, hue, saturation, lightness, tints, and shades). It's a lot to learn.

If you're just getting started, I can offer you two tips that will save you time. The first tip is to do all of your design work in grayscale first and add color last. That is, figure out the copywriting, layout, and typography, and make the design work without any color. At the very end, when everything else is in place, you can add in some color, and even then, only with purpose [Kennedy 2014]. Think of adding color like painting a house: you should do it after you've put up the walls, windows, and doors, and not before. It's easier to experiment with different color schemes when the rest of the design in place, as it allows you to deliberately choose colors as an accent, set a mood, or bring out a particular theme. For example, the résumé we've been working on has been black and white the entire time. It's now easy to toss in a single color as a highlight, as shown in Figure 3-31.

Notice how this color scheme only makes sense once the layout (two columns) and font choices (a thin Helvetica Neue with a large font size and lots of letter spacing) are in place. Had I tried to add color to the original design, I would've probably done something different and had to change it anyway once the layout and typography were in place.

With hello-startup.net, I did the entire design in grayscale, and I can allow pictures in the design to influence the colors. For example, the cover image I got for the book had a gray reflection and green text, so I used those two colors throughout the design, as shown in Figure 3-32.

Yevgeniy

BRIKMAN

ybrikman.com

SUMMARY **Programmer, writer, speaker, traveler.**
I love to build beautiful software and products.

EXPERIENCE **Founder, *Atomic Squirrel***
2015 – Now
Atomic Squirrel specializes in helping startups get off the ground.

Author, *O'Reilly Media*
2014 – 2015
Wrote the book *Hello, Startup*.

Staff Software Engineer, *LinkedIn*
2009 – 2014
Led the infrastructure team that brought the Play Framework to LinkedIn. Created and edited the LinkedIn Engineering Blog. Ran the open source program and hackdays.

Software Engineer, *TripAdvisor*
2008 – 2009
Built core features of the site using Java, Velocity, CSS, and JS.

Software Engineer, *Cisco Systems*
2006 – 2008
Built VoIP contact center software for the CVP team using Java, Lucene, JSP, Struts, CSS, and JS.

EDUCATION **Master of Engineering in CS, *Cornell University***
2005 – 2006

Bachelor of Science in CS, *Cornell University*
2002 – 2005

Figure 3-31. The résumé with a splash of color as a highlight

Figure 3-32. Letting the gray and green colors in the cover image drive the colors in the rest of the design

The second tip is to use palettes put together by professionals instead of trying to come up with your own. You can, of course, copy the color schemes used on your favorite websites, but there are also tools dedicated specifically to helping you work with colors. For example, Adobe Color CC and Paletton can generate a color scheme for you using color theory (e.g., monochromatic, adjacent colors, triads). Adobe Color CC, COLOURlovers, and Dribbble's color search also allow you to browse through premade color schemes.

A QUICK REVIEW OF VISUAL DESIGN

Figures 3-33 and 3-34 show the progression of the résumé and hello-startup.net designs, respectively. Take a minute to look through these images and consciously name what changed between them.

Figure 3-33. The progression of the résumé design

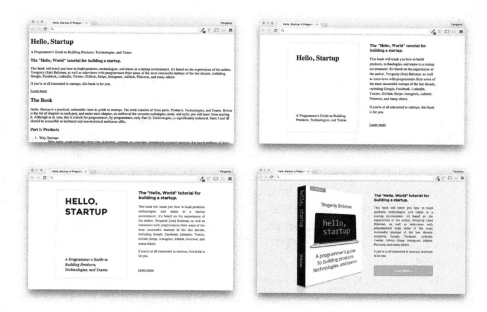

Figure 3-34. The progression of the hello-startup.net design

Hopefully, you were able to spot the following aspects of visual design:

- Top left: copywriting
- Top right: layout (alignment and proximity)
- Bottom left: typography (measure, leading, typefaces, fonts)
- Bottom right: contrast and colors

Finally, all the steps are based on templates, font combinations, and color palettes I found online, so at the center of it all is design reuse.

The MVP

The first design challenge you'll have at your startup is building the initial version of your product. Even if you've come up with a great idea and validated it with real customers, resist the temptation to lock yourself in a room for a year to design and build the perfect product. Remember, a product is not just one idea but a constant cycle of new problems, new ideas, and execution. Execution is expensive, so you need to validate each new problem and idea as quickly and cheaply as possible with customers. The best way to do that is to build what's known as a *minimum viable product*, or MVP.

MVP is a term that's often misinterpreted. "Minimum" is often misread as "ship something—anything—as soon as humanly possible," which misleads people into recklessly focusing on time to market above all else. "Viable" is often incorrectly understood as "enough features for the product to function," which misleads people into building many features that are unnecessary and omitting the ones that actually matter. And "product" incorrectly suggests that the MVP must be a product, so people often overlook simpler, cheaper ideas for an MVP.

The term MVP was popularized by Eric Ries's book *The Lean Startup*, which has a proper definition: an MVP is "a version of a new product which allows a team to collect the maximum amount of validated learning about customers with the least effort" [Ries 2011a, 103]. The point of an MVP is *learning*. The goal is to find the cheapest way to validate a hypothesis with real customers.

The "minimum" in MVP means eliminating anything that does not directly help you validate the current hypothesis. For example, when 37signals first launched their project management tool, Basecamp, their MVP did not include the ability to bill customers. The hypothesis they were validating was that customers would sign up for a web-based project management tool with a clean user interface. A billing system does not help validate that hypothesis so it can be eliminated from the MVP and added later (if customers actually start signing up). On the other hand, they invested time in coming up with a clean and simple design for the MVP, as that was an essential part of the hypothesis they were testing.

The "viable" in MVP means that the MVP has everything it needs for customers to accept it. The MVP might have bugs, it might be missing features, it might be ugly, and it might not even resemble the actual product you ultimately want to build, but it has to solve a problem the customer cares about. See Figure 3-35 for a great demonstration of the difference between a non-viable and viable MVP.

Figure 3-35. How to build an MVP that's viable (image by Henrik Kniberg [Kniberg 2013])

And finally, the "product" in MVP really means "experiment." It could be a working prototype of your product or something simpler, such as as a landing page with a demonstration video, just as long as it can validate your hypothesis (see "Types of MVPs" on page 128 for more information).

Building an MVP is not a one-time activity. For one thing, you will most likely have to build multiple MVPs before you find one that works. But even more importantly, building MVPs is more of a way of thinking than just an activity you do early in the life cycle of a product. Think of it like placing little bets instead of betting the house every time you play a game of cards. Whether you're trying out ideas for a new product that no one has ever used or adding new features to an existing product that has lots of traction, you should use the MVP mindset, which can be summarized as:

1. Identify your riskiest, most central assumption.

2. Phrase the assumption as a testable hypothesis.

3. Build the smallest experiment (an MVP) that tests your hypothesis.

4. Analyze the results.

5. Repeat step 1 with your new findings.

No matter how confident you are in an idea, always try to find the smallest and cheapest way to test it, and always try to keep projects small and incremental. Research by the Standish Group on over 50,000 IT projects found that while three out of four small projects (less than $1 million) are completed successfully, only one in 10 large projects (greater than $10 million) are completed on time and on budget, and more than one out of three large projects fail completely [The Standish Group 2013, 4].

> *The Standish Group has categorically stated with much conviction—backed by intense research—that the secret to project success is to strongly recommend and enforce limits on size and complexity. These two factors trump all others factors.*
>
> **—[THE STANDISH GROUP 2013, 4], THE CHAOS MANIFESTO 2013**

Let's now take a look at the different types of MVPs you can build.

TYPES OF MVPS

An MVP doesn't have to be an actual product. It just has to be something that can validate a hypothesis when a customer uses it. Here are the most common types of MVPs:

Landing page

An easy, cheap, and surprisingly effective MVP is a simple web page that describes your product and asks the user for some sort of commitment if they are interested, such as providing their email address to get more info or placing a pre-order. The general idea is to describe the most ideal vision of your product and see how much traction you can get, even if the product does not yet exist. If the most idealized description of your idea can't convince a few people to sign up for your mailing list, you may want to rethink things. For example, Buffer, a Social Media Management app, started as a landing page that showed a description of the product idea, some pricing details, and a way to sign up for a mailing list to get more info, as shown in Figure 3-36. They got enough sign-ups, and just as importantly, enough clicks on the pricing options, to have enough confidence to build the actual product.

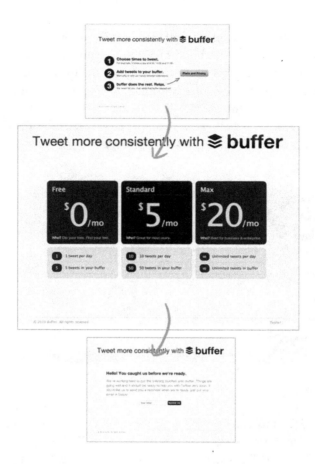

Figure 3-36. The Buffer MVP [Gascoigne 2011]

Because the text and images on a landing page are quicker to update than a working product, a landing page is one of the most efficient ways to hone in on the right design, message, and market. You can experiment with different wording, target different customer segments, try out different pricing strategies, and iterate on each one until you find a sweet spot (see Chapter 4 for how to measure the performance of each iteration). You can host your own landing pages on AWS or GitHub Pages, or use one of the many tools custom-built for landing pages, such as LaunchRock, Optimizely, Lander, or LeadPages.

Explainer video

Before Drew Houston started building DropBox, he wanted to be sure he wasn't spending years building a product nobody wanted. Even building a simple prototype that users could try on their own computers would have taken a long time, because it would have required building a reliable, high-performance online service to store all the data. Instead, Houston built a much simpler MVP: a landing page with a sign-up form, plus a four-minute explainer video (*http://bit.ly/dropbox-intro*), as shown in Figure 3-37.

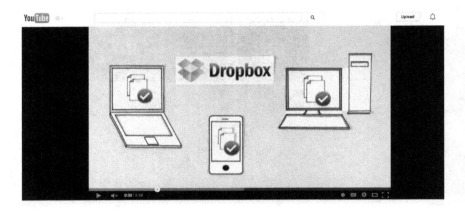

Figure 3-37. The DropBox explainer video

The video was an effective way to show the product in action rather than just describe it, and it included some Easter eggs (e.g., references to *XKCD* and *Office Space*) for the tech-savvy viewer. Houston put the video on Hacker News and Digg, and within 24 hours, the landing page got hundreds of thousands of views and 70,000 sign-ups. This gave Houston the confidence that it was worth building the actual product [Ries 2011b]. Tools such as PowToon, GoAnimate, and Camtasia allow you to make an explainer video for free or on a small budget.

Crowdfunding

Crowdfunding sites such as Kickstarter or Indiegogo are a bit like a landing page with an explainer video, except instead of email addresses, interested customers give you money to support your project. In other words, this is a way to get customers to buy your product before you build it, which is the best validation you can get. One of the most successful Kickstarter campaigns of all time was for the Pebble watch (*http://bit.ly/pebble-ewatch*), which raised $10 million from 68,000 backers with little more than a prototype [Gorman 2013], as shown in Figure 3-38.

Figure 3-38. Pebble raised $10 million on Kickstarter before building the product

Wizard of Oz

A Wizard of Oz MVP is one that looks like a real product to a user but behind the scenes, the founders are doing everything manually. For example, when Nick Swinmurn wanted to test his idea for Zappos, a place to buy shoes online, he went around to local shoe stores, took pictures of the shoes they had in stock, and put the pictures up on a website that looked like a real online shoe store, as shown in Figure 3-39.

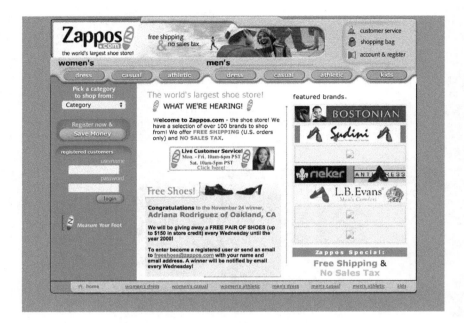

Figure 3-39. A screenshot of Zappos.com from 1999 via the Internet Archive

When a user placed an order, Swinmurn went back to the local shoe store, bought the shoe, and shipped it to the customer. This allowed Swinmurn to validate his hypothesis that people would be willing to buy shoes on the Internet without having to invest in a huge inventory of shoes, an automated ordering system, a factory to stock and deliver the shoes, and so on [Hsieh 2013, 58]. Pay no attention to the man behind the curtain.

Piecemeal MVP

A piecemeal MVP is similar to the Wizard of Oz MVP, except some of the manual pieces are automated as cheaply as possible with existing, off-the-shelf tools. For example, to create the Groupon MVP, Andrew Mason put a custom skin on a WordPress Blog (see Figure 3-40), used FileMaker to generate coupon PDFs, and sent them out using Apple Mail [Mason 2010].

Figure 3-40. A screenshot of groupon from 2009 via the Internet Archive

Check out *http://www.hello-startup.net/resources/mvp* for a list of tools you can use to build an MVP. Whatever type of MVP you end up building, the key is to ensure that you build something that is minimal but still viable. And the best way to do that is to focus on your differentiators.

FOCUS ON THE DIFFERENTIATORS

In a talk called "You and Your Research" (which has often been nicknamed "You and Your Career," as it has advice that applies to almost any career and not just research), Richard Hamming, a notable mathematician at Bell Labs, describes how he started sitting with the chemistry researchers at lunch:

> I started asking, "What are the important problems of your field?" And after a week or so, "What important problems are you working on?" And after some more time I came in one day and said, "If what you are doing is not important, and if you don't think it is going to lead to something important, why are you at Bell Labs working on it?" I wasn't welcomed after that; I had to find somebody else to eat with!

—[HAMMING 1995], RICHARD HAMMING, "YOU AND YOUR RESEARCH"

Richard Hamming did important work at Bell Labs because he intentionally sought out important problems, and not just comfortable ones. Although his method of questioning can make people uncomfortable, it's something we should all apply to our lives. What's important in your field? What are you working on? Why aren't those one and the same?

The same reasoning applies to building an MVP. What is important in your product? What are you actually building in the MVP? Why aren't those one and the same? The most important aspect of a product is its *differentiators*: those features that separate it from all the other alternatives. People often refer to differentiators as the "competitive advantage," but that phrase makes it seem like any advantage, no matter how marginal, is enough. It's not. Your differentiators need to be much, much better than the competition. You're looking not for a 10% improvement, but a 10x improvement. Anything less, and most customers simply won't think it's worth the effort to switch.

Therefore, it's important to ask yourself, "what two or three things does my product do exceptionally well?" Once you identify this small number of core features, build your MVP around them and ignore just about everything else. For example, when Google first launched Gmail, its differentiators were 1 GB of storage space (in an era when most other email providers only gave you 4 MB) and a zippy user interface (it had conversation view, powerful search features, and used Ajax to show new emails instantly instead of having to refresh the page). Almost all other features, such as a "rich text" composer and address book, were minimal or absent [Buchheit 2010] but it didn't matter, as the differentiators were so compelling that it made all other email services look primitive.

Another great example was the original iPhone. Apple is known for building complete, polished, end-to-end solutions, but in many ways, the original iPhone was an MVP. It didn't have an App Store, GPS, 3G, a front-facing camera, a flash for the rear-facing camera, games, instant messaging, copy and paste, multitasking, wireless sync, Exchange email, MMS, stereo Bluetooth, voice dialing, audio recording, or video recording. Despite all that, the iPhone was still years ahead of any other smartphone because Apple relentlessly focused on doing a few things exceptionally well: the multi-touch user interface, the hardware design, and the music and web surfing experience were at least ten times better than any other phone. And customers loved it.

Getting customers to love your product, not just like it, is a huge advantage. It's much easier to take a product that a small number of users love and get a lot more users to love it than it is to take a product that a large number of users like and get them to love it [Graham 2008]. To take users from "like" to "love," you need to sweep them off their feet. You need to "wow" them. Think of the last time something made you say "wow." It probably took somebody going above and beyond to delight you. It probably took something exceptional, and the simple fact is that doing exceptional things takes a lot of time. So if you want users to love you, instead of doing a merely competent job at many things, choose a few of them and knock them out of the park.

How do you know which features to focus on? One way to figure it out is to write a blog post announcing the product launch *before* you build anything. What are the two or three key items you're going to highlight in that blog post? What features will you show off in the screenshots? What will be the title of the blog post? Good blog posts are short, so this exercise will help you tease out what features really matter to make your product look enticing. Those are the must-haves for the MVP. Everything else is optional. In fact, everything else is not only optional, but oftentimes, detrimental. Every extra feature has a significant cost (see "Simplicity" on page 92), so unless it's absolutely essential for delighting customers or validating your hypothesis, it doesn't belong in the MVP.

Once you've figured out your differentiators and built an MVP around them, you can use it to validate your hypotheses. Perhaps the most important validation of all is getting customers to buy the MVP.

BUY THE MVP

One of your goals with the MVP, even at a very early stage, is to get customers to *buy* your solution. Note the emphasis on the word "buy." Many people will tell you they "like" an idea, and they might even mean it, but there is a huge difference between liking something and being committed to buying it. It costs more than just money to buy a new product—it also costs time [Traynor 2014]. It takes time to convince your family (in the case of a consumer product) or your co-workers (in the case of an enterprise product) that the product is worth it, it takes time to install or deploy it, it takes time to train yourself and others to use it, and it takes time to maintain and update it in the future. The time aspect applies even if your product is free for some of your users (e.g., an ad-supported website or a freemium service), so no matter what pricing strategy you're considering, your goal is to get a firm commitment to buy the product.

Every type of MVP you saw earlier, even the most minimal ones, provides an opportunity to buy. This is obviously the point of a crowdfunded MVP, but you can also have a pre-order form on a landing page MVP, and you can charge money for a Wizard of Oz, even if you have to accept payment in cash. You can tweak the price until you find a sweet spot, but don't give it away for free. In fact, tweaking the price is a great way to see just how serious a customer is about using your product:

> I ask [my customers], "If the product were free, how many would you actually deploy or use?" The goal is to take pricing away as an issue and see whether the product itself gets customers excited. If it does, I follow up with my next question: "Ok, it's not free. In fact, imagine I charged you $1 million. Would you buy it?" While this may sound like a facetious dialog, I use it all the time. Why? Because more than half the time customers will say something like, "Steve, you're out of your mind. This product isn't worth more than $250,000." I've just gotten customers to tell me how much they are willing to pay. Wow.

—[BLANK 2013, 52], STEVE BLANK, *THE FOUR STEPS TO THE EPIPHANY*

What kind of customer would commit to buying a product that doesn't exist? Or, even if you have a working prototype, what kind of customer is willing to do business with a brand-new startup despite all the bugs, performance problems, missing features, and the fact that you might be out of business in a few months? In the book *Diffusion of Innovations*, Everett Rogers groups customers into five categories [Rogers 2003, chap. 7]:

1. *Innovators* are willing to take risks on new technologies because technology itself is a central interest in their life, regardless of its function, and they are always on the lookout for the latest innovations.

2. *Early adopters* are also willing to take risks on new technology, not because of an interest in the technology but because they find it easy to visualize the benefits the technology would have in their lives.

3. *Early majority* customers are driven by a need to solve a specific problem. They are able to envision how a new technology could be a solution, but they also know many new innovations end up failing, so they are willing to wait and see if it works out for others before buying it for themselves.

4. *Late majority* customers also have a specific problem to solve, but they are not comfortable using a new technology to solve it. They will wait until a technology is mature, has established itself as a standard, and has a support network around it before buying.

5. *Laggards* avoid new technologies as much as they can. They are the last to adopt a new innovation and usually only do so because they have no other choice.

The number of customers in each category roughly follows a bell curve, as shown in Figure 3-41.

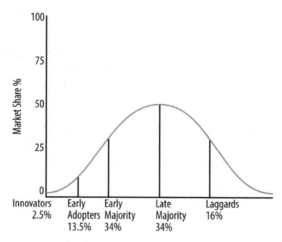

Figure 3-41. Diffusion of innovations [Diffusion of Ideas 2012]

To be a successful company, you usually have to sell to the early and late majority, but you won't be able to get there until you've convinced the innovators and early adopters. That is, innovation diffuses from left to right in the bell curve in Figure 3-41, and you can't skip to a new category until you've been successful with a previous one. And because each category of customers is looking for something different, it is essential to understand what kind of customer you're targeting or else you'll end up with the wrong product, marketing strategy, and sales process.

What the early adopter is buying [...] is some kind of **change agent***. By being the first to implement this change in their industry, the early adopters expect to get a jump on the competition, whether from lower product costs, faster time to market, more complete customer service, or some other comparable business advantage. They expect a radical discontinuity between the old ways and the new, and they are prepared to champion* *this cause against entrenched resistance. Being the first, they also are prepared to bear with the inevitable bugs and glitches that accompany any innovation just coming to market.*

—[MOORE AND MCKENNA 2006, 25], GEOFFREY MOORE AND REGIS MCKENNA,
CROSSING THE CHASM

Your goal in the early days of a startup, when you're still validating the problem and solution, is to find the right early adopters. These are the kinds of customers who will commit to buying your solution long before it's ready because they believe in your vision rather than the specific product. Steve Blank calls this group of customers *earlyvangelists* and provides the following handy list to help identify them:

- *They have a problem or need.*

- *They understand they have a problem.*

- *They're actively searching for a solution and have a timetable for finding it.*

- *The problem is so painful that they've cobbled together an interim solution.*

- *They've committed, or can quickly acquire, budget dollars to purchase.*

—[BLANK 2013, 35], STEVE BLANK, THE FOUR STEPS TO THE EPIPHANY

If you can find a customer who has already hacked together their own interim solution, that may be the best indicator of all because then you know you've found a real problem and a strong lead. Every industry has earlyvangelists, though there usually aren't that many. That said, at this early stage, when you have no product and no customers, getting even a single customer is a huge win. Before you can get to thousands or millions of customers, you need to get 1, then 10, and then 100. To do that, you might have to do things that don't scale.

DO THINGS THAT DON'T SCALE

One of the most common pieces of advice Y Combinator gives to startups is to "do things that don't scale." That is, in the early days of a startup, you might have to do many things manually, such as hiring, recruiting users, and customer service. This will feel inefficient, especially to programmers, who will be tempted to yell "But that won't scale!" But manual labor is often the only way to get the fly wheel started, and only once it's really going do you need to worry about scaling. For example, the founders of Airbnb went door to door in New York to recruit early users and even helped them photograph their apartments [Graham 2013]. The founders of Homejoy, a startup that helps customers find home cleaning services, initially went around to customers' homes and did all the cleaning themselves [Cheung Adora 2014]. The founders of Pinterest recruited their first users by going to coffee shops and personally asking strangers to try the product. They would also go to Apple stores and set all the browsers to the Pinterest home page [Altman 2014a]. The employees of Wufoo, a startup that helps users create online forms, used to send handwritten thank-you notes to every single customer:

> Perhaps the biggest thing preventing founders from realizing how attentive they could be to their users is that they've never experienced such attention themselves. Their standards for customer service have been set by the companies they've been customers of, which are mostly big ones. Tim Cook doesn't send you a hand-written note after you buy a laptop. He can't. But you can. That's one advantage of being small: you can provide a level of service no big company can.
>
> Once you realize that existing conventions are not the upper bound on user experience, it's interesting in a very pleasant way to think about how far you could go to delight your users.

—[GRAHAM 2013], PAUL GRAHAM, CO-FOUNDER OF Y COMBINATOR

When you're a tiny startup and still validating your ideas, you can afford to do things that don't scale to get your first customers. If the idea works, you can make the process more scalable through automation later. But if it doesn't work (and most ideas don't), then you've saved an enormous amount of time by not building a bunch of automation for the wrong thing. Also, by getting directly involved in the nitty-gritty details of your business, you become a domain expert, which as you saw earlier, is essential for coming up with great ideas.

Recap

A user interface is like a joke. If you have to explain it, it's not that good.

—[LEBLANC 2014], MARTIN LEBLANC, FOUNDER OF ICONFINDER

Design is an essential skill because the user interface *is* the product. The good news is that the design process is iterative: any design can be incrementally improved and any person can incrementally improve their design skills. The best thing you can do is to start reusing existing designs, writing user stories, and designing for personas. With practice, you can learn copywriting, layout, typography, contrast, repetition, and colors. By giving your product a personality, especially a polite one that is responsive, considerate, and forgiving, you can build a design that resonates emotionally. And by frequently running usability tests, you can get direct feedback on how you're progressing.

However, no matter how good your design is, there is no way to be sure if it will be successful. Therefore, the best strategy is to constantly be running small experiments and adjusting them based on feedback from real users. Do a little market research, talk to potential customers, release a quick MVP, learn from your users' reactions, and then repeat again and again.

> I'm the author of Amazon's best-selling interview book, but it all started with a little 20-page PDF. Honestly, it wasn't very good. I'm embarrassed to look at it now. It was good enough to act as an MVP, even though I didn't think about it that way at the time. It ended up testing the market, establishing that there was a real demand, and from there I could expand on it. It also got me very early feedback on what matters.
>
> There was one other company I started that was much the same thing. It started small, and then by accident, I realized I had a company.
>
> It's so easy to hear an idea from yourself or someone else and cross it off as being a bad idea for various reasons. I could tell you a million reasons for why my company would fail. And yet, it succeeds despite those reasons (and perhaps because of them, in some cases).
>
> The truth is that it's so hard to predict what will and won't work. An MVP allows you to try something out relatively quickly and cheaply. Those results often mean more than your other predictions.
>
> **—[MCDOWELL 2015], GAYLE LAAKMANN MCDOWELL, FOUNDER AND CEO OF CAREERCUP**

A lot of people find this hectic, trial-and-error approach unsettling. It's tempting to look at a successful product and assume that it appeared in the creator's head exactly as you see it now, fully formed, beautiful, and complete. But that's like seeing Michael Jordan looking smooth and dominant on the basketball court and assuming he came out of the womb 6'6" and 216 lbs, with the ability to dunk and an unstoppable fade-away shot.

> *I've missed more than 9000 shots in my career. I've lost almost 300 games. 26 times, I've been trusted to take the game winning shot and missed. I've failed over and over and over again in my life. And that is why I succeed.*
>
> **—[GOLDMAN AND PAPSON 1999, 49], MICHAEL JORDAN**

Any time you hold a polished product in your hand, remember that what you're looking at is the final iteration of thousands of trials and errors that included many missteps, pivots, redesigns, and compromises. And the entire way, the company that built it was probably struggling to survive and hoping it could find a working combination before going out of business.

> *Starting a company is like throwing yourself off the cliff and assembling an airplane on the way down.*
>
> **—[CHANG 2013], REID HOFFMAN, CO-FOUNDER AND CHAIRMAN OF LINKEDIN**

This is what it means for a startup to be in "search mode." It is a frantic race against time to find a problem worth solving and a solution that's worth building, and the best way to make that happen is not to hope for a eureka moment but to use an iterative, experimental process.

Data and Distribution

In the previous chapter, you saw how to design a minimum viable product (MVP) around your startup ideas. In this chapter, we're going to look at how to grow the MVP using data and distribution.

Data is how you take a bunch of assumptions and guesses and turn them into concrete, actionable facts. I'll describe why measuring is almost always better than not measuring, introduce a list of the metrics you should be tracking at every startup, and explain how to use those metrics to make better decisions using data-driven development.

Distribution is how users find your product. It doesn't matter if you've created an incredible product if no one actually knows it exists. I'll review the most common distribution strategies used by startups, including word of mouth, marketing, sales, and branding.

Data

It's the product manager's job to articulate two simple things:

- *What game are we playing?*

- *How do we keep score?*

Do these two things right, and all of a sudden a collection of brilliant individual contributors with talents in engineering, operations, quality, design, and marketing will start running in the same direction. Without it, no amount of prioritization or execution management will save you.

—[NASH 2011], ADAM NASH, PRESIDENT AND CEO AT WEALTHFRONT

If you want to build a successful product, you have to know what game you're playing and how to keep score. For a company, the "game" is just another way of saying "mission," which I will discuss later in the book in "Core Ideology" on page 386. In this chapter, I'm going to focus on how to keep score. Although there are times when the only meaningful gauge of progress is gut feel—such as observing how happy users are in a usability study—a better way to keep score in most situations is by gathering and analyzing data.

One of the strengths of modern software startups is that it is very easy to collect data on every aspect of your business. Using tools like Google Analytics, KISSmetrics, and New Relic (see "Monitoring" on page 374 for the full list), you can track where users are coming from, how they are using your product, which features are generating the most revenue, what parts of your tech stack have the best performance, and so on. Instead of blindly guessing, you can use this data to make informed decisions about what products to build, what distribution channels to use, and how to evolve your technology. Making good use of data for decision making is largely a game of measurement:

Measurement: a quantitatively expressed reduction of uncertainty based on one or more observations.

—[HUBBARD 2010, 23], DOUGLAS W. HUBBARD, *HOW TO MEASURE ANYTHING*

Notice that the definition of measurement is not about *eliminating* uncertainty but merely *reducing* it. You can never completely eliminate uncertainty. Nothing in business, or anywhere in life, is ever completely certain, and no measurement is perfect. But just because the measurement is not exact or there is still some doubt does not mean that it is worthless. Imperfect measurements are typically better than doing no measurement and going with your opinion—even if it's an expert opinion. Researchers at the University of Michigan have compiled hundreds of studies that show that basic measurement and quantitative analysis routinely outperforms human experts:

- *In predicting college freshman GPAs, a simple linear model of high school rank and aptitude tests outperformed experienced admissions staff.*

- *In predicting the recidivism of criminals, criminal records and prison records outperformed criminologists.*

- *The academic performance of medical school students was better predicted with simple models based on past academic performance than with interviews with professors.*

- *In a World War II study of predictions of how well Navy recruits would perform in boot camp, models based on high school records and aptitude tests outperformed expert interviewers. Even when the interviewers were given the same data, the predictions of performance were best when the expert opinions were ignored.*

—[HUBBARD 2010, 225], DOUGLAS W. HUBBARD, *HOW TO MEASURE ANYTHING*

Human beings, even experts, are wrong very, very frequently. Data and measurement are some of the best tools for getting things right. If you're not an expert on data analysis, don't worry. For most of the things you need to measure in a startup, you don't need sophisticated tools or methods. Your goal is not to be published in a scientific journal but to gather data that increases the odds that you're making good decisions. To do that, simple, imperfect methods are usually good enough.

Moreover, as is a common theme in this book, measurement is an iterative process. You don't have to set up the perfect tracking and analytics system from day one. You don't have to measure everything to get value out of measuring. In fact, you usually get the most bang for the buck off of the initial few measurements, and then diminishing returns with more and more elaborate methods. Start small, perhaps by tracking just a single metric (see "The magic number" on page 149), and then gradually evolve your approach to measure more and more.

Of course, not everything that can be measured should be measured. For each type of data X, ask yourself two questions:

1. If I could measure X, is there at least one concrete decision it would affect?

2. Is that decision worth more than the cost to measure X?

If you can't answer "yes" to both questions, then it's not worth measuring X. That said, most people are surprised by what can be measured with minimal cost and effort. The book *How to Measure Anything* shows how to quantify a variety of concepts, including ones that seem fuzzy and unmeasurable, such as product quality, brand perception, security, and risk [Hubbard 2010].

Anything can be measured. If a thing can be observed in any way at all, it lends itself to some type of measurement method. No matter how "fuzzy" the measurement is, it's still a measurement if it tells you more than you knew before. And those very things most likely to be seen as immeasurable are, virtually always, solved by relatively simple measurement methods.

—[HUBBARD 2010, 3], DOUGLAS W. HUBBARD, *HOW TO MEASURE ANYTHING*

Let's take a look at some metrics that you'll want to track at almost every startup.

WHAT METRICS TO TRACK

The numbers that matter to a startup will vary from company to company, but there are several types of metrics that just about everyone will need to track:

- Acquisition
- Activation
- Retention
- Referral
- Revenue
- The magic number

The first five metrics—acquisition, activation, retention, referral, and revenue—come from Dave McClure's "Startup Metrics for Pirates," and are easy to remember by the acronym AARRR [McClure 2007].[1] The last metric, the magic

---

1 Just about all of these metrics can be tracked in mobile apps and on the web using Google Analytics (GA). It's free and simple to use, so it's a great choice when starting out.

number, is derived from the first five, and it's a great way to get a global view of how your startup is doing.

Acquisition

The first metric you should care about is acquisition, or how users find your product. As I'll discuss in "Distribution" on page 159, it doesn't matter how great your product is if no one can find it. To help people find it, you can use distribution channels such as search engines, advertising, blogs, email, TV, and social networks. Because acquisition is the top of the funnel, it's the first and often the toughest bottleneck for growth. The only way to make it work is to try many different experiments across many different acquisition channels and to carefully track which ones are working and which ones aren't.

Activation

Once users have found your product, the next thing to track is activation, which is a measure of how many users engage with your product by signing up for an account, inviting a friend, performing a search, or making a purchase. If you have the wrong messaging, your design doesn't make it obvious what the user needs to do, or if your acquisition channel is bringing in the wrong audience, the user might *bounce*, or leave the product immediately after seeing it, without performing any actions.

In general, as you make your product better and improve your acquisition targeting, the activation rate should go up and the bounce rate should go down. This is one area where you can do heavy A/B testing (which we'll discuss in "Data-driven development" on page 152) to improve your numbers. Also, make sure to break down the activation numbers by acquisition channel to see if certain channels are leading to higher activation rates than others. Perhaps users who come in through Facebook ads have an 80% bounce rate, while users who come in through Google search have only a 50% bounce rate. If so, you know you need to tweak your ad targeting on Facebook or stop using ads entirely and double down on improving your search ranking.

Retention

The next stage is getting activated users to come back and use your product again. In some ways, this is also acquisition, but retention typically uses different channels and therefore should be tracked separately. Most users have lots of things fighting for their attention, so they will not remember to keep using your app or come back to your website unless you go out of your way to remind them.

This is why almost everyone wants you to sign up for their email newsletter, why every company maintains a blog full of useful tips and advice, why every mobile app wants to send you notifications, and why many games have time-based features that require you to keep coming back so you don't lose progress. Even users that have activated still need to see a product many times before it sticks and becomes a part of their routine.

You'll want to track how many of your visitors return after a week, a month, and a year. And just as some of your acquisition channels will work better than others, you'll want to track which of your retention channels is most effective at getting users to come back. Finally, make sure to break the retention numbers down across activation and acquisition dimensions. For example, if you're building a product with social features, you might find that retention is higher among users who were invited by a friend than users who came in as a cold sign-up. This is why most social applications make such an effort to get you to invite your friends and to connect with users during the initial activation flow.

Referral

The topic of inviting friends brings us to referral metrics. In a sense, this is also another form of acquisition, but one that's focused on one specific channel: existing users of your product helping you acquire new users. It's worth calling out separately because just about every product in the world, no matter what other distribution channels it uses, still relies heavily on word of mouth (see "Word of mouth" on page 160). This is why many companies offer rewards for referring your friends, such as DropBox offering 500MB of free storage space for each friend you get to sign up.

Referral metrics are not only important as a source of acquisition, but also as a proxy for measuring the quality of your product. You wouldn't recommend a product to your friend unless you liked it, so referrals going up is often a great way to measure that your product is getting better. This is why knowing where referrals came from is essential, and why "how did you hear about us?" is a very common question on registration forms.

Revenue

You should be tracking how much money you're making and what channels it's coming through, such as sales, subscriptions, ads, or biz dev. You will probably want to use your revenue numbers to calculate the *customer lifetime value* (CLV), which is an estimate of how much money you'll make from a single customer over the lifetime of your relationship with them (if you Google around, you can find a number of simple formulas for calculating CLV). For a business to be successful, your CLV must be greater than your acquisition costs, so track these two metrics carefully.

Also, don't forget to break down your revenue numbers across the other metrics. For example, if you look at mobile games produced by companies like Zynga, you'll find that half of the revenue comes from just 0.15% of the players. These players are known as "whales" and understanding what acquisition, activation, retention, and referral strategies attract more whales is the only way to succeed in such a business [Johnson 2014].

The magic number

Every company has a "magic number": some metric that, when the user crosses it, they have an "a-ha" moment and finally "get" the product. For example, for Facebook, the leading indicator that a new user will become a highly engaged user is the magic number of connecting with 7 friends within 10 days of registering [Palihapitiya 2013]. At Twitter, a new user is likely to become an active user once they follow 30 people [Elman 2011]. At Slack, once a team exchanges 2,000 messages, 93% of them remain Slack users [First Round Review 2015]. Identifying a magic number allows your team to focus on a single clear, concrete, easily measurable goal, which simplifies decision making across the company. Will this project significantly affect our magic number? If yes, let's do it. If not, shelve it for later.

Andrew Chen posted a great guide on Quora on how to identify the magic number for your company [Chen 2013]. The first step is to figure out what the *success metric* is for your company. When the success metric is going up, your business is succeeding, and when it's going down, your business is failing. This will vary for every company, but it should be pretty obvious. Facebook and Twitter get most of their revenue from ads, so their success metrics are very closely tied to user engagement (e.g., how many times the user comes back to the site over a 28-day period). Slack is a subscriptions product, so its success might be tied to what percentage of users are paying customers. Etsy is an e-commerce company, so its success metric is probably tied to how many transactions happen on the site.

Once you've figured out the success metric, the second step is to determine which user actions correlate with an increase in your success metric. Grab a representative subset of your users and plug all the data you have on them (e.g., the acquisition metrics, activation metrics, etc.) into a giant spreadsheet. Once you

plot the user activity metrics against your company's success metric, you'll sometimes get lucky and find a very obvious correlation. For example, if you plot the
number of people a Twitter user is following versus the number of consecutive
days they log in, you get the graph in Figure 4-1, and it's obvious that the tipping
point is around 30–40 on the y-axis. Sometimes it's not as obvious, and you'll
have to run a regression to find a good correlation.[2]

---

2 See [Cook 2013] for an example.

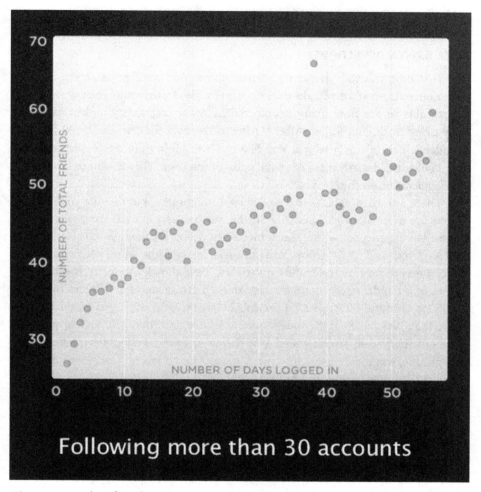

Figure 4-1. Number of people a Twitter user is following versus how many days in a row they log in [Elman 2011]

You don't need to find a perfect correlation and you don't want to define your magic number as a collection of 25 different factors. Your magic number needs to be inspiring and easy to reason about, so prefer a metric that's simple and explains most of the variation to one that explains a little more of the variation but at the expense of significantly more complexity. Whatever metric you select as your magic number, the final step is to test it and make sure that it affects your success metric the way you expect. In other words, you need to show cause and effect rather than just correlation, which is usually best done through A/B testing, a key part of data-driven development.

DATA-DRIVEN DEVELOPMENT

The first time you start gathering metrics about your business is an eye-opening experience. Even if all you do is hook up Google Analytics to your website, it's remarkable to see how many people visited, what pages they looked at, where they came from, and so on. After staring at the data for a while, you'll begin to wonder which of the products and features you built were successful and how you could use data to increase your odds of success. This is where *data-driven development* comes into play.

There are many aspects to data-driven development, but the one you're going to use the most often is called *A/B testing*. An A/B test is marketing jargon for a controlled experiment where the subjects are randomly divided into two groups, an "A" group and a "B" group, with all variables kept the same between the two groups except for one independent variable. This allows you to try two different values of the independent variable, one in each group, and see if it has any statistically meaningful effect on that group's behavior. Of course, you could also test more than two values of the independent variable, but then you have to switch to different marketing jargon called *split testing* or *bucket testing*, where instead of two groups, you divide users into many groups (or "buckets") and test a different value of the independent variable on each one.

For example, around 2009, LinkedIn was working on a new design for the subscriptions page, where users could sign up for a premium account. The design called for a large image of a happy person right at the top. But what person should we use? We could have let the designer choose it based on gut feel, but we decided to bucket test it. We had four stock photos to choose from, so we randomly divided LinkedIn members into four buckets, buckets A, B, C, and D, and showed each user one of the images in Figure 4-2. Which bucket do you think performed the best?

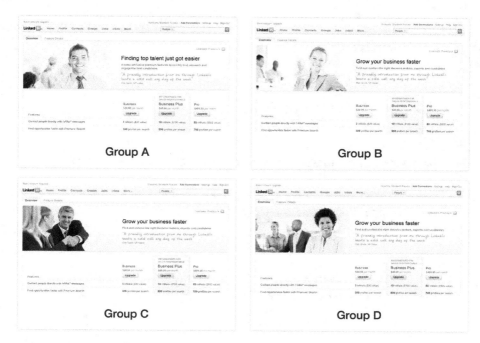

Figure 4-2. LinkedIn subscriptions bucket test

It turns out that bucket C significantly outperformed the others. The image of the gray-haired gentleman must have inspired confidence in our users, as we had far more people subscribe when he appeared on the screen. Think about that: we made more money just by using bucket testing instead of gut feel.

Once you've tasted success with A/B testing, you won't be able to go back. You'll realize how much more effective your decision making can be when powered by data, and you'll want to incorporate data into every aspect of your product development process.

Incorporating data into the product development process

Here is how Etsy used to develop products:

1. *Build feature.*

2. *Rent warehouse for launch party.*

3. *Release feature.*

4. *Launch party.*

5. *Wait 20 months.*

6. *Delete feature for lack of usage.*

—[MCKINLEY 2014A], DAN MCKINELY, SOFTWARE ENGINEER AT ETSY AND STRIPE

In my experience, this description applies not only to Etsy but to the vast majority of companies. Figure 4-3 shows a rough diagram of this product development process.

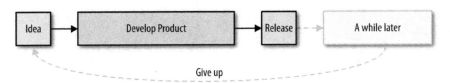

Figure 4-3. Typical product release process (diagram based on a talk by Dan McKinely [McKinley 2014a])

The odds of building a successful product this way are low. Even worse, sometimes you can't even tell if you were successful or not. Let's say you redesign your website, and a week later your activation numbers are up by 10%. It's possible the redesign caused the uptick but it's also possible that the real cause was something entirely unrelated, such as a change to your website's ranking on Google search. With this product release process, there's no way to be sure.

One way to solve this problem is to run an A/B test. Instead of releasing the new feature to all users, you randomly partition users into either group A, which is a control group that doesn't see the new feature, or group B, which is the experimental group that does get to see it.[3] After some amount of time, depending on how long it takes you to get enough website visitors for the results to be statistically meaningful,[4] you look at the metrics for group B and see if they are

---

3 Check out *http://www.hello-startup.net/resources/mvp/* for a list of A/B testing tools.

4 Check out *http://www.experimentcalculator.com/* to calculate the appropriate duration for an A/B test.

any different from those of group A. If they are, the new feature is the most likely cause, as that should be the only variable that changed between the two groups.

If the new feature gets your metrics to improve, you can roll it out to all users. If not, then you throw it away and go back to the drawing board. This gives you the slightly better product development process shown in Figure 4-4.

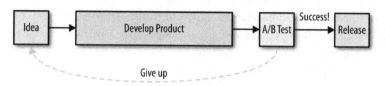

Figure 4-4. *Typical product release process with A/B testing at the end (diagram based on a talk by Dan McKinely [McKinley 2014a])*

The remarkable thing is that when you use this process and A/B test just before a release, you are likely to find that most of your features either hurt your metrics or have no impact. This is exactly what Etsy found when they started A/B testing. It's a pattern I saw at LinkedIn and at almost every single startup I talked to for this book. All of these companies are spending months or years and millions of dollars on developing new products, and in many cases, no one uses them and they throw them away after a year or two.

There are many reasons why a product might fail, but one of them is what Tim Harford calls *the God complex*. Many people, especially experts, hold the belief that they can solve almost any problem just by thinking very hard about it. They come up with elaborate product ideas, or clever engineering designs, or fancy diagrams and equations on a piece of paper, and await success. Except in the vast majority of cases, the success never comes. That's because the world we live in is immensely complicated. We are constantly dealing with systems that are beyond any individual's understanding, such as the free market economy, or the human mind, or a distributed computer system. The problems that affect these systems are too complicated to solve through reason alone.

I'm not trying to say we can't solve complicated problems in a complicated world. We clearly can. But the way we solve them is with humility—to abandon the God complex and to actually use a problem-solving technique that works. And we have a problem-solving technique that works.

Now you show me a successful complex system, and I will show you a system that has evolved through trial and error.

—[HARFORD 2011], TIM HARFORD, ECONOMIST

Instead of intelligent design, we need evolution. That means letting go of the God complex and admitting to yourself that you don't know the right answer. This is hard because schools condition you to think that there is a right answer to every problem and that you can get it just by thinking hard. And while that's true of the simple, constrained, cookie-cutter problems you do in school, the type of problems you deal with in the business world have no easy, obvious solutions. Company after company has found that the only way to survive in such a world is to try as many things as possible and see what works.

In examining the history of the visionary companies, we were struck by how often they made some of their best moves not by detailed strategic planning, but rather by experimentation, trial and error, opportunism, and —quite literally—accident. What looks in hindsight like a brilliant strategy was often the residual result of opportunistic experimentation and "purposeful accidents."

—[COLLINS PORRAS 2004, 141], JIM COLLINS AND JERRY I. PORRAS, *BUILT TO LAST*

Note that trial and error is not the same thing as blind guessing. You still try to reason through problems as best you can, but you acknowledge that some of your assumptions are wrong and that the only way to find out which ones is through trial and error. And as scientists have known for centuries, the proper way to do trial and error is through controlled experiments.

Data-driven development through controlled experiments

Building out an entire feature or product only to see that it has no impact after you run an A/B test is expensive and painful. Is there a way to avoid all this wasted effort? Well, just as you can't eliminate all uncertainty with measurement, you can't eliminate all wasted effort when building products, but you can reduce it. To do that, you need to use data and controlled experiments throughout your entire development process. As shown in Figure 4-5, instead of investing in building out the whole product right up front, you use an iterative methodology:

1. Build an MVP.

2. A/B test it.

3. Analyze the results and make one of three decisions:

    a. Refine: the numbers look good enough to justify developing the MVP further. Go back to step 1.

    b. Release: the numbers look great and the product is done. Release it to everyone.

    c. Give up: the numbers are not good enough to justify continued work. Move on to the next idea.

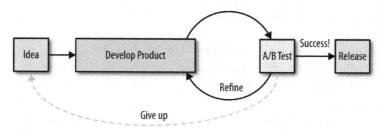

Figure 4-5. Data-driven development (diagram based on a talk by Dan McKinely [McKinley 2014a])

Instead of making a large investment in the product up front, you iteratively make small investments in MVPs that test your assumptions, gather data from each experiment, and only invest further if the numbers merit it. For example, on the first iteration, the MVP may just be a paper prototype and you use the customer validation process to chat with real customers to see if you've identified whether the prototype resonates with them (see "Customer development" on page 57). If the customer feedback looks good, the next iteration could be a Wizard of Oz MVP (see "Types of MVPs" on page 128) and an A/B test. If the A/B test shows that the MVP is having a positive impact on your metrics (especially your magic number), you could build out the prototype more fully and run another A/B test. You continue this build-validate cycle until the product is done or it's clear that the idea is not working, in which case you give up. But even if the idea doesn't work out, with a data-driven process, you find that out earlier and significantly reduce wasted effort. Speed wins.

Data-driven development strengths and weaknesses

"Design like you're right. Read the data like you're wrong."

—[LILLY 2015], JOHN LILLY, PARTNER AT GREYLOCK

Data-driven development will reveal if something you built is working, but it's up to you to interpret the data and understand why that's the case. Data-driven development is superb at comparing options, but it's up to you to come up with the options in the first place. And data-driven development is the perfect way to incrementally improve a product, but it's up to you to make massive jumps to avoid getting stuck in local maxima. In short, data-driven development works best when you combine the strengths of a human being (i.e., creativity and insight) with the strengths of a computer (i.e., data collection and measurement). Use data as a way to *inform* your decision-making process and not as a way to *replace* it.

Besides informing your product development process, you can also use data as an ingredient for building *data products*. For example, one of the most recognizable features on LinkedIn is People You May Know (PYMK), a recommendation system that tries to predict who else you might know on the site. PYMK generates recommendations by processing a vast amount of data, including connection data (e.g., if Alice knows Bob and Bob knows Carole, perhaps Alice knows Carole, too), education and work data (e.g., if Alice and Bob were at the same school or company at the same time, they are more likely to know each other), and geographical data (e.g., if Alice and Bob are in the same city, they are more likely to know each other). It also feeds user behavior data (i.e., whether a user clicked on one of the recommendations or not) into the recommendation engine as feedback (i.e., reinforcement learning).

Data products can be a powerful differentiator. For example, PYMK is responsible for more than half the connections on LinkedIn. Amazon has reported that 35% of product sales come from its recommendation system [Marshall 2006]. And Netflix is known for its movie recommendation system, in part because it makes great recommendations and in part because they held a competition where they offered $1 million to anyone who could build a better system.[5]

---

5 The details of the competition are posted online (*http://www.netflixprize.com/*).

Distribution

So far, we've talked about all the ways to build a great product: you need a great idea, you need to build a cheap MVP, you need to come up with a simple design, and you need to use data to inform your decisions. Unfortunately, even if you manage to put together an amazing product, the best product does not always win.

In the late 90s, TiVo came out with the first consumer DVR and developed a very loyal following of customers who raved about the ability to pause and rewind live TV and schedule recordings of all of their favorite shows. But by 2008, TiVo's market share in the DVR space was a mere 6%. The other 94% was dominated by cable companies who sold DVRs that, by all accounts, were inferior to TiVo (fewer features, worse user experience). However, the cable companies had a superior distribution strategy: they offered the DVR as an upgrade to the cable box that their customers were required to get anyway [Machefsky 2008].

In the early 80s, Microsoft's DOS operating system was not as powerful or user friendly as Apple's operating system, but while Apple kept its software proprietary and only allowed it to be distributed on Apple hardware, Microsoft licensed its operating system to anyone who would buy it. And buy it they did. Dozens of desktop manufacturers, including IBM and all the IBM PC clones, licensed Microsoft's operating system and flooded the market with cheap PCs. By 2000, Microsoft had replaced DOS with Windows, and while it was still arguable whether it was as good as Apple's OS, it controlled 97% of the market [Yarow 2012].

If we lived in a world with perfect information, the best product would always win. But we don't live in such a world. These days, there are way too many things vying for our attention and there's simply no way for any customer to be aware of even a fraction of the products out there. And if the customer doesn't know you exist, it doesn't matter how good your product is. Therefore, it's not the best product that wins, but the product the customer thinks is best. Making customers aware of your products and influencing how they perceive them is known as *distribution*.

The saying "If you build it, they will come" is not true. There is no such thing as a product that sells itself. If you want to succeed, you have to build not only a product, but also a way to distribute it.

It's better to think of distribution as something essential to the design of your product. If you've invented something new but you haven't invented an effective way to sell it, you have a bad business—no matter how good the product.

—[THIEL 2014, 130], PETER THIEL, *ZERO TO ONE*

Let's take a look at the four most common distribution channels for startups:

- Word of mouth
- Marketing
- Sales
- Branding

WORD OF MOUTH

The most powerful way to spread the message about your product is for you not to spread it at all. Instead, let your customers do it. No company can afford to pay for every marketing contact, so just about every company relies on some form of word-of-mouth distribution [Moore and McKenna 2006, 36-37]. That is, someone who is a customer recommending your product to someone who is not a customer. There are three things you can do to increase distribution through word of mouth:

- Build a better product
- Provide great customer service
- Build viral loops into your product

Build a better product

Although no product can truly sell itself, you can come close to this ideal by building a product so good that customers can't stop talking about it. For example, CrossFit is a fitness company and training program that was founded in 2000. Now, 15 years later, it is one of the fastest-growing sports of all time, with more than 10 million CrossFitters working out at over 10,000 affiliates across the world [Oh 2014] (for comparison, it took McDonald's 33 years to get to 10,000 affiliates [History of McDonald's 2015]). One of the reasons that CrossFit has grown so quickly is that it's like no other fitness program out there. Instead of promising you abs in five minutes by doing the same workout every day on fancy exercise machines in an air-conditioned gym, CrossFit promises you a lot of hard work in the form of intense and constantly varied full-body workouts that mix all aspects of fitness (running, lifting, gymnastics) and are done in unadorned buildings, garages, and parking lots using barbells, kettlebells, gymnastics rings, ropes, sleds, tractor tires, and sledge hammers. It is so wildly different than other fitness programs that CrossFitters cannot shut up about it. Or as the joke goes, "How can you tell that someone does CrossFit? Don't worry, they'll tell you."

Notice that what makes CrossFit worthy of discussing is how *different* it is. It's not about having every possible feature (as a fitness program, CrossFit has plenty of gaps and weaknesses), but about being exceptional at a small number of features (see "Focus on the differentiators" on page 133). Focusing on your differentiators is not only important for building a great MVP but also for increasing the odds that customers will notice your product because it stands out from the rest.

In his TED Talk "How to Get Your Ideas to Spread," Seth Godin has a great analogy for this idea [Godin 2003]. Imagine you were driving along and saw a cow on the side of the road. Would you stop and take notice? Probably not. You've seen cows plenty of times in your life, so you'd just keep on driving. But if you saw a purple cow, you'd almost certainly pull over and take some pictures. Why? Because a purple cow is *remarkable*. It works the same way for products. Consumers are so overloaded with product choices and marketing messages that the only way you're going to get them to pay attention to you—and just as importantly, get their friends to pay attention to you—is if you do something remarkable. You have to stand out and give people something worth talking about.

Provide great customer service

No matter how hard you try to build an amazing product, you won't get everything right. Customers will have questions. They will run into bugs. They will find corner cases and make requests for new functionality. This is where customer service comes in. It might seem strange to lump customer service into a discussion about distribution, but many companies have found that if you do customer service exceptionally well, you can turn it into your differentiator and get powerful word-of-mouth effects:

> *Over the years, the number one driver of our growth at Zappos has been repeat customers and word of mouth. Our philosophy has been to take most of the money we would have spent on paid advertising and invest it*

into customer service and the customer experience instead, letting our customers do the marketing for us through word of mouth.

I personally think it's kind of funny when I attend marketing or branding conferences and hear companies talk about consumers being bombarded with thousands and thousands of advertising messages every day, because there's usually a lot of discussion among companies and ad agencies talking about how to get their message to stand out. There's a lot of buzz these days about "social media" and "integration marketing." As unsexy and low-tech as it may sound, our belief is that the telephone is one of the best branding devices out there. You have the customer's undivided attention for five to ten minutes, and if you get the interaction right, what we've found is that the customer remembers the experience for a very long time and tells his or her friends about it.

—[HSIEH 2013, 143], TONY HSIEH, *DELIVERING HAPPINESS*

If you really want to be exceptional at customer service, it's usually not enough to have a separate, outsourced customer service department. Zappos makes every employee participate in customer service (see "Culture fit" on page 476). Similarly, every engineer at Stripe, and even the founders, do customer support on a biweekly rotation [Maccaw 2012]. How can you possibly scale a company if the engineers are doing customer service? Well, as we've discussed before, in the early days of a company, it's perfectly fine to do things that don't scale. But involving everyone in customer service can scale surprisingly far, as it not only gets you loyal customers who spread the product by word of mouth but also helps you build a better product by making the people who write the code feel the pain of the customers that use it. For example, Paul English, the cofounder of KAYAK, installed a customer support phone line in the middle of the engineering floor. People would often ask him "Why would you have high-paid engineers answering customer phone calls?" and his response was, "Well, after the second or third time that the phone rings, and the engineer gets the same problem, they stop what they're doing, they fix the bug, and they stop getting phone calls about it" [Hale 2014].

We talked in Chapter 3 about using customer development to constantly validate assumptions with real customers by getting out of the building. Customer service has the same benefits, except in this case, the customers come to you. Make it easy for them by making sure there is a feedback email address or phone number in an obvious place in your product and/or by using tools such as Zen-Desk, Groove, and Get Satisfaction to manage communication with your users.

Build viral loops into your product

Many people are talking about using a "viral marketing strategy" these days, but the truth is that there is no such thing. A blog post or video that "goes viral" on all the social networks isn't a marketing strategy but dumb luck. You can't predict it, you can't control the audience that sees it, and you can't turn it into a sustainable strategy for distribution. Virality is no more than another way of saying word of mouth. If you want to encourage word of mouth beyond the mechanisms we already discussed (building a better product and providing great customer service), then what you need is not a viral marketing strategy, but to build a *viral loop* into your product.

A viral loop is a feature in the product that gives current users an incentive to recruit new users. The new users, in turn, have an incentive to invite even more users, spreading your product like a virus. For example, in the late 90's, PayPal offered current users $10 for every friend they referred and new users got $10 for signing up. The bet was that once users signed up, they'd be hooked on the service and would be sending enough money back and forth to cover the $20 acquisition cost per user. It was a huge risk and probably not one many other companies should try to copy, but it paid off for PayPal, propelling growth to as much as 7%–10% per day until the service had over 100 million users [Masters 2012, sect. III].

Some viral loops require no user intervention at all. For example, when Hotmail first launched in 1996, they were one of the world's first free web-based email services, but they were struggling to find a way to communicate that message to a large number of users. They decided to try a viral tactic: each time a user sent an email, Hotmail automatically added a signature to the bottom of the email that included a link with the text "Get your free email at Hotmail." When someone received an email from a Hotmail user, they would see that (a) the sender, who was often someone they trusted, was a user, (b) the service worked, and (c) the service was free. As soon as the signature went live, Hotmail's growth took off. They started adding thousands of users per day, a million within six months, 2 million a few weeks after that, and so on [Penenberg 2009, chap. 4].

The most powerful viral loops are those that are an intrinsic part of using the product. If you have a product where a customer doesn't get value out of it unless someone else uses it, such as telephone, video chat, or messaging, then inviting new customers becomes an inherent part of using the product, and you have a chance for rapid viral growth. However, there is a catch. How do you get the initial customers to sign up? How do you convince someone to buy a telephone when no one else has a telephone and there is no one to call? This is known as the *cold start problem*. Products like the telephone are subject to Metcalfe's Law: the value of the product is proportional to the square of the number of users (n^2). That means it's hard to get such a product started (0^2 is 0), but once you get the ball rolling, you get strong *network effects*, where every new user significantly increases the value of the network, which attracts more new users, which increases the network value even more, and so on.

Social networks are a classic example of the power of intrinsic viral growth and network effects. The whole point of social networking is to connect with other people, so sending invites is an inherent part of using the product, leading to explosive growth. At the end of 2014, LinkedIn had 347 million members [LinkedIn 2014] and Facebook had nearly 1.4 billion [Facebook 2014]. How did these networks solve the cold start problem? First, they made it easy to invite non-members to the service by allowing you to import contacts from your email, phone, and other existing networks (it's easier to build a viral software product because new users don't need to purchase anything physical, such as a phone). Second, they offered users something valuable even before the network was large. For example, even when LinkedIn had very few members, it was still useful as a public place to store your résumé so that potential employers and business partners could find you.

These examples should dispel a few myths about viral loops. First, they are not free. It always costs something to build a viral loop into the product, and if the viral mechanism isn't an inherent part of the user experience, you might have to pay for each new user, as in the case of PayPal. Second, while almost every product can benefit from word of mouth, not every type of product will be able to include a viral loop. Here are some questions you should ask:

- *How can a user create content that reaches another user?*

- *How does a user's experience get better the more people they are connected to on it?*

- *How does a user benefit from reaching out to a non-user?*

—[NASH 2012], ADAM NASH, PRESIDENT AND CEO AT WEALTHFRONT

If your product is inherently social—that is, it is meant to be used by multiple people collaboratively, such as a social network, a file sharing service, or a payments app—the answers to these questions are typically easy. If not, then building a sustainable viral loop is likely to be difficult. To see if it's worth your time, you can do some back-of-the-envelope calculations to see what kind of payoff you might get.

The first step is to estimate your *viral coefficient*. The viral coefficient (AKA viral factor) is a number that answers the following question:

Given that I get a new customer today, how many new customers will they bring in over the next N days?

—[NASH 2012], ADAM NASH, PRESIDENT AND CEO AT WEALTHFRONT

The number N represents a reasonable *cycle time* for your business. That is, how long does it typically take for a new customer to send out invites and for the recipients to respond to them? For example, for a product like Facebook, a reasonable guess might be $N = 1$ day because a new user will typically send out all their invites right after registering, and because the invites go out by email and mobile notifications, the recipients are likely to see and respond to them that same day. On the other hand, for a product like SlideShare, a new user may post a slide deck and share it with their friends right after registering, but the friends probably won't sign up for SlideShare until they have their own slide deck to share, which might not be until many months later, so perhaps $N = 180$ days.

To calculate your viral coefficient (K), you need to take the number of invites (I) your users send every N days (i.e., how many times a current user performs an action that could potentially recruit a new user, such as sending an invite on a social network) and multiply it by the average conversion rate (C) on those invites (i.e., what percentage of the invites are accepted).

$$K = I \times C$$

For example, let's say you launched your product today and 1,000 people signed up. You look at the metrics and find that those 1,000 users sent 5,000 invites shortly after registering, or an average of $I = 5$ invites per user. Those invites get a lot of clicks the first few days, tailing off to zero after about a week, so your cycle time is $N = 7$ days. At the end of that week, you've found that the invites got 500 new users to sign up, so your conversion rate is $C = 500 / 5,000 = 0.1$. That gives you a viral coefficient of $K = I \times C = 5 \times 0.1 = 0.5$. Assuming these numbers hold, you will have $1,000 \times 0.5 = 500$ new users after the first week, $500 \times 0.5 = 250$ new users after the second week, and so on:

$$1,000 + (1,000 \times 0.5) + \left(1,000 \times 0.5^2\right) + \left(1,000 \times 0.5^3\right) + \ldots$$

For a viral coefficient of K and a cycle time of N, you can calculate the number of users T days after launch as:

$$Users(T) = \sum_{i=0}^{T/N} Users(0) \times K^i$$

If you remember your high-school math, this is a geometric series, and the sum of the first x terms of this geometric series can be expressed as:

$$Users(0) \times \frac{1 - K^x}{1 - K}$$

If $K < 1.0$, as x approaches infinity, K^x will go to 0, reducing the equation to:

$$Users(0) \times \frac{1}{1 - K}$$

If you plug in your viral coefficient of $K = 0.5$, you'll see that this geometric series converges to double the number of users you started with. Similarly, if you plug in $K = 0.67$, you will see that it triples your users; $K = 0.75$ will quadruple your users, and so on. This means that a viral coefficient between 0 and 1 can be thought of as a fixed multiplier, as shown in Figure 4-6. When you combine it with other sustainable distribution strategies, viral growth is a powerful way to amplify your reach.

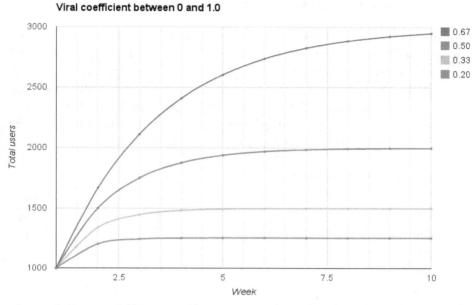

Figure 4-6. User growth if you start with 1,000 users and a viral coefficient between 0 and 1.0

But what if you had a viral coefficient of 1.0 or greater? For example, if you had a viral coefficient of 1.5, then the initial 1,000 users would bring in (1,000 * 1.5) = 1,500 users the next week. Those users, in turn, would bring in (1,500 * 1.5) = 2,250 users the week after, and then 3,375 the week after that, and so on. If you continue this pattern, you get exponential growth and before long, every human on earth is using your product. This is obviously unrealistic. In the real world, no product can maintain a viral coefficient above 1.0 for more than a short period of time, and most products have a coefficient that is much smaller:

True viral growth is incredibly rare. It took me a while to appreciate this: very few products have sustained a viral factor over 1 for any meaningful period of time. But if we shouldn't bet on a viral factor greater than 1, what should we use in our model? From discussions with other entrepreneurs, investors, and growth hackers, I've learnt the following: for a consumer internet product, a sustainable viral factor of 0.15 to 0.25 is good, 0.4 is great, and around 0.7 is outstanding.

—[VOHRA 2012], RAHUL VOHRA, CO-FOUNDER OF RAPPORTIVE

Because very few products can sustain a viral factor over 1.0, you can't rely solely on a PR push and viral growth. You need some other sustainable distribution mechanism. For example, let's say your product gets 10,000 visitors per week via Google search (see "SEO" on page 171), and that you're able to get 500 of these visitors to register. Take a look at Figure 4-7 to see what happens when you combine your initial 1,000 users from the PR push, plus the 500 users who register from search, plus a variety of different viral coefficients.

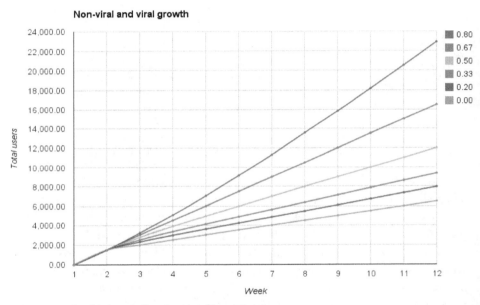

Figure 4-7. Combining viral and non-viral growth

If your product isn't viral at all, after 12 weeks, you have a little over 6,500 users. If you have a viral coefficient of 0.5, you'll have roughly 12,000 users, and if you're really crushing it and have a viral coefficient of 0.8, you'll have almost 23,000 users. Note that this calculation doesn't take into account many factors, such as user retention (e.g., every week, some percentage of users stop using your product) and the way the viral coefficient changes over time (e.g., the calculation assumes that new users send invites when they join, but never after that). For a more complete discussion of how to model viral growth, as well as some handy spreadsheets you can use to do all the calculations for you, check out Rahul Vohra's series of posts on "How to Model Viral Growth" [Vohra 2012].

MARKETING

Let's now turn our attention from word of mouth, where new customers find out about your product from existing customers, to marketing, where new customers find out about your product directly from you. There are many different ways to market a product, so we'll just take a brief look at some of the most common ones used by startups:

- Advertising
- PR and media
- Email
- SEO
- Social media
- Inbound marketing

Advertising

Advertising is almost synonymous with marketing. You figure out where your potential customers are already directing their attention and you pay money to put a message about your product there. The good thing about advertising is that it works. The bad thing about advertising is that everyone knows it works. Advertising is a $220 billion industry in the United States alone [Advertising Spending in the United States 2014], and anywhere you turn, there are ads vying for your attention. There are commercials on TV, the radio, airplanes, billboards, and the sides of buses; there are product placements and celebrity endorsements in every movie and show; there are ads in every newspaper, magazine, stadium, movie theater, and concert hall; there are ads on park benches and sidewalks, on T-shirts and hats, on stickers and decals; and, of course, there are ads on your computer and smartphone in the form of banner ads, floating ads, search ads, sponsored updates in newsfeeds, mobile ads, and all manner of interstitial ads that you have to wade through to watch a video or read an article.

If you're going to spend money on advertising, you have to set up detailed tracking of your acquisition channels so you can tell if the advertising is working or not (see "Acquisition" on page 147). This is easier to do with online advertising, where you can usually tell if the user came through an ad click, and if they did, see how much that ad cost you and how much money that user made you in return. Although more difficult, it's also possible to track traditional ads such as TV commercials. One option is to use promo codes. For example, in each ad campaign, you can tell users to enter a specific promo code to get a discount, which gives users an incentive to come and check you out, and gives you the ability to track where they came from. Another option is to use consumer surveys. For example, when TripAdvisor launched a series of TV ads, it sent out surveys to its users to see how many people the campaign had reached and the effect it had on them [Schaal 2015].

Although surveys and promo codes are not as accurate as online tracking, your goal is not perfect data but just a reduction in uncertainty. Make sure to measure both where users came from and who they are, as you need to be sure not only that your advertising is reaching an audience but that it's reaching the right audience, which is often tricky to do with broadcast mediums like television and billboards.

PR and media

Besides advertising, public relations (PR) is another great way to get a message about your product in front of a large audience. To do that, you have to build relationships with people in the TV and movie industries, journalists, bloggers, and celebrities. Of course, if you do something that's remarkable (or something that's remarkably bad), sometimes they'll talk about you even if you don't ask.

For most startups, PR events are unpredictable, occasionally negative, and rarely a sustainable distribution strategy. They are a great way to get a spike in traffic, but after a few days, the spike usually dies down and you need to start all over again.

Email

When done right, email marketing is incredibly effective. When done wrong, it's just spam. The wrong way to use email is *direct marketing*, where you buy an email list and send a mass email to a bunch of strangers who have never heard of you. This is not a sustainable strategy, as the click-through rate (CTR) on such emails is miniscule (typically just a fraction of a percent) and your emails quickly get classified as spam by most major email carriers. This could end up hurting your company's reputation so you'll only be able to send a few campaigns of this sort.

A better way to use email is to build an email list of users who opt in to receive information about your product. For example, you could give users a way to sign up for a newsletter on your landing page (see "The MVP" on page 125). Customers often take a long time to make a purchase decision and they may have to see the product over and over again before they warm up to it. Sending an occasional reminder email with useful information can be a great way to turn a warm lead into a paying customer. Compared to direct marketing, this approach will get you a slightly higher CTR (maybe 1%) and your emails are less likely to be categorized as spam.

The best way to use email is to send personalized emails in response to user actions or events the user cares about. For example, every time someone tags you in a photo on Facebook, you get an email. I don't know about you, but my CTR on such emails is pretty much 100%, as I have to make sure it's not an image I'll regret. In 2011, LinkedIn launched the "Year in Review" email, an annual email that shows you photos of all of your colleagues who made significant career changes over the last year. The CTR on this email was astronomical, as many users clicked on more than one link in the email (CTR > 100%?) to find out who got a new job or a promotion.

The important thing to realize about email is that it's not a good tool for getting new users (acquisition), but it's one of the best tools for engaging existing users (activation, retention, referral, and revenue). There are many different kinds of emails you can send, such as welcome emails, onboarding emails, re-engagement emails, and referral campaigns. Check out the sendwithus "How to Send Email Like a Startup" guide (*https://www.sendwithus.com/resources/guide/*) for more info.

SEO

Search Engine Optimization (SEO) is optimizing your website so that it ranks highly in search results. Google saw 1.2 trillion searches in 2012 [Google Zeitgeist 2012] and many large businesses have been built by carving out a slice of this massive query volume. If your product has a large amount of unique and valuable content, such as user reviews (e.g., TripAdvisor), discussion forums (e.g., Reddit), Q&A (e.g., Stack Overflow), or reference material (e.g., Wikipedia), you may be able to drive thousands or millions of page views more or less for free through SEO. And not only does this get you a large amount of fairly sustainable traffic, but it's often traffic that converts well because it represents people who were searching for the exact kind of content you have.

The catch is that the ranking algorithm used by Google and all other search engines is kept secret. Google has published an SEO starter guide (*http://bit.ly/seo-start-guide*) and there are many other resources with SEO tips and tricks,[6] but there is no guarantee that these correspond to the way the ranking algorithm actually works. Making things even harder is that Google changes its ranking algorithm more than 500 times per year, and although most of the changes are minor, some can have a dramatic effect on your ranking.[7] This means that SEO isn't entirely free: you have to put in work up front to optimize your site and you have to stay up to date with the ranking-algorithm changes to keep your site at the top of the results pages. And, of course, you have to compete with all the other websites that are trying to do the same.

The good thing about SEO is that the ranking algorithms generally reward behavior you should be doing anyway. For example, the most important "optimization" you can do is to have a lot of high-quality content on your website—that is, you need to build a better product (see "Build a better product" on page 160). If you do, a lot of other websites will link to you, and when users click to your website, they won't bounce immediately—both factors that increase your page rank. All the other optimizations, such as tweaking header titles, URLs, domain names, and meta tags, are also useful but won't have nearly as big of an impact as building a better product.

Social media

Many companies are turning to social media for distribution, and for good reason, as social networks have massive and highly engaged audiences. Building a following on Facebook, Twitter, LinkedIn, Instagram, Pinterest, and similar sites is a great strategy for engaging users you already have—it's like a more modern version of the email newsletter. Even better, social media allows you to engage with users on an individual level, which makes it an effective customer service tool. The only thing it's not particularly good at is user acquisition. When you share something on Twitter or Facebook, your existing followers will see it, but no new users will unless someone reshares it. Occasionally, some of your content might get a huge number of reshares and "go viral," which can put your product in front of a lot of new users. However, this is much like a PR push, where it's a

---

6 Moz has a pretty good SEO Best Practices guide (*http://moz.com/learn/seo/on-page-factors*).

7 Moz maintains a "change history" (*http://moz.com/google-algorithm-change*) for Google's ranking algorithm.

one-time boost that's too unpredictable to rely on as a sustainable form of user acquisition.

Inbound marketing

Inbound marketing is about trying to attract customers' attention using content they find valuable rather than trying to buy customers' attention, as with advertising. Think of it as trying to bring customers *in* using a honeypot (*inbound marketing*), rather than sending your marketing messages *out* using a loudspeaker (*outbound marketing*). Your honeypot can be in the form of a blog, a podcast, a video, a book, or a set of open source tools, and you usually combine it with SEO and social media sharing to help customers find it. The key idea behind inbound marketing is not to try to sell something to the customer, but to try to teach them.

> Teach and you'll form a bond you just don't get from traditional marketing tactics. Buying people's attention with a magazine or online banner ad is one thing. Earning their loyalty by teaching them forms a whole different connection. They'll trust you more. They'll respect you more. Even if they don't use your product, they can still be your fans.
>
> —[FRIED AND HANSSON 2010, 173], JASON FRIED AND DAVID HEINEMEIER HANSSON, *REWORK*

Inbound marketing is an especially useful strategy for startups, as they can't compete with the ad budgets of larger companies but can produce valuable content. sendwithus is a great example. They run a blog that has tips on email marketing; they publish a free, comprehensive guide called "How to Send Email Like a Startup," and they give away lots of email tools (e.g., templates, components, layouts) for free.[8] If you're searching for help with sending email, you're more likely to click on free, valuable content than an ad or any overt message trying to sell you a product. As you read the sendwithus blog and use their tools, an association will slowly form in your mind between sendwithus and email. You'll start to think of them as the experts on email. They will be your go-to when you have questions. And then, one day, when you do need a paid email product, you are more likely to become their customer.

---

8 See *https://www.sendwithus.com/resources/*.

SALES

Marketing is about getting the customer to the door (acquisition). Sales is about closing the deal and getting the customer to make a purchase (revenue). If you have a "self-serve" product, such as a website where customers can plug in their credit card information to make a purchase, then your sales and marketing process are largely one and the same. However, there are many kinds of products where sales requires human intervention—a salesperson to take the customer through the process, answer questions, and hash out the details in a contract. Roughly 14 million people in the United States are employed in sales [Sales and Related Occupations 2013], which is nearly 5% of the population. The reason it's such a popular profession is that sales is fundamental to the success of most businesses, and even more generally, to the success of most things in life.

> *The most fundamental reason that even businesspeople underestimate the importance of sales is the systematic effort to hide it at every level of every field in a world secretly driven by it.*
>
> **—[THIEL 2014, 129], PETER THIEL, *ZERO TO ONE***

Just about every profession involves sales. The CEO of a company is, in may ways, a salesperson, selling the company's vision to customers, investors, shareholders, and employees. If you're in marketing or politics, you also spend most of your time selling. And even if you're a programmer, every time you interview for a job, negotiate an offer, or try to convince your team to adopt a new technology, you're also a salesperson. Of course, none of these jobs have "sales" in the title, because it's one of those games we all play where you can't acknowledge the game itself, or it falls apart. If you admit that you're flirting with someone, you probably won't get a date, and if you admit that you're trying to sell something, you probably won't close the deal. No one wants to be sold to, but everyone wants to buy something, which is what makes sales such a difficult profession.

> *How do you learn sales? Convince somebody to go use your product. It's like in* **The Wolf of Wall Street***: try to sell me this pen. Seriously, try it out. How would you do it? How would you make this pen important to me? Once you learn that, you'll know how to sell.*
>
> **—[SHOUP 2015], MATTHEW SHOUP, PRINCIPAL NERD AT NERDWALLET**

If you've founded a startup, selling your product—even if (or especially if) you're not a salesperson by trade—is a valuable exercise. Before you hire a sales team and before you spend a bunch of money on marketing, you should get out of the building, talk to customers in person, and try to sell your product (see "Customer development" on page 57). Only after you've made a few sales yourself, and thereby figured out what's important to the customer and what sales strategy works, should you worry about hiring a separate sales team (see "Do things that don't scale" on page 139).

Once you do reach that stage, the type of sales team you need depends largely on your product. Broadly speaking, there are three categories of sales:

1. *Automated sales* are self-serve systems where a customer can make a purchase without talking to a human representative, such as a checkout form on a website like Amazon.com.

2. *Inside sales* are salespeople who do most of their sales in their employer's workplace. One common type of inside sales is a salesperson who works in a store or dealership and sells products over the counter, such as an employee of an Apple store. Another common type is a salesperson who works in an office and sells products over the phone, email, chat, and web conferencing. For example, many Software as a Service (SaaS) products, such as SalesForce, allow you to sign up for a trial or basic versions of the product online (automated sales) and if you want the more powerful version of the product, you can reach out to a sales representative by phone or email (inside sales).

3. *Outside sales* are salespeople who do most of their work at the customer's workplace. They schedule in-person meetings with customers, give them on-site demos, and spend most of their time traveling to customer sites to talk directly with the relevant stakeholders.

Automated sales are the most scalable and cost-efficient option, but they generally only work for low-price products (less than $1,000). Outside sales is far more expensive and far less scalable—you have to hire a sales team and pay for their travel expenses, and each salesperson can only work with one customer at a time—but the personal attention allows you to sell much more expensive products that no one will order via an online checkout form ($100,000 and up). Inside sales falls somewhere in between. It costs more to run an inside sales team than an automated sales system, but not as much as an outside sales team, as an inside sales person in a store or making calls from an office can interact with many customers per day. This personal interaction with customers allows an inside sales team to secure larger deals than automated sales, but not as large as a dedicated outside sales team (deals in the $1,000 to $100,000 range are typical).

BRANDING

Earlier, I mentioned that it's not the best product that wins but the product the customer thinks is the best that wins. How a customer thinks about your company—if they think about it at all—is your *brand*, and trying to influence that perception is called *branding*. Branding is not a single strategy or marketing campaign, but the sum of all the ways you interact with the customer: it's what your company logo looks like, what you say in your tagline, how you present the company in your ads, what sort of expertise you give away in your inbound marketing, how your website looks, how your business cards look, what tactics your sales team uses, and how customer service treats the customer. Just as differentiators separate your products from other products, you brand needs to separate your company from other companies.

Red Bull makes sugary, caffeinated soda drinks, but its brand is something completely different. For example, the Red Bull website (*http://www.redbull.com*), as shown in Figure 4-8, shows a guy racing a dirt bike, college students at a party, and someone jumping off a mountain. The company runs a Red Bull TV channel that shows adventure sports like BASE jumping, free running, ice climbing, and whitewater kayaking; it owns a number of sports teams, including the New York Red Bulls (soccer), Infiniti Red Bull Racing (Formula One), and Team Red Bull (Nascar); and it sponsors events such as Red Bull Road Rage (an extreme downhill bike competition), Red Bull X-Fighters (freestyle motocross stunt competitions that take place in bullrings), and Red Bull Stratos (a space-diving project involving skydiver Felix Baumgartner, who did a free fall from 24 miles up and achieved speeds of over 800 mph) [Red Bull 2015]. When you think of Red Bull, you don't think of a drink but of extreme activities. That's its brand.

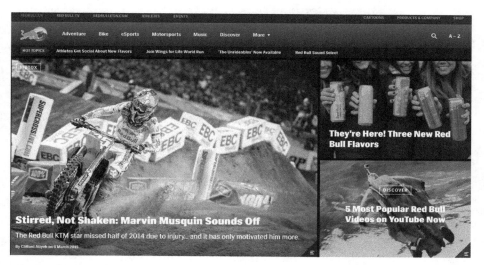

Figure 4-8. The Red Bull website

The thing to notice is that branding has very little to do with concrete products. It's all about emotions and beliefs. It's about why the company exists and not what it does (see "Core Ideology" on page 386). For example, Nike ad campaigns are not about shoes or air soles but about honoring great athletes and great athletics. Similarly, one of Apple's most successful ad campaigns, "Think Different," was not about computers, or CPU speeds, or why Apple was better than Microsoft but about answering the questions "Who is Apple and what do they stand for?" [Jobs 2007]:

> *Here's to the crazy ones. The misfits. The rebels. The troublemakers. Round pegs in the square holes. The ones who see things differently. They're not fond of rules and they have no respect for the status quo. You can quote them, disagree with them, glorify or vilify them. About the only thing you can't do is ignore them. Because they change things. They push the human race forward. And while some may see them as the crazy ones, we see genius. Because the people who are crazy enough to think they can change the world are the ones who do.*

—[JOBS 2007], APPLE

In just two words, "think different," you know exactly what Apple is all about and why you should care. Crafting such a clear, compelling message is not easy, but just as copywriting is the most important aspect of product design (see "Copywriting" on page 98), it's also the core of marketing. A great example of this is the tagline for a product. It has to be remarkable to catch people's attention, show how you're different, and be short and simple. For example, consider the slogan for the original iPod:

1,000 songs in your pocket.

—[LIST OF APPLE INC. SLOGANS 2015], TAGLINE FOR THE ORIGINAL IPOD

The iPod came out in an era when most people lugged around their music collection in massive CD wallets, where each CD held about 12 songs. The idea that you could have a music player that held 1,000 songs and still fit it into your pocket was remarkable.

In some sense, your brand is a promise that you're going to change the customer's life: "If you go with our company, here's what you will be able to do." Red Bull promises you the energy to do extreme activities. Apple promises you the technology that will allow you to think different. Note that the promise is not about what the product can do (features) but what the customer can do with your product (benefits). It's a critical difference, as illustrated in Figure 4-9, but once you deeply grok it, you'll find it easier to craft effective messaging.

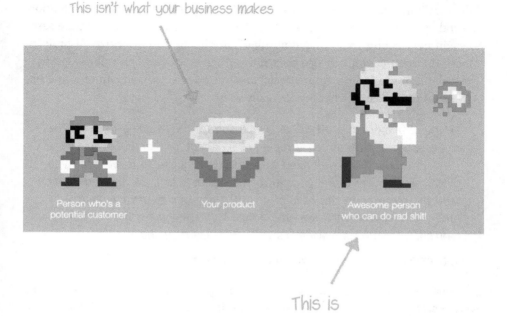

Figure 4-9. Features versus benefits (image courtesy of Samuel Hulick (http://bit.ly/hulick-fvb))

Recap

Y Combinator's motto is "make something people want." These four simple words manage to capture almost everything you need to know about building a successful startup. In Chapter 2, we talked about how to come up with ideas, and in Chapter 3, we covered how to design a basic product around them. These are, respectively, the "make" and "something" portion of "make something people want." In this chapter, we looked at the other two words in that motto, "people" and "want," in the form of "data" and "distribution," respectively.

If we have data, let's look at data. If all we have are opinions, let's go with mine.

—JIM BARKSDALE, FORMER CEO OF NETSCAPE

Data is how you know you're making something *people* want. Almost every decision you make can be improved by measuring and reducing your uncertainty. You can get a sense of how every aspect of your product is doing by carefully tracking your pirate metrics (AARRR): acquisition, activation, retention, referral, and revenue. And you can get your entire team aligned along the same mission by defining your "magic number" and using it to prioritize all projects. Most importantly, you can use data not only to track how past decisions have worked out but to inform future decisions. Put aside your God complex and use A/B testing to measure what people really want.

> Think of a "perfect product" as a mousetrap. You're going to catch the mouse, because it's a mousetrap and it's perfect for that, but even if it's a perfect product, you still need to attract the mouse to it. So what you really need to make the mousetrap successful is to think about the **bait** and the **placement**. You have to use the right food to attract the mouse and you have to put the trap in the right location, against the wall, where you know the mouse is living. It's all about placement and bait.
>
> —[SHOUP 2015], MATTHEW SHOUP, PRINCIPAL NERD AT NERDWALLET

Distribution is how you make something people *want*. To want something, your customer has to know it exists and find it desirable. This doesn't happen on its own, so you have to use the right placement and bait, which in the startup world consists of word of mouth, marketing, sales, and branding. When you're just starting out, your distribution strategy should mostly consist of the founders personally making sales. As the company grows, word of mouth, marketing, and branding will be necessary to scale. Which one you use depends on the type of product you're building. Table 4-1 has a few examples from the real world.

Table 4-1. *Primary distribution channels based on product*

Number of customers	Type of product	Price range	Example company	Distribution strategy
1,000,000,000	Physical goods	$1–$10	Coca-Cola	Marketing (advertising)
1,000,000,000	Ads	$1–$10	Facebook	Word of mouth (network effects and virality)
100,000,000	Physical goods	$10–$100	Johnson & Johnson	Marketing (advertising)
100,000,000	Ads	$10–$100	TripAdvisor	Marketing (user-generated content and SEO)
10,000,000	Video game	$100–$1000	Blizzard	Marketing (advertising) and word of mouth (virality)
1,000,000	Software as a Service	$1,000–$10,000	sendwithus	Marketing (inbound marketing)
100,000	Enterprise support	$10,000–$100,000	MongoDB	Sales (inside sales)
10,000	Data analysis	$100,000+	Cloudera	Sales (outside sales)

Putting it all together, if you get the right idea, design, data, and distribution, you'll be able to make something people want.

- *An idea is not a design*

- *A design is not a prototype*

- *A prototype is not a program*

- *A program is not a product*

- *A product is not a business*

- *A business is not profits*

- *Profits are not an exit*

- *And an exit is not happiness.*

—[SELLERS 2011], MIKE SELLERS, SERIAL ENTREPRENEUR

PART II

Technologies

Choosing a Tech Stack

Thinking about tech stacks

Which programming language should you use? Which web framework? How do you store data? What tech stack should you use at your startup?

A tech stack is a tool. It's a means to build a product, not an end in and of itself. Do not go with a technology just because it sounds cool or looks fun. Choose a technology that will give you leverage. To do that, you should keep in mind *the golden rule of tech stacks*:

> A good tech stack is one that scales faster than the people required to maintain it.

Your goal is to be able to scale your tech stack to more users, traffic, data, and code by throwing money or hardware, rather than manpower, at the problem. If every time your user base doubles, you can just pay for a few more servers and everything keeps working, you're in good shape. On the other hand, if you have to double the size of your team, you might need a change. Remember, startups are about people, and although technology is the focus of this chapter, the most important thing about that technology is what kind of leverage it gives to the people using it.

A great example of leverage is the WhatsApp team, which built a tech stack around Erlang that could support 70 million Erlang messages per second, 450 million users, 50 billion messages per day, and 7.2 trillion messages per year.[1] And they did all this with a team of just 32 engineers [Hoff 2014].

Of course, the WhatsApp story does not mean everyone should use Erlang. Successful startups have been built on almost every conceivable technology, and in this chapter, I will help you figure out what tech stack will give you leverage at

---

1 For reference, the number of SMS messages sent per year sent across all telecoms globally is 7.5 trillion [Evans 2014].

your startup. First, I'll describe how to make the initial tech stack choice and how to evolve it over time. Next, I'll present the trade-offs you'll need to consider before you decide whether to build technology in-house, buy commercial software, or use open source. Finally, I'll dive into the details of three of the most common technical decisions for startups: the programming language, the server-side framework, and the database. We'll discuss some of the other aspects of the tech stack, including how you build, deploy, and monitor your code, in Chapter 8.

Evolving the tech stack

One of the major themes in this book is that great companies are the result of evolution and not intelligent design. The same is true of the tech stacks at those companies. Although we like to think of technology as the result of meticulous planning, like a city carefully laid out in a grid pattern according to a blueprint, the reality is that most tech stacks are the result of organic growth, and look more like a sprawling jungle, full of the random roots and offshoots that were necessary to survive. This is because it's almost impossible to predict what technical challenges you'll face in the future, and it's wasteful to build things you don't need. Therefore, the only thing you can do is start with a small and simple tech stack and create a process that will allow you to adapt it as necessary to new pressures from the environment, such as the need to handle increased traffic, new employees, and new features. In other words, you should focus more on how to build a tech stack that you can evolve over time and less on what is the "best" tech stack now.

In fact, there is no "best" tech stack. Selecting a technology without considering the type of product, team, and company culture is like deciding what furniture to buy before you've bought a house, set a budget, or figured out who you are going to live with. Context matters.

For example, a company like Google has to maintain a tech stack that supports incredible scale. Google engineers have to be careful that their web crawlers don't overwhelm tiny websites; they have to come up with meticulous plans for projects because they are dealing with petabytes of data; and they have to be deliberate with the testing methodology for their ranking algorithms because hundreds of millions of users are using the search results to guide their daily lives. On the other hand, the tech stack for a startup like AdMob back in 2007 had completely different requirements:

> When I went to AdMob [after leaving Google], my first impulse was like oh, garbage, garbage, garbage. I wasn't saying any of this, because the more important lesson to learn as a leader is to shut your mouth and listen before you start talking. But, in my head, I'm thinking, we wouldn't do this at Google and we wouldn't do this at Google and we wouldn't do this at Google. After running this script inside your head a bunch of times, you realize that you're not at Google and you're trying to solve a different problem and you have a different engineering culture—and all of this is good. It's really good.
>
> At AdMob, we were in this environment where the market was changing so quickly that there were first-mover benefits to be had on almost a monthly basis. To be successful, we needed to be unbelievably Agile. So we rigged our entire system for agility: we hired people who were adrenaline junkies; we made sure in your first week that you could write code and get it pushed into production. If you couldn't do that, we had a real hard conversation with you at the beginning of your second week whether this was really the right environment for you.
>
> We encouraged people to take what other folks might have seen as insane levels of risk. Every engineer in the company had root access on thousands of machines. It was perfectly fine for an engineer to go in and pull a machine out of rotation and deploy a new ads server onto it. And it was perfectly OK for their deployment to break—and it could break spectacularly—and the reason it could do that is that we had engineered the entire system to watch the critical things that we expected out of all of the software and if something was critically failing, there was a sniper that would shoot the bad actor and send a notification to somebody to come and clean up the mess.
>
> So, we did that for queries on our core database, we did it for the ad serving processes in production, we did it for the way that we hired, the way that we ran our software development process, the way that we built our safety nets. We built this environment that encouraged risk taking. It let us grab these crazy first mover advantages. It even went down to the structure of the team: we tried to have as little team structure as humanly

possible. We wanted to be able to finish things and move on to the next thing and not have these affiliations to code and to managers and to these sort of artificial constructs, because, again, agility was important.

I remember it was June 2008 when Steve Jobs announced at WWDC that the iPhone was going to have an app store. I think everybody had known about it since March of that year when they announced a beta program, but we weren't in the beta program, so we didn't know any of the details. I wanted to see the live blogs for the keynote so much that I stayed at home on that day so I wasn't in traffic while it was going down. I remember watching this live blog where Steve is unveiling all the details of how the app store is going to work and what developers are going to be able to build, and at the end of the WWDC, my phone rang immediately—it was Omar, the CEO of the company, and he was like, "Did you just watch Steve's keynote?" And I was like, "Yup." And he was like, "We have to get on this. We've got to build an ads SDK for the app store, and we need to get it done before the app store launches."

Well, the app store was going to launch **six weeks later.** *This was June and I think the app store was launching mid-July. And by the end of the day, because we had created this capability for agility, we had assembled an entire team, six people, and we were like, "We need to build this, we need to build it so it's awesome, and we need to be the first company that has an in-app advertising SDK, and we need it done immediately. You have six weeks."*

And this team, they weren't flustered. No one was flustered about being pulled off of their job, nothing failed as a consequence of them being pulled off, and they had a blast. They crushed getting this thing out of the door. We got it done in six weeks, we launched, we ran press concurrent with the launch of the app store, and within six months, it had become our biggest line of business.

—[SCOTT 2014], KEVIN SCOTT, SVP AT LINKEDIN, VP AT ADMOB, DIRECTOR AT GOOGLE

Without knowing your exact context, there is no way for me to make specific technology recommendations in this chapter. Instead, my goal is to give you the vocabulary for reasoning about these decisions, to make you aware of the trade-offs involved, and to reveal how other companies have made these decisions in the past.

Let's start with the very first decision you need to make: how do you choose the initial tech stack for a startup? I can answer that with just five words: go with what you know. From the interviews I did for this book, I can tell you that just about every single startup selects whatever technology the founding team already knows best. LinkedIn was built with Java because the founding team knew Java [Dellamaggiore 2014]; GitHub's founders were all Ruby developers, so they built the site with Ruby [Holman 2014]; Twitter used Rails primarily because they had a lot of early employees who were familiar with it [Larson 2014]; Foursquare started out in PHP because that's what co-founder Dennis Crowley knew [Ortiz 2014]; Pinterest used Python because the founding team was familiar with it [Chou 2014].

It can be fun to learn a new technology that promises all sorts of theoretical benefits, but your goal in the early days of a startup is to learn what your users want, and anything that takes time away from that is a waste. During those early days, your product has few users and little code, so scalability will not be much of a challenge, and all that matters is that you can iterate as quickly as possible (see "Speed Wins" on page 51). If you're a Java guru, go with Java; if you love Ruby on Rails, use Ruby on Rails; if you've been using MySQL for years, go with MySQL. A good tech stack, violently executed now, is better than a perfect tech stack next week.[2]

Of course, if your startup is successful enough to survive until "next week," you might have to evolve your tech stack to meet new requirements. For example, Twitter started as a Ruby on Rails shop, but when they got bigger, they had to migrate to Scala and the JVM [Humble 2011]. HubSpot migrated from .Net and SQLServer to the JVM and MySQL, Hadoop, and HBase [Milstein 2013]. Coursera is currently migrating from PHP to Scala [Saeta 2014]. LinkedIn has tried almost a dozen technologies throughout its history, including Java Servlets, Groovy on Rails, JRuby on Sinatra, Java and SpringMVC, JavaScript and Node.js, and Scala and the Play Framework.

The trick is not the initial choice of technology. The initial decision is guaran-fucking-teed to be wrong... eventually. The only question is how long it's going to take to be wrong. The trick is recognizing when you hit

---

2 A salute to General Patton.

that inflection point where you need to have the courage to just kill the thing rather than apply Band-Aid after Band-Aid after Band-Aid to it to keep it alive.

Having that discipline is super important. I think, by far and away, that's more important than trying to read the zeitgeist and get into an infinite design analysis loop to figure out the best initial technology decision. Instead, make sure that you're building yourself and your environment to adapt to change and you know when the time is right to rebuild.

—[SCOTT 2014], KEVIN SCOTT, SVP AT LINKEDIN, VP AT ADMOB, DIRECTOR AT GOOGLE

Knowing when it is time to change the tech stack is fundamentally a question of scale. When you are violating the golden rule of tech stacks—finding yourself scaling people faster than technology—it's time to reevaluate. If building new features takes longer than you expect and each new release is breaking more features than it adds, it might be time for a change. Sometimes a simple change, such as optimizing database queries or adding a cache, will be enough. Sometimes you have to swap out larger parts of your tech stack, such as migrating to a different database. But be wary of stop-the-world, ground-up rewrites.

Pausing all development to rewrite your code on a completely new tech stack is a massive risk. It has been described as the "single worst strategic mistake that any software company can make" [Spolsky 2000] and "startup suicide" [Blank 2011]. When you throw away old code, you're throwing away years of learning and bug fixes. While doing a rewrite, you'll end up repeating many of the same mistakes, plus lots of new ones. You'll realize that rewriting the code on the shiny new technology is only a tiny fraction of the problem, and most of your time will instead be spent retraining team members on the new way of doing things, convincing them that the new way is better, updating documentation, dealing with data migration issues, integrating the technology into the build and deploy system, setting up monitoring, and figuring out how to debug the new technology. A rewrite is the ultimate example of Hofstadter's Law: it always takes longer than you expect, even when you take into account Hofstadter's Law [Hofstadter 1999, 152]. Meanwhile, your product is stuck in the mud and your competitors are passing you.

So how can you evolve your tech stack without killing your startup? The answer is *incrementalism*. The idea is to break up the work into small, isolated steps, each of which has value by itself [Milstein 2013]. Not all "small steps" are created equal, so be wary of *false incrementalism*:

> *False incrementalism is breaking a large change up into a set of small steps, but where none of those steps generate any value on their own. [...] Fortunately, there's a very simple test to determine if you're falling prey to the False Incrementalism: if after each increment, an Important Person were to ask your team to drop the project right at that moment, would the business have seen some value? That is the gold standard.*

—[MILSTEIN 2013], DAN MILSTEIN, CO-FOUNDER OF HUT 8 LABS

In short, even when you have to make major changes to your tech stack, the best way to accomplish them is to gradually evolve what you have now, rather than throw everything away and try to come up with a replacement from scratch (i.e., evolution beats intelligent design). In some ways, this is like changing the wheels of a car while it's still moving. But in the startup world, there is no breakdown lane—if you pull over, you're dead.

For example, around 2011, LinkedIn was going through a period of hypergrowth, both in terms of site traffic and the number of employees, and the infrastructure was buckling under the load. I was part of the service infrastructure team and we knew we had to make some significant changes to be able to scale the tech stack to the rapidly growing demands. Other teams worked on the massive changes we needed for delivering the code (see Chapter 8), while my team worked on improving how we wrote the code in the first place. We ended up kicking off a project to migrate LinkedIn to the Play Framework.[3] Table 5-1 shows the incremental steps we followed to arrive at this decision and how we performed the actual migration, including what would happen at each stage of the project if it succeeded or why it would be worth doing even if it was canceled.

---

3 See The Play Framework at LinkedIn (*http://bit.ly/li-play*) for more info.

Table 5-1. Incrementally migrating LinkedIn to the Play Framework

Stage	If project succeeds	If project gets canceled	Actual result
Stage 1: talk to dev teams to figure out their biggest pain points and find an "early adopter team" willing to try new technology as a solution.	We find out how to prioritize our infrastructure work.	We know what's hurting teams and put it on the backlog until we can get resources to work on it.	We found out the productivity and performance of our web framework was causing significant pain and decided to try the Play Framework as a solution.
Stage 2: build the minimal number of integration points to use Play at LinkedIn.	We end up with the basic integration code to support Play apps at LinkedIn.	The lessons we learned and some of the integration code would be useful for any framework we introduced in the future.	We hooked Play into our monitoring, deployment, and configuration tools.
Stage 3: work with the early adopter team to rewrite one of their services on top of Play.	At least one team benefits from increased productivity and performance.	At least one team benefits from increased productivity and performance.	We rewrote the LinkedIn Polls back-end on Play.
Stage 4: go back to stage 1.	We find more teams interested in migrating to Play and build any new integration points they need.	We find out other teams have different pain points and shift our focus to solving those.	We migrated 80+ services to Play, including the Home Page, Jobs, Recruiter, and Pulse. The migration is still on-going.

You might have noticed that this is an iterative product development process similar to what we discussed in Part I of this book. This process allowed us to incrementally move parts of the site onto Play, gradually picking up performance and productivity benefits, all without the risk of having to pause all work for a major rewrite. Each step was valuable by itself so if at any point we had to stop the project, it would still have been worth doing.

One of the reasons the Play project was successful was that we didn't have to develop an entirely new web framework from scratch. Instead of building a massive piece of infrastructure in-house, which would have been hard to do incrementally, we were able to use open source and even get a commercial support contract.

Build in-house, buy commercial, or use open source?

For every part of your tech stack, you will need to decide if you will build it in-house, buy a commercial product, or use open source.

BUILD IN-HOUSE

Building a project in-house gives you full control. You own the code and data, you can customize the project to your needs, you can release new features whenever you like, and you decide how the project evolves in the future. For one-off, custom products, such as the user interface of a website, and for anything that is your differentiator, such as Google's PageRank algorithm, building in-house is your only option. But when it comes to reusable libraries or infrastructure, proprietary software comes with a heavy cost: developer time.

Most developers only think about the time it takes to write the initial version of a project—and they usually vastly underestimate how long that will take—but this is only a tiny fraction of the total cost. These developers also have to maintain the project in the long term, evolving it to meet new requirements, fixing bugs, and creating documentation. Whenever something goes wrong, those same developers—if they are still at your company—are responsible for answering all questions and providing 24/7 support. Stack Overflow can't help you with proprietary code, there is no community to contribute plug-ins or extensions, and there is no one you can hire who is already an expert in the project. In fact, most developers don't like learning proprietary systems because they won't be able to use that knowledge anywhere else in their career.

BUY A COMMERCIAL PRODUCT

Commercial products allow you to trade developer time for money. An external vendor takes care of writing all the code, fixing bugs, and creating documentation. And because there is a whole company dedicated to this one product, they can assign a lot more people to it than your startup. Some vendors also offer support contracts, so you can pay money to customize the product, prioritize bug fixes, and get help 24 hours a day. Some commercial products even have a community around them. A product community can be a great source of testimonials, developers who already know how to use the software, plug-ins, and extensions, and help in the form of Stack Overflow, mailing lists, blog posts, and talks. And a product built by a reputable vendor that is being used successfully at a dozen companies is a safer bet than a completely unproven project you start internally. Most startups make very heavy use of commercial software, especially SaaS offerings such as Slack (a platform for team communication), PagerDuty (a monitoring and alerting tool), Amazon EC2 (cloud hosting), Zenefits (online HR software), Salesforce (customer relationship management), and many others.

Commercial software comes with its own costs. Some come in the form of a bill that the vendor sends you. Others are less obvious. For example, the vendor owns the code, so you can't see it, judge its quality, tell if it's secure, reference it when debugging problems, or control how it evolves in the future. If you don't have access to the code, and in the case of SaaS products, the data, then migrating to a different technology can be very difficult (this is known as *vendor lock-in*).

> *The brutal truth is this: when your key business processes are executed by opaque blocks of bits that you can't even see inside (let alone modify) you have lost control of your business. You need your supplier more than your supplier needs you—and you will pay, and pay, and pay again for that power imbalance.*
>
> **—[RAYMOND 2001, 152], ERIC S. RAYMOND, AUTHOR OF** *THE CATHEDRAL & THE BAZAAR*

In short, every time you use a commercial product, you are betting a part of your company on a third party that you don't control. What happens if that vendor goes out of business in a few months? Or gets acquired by a competitor? These are serious risks, so be wary of using unproven vendors for critical parts of your business, such as data storage.

USE OPEN SOURCE

Open source projects give you many of the benefits of commercial products, but without many of the risks. With open source, there is a community of developers who are responsible for writing the code, fixing bugs, creating documentation, and building plug-ins and extensions. This community is a powerful resource for getting help: you can get your questions answered on Stack Overflow and mailing lists, learn best practices from blog posts and talks, and hire developers who are already experts with many of the projects. In fact, most developers love working on open source because they can reuse that knowledge later in their careers and any contributions they make become part of their public résumé (see "Why you should share" on page 517). For popular projects, the open source community is much larger than any single company. For example, as of 2014, 702 people have committed code to Django, 2,469 people have committed code to Ruby on Rails, and there are thousands of plug-ins available for each framework. If your startup is thinking of writing its own web framework, how many people do you think you'll be able to dedicate to it?

The downside to open source is that it's mostly done on a volunteer basis, which is effective at getting large numbers of developers from many companies to work together (see "Autonomy" on page 406), but not as effective if you need any sort of guarantee, such as getting a specific bug fixed, or getting a new release by a specific deadline, or even getting assurance that the project will continue to be developed at all. Sometimes the maintainer of an open source project will abandon it entirely. Sometimes the maintainer will even delete the project (e.g., after FoundationDB was acquired by Apple, they deleted all of their GitHub repos). Sometimes the community around the project will splinter and break off in several different directions (e.g., complaints around Joyent's governance of Node.js led to a fork called io.js). Sometimes open source projects aren't nearly as "open" as you'd think, and there is often confusion about licenses (e.g., most commercial companies have to avoid software with a GPL license), trademarks (e.g., Joyent owns the Node.js trademark, so forks of Node.js cannot use "Node" in the name), and copyrights (e.g., there are open source implementations of Java and yet Oracle claims to have a copyright on the Java APIs and is suing Google for copying those APIs in Android).

Just like commercial software, using open source means you are risking a part of your company on a third party that you don't entirely control. Unlike commercial software, having access to the source code mitigates some of that risk. If you have the code, you can contribute patches or plug-ins, create custom builds if the release cycle is too slow, fork the project if it starts moving in the wrong direction, or migrate to a totally different project if necessary (no vendor lock-in). And because everyone else is looking at the source code, too, there is evidence that open source projects have higher quality [Coverity, Inc. 2013] and fewer security problems [Renolds and Wyat 2011] than proprietary projects. It's easier to gauge the quality of an open source project because you can read the code and take into account how many companies are using it, the reputation of the maintainers, how many watchers or forks there are, and how many resources are available online. And if you need help, there are companies dedicated to providing commercial support for open source projects, such as RedHat, Typesafe, Joyent, Cloudera, and Hortonworks.

TECHNOLOGIES YOU SHOULD NEVER BUILD YOURSELF

There are certain technologies that are so complicated, error-prone, and time consuming to build yourself, and solved so well in the open source or commercial world that, as a startup, you should never build them yourself. Here's a partial list:

- Security: cryptography, password storage, credit card storage
- Web technologies: HTTP servers, server-side and client-side frameworks
- Data systems: databases, NoSQL stores, caches, message queues
- Software delivery: version control, build systems, deployment automation
- CS 101: basic data structures (map, list, set), sorting algorithms
- Libraries for common data formats: XML, HTML, CSV, JSON, URLs
- Utility libraries: date/time manipulation, string manipulation, logging
- Operating systems
- Programming languages

The only reason you would ever build one of these systems from scratch is either (a) you're using it as a personal side project for learning or (b) your startup has extremely unique requirements for one of these technologies. The latter case is uncommon. If you're in the business of selling a database or you're operating at a scale unmatched by any other company, it might make sense to implement your own, but otherwise, use an off-the-shelf solution.

Google was very a much a "not invented here" stack. Everything was written in-house. I don't think I used a single open source tool or library except maybe gcc when I was at Google. I think part of the reason was that Google was five years or more ahead of everyone else in the industry. The stuff that Google was building, things like MapReduce, using tons of cheap commodity hardware for running distributed systems—they basically invented or popularized a lot of that stuff. It's all industry-standard now, but much of it just didn't exist before Google. I feel like Google was just enough ahead of everyone else that they had to build it, and then maybe it became self-reinforcing, because we've got this not-invented-here culture that's worked for us.

—[LARSON 2014], BRIAN LARSON, SOFTWARE ENGINEER AT GOOGLE AND TWITTER

BUILD IN-HOUSE, BUY COMMERCIAL, OR USE OPEN SOURCE SUMMARY?

For a startup, using open source is usually the best choice, closely followed by using a commercial product. Building infrastructure in-house should be treated as a last resort that you use only when you have no other options. This can be hard to remember, as many developers get excited at the chance to build a complicated piece of infrastructure, and will be quick to claim that no existing technology fits their needs. But given that there are more than 10 million open source repositories to choose from [Doll 2013], and developer time is the most scarce and expensive resource at a startup, you cannot afford to spend time reinventing the wheel when there is an off-the-shelf solution readily available. Use the flowchart in Figure 5-1 to determine whether to build in-house, buy a commercial product, or use open source.

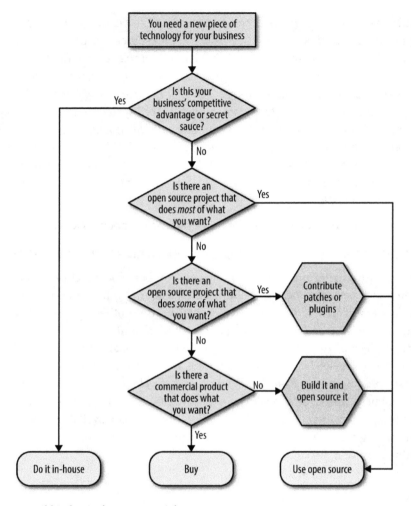

Figure 5-1. Build in-house, buy commercial, or use open source

Choosing a programming language

The programming language is often the first technical decision you'll make at a company. It's also the one that has the most influence on all the other decisions. The "go with what you know" principle means that most startups initially use whatever language the founders know best. However, as a startup grows and evolves, it's not uncommon to introduce other languages. For example, Twitter started out as a Ruby shop, but for the last several years have been migrating many of their services to Scala [Humble 2011]. But why Scala? Why not Python or Java or Haskell or some other language? To answer this question, you need to understand the key ways programming languages differ from one another, including programming paradigms, performance, problem fit, culture fit, and productivity.

PROGRAMMING PARADIGMS

Each programming language has a different philosophy for how to solve problems. Think of the paradigms of a programming language as the vocabulary and grammar of the language. They determine both how you say things and what things you can say. There has been little conclusive evidence that any one paradigm is better than the others,[4] but some ideas will be easier to express in certain paradigms than others. In the next few sections, I'll discuss the trade-offs of a few of the most popular paradigms, including object-oriented programming, functional programming, static typing, and automatic memory management.

Object-oriented programming

Object-oriented programming (OOP) tries to model the world as objects—that is, data structures that package together both data and behavior. OOP has been the dominant programming paradigm for the last two decades, used in some of the most popular programming languages in the world, including C++, C#, Java, JavaScript, Ruby, and Python.

Part of the reason for its popularity is that objects and methods often map nicely onto the real world of nouns and verbs. It's intuitive to reason about a Car class with a move method that knows how to update the internal state of the Car. OOP also helps reduce coupling by encouraging *information hiding*, where an object does not give other objects access to its internal implementation details, which are likely to change. Instead, the rest of the program must interact with the object via its public methods, which are a more stable interface.

There are two main problems with OOP. First, there is no consensus on what "object oriented" really means or how to do it correctly. Every OOP

---

4 There is a small amount of evidence which indicates that static typing and functional programming lead to modest improvements in productivity, but the differences between these paradigms tend to be vastly overshadowed by the differences in ability between individual programmers [Luu 2014].

language and programmer does it differently.[5] Second, most OOP languages encourage the use of mutable state and side effects (see Chapter 6), which makes it harder to reason about, maintain, and test code, especially in concurrent environments.

Functional programming

Functional programming languages try to model the world as the evaluation of functions and, unlike OOP languages, they significantly limit the use of mutable data and side effects. The focus is on building complex code by composing simple, pure functions and using a more declarative style of programming where you describe what you want rather than how to get it. This makes it easier to reason about, maintain, and test the code (I'll discuss this topic in more depth as part of "Functional programming" on page 268). Popular functional programming languages include Haskell, the Lisp family (e.g., Scheme and Clojure), and Scala, which is a hybrid OOP and functional language.

Why isn't functional programming as popular as OOP? There are two primary reasons. The first reason is that functional programming has a steep learning curve. Category theory, monads, monoids, applicatives, and functors are harder to get started with than "objects that do things" and "Cat extends Animal," and not enough has been done to make the mathematical roots of functional programming more accessible to the public. The second reason is that, by design, functional programming is removed from the real world. It moves away from side effects and state, but most programs exist solely to maintain state and have interesting side effects. Functional programming also moves away from the underlying hardware architecture—for example, it uses recursion instead of loops, immutable data instead of mutable data, garbage collection instead of manual memory management, lazy evaluation instead of eager evaluation—which makes it harder to predict the performance of functional code. There are ways to mitigate or even eliminate the performance penalty, such as using persistent data structures and tail-call optimization, but they often increase the burden on the programmer.

---

5 Alan Kay, one of the inventors of object-oriented programming, on the two most popular OOP languages: "I made up the term *object-oriented*, and I can tell you I did not have C++ in mind" and "Java is the most distressing thing to hit computing since MS-DOS" [Kay 1997].

Static typing

In programming, each piece of data has a *type* that determines how to store it in memory, what values it could have, and what operations can be performed on it. For example, in some languages, if a value is an *int*, it means it should be stored on the stack as a 32-bit signed two's complement integer, the possible values are -2^{31} to 2^{31}-1, and the valid operations are add, subtract, multiply, divide, and remainder. *Dynamically typed languages* only check types at runtime, such as throwing an error if you try to access an array index that is out of bounds. *Statically typed languages* have the ability to catch certain type errors at compile time, such as the compiler failing the build if you are trying to assign a String to an int.

A static type system is like a compiler-enforced suite of automated tests that are guaranteed to be up to date and correct (see "Automated Tests" on page 296). While you can (and should) write automated tests even when using a statically typed language, the type system can save you a lot of time by catching a large subset of bugs automatically. Static typing also provides a lot of useful information to anyone reading the code. That includes developers, who can use type signatures as a form of documentation; IDEs, which can use type signatures to make it easier to build code navigation, refactoring, and auto-complete features; and the compiler, which can use type signatures to optimize the code.

But static typing is not a silver bullet. Statically typed code must be compiled, which takes time and slows down iteration speed. And no matter how much time you spend compiling, only a subset of code "correctness" can ever be checked statically. As type systems become more powerful, this subset increases, but it usually comes at the cost of an exponential increase in the complexity of the type system. You are forced to learn a whole language—generics, covariance, contravariance, existential types, uniqueness types, union types, dependent types, self-recursive types, type classes, type bounds, higher kinded types, phantom types, structural types—and the overhead of using this language can sometimes outweigh the benefits. This is especially true for certain types of problems, such as domain-specific languages (DSLs) and metaprogramming, which exceed the flexibility and expressiveness of most type systems.

Automatic memory management

Low-level, systems programming languages, such as C and C++, require the programmer to manually manage memory allocation and deallocation. Most high-level programming languages, such as Java, Ruby, and Python, support automatic memory management, which allows programmers to focus on the actual problems they are solving instead of the underlying memory architecture of the computer. This improves productivity and prevents a large class of bugs, such as forgetting to free memory you're no longer using (memory leak) or freeing memory at the wrong time (dangling pointer and double free bugs).

Unfortunately, automatic memory management comes at a cost. The most common way to automatically deallocate memory is *garbage collection (GC)*, where you periodically run a *collector* that scans all allocated memory and reclaims anything no longer in use. The problem is that running the collector consumes CPU and memory resources. It is possible to reduce the overhead with tuning, but it may still be too much for memory-intensive programs, such as a high-performance in-memory cache. Many garbage collection algorithms also require that the entire program pause during a collection. This means garbage-collected languages are not a good choice for real-time applications—that is, applications that must always respond in a very short time (i.e., a shorter time period than a typical GC pause).

PROBLEM FIT

In theory, all modern programming languages are Turing-complete, so they are all equivalent. In practice, certain types of problems are much easier to solve in some programming languages than others. For example, languages with strong metaprogramming capabilities, such as Clojure and Ruby, make it easy to define custom DSLs. Erlang is particularly effective at building fault-tolerant, distributed systems. Assembly and C are usually your only options for low-level, real-time, or embedded systems.

The community around the language has a significant impact on problem fit. For example, C++ and Python have a huge number of computer vision libraries. Matlab, Mathematica, and R come with comprehensive libraries for math, graphing, and statistics. PHP, Ruby, Python, JavaScript, and Java have vast ecosystems of libraries and frameworks for building web applications. For certain problem domains, selecting the right language can give you a huge productivity boost because a lot of the code is already written for you.

PERFORMANCE

The programming language is usually not the bottleneck for most companies (see Chapter 7). However, in certain cases, especially with enough load, the language does matter. The two most common performance bottlenecks in programming languages are garbage collection and concurrency.

Garbage collection, as we discussed in "Programming paradigms" on page 199, consumes CPU and memory and can pause program execution. Some garbage-collection algorithms are more mature and tunable than others. For example, the JVM is well known for having one of the better garbage collectors in the world, while the Ruby VM's garbage collector is known for numerous performance problems.[6] However, neither language can compare performance-wise to languages where there is no garbage collection. If your application cannot tolerate any GC pauses or any CPU or memory overhead, then you may want to use a language with manual memory management, such as C or C++.

With concurrency, the most important factors are what concurrency constructs are supported by the language and how it handles I/O. For example, Ruby supports threads, but it has a *Global Interpreter Lock (GIL)*, which means that only one thread at a time can execute. Moreover, most popular Ruby libraries perform synchronous I/O, blocking the thread while waiting for a disk read or a network call to return. The result is that Ruby is not an efficient language for dealing with lots of concurrency. There are workarounds, such as running multiple Ruby processes (e.g., one per CPU core), using non-blocking libraries (e.g., EventMachine), or using a different VM (e.g., JRuby), but they all involve trade-offs and overheads.

This is one of the reasons Twitter moved off of Ruby and onto the JVM. The JVM has full support for multithreading with no global interpreter lock. It also has full support for non-blocking I/O and a variety of concurrency constructs, including threads and locks, Futures, Actors, and Software Transactional Memory. The move from Ruby to Scala helped Twitter reduce search latencies by three-fold and CPU usage by half [Humble 2011].

PRODUCTIVITY

While programming language performance is important, programmer performance is a bigger bottleneck for most startups. Look for a language that lets you get the most done in the least amount of time. Productivity consists of two main

---

6 Ruby 2.1 made great improvements to garbage collection [Saffron 2014], but there are still many lingering issues [Robertson 2014].

aspects: how much existing code you can reuse and how fast you can create new code.

The amount of existing code is determined by the popularity of the language and the size of its community. Popular languages will have more learning resources, more people you can hire who already know the language, and more open source libraries you can use. Mature languages also come with an ecosystem of productivity tools, such as IDEs, profilers, static analysis tools, and build systems. The more code you reuse, the less code you have to write and maintain yourself.

How fast you can create new code depends on three factors. The first factor is experience. The more experience you have with a language, the more productive you'll be, so look for languages you and your team already know and those that are well documented and easy to learn. The second factor is the feedback loop, which is how long it takes to see the effect of a code change. If you have to wait several minutes for code to compile or redeploy, you will be less productive than if you only have to wait a few seconds for a page to refresh or script to rerun. Look for languages that support hot reload, an interactive coding environment (such as a read-eval-print loop, or REPL), fast compile times, and fast automated tests. The third factor is the expressiveness of the language, which is a measure of how many lines of code it takes to implement any given idea. The more lines of code you have to write and maintain, the more bugs you'll have and the slower you'll go (see "Split up the code" on page 323). In general, you should choose the most high-level and concise language you can that still fits your other requirements.

FINAL THOUGHTS ON CHOOSING A PROGRAMMING LANGUAGE

When you choose a language, you're choosing more than a set of technical trade-offs—you're choosing a community. It's like choosing a bar. Yes, you want to go to a bar that serves good drinks, but that's not the most important thing. It's who hangs out there and what they talk about. And that's the way you choose computer languages. Over time the community builds up around the language—not only the people, but the software artifacts: tools, libraries, and so forth. That's one of the reasons that sometimes languages that are, on paper, better than other languages don't win —because they just haven't built the right communities around themselves.

—[SEIBEL 2009, 174], JOSCHUA BLOCH, DISTINGUISHED ENGINEER PASS:[
]AT SUN MICROSYSTEMS, CHIEF JAVA ARCHITECT AT GOOGLE

Although there are hundreds of programming languages to choose from, there are only a handful of languages that are mature enough and have a large enough community to make them viable choices for a startup. Here is the list as of 2015, ordered alphabetically, based on programming language popularity indexes (TIOBE (*http://bit.ly/TIOBE-index*), LangPop (*http://langpop.com/*), and RedMonk (*http://bit.ly/redmonk*)), the Stack Overflow Developer Survey (*http://bit.ly/so-survey*), and my own experience:

- C family (C, C++, C#)
- Go
- Groovy
- Haskell
- Java
- JavaScript
- Lisp family (e.g., Clojure or Scheme)
- Perl
- PHP
- Python
- Ruby
- Scala

You can quickly shorten this list by applying three filters: problem fit, programming paradigm, and performance requirements. For example, a startup building computer-vision and machine-learning systems would limit this list to just three languages based on problem fit: C++, Java, and Python. If that startup preferred static typing, they would knock Python off the list. Finally, if they were building a high-performance, real-time system, they would not be able to use garbage collection, so they would be left with C++.

If after applying the first three filters, you still have multiple languages to choose from, you should choose the language that makes you the most productive. For example, a startup that is building web applications will most likely find that Java, JavaScript, PHP, Python, Ruby, and Scala are the best fit for this problem. If the team prefers dynamic typing, they might remove Java and Scala from the list. And if a few of them already know Python and found a few Django plugins that will save them lots of time, then Python will be their best choice.

Choosing a server-side framework

Should you use a framework at your startup? Some programmers will tell you that frameworks are too heavy and complicated so you should use libraries instead. But what's the distinction between a library and a framework? The typical answer is *inversion of control*: you plug libraries into your code and call out to them, whereas you plug your code into frameworks and they call out to you. This is also known as the *Hollywood principle*: don't call us, we'll call you [Fowler 2005]. If you're building a web service, unless you're calling socket.accept and writing your own HTTP parsing code, you are always plugging your code into some sort of framework that calls you. That might be a full-stack framework like Ruby on Rails, where you plug in a controller to handle requests, or something more minimal, like a raw HTTP server, where you plug in a function to handle HTTP messages. In either case, you can't not have a framework [Florence 2014].

So it's usually not a question of libraries versus framework but *minimal framework* versus *full-stack framework*. A full-stack framework, such as Ruby on Rails, is one that has default solutions built in for the most common tasks, such as routing, data modeling, view rendering, internationalization, configuration, and testing. A minimal framework, such as Sinatra, is one that gives you just enough functionality to get started—perhaps just the HTTP routing—and has little else built in, leaving it up to you to figure out how to handle all the common tasks.

For small projects, prototypes, and experimentation, a minimal framework can be great. For example, the "Hello, World" for Sinatra is just five lines of Ruby code:

```ruby
require 'sinatra'

get '/hi' do
  "Hello, World!"
end
```

If the task is small and simple, a framework that is easy to learn and gets out of your way is a big advantage. You grab just the libraries you need (perhaps a templating engine and a library for handling JSON), toss them in, and get something out the door quickly. However, as the project grows in size and importance, you will realize that you need a way to handle configuration, testing, security, static assets, monitoring, and database access, and so you'll start bolting more and more libraries onto your minimal framework. In the end, all you've done is create a full-stack framework, except yours is proprietary and doesn't have documentation, testing, or an open source community to back it.

> *Any sufficiently complicated collection of libraries contains an ad hoc, informally-specified, bug-ridden, slow implementation of half of a full-stack web framework.*[7]

There is a reason full-stack frameworks include all those built-in features: most real-world applications need them. Even if you aren't actively using the features now, having them built in adds little cost, so avoiding them because they somehow "feel heavyweight" is short sighted. Of course, not every built-in solution will fit your needs, so you should look for frameworks where the defaults work for you 80%–90% of the time, but when they don't, you can easily replace them with a custom library. For example, the Play Framework is a full-stack Java/Scala framework, but most of the functionality, such as database access, view rendering, caching, and internationalization, is pluggable. You can even replace core features such as routing with a single class:

```
public class Global extends GlobalSettings {
  @Override
  public Action onRequest(Request request, Method actionMethod) {
    return handleRequestWithCustomRoutingLogic(request);
  }
}
```

If you're using a web framework to build something important to your business—something that's more than a prototype—the best choice is usually a modular full-stack framework. That way, you get the best of both worlds: a documented, community-supported, open source framework where the defaults

---

7 A hat tip to Greenspun's tenth rule of programming, which states, "Any sufficiently complicated C or Fortran program contains an ad hoc, informally-specified, bug-ridden, slow implementation of half of Common Lisp."

do a good job of handling most use cases, plus the ability to plug in custom libraries for a few special cases.

To help you choose a good full-stack framework, we'll look at problem fit, the data layer, the view layer, testing, scalability, deployment, and security.

PROBLEM FIT

Some web frameworks are specialized for solving specific types of problems. For example, Ruby on Rails and Django streamline the process of building *CRUD applications* (that is, those that perform basic create/read/update/delete operations on a relational database) with built-in support for database migrations, database client libraries, view rendering, routing, and scaffolding. Many Node.js frameworks, such as derby.js and express.io, are built specifically for real-time web applications that use web sockets. The DropWizard framework is custom-tailored for building RESTful API servers: it has built-in support for configuring RESTful routing, implementing resources, generating API documentation, and monitoring. If you're not sure whether the framework fits your needs, you probably don't understand the framework, or your own requirements, well enough. Do more research and build some prototypes.

DATA LAYER

Much of the work you do in a server-side framework is parsing, transforming, and serializing data, so look for frameworks that give you powerful data manipulation tools. When you're building a backend service, you mostly deal with data from databases, which I'll discuss in "Choosing a database" on page 219, and data from clients. Data from clients is usually in the form of URLs, JSON, and XML. For example, consider the following HTTP request:

```
Method: POST
Path: /article/5/comments
Headers: Content-Type: application/json;
Body: {userId: 10, text: "Thanks for sharing!"}
```

To handle this request in Ruby on Rails, you could add the following entry to the *routes.rb* file:

```
post '/article/:articleId/comments', to: 'Comments#create'
```

And you could create the following controller to handle the request:

```
class CommentsController < ApplicationController
  def create
```

```
    comment = Comment.create(
      articleId: params[:articleId],
      userId: params[:userId],
      text: params[:text])
    render :json => comment
  end
end

class Comment < ActiveRecord::Base
end
```

It takes only a few lines of code, but consider how much data manipulation Ruby on Rails is doing for you under the hood:

1. Rails parsed the URL path based on the pattern in *routes.rb* so you can extract articleId from the params hash.

2. Because the Content-Type header was "application/json", Rails automatically parsed the body of the request as JSON, so you can also extract userId and text from params.

3. Making the Comment class extend from ActiveRecord::Base allows you to save the comment data to the database with a single call to the create method.

4. When you call render :json, Rails automatically converts the comment object to JSON, adds the proper Content-Type headers, and sends a response back to the browser.

Look for frameworks that make working with data this easy.

VIEW LAYER

Most web frameworks come with a templating library for rendering HTML. When evaluating templating libraries, some of the things to consider are built-in view helpers, server-side versus client-side, and logic versus logic-less.

Built-in view helpers

Just as there are full-stack frameworks, there are also full-stack templating libraries that come with a suite of helpers for all common view tasks. For example, Ruby on Rails ERB templates come with helpers for i18n (internationalization), generating URLs to controllers in the app, generating URLs to static content (e.g., CSS, JS, images), form rendering, and template composition (i.e., reusable layouts and partials).

Server-side versus client-side

Most templating technologies, such as Rails ERB templates, Django templates, and JSPs, are used server-side. Your server fetches some data from a database, feeds it into a template to generate HTML, and sends this HTML to the web browser, as shown in Figure 5-2.

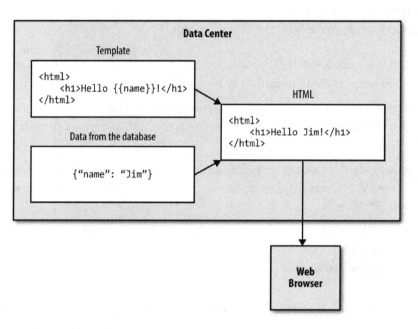

Figure 5-2. Server-side rendering

An alternative that has become more popular in recent years is to use a templating technology that can compile into JavaScript, such as Mustache.js, so you can do most of the rendering client-side. You still need a little server-side rendering so you can send the web browser a skeleton HTML page, but all that page contains is the data you fetched from the database, typically embedded as JSON, plus a link to the JavaScript code. When the browser executes the JavaScript code, it will fetch the client-side template, feed the JSON data into it to generate HTML, and inject the HTML into the DOM, as shown in Figure 5-3.

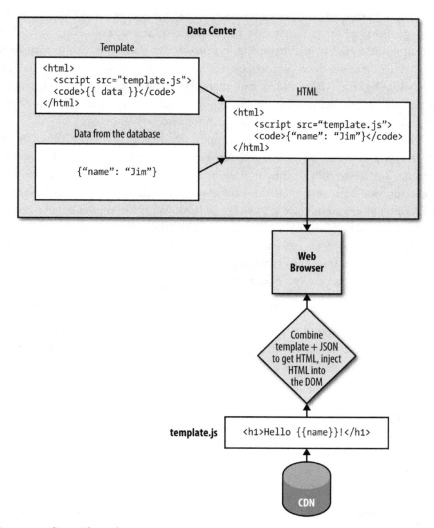

Figure 5-3. Client-side rendering

Client-side templating is great for rich JavaScript applications where, instead of reloading the page, you fetch data via Ajax and use client-side rendering to redraw small parts of the page. There are potential performance gains, too, as most of the markup is in a JavaScript file, which can be served from a content delivery network (CDN) to reduce latency, and cached in the browser, so you never have to load the same markup twice. Unfortunately, there are also potential performance costs. Most browsers are optimized for rendering HTML on the initial page load, whereas client-side rendering requires downloading JavaScript, parsing it, executing it, and inserting the result into the DOM. Some companies have been able to get good performance from client-side rendering, such as Facebook with BigPipe [Jiang 2010], but many companies have struggled, such as Twitter, which tried client-side rendering, but found that moving back to server-side rendering reduced initial page load time by 80% [Webb 2012].

The ideal solution might be to support rendering the same templates on both server and client. Node.js is a server-side JavaScript engine that has become a popular platform for web apps in part because it allows you to execute the same JavaScript code both server-side and client-side, a technique known as *Isomorphic JavaScript*. For example, for the initial page load, you could render Mustache templates server-side in Node.js, but for all clicks in the browser after that, you could use the same Mustache templates to redraw parts of the page with client-side rendering. Node.js frameworks such as rendr, meteor.js, and derby.js try to make it easy to share code between client and server.

Logic versus logic-less templates

Most templating languages consist of HTML markup plus a special syntax for including arbitrary code from a general-purpose programming language. For example, Ruby on Rails comes with ERB templates, and any code wrapped in <% %> blocks will be executed as Ruby code:

```
<p>Regular HTML markup</p>

<%
  text = "Arbitrary Ruby code"
  puts text
%>
```

Some programmers have abused this ability and crammed HTML markup, JavaScript code, database calls, and other business logic into a single file (e.g., *my-entire-app.php*). This has made maintenance, reuse, testing, and reasoning about the code extremely difficult. To enforce a separation of concerns, some developers began using *logic-less templates*, which are designed solely for HTML markup and restrict the syntax for including other code. For example, one of the most popular logic-less templating libraries is Mustache.js, where the only special syntax is variable lookups (e.g., {{variable_name}}) and basic loops and conditionals (e.g., {{#conditional_variable_name}}):

```
<p>Regular HTML markup</p>
<p>This is a {{variable}} lookup.</p>
<p>This is {{#is_enabled}}conditional text{{/is_enabled}}</p>
```

The downside to logic-less templates is that there is such a thing as *view logic*. For example, if you need to label alternate rows of a table with a different CSS class name, you need a loop construct that gives you access to the index and the ability to check if that index is odd or even. Logic-less templates force you to handle this type of logic by implementing custom helper functions, which often leads to re-implementing large parts of a full programming language in helper syntax.

TESTING

One of the first things you should try with a web framework is to write several automated tests for your code (see "Automated Tests" on page 296 for more information). It's a good sign if the framework has clear documentation on how to write tests and comes with libraries and helpers for common test tasks (e.g., using an in-memory DB or issuing fake requests). It's a bad sign if it's hard to write unit tests because the framework uses global state or is tightly coupled to slow dependencies (e.g., the app and database must be started to write any tests). It's a terrible sign if there is no documentation on how to write tests and if the source code for the framework itself does not include lots of automated tests.

SCALABILITY

Web frameworks are rarely the scalability bottleneck in an application (see Chapter 7), so you're usually better off selecting a framework that is fast in terms of developer productivity rather than fast in terms of serving requests. That said, if you're worried about performance, you need to understand if your application is I/O bound or CPU/memory bound.

I/O bound

Many web frameworks, such as Ruby on Rails, Servlets, and Django, assign one thread (or process) to each request and block that thread while waiting on I/O, such as a response from a database or a remote web service. If you have too few threads, it's easy for all of them to become tied up waiting for I/O, preventing any new requests from being processed even though most of your threads are just idly waiting. If you have too many threads, you'll incur a significant overhead from extra memory usage and context switching. Figuring out the right number of threads is hard because it depends on the load on your server and the latencies of downstream dependencies, all of which are constantly changing. And if you pick the wrong number, a small increase in latency in one downstream dependency could cause latency increases and failures to cascade throughout the data center [Brikman 2013a].

A more efficient way to deal with I/O is to use a web server built around non-blocking I/O, such as Node.js or Netty. Instead of blocking a thread while waiting for I/O to complete, you register a callback (or promise), and the thread can go on and process other requests. When the callback fires, the thread can pick the request up again and finish processing it. Because I/O takes several orders of magnitude longer than anything in-process,[8] handling it asynchronously allows you to make more efficient use of the resources on your server. Non-blocking servers typically need just one thread (or process) per CPU core and are less sensitive to downstream latency.

CPU/memory bound

Although most web apps are I/O bound, if your service performs very little I/O, then it might be CPU bound or memory bound. In that case, to maximize performance, you need a framework (and language) that is fast for pure computation and has minimal overhead. As with all questions of performance, the only way to find the answer is through performance testing and measurement. See the TechEmpower web framework benchmarks[9] as a starting point and read Chapter 7 for more information on measuring performance.

DEPLOYMENT

To deploy your code, you'll have to figure out how to build, configure, and monitor it.

The build process includes compiling the code, compiling static assets (e.g., sass, less, CoffeeScript), running tests, and packaging the app for production deployment. Parts of the build process may happen during development, too, such as re-compiling a CoffeeScript file every time you refresh the page. Don't use any web framework unless you understand how to integrate its build process into your tech stack (see "Build" on page 353 for more information).

After building the app, you need to configure it for production deployment. Look for frameworks that are already in use at other companies so you can learn

---

8 See "Latency Numbers Every Programmer Should Know" (*http://bit.ly/latency-prog*) for more details.

9 *http://www.techempower.com/benchmarks/*

from their experience. For example, how do you run the framework so it uses all the CPU cores on a single server? How do you load balance across multiple servers? How do you configure the web framework to handle SSL termination and static content serving, or should those be offloaded to a separate web server? Most frameworks have a configuration system that lets you tweak parameters like SSL settings, static content settings, and memory settings. Make sure the config-uration system is well documented, the configuration files are stored in version control just like the rest of your code, and that there is an easy way to use differ-ent configuration files in different environments (see "Application configuration" on page 367).

Once you figure out how to deploy the code in production, you need moni-toring to keep it running. Logging is the most basic form of monitoring, so make sure you understand the type of logging built into the framework and how to tweak log levels, log formats, and logfile rotation and storage. You also want to be able to monitor metrics such as QPS, latency, what URLs are being hit, error rates, and CPU and memory usage. Some frameworks expose these automati-cally or through a plug-in; others integrate with third-party services and dash-boards (see "Monitoring" on page 374).

SECURITY

Security is hard. It's one of the top items on the list of "Technologies you should never build yourself" on page 196. You should use frameworks where the secu-rity features are built in, open source, and battle tested. These cannot be features you bolt on later—the framework needs to be *secure by default* so that doing some-thing insecure is difficult or impossible. Take the time to familiriaze yourself with the common web security practices—The Open Web Application Security Project (OWASP) (*https://www.owasp.org/*) is a good place to start. In this section, I'll briefly introduce the basics: authentication, CSRF attacks, injection attacks, and security advisories.

Authentication

The first rule of password storage is: You do not store passwords as plain text. The second rule of password storage is: YOU DO NOT STORE PASS-WORDS AS PLAIN TEXT.

It is a bad idea, I dare say even immoral, to store passwords without a deep understanding of how to do it safely. It's not only a risk for your users but also for everyone on the Internet, as people reuse the same passwords in multiple places. Do not take password storage lightly. Do not come up with your own password storage scheme. And never store passwords as plain text.

The bare minimum for safely storing passwords is:

- Use proper password fields in the client interface.
- Only send passwords over SSL connections.
- Create a long, unique, random salt for each password.
- Combine the password and salt, and hash them using a cryptographically secure hash function, such as bcrypt.
- Store the salt and the hash, and throw away the original password.

Don't touch a user's password until you understand why all these steps are necessary and how to implement them.[10] In addition to passwords, you also need to know how to securely manage session information, including how to properly generate session IDs, store session cookies, and handle session expiration.[11] It's best if you don't implement these pieces yourself, but instead find a framework that has thoroughly tested open source libraries for all of these tasks.

CSRF attacks

A cross-site request forgery (CSRF) attack is where a malicious website gets a user to perform unwanted actions on a trusted website. For example, imagine you visit *win-an-ipad.com*, a website that asks you to enter some data in a form and submit it for a chance to win an iPad. What you don't know is the form actually submits to *amazon.com*, a website you trust and are logged into. If Amazon had no CSRF protection and the attacker crafted the form correctly, Amazon would interpret the form submission as you making a purchase because the browser sends your Amazon cookies along with that submission.

To protect against a CSRF attack, your web framework should have a mechanism to generate a short-lived random token for each user, store it in a cookie, and reject any form submission where the token in the body doesn't match the token in the cookie. When you render a legitimate form on your own website, you can easily include the token as a hidden form field. However, when attackers

---

10 Password Storage Cheat Sheet (*http://bit.ly/owasp-cheat*) is a good starting point.

11 See the OWASP Session Management Cheat Sheet (*http://bit.ly/owasp-manage*) for more information.

try to render a malicious form on their website, they cannot read your cookies, so they will not be able to guess the right token value to include in the form.

Code injection attacks

A code injection attack is when a malicious user is able to get your application to execute their code. This is possible if you don't correctly sanitize user-generated data. The three most common types of injection attacks are cross-site scripting, SQL injection, and eval injection.

A cross-site scripting (XSS) attack is possible when you put unsanitized user-generated data into a web page, which allows an attacker to execute arbitrary code on that page, such as stealing a user's cookies. To protect against XSS attacks, your templating technology should escape HTML characters by default and have a way to escape other character classes (e.g., JavaScript, XML) when necessary. See the OWASP XSS Prevention Guide (*http://bit.ly/xss-sheet*) for more info.

A SQL injection attack (*http://bit.ly/sql-attack*) happens when you put unsanitized user-generated data into a SQL query. This allows an attacker to make arbitrary modifications to your database, such as deleting all your tables. Make sure the library you are using to talk to your database sanitizes all query parameters by default.

Eval injection is when you put unsanitized user-generated data into an `eval` statement, which allows an attacker to run arbitrary code on your servers, such as taking them over or stealing user data. By `eval`, I mean any language construct that takes a `String` and executes it as arbitrary code. There are no safe ways to protect against an eval injection attack through sanitization, so you should never use `eval` with user-generated data.[12] In fact, `eval` also makes it harder to reason about your code and may cause performance problems, so as a general rule, you should avoid it at all costs. This is easy enough to do in your own code, but you never know if it is used in a framework or library you depend on. Most statically typed languages do not support any form of eval, which makes them inherently safer against these types of attacks.[13]

---

12 For example, you can write *any* JavaScript code using *just* the characters ()[]{}!+ [Palladino 2012].

13 It's possible to mimic `eval` in some statically typed languages, but you have to jump through a lot of hoops, so it is extremely uncommon. On the other hand, `eval` is used much more frequently in dynamic languages, which leads to severe security holes. For example, a single `eval` used deep inside a routing class made every Ruby on Rails installation in the world vulnerable to arbitrary code injection [Schneeman 2013].

Advisories

Most popular web frameworks have a system to notify users if a serious security flaw has been uncovered. For example, there is the Ruby on Rails Security List (*http://bit.ly/ruby-sec-list*) and the Node Security Project (*https://nodesecurity.io/*). All frameworks have security issues from time to time, so it is critical that you can recover quickly after a vulnerability has been found. Look for frameworks that take security seriously and sign up for their advisories immediately.

FINAL THOUGHTS ON CHOOSING A SERVER-SIDE FRAMEWORK

The biggest driving factor for choosing a framework is the size of the community around it, as it affects your ability to hire, find learning resources, and leverage open source libraries and plug-ins. As of 2015, here are some of the most popular and mature frameworks, broken down by programming language and ordered alphabetically, based on HotFrameworks (*http://hotframeworks.com/*) and my own experience:

- C#: .NET
- Clojure: Ring, Compojure, Hoplon
- Go: Revel, Gorilla
- Groovy: Grails
- Haskell: Snap, Happstack, Scotty
- Java: Spring, Play Framework, DropWizard, JSF, Struts
- JavaScript: express.js, sails.js, derby.js, geddy.js, koa, kraken.js, meteor
- Perl: Mojolicious, Catalyst, Dancer
- PHP: Laravel, Phalcon, Symfony, CakePHP, Yii, Zend
- Python: Django, Flask
- Ruby: Ruby on Rails, Sinatra
- Scala: Play Framework, Spray

You can quickly cut this list down by applying three filters: programming language, problem fit, and scalability. For example, if your team prefers writing everything in Java, your options are Spring, Play Framework, DropWizard, JSF, and Struts. If your goal is to build a RESTful API server, then Spring, Play

Framework, and DropWizard will be the best fit. And if you know this app will be I/O bound, the non-blocking I/O model of Play Framework makes it the best choice.

If after the first three filters, you still have several options, then it's a question of selecting the framework that best fits your deployment, security requirements, data, templating, and testing needs.

Choosing a database

Modern Internet companies are dealing with more data than ever before. Consider the amount of data created and exchanged on the Internet in just one minute:

- 100 hours of video are uploaded to YouTube [YouTube Statistics 2014]

- 19,000 downloads from Apple's App Store [Nerney 2012]

- 276,000 photos are uploaded to Snapchat [Van Hoven 2014]

- 350,000 tweets are posted on Twitter [Mirani 2013]

- 3,000,000 likes on Facebook [Tepper 2012]

- 44,000,000 messages sent on WhatsApp [Bushey 2014]

- 204,000,000 emails are sent [Knoblauch 2014]

Even more astonishing is that all of these numbers are growing exponentially—the amount of data created worldwide is doubling every year [Turner 2014]. To handle all of this data, there has been an explosion of data storage systems in the last 15 years. So the good news is that your startup has many data storage options to choose from.

The bad news is that your startup has many data storage options to choose from. The number of buzz words and concepts can be overwhelming. Should you use SQL or NoSQL? Schema or schema-less? MySQL or MongoDB? Redis or Riak? To help answer these questions, I'll do a brief overview of the most common types of data systems used by startups: relational databases and NoSQL databases. After that, I'll review a list of trade-offs to consider when choosing between them, including reading data, writing data, schemas, scalability, and maturity.

RELATIONAL DATABASES

Relational databases have been the dominant data storage solution since the 1980s. The most popular ones include Oracle, MySql, PostgreSQL, MS SQL Server, and SQLite. A relational database stores data in *tables, rows,* and *columns.* Each table represents a collection of related items, where each item is stored in a row, and each row in a table has the same columns. For example, imagine you're working on a website for a bank, and you need to store data about the customers. You could create a `customers` table where each row represents one customer as a tuple of `customer_id`, `name`, and `date_of_birth`, as shown in Table 5-2.

Table 5-2. customers

customer_id	name	date_of_birth
1	Brian Kim	1948-09-23
2	Karen Johnson	1989-11-18
3	Wade Feinstein	1965-02-29

Relational databases require you to define a *schema* to describe the structure of each table. This is typically done using Structured Query Language (SQL) as the data definition language:

```
CREATE TABLE customers (
    customer_id     INT NOT NULL PRIMARY KEY,
    name            VARCHAR(128),
    date_of_birth   DATE
);
```

The schema allows the relational database to enforce a variety of *integrity constraints.* For example, in the preceding schema, each column has a type (`INT`, `VARCHAR`, `DATE`) which the database will use to verify every write. The `customer_id` column is also labeled as `NOT NULL PRIMARY KEY`, so the database will ensure that the column always has a value and that each `customer_id` appears at most once in the table (i.e., it can be used as a unique identifier for the row).

Relational databases also use SQL as the data manipulation language. For example, here is how you can insert one row into the `customers` table:

```
INSERT INTO customers (customer_id, name, date_of_birth)
VALUES              (1, "Brian Kim", "1948-09-23");
```

And here is how you can use SQL to query the database to find the customer with the name "Brian Kim":

```
SELECT * FROM customers WHERE name = 'Brian Kim';
```

Relational databases allow you to create *indices* over any of the columns, or even *compound indices* over multiple columns, to speed up these sorts of search queries. They also allow you to work with multiple tables at the same time. For example, imagine that each customer of the bank has a checking and/or savings account with a balance. To represent this data, you could create the accounts table shown in Table 5-3.

Table 5-3. accounts

account_id	customer_id	account_type	balance
I	I	checking	500
2	2	checking	8,500
3	I	savings	2,500
4	3	checking	160

Notice how the customer_id column is a reference to IDs in the customers table. You can express this relationship by labeling the customer_id column as a *foreign key*:

```
CREATE TABLE accounts (
    account_id      INT NOT NULL PRIMARY KEY,
    customer_id     INT FOREIGN KEY REFERENCES customers(customer_id),
    account_type    VARCHAR(20),
    balance         INT
);
```

Now the database will throw an error if you try to insert a row into the accounts table with a customer_id that isn't in the customers table:

```
INSERT INTO accounts (account_id, customer_id, account_type, balance)
VALUES                (1, 555, "checking", 500)

-- Error: Cannot add or update a child row: a foreign key constraint fails
```

You can also use SQL to run queries across multiple tables, known as a JOIN. For example, here is how you can find the names of customers who have a balance of at least $1,000:

```
SELECT customers.name
FROM customers JOIN accounts
ON customers.customer_id = accounts.customer_id
WHERE accounts.balance > 1000
```

NOSQL DATABASES

NoSQL, which stands for *Not Only SQL,* is a fuzzy term that refers to databases that do not use SQL—that is, they do not use the relational model. There are many types of non-relational databases, most of which failed to gain wide adoption, such as object databases in the 90s and XML databases in the early 2000s. NoSQL refers to a new breed of databases that were built in the late 2000s, primarily by Internet companies struggling to adapt relational databases to unprecedented demands in performance, availability, and data volume.

The early inspirations for NoSQL included Google's 2006 paper on BigTable, a distributed storage system that was designed to handle "petabytes of data across thousands of commodity servers" [Chang, et al. 2006], and Amazon's 2007 paper on Dynamo, a "highly available key-value storage system that some of Amazon's core services use to provide an always-on experience" [DeCandia et al 2007]. The actual term *NoSQL* came after these papers, originating as a Twitter hashtag (#NoSQL) for a 2009 meetup in San Francisco (*http://bit.ly/nosql-meetup*) to discuss "open source, distributed, non-relational databases."

The meetup's description is probably the best definition that we have of NoSQL: open source databases that are designed to run on clusters of servers and do not use the relational model. The most common types of NoSQL databases are key-value stores, document stores, column-oriented databases, and graph databases.

Key-value stores

Key-value stores are optimized for a single use case: extremely fast lookup by a known identifier. They are effectively a hash table that is distributed across many servers and persisted to disk. Popular examples include Redis, DynamoDB, Riak, and Voldemort.

The API for most key-value stores usually consists of just two functions, one to insert a key-value pair and one to look up a value by key. Here is an example using the put and get functions in Voldemort:

```
> put "the-key" "the-value"
> get "the-key"
version(0:1): "the-value"
```

Key-value stores do not use schemas, so you can store any kind of value you want. Unfortunately, because most key-value stores treat the values as opaque blobs, they cannot support any query mechanism other than lookups by primary key.

Document stores

Document stores are similar to key-value stores in that they allow you to store key-value pairs. The difference is that the document store is aware of the format of the value, so it can support more advanced query functionality. Popular document stores include MongoDB, CouchDB, and Couchbase.

Let's look at a quick example using MongoDB. MongoDB allows you to store JSON *documents* in *collections*, somewhat analogously to how a relational databases allow you to store *rows* in *tables*. MongoDB has no predefined schema for documents, so you can store any JSON data you want. For example, here is how you can use the save command to store a JSON document in a collection called people:

```
> db.people.save(
{_id: "the-key", name: "Ann", age: 14, locationId: 123})
```

In MongoDB, every document has a field called _id, which is used as the key. In the preceding example, the _id is explicitly set to "the-key", but you can also allow MongoDB to auto-generate the _id field for you by just not including it when you call save:

```
> db.people.save({name: "Bob", age: 35, locationId: 456})
```

You can now see all the documents in the people collection using the find command:

```
> db.people.find()
{"_id": "the-key", "age": 14, "name": "Ann", "locationId": 123}
{"_id": ObjectId("545bdc1e"), "age": 35, "name": "Bob", "locationId": 456}
```

You can also look up a specific document by ID almost as efficiently as in a key-value store:

```
> db.people.find({"_id": "the-key"})
{"_id" : "the-key", "age": 14, "name": "Ann", "locationId": 123}
```

Unlike key-value stores, document databases can also perform lookups by any field inside a document. For example, here is how you can find all the documents where the name field is set to "Ann":

```
> db.people.find({"name": "Ann"})
{"_id": "the-key", "age": 14, "name": "Ann", "locationId": 123}
```

Many document databases even support indexing the fields within a document, known as a *secondary indices*, to make searches much faster. Unfortunately, JOIN queries are usually not supported. For example, let's say you had another collection called locations:

```
> db.locations.find()
{"_id": 123, "city": "Boston", "state": "Massachusetts"}
{"_id": 456, "city": "Palo Alto", "state": "California"}
```

The only way to fetch a person and the name of where they live is to use two sequential queries in your application code: one to fetch data from the people collection and then a second to fetch location data from the locations collection. One alternative is to denormalize the data, and instead of storing locationId in each document in the people collection, you could store the city and state directly. This will make reads simpler and faster, because you'll only need a single query, but it will make updates more complicated, error prone, and slower, because you have redundant data. For example, if a city were renamed, you'd have to update every entry in the people collection with the new name instead of just a single entry in the locations collection.

Column-oriented databases

Popular column-oriented databases include HBase and Cassandra. On the surface, they look similar to a relational database because they store data in tables that consist of rows and columns. Cassandra even has schemas for tables and a query language called CQL that looks similar to SQL. The major difference is that relational databases are typically *row-oriented*, which means they are optimized for operations across many rows of data, while *column-oriented* databases are optimized for operations across many columns. For example, consider the books table as shown in Table 5-4.

Table 5-4. books

id	title	genre	year_published
1	Clean Code	tech	2008
2	Code Complete	tech	1993
3	The Giver	sci-fi	1993

How does this data get stored on the hard drive? In a relational database, the values in each row will be kept together, so conceptually, the serialized data might look something like this:

```
1:Clean Code,tech,2008;2:Code Complete,tech,1993;3:The Giver,sci-fi,1993;
```

All the columns for a single row are laid out sequentially. Compare this to the way a column-oriented store might serialize the same data:

```
Clean Code:1,Code Complete:2,The Giver:3;tech:1,2,sci-fi:3;2008:1,1993:2,3;
```

In this format, all the values in a single column are laid out sequentially, with the column values as keys (e.g., computers), and the IDs as values (e.g., 1,2). Now consider the following query:

```
SELECT * FROM books WHERE year_published = 1993;
```

Because this query uses SELECT *, it will need to read every column for any matching rows. Hard drives perform best for sequential reads, so this query will be most efficient with the row-oriented storage, where all the columns for a row are next to one another. Compare that to the following query:

```
SELECT COUNT(*) FROM books WHERE year_published = 1993;
```

This query uses SELECT COUNT(*), so it will only need to read the values in the year_published column. These kinds of aggregate queries are more efficient in a column-oriented database, where all the values for a single column are next to one another.

Graph databases

Graph databases represent data as nodes that are connected by directed edges. While other NoSQL data stores were primarily motivated by the need to run on clusters, most graph databases run on a single node, and are motivated by the need to efficiently store, query, and navigate relationship data. Popular graph databases include Neo4j and Titan.

Consider the example graph in Figure 5-4.

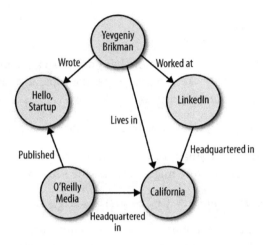

Figure 5-4. Example graph

To create the nodes of this graph in Neo4j, you can use the CREATE command:

```
CREATE
  (yevgeniy { name: "Yevgeniy Brikman" }),
  (oreilly { name: "O'Reilly Media", industry: "publishing" }),
  (california { name: "California" }),
  (linkedin { name: "LinkedIn", industry: "social networking" }),
  (hello { name: "Hello Startup", yearPublished: 2015 })
```

You can also use CREATE to connect the nodes with edges:

```
CREATE
  (yevgeniy)-[:WROTE]->(hello),
  (yevgeniy)-[:LIVES_IN]->(california),
  (yevgeniy)-[:WORKED_AT]->(linkedin),
  (oreilly)-[:PUBLISHED]->(hello),
  (oreilly)-[:HEADQUARTERED_IN]->(california),
  (linkedin)-[:HEADQUARTERED_IN]->(california)
```

There are no predefined schemas, so nodes and edges can be created with arbitrary properties. You can use the MATCH command to query the graph based on these properties, such as this query to find a node with the name property set to "Yevgeniy Brikman":

```
MATCH (person)
WHERE person.name = "Yevgeniy Brikman"
RETURN person
```

This query returns one node:

```
(8 {name:"Yevgeniy Brikman"})
```

You can also query the relationships between nodes. For example, here is how you can find companies headquartered in California:

```
MATCH (company)-[:HEADQUARTERED_IN]->(location { name: "California" })
RETURN company
```

You get back two nodes:

```
(9 {name:"O'Reilly Media", industry: "publishing"})
(10 {name:"LinkedIn", industry: "social networking"})
```

You can go even deeper, such as finding books written by people who live in California:

```
MATCH (book)<-[:WROTE]-(person)-[:LIVES_IN]->(location { name: "California" })
RETURN book
```

Which in this case returns one node:

```
(11 {name:"Hello, Startup", yearPublished: 2015})
```

READING DATA

In the introduction to relational and NoSQL databases, you saw trade-offs between the types of query models supported, as shown in Table 5-5. Relational and graph databases are a great choice for general-purpose data storage because their flexible query models can handle the ever-changing access patterns of most startups. Other NoSQL databases are great choices for special-purpose data storage that fits specific access patterns.

Table 5-5. Query models

Database type	Access patterns	JOIN	Indexes
Relational	Very flexible query model	Yes	Primary, secondary, compound
Key-value	Primary key lookup	No	Primary
Document	Primary, secondary key lookup	No	Primary, secondary
Column-oriented	Operations on a single column	No	Primary, secondary
Graph	Very flexible query model	Yes	Primary, secondary

Another trade-off to consider when reading data is how that data is represented. For example, consider the following Java class:

```java
public class Person {
  private long id;
  private String name;
  private int age;
  private List<String> skills;
}
```

It's easy to represent the Person class as an analogous JSON document:

```json
{
  "_id": 123,
  "name": "Linda",
  "age": 35,
  "skills": ["Java", "Scala", "Ruby"]
}
```

With a key-value store or a document database, you could save or retrieve this JSON document in just a single command:

```
> db.people.save(
{_id: 123, name: "Linda", age: 35, skills: ["Java", "Scala", "Ruby"]})
> db.people.find({_id: 123})
{_id: 123, name: "Linda", age: 35, skills: ["Java", "Scala", "Ruby"]}
```

On the other hand, the normalized representation of this data in a relational database looks quite a bit different, as shown in Tables 5-6, 5-7, and 5-8.

Table 5-6. people

person_id	name	age
12345	Linda	35

Table 5-7. skills

skill_id	skill_name
1	Java
2	Scala
3	Ruby

Table 5-8. people_skills

person_id	skill_id
12345	1
12345	2
12345	3

To fetch the data for a single `Person` object, you need a query that `JOIN`s three tables:

```
SELECT people.person_id, people.name, people.age, skills.skill_name
FROM people
  JOIN people_skills ON people.person_id = people_skills.person_id
  JOIN skills ON skills.skill_id = people_skills.skill_id
WHERE people.person_id = 12345
```

This query returns three rows, as shown in Table 5-9, that you then have to carefully parse into the fields of the `Person` class.

Table 5-9. Query result

person_id	name	age	skill_name
12345	Linda	35	Java
12345	Linda	35	Scala
12345	Linda	35	Ruby

Even for a simple class, it is complicated to map from the relational representation to the in-memory representation. This is known as an *impedance mismatch*. Many *object-relational mapping (ORM)* tools have been built to try to solve this problem, such as ActiveRecord and Hibernate, but they are often the source of controversy, blamed for exposing leaky abstractions and causing performance problems. This is not because those particular ORM tools are bad, but because the mapping problem is inherently hard. Any solution you can come up with will involve serious, painful trade-offs [Atwood 2006b].

For many startups, when the application is small and the performance requirements are low, it's worth using an ORM, as it will likely handle 80%–90% of use cases without issues. It's important to realize that using an ORM does not mean you can ignore the underlying details of how a relational database works. You still need to understand relational data modeling, normalization, indexing, joins, and query tuning so you know how to store your data correctly and handle the 10%–20% of use cases that the ORM struggles with.

As your startup grows, it's possible the ORM success rate will drop well below 80%. At this point, you have two options: either abandon objects (drop the "O") or abandon relational databases (drop the "R"), and you will no longer have a mapping problem [Atwood 2006b]. If you want to go with the first option, instead of objects you can represent the data in memory using a relational or functional model. For example, you could use a *functional-relational mapper (FRM)*, such as Typesafe Slick, instead of an ORM. If you want to go with the second option, you can switch from a relational database to a NoSQL store. As you saw before, the representation of data in a key-value or document store can be analogous to its representation in memory, so the mapping problem is easier. The only bad option is to try to write your own ORM, as you will almost certainly end up with a worse solution than the open source ORM tools that have been under development for years.

WRITING DATA

Most NoSQL databases are optimized for working on *aggregates*: a single value in a key-value store, a single document in a document store, or a single column in a column-oriented database.[14] While writing a single aggregate is usually easy and guaranteed to be atomic, NoSQL databases give you no guarantees when trying to write multiple aggregates.

For example, imagine you were building a bank website and you needed to store the balance for each account as shown in Table 5-10.

---

14 The term "aggregates" comes from [Sadalage and Fowler 2012, 14]. Graph databases are not optimized for aggregates, so they are excluded from this discussion.

Table 5-10. accounts

account_id	balance
I	500
2	8,500
3	2,500

In a key-value store such as Voldemort, inserting a single value (a single aggregate) is easy:

```
> put "4" "5,000"
```

However, updating existing data can be harder. To update a bank account balance, you might have to make one request to fetch the current value, calculate the new value in your application code, and then make a second request to save the new value (note that this operation is not atomic).[15]

In a document database, updating a single account (a single aggregate) is easier. For example, to subtract $100 from an account, you can use MongoDB's update function and the increment operator, $inc:

```
> db.accounts.update({_id: 1}, {$inc: {balance: -100}})
```

In a relational database, updating a single account is also straightforward:

```
UPDATE accounts
SET balance = balance - 100
WHERE account_id = 1
```

But what if this bank charged a $100 annual fee and you wanted to subtract $100 from every account? You could do this in MongoDB by setting the multi option to true:

```
> db.accounts.update({}, {$inc: {balance: -100}}, {multi: true})
```

The catch is that updates to more than one account (more than one aggregate) do not happen atomically. A customer with multiple accounts could open the bank website and see that one of their accounts has had $100 deducted, but

---

15 Some key-value stores, such as Redis and Riak, support a limited set of data types for the values, such as string, integer, set, list, and map. This gives you the ability to make certain types of updates in one round-trip, such as incrementing an integer value with the INCR command in Redis.

the other has not. In a relational database, this could never happen because all updates are atomic:

```
UPDATE accounts
SET balance = balance - 100
```

This becomes an even bigger problem when you need transactional semantics. For example, if you want to transfer $100 from account 1 to account 2, in most NoSQL databases, you would need to issue two separate updates:

```
> db.accounts.update({_id: 1}, {$inc: {balance: -100}})
> db.accounts.update({_id: 2}, {$inc: {balance: 100}})
```

The problem is that these two updates do not happen atomically, so what happens if something goes wrong in the middle? For example, if you withdraw money from account 1 and the database crashes before you can add it to account 2, then that money disappears into thin air. If you wanted to do this update atomically with a NoSQL database, you'd have to manually implement two-phase commits in your application code, which is complicated and error prone.

Most relational databases solve this problem for you automatically if you wrap the updates in a transaction:

```
START TRANSACTION;
  UPDATE accounts
  SET balance = balance - 100
  WHERE account_id = 1;

  UPDATE accounts
  SET balance = balance + 100
  WHERE account_id = 2;
COMMIT;
```

This allows you to perform several updates across multiple rows or even tables, and either all of the updates succeed or all of them get rolled back.

SCHEMAS

Most NoSQL databases advertise themselves as *schema-less*, while relational databases require you to define a schema up front. This distinction is a bit misleading. While a NoSQL database may not care about the schema of your data, at some point your application will need to know the format of the data to be able to read it. For example, consider the following Java code to read a document from MongoDB:

```
DBCollection books = db.getCollection("books");
BasicDBObject query = new BasicDBObject();
query.put("author", "Yevgeniy Brikman");

DBObject book = books.findOne(query);

String title = (String) book.get("title");
int pages = ((Number) book.get("pages")).intValue();
Date datePublished = (Date) book.get("datePublished");
```

In order to issue a meaningful query and parse the results, the Java code has to know the name of the fields (author, title, pages, datePublished) and the types of each of those fields (String, int, Date). This is the schema! In other words, it's not a question of schema versus schema-less, but a question of whether the schema is explicit and enforced by the database or implicit and enforced by the application code.

Having the database enforce the schema helps to automatically prevent a large class of errors, similar to static typing in a programming language. For example, the relational database can ensure that your queries don't have typos in the names of the tables or columns, that you don't store the wrong data type in a column, that strings do not exceed predefined size limits, that primary key IDs are unique, and that foreign keys refer to valid IDs in other tables. These same integrity checks are necessary in the NoSQL world as well, but you have to implement them manually in your application code. Letting a well-tested relational database do them for you automatically is usually safer, especially as that ensures the schema is enforced in one place instead of distributed among every bit of application code that talks directly to the NoSQL database. The schema also acts as a form of documentation for any developer trying to understand what kind of data they are dealing with.

There are two cases where the schema-less approach is advantageous. The first case is when you need to store unstructured or non-uniform data. For example, user-generated data, event-tracking data, and log messages may have irregular or unpredictable formats. If you stored this data in a relational database, you might end up with lots of NULL columns, columns with meaningless names (e.g., col1, col2, col3), or columns that store "blobs" (e.g., putting a JSON document into a column), all of which are anti-patterns in the relational world.

The second case is when doing data migrations. To change the type of data you store in a relational database, you have to update not only your application code but also the schema. Depending on the database and how much data you have, adding or removing columns, tables, or integrity constraints can be expensive and tricky to do without downtime. With a NoSQL database, all you have to do is update your application code to be able to handle both the new data format and the old one, and your migration is done. Or, to be more accurate, your migration has just started, and it will happen incrementally as new data gets written. For example, if you were storing book data in MongoDB and you renamed the pages field to pageCount, you'd have to update the Java code as follows:

```
int pages;

if (book.containsKey("pages")) {
  pages = ((Number) book.get("pages")).intValue();
} else {
  pages = ((Number) book.get("pageCount")).intValue();
}
```

This makes it easier to do an incremental, zero-downtime migration, as you can handle both the old field name for all the existing books in the database and the new field name for any new books you write to the database. However, after a few migrations, these types of if statements can make the application code hard to maintain. Therefore, you may have to do some extra work to create a background script that will speed up the migration, allowing you to clean up the code for the old format before it gets too messy.

SCALABILITY

Scalability was one of the main motivations for NoSQL.[16] Companies like Google and Amazon were facing availability and performance requirements that exceeded the capabilities of any single server. They had reached the limits of *vertical scaling* (i.e., adding more RAM or CPU to a single server), so they needed systems that could run on a cluster of servers that could be scaled *horizontally* (i.e., adding more servers).

Once you go from storing data on a single server to multiple servers, you are dealing with a *distributed system*. All distributed systems are subject to the CAP theorem, which states the following:

It is impossible for a distributed computer system to simultaneously provide all three of the following guarantees:

---

16 Except for graph databases, which had a different motivation: the need to efficiently store and query relationship data.

- *Consistency (all nodes see the same data at the same time)*

- *Availability (a guarantee that every request receives a response about whether it succeeded or failed)*

- *Partition tolerance (the system continues to operate despite arbitrary message loss or failure of part of the system)*

—[CAP THEOREM 2014]

Consistency (C), availability (A), partition tolerance (P): choose two. In practice, it's always possible that a server will fail or the network will drop messages, so all distributed systems *must* choose P—that is, you can't sacrifice partition tolerance [Hale 2010]. So the real question is, in the presence of network partitions, do you maintain consistency or availability?

Some systems, such as MongoDB, HBase, and Redis, always try to keep the data consistent on all nodes, so in the case of a network partition, they might lose availability. Other systems, such as Voldemort, Cassandra, Riak, and CouchDB, are *eventually consistent*, which means that during a network partition, they will remain available, but different nodes may end up with different data and the conflicts will have to be resolved later. In fact, even without a partition, propagating data in a distributed system always takes time, so even during normal operation, eventually consistent systems may have different data in different nodes at least for a short amount of time.

There are two primary strategies for building a distributed data system that can scale horizontally: replication and partitioning [Kleppmann 2015, part 2].

Replication

Replication involves copying the same data to multiple servers or *replicas*. One of the key benefits of replication is fault tolerance. Servers and hard drives fail all the time, so no matter what database technology you pick, you need to ensure that a copy of your data is in more than one place to prevent downtime and data loss. The bare minimum is replicating data to a *standby replica*, which doesn't serve any live traffic but can be swapped in if the primary database goes down. You can also replicate data to one or more *active replicas*, which serve live traffic, thereby allowing you to horizontally scale your database by adding more replicas.

There are two general ways to use replication for scalability: *master/slave replication* and *multi-master replication* [Kleppmann 2015, chap. 5].

In master/slave replication, as shown in Figure 5-5, all writes go to a single node (the master), which propagates those changes to one or more replicas (the slaves). All reads go to the replicas.

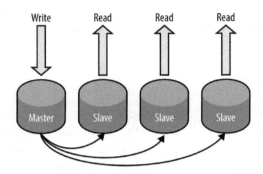

Figure 5-5. Master/slave replication

In multi-master replication, as shown in Figure 5-6, all nodes are equal, so they can accept reads or writes, and propagate the changes to all of their peers.

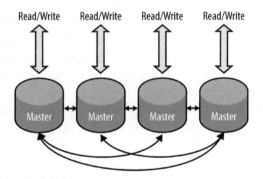

Figure 5-6. Multi-master replication

Master/slave replication primarily allows scaling for more read traffic, while multi-master replication allows scaling for both read and write traffic. So why not use multi-master replication in all cases? The answer is complexity. Systems with a single writer (a single master) are easier to reason about and maintain, and because most databases see much more read traffic than write traffic, master/slave replication is enough to handle many scalability challenges. However, if a single master is becoming a bottleneck for writes, then the complexity of multi-master replication might be worth it.

The complexity arises from the fact that a system with multiple writers could simultaneously see two different updates to the same piece of data on two different nodes. This is known as a *conflict*, and systems that use multi-master replication have to implement a *conflict resolution strategy*. In some cases, merging the writes together can work. For example, Amazon uses the Dynamo database to store shopping cart data, where it makes sense to merge conflicting writes together, because they just represent everything the user has added to the shopping cart. Other strategies include *last write wins*, where values with a newer timestamp or vector clock overwrite older ones, and *user specified*, where all conflicting versions are saved and the client code has to decide which one to keep when it reads the data.

Partitioning

Whereas replication is copying the same data to multiple servers, partitioning is copying different subsets of the data to different servers. The goal of partitioning is to divide your data set between n servers so that each one only has to handle $1/n^{th}$ of the total load. You can horizontally scale by adding more nodes, further reducing the load on each one. However, if you don't partition your data correctly, then one node will receive more load than the others. This is known as a *hot spot* and it will become a bottleneck for your scaling efforts. To avoid such bottlenecks, you need to select the right partitioning strategy. The two main options are *vertical partitioning* and *horizontal partitioning*.

Vertical partitioning involves splitting up unrelated types of data, such as moving columns into separate tables or tables into separate databases. For example, let's say you're building a bank website with just two pages: one for managing your savings account and one for managing your checking account. As an initial design, you might store all the user data in a table called users, as shown in Table 5-11.

Table 5-11. users

user_id	username
1	alice123
2	bob456
3	jondoe

And you'll store all the account data in a table called `accounts`, as shown in Table 5-12.

Table 5-12. accounts

account_id	user_id	type	balance
I	I	checking	100
2	I	savings	500
3	2	checking	1500
4	3	savings	250

If the website becomes popular and the `accounts` table becomes so large that the database struggles to keep up with the load, one solution is to vertically partition the data by storing the checking and savings account data in two separate tables: `checking`, as shown in Table 5-13 and `savings`, as shown in Table 5-14.

Table 5-13. checking

account_id	user_id	balance
I	I	100
3	2	1500

Table 5-14. savings

account_id	user_id	balance
2	I	500
4	3	250

You can store these tables in separate databases, as shown in Figure 5-7.

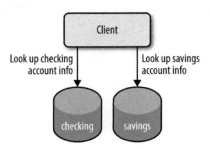

Figure 5-7. Vertical partitioning

Because each page of the website shows either the checking account or the savings account but not both, each database now only has to deal with a fraction of the requests. Moreover, each database doesn't have to compete with the other for CPU, memory, and disk space. However, partitioning always comes at a cost. For example, you lose the ability to do JOINs. If you wanted to fetch the username and total balance for a given user_id, instead of a single query with a JOIN, you'd have to make three separate requests, putting load on all partitions instead of just one. You also lose the ability to automatically enforce foreign key constraints, such as the user_id column in the checking and savings tables. Vertical partitioning also doesn't help if a single table gets too big. For example, if the bank website becomes very popular, just the checking table alone might overwhelm a single server.

An alternative is horizontal partitioning (AKA *sharding*), where you divide up the rows of a single table across separate partitions (AKA *shards*). For example, if your bank website had 10 servers and 1 million users, you could partition the original accounts and users tables by user_id so that user_id 0 - 100,000 was on server 0, 100,001 - 200,000 was on server 1, and so on up to server 9, as shown in Figure 5-8.

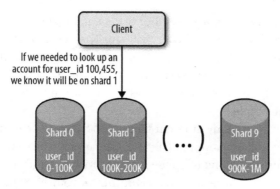

Figure 5-8. Horizontal partitioning

This strategy works very well for any page that needs the data for a single user because all of that data will be on a single shard. For example, whereas a vertical partitioning scheme needed three requests to fetch the username and total balance for a single user_id, with this horizontal partitioning scheme, you need to send just a single query to that user's shard:

```
SELECT users.username, SUM(accounts.balance)
FROM users JOIN accounts ON users.user_id = accounts.user_id
WHERE users.user_id = 100455
```

If most of your requests are for just one user at a time, then each shard will only have to deal with 10% of the load, and you'll still be able to use JOINs and foreign key constraints. If the number of users grows, you can scale horizontally by adding more shards.

But there are some serious drawbacks, too. For example, what if you want to find all users who have at least $500 in their accounts? There is no way to know ahead of time which shards those users will be on, so you'll have to perform a *scatter gather query* that fans out to all partitions, putting load on all of your shards instead of just one. Horizontal partitioning also makes it more complex to generate IDs. With a single database, it's easy to use an incrementing counter, but with multiple databases, you have to do extra work to avoid conflicts.[17] Making this even more difficult is the fact that your data and your access patterns will change over time, so a partitioning that was fair initially may have hot spots in the future. Changing the partitioning strategy, known as *rebalancing*, can be difficult and expensive, as it requires moving a lot of data around.

FAILURE MODES

At some point, every data store, whether that's a manually sharded MySQL setup or an auto-sharded MongoDB cluster, will fail. The question is, how many different ways can the system fail and how easy is it to understand and fix each one? Usually, simpler solutions are easier to fix, and many NoSQL solutions, especially those that support multiple writers, auto-sharding, and auto rebalancing, are anything but simple.

The complexity of many different failure modes was one of the main reasons Pinterest had to abandon MongoDB and Cassandra while scaling the website from zero to tens of billions of page views per month [Hoff 2013]. For example, what happens if the auto-rebalancing algorithm in your NoSQL store has a bug? One possible outcome is that the replication simply gets stuck and eventually, consistent becomes never consistent. Another possible outcome is that the cluster becomes unbalanced and even though you have 10 nodes, all the traffic goes to 1. A third possible outcome is that the broken rebalancing algorithm sprays bad data into all of your nodes and all of your data becomes completely corrup-

---

17 See [Krieger 2011] for a good overview of your options.

ted. And worst of all, when you go to fix these issues by updating to a new version of the NoSQL software, you uncover yet another failure mode: in a distributed system where all the nodes need to communicate with one another, such as a NoSQL store with multi-master replication, if the new version of the software has an incompatible change in the protocol it uses for communication, it can make it impossible to upgrade your cluster without taking the whole thing down.

MATURITY

Your company's data is one of the most important parts of your business. It will most likely outlive any feature, or any app, and perhaps even the company itself. You can change programming languages, web frameworks, and rewrite the code a hundred times, but the data you've gathered is a constant. You will need to move this data around (e.g., feed it into a data warehouse, Hadoop cluster, or search index), back it up, and monitor it, all of which is difficult to do without a mature ecosystem of tools. Therefore, you need to store your data in a manner that is safe, reliable, and well-supported so that it can survive for a long time. George Soros, a famous investor, is known for saying that "good investing is boring." I propose that good data storage is boring.

> Early on, we started trying a lot of different databases at GitHub, but in the last two or three years, we've been removing them and just using MySQL. MySQL has been in development for around 20 years. It's got its horrible parts, but we know what those are. It's pretty stable, and most importantly, we know how to scale it. We've been doing it since the start of the company, so it's a known factor.
>
> We've been trying to remove more and more things to simplify our stack as much as possible. As sexy as that new database may be, it's not as sexy as stability. People love uptime. Uptime is great. So we've just been getting more and more boring with our technology choices all the time and couldn't be happier about that.

—[HOLMAN 2014], ZACH HOLMAN, SOFTWARE ENGINEER AT GITHUB

Data storage technologies take a long time to mature. Consider the initial release dates for some of the most popular relational databases: Oracle came out in the 1970s, Microsoft SQL Server in 1989, and MySQL and PostgreSQL came out in 1995. These databases have been under constant development for 20–40 years and are still working to improve their safety, reliability, and performance. Data storage is not a problem that can be solved quickly, so I propose the following rule of thumb:

General-purpose data storage technology takes 10 years to mature.[18]

At the time of writing this book in 2014, the average NoSQL store is roughly six years old. Here are the release dates of some of the most popular ones: CouchDB came out in 2005, HBase in 2006, Neo4j in 2007, Cassandra in 2008, and MongoDB, Redis, Riak, and Voldemort came out in 2009. Many companies have reported problems with NoSQL immaturity. For example, MongoDB has been the source of controversy for years, with claims that its fault tolerance approach is broken by design [Gün Sirer 2013] a number of companies have moved away from it, including Pinterest [Hoff 2013], Urban Airship [Schurter 2011], Etsy [McKinley 2012], Viber [Ish-Shalom 2014], and Bump [Doug 2012]. But MongoDB is not alone. Twitter, Facebook, and Pinterest abandoned Cassandra [North 2011]; Instagram [Branson 2014] and Viber [Leonard 2014] abandoned Redis; and Signal Engage [Wood 2012] and Canonical [Lord 2011] had to abandon CouchDB. This is not to say that NoSQL databases are a bad choice, but they are a more risky choice, and data storage is usually not the place you want to take risks.

FINAL THOUGHTS ON CHOOSING A DATABASE

When choosing a data store, the most important consideration is maturity. You can work around limitations in a programming language or a server-side framework, but you cannot work around data loss. By that measure alone, relational databases should be the default option for any data storage decision. Start by modeling your problem with a relational database and see how far you can get before you run into walls. And don't be surprised if you don't hit a wall for a long time, because relational databases are remarkably flexible. For example, you can use them with standard relational schemas and integrity constraints and take advantage of a query language that supports indices, transactions, and JOINs. Or you can use them as a schema-less key-value store [Entity–attribute–value Model

---

18 It may not just be data storage, but any complicated piece of software takes this long. As Joel Spolsky wrote, "Good Software Takes Ten Years. Get Used To it" [Spolsky 2001].

2014]. Or as a cube, star, or snowflake shaped offline analytics store [Online Analytical Processing 2014]. Or even as a fast JSON document store.[19]

If you do hit a wall with a relational database, it will most likely be because your data volume and availability requirements have exceeded the capacity of a single server. At this point, your priority is to identify the simplest solution that will scale. In order of increasing complexity, here are the most common options:

- Optimize the data storage format and queries on your existing database.

- Set up a cache in front of the database (e.g., memcached).

- Set up master/slave replication.

- Vertically partition unrelated tables.

- Horizontally partition a single table.

- Set up multi-master replication.

In general, avoid partitioning your data and stick with a single-writer for as long as possible. A sharded, multi-master system has more failure modes and makes it more complicated to do JOINs, transactions, enforce integrity constraints, migrations, updates, backups, and ID generation. The problem with many NoSQL databases is that they force you to make all these sacrifices up front, even though most use cases don't warrant it. And even in cases where the sacrifices are necessary, doing it with a relational database can get you quite far— Facebook has a cluster of 4,000 MySQL nodes that can handle 60 million queries per second [Harris 2011]. That said, while relational databases were originally designed for running on a single server, most NoSQL databases were designed for the express purpose of running on a cluster. They usually have built-in tools for tuning the trade-offs between consistency and availability, the replication factor, and the number of partitions. In some cases, this will mean a NoSQL store is the simplest solution for your requirements.

There are two trends to watch out for in the future. The first trend is the NoSQL ecosystem becoming more mature. Over the years, many bugs will be fixed, reliability will increase, and as an industry, we will have a better understanding of where each data store excels and fails, so NoSQL might become the

---

19 Native support for JSON documents is available in PostgreSQL [JSON types] and MySQL [Wendel 2013], and the PostgreSQL version may be faster than MongoDB [Linster 2014].

simplest solution for many more use cases. The second trend is the emergence of *NewSQL databases*, which are data stores designed to run on a cluster while still supporting the relational model (schemas, SQL, JOINs, indices, transactions) [NewSQL 2015]. These types of databases started appearing around 2011, so they are even less mature than NoSQL databases, but it'll be interesting to see how they develop. Examples include Google Spanner, VoltDB, FoundationDB, and Clustrix.

Recap

If you're building a startup, the initial choice of tech stack is easy: go with what you know. Use as many open source and commercial technologies as you can and only build in-house the pieces that represent your company's "secret sauce." If you are lucky enough to grow your company beyond this initial stage, your choices get a little more complicated.

Here are the key trade-offs to consider when evaluating a programming language:

Programming paradigms
> Is it an object-oriented or functional programming language? Does it support static typing or automatic memory management?

Problem fit
> For example, C is particularly good for embedded systems, Erlang for fault-tolerant distributed systems, and R for statistics.

Performance
> How does the language handle concurrency? Does the language use garbage collection and how tunable is the collector?

Productivity
> How popular is the language? How many frameworks and libraries are available for it? How concise is it?

Here are the key trade-offs to consider when evaluating a server-side framework:

Problem fit
> For example, Rails is particularly good for CRUD applications, DropWizard for RESTful API servers, and Node.js for real-time webapps.

Data layer

Does the framework help you manipulate URLs, JSON, and XML?

View layer

Are there many built-in templating helpers? Does it use server-side or client-side rendering? Does it allow logic or is it logic-less?

Testing

Is it easy to write unit tests for apps built on top of the framework? Is the framework itself well-tested?

Scalability

Does the framework use blocking or non-blocking I/O? Have you benchmarked the framework with your use cases?

Deployment

Do you know how to integrate the framework into your build? Do you know how to configure, deploy, and monitor it in production?

Security

Is there an built-in, well-tested way within the framework to handle authentication, CSRF, code injection, and security advisories?

Here are the key trade-offs to consider when evaluating a database:

Database type

Is it a relational database or a NoSQL store (key-value store, document store, column-oriented database, or graph database)?

Reading data

Do you need to look up data by primary key or secondary key? Do you need JOINs? How do you map the data into an in-memory representation?

Writing data

Do your writes update just a single aggregate or many? Do you need atomic updates or transactions?

Schemas

Is the schema stored explicitly in the database or implicitly in your application code? Is your data uniform or unstructured?

Scalability

> Can you get by with just vertically scaling your database? If not, does the database support replication, partitioning, or both?

Failure modes

> How many different ways can the system fail? How easy are the failures to debug?

Maturity

> For how long has this database been in development? How many companies are using it? How rich is the ecosystem of supporting tools?

Finally, when thinking about your tech stack as a whole, it's worth mentioning that many companies have moved away from a single, monolithic tech stack, where you have a single programming language, framework, and data storage solution for all use cases, and towards a model of *polyglot programming*, where you use different technologies for different use cases. That is, you build a tech stack on top of a number of different services, where each service is written using different languages and frameworks, is deployed to different servers, talks to different data stores, and communicates with other services via remote messages (see "Services" on page 327). For example, an e-commerce website might consist of the following pieces:

- A frontend service built with JavaScript and Node.js that makes non-blocking JSON-over-HTTP calls to fetch data from the backends.

- A RESTful backend service built with Python and Flask that stores product and user data in PostgreSQL.

- A RESTful backend service built with Java, DropWizard, Lucene, and Redis that manages a search index.

- An HBase cluster for offline analytics.

The advantages of this polyglot model are that you can use the best tools for each task, and that you can break up the code into isolated, loosely coupled components. However, there is significant overhead with learning, deploying, and maintaining so many different technologies, so it's typically only worth it for larger companies that need to scale beyond the capacity of a single monolithic codebase. See "Split up the code" on page 323 for a deeper look at all the trade-offs.

Clean Code

Code is for people

Programming is the art of telling another human what one wants the computer to do.

—DONALD KNUTH

As a programmer, you'll spend less than 50% of your working hours on coding tasks [Orsini 2013]. Of the time spent coding, the ratio of reading code to writing code is well over 10:1. And of the tiny fraction of time you actually spend writing code, 80% or more of it will be maintenance code: that is, modifying or fixing code that already exists [Martin 2008, xx]. If you work eight hours a day, you'll be lucky to spend five minutes writing new code (see Figure 6-1). It turns out that your job as a programmer isn't to write code but to understand code.

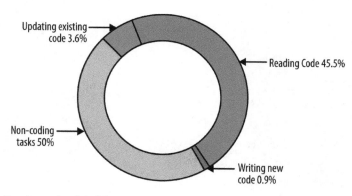

Figure 6-1. Developer time breakdown

This is why clean code matters. *Clean code* is code that is optimized for human understanding. Remember, startups are about people, so the most important thing about code is not how fast it runs or what algorithm it uses, but the impact it has on the people that use it. You should write clean code not for idealistic reasons, not because some book says you have to (not even this one), not because spaces are prettier than tabs—but because you will spend the vast majority of your time as a programmer understanding and maintaining code. Make it easy on yourself.

Let's try an experiment. Imagine you come across this Java code:

```java
public class BP {
public void cvt(File i,File o) {
BufferedReader r=null;
BufferedWriter w;
String l,j="[";
String[] p;
try {
r=new BufferedReader(new FileReader(i));
} catch (FileNotFoundException e) {}
try{
while ((l=r.readLine())!=null){
p=l.split(",");
if(!p[3].equals("fiction")&&!p[3].equals("nonfiction"))continue;
j+="{";
j+="title:\""+p[0]+"\",";
j+="author:\""+p[1]+"\",";
j+="pages:\""+Integer.parseInt(p[2])+"\",";
j+="category:\""+p[3]+"\"";
j+="},";
}
try {
r.close();
} catch(IOException e) {}
} catch(IOException e) {}
j+="]";
try {
w=new BufferedWriter(new FileWriter(o));
w.write(j);
w.close();
} catch (IOException e) {}}}
```

What does it do? No, really, pause for a few seconds and try to figure it out. It's less than 30 lines of code and the functionality is very simple. Have you understood it yet?

I bet you glanced at the code snippet and gave up immediately. Because this is just some code in a book and not your real job, you have that luxury. But some day, you won't. Some day, you'll run across code like this at work. You'll learn that it was written by someone no longer at the company, there's no documentation, and the code is responsible for a critical part of your business. Oh, and it's full of bugs and it's your job to fix it. On days like these, you'll realize the importance of clean code.

In this chapter, I'll introduce the basic principles of clean code, including code layout, naming, don't repeat yourself (DRY), the single responsibility principle (SRP), functional programming, loose coupling, high cohesion, comments, and refactoring. I won't cover every possible clean code topic, nor every nuance and exception, and I won't focus much on theory. Instead, this is a practical guide to the most common code quality problems you're likely to hit at a startup.

The code example at the beginning of this chapter exhibits almost all of these problems. As you read on, you'll find solutions for each problem, use them to improve the code example, and eventually end up with something that's easy to understand. The solutions you see here won't work for every use case, but the same problems show up just about everywhere, so the goal in this chapter is to help you recognize the problems by walking you through a number of concrete examples. In other words, get ready to read a whole bunch of code.

Code layout

As a reader of the English language, you expect the writing in this book to follow certain rules: words are grouped into sentences by periods, sentences are grouped into paragraphs by line breaks, paragraphs are grouped into chapters by section headings, section headings use larger fonts, quoted text is indented, and tangential discussions appear at the bottom of the page as footnotes.

> The tools of grammar haven't survived for so many centuries by chance; they are props the reader needs and subconsciously wants.
>
> **—[WILLIAM ZINSSER, 233], WILLIAM ZINSSER, *ON WRITING WELL***

Although programming hasn't been around for nearly as long as writing, readers of your code still expect you to follow certain code layout rules to make it clear how your program is structured. For example, in most curly brace languages (e.g., Java, C, JavaScript), readers expect you to wrap blocks of code in curly braces, to indent the contents of each block, and to separate functions with newlines. If you break these rules, the productivity and comprehension of the reader drops sharply.

The Fundamental Theorem of Formatting says that good visual layout shows the logical structure of a program. Making the code look pretty is worth something, but it's worth less than showing the code's structure.

—[MCCONNELL 2004, 732], STEVE MCCONNELL, *CODE COMPLETE*

Let's look at what happens when you get code layout wrong. In February 2014, a huge security hole was found in the way Apple's Safari web browser verified SSL server keys [Langley 2014]:

```
static OSStatus SSLVerifySignedServerKeyExchange(
  SSLContext *ctx,
  bool isRsa,
  SSLBuffer signedParams,
  uint8_t *signature,
  UInt16 signatureLen)
{
  OSStatus        err;
  ...

  if ((err = SSLHashSHA1.update(&hashCtx, &serverRandom)) != 0)
    goto fail;
  if ((err = SSLHashSHA1.update(&hashCtx, &signedParams)) != 0)
    goto fail;
    goto fail;
  if ((err = SSLHashSHA1.final(&hashCtx, &hashOut)) != 0)
    goto fail;
  ...

  err = sslRawVerify(...);

fail:
  SSLFreeBuffer(&signedHashes);
  SSLFreeBuffer(&hashCtx);
  return err;
}
```

Have you spotted the bug? It's the two **goto** statements in a row:

```
  if ((err = SSLHashSHA1.update(&hashCtx, &signedParams)) != 0)
    goto fail;
    goto fail;
```

This code has two layout mistakes. First, it does not wrap the body of each if statement in curly braces. Second, the indentation is wrong, which could mislead you into thinking that both goto statements are part of the body of the if statement, when in reality, only the first one is. If you fix both layout mistakes, the bug is more obvious:

```
if ((err = SSLHashSHA1.update(&hashCtx, &signedParams)) != 0) {
    goto fail;
}

goto fail;
```

The second `goto` statement will always execute, skipping all the checks that are below it (including the critical `sslRawVerify` check), and jumping execution over to the `fail` label:

```
fail:
    SSLFreeBuffer(&signedHashes);
    SSLFreeBuffer(&hashCtx);
    return err;
```

The `fail` label returns `err`, which is set to zero at this point, indicating to the caller that the checks all passed even though they didn't actually happen. This bug, appropriately nicknamed "gotofail," left millions of iOS and OS X devices vulnerable to man-in-the-middle attacks. Layout was not the only thing wrong with this code, and code layout bugs are usually not this severe, but it's a useful reminder that code layout is less about making the code pretty and more about revealing the structure of the code.

Your team should enforce a set of conventions about code layout, including the use of whitespace, newlines, indentation, and curly braces. Although programmers love to debate spaces versus tabs and where the curly brace should go, the actual choice isn't that important. What really matters is that you are consistent throughout your codebase. Formatting tools are available for most text editors and IDEs, and as pre-commit hooks for version control systems to help you enforce a common code layout.

A good example of layout conventions is the Google Java Style Guide. You can use it to improve the layout of the code snippet at the beginning of the chapter:

```
public class BP {
    public void cvt(File i, File o) {
        BufferedReader r = null;
        BufferedWriter w;
        String l, j = "[";
        String[] p;
```

```
try {
  r = new BufferedReader(new FileReader(i));
} catch (FileNotFoundException e) {}

try {
  while ((l = r.readLine()) != null) {

    p = l.split(",");
    if (!p[3].equals("fiction") && !p[3].equals("nonfiction")) {
      continue;
    }

    j += "{";
    j += "title:\"" + p[0] + "\",";
    j += "author:\"" + p[1] + "\",";
    j += "pages:\"" + Integer.parseInt(p[2]) + "\",";
    j += "category:\"" + p[3] + "\"";
    j += "},";
  }

  try {
    r.close();
  } catch (IOException e) {}
} catch (IOException e) {}

j += "]";

try {
  w = new BufferedWriter(new FileWriter(o));
  w.write(j);
  w.close();
} catch (IOException e) {}
  }
}
```

Just by adding whitespace in the correct places, you can start to see the structure of the code: there is a class called BP with a single method called cvt that seems to read in a file called i, loop over its contents while building a String called j, and then writes j out to a file called o. You can understand a little more now, but to go further, you'll need better variable, function, and class names.

Naming

Every codebase defines its own language that consists of class names, method names, variable names, function names, package names, filenames, and folder names. If code layout is the grammar, the names in your code are the vocabulary. They are the words you use to think about the code. Good names should answer all the big questions, be precise and thorough, reveal intent, and follow conventions.

ANSWER ALL THE BIG QUESTIONS

The name of a variable, function, or class should answer all the big questions. It should tell you why it exists, what it does, and how it is used.

—[MARTIN 2008, 18], ROBERT C. MARTIN, *CLEAN CODE*

The code snippet from the beginning of the chapter is incomprehensible because there are no names and no concepts for your mind to grasp onto:

```
public class BP {
  public void cvt(File i, File o) {
    BufferedReader r = null;
    BufferedWriter w;
    String l, j = "[";
    String[] p;
```

Names that are too short (e.g., i, o, r, j) convey no information. Abbreviated names (e.g., BP, cvt) might make sense to you while you're writing the code, but why force others to have to work hard to decipher these names when reading your code? Developers spend more time reading code than writing it, so the time spent figuring out a cryptic name can be significant, whereas the time saved by typing fewer characters is negligible, especially with the auto-complete support in modern text editors and IDEs. Make names as long as they need to be to answer the what, why, and how of the code.

Here is a first try at improving the names:

```
public class BookParser {

  public void convert(File inputCsv, File out) {
    BufferedReader reader = null;
    BufferedWriter writer;
    String tmp, data = "[";
    String[] parts;
```

This small change should improve your understanding of the code. From the class name BookParser, you can guess that it's dealing with parsing data about books, and from the method name convert and the parameter names inputCsv and out, it looks like it's converting book data from CSV format to some sort of output format.

BE PRECISE

You want to choose names that describe exactly what the piece of code is doing and why. For example, you should be precise with opposites. If you have a method called open(), the complementary method should be called close(); if you have an input, you should usually also have an output [McConnell 2004, 172]. The convert function is inconsistent with opposites, as it has a parameter it reads called inputCsv and a parameter it writes called out. You can make the purpose of the parameters clearer by calling them inputCsv and ouputJson:

```
public void convert(File inputCsv, File outputJson) {
```

Now you can guess that the purpose of the function is to convert book data from CSV format to JSON format. You can use this knowledge to make the names of the variables reader and writer more precise by renaming them to csvReader and jsonWriter:

```
BufferedReader csvReader = null;
BufferedWriter jsonWriter;
```

You should also avoid vague variable names like tmp, data, and parts:

```
String tmp, data = "[";
String[] parts;
```

These names are so generic that you could use them to store any type of data. They give no hint as to what the variables are used for or why they exist, so they are little better than the single letter names from before. The code becomes a little clearer if you rename them to line, json, and fields, respectively:

```
String line, json = "[";
String[] fields;
```

Choose your words wisely. There are always better options than vague terms like temp, num, and data. And you should prefer words over numerals. Instead of subtotal1 and subtotal2, use names that make it clear what the values represent, such as subtotalWithShipping and subtotalWithShippingAndTax. Develop a good vocabulary, and don't be afraid to use a thesaurus.

BE THOROUGH

Names should thoroughly capture the what, why, and how. The names in the BookParser class are better than before, but they are still missing some details.

For example, the method name `convert` doesn't tell you what is being converted. A more thorough name would be `convertCsvToJson`:

```
public void convertCsvToJson(File inputCsv, File outputJson) {
```

If being thorough leads to names that are comically long, it's usually a sign that the thing you're naming has too many responsibilities (see "Single Responsibility Principle (SRP)" on page 266). For example, if the `BookParser` code not only converted the CSV file to JSON, but also deleted the CSV file and generated a report, you'd have to change the name to something like `convertCsvToJsonAnd-DeleteCsvFileAndGenerateReport`. The fact that this name is so long is a sign that the code is doing too much. The solution isn't to use abbreviations or acronyms, but to break the responsibilities up into three separate functions, each with their own name, such as `convertCsvToJson`, `cleanupCsvFile`, and `generateReport`.

You should also be thorough in capturing how a variable, function, or class should be used. For example, it's not obvious what data should be stored in the `line` and `fields` variables. What kinds of lines are these? Lines of code? Lines of music? Fishing lines? Everything becomes clearer if you name the variables `csvLine` and `csvFields`, respectively:

```
String csvLine, json = "[";
String[] csvFields;
```

Names that are more thorough not only make it easier to read the code, but also help prevent bugs. For example, consider the following code:

```
double totalWeight = packagingWeight +
                    (itemWeight * numberOfItems);
```

See anything wrong? What if you have the same code, but with different variable names:

```
double totalWeightInLbs = packagingWeightInLbs +
                    (itemWeightInKgs * numberOfItems);
```

Now it's obvious that there is a bug, as you shouldn't be mixing kilograms (`itemWeightInKg`) and pounds (`packagingWeightInLbs`) in the same calculation. By being thorough, you can encode information in variable names that makes wrong code look wrong.[1] Including units in a variable name is one example (e.g., lengthInMeters is better than just length), but anything that encodes how a variable should be used is helpful (e.g., csvLine is better than just line).

Note that the information you encode in the variable name should not be redundant with anything you encode in the type system (if you're using a statically typed language). For example, the following name would be redundant:

```java
String csvLineString; // Redundant variable name
```

You don't need the word "String" in the variable name because it is already specified as part of the type, so the compiler will automatically enforce it for you. On the other hand, indicating the InLbs in totalWeightInLbs and the InKgs in itemWeightInKgs is not redundant because both variables are doubles and the type system can't tell they represent different units of measurement.

REVEAL INTENT

Good names should reveal intent. Whereas a computer only cares about *what* the code does, a human being cares about *why* the code is doing it. For example, the BookParser code is littered with numbers that give no hints as to why they are there:

```java
if (!csvFields[3].equals("fiction") &&
    !csvFields[3].equals("nonfiction")) {
  continue;
}

json += "{";
json += "title:\"" + csvFields[0] + "\",";
json += "author:\"" + csvFields[1] + "\",";
json += "pages:\"" + Integer.parseInt(csvFields[2]) + "\",";
json += "category:\"" + csvFields[3] + "\"";
json += "},";
```

What's special about the third index of csvFields? Why compare csvFields[3] to "fiction" and "nonfiction"? And what's in csvFields[0], csvFields[1], etc.? It's a good idea to replace these *magic numbers* with named constants. One way to define constants in Java is to use an enum:

---

[1] As described by Joel Spolsky in a blog post of the same name [Spolsky 2005b], this was the original intention of Hungarian notation.

```
public enum CsvColumns {
  TITLE, AUTHOR, PAGES, CATEGORY
}
```

In an enum, each constant has a name as well as an ordinal based on the order in which it was defined. For example, CsvColumns.TITLE.ordinal() is 0 and CsvColumns.PAGES.ordinal() is 2. Here is how you can replace the magic numbers in BookParser with the CsvColumns enum:

```
String title = csvFields[TITLE.ordinal()];
String author = csvFields[AUTHOR.ordinal()];
Integer pages = Integer.parseInt(csvFields[PAGES.ordinal()]);
String category = csvFields[CATEGORY.ordinal()];

if (!category.equals("fiction") && !category.equals("nonfiction")) {
  continue;
}

json += "{";
json += "title:\"" + title + "\",";
json += "author:\"" + author + "\",";
json += "pages:\"" + pages + "\",";
json += "category:\"" + category + "\"";
json += "},";
```

Introducing better names makes it more clear that each line of the CSV file should contain four columns (title, author, pages, and category) and that the category column must have the value "fiction" or "nonfiction." This suggests that you could introduce another enum for the category column:

```
public enum Category {
  fiction, nonfiction
}
```

You can use the valueOf function to automatically convert a String to the corresponding enum value (or throw an exception if no matching value is found) so that you no longer have to explicitly compare category to "fiction" and "nonfiction":

```
Category category = Category.valueOf(csvFields[CATEGORY.ordinal()]);
```

FOLLOW CONVENTIONS

More important than following any particular naming rule is to follow the rules consistently throughout the project. Do you call the variable recordNum in one place and numRecords in another place? Do you call the interface PaymentProces-sor or IPaymentProcessor and the implementation CreditCardPaymentProcessor or CreditCardPaymentProcessorImpl? Are you using the shared vocabulary of design patterns, such as factory, builder, decorator, and visitor for object-oriented programming and monad, iteratee, reader, and lens for functional program-ming?

In most cases, you should follow the conventions of your programming lan-guage. For example, to read Ruby code, you should know that the convention is to use snake case for method and variable names (e.g., my_method_name and my_variable_name), upper camel case for class names (e.g., MyClassName), screaming snake case for constants (e.g., MY_CONSTANT_NAME), end method names with a question mark if they return a boolean (e.g., is_empty?), and end method names with an exclamation mark if they cause mutation, have side effects, or are destructive (e.g., fire_missles!). You should establish the coding conventions for your team (including rules for naming), write them down, and enforce them throughout the codebase.

> If I look at a single file and it's written by 10 different engineers, it should be almost indistinguishable which part was written by which person. To me, that is clean code. The way you do that is through code reviews[2] and publishing your style guide, your patterns, and your language idioms. Once you learn them, everybody is way more productive because you all know how to write code the same way. At that point, it's more about *what* you're writing and not *how* you write it.
>
> **—[DELLAMAGGIORE 2014], NICK DELLAMAGGIORE,**
> **SOFTWARE ENGINEER AT LINKEDIN AND COURSERA**

NAMING IS HARD

> *There are only two hard things in computer science: cache invalidation and naming things.[3]*
>
> **—PHIL KARLTON**

---

2 See "Code reviews" on page 329.

3 Alternatively: "There are only two hard things in computer science: cache invalidation, naming things, and off-by-one errors."

Good names heavily depend on the context. You often have to become an expert in the product domain, your tech stack, and your team's culture and conventions before you can come up with good names. When writing a new function, I sometimes have to start with a meaningless name like foo, implement the body, test it a few times, and only then do I understand enough about what it does to give it a reasonable name. Sometimes even that name won't be right, and days later, once I have a deeper understanding of the problem space, I can come back and change the name to something even better. Naming is so important that we'll come back to it again several times in this chapter. But first, let's talk about error handling.

Error handling

The BookParser code silently swallows errors, such as an empty catch block when trying to read inputCsv:

```
try {
  csvReader = new BufferedReader(new FileReader(inputCsv));
} catch (FileNotFoundException e) {}
```

It also silently swallows exceptions if there was a failure to write the JSON to disk:

```
try {
  jsonWriter = new BufferedWriter(new FileWriter(outputJson));
  jsonWriter.write(json);
  jsonWriter.close();
} catch (IOException e) {}
```

If you run this code and no JSON file is created, the lack of proper error handling makes debugging hard. You won't know if the code failed to read the CSV file, if there were no valid records in the CSV, if the path to the JSON file was invalid, or if the hard disk was out of space. Every program has different error handling requirements, but silently swallowing errors is never one of them.

Clear error messages are a hallmark of clean code. You can throw exceptions, make error messages a part of the return value, or log errors. Just don't fail silently. Because the BookParser deals with business data, and you usually want to keep data as pristine as possible, it's a good idea to loudly fail the entire conversion process if you hit any sort of error. You can do this by removing all of the useless try/catch blocks and allowing exceptions to propagate upward to the caller:

```java
public void convertCsvToJson(File inputCsv,
                             File outputJson) throws IOException {
  try (
    BufferedReader csvReader =
      new BufferedReader(new FileReader(inputCsv));
    BufferedWriter jsonWriter =
      new BufferedWriter(new FileWriter(outputJson))
  ) {
    String csvLine, json = "[";
    String[] csvFields;

    while ((csvLine = csvReader.readLine()) != null) {
      csvFields = csvLine.split(",");

      String title = csvFields[TITLE.ordinal()];
      String author = csvFields[AUTHOR.ordinal()];
      Integer pages =
        Integer.parseInt(csvFields[PAGES.ordinal()]);
      Category category =
        Category.valueOf(csvFields[CATEGORY.ordinal()]);

      json += "{";
      json += "title:\"" + title + "\",";
      json += "author:\"" + author + "\",";
      json += "pages:\"" + pages + "\",";
      json += "category:\"" + category + "\"";
      json += "},";
    }

    json += "]";

    jsonWriter.write(json);
  }
}
```

The only try block left is the try-with-resource statement, which ensures that the files you opened for reading and writing (csvReader and jsonWriter) will be closed correctly, even if an exception is thrown. This makes convertCsvToJson easier to debug, as all errors will be clearly reported, and easier to read, as you no longer have try/catch blocks all over the place.

Don't Repeat Yourself (DRY)

Every piece of knowledge must have a single, unambiguous, authoritative representation within a system.

—[HUNT AND THOMAS 1999, 27], ANDREW HUNT AND DAVID THOMAS,
THE PRAGMATIC PROGRAMMER

Avoiding duplication is one of the most fundamental principles of clean code. Ironically, the idea of avoiding duplication comes up again and again under many different names: don't repeat yourself (DRY), single point of truth, once and only once. Duplication can arise in any part of your technology, including the architecture, code, tests, process, requirements, and documentation, and it can arise for any number of reasons:

- You need to represent the same information in multiple ways, such as listing the same columns in your database schema, database access layer, HTML markup, and CSS.

- Language limitations, such as specifying getters and setters in Java.

- Lack of denormalization, such as derived data in a database table.

- Lack of time, leading to copying and pasting of code.

- Lack of awareness, such as multiple developers creating their own String-Util classes in a large codebase because they didn't know a similar one already existed (and because they didn't know there was an even better version available as an open source library).

Duplication is not only a waste of time because you reimplement the same thing more than once, but also a hindrance to understanding and maintaining code. If your code is not DRY, every time you need to answer a question about it, you might have to look in more than one place; every time you have to change it, you have to make sure not to miss any of the duplicates; and if one of the duplicates goes out of sync, you'll end up with contradictions and bugs.

If you find yourself writing the same code over and over again or if making a small change requires touching half your codebase, you need to find a way to make your code more DRY. In particular, if you have to repeat the same *process* over and over again, then you need to build automation. If you have the same *logic* in more than one place, then you need to build abstractions that allow you to share a single implementation [Henney 2010, 60-61].

For example, consider how the BookParser code constructs JSON:

```
String csvLine, json = "[";
while ((csvLine = csvReader.readLine()) != null) {

    // ...

    json += "{";
    json += "title:\"" + title + "\",";
    json += "author:\"" + author + "\",";
    json += "pages:\"" + pages + "\",";
    json += "category:\"" + category + "\"";
    json += "},";

}

json += "]";
```

There is a lot of duplication here: there are multiple copies of the code to wrap JSON elements in brackets ([] or {}) and there are multiple copies of the code to create a key-value entry in a JSON object. All this duplication has led to several bugs. Have you spotted them? One is a classic copy/paste error. The pages variable, which is an Integer, should not be wrapped in quotes when inserted into JSON:

```
json += "pages:\"" + pages + "\",";
```

The second bug is that the last element in the JSON array will have an extra trailing comma:

```
json += "},";
```

You could fix these bugs, but that would leave the biggest duplication of all: JSON and CSV are common data formats and there is no reason you should have to write code from scratch to deal with them. *Reinventing the wheel* is one of the most common and unnecessary forms of duplication. Whenever possible, you should use open source libraries instead (see "Build in-house, buy commercial, or use open source?" on page 193). For example, you can make the code more DRY and robust by writing the JSON using Java's Jackson library (*http://jack son.codehaus.org/*). Because Java is a class-based, object-oriented language, the canonical way to represent data is to create a class:

```
public class Book {
  private String title;
  private String author;
  private int pages;
  private Category category;

  // (Constructor and getters omitted)
}
```

Instead of manually building a JSON String, you build up a List of Book objects:

```
List<Book> books = new ArrayList<>();

while ((csvLine = csvReader.readLine()) != null) {
  csvFields = csvLine.split(",");

  String title = csvFields[TITLE.ordinal()];
  String author = csvFields[AUTHOR.ordinal()];
  Integer pages =
    Integer.parseInt(csvFields[PAGES.ordinal()]);
  Category category =
    Category.valueOf(csvFields[CATEGORY.ordinal()]);

  books.add(new Book(title, author, pages, category));
}
```

The Jackson library can convert most Java classes into an equivalent JSON representation, using the field names in the class as keys in the JSON. Using the Jackson ObjectMapper class, it takes just two lines of code to convert the List of Book objects into a JSON file:

```
ObjectMapper mapper = new ObjectMapper();
mapper.writeValue(outputJson, books);
```

Similarly, you can use the Apache Commons CSV library (http://commons.apache.org/proper/commons-csv/) to simplify the CSV parsing. The CSVParser class can read a CSV file using the parse method and assign labels to each column using the withHeader method:

```
List<CSVRecord> records = CSVFormat
  .DEFAULT
  .withHeader(TITLE.name(), AUTHOR.name(),
              PAGES.name(), CATEGORY.name())
  .parse(new FileReader(inputCsv))
  .getRecords();
```

Now, instead of manually splitting each line on a comma and fussing with column indices, you can loop over the records you got from the CSVParser and read each column in by name:

```
for (CSVRecord record : records) {
  String title = record.get(TITLE);
  String author = record.get(AUTHOR);
  Integer pages = Integer.parseInt(record.get(PAGES));
  Category category = Category.valueOf(record.get(CATEGORY));

  books.add(new Book(title, author, pages, category));
}
```

Instead of handcrafted, buggy code, you are now leveraging popular, battle-tested open source libraries. The code is shorter, looks more like idiomatic Java, and has fewer bugs and less duplication. Here's the whole convertCsvToJson function:

```
public void convertCsvToJson(File inputCsv,
                             File outputJson) throws IOException {
  List<Book> books = new ArrayList<>();
  List<CSVRecord> records = CSVFormat
    .DEFAULT
    .withHeader(TITLE.name(), AUTHOR.name(),
                PAGES.name(), CATEGORY.name())
    .parse(new FileReader(inputCsv))
    .getRecords();

  for (CSVRecord record : records) {
    String title = record.get(TITLE);
    String author = record.get(AUTHOR);
    Integer pages = Integer.parseInt(record.get(PAGES));
    Category category = Category.valueOf(record.get(CATEGORY));

    books.add(new Book(title, author, pages, category));
  }

  ObjectMapper mapper = new ObjectMapper();
  mapper.writeValue(outputJson, books);
}
```

Single Responsibility Principle (SRP)

The *single responsibility principle* (SRP) states that every class, function, and variable should have only one purpose. Or, to look at it from a different perspective, every class, function, and variable should have one, and only one, reason to change [Martin 2005]. For example, the convertCsvToJson function violates the single responsibility principle. If you needed to read the CSV data in a different way (e.g., from the network instead of from disk), parse the CSV format in a different way (e.g., a new column was added), or write the JSON output in a different way (e.g., write it to the console instead of to disk)—all of these would be reasons to change convertCsvToJson. That's too many responsibilities for a single function, and every time you go to change any of one of them, you risk breaking all the others.

One way to improve this is to move each responsibility into a separate function. First, you take the code for converting a single row of CSV format into a Java object and put it into a separate function called parseBookFromCsvRecord:

```java
public Book parseBookFromCsvRecord(CSVRecord record) {
    String title = record.get(TITLE);
    String author = record.get(AUTHOR);
    Integer pages = Integer.parseInt(record.get(PAGES));
    Category category = Category.valueOf(record.get(CATEGORY));

    return new Book(title, author, pages, category);
}
```

Next, you can create a function called parseBooksFromCsvFile that will read a CSV file and use parseBookFromCsvRecord to convert it into a List of Book objects:

```java
public List<Book> parseBooksFromCsvFile(File inputCsv)
  throws IOException {

List<CSVRecord> records = CSVFormat
  .DEFAULT
  .withHeader(TITLE.name(), AUTHOR.name(),
              PAGES.name(), CATEGORY.name())
  .parse(new FileReader(inputCsv))
  .getRecords();

List<Book> books = new ArrayList<>();

for (CSVRecord record : records) {
  books.add(parseBookFromCsvRecord(record));
}

return books;
}
```

Finally, move the code that converts the `List` of `Book` objects to JSON into a separate function called `writeBooksAsJson`:

```java
public void writeBooksAsJson(List<Book> books,
                            File outputJson) throws IOException {
  ObjectMapper mapper = new ObjectMapper();
  mapper.writeValue(outputJson, books);
}
```

Each of these three helper functions has a single responsibility, and if one of the responsibilities changes, you can change just the function associated with it without much risk of affecting the other responsibilities in the code. And if you put the helpers together, you can reduce `convertCsvToJson` to just two lines of code:

```java
public void convertCsvToJson(File inputCsv,
                            File outputJson) throws IOException {
  List<Book> books = parseBooksFromCsvFile(inputCsv);
  writeBooksAsJson(books, outputJson);
}
```

Functional programming

Following the single responsibility principle has led to a design where you have several short, simple, standalone functions. Each one is easy to read, maintain, and test. And you can combine several of these functions to create a new function with more complicated behavior. This is the basis of functional programming: you use functions and function composition as the building blocks of your application. The key is to design the functions in a way that makes composition safe and easy.

Functional programming is a big topic and Java is not the ideal language for it, so this section is just a brief introduction to some of the basic ideas behind functional programming and an explanation of how these ideas lead to cleaner code (see "Recommended reading" on page 529 for a deeper look). The concepts I'll introduce are immutable data, higher-order functions, and pure functions.

IMMUTABLE DATA

Consider the following code:

```java
public class Groceries {
  public List<String> shoppingList = new ArrayList<>();

  public void fillShoppingList() {
```

```
shoppingList.add("milk");
shoppingList.add("eggs");
shoppingList.add("bread");

if (!isOnDiet()) {
  addCandy(shoppingList);
}

if (isXmas()) {
  addXmasFoods(shoppingList);
}
  }
}
```

If you call the fillShoppingList function, what will be the value stored in the shoppingList field? Initially, the shoppingList field is empty. Then it has the values ["milk", "eggs", "bread"]. After that, it's less clear. The addCandy and addXmasFoods methods get a reference to shoppingList, so you'd have to read the code in those functions to see what they do with it. Actually, because shoppingList is a field of the Groceries class, any method in the class could modify it, so you'd also have read all the code in isOnDiet and isXmas. And because shoppingList is a public field, it could be modified by anyone who has access to the Groceries class. That means you can't be sure of the value in shoppingList unless you crawl through the entire codebase. If during the search, you find that the Groceries class is used in a multithreaded environment, then there is no way to know what's in shoppingList because its value depends on the non-deterministic order of thread execution.

In other words, even in this tiny code snippet, it's hard to reason about shoppingList because it is a *mutable variable*. Mutable variables are pointers to a location in memory where different values may be stored at different times. Thinking about time is hard. You have to keep the state of shoppingList in your head as you read through all the code and try to juggle all possible timelines to figure out its value. As the scope of a mutable variable increases, and as you introduce concurrency, the number of possible timelines increases exponentially, and it becomes impossible to follow the code.

A better approach is to use *immutable variables*. An immutable variable is just an identifier for a fixed value that can never change.[4] In most functional pro-

---

4 For a more nuanced look at value, state, identity, and time, see Rich Hickey's talk "Are We There Yet?" [Hickey 2009].

gramming languages, such as Haskell, immutable variables are the default. Once you've associated a variable name with a value, it can never be changed. For example, if you set a variable called x to the value 5 and later try to change it to the value 6, you get a compile error:

```
x = 5
x = 6 -- compile error!
```

In non-functional programming languages, mutability is the default, but there is usually a way to mark a variable as immutable. For example, in Java, you can declare a variable as final so that once you give it a value, it can never be changed:

```
final int x = 5;
x = 6; // compile error!
```

If you have an object instead of a primitive, it's best practice to make all the fields in the object immutable:

```java
public class Person {
  private final String name;
  private final int age;

  public Person(String name, int age) {
    this.name = name;
    this.age = age;
  }

  public String getName() {
    return name;
  }

  public int getAge() {
    return age;
  }

  public Person withName(String newName) {
    return new Person(newName, age);
  }

  public Person withAge(int newAge) {
    return new Person(name, newAge);
  }
}
```

Notice how all the fields in the `Person` class are declared as `final`. Also, while there are the usual getter methods, instead of setter methods, there are `withX` methods that return new instances of the `Person` class. You've probably worked with immutable classes like this many times before. For example, in Java, the `String` class is immutable. The only thing you can do with immutable variables is perform computations on them that generate new values:

```
newValue = someComputation(oldValue);
```

In the `String` class, all the methods that imply a modification to the `String` actually return a new `String`:

```
String str1 = "Hello, World!";
String str2 = str1.replaceAll("l", "");

// str1 is still "Hello, World!"
// str2 is "Heo, Word!"
```

Most languages also have immutable implementations of common data structures. For example, for Java, the Google Guava library (*https://github.com/google/guava*) provides immutable versions of `Set`, `Map`, and `List`:

```
List<String> shoppingList =
    ImmutableList.of("milk", "eggs", "bread");
```

While there are some problems that can only be solved with mutation, the vast majority of code can, and should, be written with immutable variables. The general strategy is to start with an initial value and instead of changing it in place, you transform it one step at a time into a series of new *intermediary values* until you get to some desired result:

```
originalValue = getOriginalValue();

intermediateValue1 = computation1(originalValue);
intermediateValue2 = computation2(intermediateValue1);
intermediateValue3 = computation3(intermediateValue2);

desiredResult = finalComputation(intermediateValue1,
                                 intermediateValue2,
                                 intermediateValue3);
```

Notice how in the preceding pattern, you never modify any old values, but always generate new intermediary values from each computation. You could use this strategy to make it easier to reason about the `Groceries` class:

```
public List<String> buildShoppingList() {
  List<String> basics =
    ImmutableList.of("milk", "eggs", "bread");
  List<String> candy =
    !isOnDiet() ? getCandy() : emptyList();
  List<String> xmas =
    isXmas() ? getXmasFoods() : emptyList();

  return new ImmutableList.Builder<String>()
    .addAll(basics)
    .addAll(candy)
    .addAll(xmas)
    .build();
}
```

The idea is store the result of each food "computation" in a local intermediary `List` that you never change. At the end, you concatenate all the `List`s into a new `List` and return it from the function. Because each intermediary `List` has a name, the logic is easier to read. And because everything is immutable, the logic is now entirely local to the `buildShoppingList` function. No other function, class, or thread can have any impact on the result. With immutable data, there are no timelines to juggle.

HIGHER-ORDER FUNCTIONS

It's easy to make all the variables immutable in the `buildShoppingList()` method because you know the number of "computations" you want to perform ahead of time, so you can assign each one to a named, intermediary, immutable variable and concatenate them all together at the end. But what do you do if you have a dynamic number of computations to perform? For example, in the `parseBooksFromCsv` method of the `BookParser` code, the number of records depends on the contents of the CSV file:

```
public List<Book> parseBooksFromCsvFile(File inputCsv)
  throws IOException {

List<CSVRecord> records = CSVFormat
  .DEFAULT
  .withHeader(TITLE.name(), AUTHOR.name(),
              PAGES.name(), CATEGORY.name())
  .parse(new FileReader(inputCsv))
```

```
    .getRecords();

List<Book> books = new ArrayList<>();

for (CSVRecord record : records) {
  books.add(parseBookFromCsvRecord(record));
}

return books;
}
```

The number of "computations" (i.e., calls to `parseBookFromCsvRecord`) you have to do is not known ahead of time, so how can you build up the `List` of `Book` objects without mutation?[5] One solution is to use *higher-order functions*, which are functions that take other functions as parameters.

In version 8, Java added support for higher-order functions, such as `map`, `filter`, and `reduce`, as part of the `Stream` API. To see it in action, let's compare how you would multiply all the even numbers in a `List` of `Integers`. Here is an imperative solution:

```
List<Integer> numbers = Lists.newArrayList(1, 2, 3, 4, 5);
int product = 1;

for (int i = 0; i < numbers.size(); i++) {
  int number = numbers.get(i);
  if (number % 2 == 0) {
    product = product * number;
  }
}

// product now has the value 8
```

The imperative solution forces you to focus on low-level, error-prone details like iteration, list indices, and maintaining a mutable variable to calculate the product. Here is a functional solution for the same problem:

```
List<Integer> numbers = ImmutableList.of(1, 2, 3, 4, 5);
final int product = numbers
  .stream()
```

---

5 In this particular case, the fact that `books` is a mutable variable is not a cause for concern. It's a local variable that isn't passed to any other functions, and the code is short. Depending on the coding conventions in your project, it might be reasonable to leave it this way. However, code like this tends to get longer and more complicated, so if you're refactoring the code anyway or you're writing something similar from scratch, it's a good idea to get into the habit of using immutable variables when you can.

```
.filter(number -> number % 2 == 0)
.reduce((a, b) -> a * b)
.orElse(1);

// product now has the value 8
```

The functional solution lets you focus on the high-level details, such as how to identify even numbers and how to multiply two numbers together, all without having to maintain any mutable variables yourself. You can use higher-order functions to remove mutation from the parseBooksFromCsv function:

```
public List<Book> parseBooksFromCsvFile(File inputCsv)
  throws IOException {

List<CSVRecord> records = CSVFormat
  .DEFAULT
  .withHeader(TITLE.name(), AUTHOR.name(),
              PAGES.name(), CATEGORY.name())
  .parse(new FileReader(inputCsv))
  .getRecords();

return records
  .stream()
  .map(this::parseBookFromCsvRecord)
  .collect(Collectors.toList());
}
```

PURE FUNCTIONS

Using immutable data and higher-order functions makes the code easier to understand and maintain. But to get the most advantage out of functional programming, you need to use *pure functions*. A function is pure if:

- The function is idempotent: given the same input parameters, the function always returns the exact same result.
- The function does not have *side effects*: that is, it does not depend on or modify the state of the outside world in any way. Examples of side effects include changing a global variable, writing to the hard disk, reading user input from the console, or receiving data over the network.

The only thing a pure function can do is transform its input parameters and return a new value. This not only makes it easy to reason about pure functions but also makes them easy to compose. As long as the return value of one pure function is a valid parameter for another pure function, it's always safe to compose them:

```
result = pureFunction3(pureFunction2(pureFunction1(val)));
```

Functions with side effects are harder to compose. For example, the convertCsvToJson function in BookParser reads from and writes to the filesystem, so it is not pure:

```
public void convertCsvToJson(File inputCsv,
                             File outputJson) throws IOException {
```

Notice how the signature has no return value (it's a void function), which is a classic sign that a function has a side effect.[6] Without a return value, composing this function with another function is difficult. The functions would have to communicate via the filesystem or shared mutable variables, both of which are more complicated and error prone than using parameters and return values.

Even if the function has a return value, but still has side effects, it will be harder to reason about and compose. For example, to reason about the behavior of convertCsvToJson, it's not enough to look at the code inside of it or its signature. You also have to know the state of the outside world. For example, does the input CSV file exist? Do you have permission to read it? What if someone starts overwriting the file while you're reading it? Does the JSON file already exist? Do you have permissions to write to it? What if someone starts writing to it at the same time that you do? Is there enough disk space on the hard drive to write the JSON file?

Mutable data forces you to juggle multiple timelines in your head. Side-effecting functions force you to juggle multiple timelines and multiple possible global states in your head. Composing several side-effecting functions can cause all of these timelines and states to interact with one another, which leads to an exponential increase in complexity.

I think the lack of reusability comes in object-oriented languages, not functional languages. Because the problem with object-oriented languages is they've got all this implicit environment that they carry around

---

6 In fact, if there is no return value, the only thing a function can do is perform a side effect.

with them. You wanted a banana, but what you got was a gorilla holding the banana and the entire jungle.

If you have referentially transparent code, if you have pure functions— all the data comes in its input arguments and everything goes out and leaves no state behind—it's incredibly reusable.

—[SEIBEL 2009, 213], JOE ARMSTRONG, CREATOR OF ERLANG

You'll find it easier to reason about and reuse your code if you write most if it as pure functions. Of course, if you want the code to do anything useful, your code has to interact with the real world at some point, so you can't completely get rid of side effects. The best you can do is to control and manage them.

In a programming language like Haskell, only the runtime is allowed to perform side effects. If you try to execute a side effect directly in your own code, you will get a compile error. For example, consider the following pseudocode:

```
def main():
  someSideEffect()
```

If this were Haskell code, it would not compile because you're trying to execute a side effect directly. To make it work, you need to wrap the side effect in a type called IO, which won't execute the side effect until you return it from the main method and the Haskell runtime executes it for you:[7]

```
def main():
  return IO(someSideEffect)
```

Since Haskell is a statically typed language, the IO type is part of the function signature, which means side effects are first-class citizens of the language and you can pass them around, compose them, and have the compiler check them:

```
main:: IO ()
```

In most other languages, such as Java, side effects are largely invisible. Any function, no matter what is in its signature, can make network calls, change global variables, and launch missiles. Other than switching to a pure functional language, there is no easy fix for this. The best you can do is to try to isolate code

---

7   IO is actually a *monad*, which is a general-purpose structure for wrapping and unwrapping arbitrary computations (not just side effects) in a way that makes composition, chaining, and decoration easy.

with side effects to as few places as possible and to do your best to make sure the method signature and documentation accurately reflect any side effects. In some cases, you can emulate the Haskell approach by pushing the side effects toward the entry point of your application, such as the `main` method in a command-line application or an HTTP request handler in a web server.

For example, there is no need for the `BookParser` class to read and write files. The purpose of the class is to parse CSV data and convert it to JSON data, but the fact that this data starts or ends on a hard disk is irrelevant. You can change the code to take the CSV data as a `String`, return JSON data as a `String`, and avoid touching the filesystem entirely:

```java
public class BookParser {

    public String convertCsvToJson(String csv) throws IOException {
        List<Book> books = parseBooksFromCsvString(csv);
        return writeBooksAsJsonString(books);
    }

    public List<Book> parseBooksFromCsvString(String csv)
        throws IOException {

        List<CSVRecord> records = CSVFormat
            .DEFAULT
            .withHeader(TITLE.name(), AUTHOR.name(),
                        PAGES.name(), CATEGORY.name())
            .parse(new StringReader(csv))
            .getRecords();

        return records
            .stream()
            .map(this::parseBookFromCsvRecord)
            .collect(Collectors.toList());
    }

    public Book parseBookFromCsvRecord(CSVRecord record) {
        String title = record.get(TITLE);
        String author = record.get(AUTHOR);
        int pages = Integer.parseInt(record.get(PAGES));
        Category category = Category.valueOf(record.get(CATEGORY));

        return new Book(title, author, pages, category);
    }

    public String writeBooksAsJsonString(List<Book> books)
        throws JsonProcessingException {

        ObjectMapper mapper = new ObjectMapper();
```

```
    return mapper.writeValueAsString(books);
  }
}
```

Now, every function in `BookParser` is pure: each one reads in some input parameters, transforms them, and returns a value, without any side effects along the way. This makes the functions easy to read, maintain, and reuse. It also allows `BookParser` clients to control how they feed in CSV data and what they do with the JSON output, so you can use this code in a wider variety of contexts. For example, here is how you can use `BookParser` from the command line:

```java
public class Main {
  public static void main(String[] args) throws IOException {
    String inputCsv = args[0];
    String outputJson = args[1];

    String csv = IOUtils.toString(new FileInputStream(inputCsv));
    String json = new BookParser().convertCsvToJson(csv);

    IOUtils.write(json, new FileOutputStream(outputJson));
  }
}
```

All the side effects that used to be in `BookParser`—that is, reading from and writing to disk—are now isolated to the `main` method, which, as the entry point to the app, is a natural place to put your I/O. The fact that all of `BookParser` functions are now pure also makes it easy to write unit tests for them. For example, here's a simple JUnit test for the `convertCsvToJson` function (see "Automated Tests" on page 296 for more information):

```java
@Test
public void testConvertCsvToJson() throws Exception {
  String csv = "Code Complete,Steve McConnell,960,nonfiction";

  String expected = "[{\"title\":\"Code Complete\"," +
                      "\"author\":\"Steve McConnell\"," +
                      "\"pages\":960," +
                      "\"category\":\"nonfiction\"}]";

  String actual = new BookParser().convertCsvToJson(csv);
  Assert.assertEquals(expected, actual);
}
```

This unit test is easier to write when you don't have to worry about side effects: no mucking around with CSV or JSON files on the hard drive, no chance of tests overwriting each other's files when running in parallel, and no need to clean up any files when you're done.

Loose coupling

Consider the NewsFeed class:

```java
public class NewsFeed {
  List<Article> getLatestArticlesSharedByUser(User user) {
    long userId = user.data().getProfile().getDatabaseKeys().id;
    List<Article> articles = GlobalCache.get(userId);

    if (articles == null) {
      Date oneMonthAgo = new DateTime().minusDays(30).toDate();

      String query =
        "select * from articles where userId = ? AND date > ?";
      articles = parseArticles(DB.query(query, userId, oneMonthAgo));

      GlobalCache.put(userId, articles);
    }

    return articles;
  }
}
```

The getLatestArticlesSharedByUser method in the NewsFeed class tries to fetch the articles shared by a given user in the last 30 days, looking first in a cache and falling back to a database call in the case of a cache miss. There are many problems with this code. A good way to see them is to try to write a unit test (see "Test-driven development (TDD)" on page 306 to learn more about how tests lead to better design):

```java
@Test
public void testGetLatestArticlesSharedByUserFromDB() {
  // Start with an empty cache so everything is a cache miss
  GlobalCache.reinit();
  // Start with an empty DB
  DB.reinit();

  // Create two recent articles
  Article article1 = new Article("Recent Article 1");
  Article article2 = new Article("Recent Article 2");

  // Create User object
  long userId = 5;
  User user = createMockUser(userId);
```

```
// Insert the articles into the database
String insertStatement =
  "insert into Articles(userId, title, date) values ?, ?, ?";
DB.insert(insertStatement, userId,
          article1.getTitle(), new Date());
DB.insert(insertStatement, userId,
          article2.getTitle(), new Date());

// Make sure the newsfeed returns the two articles
List<Article> actualNews =
  new NewsFeed().getLatestArticlesSharedByUser(user);
List<Article> expectedNews =
  Arrays.asList(article1, article2);

assertEquals(expectedNews, actualNews);
}
```

Consider how many of the internal implementation details and assumptions of the NewsFeed code are copied into the TestNewsFeed class just to get a test to pass:

- The test code has to know to call GlobalCache.reinit() so the cache lookup in getLatestArticlesSharedByUser doesn't blow up on an uninitialized cache. If some day the NewsFeed class uses a different caching strategy, the test code would break.

- The test code implicitly knows to call DB.reinit() to make sure the database is up and running, the schema is installed, and the tables are all initially empty (i.e., have no records from other tests). The test also has explicit knowledge of the database schema so it can insert mock articles using DB.executeInsert(). If some day the NewsFeed class changes how it stores data, such as a different database schema or using a key-value store instead of a database, the test code would break.

- The TestNewsFeed class has to know that getLatestArticlesSharedByUser extracts the user ID from the User object, so it can carefully craft a User object and list of articles that have the same user ID. If some day the User object changed or the NewsFeed class used a different cache key (e.g., the hashCode of the User class), the test code would break.

- The test duplicates the knowledge that getLatestArticlesSharedByUser defines "latest" as articles from the last 30 days. It uses this knowledge to ensure the dates on the articles it inserts into the database will be picked up by the query code inside of `getLatestArticlesSharedByUser`. If some day the `NewsFeed` changed the definition of "latest" (e.g., articles form the last five days), the test code would break.

- The `NewsFeed` class is using `GlobalCache` to store a mapping of user ID to latest articles and just assumes no one else uses this cache. However, the cache is global, so some day a developer working in a completely different part of the codebase could come along and store a different type of data in the cache, which would cause the `NewsFeed` code to break.

Every time you need to change the `NewsFeed` class, even if you're only changing an internal implementation detail that has no external impact, you will probably have to update the test code as well. Worse yet, all clients of the `NewsFeed` class will have to make many of the same assumptions as the test code, so you'll have to update them, too. In software, the degree to which two modules depend on each other is known as *coupling*. If you frequently have to update one module whenever you update another, the modules are *tightly coupled*, which usually means the code is brittle and hard to maintain.

Clean code should follow the *dependency inversion principle* [Martin 1996]:

- High-level modules should not depend upon low-level modules. Both should depend upon abstractions.

- Abstractions should not depend upon details. Details should depend upon abstractions.

The `NewsFeed` class is an example of four common violations of the dependency inversion principle that lead to tight coupling:

- Internal implementation dependencies: the `User` class.

- System dependencies: time.

- Library dependencies: the `DB` class.

- Global variables: the `GlobalCache` class.

INTERNAL IMPLEMENTATION DEPENDENCIES

Consider how the `NewsFeed` class extracts the user ID from the `User` class:

```
long userId = user.data().getProfile().getDatabaseKeys().id;
```

A long chain of method calls and field lookups is usually a sign of tight coupling.[8] In this case, because the `NewsFeed` class is reaching deep into the internals of the `User` class, any time the `User` class changes, (e.g., you change the name of the `id` field or start storing users in a key-value store instead of a database), you'll have to update `NewsFeed` as well.

This is a violation of the dependency inversion principle because the `NewsFeed` class depends on low-level implementation details of the `User` class instead of a high-level abstraction for how to get the user ID. It's also a case where introducing more names leads to cleaner code, such as exposing a `getId()` method in the `User` class:

```
public long getId() {
  return data().getProfile().getDatabaseKeys().id;
}
```

Relying on the higher-level abstraction of `getId()` reduces coupling. Under the hood, you can implement the `getId()` method in the `User` class however you want, and change the implementation any time, without having to change the `NewsFeed` class or any other client.

SYSTEM DEPENDENCIES

Consider this line in `getLatestArticlesSharedByUser`:

```
Date oneMonthAgo = new DateTime().minusDays(30).toDate();
```

The call to `new DateTime()` looks up the current date and time, so `getLatestArticlesSharedByUser` is not idempotent: it will behave differently every single time you run it. The dependency on the system clock makes testing and reasoning about the code harder.

---

8 This does not apply to code that is designed for chaining method calls together, as these usually return the same data type each time rather than navigating into the internals of a class. For example, it's fine to chain method calls when doing functional transformations on collections (e.g., `list.filter(i → i > 5).map(i → i + 2).sum()`) and builder classes (e.g., `CacheBuilder.newBuilder().maximum-Size(1000).expireAfterWrite(10, TimeUnit.MINUTES).build()`).

A better design is to *inject* dependencies. That is, you invert the dependency relationship by having the client pass in the dependency instead of hardcoding it inside of getLatestArticlesSharedByUser. Whenever possible, the best way to inject dependencies is to pass them in as function parameters, as it's easier to reason about a function if all of its dependencies are visible in the function signature. For example, you could add a date parameter called since and rename the function to getLatestArticlesSharedByUserSince to reflect that it will return all articles shared by the given user since a specified date:

```
List<Article> getLatestArticlesSharedByUserSince(User user,
                                                 Date since) {
  List<Article> articles = GlobalCache.get(user.getId());

  if (articles == null) {
    String query =
      "select * from articles where userId = ? AND date > ?";

    articles = parseArticles(DB.query(query,
                                      user.getId(),
                                      since));
    GlobalCache.put(user.getId(), articles);
  }

  return articles;
}
```

The function no longer has a dependency on the system clock, so its behavior is idempotent, making it easier to understand and test. It's also more flexible. In the future, if you have a use case that wants articles from the last 60 days instead of the last 30 days, you can just pass in a difference since parameter instead of having to write a new function.

LIBRARY DEPENDENCIES

The NewsFeed class uses a library called DB to access the database:

```
String query =
  "select * from articles where userId = ? AND date > ?";
articles = parseArticles(DB.query(query, userId, oneMonthAgo));
```

The NewsFeed code shouldn't care, or know, that articles are stored in a database. All it cares about is that it has some way of fetching articles that match specific criteria—what happens under the hood is somebody else's problem. In other words, this code violates the dependency inversion principle: the NewsFeed class depends on the low-level details of database access instead of a high-level abstraction for retrieving articles. To define an abstraction in Java, you can use an *interface*:

```
public interface ArticleStore {
  List<Article> getArticlesForUserSince(long userId, Date since);
}
```

How do you inject an `ArticleStore` instance into the `NewsFeed` class? You could pass it in as a parameter to the `getLatestArticlesSharedByUserSince` function, but this would lead to a verbose and confusing API. Depending on the programming language, there are many other ways to inject dependencies. In Java and other object-oriented languages, an easy way to inject dependencies is to pass them in as constructor parameters. Java also has libraries and frameworks dedicated to dependency injection, often called inversion of control (IoC) containers, such as Spring and Guice. In Scala, you could inject dependencies via the cake pattern, and in Haskell, you might use function currying or the reader monad pattern. Whatever technique you pick for dependency injection, the goal is to make the dependency a visible and explicit part of the API.

Let's use constructor injection for the `NewsFeed` example, which makes it obvious to any user of the class that it depends on a way to fetch article data:

```
public class NewsFeed {
  private final ArticleStore articleStore;

  public NewsFeed(ArticleStore articleStore) {
    this.articleStore = articleStore;
  }

  List<Article> getLatestArticlesSharedByUserSince(User user,
                                                   Date since) {
    List<Article> articles = GlobalCache.get(user.getId());

    if (articles == null) {
      articles =
        articleStore.getArticlesForUserSince(user.getId(), since);
      GlobalCache.put(user.getId(), articles);
    }

    return articles;
  }
}
```

This decouples the implementation details of how to fetch article data from the implementation details of the NewsFeed itself. Now you can pass in a DatabaseArticleStore that implements the ArticleStore interface by issuing queries to a relational database, or a DocumentArticleStore that issues queries to a document database, or even an InMemoryArticleStore that stores the articles in an in-memory HashMap, which might be useful for testing. The power of abstraction is that you can make any changes you want to the implementation of the ArticleStore without having to modify the NewsFeed code.

A tricky question is, which libraries should you expose as dependencies? For example, the BookParser code used the Jackson library for converting Java objects to JSON and the Apache Commons CSV library for parsing CSV files. Should you inject those libraries as dependencies, too? As a rule of thumb, you should prefer an injected abstraction over a concrete implementation for libraries that:

- Have side effects.
- Behave differently in different environments.

For example, in the BookParser code, you do not need to inject the Jackson or Apache Commons CSV libraries because (a) you're only working with in-memory Strings so there are no side effects and (b) the libraries behave identically in all environments. On the other hand, in the NewsFeed code, you should make the ArticleStore an injected dependency because (a) it may communicate with a remote database via network I/O, and (b) you may use different databases in different environments, or even a mock database at test time.

GLOBAL VARIABLES

The most problematic dependency in the NewsFeed class is the use of the GlobalCache class:

```
List<Article> articles = GlobalCache.get(userId);

// ...

GlobalCache.put(userId, articles);
```

As its name implies, GlobalCache is a *global variable*: that is, mutable state that can be accessed from anywhere in the codebase. What happens if a user of NewsFeed forgets to initialize GlobalCache before calling getLatestArticlesSharedByUserSince? What if more than one user initializes GlobalCache? What if the NewsFeed is being used across more than one thread? What if some unrelated code starts using GlobalCache to store a different list of articles for the user? Or doesn't use userId as the key?

Global variables are dangerous. By definition, they are accessible everywhere, so when you use them, you are increasing coupling throughout your entire codebase. Global variables appear in different forms in different languages, such as the static keyword in Java, the window scope in JavaScript, variable names that start with $ in Ruby, the global keyword in PHP and Python, or a mutable singleton in any language. Avoid global variables whenever you can—there is almost always a better solution.

If you're working with legacy code and are stuck with global variables, then you can reduce the damage by following the dependency inversion principle. The NewsFeed class does not need to know the low-level details of how to cache something. All it needs is a high-level abstraction for caching. Let's define an interface for a passthrough cache:

```
public interface PassthroughCache<K, V> {
  V getOrElseUpdate(K key, Supplier<V> valueIfMissing);
}
```

This interface has just one method, which returns the value for a given key, or if no value is associated with the key, stores the value generated by the valueIfMissing function and returns that. Under the hood, if you really wanted to, you could implement this with a global variable (e.g., GlobalCache), but a better idea is to use an instance of an in-memory cache or a distributed cache (e.g., memcached). Using an abstraction means the NewsFeed code does not need to know or care. Loose coupling let's you choose any implementation you want and safely change your mind later.

Let's inject the cache abstraction into the NewsFeed constructor:

```
public class NewsFeed {
  private final ArticleStore articleStore;
  private final PassthroughCache<Long, List<Article>> cache;

  public NewsFeed(ArticleStore articleStore,
                  PassthroughCache<Long, List<Article>> cache) {
    this.articleStore = articleStore;
    this.cache = cache;
  }
}
```

```
List<Article> getLatestArticlesSharedByUserSince(User user,
                                                 Date since) {
    return cache.getOrElseUpdate(
        user.getId(),
        () -> articleStore.getArticlesForUserSince(user.getId(),
                                                   since));
    }
}
```

You've now inverted all the dependencies in the NewsFeed code, reducing coupling, and making the code easier to maintain and test. Here is an updated version of the unit test from earlier:

```
@Test
public void testGetLatestArticlesSharedByUserSince() {
    List<Article> expected = Arrays.asList(
        new Article("Article 1"), new Article("Article 2"));
    NewsFeed newsFeed =
        new NewsFeed(new MockArticleStore(expected),
                     new AlwaysEmptyCache());

    User user = createMockUser(5);
    Date since = new Date();
    List<Article> actual =
        newsFeed.getLatestArticlesSharedByUserSince(user, since);

    assertEquals(expected, actual);
}
```

This test code is easier to read, it's less likely to break due to internal changes to the NewsFeed class, and you can safely run many such tests in parallel.

High cohesion

Consider the following sentence from Noam Chomsky's thesis: "Colorless green ideas sleep furiously" [Chomsky 2002, 15]. Chomsky presented it as an example of a sentence that is grammatically correct but completely nonsensical. The words are unrelated and the result is an incoherent sentence.

Now, consider the following class:

```
public class Util {
    void generateReport() { /* ... */ }
    void connectToDb(String user, String pass) { /* ... */ }
    void fireTheMissles() { /* ... */ }
}
```

This is an example of a class that is technically correct but completely nonsensical. The methods are unrelated and the result is a class with *low cohesion*.

Cohesion comes from the same root word that "adhesion" comes from. It's a word about sticking. When something adheres to something else (when it's adhesive, in other words) it's a one-sided, external thing: something (like glue) is sticking one thing to another. Things that are cohesive, on the other hand, naturally stick to each other because they are of like kind, or because they fit so well together. Duct tape adheres to things because it's sticky, not because it necessarily has anything in common with them. But two lumps of clay will cohere when you put them together, and matched, well-machined parts sometimes seem to cohere because the fit is so precise.

—[VANDERBURG 2011], GLENN VANDERBURG,
DIRECTOR OF ENGINEERING AT LIVINGSOCIAL

The word "util" in the name of a class is a classic sign of low cohesion. Classes with the word util in the name are typically a hodgepodge of unrelated functions that didn't seem to fit anywhere else. But low cohesion isn't always as obvious as the Util class above. Let's look at a more real-world example:

```
public interface HttpClient {
  byte[] sendRequest(String url,
                     Map<String, String> headers,
                     byte[] body);
  Document getXml(String url);
  int postOnSeparateThread(String url,
                           String body,
                           ExecutorService executor);
  void setHeader(String headerName, String headerValue);
  boolean statusCode();
}
```

The methods in this fake HttpClient interface are more closely related than those of the Util class, as all of them are involved with sending HTTP requests. However, these methods also have low cohesion because they operate at many different levels of abstraction:

- sendRequest uses byte arrays for the request and response bodies; postOnSeparateThread uses a String for the request body and doesn't return a response body (it only returns a status code); and getXml doesn't have a request body and returns an XML Document for the response body.

- postOnSeparateThread deals with low-level threading details (via the ExecutorService), but none of the other methods do.

- The setHeader and statusCode methods imply HttpClient is mutable and can store state for the next request or from the previous response. It's not clear how this interacts with other methods, especially sendRequest, which takes a Map of HTTP headers as one of its parameters.

Clean code should have *high cohesion*: all the variables and methods should be related, everything should operate at the same level of abstraction, and the pieces should fit neatly together. For example, here is a more coherent version of the HttpClient interface:

```
public interface HttpClient {
  HttpResponse sendRequest(HttpRequest request);
}

public interface HttpRequest {
  URL getUrl();
  Map<String, String> getHeaders();
  byte[] getBody();
}

public interface HttpResponse {
  Map<String, String> getHeaders();
  byte[] getBody();
}
```

This new HttpClient API has just a single method for sending requests. All the other logic will be handled in other classes. For example, the details about HTTP headers, URLs, and bodies are handled in HttpRequest and HttpResponse. If you wanted to deal with requests at a higher level than manually setting HTTP headers and working with byte arrays for the request body, you could create an HttpRequestBuilder class:

```
public class HttpRequestBuilder {
  public HttpRequest postJson(String url,
                              String json) throws Exception {
    return new BasicHttpRequest(
      url,
      ImmutableMap.of("Method", "POST",
```

```
                        "Content-Type", "application/json"),
        json.getBytes("UTF-8"));
    }
}
```

If you wanted a higher level way to deal with response bodies that didn't involve byte arrays, you could create an `HttpResponseParser` class:

```
public class HttpResponseParser {
  public Document asXml(HttpResponse response) {
    return DocumentBuilder.parse(
      new ByteArrayInputStream(response.getBody())));
  }
}
```

Anything to do with the threading could be handled by the `HttpClient` implementation:

```
public class ThreadedHttpClient implements HttpClient {
  private final ExecutorService executor;

  public ThreadedHttpClient(ExecutorService executor) {
    this.executor = executor;
  }

  public HttpResponse sendRequest(HttpRequest request) {
    try {
      return executor.submit(() -> doSend(request)).get();
    } catch (Exception e) {
      throw new HttpClientException(e);
    }
  }
}
```

Instead of one large `HttpClient` class that handles many unrelated tasks, you now have several smaller classes that each handle a few highly related tasks. The move from a monolith to a number of focused, highly cohesive classes is a standard pattern in clean code.

Comments

Don't comment bad code—rewrite it.

—[KERNIGHAN AND PLAUGER 1978, 144], BRIAN W. KERNIGHAN AND P. J. PLAUGER,
THE ELEMENTS OF PROGRAMMING STYLE

I've intentionally put off comments until the very end. The code itself should tell you almost everything you need to know. If the code doesn't do that, your priority should be to improve the code before you bother with any sort of comments.

Now that the `BookParser` code is reasonably clean, you can add a comment to explain anything that cannot be captured in the code, such as why the code exists in the first place, any assumptions you're making about inputs or outputs, and examples. Because this is Java, you can format the comment using JavaDoc:

```java
/**
 * Convert book data in CSV format to JSON format. The CSV should
 * be using the RFC4180 format and contain 4 columns on each row:
 * author, title, pages, category. Pages must be an integer.
 * Category must be one of "fiction" or "nonfiction".
 *
 * For example, for the following CSV:
 *
 * George R.R. Martin, Game of Thrones, 864, fiction
 * Tor Norretranders, The User Illusion, 480, nonfiction
 *
 * You will get back the following JSON:
 *
 * [
 *   {
 *     "author": "George R.R. Martin",
 *     "title": "Game of Thrones",
 *     "pages": 864,
 *     "category": "fiction"
 *   },
 *   {
 *     "author": "Tor Norretranders",
 *     "title": "The User Illusion",
 *     "pages": 480,
 *     "category": "nonfiction"
 *   }
 * ]
 *
 * @param csv A String that contains book data in CSV format.
 * @return A String containing the JSON representation of the book data.
 * @throws IOException If the CSV has an invalid format.
 */
public String convertCsvToJson(String csv) throws IOException {
```

Comments are a part of documentation, which we discuss in detail in "Documentation" on page 334.

Refactoring

In this chapter, we've been incrementally improving the `BookParser` code, making one small change at a time to its internal implementation details. This is known as *refactoring*. Refactoring is the process of changing the structure of code without changing its external behavior. It is a coding task that affects only the "nonfunctional" aspects of the software: from the outside, the code does the same thing, but internally, you have improved its design [Fowler et al. 1999, xvi].

The reason refactoring is necessary is because you won't get the design right the first time. Just like the first draft of an essay, the first draft of your code will be messy, incomplete, and in need of a rewrite. The `BookParser` example was intentionally ugly, but the first version of any implementation will always have problems. As you write the code, you begin to understand the problem better. The essence of refactoring is going back to your code and improving it based on this new understanding.

> A programming language is for thinking of programs, not for expressing programs you've already thought of.

—[GRAHAM 2004A, 22], PAUL GRAHAM, CO-FOUNDER OF Y COMBINATOR

Writing code, or prose, is an iterative process. It can take many drafts to write a good essay and it can take many drafts to write good code. This means that refactoring is not a separate task—it's not something you do during a "cleanup phase" of a project (which never comes). Refactoring is the very core of writing software, and it should be something you are doing constantly.

> I'm a real believer in pure refactoring, followed by pure expansion. You clean up your code until adding the next increment of functionality will be easy, but without any change in behavior. Then you add that next increment of functionality. Then you repeat the whole process.

—[THOMPSON 2014], DEAN THOMPSON, CTO OF NOWAIT

In *On Writing Well*, William Zinsser wrote that "rewriting is the essence of writing well" [Zinsser 2006, 83]. I would like to propose that refactoring is the essence of programming well.[9]

Recap

Once you've internalized the principles in this chapter, you'll find that writing clean code takes roughly the same amount of time as writing ugly code, reading clean code takes an order of magnitude less time than reading ugly code, and updating clean code takes two orders of magnitude less time than updating ugly code. And because the ratio of reading and updating code to writing new code is roughly 50:1, it's a no brainer: write clean code, always.

That said, ugly code finds its way into every project. As the products, people, and ecosystem around your code changes, the decisions you made in the past might not scale to handle the needs of the future. So you not only need to write clean code in the first place, but you will have to constantly refactor your code to adapt it to new requirements. Refactoring is another example of how everything at a startup, including the code, is more about evolution than up-front design.

If you don't keep things clean—if you don't evolve your code—you end up with technical debt. And just like real debt, the longer you wait to pay it back, the more interest it will accrue. The productivity costs of technical debt are well known, but there is also a human cost.

Quality isn't purely an economic factor. People need to do work they are proud of.

—[BECK AND ANDRES 2004, 33], KENT BECK AND CYNTHIA ANDRES,
EXTREME PROGRAMMING EXPLAINED

Technical debt is depressing. Think of the original `BookParser` code at the start of the chapter: your brain refused to look at it. Imagine if working with code like that on a daily basis was your job. A big enough salary might persuade you to do it, but no amount of money will make you happy about it. Remember, startups are about people, and the real cost of technical debt is not the problems it causes with more bugs or missed deadlines but the pain it causes for people.

---

9 See "Refactoring: Improving the Design of Existing Code" [Fowler et al. 1999] for a nice guide to refactoring.

In many ways, programming is a craft. You get a deep sense of fulfillment from selecting the right tools, working hard, and building something beautiful. Not just beautiful on the outside for how it looks to a user, but also beautiful on the inside for the way it works. An elegant solution makes programmers happy. An ugly cludge makes programmers sad. And sad programmers are less productive, less effective, and eventually leave companies.

Worst of all, technical debt begets technical debt. Once you allow a small amount of ugly code into your system and do nothing to fix it, a whole lot more is likely to follow, until the whole structure begins to crumble. This is typically known as the parable of the broken window:

> In inner cities, some buildings are beautiful and clean, while others are rotting hulks. Why? Researchers in the field of crime and urban decay discovered a fascinating trigger mechanism, one that very quickly turns a clean, intact, inhabited building into a smashed and abandoned derelict.
>
> A broken window.
>
> One broken window, left unrepaired for any substantial length of time, instills in the inhabitants of the building a sense of abandonment—a sense that the powers that be don't care about the building. So another window gets broken. People start littering. Graffiti appears. Serious architectural damage begins. In a relatively short space of time, the building becomes damaged beyond the owner's desire to fix it, and the sense of abandonment becomes reality.
>
> —[HUNT AND THOMAS 1999, 4-5], ANDREW HUNT AND DAVID THOMAS,
> *THE PRAGMATIC PROGRAMMER*

The broken window theory applies to code as much as it applies to buildings. If your codebase is full of ugly hacks and messy code, each new developer is more likely to contribute to the mess than to clean it up. As the quantity of ugly code grows, it gets harder and harder to clean it up, so the problems will only accelerate. Fix broken windows as quickly as possible. Write clean code, always. Then rewrite it to be even cleaner.

Scalability

Scaling a startup

In this chapter, I'll discuss the two types of scalability you need to think about at a startup. The first type is scaling your coding practices to handle more developers, more code, and more complexity. The second type is scaling the performance of your code to handle more users, more traffic, and more data.

Scaling a startup is a bit like shifting gears in a car with a manual transmission. Scaling too early is like shifting into a high gear while the car is moving at a low speed: the gears will grind and you may stall out completely. Scaling too late is like flooring the gas pedal while staying in low gear: you put a lot of stress on the engine, push it into the red, and if you keep it up too long, you'll overheat without ever hitting top speed. You have to scale and you have to shift gears at the right time to keep things moving smoothly.

The most important thing to understand is that scalability isn't a boolean property. You can't say a practice or a system is or isn't scalable. The most you can say is that, under certain conditions, it's scalable along certain dimensions, up to a certain point. The scalability practices that work for a 10-person company will not work for a 1,000-person company, and the database that scales to 100 queries per second and gigabytes of data won't scale to 10,000 queries per second and petabytes of data. To go faster, you need to shift to completely different gears.

Most of this chapter will focus on scaling coding practices because they become important early in the life of a company and affect every startup. They are like the low gears of a car: you have to shift through them before you can worry about the higher gears, such as scaling for performance, which typically only affects companies later in their lives when they have achieved significant traction.

Scaling coding practices

Programming can be scary. One of the underappreciated costs of technical debt is the psychological impact it has on developers. There are thousands of programmers out there who are scared of doing their jobs. Perhaps you're one of them.

You get a bug report at three in the morning and after digging around, you isolate it to a tangled mess of `if` statements, `for` loops, global variables, short variable names, and confusing patterns. There is no documentation. There are no tests. The developer who originally wrote the code no longer works at the company. You don't understand what the code is doing. You don't know all the places it gets used. You are afraid.

You still have scars from the time you tried to fix one bug only to reveal three more; the "trivial" change that took two months; the tiny performance tweak that brought the whole system down and pissed off all of your coworkers. You start to massively bloat the time estimates for projects and find yourself frequently saying "It's too expensive" or "It's impossible." You have a feeling of dread every time you have to make a code change.

In a startup, everything is constantly changing. If you've gotten to the point where you're afraid to change your code, it means you need to scale your coding practices to adapt to growth. The four most important coding practices to deal with a growing codebase and developer team are:

- Automated tests
- Split up the code
- Code reviews
- Documentation

AUTOMATED TESTS

Automated tests give you the confidence to make changes. While the rest of your world is full of fear and uncertainty, automated tests are always there for you as a stable and calming presence. They are the reliable friend who is there at three in the morning when you need them. They are the guardians of your code. They are, with my deepest apologies to George R.R. Martin, the Night's Watch of the programming world:

Night gathers, and now my watch begins. It shall not end until my dele-
tion. I shall permit no null-pointer exceptions, allow no off-by-1 errors,
accept no infinite loops. I shall deploy to no production server and win no
glory. I shall live and die by my assertions. I am the mock object in the
darkness. I am the watcher on the CI server. I am the shield that guards
the realms of programmers. I pledge my life and honor to the automated
test suite, for this night and all the nights to come.

Automated tests give you the benefit of an iterative code-test cycle that gives
you confidence every time you make a change that things are still working. You
don't have to keep the state of the whole program in your head. You don't have to
worry about breaking other people's code. You don't have to repeat the same boring, error-prone manual testing over and over again. You just run a single test
command and get rapid feedback on whether things are working.

A primer on automated testing

If you're new to automated testing, here's a quick primer to get you started.
Imagine you needed to write a function that reverses the words in a sentence:

```
reverseWordsInSentence("startups are great");
// Returns: "sputrats era taerg"
```

Here's a first try at an implementation in Java:

```java
public class TextReverse {
  public static String reverseWordsInSentence(String sentence) {
    StringBuilder out = new StringBuilder();
    String[] words = sentence.split(" ");

    for (int i = 0; i < words.length; i++) {
      String word = words[i];
      StringBuilder reversed = new StringBuilder(word).reverse();
      out.append(reversed);
      out.append(" ");
    }

    return out.toString();
  }
}
```

How do you know if this code works? Well, you could stare at it for a while
and just decide that it works. Or maybe you decide to do some manual testing by
clicking around in a UI and visually checking the results. With the TextReverse

example, there is no UI, so you could add a main method to this code that prints out the results to the console:

```
public static void main(String[] args) {
  System.out.println(reverseWordsInSentence("startups are great"));
}
```

If you run this code, you'll see the output:

```
sputrats era taerg
```

From a quick visual inspection, things seem to be working. You're done, right? Not quite. Instead of a visual inspection and instead of a main method, what if you wrote code to check your code? To do this, you can use a test framework. There are test frameworks for every programming language, such as JUnit for Java. With most testing frameworks, you put your test code into a separate class so it isn't mixed up with the production code. Here is an example JUnit test class for TextReverse:

```
public class TestTextReverse {
  @Test
  public void testReverseThreeNormalWords() {
    String expected = "sputrats era taerg";
    String actual = reverseWordsInSentence("startups are great");
    assertEquals(expected, actual);
  }
}
```

With JUnit, you mark methods that contain tests with the @Test annotation and you use assert functions to fail the test if certain conditions aren't met. Here's what you'll see in your console if you run this test:

```
JUnit version 4.11
Time: 0.068

There was 1 failure:
1) testReverseThreeNormalWords
   (com.hello.startup.reverse.TestTextReverse)

org.junit.ComparisonFailure:

expected:<[sputrats era taerg]> but was:<[sputrats era taerg ]>

at org.junit.Assert.assertEquals(Assert.java:115)
at org.junit.Assert.assertEquals(Assert.java:144)
at com.hello.startup.reverse.TestTextReverse.
```

```
testReverseThreeNormalWords
(TestTextReverse.java:14)

FAILURES!!!
Tests run: 1,  Failures: 1
```

Oops, it looks like the test failed. Looking at the stack trace, you can see that it was the assertEquals call that failed, and looking at the error output, you can see the cause: it was expecting "sputrats era taerg", but instead got "sputrats era taerg " (note the trailing space). The problem is that manually looping over a List and concatenating Strings is error prone. You saw this exact problem in Chapter 6 with the BookParser example and the solution was to use higher-order functions to handle looping (via map) and concatenation (via collect):

```
public static String reverseWordsInSentence(String sentence) {
  return Arrays
    .stream(sentence.split(" "))
    .map(word -> new StringBuilder(word).reverse())
    .collect(Collectors.joining(" "));
}
```

If you rerun the tests against this new version of the code, you'll see the following:

```
JUnit version 4.11
..
Time: 0.061

OK (1 tests)
```

Excellent. The test passed. Problem solved. But wait, what about the case where there is more than one space between words? You can add another test case to find out:

```
@Test
public void testReverseWordsWithTabsAndLeadingWhitespace() {
  String expected = "sputrats era taerg";
  String actual = reverseWordsInSentence("   startups are\tgreat");
  assertEquals(expected, actual);
}
```

When you rerun the tests, you'll see:

```
JUnit version 4.11
Time: 0.068
```

```
There was 1 failure:
1) testReverseWordsWithTabsAndLeadingWhitespace
   (com.hello.startup.reverse.TestTextReverse)

org.junit.ComparisonFailure:

expected:<[sputrats era taerg]> but was:<[    sputrats taerg era]>

at org.junit.Assert.assertEquals(Assert.java:115)
at org.junit.Assert.assertEquals(Assert.java:144)
at com.hello.startup.reverse.TestTextReverse.
    testReverseWordsWithTabsAndLeadingWhitespace
    (TestTextReverse.java:23)

FAILURES!!!
Tests run: 2,  Failures: 1
```

Uh-oh, another bug. This time, the code isn't handling whitespace correctly, such as tabs and leading and trailing spaces. Here's a fixed version:

```
public static String reverseWordsInSentence(String sentence) {
  return Arrays
    .stream(sentence.trim().split("\\s+"))
    .map(word -> new StringBuilder(word).reverse())
    .collect(Collectors.joining(" "));
}
```

Now, rerun the tests one more time and you'll see that both of them pass:

```
JUnit version 4.11
..
Time: 0.063

OK (2 tests)
```

On a tiny, simple function like reverseWordsInSentence, manually inspecting the code and its output missed several bugs. As the codebase grows, manual testing becomes even less effective. Even at a small startup, most products have too many use cases and corner cases to thoroughly test by hand. In addition to the two tests just shown, you'd want to add tests that check TextReverse across all normal use cases and corner cases: empty string, single word, short strings, long strings, a string with nothing but whitespace, and strings with newlines and carriage returns. It would take too long to check all these cases by hand, but when you have automated tests, it takes just a fraction of a second to run them (the preceding tests took 0.063 seconds).

Automated tests are fast enough that it makes sense to rerun them after every single change. You should also run your tests after every check-in as part of the build process (see "Build" on page 353). This ensures that your code continues to work months and years after you wrote it, no matter who is working on it or what other changes have happened. Using tests during development and running them at build time allows you to make changes quickly while remaining confident that you're not breaking anything. The key word here is *confidence*: just because the tests pass doesn't guarantee your code has no bugs. No form of testing can guarantee your code is bug-free, so it's really a game of probability. You can increase the probability that your code is bug-free by learning to write high-quality tests.

One of the ways to determine the quality of your tests is to calculate what percentage of the production code gets executed while the automated tests are running. This measure is called *code coverage* and there are tools for most programming languages that will automatically calculate your code coverage percentage, and even show you which parts of the code are and aren't covered. For example, you can use JaCoCo for Java, as shown in Figure 7-1.

Figure 7-1. JaCoCo code coverage

Lines in green were executed by automated tests; lines in yellow were if statements where only some of the branches were executed; and lines in red were not executed at all. If your tests only execute 20% of your code, then you can't have too much confidence that there aren't bugs in the other 80%. On the other hand, if you execute 80% of the code paths in your code and can't find bugs, there is a much higher probability that your code is bug-free.

Types of automated tests

There are many different types of automated tests, including unit tests, integration tests, smoke tests, acceptance tests, and performance tests. Most real-world applications need a mixture of all the different test types because each one serves a different purpose and can catch different types of bugs. Let's look more closely at the different types:

Unit tests

Unit tests verify the functionality of a single, small unit of code. The definition of *unit* varies, but it's usually a single function, or at most, a class. For example, the tests for the `TextReverse` code are all unit tests for a single function called `reverseWordsInSentence`.

Unit tests are an integral part of the coding cycle: make a change, run the tests, make a change, run the tests. Each time the tests pass, you get feedback that you haven't broken anything. This feedback loop needs to be fast, taking no more than a few seconds to run the whole unit test suite. Therefore, unit tests are typically not allowed to have any side effects. That is, no reading or writing to disk, no network calls, no database calls, no access to global state. Setting up and communicating with such dependencies takes too long. If the unit you're testing has such a dependency, you should replace it with a test double, as I'll discuss in "Test doubles" on page 304.

Unit tests should be your first line of defense, used many times during development to build out each incremental piece of code. They are fast and reliable because they have no external dependencies. They give you confidence that the small building blocks of your application are working correctly before you put them together.

Integration tests

Just because a unit works correctly in isolation does not guarantee that multiple units will work correctly when you put them together. This is where integration tests come in. There is a wide spectrum of integration tests, from those that test the interaction of just a couple classes or modules all the way up to testing how entire subsystems work together, such as verifying that your backend server can correctly work with a real database. Unlike unit tests, integration tests are allowed to have side effects and depend on the outside world. You should still use test doubles to replace any dependency not directly relevant to the test, but if you're testing how two subsystems interact, you'll need to deploy both and have them talk to each other.

The downside to deploying real dependencies is that integration tests take longer to run, so you won't use them as often in the development environment. The upside is that even if they only run in your build after a check-in, they will still catch many errors that slip by unit tests, such as incompatible APIs between subsystems.

Acceptance tests

Unit tests and integration tests primarily verify the behavior of the code from the perspective of the developer, answering the question, "Is the code working correctly?" Acceptance tests verify the behavior of the product from the perspective of the customer, answering the question, "Does the code solve the right problem?" There is no bigger waste than a startup that writes perfectly correct code that passes all the unit and integration tests, but doesn't actually do what the customer wants [Freeman and Pryce 2009, 7].

A typical acceptance test describes what a user does and how your product reacts to it. For example, you might use Selenium (*http://www.sele niumhq.org/*) to automate clicks in a web browser to check that when a user clicks the "like" button, the number of likes increases by 1. Whereas an integration test might verify the interaction of a few isolated subsystems, an acceptance test is an *end-to-end test* that verifies that all the pieces of your tech stack come together correctly to form a working product.

The downside of an end-to-end test is that you need to have all of your subsystems deployed, so the tests can be complicated to write and slow to execute. The benefit of an end-to-end test is that by running in a production-like environment, a small number of tests can execute a massive amount of production code and flush out issues that other tests cannot, such as bugs in deployment, configuration, service communication, and the UI.

Performance tests

Most unit, integration, and acceptance tests verify the correctness of a system under ideal conditions: one user, low system load, and no failures. The real world is quite a bit messier. Your app might have to deal with thousands of concurrent users; your servers will be constrained in terms of CPU, memory, and bandwidth; and your system will have to deal with a variety of error conditions, such as slow or unresponsive services, servers going down, hard drives failing, and network problems.

The goal of performance testing is to verify the stability and responsiveness of a system in the face of heavy load and failures. Performance tests span the gamut from unit tests to end-to-end tests. For example, you could stress test a single sort function to figure out which algorithm yields the best performance; you could performance test a search service to measure its latency when it's handling 1,000 queries per second; or you could run an end-to-end performance test where you bombard a frontend server with requests and see where it *red lines*—that is, at what point does the server start dropping requests, and is it because the server itself is out of resources or is it a problem further downstream, such as a database? We discuss performance more in depth in "Scaling performance" on page 341.

Test doubles

When writing automated tests, especially unit tests and integration tests, you typically want to test each unit or component in isolation so that if you hit an error, you can be confident the cause is within that unit or component and not in one of its dependencies. To make that possible, you can swap in a *test double* instead of the real dependency at test time, a bit like a stunt double might take the place of an actor in an action scene. Test doubles implement the interface of a dependency in a way that is convenient and fast enough for testing. There are several kinds of test doubles, including fakes, stubs, and mocks, although many people just use the term *mock* in all cases.[1] For example, consider the NewsFeed class:

```
public class NewsFeed {
  private final ArticleStore articleStore;

  public NewsFeed(ArticleStore articleStore) {
    this.articleStore = articleStore;
```

---

1 See *xUnit Test Patterns: Refactoring Test Code* [Meszaros 2007] for the formal definitions.

```
  }

  public List<Article> getLatestArticlesForUser(long userId) {
    List<Article> rawArticles = articleStore.get(userId);
    return sortAndFilter(rawArticles);
  }
}
```

The function **getLatestArticlesForUser** retrieves articles from a distributed key-value store, as defined by the **ArticleStore** interface:

```
public interface ArticleStore {
  List<Article> get(long userId);
  void put(long userId, List<Article> articles);
}
```

If you wanted to unit test the **getLatestArticlesForUser** function, firing up a real distributed key-value store would take too long, so instead you could create a test double of the **ArticleStore** interface that uses an in-memory **ConcurrentHashMap** under the hood:

```
public class InMemoryArticleStore implements ArticleStore {
  private final Map<Long, List<Article>> store =
    new ConcurrentHashMap<>();

  public List<Article> get(long userId) {
    return store.get(userId);
  }

  public void put(long userId, List<Article> articles) {
    store.put(userId, articles);
  }
}
```

You can use this test double to write a unit test for **getLatestArticlesForUser**:

```
public class TestNewsFeed {
  @Test
  public void testGetLatestArticles() {
    long userId = 5;

    ArticleStore articleStore = new InMemoryArticleStore();
    articleStore.put(userId, createFakeArticles());

    NewsFeed newsFeed = new NewsFeed(articleStore);
```

```
List<Article> actualArticles =
  newsFeed.getLatestArticlesForUser(userId);

// .. check actualArticles contains fake articles
  }
}
```

The InMemoryArticleStore is not only fast enough for unit testing, but it also allows you to control its behavior (e.g., return specific values at test time) so you can verify that getLatestArticlesForUser handles all cases correctly. Note that it's easier to use test doubles if the code you're testing exposes all of its dependencies and relies on high-level abstractions. See the discussion of the dependency inversion principle in "Loose coupling" on page 279 for more information.

Test-driven development (TDD)

The mere act of trying to write tests for your code will force you to take a step back and ask some important questions: How do I structure the code so I can test it? What dependencies do I have? What are the common use cases? What are the corner cases?

If you find that your code is hard to test, it's almost always a sign that it needs to be refactored for other reasons, too. For example, if the code uses lots of mutable state and side effects, it will not only be hard to test but also hard to reuse and reason about the code (see "Functional programming" on page 268). If the code is difficult to test because it has many complex interactions with its dependencies, then it's likely that the code is too tightly coupled and will be difficult to change (see "Loose coupling" on page 279). If the code is hard to test because there are too many use cases to cover, then that's a sign that the code is doing too much and needs to be broken up (see "Single Responsibility Principle (SRP)" on page 266).

In other words, tests not only help you write correct code but they provide feedback that leads to a better design. You get the most benefit from this feedback if you write the test code *before* you write the implementation code. This is known as *test-driven development* (TDD). The TDD cycle is:

1. Add tests for the new functionality.

2. Run all the tests. The new tests should fail, but all other tests should pass.

3. Implement the new functionality.

4. Rerun the tests. Everything should now pass.

5. Refactor the code until you have a clean design.

Let's review an example of using TDD. Imagine you need to write a function that reads in a file, counts how many times each word appears in the file (while skipping *stop words* like "to," "the," and "and"), and prints out the words in sorted order from most to least occurrences. For example, if you have a file called *four-words.txt* with the following contents:

```
Hello! Hello startup people! Hello startup world!
```

Then the function should print the following results:

```
hello (3)
startup (2)
people (1)
world (1)
```

Here's a first guess at the signature for the function:

```
public class WordCount {
  public void printWordCounts(File file) {
  }
}
```

Because you're trying to do TDD, before you fill in the implementation, try to come up with some test cases:

```
public class TestWordCount {
  @Test
  public void testPrintWordsCountOnFourWords() {
    WordCount wordCount = new WordCount();
    wordCount.printWordCounts(new File("four-words.txt"));
    // Uh-oh... How do you check the results?
  }
}
```

As soon as you try to write the test case, a problem becomes obvious: if the function only prints the results to stdout, there is no return value. This not only makes it hard to test the function, but is also a sign of a bad design, as there is no way to reuse this function for any other task. For example, if you wanted to show the word counts on a web page or save the word counts to a file, you'd have to rewrite printWordCounts. Fortunately, by using TDD, you catch this issue early, so the only thing you need to rewrite is the function signature:

```java
public class WordCount {
  public Map<String, Integer> calculateWordCounts(File file) {
    return null;
  }
}
```

The function is now called `calculateWordCounts` and instead of printing to stdout, it returns a `Map` of word to count. You still leave the implementation blank and try again to write the tests:

```java
@Test
public void testCalculateWordsCountOnFourWords() {
  WordCount wordCount = new WordCount();

  Map<String, Integer> actual =
    wordCount.calculateWordCounts(new File("four-words.txt"));

  Map<String, Integer> expected =
    ImmutableMap.of("hello", 3,
                    "startup", 2,
                    "people", 1,
                    "world", 1);

  assertEquals(expected, actual);
}
```

All right, you have the first unit test. Run it to make sure that it fails:

```
There was 1 failure:

1) testPrintWordsCountOnFourWords
   (com.hello.startup.wordcount.TestWordCount)

java.lang.AssertionError:
Expected :{hello=3, startup=2, people=1, world=1}
Actual   :null
```

Whether you are writing tests before the implementation or after, you should always check that a test fails right after writing it. This ensures that the test is checking the behavior you're interested in and not failing (or passing!) for the wrong reasons. Moreover, this gives you a chance to check that the test shows a clear error message when it fails [Freeman and Pryce 2009, 42].

You should write a few more test cases to make sure that you fully understand the problem. One good test case is to check that `calculateWordCounts` ignores stop words like "to," "the," and "and." Here's a new test file called *four-words-plus-stop-words.txt*:

Hello! Hello to the startup people! And hello to the startup world!

This file is identical to *four-words.txt*, except it adds the stop words "to," "the," and "and." But wait, how do you know that the WordCount class will treat "to," "the," and "and" as stop words? The initial API for the class does not expose the stop words, which implies they are hidden within as an implementation detail. This will make testing harder, as a change to this implementation detail could break your test cases. Moreover, this design makes WordCount less flexible, as the list of stop words may be different for different use cases.

The solution is to follow the dependency inversion principle (see "Loose coupling" on page 279) and to inject the list of stop words into the WordCount API:

```java
public class WordCount {
  private final Set<String> stopWords;

  public WordCount(Set<String> stopWords) {
    this.stopWords = stopWords;
  }

  public Map<String, Integer> calculateWordCounts(File file) {
    return null;
  }
}
```

Now you can write a test case for *four-words-plus-stop-words.txt* and be confident that WordCount will use the stop words you specify:

```java
@Test
public void testCalculateWordCountsIgnoresStopWords() {
  Set<String> stopWords = ImmutableSet.of("and", "the", "to");
  WordCount wordCount = new WordCount(stopWords);

  Map<String, Integer> actual = wordCount.calculateWordCounts(
    new File("four-words-plus-stop-words.txt"));

  Map<String, Integer> expected =
    ImmutableMap.of("hello", 3,
                    "startup", 2,
                    "people", 1,
                    "world", 1);

  assertEquals(expected, actual);
}
```

After writing this second test case, another problem becomes apparent: the stop words are defined directly in the test code, but the text you're processing is defined in files. Having to go back and forth between the two makes it harder to understand the test case. As usual, the difficulty in testing also brings up a larger design problem: the `calculateWordCounts` function has no reason to read a file. Reading files introduces side effects (I/O), which makes the code harder to reason about. It also makes the code less flexible, as you may want to calculate word counts on text in a database or a remote web service instead of a file.

A more flexible design for `calculateWordCounts` would be to take in a `String` of text instead of a `File`:

```java
public Map<String, Integer> calculateWordCounts(String text) {
  return null;
}
```

This makes `calculateWordCounts` a pure function (see "Pure functions" on page 274). One of the benefits is that this makes it easier to write test cases:

```java
public class TestWordCount {
  final Set<String> stopWords = ImmutableSet.of("and", "the", "to");
  final WordCount wordCount = new WordCount(stopWords);

  @Test
  public void testCalculateWordCountsOnFourWords() {
    String text =
      "Hello! Hello startup people! Hello startup world!";
    Map<String, Integer> actual =
      wordCount.calculateWordCounts(text);

    Map<String, Integer> expected =
      ImmutableMap.of("hello", 3,
                      "startup", 2,
                      "people", 1,
                      "world", 1);

    assertEquals(expected, actual);
  }

  @Test
  public void testtestCalculateWordCountsIgnoresStopWords() {
    String text =
      "Hello! Hello to the startup people! " +
      "And hello to the startup world!";
    Map<String, Integer> actual =
      wordCount.calculateWordCounts(text);

    Map<String, Integer> expected =
      ImmutableMap.of("hello", 3,
                      "startup", 2,
```

```
                    "people", 1,
                    "world", 1);

    assertEquals(expected, actual);
  }

}
```

Run the test cases again to make sure you get good error messages:

```
There were 2 failures:

1) testCalculateWordCountsOnFourWords
   (com.hello.startup.wordcount.TestWordCount)

java.lang.AssertionError:
Expected :{hello=3, startup=2, people=1, world=1}
Actual   :null

2) testCalculateWordCountsIgnoresStopWords
   (com.hello.startup.wordcount.TestWordCount)

java.lang.AssertionError:
Expected :{hello=3, startup=2, people=1, world=1}
Actual   :null
```

You should add a few more test cases, such as one for an empty string and one that includes multiple types of whitespace and punctuation, but for this example, the two tests above will be enough to get started. You can now start implementing calculateWordCounts to get these tests to pass. Here's a first try:

```java
public Map<String, Integer> calculateWordCounts(String text) {
  String[] words = text.split("\\s+");

  Map<String, Integer> counts = new HashMap<>();
  for (String word : words) {
    if (!stopWords.contains(word)) {
      Integer count = counts.get(word);
      counts.put(word, count == null ? 1 : count + 1);
    }
  }

  Comparator<String> sortByValue =
    (key1, key2) -> counts.get(key2).compareTo(counts.get(key1));

  Map<String, Integer> sortedCounts = new TreeMap<>(sortByValue);
  sortedCounts.putAll(counts);
```

```
    return sortedCounts;
}
```

This code splits the text into words on whitespace characters, loops over the words, uses a HashMap to count the ones that are not stop words, and then uses a TreeMap with a custom Comparator to sort the words by count. This looks like a reasonable implementation, but you should run the tests to see what they think of it:

```
FAILURES!!!
Tests run: 2, Failures: 2
```

It looks like there are bugs. To understand what's wrong, take a look at one of the test failures in detail:

```
1) testCalculateWordCountsOnFourWords
   (com.hello.startup.wordcount.TestWordCount)

java.lang.AssertionError:
Expected :{hello=3, startup=2, people=1, world=1}
Actual   :{Hello=2, startup=2, Hello!=1, people!=1, world!=1}
```

Right away, you can see that there is a bug with punctuation, as there are words like "Hello!" and "people!". It looks like you need to split the text not only on whitespace characters ("\\s") but also punctuation characters ("\p{Punct}"). You can give this regular expression a name:

```
private static final String PUNCTUATION_AND_WHITESPACE =
    "[\\p{Punct}\\s]+";
```

And use it in calculateWordCounts:

```
String[] words = text.split(PUNCTUATION_AND_WHITESPACE);
```

Rerun the tests:

```
FAILURES!!!
Tests run: 2, Failures: 2
```

Look at one specific test failure to understand what's going on:

```
1) testCalculateWordCountsOnFourWords
   (com.hello.startup.wordcount.TestWordCount)

java.lang.AssertionError:
```

```
Expected :{hello=3, startup=2, people=1, world=1}
Actual   :{Hello=3, startup=2, world=1}
```

You can see that the punctuation problem is fixed, but now there are two new problems. First, the code isn't handling capitalization correctly, so "Hello" and "hello" are treated as different words. Second, the word "people" has disappeared, but it's not obvious where. It is tempting to use a debugger or some println statements to figure out what's going on, but if the error message from the test case isn't enough to figure out what's wrong, it might be a sign that something is wrong with the design of the code. If you break down the code in calculateWordCounts, you'll see that it performs two separate tasks:

- Parsing words: splitting a string into words and removing stop words.

- Counting words: counting occurrences and sorting by count.

A classic sign that a function has too many responsibilities (see "Single Responsibility Principle (SRP)" on page 266) is that you find a bug during testing and it's hard to tell which part of the function is causing the bug. The solution is not to use debugging tricks but to break up all the different parts into separate functions so that you can think about and test each one separately. Imagine you split calculateWordCounts into two functions:

- splitTextIntoNormalizedWords

- countOccurrences

The first function processes words but has nothing to do with counting them. The second function counts things, but those things don't necessarily have to be words. If you added these functions to the WordCount class, you would end up with an API that has low cohesion (see "High cohesion" on page 287). Some programmers solve this dilemma by marking the helper methods as protected, so that they aren't a visible part of the API, but tests can still access them. This is better than nothing, but internally, the class would still be incoherent, so a better approach is to put these functions into their own classes where they can be part of a cohesive public API.

For example, you could create a WordParser class that solely deals with processing words in text. Continuing with the TDD process, you should make a first guess at the API for the class, but leave the implementation empty for now:

```
public class WordParser {
  public List<String> splitTextIntoNormalizedWords(String text) {
    return null;
  }
}
```

What should you test about this code? Start with four use cases:

- Splitting words based on any whitespace or punctuation.

- Converting all words to lowercase.

- Handling empty strings.

- Removing stop words.

The fourth item sounds familiar. Just thinking about how to test a class with stop words helps you realize that you need to inject the list of stop words into the WordParser class:

```
public class WordParser {
  private final Set<String> stopWords;

  public WordParser(Set<String> stopWords) {
    this.stopWords = stopWords;
  }

  public List<String> splitTextIntoNormalizedWords(String text) {
    return null;
  }
}
```

Now you can write the four test cases:

```
public class TestWordParser {
  final Set<String> stopWords = ImmutableSet.of("and", "the", "to");
  final WordParser wordParser = new WordParser(stopWords);

  @Test
  public void testSplitTextIntoNormalizedWordsWithPunctuation() {
    String text =
      "Hello! Can you hear me? This should, um, ignore punctuation.";
```

```java
    List<String> expected = ImmutableList.of(
      "hello", "can", "you", "hear", "me",
      "this", "should", "um", "ignore", "punctuation");
    List<String> actual =
      wordParser.splitTextIntoNormalizedWords(text);

    assertEquals(expected, actual);
  }

  @Test
  public void testSplitTextIntoNormalizedWordsEmptyString() {
    List<String> out = wordParser.splitTextIntoNormalizedWords("");
    assertEmpty(out);
  }


  @Test
  public void testSplitTextIntoNormalizedWordsDifferentWhitespace() {
    String text =
      "Hello\nthere!\t\tIs this    working?";
    List<String> expected =
      ImmutableList.of("hello", "there", "is", "this", "working");

    List<String> actual =
      wordParser.splitTextIntoNormalizedWords(text);

    assertEquals(expected, actual);
  }

  @Test
  public void testSplitTextIntoNormalizedWordsRemovesStopWords() {
    String text =
      "Hello to you and all the best!";
    List<String> expected =
      ImmutableList.of("hello", "you", "all", "best");

    List<String> actual =
      wordParser.splitTextIntoNormalizedWords(text);

    assertEquals(expected, actual);
  }

}
```

When you run them, they all fail as expected:

```
FAILURES!!!
Tests run: 4,  Failures: 4
```

Next, copy the implementation that was originally in the `WordCount` class and see if it passes these tests:

```
private static final String PUNCTUATION_AND_WHITESPACE =
  "[\\p{Punct}\\s]+";

public List<String> splitTextIntoNormalizedWords(String text) {
  return ImmutableList.copyOf(text.split(PUNCTUATION_AND_WHITESPACE));
}
```

The bad news is that when you run the tests on this version, all four of the tests still fail. The good news is that you are testing isolated functionality instead of all of `WordCount`, so the error messages from the tests are more helpful:

```
java.lang.AssertionError:
Expected :[hello, there, is, this, working]
Actual   :[Hello, there, Is, this, working]
```

A-ha, the code isn't handling capitalization. You can use Java 8 Streams (see "Higher-order functions" on page 272) to convert each word to lowercase:

```
public List<String> splitTextIntoNormalizedWords(String text) {
  return Arrays
    .stream(text.split(PUNCTUATION_AND_WHITESPACE))
    .map(String::toLowerCase)
    .collect(Collectors.toList());
}
```

When you run the tests again, two tests pass, but two still fail:

```
1) testSplitTextIntoNormalizedWordsEmptyString
   (com.hello.startup.wordcount.TestWordParser)
2) testSplitTextIntoNormalizedWordsRemovesStopWords
   (com.hello.startup.wordcount.TestWordParser)
```

You can tell just from the names of the failing tests that the problems are obvious. You need to filter out empty strings and stop words:

```
public List<String> splitTextIntoNormalizedWords(String text) {
  return Arrays
    .stream(text.split(PUNCTUATION_AND_WHITESPACE))
    .map(String::toLowerCase)
    .filter(word -> !word.isEmpty() && !stopWords.contains(word))
    .collect(Collectors.toList());
}
```

When you run the tests again, they all pass.

Next up is counting occurrences. Before running off and implementing a custom countOccurrences function, you should pause to think for a moment. Counting things is a common activity. Perhaps someone has already solved this problem? It turns out that in the Java world, a solution is readily available in the form of the MultiSet class in Google's Guava library (*http://bit.ly/multiset-class*). Guava is a popular, well-tested, and robust library, and the MultiSet is built explicitly for counting so it's a better fit for the WordCount API than a simple Map.

You can now update the WordCount class to use the WordParser and MultiSet classes:

```
public class WordCount {
  private final WordParser parser;

  public WordCount(WordParser parser) {
    this.parser = parser;
  }

  public Multiset<String> calculateWordCounts(String text) {
    List<String> words =
      parser.splitTextIntoNormalizedWords(text);
    ImmutableMultiset<String> counts =
      ImmutableMultiset.copyOf(words);
    return Multisets.copyHighestCountFirst(counts);
  }
}
```

This code injects the WordParser as a dependency and uses it to get the list of normalized words. It then calls ImmutableMultiset.copyOf to count the words and Multisets.copyHighestCountFirst to sort those counts from highest to lowest. The entire calculateWordCounts function is now just three lines long.

You can now update the tests for WordCount to make sure everything works:

```
public class TestWordCount {
  private final Set<String> testStopWords =
    ImmutableSet.of("the", "and", "to");
  private final WordParser wordParser = new WordParser(testStopWords);
  private final WordCount wordCount = new WordCount(wordParser);

  @Test
  public void testCalculateWordCountsOnFourWords() {
    String text =
      "Hello! Hello startup people! Hello startup world!";
    Multiset<String> actualCounts =
      wordCount.calculateWordCounts(text);
```

```
    Multiset<String> expectedCounts = ImmutableMultiset
      .<String>builder()
      .addCopies("hello", 3)
      .addCopies("startup", 2)
      .addCopies("people", 1)
      .addCopies("world", 1)
      .build();

    assertEquals(expectedCounts, actualCounts);
  }

  @Test
  public void testCalculateWordCountsIgnoresStopWords() {
    String text =
      "Hello! Hello to the startup people! " +
      "And hello to the startup world!";
    Multiset<String> actualCounts =
      wordCount.calculateWordCounts(text);

    Multiset<String> expectedCounts = ImmutableMultiset
      .<String>builder()
      .addCopies("hello", 3)
      .addCopies("startup", 2)
      .addCopies("people", 1)
      .addCopies("world", 1)
      .build();

    assertEquals(expectedCounts, actualCounts);
  }
}
```

Next, run all the WordParser and WordCount tests:

```
JUnit version 4.11
..
Time: 0.156

OK (6 tests)
```

All of the tests pass! By following a test-code-test cycle, you've ended up with clean, reusable, well-tested code. Notice that instead of planning the design up front, you can allow it to grow—to emerge— based on iterative feedback from the tests. In other words, clean code is more the result of evolution than intelligent design. And it's not scary to evolve this code further because it takes just 0.156 seconds to run the tests and see if you've broken anything.

Of course, these tests are fast because they are all unit tests. In the real world, TDD also means writing integration tests, acceptance tests, and performance tests first. Thinking about integration tests up front forces you to consider how to deploy your systems and how they will communicate with one another. Thinking about acceptance tests up front forces you to think about whether you're building the right product and solving real user problems. Thinking about performance tests up front forces you to think about where your bottlenecks are and what metrics you should expose to identify them.

> *Including the deployment step in the testing process is critical for two reasons. First, this is the sort of error-prone activity that should not be done by hand, so we want our scripts to have been thoroughly exercised by the time we have to deploy for real. One lesson that we've learned repeatedly is that nothing forces us to understand a process better than trying to automate it. Second, this is often the moment where the development team bumps into the rest of the organization and has to learn how it operates. If it's going to take six weeks and four signatures to set up a database, we want to know now, not two weeks before delivery.*
>
> **—[FREEMAN AND PRYCE 2009, 32], STEVE FREEMAN AND NAT PRYCE,**
> ***GROWING OBJECT-ORIENTED SOFTWARE, GUIDED BY TESTS***

Writing tests up front increases the chances that you'll have thorough test coverage, because it forces you to write code incrementally. Tests can be tedious to write, so it's easier if you only have to do a few at a time: write a few tests and then a little bit of implementation, then a few more tests, then a little more implementation, and so on. It's less effective to write thousands of lines of implementation code and then try to do a marathon session of writing test cases for all of it. You'll get bored. You'll also miss many corner cases because you'll forget the nuances of implementation code you wrote many days earlier.

Most importantly, TDD helps you make sure that you're writing the right code by forcing you to think through the problem from the end result backward rather than jumping straight into coding and getting lost in implementation details. You focus on *what* you're building rather than *how* you're building it. And you do it with a fast feedback loop that leads to a higher quality design. Speed wins.

What should you test?

Tests are important. They are one of the most powerful tools for quickly building high-quality software. But tests are not free. It takes time to write the tests, update them when code changes, and optimize them so they run quickly and reliably. You have to set up a test framework for backend servers, another one for frontend servers, and one more for client-side code. You have to wire everything into a CI job that runs after every check-in. In most cases, automated tests are so valuable that this overhead is worth it. In some cases, it is not.

Very few of the startups I talked to had thorough automated tests or used TDD in their early days. That doesn't imply that these startups wouldn't have been even more successful if they did a better job with testing, but it does suggest that automated tests are not a strict requirement for startup success. An early-stage startup might build 10 different products and throw away 9 of them (or sometimes, all 10 of them). Writing well-designed and thoroughly tested code is not as valuable if you're going to throw 90%+ of it away. At an early-stage company, skipping tests can sometimes be an acceptable trade-off if it allows you to get feedback from users faster (see "Speed Wins" on page 51).

I can already hear TDD enthusiasts screaming "but a codebase without tests won't scale!" And they are right. But early-stage startups must routinely do things that don't scale (see "Do things that don't scale" on page 139). Almost every startup I talked to had to invest heavily in automated tests to be able to scale once it got past a certain size—but not before that. The key question is, how do you know when you've gone from one stage to the other? How can you tell when it's time to invest in automated testing?

In theory, the answer is simple: you need automated tests when you no longer have enough confidence in your code to make changes quickly. If you are hesitant to add a new feature, or you are nervous about deploying a new piece of code, or every release breaks more features than it adds, you need tests. In practice, the answer comes down to continuously evaluating your testing strategy and making trade-offs between several factors: the cost of bugs, the likelihood of bugs, and the cost of testing. Let's take a closer look:

The cost of bugs

> If you're building a prototype that you'll most likely throw away in a week, the cost of bugs is low. If you're building a payment processing system, the cost of bugs is very high—you don't want to charge a customer's credit card twice or for the wrong amount. Bugs are also costly in any system that touches data storage (i.e., any code that can delete or corrupt user data) and any code related to security (e.g., authentication, authorization, encryption). Although the startups I talked to varied wildly in their testing practices, just about every single one identified a few parts of their code, such as pay-

ments, security, and data, that were very heavily tested from day one because they simply were not allowed to break.

The likelihood of bugs

As a codebase gets larger, it is less likely that you can keep it working solely through manual testing. Similarly, as you increase the number of people working on the same code, automated tests become crucial to avoid integration bugs and as a way to document what the code should do (see "Documentation" on page 334). It's also worth mentioning that some technical problems are inherently more complicated, so you'll need more tests to solve them correctly. For example, you might want to write automated tests if you're solving complicated math problems or writing your own distributed consensus algorithms.

The cost of testing

Setting up unit tests these days is practically free. There are high-quality unit-testing frameworks for almost every programming language and most build systems have built-in support for unit testing. The cost is so low, the tests run so fast, and the improvement to code quality and correctness is so high that it is almost always worth writing unit tests. On the other hand, integration tests, acceptance tests, and performance tests are each progressively more expensive to set up. These types of tests are more use-case specific, so it's up to you to figure out how to automatically deploy code, initialize data stores, and wire everything together. These are all valuable tasks you'll have to solve anyway, but in some cases, the overhead may outweigh the benefits.[2]

Automated testing best practices

Although TDD is the gold standard, almost any type of automated testing is better than manual testing. If you're working on something that doesn't fit the TDD model,[3] writing tests shortly after you write the code is still valuable. If you're

---

2 This is especially true for testing client-side code, such as web and mobile apps. These tests tend to be slow to run and hard to maintain as minor UI changes can cause test failures. Also, there are few automated tools that can match manual testing for certain types of tasks, such as verifying that the UI "looks right."

3 The most common case where TDD is a poor fit is "exploratory coding." That is, you don't know what you're building and you are just exploring the problem space by coding and messing with data. If you don't know what result you're looking for, you can't write a test for it.

working on an existing codebase that doesn't have any tests, there is no time like the present to add some. And if you're fixing a bug, the best way to get started is to write a failing test that reproduces the bug (test-driven bug fixing). That proves you understand the cause of the bug and, after you fix it, leaves you with an automated test that will prevent the bug from coming back.

Also, automated tests should be, well, automated. That is, you should be able to run all of your tests with a single command, with no manual intervention, and preferably as part of your build process (see "Continuous Integration" on page 358). It should take no more than a few seconds to run the unit tests, and no more than a few minutes for all the integration tests, acceptance tests, and performance tests.[4] A giant test suite that takes many hours is nearly worthless, as it will only give you feedback once per day, which is little better than the productivity of 60s-era programmers submitting punch cards to be run in a mainframe overnight. Either make your tests fast (reduce dependencies, parallelize them, run them on a cluster) or delete them, as a slow test suite will usually cause more harm than good (see "Manual delivery: a horror story" on page 351).

The only thing worse than a slow test suite is an unreliable test suite. Tests that fail intermittently or behave non-deterministically are harmful because they decrease your confidence when changing the code. And if you don't fix transient failures immediately, they will undermine the value of your entire test suite. If you keep seeing test failures that seem to come and go of their own accord, then you'll get used to ignoring failures, and like the boy who cried wolf, no one will know when you've hit a real problem. Fix or delete flaky tests immediately. In fact, try to avoid writing them in the first place by watching out for the cause of most transient test failures: time. Be extra careful when writing tests that depend on asynchronous events in a UI, random numbers, the system clock, eventually consistent data stores, caches with TTLs, or the execution order in a multithreaded program.

---

4 *Endurance tests* are an exception, as they are specifically designed to see how a system handles load over a long period of time. These should be run outside of the build process.

SPLIT UP THE CODE

*Software development doesn't happen in a chart, an IDE, or a design tool;
it happens in your head.*

—[SUBRAMANIAM AND HUNT 2006, 11], VENKAT SUBRAMANIAM AND ANDY HUNT,
PRACTICES OF AN AGILE DEVELOPER

Earlier in the book, I discussed that the design of a product has to be simple to accommodate the limitations of the human mind. If you have too much information in a product—too many features, too much text, too many buttons, too many settings—it overwhelms human memory and the product becomes unusable (see "Simplicity" on page 92). The same principle applies to code. If you have too much code in one place, it overwhelms the programmer's memory, and the codebase becomes harder to reason about. It doesn't take much code either. Just a couple thousand lines, the size of a small iPhone app or JavaScript library, is more than most people can keep in their head.

Although most programmers believe their job is to write code, the reality is that, in many ways, code is the enemy. The more of it you have, the slower you go. Defect density—how many bugs you have per thousand lines of code—significantly increases with project size, so a project with twice as many lines of code will typically have more than twice as many bugs [McConnell 2004, 651] and will be more than twice as difficult to plan, build, test, and maintain. Imagine if every line of code you wrote was printed on paper and you had to carry it with you in a backpack everywhere you went. As the codebase grew, the reams of paper would slow you down more and more until your progress ground to a halt.

The worst thing that can happen to a codebase is size [Yegge 2007], so you should strive to keep your codebase as small as possible. In part, you do this by delegating as much work as you can to open source and commercial libraries that are outside of your codebase (see "Build in-house, buy commercial, or use open source?" on page 193). In part, you do this by using a programming language and coding style that is concise and reduces boilerplate and repetition (see Chapter 6). But to some extent, as the company and product grows, the codebase will inevitably grow with it, and you'll need to adopt new techniques to deal with it.

The best solution is to split up the code into multiple "pieces" in such a way that you can reason about one piece at a time and safely ignore the others. This is known as *abstraction*. You do it all the time, even outside of programming. For example, when you try to paint something from memory, such as an orange, you find that the image of an orange in your head is a simplified abstraction that's missing many of the details. (see "Design is iterative" on page 73). For most purposes, this version of an orange is good enough because you don't need to be aware of every minute detail, such as its exact color and texture, in order to be able to find one and eat it. A good abstraction should satisfy two properties: information hiding and composability.

Information hiding means the abstraction should be simpler than whatever details are behind it, just like the image of an orange in your head is simpler than all the details of the real fruit. One way to think of it is that the surface area of the abstraction (i.e., the interface it exposes to the outside world) should be smaller than its volume (i.e., the implementation details it hides inside) [Milewski 2014]. In the real world, the surface area of an object grows with the square of its size, whereas the volume grows with its cube. Similarly, in the software world, the amount of information in the implementation details grows very quickly, so to prevent it from overwhelming your mind, you want an abstraction that presents a smaller and simpler interface.

Composability means you can combine multiple abstractions in such a way that you get a new abstraction, which, in turn, can be combined with still other abstractions. This way, you can start with simple pieces and incrementally build up complexity, one abstraction layer at a time. It's a bit like building a house out of Legos. You start with hundreds of individual pieces, each of which is simple, but there are so many that it's difficult to mentally organize them. Therefore, you assemble a dozen pieces into a floor, another dozen into walls, and another dozen into a ceiling. Now, instead of dozens of items to keep track of, you have just a handful: a floor, a few walls, and a ceiling (information hiding). Even better, you can combine these pieces into the first floor of a house. This floor, in turn, can be combined with other Lego structures (e.g., a staircase, other floors, a garage) to create larger and larger structures (composability).

In programming, there are many different kinds of abstractions. We'll just look at the three most common ones:

- Interfaces and modules

- Versioned artifacts

- Services

Interfaces and modules

Most programming languages allow you to define *interfaces*, which specify the set of operations you are allowed to perform on a piece of code, as well as *modules*, which group related interfaces together. Depending on the language, the interface can be a function signature, the public methods in a class, or an abstract interface or trait; and a module can be a package, namespace, or library. As you saw in Chapter 6, well-defined interfaces and modules are the backbone of clean code.

Versioned artifacts

Modules and interfaces are an effective way to split up the code, but as the codebase continues to grow, there is a tendency for all the modules to become tangled together. The codebase starts to resemble a box full of wires. You reach in to pull out a single cable but everything is so intertwined that you end up pulling up almost everything in the entire box. There are some programming practices you can use to reduce this coupling (see "Loose coupling" on page 279), but as a codebase gets larger, it becomes almost unavoidable.

One possible solution is to break up the codebase so that instead of modules depending on the *source code* of other modules (*source dependencies*), they depend on *versioned artifacts* published by other modules (*versioned dependencies*). Just about everyone does this already with open source libraries. To use jQuery in your JavaScript code or Google Guava in your Java code, you don't depend on the source code of those open source libraries, but on a versioned artifact they provide, such as *jquery-1.11-min.js* or *guava-14.0.jar*. You can use the same approach within your own codebase. This usually means changing your build system to publish versioned artifacts after each build and to pull in versioned dependencies instead of source dependencies (see "Build tool" on page 357). In fact, once you've moved all of your dependencies from source dependencies to versioned dependencies, you could even put the source code of each module into a separate repository so it can be developed in isolation (see "Version control" on page 353).

LinkedIn used to keep all of its code in a single monolithic repository with source dependencies between all the modules, but once it grew to millions of lines of code across thousands of modules, a number of problems emerged (see "Manual delivery: a horror story" on page 351). So for the last few years, the company has been breaking up the codebase into multiple repositories with versioned dependencies between them. Twitter has gone the other way: they started with many separate repositories and versioned dependencies between them and now they are trying to collapse everything down into a single repository with source dependencies. Why are the two companies moving in opposite directions?

The answer is that there are a number of non-trivial trade-offs to consider. Here are the advantages of multiple repositories with versioned dependencies:

Isolation
> With versioned dependencies, you are isolated from changes to other modules until you choose to upgrade to a new version, and there is no chance that a change to an unrelated module breaks your build or causes bugs in your code.

Coupling
> Keeping all your code in separate repositories and only allowing explicit, versioned dependencies tends to reduce coupling. Moreover, it makes it easier to open source your code because separate, versioned repos is the model used by all open source projects.

Build times
> If all the code is in one repo, then each module you add increases the build time (at least) linearly, and once you get to millions of lines of code, a build can take many hours. You can mitigate this problem by keeping each module in a separate repo so that the build time for each one stays fairly constant and fast.

And here are the disadvantages of multiple repositories with versioned dependencies:

Continuous integration
> With versioned dependencies, you don't find out about bugs and incompatibilities in your dependencies until you upgrade to a new version, which might not be until months after the broken change went in. In other words, you lose many of the advantages of continuous integration (see "Continuous Integration" on page 358).

Dependency hell
> With versioned dependencies, many different kinds of dependency problems are possible: dependency conflicts, circular dependencies, diamond dependencies, and so on. Backward compatibility becomes a strict requirement of all module APIs. Upgrading to new versions of libraries can be painful and time consuming.

Global changes

> With multiple repositories, making global changes is difficult and cannot be done atomically. You have to use special tools to search across all of your repositories, check out each repo that matches your search, update dependency versions and code in each repo, and then try to commit your changes back, all while dealing with dependency hell.

In general, if your code consists of a number of isolated modules and the majority of your changes are *within* individual modules (i.e., your company resembles a number of separate open source projects), then multiple repositories with versioned dependencies will allow you to go faster. However, if you regularly need to make global changes across many modules, then a single repository with source dependencies will be the better option, especially if you mitigate some of the downsides, such as slow builds, by heavily investing in tooling (e.g., Google uses a gigantic distributed cluster for compiling and testing its code [Hammant 2013]).

Services

Another way to split up the codebase is to group related functionality into *services*. That is, you put certain types of functionality behind a process and instead of function calls, you communicate with it via messages. There are many different models for building a tech stack out of standalone services, including service-oriented architecture (SOA), microservices, and actor systems. For example, at LinkedIn, we had an architecture that resembled microservices, where there were separate services for storing profile data (i.e., the name, education, and experience details for each user), company data (i.e., the name, location, and images for a company), cloud data (i.e., how users and companies are interconnected), and so on. Each service was owned by a different team, developed in isolation in a separate repository, deployed on separate hardware, and handled communication with other services via RESTful HTTP calls.

Just as there are many trade-offs with splitting up a codebase into multiple repositories, there are many trade-offs with splitting it up into multiple services. Here are the advantages of services:

Isolation

> It's nice to be able to build, test, and deploy a small, standalone service without having to worry about the rest of the codebase. Also, service boundaries work well as code ownership boundaries, which allow teams to work

independently from one another. This is important for dividing up the work in a growing company.

Technology agnostic

Whereas modules can only be shared within a single language (e.g., a Java module can only be called from other Java code), you can use any language you want to build a service, because a remote endpoint (e.g., HTTP) can be used by any language. If your company needs to use multiple programming languages (e.g., because of an acquisition or while migrating to a new tech stack), services may be your only option for sharing functionality.

Performance

If your product has enough traffic or data, multiple services might be the only way to achieve acceptable performance. For example, some functionality might need a single server with lots of memory, while other types of functionality will need a cluster of servers with fast CPUs. By splitting the functionality across different services, you can scale each one independently.

And here are the disadvantages of services:

Operational complexity

Instead of deploying one type of service, you now have many different types, each with their own requirements and technologies. Moreover, these services talk to one another in complicated ways, so you need mechanisms for service discovery, load balancing, and analyzing the call graph, all of which are expensive to build and maintain.

Error handling

While a call to a local function always succeeds, a call to a remote service can fail because of network problems, because the service is down, or it might simply take too long. With services, all of your code now needs to handle a whole new class of errors.

Performance overhead

Remote calls take several orders of magnitude more time than local function calls, so you have to re-organize your code to minimize the latency overhead (e.g., batching, de-duping, pre-fetching, caching). There is also CPU and memory overhead with serializing and deserializing remote requests.

I/O

If you use blocking I/O for remote calls, then you have to manage thread pools for each service, which increases operational overhead and can cause performance problems. If you use non-blocking I/O, you avoid some of these issues, but now you have to use a different coding style built around callbacks or promises (see "Play Framework: Async I/O without the Thread Pool and Callback Hell" [Brikman 2013a]).

Backward compatibility

You cannot delete or rename a service API, or even a single parameter of an API, as it's possible some client out there is still using the old version. This means you can't just refactor a service API; you have to make versioned changes and maintain old versions for a potentially long time, which increases maintenance overhead.

In general, services entail a massive overhead, so you're best off avoiding them until you have no other choice. That is, if you really need your teams to be able to work independently from one another or to be able to use different programming languages, or if a single monolithic app simply can't handle the load anymore (see "Scaling performance" on page 341), then you should move to services, but only if you can afford to put in the considerable work to operationalize them.

CODE REVIEWS

Every page in this book has been checked over by an editor. Why? Because even if you're the smartest, most capable, most experienced writer, you can't proofread your own work. You're too close to the concepts, and you've rolled the words around your head for so long you can't put yourself in the shoes of someone who is hearing them for the first time. Writing code is no different. In fact, if it's impossible to write prose without independent scrutiny, surely it's also impossible to write code in isolation; code has to be correct to the minutest detail, plus it includes prose for humans as well!

—[ORAM AND WILSON 2010, 329], JASON COHEN,
FOUNDER OF WP ENGINE AND SMART BEAR SOFTWARE

If clean code is about making your code easier to understand for other programmers, then the best way to make sure you're succeeding is to actually show it to other programmers. Having your code reviewed by someone else is one of the most effective tools for catching bugs. A study of a team of 11 programmers found that the programs they developed without code reviews averaged 4.5 errors per 100 lines of code, while those developed with code reviews averaged 0.82 errors per 100 lines of code, a reduction in error rate of over 80% [Freedman and Weinberg 1990]. Another study found that while unit and integration tests each catch about 30%–35% of bugs, design and code reviews can catch 55%–60% of bugs [Jones 1996].

Besides catching bugs, code reviews have another important benefit: they are an efficient mechanism to spread knowledge, culture, training, and a sense of ownership throughout the team. Everyone that participates in code reviews will see benefits. Senior engineers can use code reviews to mentor junior engineers. Junior engineers can participate in code reviews to learn the codebase and to contribute important questions. If the new developer doesn't understand the code, it might be because the developer is inexperienced, but it could also be that the code is confusing.

There are four types of code review: design reviews, pair programming, pre-commit reviews, and static analysis.

Design reviews

Before you start working on a large new project, it's a good idea to come up with a design and gather feedback from your team. This is a good way to give your team a chance to suggest improvements, warn you about potential problems, and discuss how your work fits with what everyone else is doing. You don't need to spend three months writing a 300-page specification, but a few hours of thinking through ideas can save you weeks of coding down the line (see "Readme-driven development (RDD)" on page 339). Keep design reviews light, friendly, and make sure everyone participates: senior engineers should have their designs reviewed by junior engineers and vice versa.

> For our design process, we just use Google Docs for everything at Coursera. You write up a straw-man, RFC-like proposal that describes what you're thinking about, along with a bunch of open-ended questions. You throw it over the wall to the entire engineering team and they just spam the hell out of it, ripping it to shreds with comments. You get tons of great feedback from your peers and everyone gets to provide their input. That makes you better and makes for a better design in the end. I find it really valuable for junior engineers to observe (or even participate in) the design

process and get better at architecture. Eventually, all the comments get resolved and you'll have a rough draft of the design. The whole process is asynchronous and rarely takes more than a day or two.

—[DELLAMAGGIORE 2014], NICK DELLAMAGGIORE,
SOFTWARE ENGINEER AT LINKEDIN AND COURSERA

Pair programming

Pair programming is a development technique where two programmers work together at one computer. One person is the driver and responsible for writing the code, while the other is the observer, and responsible for reviewing the code and thinking about the program at a higher level. The two programmers regularly switch roles [Beck and Andres 2004, 42].

The result is a constant code review process. It takes some time to get used to it, but with another developer nearby, you are always focused on how to make it clear what your code is doing, and you have a second set of eyes to catch bugs. Although pairs of developers spend an average of 15% more time on programs than individuals, the resulting code has about 15% fewer defects and a higher quality design [Cockburn and Williams 2001, 3]. In addition, because more than one person is familiar with the code, it'll be easier to maintain it in the future.[5]

You don't need to do pair programming for every line of code, but it is a valuable exercise any time you are working on a tricky or business-critical part of the codebase. Pair coding is also a great way to interview candidates (see "The interview" on page 487) and to onboard new hires.

Pre-commit reviews

Once you've finished writing and testing a piece of code and are ready to commit it, it's a good idea to submit it to the team for a final review. The pre-commit review gives everyone a chance to see what you've built, ask questions, and identify errors. You should use an online tool to track code review comments so you can go back to them later when debugging or trying to understand the context behind a piece of code. Good code review tools include GitHub, which includes a code review as part of the pull request process, ReviewBoard, and Phabricator.

---

5 Pair programming increases your *bus factor*. The bus factor is a measure of how many individuals you could lose—because they were hit by a bus, or perhaps something less drastic, like going on vacation or leaving the company—before you are unable to proceed with a project. A high bus factor is a good thing.

Static analysis

In addition to having people review your code, it's a good idea to use automated tools to check your code as well. For languages that are compiled, the most important tool is the compiler itself, but there are static analysis and linter tools available for every programming language.[6] These tools can help you identify common sources of bugs, find code style issues, detect duplicate code and unused code, calculate complexity metrics to identify code that needs refactoring, find code that uses unsafe features (e.g., eval, goto), identify potential security holes, and find potential memory leaks

Most static analysis tools can be run from the command line (e.g., before you check-in) and integrated into your build system. You can even fail the build for serious static analysis errors. Ideally, you also run static analysis tools while you code. Many IDEs and text editors have static analysis built in, which means you get instant feedback as you type. For example, the folks at JetBrains showed us that using the right IDE with static analysis could've caught Apple's infamous gotofail bug (see "Code layout" on page 251), as shown in Figure 7-2.

Code review best practices

Code reviews are an essential practice that should be used at every company, but there are a few guidelines to follow to get them right.

First, it's a good idea to assign an owner to every part of the code. The owner isn't the only person who is allowed to change that part of the code, but they are responsible for knowing how it works and keeping it running. This means they get to decide what changes can go in, who can review them, what coding standards to enforce, and when the code can be deployed.

---

6 See the List of tools for static code analysis (*http://bit.ly/sca-list*).

 **JetBrains AppCode**
@appcode

Tip of the day: Detecting unreachable code is easy with AppCode. Can your IDE do the same?

```
static OSStatus
SSLVerifySignedServerKeyExchange(SSLContext *ctx, bool isRsa, SSLBuffer signedParams,
        uint8_t *signature, UInt16 signatureLen)
{
    OSStatus        err;
    //...

    if ((err = SSLHashSHA1.update(&hashCtx, &serverRandom)) != 0)
        goto fail;
    if ((err = SSLHashSHA1.update(&hashCtx, &signedParams)) != 0)
        goto fail;
        goto fail;
    if ((err = SSLHashSHA1.final(&hashCtx, &hashOut)) != 0)
        goto fail;

    //...  Unreachable code

fail:
    SSLFreeBuffer(&signedHashes);
    SSLFreeBuffer(&hashCtx);
    return err;
}
```

Figure 7-2. Static analysis in an IDE [JetBrains AppCode 2014]

Second, you need to establish a good code review culture by writing down your code review guidelines ahead of time. These guidelines should include a checklist of things a reviewer should look for, such as whether the code is easy to read, follows the team's coding conventions, and includes tests. The guidelines should also define the code of conduct in a code review. Code reviews are not about showing off your knowledge, making fun of someone else's code, or placing blame. They are a learning tool that makes everyone on the team better and makes everyone feel (and act) like an owner. To make sure everyone is on the same page, the code review guidelines should define what code must be reviewed (e.g., all of the code or just the mission-critical parts), when the code must be reviewed (e.g., before every commit, before merging a branch, or during a weekly review session), who has to get their code reviewed (e.g., everyone, no matter how senior), who is responsible for giving review comments (e.g., everyone, no matter how junior), and what types of comments are appropriate (e.g., take the time to note the good things about the code and not just the bad, never personally insult the submitter, don't be afraid to admit you don't understand something).

Third, keep reviews small. It's easy to review a 10-line change, but nearly impossible to review 1,000 lines. This means you should encourage developers to make changes in small, incremental commits, which also happens to be a good way to reduce the chance of bugs, merge conflicts, and late integration issues.

DOCUMENTATION

Documentation is essential for scaling a codebase and a developer team, but it's useful even if you're a team of one. Writing documentation, just like writing automated tests, can dramatically improve the quality of your code. If you force yourself to see the project from the end user's perspective, you'll come up with a better design. And if you spend an hour describing the right solution in prose, you'll save yourself a week of building the wrong solution in code.

By "documentation," I don't just mean a reference manual, but all the pieces that go into making your software learnable, including written documentation (readmes, tutorials), code documentation (type system, comments), and community documentation (Q&A sites, mailing lists). Each type of documentation solves a different problem, so most projects should include a mix of all types.[7]

Written documentation

Written documentation consists of the readme, tutorials, reference manuals, and project websites.

The *readme* is the most important document in your codebase. It is the introduction to a project that outlines what the project does, shows examples, and explains how to get started, how to contribute, and where to get more info. I'll

---

7 See "You Are What You Document" [Brikman 2014b] for examples of projects with great documentation.

come back to the readme in more detail in "Readme-driven development (RDD)" on page 339.

If the readme gets the user in the door, the *tutorial* shows them how to walk around. The goal is to take the user, step by step, through the typical development flow and to highlight the idiomatic patterns, best practices, and unique features of the project. You don't have to go too in-depth. Instead, at each step of the tutorial, provide links to where the user can find more information. For small, simple projects, you may be able to squeeze a tutorial into the readme itself, but larger projects will want to use a wiki, blog post, standalone web page, slide deck, or even a recorded video. If you want to take it a step further, try to put together an interactive tutorial. For example, the Tour of Go tutorial (*http:// tour.golang.org/*) lets you try the Go programming language directly in the browser without installing anything. Most developers learn best by doing, so a step-by-step guide that lets the developer participate is a powerful learning tool.

After the new user gets their foot in the door with the readme and takes a few steps by following the tutorial, they will know enough to start asking questions. This is where the *reference manual* comes into play. In this part of the documentation, you can cover all the major topics in depth. Just remember that the goal of a reference manual is to answer questions, so make sure to organize the information in a way that is easy to search and navigate.

Finally, a *project website* can be a great example of documentation as marketing [Holman 2011]. You can give your project its own home with a custom look and feel, and content that is linkable, shareable, and searchable. The easiest way to create a website for your project is with GitHub Pages (*https:// pages.github.com/*): create a repo on GitHub, put a few static HTML files in it, commit the code, and you have your own landing page on the github.io domain.

Code documentation

There's really no such thing as "self-documenting code." The code can only show you what it does, and not what it's supposed to do or why it does it [seibel 2009, 232], so every project needs written documentation. That said, the code itself is a critical source of information, as it shows you how things actually work. The most important aspects of code documentation are comments, the type system, and example code.

Comments are written documentation within the code. Clean code does not need many comments. Almost everything you need to say should be said in the code itself. If you come across some incomprehensible code, the fix is not to add explanatory comments but to refactor the code until it can be understood on its own terms. The classic example is a long method body where someone has inserted a comment every 10–15 lines to help the reader figure out what's going on. A better solution is to break up the code into multiple methods, each with a clear signature (method name, parameter names, and types) that removes the need for most of the comments. That said, the need for comments will never go away entirely because, depending on the programming language, there are certain types of information that cannot be captured by the code, such as background information (e.g., "this function uses algorithm X based on the paper..."), assumptions you're making about the inputs (e.g., preconditions like "the start parameter must be a non-negative integer"), guarantees you're providing for the outputs (e.g., postconditions like "the returned value will never be null"), explanations of any side effects (e.g., "this function will store the uploaded data in a temporary file"), and explanations for ugly or unintuitive code that cannot be fixed (e.g., "this is a workaround for bug X that cannot be fixed until the next release").

> *The proper use of comments is to compensate for our failure to express ourself in code. Note that I used the word failure. I meant it. Comments are always failures. We must have them because we cannot always figure out how to express ourselves without them, but their use is not a cause for celebration.*
>
> **—[MARTIN 2008, 54], ROBERT C. MARTIN, *CLEAN CODE***

An aspect of code that reduces the need for comments is the *type system*. In statically typed languages, the type system not only prevents a certain class of errors automatically but also reduces the amount of documentation you have to write. For example, consider the type signature of the following function in Java, a statically typed language:

```
public String convertCsvToJson(String csv)
```

Here is the analogous function signature in Haskell, a statically typed language with a stronger and stricter type system than Java:

```
convertCsvToJson :: String -> String
```

And here is the analogous function signature in JavaScript, a dynamically typed language:

```
function convertCsvToJson(csv)
```

What type of value does this function expect for the input parameter csv? In Haskell and Java, it's clear that the function expects a String. In JavaScript, you have no idea what type of value the function expects: it could be looking for a File, a String, a function, or even behave differently based on the types or number of parameters, and you won't know unless the author of the function documents it. What type of data does the function return? In Java, it will return a String or possibly null. In Haskell, you know that it returns a String (Haskell does not have null). In JavaScript, there is no way to know what the function returns: it could be a String, a File, or it may be a void function that doesn't return any value at all. You won't know unless the author of the function documents it. Finally, does the function have any side effects? In Haskell, if you perform any I/O, the compiler will require you to return a type called IO (see "Functional programming" on page 268). Just by looking at the signature of this function, you see that it returns a String and not IO, so you can be confident that there are no side effects.[8] On the other hand, with Java and JavaScript, there is no way to know that the function doesn't internally change a global variable, write to disk, or launch missiles unless the author documents it.

When it comes to documentation, static type systems are a clear winner. Whereas a developer may be too lazy to write comments for each method, and what comments they do write tend to go out of date, the information you get from the type system is enforced by the compiler, so it's always available and always correct. And as the type system becomes more powerful, it can reduce the need for comments even more. For example, languages that support *dependent types*, such as Idris (*http://www.idris-lang.org/*), allow you to define a type such as "an integer greater than 0" or "a list with two elements," and the compiler can enforce these constraints at build time (instead of the developer just listing them as preconditions in the comments).

All that said, no matter how good your type system is or how much documentation you write, you can't force developers to RTFM.[9] Some developers prefer to learn by example—which is a polite way of saying that they like to copy and

---

8 In Haskell, there are some ways to perform I/O or side effects without changing the function signature, such as using unsafePerformIO, but as the name implies,.this is an unsafe operation that is not idiomatic and is rarely used.

9 Read the Fucking Manual.

paste. Therefore, every project should include clean and idiomatic *example code*. Automated tests are a special case of example code. Tests can be useful as documentation in that they show the expected behavior of the code for a variety of use cases and corner cases. Whereas written documentation can go out of date, as long as a test passes, you can be sure it is accurate.

Community documentation

If a project has a community around it, then the community provides another rich source of documentation in the form of project management tools, mailing lists, Q&A boards, blog posts, and talks. For example, most teams use bug tracking software (e.g., JIRA, Bugzilla, GitHub issues) and/or project management software (e.g., Basecamp, Asana, Trello), and these systems contain a lot of valuable information about the project: what you worked on before, what you're working on now, what you'll work on in the future, bugs found, bugs fixed, and so on. It's not uncommon to come across a bug report or an old wiki page while searching for information about a project, especially if it's an open source project that makes all of this information publicly available.

Discussions from Q&A sites like Stack Overflow and mailing lists like Google Groups also come up frequently in search results. For internal and proprietary projects, you can use internal mailing lists, maintain an FAQ, or install an internal Stack Overflow–style Q&A site.[10] Even the best documentation will not be able to answer everything, so cultivating community websites can be a critical part of making software learnable. Over time, these can become some of the most important parts of your project's documentation, as they inherently deal with issues where developers got stuck.

Finally, for popular open source projects, some of the best documentation comes in the form of blog posts and talks from end users, as they will reveal what's really working and what isn't. They are also great marketing for the project, as it makes it clear other people are using it. If your project is open source, growing a community around it can have a huge pay off. A small investment in "marketing" your project via good documentation, custom project pages, talks, and meetup groups, can yield huge returns in the form of free labor, cleaner code, and better branding (see "Why you should share" on page 517 for more information).

---

10 More on this on StackExchange Meta (*http://bit.ly/sx-clones*).

Readme-driven development (RDD)

Earlier in this chapter, you saw test-driven development (TDD), where you write the tests before the implementation. For a new project, there is another step that you should do even before writing the tests: you should write the readme. This is known as readme-driven development (RDD). Don't confuse it with a design-everything-up-front Waterfall process where you spend weeks working on a 300-page spec that spells out every detail. With RDD, you spend an hour thinking through a project and, most importantly, writing down your thoughts before you start coding.

RDD helps you make sure that you're building the right thing by forcing you to think about *what* you're building before you get lost in the details of *how* to build it. You might think you know what you're going to build, but something magical happens in the process of taking vague thoughts circling around in your head and putting them down on (digital) paper. Writing is a more rigorous form of thinking and it always reveals flaws in your plan. Fixing these flaws when all you've created is a few paragraphs of text is easier than having to fix them after you've written a few thousand lines of code [Preston-Werner 2010].

If you create the readme up front, you'll be able to incrementally fill out the details as you implement the rest of the project. This makes the documentation process less painful, as you can work on small pieces of it at a time while each piece of information is fresh in your mind instead of a marathon documentation session at the very end of the project where you struggle to remember all the details. Moreover, the readme itself is an invaluable tool for working with others. If you circulate the readme around your team, you'll have something concrete to discuss, especially as part of a design review (see "Design reviews" on page 330), and once you all come to an agreement, the readme can serve as documentation of who should work on what [Preston-Werner 2010].

To make it clear why RDD is valuable, let's walk through all the pieces of a readme, including the sales pitch, examples, quick start guide, and project organization details.

Sales pitch

At the top of the readme, explain very succinctly (a) what the project does and (b) why you should use it. The first point forces you to be clear about *what* you're building. The second point forces you to justify *why* you're building it and not, for example, using a library already in your codebase, or an open source library, or building something else entirely (see "Build in-house, buy commercial, or use open source?" on page 193). If you can't justify why someone should use it, you probably shouldn't build it.

Examples

After the sales pitch, show a few code snippets, UI mockups, screenshots, or architecture diagrams, that demonstrate how to use the project. This is your chance to figure out the user experience up front. Many programmers, unfortunately, skip this step and go straight into the implementation. They start fighting with the trickiest bit of code and pile layer after layer on top of it. Slowly, like a weed crawling up a tree in a jungle, they wind their way up and up until at some point, they break through the canopy, and for the first time, expose their code to the sunlight—that is, to real users. Whatever mess happens to be at the edge of this tangle of weeds becomes the user experience. In most cases, this API or UI is completely unusable, but now it's too late to fix it because there are too many branches, roots, offshoots, and code to make a meaningful change. That's why you should start with the user experience first (see Chapter 3). It's often both the hardest part of the project and the one that most determines if the project will be successful.

Quick start guide

You're not done thinking about the user experience yet. After you list a few examples, the next step is the quick start guide, where you explain how to install the project and start using it. This will force you to think about how your project will be packaged, what dependencies it has, what kind of configuration it needs, and how it will work in both development and production environments. Do not put these decisions off until the end. They are an integral part of the experience of using your product and they always take longer to get right than you expect.

One of my favorite examples is to compare the quick start guide for building a simple web app on the Spring Framework versus Node.js. The tutorial for Spring (*http://spring.io/guides/gs/rest-service/*) takes 15 minutes (if you don't make any mistakes) and includes a dozen steps where you create 8 folders and files and write 88 lines of code (yes, I counted) across 2 programming languages. With Node.js (*https://nodejs.org/*), it takes 2 steps and 15 seconds: you copy and paste 6 lines of code from the Node.js home page into a single file on your computer, and run it. Is it a surprise that

Node.js is one of the fastest-growing open source projects of all time? The quick start guide is your first impression. Make sure you get it right.

Project organization

This is the section where you explain the mechanics of working on this project. Where does the code live? How is the code organized? How are tasks and bugs tracked? How do you contribute? What are the legal considerations (license, copyright)? If you want to be able to work on this project with other people, it's essential to figure out these administrative details ahead of time.

Scaling performance

Jackson's rules of program optimization

- *Rule #1: Don't do it.*

- *Rule #2 (for experts only): Don't do it yet.*

—[BENTLEY 1988, 61], MICHAEL A. JACKSON, INDEPENDENT COMPUTING CONSULTANT

Programmers love to obsess about performance, big O notation, and scalability, and to glorify companies that are "web scale" and deal with "big data," but the reality is that for the vast majority of startups, none of these are particularly important problems. Your time is better spent on tools and practices that allow your development team to ship code faster than it is on making your servers run faster. In fact, doing things that don't scale is an important ingredient for success in the early days of a startup (see "Do things that don't scale" on page 139).

It's only after your product has traction that performance might become a bottleneck. In other words, it's a good problem to have. That said, if you're lucky enough to have such a problem, it's an important one to fix: 40% of users abandon a web page if it takes more than three seconds to load [Work 2011], and that number goes up to 57% for online shoppers and 65% for 18- to 24-year-olds [Rheem 2010]. Worst of all, 79% of visitors who had a slow experience on a website probably won't come back [Work 2011].

The basic process for thinking about performance, or software development in general, is make it work, make it right, make it fast.[11] These are sequential steps and you must do them in order. Software that does the wrong thing, even if it does it very efficiently, isn't worth much, so before you can worry about performance, you have to worry about correctness. Only after you've got clean, reliable code should you start thinking about performance tuning. Improving performance is an iterative two-step process:

1. Measure
2. Optimize

MEASURE

Here's a fun test of your Computer Science 101 fundamentals from Bjarne Stroustrup, creator of the C++ programming language [Stroustrup 2012]. I'm going to generate N random integers and you need to insert them into a list that keeps them in sorted order. For example, if I generated the numbers 5, 1, 4, 2, your list would appear as follows:

```
- []            // Initial list
- [5]           // Add 5
- [1 5]         // Add 1
- [1 4 5]       // Add 4
- [1 2 4 5]     // Add 2
```

Now I'm going to generate random indexes between 0 and the length of the list and you need to remove the element at that index from your list. For example, if I generated the indexes 1, 2, 0, 0, your list would look like this:

```
- [1 2 4 5]     // Initial list
- [1 4 5]       // Remove index 1
- [1 4]         // Remove index 2
- [4]           // Remove index 0
- []            // Remove index 0
```

Here's the question: for what values of N is it more efficient to use a linked list versus an array to store this sequence? Take a minute to think about it.

---

11 This saying is usually attributed to Kent Beck, though it's hard to find a definitive source.

Thinking back to Computer Science 101, the obvious answer is that the linked list should be better, especially as N gets larger, because random insertions and deletions in an array can require resizing the whole array, whereas in a linked list, it's a constant time operation to update a couple pointers. Unfortunately, this obvious answer is wrong. If you actually benchmark this code in C++, the array version is several orders of magnitude faster [Coppola 2014]. Now, maybe you're thinking this is because the array can do a constant time index lookup, so it can do a binary search on insertion (O(log N) instead of the linked list's O(N)) and a direct lookup on deletion (O(1) instead of the linked list's O(N)). All right, so let's change the array implementation to do a linear scan on both insertion and deletion so that it's a more apples-to-apples comparison. Now which solution do you think is faster?

Again, the obvious CS 101 answer says that it must be the linked list. And again, the obvious answer is wrong. In virtually all cases, the array implementation is 50–100 times faster than the linked list. The reason is that the linear search dominates both insertion and deletion time, and although it doesn't show up in big O analysis, linear search in an array is much faster than a linked list. Why? Because of cache coherency. All of the elements in an array are contiguous in memory and doing a linear search through them is a predictable access pattern that can be efficiently cached in the CPU's L1 and L2 cache. A linked list, on the other hand, is not a contiguous data structure, and each jump to a next or previous pointer is a random access that is typically a cache miss, so you have to go to main memory, which is about 50–100 times slower. And to make matters worse, the linked list has roughly four times the memory overhead of an array because it needs to store next and previous pointers for each element, so you have to read more data from memory than with an array.

The point of this exercise is not to convince you that you should never use linked lists but to make you realize that without measuring, there is no way to predict the performance of your code. Even with something as simple as list insertion and deletion, your intuition and the big O notation you learned in college will almost certainly lead you astray.

No programmer has ever been able to predict or analyze where performance bottlenecks are without data. No matter where you think it's going, you will be surprised to discover that it is going somewhere else.

—[MCCONNELL 2004, 604], STEVE MCCONNELL, *CODE COMPLETE*

Therefore, the first step of performance tuning is always to measure. You need to instrument your code, using monitoring tools (see "Monitoring" on page 374) as well as performance tools and profilers.[12] Do not make any performance optimizations until you've gathered hard data that identifies the biggest bottlenecks. In most cases, you will find that there are a few hot spots, usually completely unexpected ones, that account for the vast majority of the performance overhead. For example, the most common bottleneck for most startups is not the performance of the programming language, web framework, or any algorithm. Instead, it's I/O, such as remote web service calls or reading data from a hard disk. That's because I/O is several orders of magnitude slower than anything you do in memory or on the CPU, so although it's rarely captured by big O analysis, it tends to dominate performance. These are the sort of bottlenecks you want to find through profiling and where you want to spend all of your time optimizing.

OPTIMIZE

The exact techniques for writing high-performance code or building scalable systems are extremely use-case specific (see *http://www.hello-startup.net/resources/scalability* for a list of reading on scalability patterns for your domain). What I can offer here is a list of the most common high-level strategies used to improve performance and scalability:

Divide and conquer

Divide a problem into many smaller problems and solve the problems across many CPUs or servers so that each one has to do less work. Examples: multiple web servers, replicating or sharding a database, MapReduce.

Caching

Do the work ahead of time and save your results so instead of computing them on-demand, you just retrieve precomputed values from storage. Examples: database caches, denormalized schemas, distributed caches, CDNs, cookies, memoization, dynamic programming algorithms.

Laziness

Avoid doing work by putting it off until it's absolutely necessary. Examples: lazy-loading parts of a web page only when you scroll to it, optimistic locking in a database.

---

12 For a list of performance tools, see this book's website (*http://www.hello-startup.net/resources/scalability*).

Approximate correctness

In many cases, it takes less work to get an answer that is "close enough" than to get one that's exactly correct. Examples: eventual consistency, HyperLogLog, reduced durability guarantees, best-effort messaging.

Asynchrony

Instead of locking or blocking while waiting on the result of a computation, continue to do work and have the computation notify you when it's done. Examples: non-blocking I/O, event loops, lock-free data structures.

Jitter and randomization

Avoid spikes and hot spots by trying to spread the load out evenly. Examples: randomizing cache expiration dates [Solomon 2012], load-balancing algorithms (round robin, priority scheduling), algorithms for key partitioning (e.g., range partitioning, hash partitioning).

Throttling

Reject certain computations so that they don't slow down other ones. Examples: rate-limiting requests on a server or removing slow servers from the request path.

Redundancy

Kick off the same computation more than once and return the one that finishes fastest. Examples: backup or hedged requests in distributed systems [Dean and Barroso 2013], redundant servers in case of failure (e.g., hot-standby for a database).

Co-location

Move things physically closer together to reduce latency. Examples: CDNs, multiple data centers around the world, putting related servers in the same server rack.

Faster hardware

AKA *vertical scaling*. Examples: faster CPU, more RAM, more CPU cache, solid-state hard drives, faster networks, performing computations in RAM instead of on disk or in the CPU cache instead of in RAM.

Faster algorithms

Find an algorithm that allows you to do less work. Examples: binary search instead of linear search, quick sort instead of bubble sort.

Before implementing one of these strategies, you can do some back-of-the-envelope calculations to estimate which one is most likely to give you the best bang for the buck. Of course, you won't know for sure until you actually build and measure it, but building things is expensive and you can save yourself a lot of time by eliminating some obviously bad choices using basic arithmetic. To do that, you need to know the relevant metrics for all of your major systems, such as how long a primary key lookup takes in your database or the roundtrip time of a request in your data center (once again, measuring first is essential!). You can get some ballpark numbers by looking up "Latency Numbers Every Programmer Should Know" (*http://bit.ly/latency-prog*).

For example, let's say you're building a search application. The search index has grown too big to fit in memory on a single server, so you can either keep it on disk or you can partition it across 10 services, each of which can keep one-tenth of the index in memory. Is it faster to look up a query locally from the hard drive or to fan out to 10 services in parallel and have them each look up the query from RAM? Let's assume that to process the typical search query, you have to read 1 MB of data sequentially and use the following numbers in our calculations:

- A main memory reference takes about 100 ns.
- Reading 1 MB sequentially from memory takes about 12,000 ns.
- A random disk seek takes about 4,000,000 ns.
- Reading 1 MB sequentially from disk takes about 2,000,000 ns.
- A round trip in the same data center takes 500,000 ns.

With these numbers, looking up data on the local hard drive will take:

```
Latency = 1 disk seek + read 1 MB
Latency = 4,000,000 ns + 2,000,000 ns
Latency = 6,000,000 ns
```

And fanning out to 10 services in parallel and having them look up the data in memory will take:

```
Latency = 1 data center round-trip + 1 memory reference + read 1 MB
Latency = 500,000 ns + 100 ns + 12,000 ns
Latency = 512,100 ns
```

So it seems like breaking up the code into a bunch of services will be faster. But wait, what about SSD drives? Looking up their numbers, you'll see:

- A random seek in an SSD takes 16,000 ns.
- Reading 1MB sequentially from an SSD takes 200,000 ns.

With an SSD, processing the query locally would take:

```
Latency = 1 SSD seek + read 1 MB
Latency = 16,000 ns + 200,000 ns
Latency = 216,000 ns
```

So upgrading to SSDs is likely to give you the best performance. Of course, SSDs cost money, but if it saves you from having to rewrite all of your code to use remote services, it might be cheaper overall. That's because these days, programmer time is roughly three orders of magnitude more expensive than CPU time [Cook 2014]. In most cases, if you can solve a problem by buying or renting faster hardware, it'll be cheaper than solving the problem by rewriting the code.

Recap

In some respects, coding is like strength training. Strength training novices discover that almost anything they do tends to produce some results. You walk into a gym, do a few bicep curls, and your arms start to get bigger. You run a few miles a day and your waist gets smaller. This works, but only up to a point. After some amount of time, perhaps a year, you hit a wall and all progress seems to stop. You keep lifting, but you're not getting stronger and you keep running, but you're not getting thinner. The only way to make progress at this point is to start using a more advanced routine. You learn that you need to vary the volume of your weightlifting; you learn that you need to eat more protein and get more sleep; you learn that some exercises are more effective than others. The only way to get past a wall is by fundamentally changing the way you train.

It turns out that programing is similar:

> My friend Clift Norris has identified a fundamental constant that I call Norris's number, the average amount of code an untrained programmer can write before he or she hits a wall. Clift estimates this as 1,500 lines. Beyond that the code becomes so tangled that the author cannot debug or modify it without Herculean effort.

—[COOK 2011], JOHN D. COOK, *THE ENDEAVOUR*

In programming, as in lifting, you can do almost anything—copy and paste, use global variables, write no tests and no documentation—and get it to work. For a while. Eventually you hit a wall, and to get past it, you need a more advanced routine, which means following the clean coding principles and practices described in this book. And it doesn't take long to reach this wall: just the scaffolding from generating a brand-new Ruby on Rails app is about 900 lines of code, more than halfway to Norris's number.

In fact, there is more than one such wall. The Norris number represents a wall at around 1,000–2,000 lines of code. To get past it, you may have to start thinking about some of the clean-coding principles in the previous chapter, such as better naming, code layout, loose coupling, and high cohesion. At around 20,000 lines, you might hit another wall:

> I ran into the 20,000-line wall repeatedly in my first job out of college, as did my coworkers (who were all as young as I). At DreamWorks we had 950 programs for animators to use, and a line count showed that the larger ones all hovered around 20,000 to 25,000 lines. Beyond that it was just too much effort to add features.

—[KESTELOOT 2014], LAWRENCE KESTELOOT, *TEAM TEN*

To get past this one, you'll have to start scaling your coding practices, perhaps spending more time doing code reviews, automated testing, refactoring, breaking code up into smaller functions and modules, and controlling side effects. This will carry you a long way until you hit new walls when you reach hundreds of thousands or millions of lines of code:

> It seems like there's a wall at around 3–4M LOC, and really, after 3M LOC, the growth rate seems to slow down significantly no matter how many people (hundreds) or years are involved (decades).

A number of production companies have roughly this amount in pro-prietary code, +/-1M, though that may include lots of dead code. NVIDIA's core driver code base is right at 3M, though they have 1–10M more in ancillary functionality. The game vendors seem to have a bit less, in the 1.5–2M range, though arguably they have many fewer applications.

—[WEXLER 2012], DANIEL WEXLER, FOUNDER OF WEXWORKS

Codebases with hundreds of thousands or millions of lines of code need completely different practices: separate repositories, strictly controlled and backward-compatible APIs, lots of automated tests, thorough documentation, and so on.

So once again, we come back to the fact that startups are about people. Your ability to maintain a codebase is less about the technology you use and more about the inherent limitations of the human mind and psychology. If you are pri-marily writing short-lived programs of less than 2,000 lines and working by yourself, such as during the very early days of a startup where you're mostly building throwaway prototypes, you can probably get away without worrying too much about scalable coding practices. But to write something bigger, with more people, that handles more load, you have to do something fundamentally differ-ent. You have to start paying attention to all the things that help people read and write code, such as naming, code layout, cohesion, coupling, refactoring, tests, code reviews, and documentation. If you do, you'll go faster, and speed wins.

We were in a situation at Peak Strategy where we had a customer visiting the next day. He was supposed to get in at 9 or 9:30 the next morning. He was with a firm that traded commodities and commodity derivatives and it was very high-speed trading. So it was a different kind of trading than we had dealt with before and we needed to be able to demo some things for him that our software was incapable of doing. I don't remember exactly how, but somehow we got our backs to the wall on that.

So, starting early afternoon the day before he was supposed to show up, we were basically three-way pair coding to build out the chunks of the system that were missing for the demo the next day. We were feeling very keen on pure methodology at the time, so we agreed that we would use absolutely pure test-driven development, pair programming, careful refac-toring, and so on. We did that from early afternoon until 7 a.m. the next morning. We got a ridiculously kick-ass amount of output and it was all right as far as I ever knew. I mean, errors in that environment were horrible. For a quant to find a bug in the calculations performed by the tool would just be absolutely horrific. But we made a crazy amount of functional progress without introducing any bugs to speak of and had a flawless demo the next day.

When you start trying to introduce process in a software company, there is a tendency to say, "Well, I can only use good process if I'm not in a hurry. If I'm in a hurry, I just do whatever." I've tended to go back to this story as my example of how a truly good process should be able to accelerate you at every scale. A good process should be able to accelerate you for an hour, a day, or a year.

—[THOMPSON 2014], DEAN THOMPSON, CTO OF NOWAIT

Software Delivery

Done means delivered

Software isn't done when it works on your computer. It's not done when the code is clean and the tests pass. It's not done when someone gives you a "ship it" on your code review. And it's not done when you move the Post-it note into the "feature complete" column. Software is done when you *deliver* it to the user.

Many companies use a manual delivery process. I've talked to startups where developers email bits of code back and forth, manually upload new code to servers through FTP or SSH and configure each server by hand (and only one engineer in the entire company knows the magic incantations to make everything work). As you will see in the first part of this chapter, "Manual delivery: a horror story" on page 351, this ad hoc approach can cause a startup a lot of pain.

> If it hurts, do it more often.

**—[FOWLER 2011], MARTIN FOWLER, PROGRAMMER, AUTHOR,
SPEAKER AT THOUGHTWORKS**

A common theme throughout this chapter is that the best way to reduce the pain of the delivery process is, counterintuitively, to face that pain much more often. To do that, you need to build a delivery process at your startup that handles all the critical steps that come *after* you've written the code. These steps are build, deployment, and monitoring, and in this chapter, I'll show you how to do them in a fast, reliable, and automated manner.

Manual delivery: a horror story

In 2011, LinkedIn had an IPO, a valuation of $10 billion, a growth rate of two members per second, and a delivery process that was so broken that the company nearly ground to a halt. It's a common problem at almost every single hyper-growth company, but few have been brave enough to tell the story. Until now.

We were using a release train model, where every two weeks, a "train" would leave the station with new code destined for production. To get onto the train, you needed to get your code into a release branch. At the time, teams did all of their work in separate feature branches, working in total isolation from all other teams for weeks or months at time. Then three weeks before the scheduled release date, all of these feature branches would come crashing together as dozens of teams would try to merge their changes into the release branch.

The merge process was a nightmare. Developers would find that they had been coding for months on top of assumptions that were no longer true. The class you were using no longer existed; the database schema had changed; the API you used in a several dozen places had been refactored; the UI looked completely different; the JavaScript library you thought you had finally removed from the codebase was now used in ten new places. It would take days to resolve all the conflicts, and when you were done, you'd realize that so much code had changed as part of the merge process that most of the testing you did on your feature branch was worthless.

Not that we did nearly enough testing. We had tests, at least for some of the code, but there were two problems. First, the tests were slow. Really slow. The build process—compiling, running the tests, and packaging—took on the order of 10 hours. Second, the tests were not reliable. Many of them were flaky and would fail intermittently. So after each merge, we'd get roughly one build per day to see if things were working, end up with dozens of test failures, and have no way of knowing if they were due to a bug in a feature branch, a bad merge, or just a test being flaky.

Assuming we were able to stabilize the build, the next challenge was assembling the *deployment plan*, which was a wiki page maintained by hand that listed all the services that needed to be deployed in that release, what order to deploy them, and what configuration they needed. For example, let's say that on your feature branch, you modified service B to add a new endpoint and you modified service A to call that new endpoint. You'd have to remember to add both service A and B to the deployment plan, and to indicate that B must be deployed first, so the new endpoint is available for A. And if you needed to modify service B's configuration, such as increasing its thread-pool size or tweaking garbage collection settings, you'd have to remember to put those into the deployment plan as well, as all configuration was managed manually.

The rest of the deployment was manual, too. The release team would review the wiki step by step, and deploy hundreds of services and configuration changes across thousands of servers, either by hand or with fragile shell scripts. With all this manual intervention, mistakes were guaranteed. Some of the errors were obvious, but others would go unnoticed for hours or days because we had very little monitoring in place. In many cases, we were flying blind, and until a user complained, we wouldn't know something was wrong. And something was always wrong, so releases took many hours and ran late into the night. Some releases took multiple days to finish, and a few had to be canceled partway through because we just could not get the code stabilized.

At the end of 2011, as we approached a point where we could not release code at all, we kicked off Project Inversion to overhaul the release process. When we were done,[1] we were able to deploy multiple times an hour with far fewer bugs, and had a comprehensive monitoring solution to catch any errors that slipped through. How did we make such a dramatic improvement? The first step was to improve the build process.

Build

The build process consists of three pieces: version control, a build tool, and a continuous integration process that puts them together.

VERSION CONTROL

A *version control system (VCS)* lets you track changes to a set of files over time. Even if you've never used a VCS, you've probably scraped together your own system many times. Have you ever emailed a copy of a file to yourself as backup? Do you share documents with coworkers using DropBox? Do you have 15 versions of your résumé sitting on your hard drive (*resume-v1.doc, resume-v2.doc, resume-09-03-14.doc*)? These ad hoc practices might work for a few Word documents or spreadsheets, but they are not a good way to manage software.

If you're working on code, there's no getting around it: a VCS is required. There are no legitimate reasons not to use one. None. Even if you're working on a project alone, even if it's a small project, even if you've worked on it for years without using a VCS, the costs of setting one up are so low and the benefits so high that these days you have no excuses. By storing the full revision history of

---

1 It's actually an incremental, ongoing process that's never truly done, but we saw massive improvements every few months.

each file, a VCS gives you and your team superpowers. If you made a mistake, you can *revert* to the most recent version of any file. If you've found a bug, you can dig through recent *commits* and their *commit messages* to track down the change that caused it. If you're working on multiple features simultaneously, you can put them in separate *branches*. And if you need to collaborate with team-mates, you can build a workflow on top of *commit hooks*, *merging*, and *pull requests*.

The most popular options for version control as of 2015 are SVN and Git.[2] SVN is a *centralized* VCS, where the source of truth is a repository on a central server, and all developers use client software to interact with it, as shown in Figure 8-1. To get a copy of the code, you *checkout* from the central server and if you change some of that code, you *commit* the changes back to the central server.

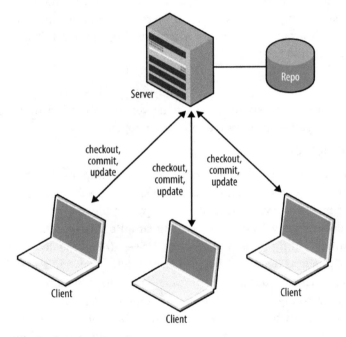

Figure 8-1. Centralized version control

Git is a *distributed* VCS, where everyone has a copy of the repository and can act as both a server and a client, as shown in Figure 8-2. You get a copy of the

---

code by *cloning* someone else's repository, you can *commit* changes to your local repository, you can send your latest commits to others by *pushing* them, and you can get their latest commits by *pulling* them.

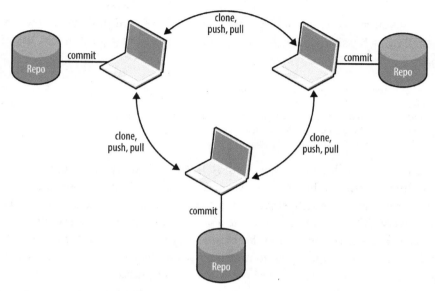

Figure 8-2. Distributed version control

In practice, even with a distributed VCS, one central node is usually treated as the official source of truth and used for all builds and releases. For example, GitHub is the source of truth for most open source projects, and you have to push your commits there for them to be "official."

Should you use a centralized or distributed VCS at your startup? For most companies, Git is probably the best choice, in part because it is distributed, and in part because it is starting to dominate the version control world due to the popularity of GitHub and open source software. That said, any VCS is better than none, so if you prefer some other tool, it's perfectly fine to use it, too. Whichever VCS you choose, there are two best practices you should follow: write good commit messages and commit early and often.

Write good commit messages

Imagine you just deployed a new version of your website to production and you find out that the search feature is broken. To try to figure out the cause, you open up the commit log and browse the changes that went into the latest release:

```
> git log --pretty=oneline --abbrev-commit
e456b8b Maybe this will do it
d98846a Fix another issue
59635e9 Fix stuff
964ce4c Initial commit
```

Can you guess which of these commits broke search? No? Well, how about the following version, which has the same commits but with different descriptions:

```
> git log --pretty=oneline --abbrev-commit
e456b8b Add alt text to all images
d98846a Improve search performance by adding a cache
59635e9 Update logo on homepage
964ce4c Initial commit
```

Now you can clearly see that commit d98846a, "Improve search performance by adding a cache" is the most likely cause of the bug. You can look at the *diff* of that commit to see exactly what changed, which will save you hours of debugging. Every VCS allows you to provide a *commit message* when checking code in. If you use them correctly, they become a critical source of information when tracking down bugs and trying to understand how code changed. That's why you should always take the time to write a good commit message.

A good commit message consists of a summary and a description. The summary is like the title of an essay: it goes all by itself on the first line and it should be short and to the point.[3] After the summary, put a new line, and in paragraph or bullet point format, explain what you changed, why you changed it, and where to find more info (e.g., links to a bug tracker, wiki, or code review) [Thompson 2013]. Here's an example:

```
Improve search performance by adding a cache

To improve the latency of our search page, we are now using
memcached to cache search results for a configurable
amount of time (default is 10 minutes). Results from
memcached come back in 1ms instead of the 100ms it takes
to hit the search cluster.

- Full design: http://wiki.mycompany.com/search-caching
```

---

3 Usually, the summary should be less than 50 characters so that it shows up nicely in tooling, such as in the git log command.

```
- JIRA ticket: http://jira.mycompany.com/12345
- Code review: http://reviewboard.mycompany.com/67890
```

Commit early and often

If you don't commit for a long time and something goes wrong, your VCS can't help you. Therefore, you should commit early and often. That way, if a problem pops up, the commits are like checkpoints that make it easier to track down the cause, and if necessary, revert back a few steps. Aim for each commit to be a *reasonably sized unit* that *fully implements* a *single purpose*. Let's break this sentence down.

Single purpose means you shouldn't fix two bugs in one commit, implement two features in one commit, or refactor existing code and implement new code in one commit. *Fully implements* means you shouldn't commit code that breaks the build or allows a user to see an unfinished feature. *Reasonably sized* means you should break your work up into small, incremental steps. Not coincidentally, this also happens to be the secret to successful test-driven development, refactoring, and code reviewing (see Chapter 7). For example, if you're working on a feature that takes several days to implement, you might break it into three commits. One commit could add failing test cases (marked as ignore, initially, so the build doesn't fail), another commit could refactor existing code to make it easy to implement the new feature, and then a final commit implements the actual feature. See "Branch by abstraction" on page 361 and "Feature toggles" on page 363 for more information on how to break up large features into small, safe commits.

BUILD TOOL

Every codebase needs a build tool to compile it, run tests, and package the code for production. There are many open source build tools available. Which one you use depends on the type of code you're trying to compile. For example, if you're working with Ruby, you'll probably want to use Rake. If you're working with Scala, you'll probably want to use SBT. If you're working with many different programming languages, Gradle may be your best bet. And if you're compiling static content, Grunt.js and Gulp have a huge number of plug-ins to take care of all the common tasks, such as concatenating or minifying CSS and JavaScript, and preprocessing CoffeeScript, Sass, and Less.

Most build systems can also help you manage dependencies. If your code depends on a third party or open source library, you should not just copy and paste that dependency's code directly into your project. If you do, you'll also have to copy/paste the entire tree of transitive dependencies. For example, if you depend on library A, and A depends on B and C, and C depends on D, E, and F, you'll have to copy the code for all of those libraries into your project. And when you go to upgrade to a new version of library A, you might discover that it is using new versions of B and C, and it has added a new dependency G, and now you have to upgrade all of those dependency trees as well.

This quickly becomes unmanageable, so most build systems allow you to specify your top-level dependencies, and they will take care of the transitive dependencies for you. For example, here is how you can specify your dependencies in Gradle:

```
dependencies {
  compile group: 'commons-io', name: 'commons-io', version: '2.4'
  testCompile group: 'junit', name: 'junit', version: '4.+'
}

repositories {
  mavenCentral()
}
```

This tells Gradle that you need the commons-io library at version 2.4 to compile your code, the junit library at version 4.0 or greater to compile the test code, and that Gradle can find these libraries in the Maven Central repository (*http://search.maven.org/*). When you compile or run your code, Gradle will automatically download these libraries, plus all their transitive dependencies, and include them on your classpath.

CONTINUOUS INTEGRATION

Imagine you're responsible for building the International Space Station (ISS), which consists of dozens of components, as shown in Figure 8-3.

ISS Configuration
As of May 2011 (ULF6 - STS-134)

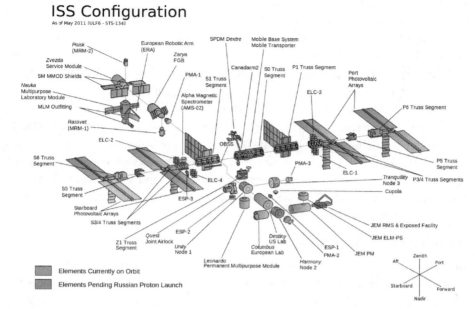

Figure 8-3. International Space Station [ISS Configuration 2011]

A separate team will build each component and it's up to you to decide how you will organize them. You have two options:

1. Come up with a design for all the components up front and then have each team go off and work on their component in isolation until it's finished. When all the teams are done, launch all the components into outer space, and try to put them together at the same time.

2. Come up with an initial design for all the components and then have each team go off and start working. As they make progress, they continuously test each component with all the other components and update the design if there are any problems. As components are completed, you launch them one at a time into outer space, and assemble them incrementally.

With option #1, attempting to assemble the entire ISS at the last minute will expose a vast number of conflicts and design problems. Team A thought team B would handle the wiring while team B thought team A would do it; all the teams used the metric system, except one; no one remembered to install a toilet.

Unfortunately, as everything has been fully built and is already floating in outer space, it will be expensive and difficult to go back and fix things. Clearly, this option will be a disaster, but this is exactly the way in which many companies build software. Developers work in total isolation for weeks or months at a time and then try to merge all their work together at the very last minute. This process is known as *late integration*, and as you saw in the LinkedIn story at the beginning of the chapter, it often leads to disaster.

A better approach, as described in option #2, is *continuous integration*, where all developers merge their work together on a very regular basis (e.g., daily or multiple times per day). This exposes problems with the design earlier in the process before you've gone too far in the wrong direction, and allows you to improve the design incrementally. The most common way to implement continuous integration is to use a *trunk-based development model*.

Trunk-based development

In a trunk-based development model, developers do all of their work on the same branch—typically `trunk`, `HEAD`, or `master`, depending on what your VCS calls it. There are no feature branches.[4] It may seem like having all developers work on a single branch couldn't possibly scale, but the reality is that it might be the only way to scale. LinkedIn moved off of feature branches and onto trunk-based development as part of Project Inversion, which was essential for scaling from roughly 100 developers to over 500. Facebook uses trunk-based development for well over 1,000 developers [Rossi 2011]. Google has been using it for many years, showing that trunk-based development can support 15,000+ developers, 4000+ projects, and 20–60 commits per minute [Micco 2012].

How can thousands of developers frequently check into the same branch without conflicts? It turns out that if you make small, frequent commits instead of huge monolithic ones, the number of conflicts is fairly small and those that do happen are desirable. That's because you'll have to deal with conflicts no matter what integration strategy you use, and it's easier to deal with a conflict representing one or two days of work (with continuous integration), rather than a conflict representing months of work (with late integration).

---

4 That is, you do not use feature branches to share code between developers. A developer can still use branches in their local environment to work on multiple features simultaneously, but when they are ready to share those changes with others, they always push them back to trunk.

Trunk-based development makes conflicts less of a problem, but what about stability? If all developers are working on the same branch, and one developer checks in code that doesn't compile or causes serious bugs, it could block all development. To prevent this, you must have a self-testing build. A *self-testing build* is a fully automated build process (i.e., you can run it with a single command) that has enough automated tests so that, if they all pass, you can be confident the code is stable (see "Automated Tests" on page 296). The usual approach is to add a commit hook to your VCS that takes each commit, runs it through the build on a continuous-integration (CI) server such as Jenkins or Travis, and rejects the commit if the build fails.[5] The CI server is your gate keeper, validating every check-in before allowing it into trunk.

> *Without continuous integration, your software is broken until somebody proves it works, usually during a testing or integration stage. With continuous integration, your software is proven to work (assuming a sufficiently comprehensive set of automated tests) with every new change—and you know the moment it breaks and can fix it immediately.*
>
> **—[HUMBLE AND FARLEY 2010, 56], JEZ HUMBLE AND DAVID FARLEY,**
> *CONTINUOUS DELIVERY*

Continuous integration is great for small, frequent commits, but how do you handle a large change? If you're working on something that will take weeks or months, how can you commit your incomplete work on a daily basis without breaking the build or accidentally releasing unfinished features to users? The answer is to use *branch by abstraction* and *feature toggles*.

Branch by abstraction

The easiest way to explain *branch by abstraction* [Hammant 2007] is with an example. Let's say you are using the Redis key-value store in your Java application and that you're accessing it using the Jedis client library:

```
Jedis jedis = new Jedis("localhost");
String value = jedis.get("foo");
```

---

5 As a nice optimization, you could run the build while waiting for a code review so by the time a reviewer takes a look, you usually know if the check-in causes any problems.

You want to replace Redis with the Voldemort key-value store, but you're using the Jedis library in thousands of places throughout your codebase. One option is to create a feature branch so you can spend several weeks in isolation changing all the clients to use the Voldemort library, and then hope you can safely merge it back in. A better option is to achieve the same isolation by using abstractions in your code. For example, you start by defining a simple interface for a key-value store:

```
public interface KeyValueStore {
  String get(String key);
}
```

You then create an implementation of this interface that uses Jedis under the hood:

```
public class JedisKeyValueStore implements KeyValueStore {
  private final Jedis jedis = new Jedis("localhost");

  @Override
  public String get(String key) {
    return jedis.get(key);
  }
}
```

You can build and test this new class directly in trunk, and because no one is using it, it's easy to do this across several small commits without breaking the build. Once the class is ready, you can begin migrating all code that uses the Jedis client to use your abstraction:

```
KeyValueStore store = new JedisKeyValueStore();
String value = store.get("foo");
```

Because this change does not affect any external behavior, you can change the clients incrementally, across many small check-ins. In the meantime, you can also implement and test a new implementation of the KeyValueStore abstraction that uses Voldemort under the hood:

```
public class VoldemortKeyValueStore implements KeyValueStore {
  private final StoreClient<String, String> client =
    new SocketStoreClientFactory(
      new ClientConfig().setBootstrapUrls("tcp://localhost:6666")
    ).getStoreClient("my_store_name");

  @Override
  public String get(String key) {
```

```
    return client.getValue(key);
  }
}
```

Again, because no one is using this implementation, you can build and test it directly in trunk, across many small check-ins. When it's ready, and all clients have been moved to the abstraction, you can begin moving them to use the new Voldemort implementation:

```
KeyValueStore store = new VoldemortKeyValueStore();
String value = store.get("foo");
```

Once again, you can do this change incrementally, in trunk. In fact, it may be a good idea to test one use case at a time with the new key-value store and look for bugs before you move the entire product over. Eventually, you'll have all the clients migrated, and you can safely remove the Jedis abstraction from the codebase.

It's worth noting that branch by abstraction is really just the dependency inversion principle in practice (see "Loose coupling" on page 279), so it's not only a way to perform a major refactor without feature branches, but in many cases also leads to cleaner code.

Feature toggles

The idea behind a feature toggle is that unfinished or risky code should be disabled by default, and that you have an easy way to enable it when it's ready [Fowler 2010]. This approach allows you to break up large features into small, incremental pieces and check in each one as soon as it's stable as opposed to completely finished. For example, while you're building a large new module for the home page of your website, you could wrap that module in an if statement:

```
private static final String NEW_HOMEPAGE_MODULE_TOGGLE_KEY =
  "showNewHomepageModule";

if (featureToggles.isEnabled(NEW_HOMEPAGE_MODULE_TOGGLE_KEY)) {
  // Show the module on the home page
} else {
  // Don't show the new module
}
```

In the code snippet above, featureToggles is a class that looks up keys, such as showNewHomepageModule, either in your application's configuration or from a remote service (e.g., key-value store). The default state for all feature toggles is off, so as long as the code compiles and passes existing tests, you can commit the code for the new module to trunk before it's done and no user will see it. When you do finish the feature, you can enable the feature in configuration or a remote service.

At LinkedIn, the remote service we used for feature toggles was called XLNT, which had a web UI that let us dynamically decide which members could see which features. For example, for the showNewHomepageModule key, we could decide to make it visible to only LinkedIn employees, or only to French-speaking members, or only to 1% of members in the United States, as shown in Figure 8-4.

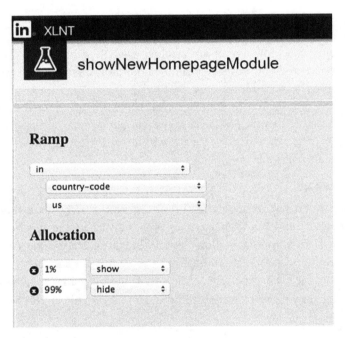

Figure 8-4. XLNT web UI

XLNT allowed us to not only have a feature be on or off but to gradually ramp the feature from completely off to 1% of members, then 10%, and finally 100%. At each step, if we found any bugs or performance problems, we could quickly ramp the feature back down.

Of course, you shouldn't wrap everything in a feature toggle.[6] Feature toggles are about managing risk, so if the risk is low, the extra complexity of if statements scattered throughout the code may not be worth it. If you do use a feature toggle, you have to be disciplined about cleaning it up once the feature has been enabled, or your codebase will be littered with branches of code that are no longer executed. At the minimum, put a TODO above each feature toggle as a reminder:[7]

```
// TODO: remove this feature toggle after the ramp on 09/01/14.
// See http://mycompany.wiki.com/new-homepage-module for more info.
private static final String NEW_HOMEPAGE_MODULE_TOGGLE_KEY =
  "showNewHomepageModule";
```

Deployment

The build system gives you a a reliable way to take your code, test it, and package it. To deploy this package to production, you need to ask four questions:

- Where are you going to deploy?
- What are you going to deploy?
- How are you going to deploy?
- When are you going to deploy?

The answers to these four questions are, respectively, hosting, configuration management, deployment automation, and continuous delivery.

HOSTING

Every startup needs to decide between *self-hosting* and *cloud hosting*. If you go with self-hosting, then you deploy your code on top of hardware that you own and manage, either in your own data center or in racks you rent in someone else's data center (known as *co-location*). If you go with cloud hosting, then you deploy

---

6 Actually, there are some things you can't easily wrap in feature toggles even if you wanted to, such as database schema changes.

7 There are TODO libraries for Ruby (*https://github.com/leanovate/doby*) and Scala (*https://github.com/andyw8/do_by*) that allow you to specify a TODO with an expiration date. When the date passes, the TODO will cause your build to fail.

your code onto virtualized servers that run on top of hardware owned and managed by a third party.

Just as most startups should use open source software instead of building their own infrastructure (see "Build in-house, buy commercial, or use open source?" on page 193), most startups, especially in the early days, should also use cloud hosting instead of building their own data center. It takes a lot of time and up-front costs to purchase and set up the hardware, and costs even more to do this in a way that is reliable and redundant, and to maintain it over time. Most startups just do not have the time or money to develop dedicated in-house expertise in hardware, power, cooling, networking, and security. For example, less than 25% of the 2011 and 2012 Y Combinator Startups were self-hosted.[8]

A cloud-hosted option from a popular provider like Amazon, Rackspace, DigitalOcean, or SoftLayer gives you much more flexibility, as you can provision servers in seconds (e.g., in response to an increase in traffic) rather than the weeks it takes to order and install your own hardware. These services have large communities around them, which means it's easy to find documentation, learn best practices, take advantage of open source plug-ins and extensions, and hire developers who know how to use them. Most of the services come with their own extensions, too, such as managed databases, load balancers, queues, and tools for security, deployment, monitoring, and analytics. In many cases, cloud hosting is also the cheapest option because instead of paying for lots of hardware up-front, you pay based on usage with the cost growing only if your company grows and becomes more successful.

The only reason to go with self-hosting is if your application has extremely high performance requirements. Most cloud-hosting providers give you virtualized servers that run on top of shared hardware. The overhead of virtualization and the need to compete with other users for resources means that applications that need maximum CPU or hard drive performance from each server might need to run their own dedicated hardware. Moreover, many cloud providers charge a premium for data storage and bandwidth, so startups dealing with large volumes of pictures, music, or videos might find cloud hosting prohibitively expensive.

---

8 For the stats, see "Chart of Y Combinator Companies' Hosting Decisions" [Franusic 2013] and [Lalonde 2012].

CONFIGURATION MANAGEMENT

Once you've figured out where to deploy your code, you need to figure out what to deploy. Although most developers only think of their application code, this is only the last item in a long list of what you have to install on each server. You usually need an operating system (e.g., Ubuntu Trusty 14.04), the programming language (e.g., Python 2.7), a monitoring agent (e.g., New Relic System Monitor 5.1.93), a configuration agent (e.g., Chef client 12.0.0), a process supervisor (e.g., Monit 5.10), web server software (e.g., Apache 2.4.10), version control software (e.g., Git 2.0.1), security software (e.g., Snort 2.9.7.0), logging software (e.g., logstash 1.4.2), SSL certificates, passwords, and SSH keys, and only after all that do you install the application code.

You have to get each piece of software just right, including the right version, or your applications could fail. Your company may have hundreds or even thousands of servers, and the configuration on each one may be different depending on the type of software you're running on it (e.g., application, database, queue, load balancer). Installing and maintaining all of this by hand is time consuming and error prone. Doing it with custom shell scripts is a little better, but still messy. The best option is to use a documented, battle-tested, and preferably open source *configuration management system*.

Configuration management can be used to describe several different kinds of systems, including application configuration, virtual machines, containers, and orchestration tools.

Application configuration

Most applications expose knobs and levers you can tweak without changing the application code, such as log settings, memory settings, and port numbers. You can usually specify different configurations in different environments (i.e., development, staging, production). For example, in Ruby on Rails, settings that apply to all environments go into *config/application.rb*:

```
config.i18n.default_locale = :en
config.assets.compress = false
```

If you want to change some of the settings in production, you can put the overrides into *config/environments/production.rb*:

```
config.assets.compress = true
```

Although it's important to be able to tweak settings in one place without touching the code and even to share settings between applications, it's possible to have too much flexibility. For example, LinkedIn's services exposed on the order of 10,000 different configuration parameters, each of which could have different values across different environments. The sheer number of settings and their non-trivial interactions led to configuration bugs on a regular basis.

In our experience, it is an enduring myth that configuration information is somehow less risky to change than source code.

—[HUMBLE AND FARLEY 2010, 40], JEZ HUMBLE AND DAVID FARLEY,
CONTINUOUS DELIVERY

Treat configuration data the same way you treat code: store it in files, put it under version control, and review and test all changes.

Virtual machines

A *virtual machine (VM)* image is like a snapshot of a fully running system that has all the software you need already installed. You run a VM image inside of a *hypervisor*, such as VMWare, VirtualBox, or Parallels, which abstracts away the underlying hardware. That way, the software running inside the VM image always sees the exact same environment, no matter what server it's on. This means you can define a VM image in your development environment that has all the software you need, and that image will run exactly the same way in the production environment, reducing the chances of "it works on my machine"–style bugs. Unfortunately, VM images are heavyweight, as running an entire operating system on virtualized hardware incurs an overhead in boot-up time and CPU and memory usage.

Containers

A *container* is like a VM in that you can define a container image that has all the software you need already installed, and that image will run exactly the same way in all environments, including development and production. However, unlike a VM, a container is very lightweight. It runs directly on the existing operating system but is able to keep its own processes, networking, and filesystem completely isolated from the underlying environment. Therefore, container images boot up quickly and have minimal CPU and memory overhead.

The most popular container tool is Docker, which lets you boot up an isolated Linux image in a fraction of a second. Docker makes it easy to run the exact same image in development and production, and because the images are so lightweight, you can run many of them—one for a database, one for an app server—on the same machine. The downside is that container technologies are tied to a specific operating system. For example, Docker only runs on Linux, as the process, filesystem, and networking isolation features are built on top of LxC (LinuX Containers) and Linux cgroups.[9]

Orchestration tools

Orchestration tools are general-purpose automation tools that let you define how to configure a server. Popular options include Chef, Puppet, Salt, and Ansible. To use these tools, you define all the servers you want to manage, either manually or through a service discovery mechanism, and write scripts or recipes for how each server should be configured. For example, with Ansible, you can define your servers in */etc/ansible/hosts*:

```
[webservers]
foo.example.com
bar.example.com

[dbservers]
one.example.com
two.example.com
three.example.com
```

You can then define a number of server *roles*, which are YAML files that list the tasks needed to configure a server to perform that role. For example, here is a webserver.yml role that specifies the configuration needed for the web servers:

```
- name: Install httpd and php
  yum: name={{ item }} state=present
  with_items:
    - httpd
    - php

- name: start httpd
  service: name=httpd state=started enabled=yes

- name: Copy the code from repository
  git: repo={{ repository }} dest=/var/www/html/
```

---

9 While developing, you can run Docker on OS X and Windows by using a virtual machine. There is even a lightweight Linux distribution that is specifically built for running Docker called boot2docker (*http:// boot2docker.io/*) which can boot up in just a few seconds and only uses 25MB of RAM.

Finally, you can create an executable `playbook` that tells Ansible to apply the `webserver` roles to the hosts you labeled as web servers in */etc/ansible/hosts*:

```
- hosts: webservers
  roles:
  - common
  - webserver
```

Popular, open source orchestration tools like Ansible come with large libraries of helpers that take care of common configuration management tasks in a single line of code, such as installing software, copying code, and providing environment-specific configurations. The result is that you can *treat infrastructure as code*. That is, your servers are defined by human-readable text files that you can store in version control, code review, share, and test.

Deployment automation

Simply defining what software should be on your servers is not enough. You also need to define how to get it there. For example, the typical steps to upgrade a single app server include notifying the monitoring system (e.g., Nagios) that the service is about to go down, removing the service from the load balancer's (e.g., HAProxy) rotation, installing and launching the new code onto the server, putting it back into the load balancer rotation, and notifying the monitoring system that it's up and running again. You'll need to run this upgrade on every one of your app servers, most likely in a rolling fashion. For example, if you have 20 app servers total, you might upgrade five at a time, while the other 15 keep running and serving live traffic.

Deploying many different kinds of code across many different kinds of servers can get complicated, so, as usual, you should never do it manually. The deployment process, like the build process, should be automated so that you can run it with a single command. This is essential not only for building a scalable deployment process but also one that is repeatable, testable, and high quality.

You can write custom shell scripts to manage automation, but it's a better idea to use an open source, battle-tested, well-documented library instead. The best options are the orchestration tools you saw earlier, including Chef, Puppet, Salt, and Ansible. For example, you saw in the previous section how to create and apply roles in Ansible using a playbook. Here is how you can extend the playbook to implement a rolling upgrade:

```
- hosts: webservers
  user: root
```

```
serial: 5

pre_tasks:
- name: disable nagios alerts for this host webserver service
  nagios:
    action: disable_alerts
    host: {{ inventory_hostname }}
    services: webserver
  delegate_to: "{{ item }}"
  with_items: groups.monitoring

- name: disable the server in haproxy
  shell: disableServer.sh myapplb/{{ inventory_hostname }}
  delegate_to: "{{ item }}"
  with_items: groups.lbservers

roles:
- common
- webserver

post_tasks:
- name: Wait for webserver to come up
  wait_for:
    host: {{ inventory_hostname }}
    port: 80
    state: started
    timeout: 80

- name: Enable the server in haproxy
  shell: enableServer.sh myapplb/{{ inventory_hostname }}
  delegate_to: "{{ item }}"
  with_items: groups.lbservers

- name: re-enable nagios alerts
  nagios:
    action: enable_alerts
    host: {{ inventory_hostname }}
    services: webserver
  delegate_to: "{{ item }}"
  with_items: groups.monitoring
```

The `serial: 5` command tells Ansible to do a rolling upgrade, applying these changes to five servers at a time. The `pre_tasks` specify tasks to run before applying any roles, so you can use them to disable Nagios and HAProxy, and the `post_tasks` specify tasks to run after, so you can use them to re-enable Nagios and HAProxy. Once again, this approach allows you to treat your infrastructure as code.

CONTINUOUS DELIVERY

Now that you understand where to deploy (hosting), what to deploy (configuration management), and how to deploy it (deployment automation), the last question is when do you deploy? The answer is: whenever you want.

Continuous delivery is a software development discipline where you build software so that it can be released to production at any time [Humble and Farley 2010]. You could release daily, several times a day, or even after every single check-in that passes the automated tests (this is known as *continuous deployment*). Continuous integration gets developers to write their code so they can merge it frequently and stay in sync with one another; continuous delivery gets developers to write their code so it can be deployed frequently and stay in sync with production.

> *Any gap between what is on a programmer's desk and what is in production is a risk. A programmer out of sync with the deployed software risks making decisions without getting accurate feedback about those decisions.*
>
> **—[BECK AND ANDRES 2004, 68], KENT BECK AND CYNTHIA ANDRES,**
> ***EXTREME PROGRAMMING EXPLAINED***

If you're used to an error-prone, manual, slow deployment process, doing it many times a day might sound painful. But as with everything else in this chapter, if it hurts, that means you need to do it more often. However, to make continuous delivery safe and practical, you first must be able to support *rollback* and *backward compatibility*.

Rollback

Even if you have many automated tests and wrap new functionality in feature toggles, bugs will still slip through. One way to deal with bugs in production is a *rollback*: that is, you deploy an older version of the code. The alternative to a rollback is to roll forward by trying to quickly release a new version of the code with a hot fix. This is risky. A rollback takes a few minutes, whereas a bug fix may take much longer, and there is no guarantee the new code will really fix the bug and not introduce new bugs. With continuous delivery, a rollback is usually a better option because it will fix the issue immediately, and if you do come up with a fix, it won't take long to deploy it.

You can make deployments and rollbacks even safer by following a *canary deployment* model. When deploying a new version of your code, you first deploy it to just a single server, called the canary. All the other servers continue to run the old code. You can then compare the canary server with an old server (as a baseline) to see if there are any bugs or performance problems. For example, at LinkedIn, we had a tool called EKG that could compare a canary and a baseline server and automatically highlight any differences in CPU usage, memory usage, latency, errors, and other metrics, as shown in Figure 8-5.

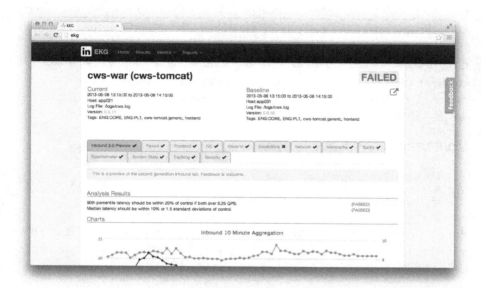

Figure 8-5. Using EKG to compare a canary and control server

If there are any issues with a canary, they only affect a small percentage of users, and you can fix them by rolling back just a single server. If everything looks OK, after a few minutes you can deploy the new version of the code to all the other servers.

Backward compatibility

Backward compatibility is almost always a requirement of distributed systems, but it becomes especially important with continuous delivery, where services may get deployed or rolled back at any time and in any order. There are two general rules for backward compatibility:

1. As a service, you cannot *delete* anything in your public API without a feature toggle.

2. As a client, you cannot *depend* on anything new in a public API without a feature toggle.

For example, if you are working on a service and your public API is RESTful and returns JSON, rule #1 means that adding new things, such as a new URL or new query string parameters, is usually safe, but you cannot delete or change a URL, rename any of the query string parameters, rename any of the fields in the JSON, or change any of the types in those fields. The only way to remove something from a public API is to wrap the removal in a feature toggle and only enable it after usage goes to zero. For a client, rule #2 means that any call to a new API in another service must be wrapped in a feature toggle, and only enabled after the new API has been deployed.

Monitoring

If you can't measure it, you can't fix it.

—DAVID HENKE, SVP ENGINEERING/OPERATIONS AT LINKEDIN

Building your code and deploying it into production is not enough. You also have to make sure it continues working after it gets there. This is where monitoring comes in. By monitoring, I mean all the tools and technologies you use to gain visibility into what your code and users are actually doing, such as logfiles, Google Analytics, and Nagios. In some ways, monitoring is the ying to the unit testing yang.

Usually, testing checks a very strong notion of correctness on a few cases, and monitoring checks a very weak notion of correctness under the real production load.

—[KREPS 2014], JAY KREPS, CO-FOUNDER OF CONFLUENT

Like unit testing, adding monitoring to your code helps you not only identify bugs but also design flaws. Code that's hard to monitor is usually also code that's hard to read, maintain, and test. Therefore, you should build an infrastructure where instrumenting your code is as easy and commonplace as writing a unit test. Unfortunately, setting up monitoring can be difficult, as the monitoring space is fragmented.

At the time of writing this book, there are hundreds of open source and commercial monitoring products, but none of them offer a comprehensive solution. The dominant player is Nagios, which was originally created in 1999—and has a UI to match. Around 2011, the #monitoringsucks hashtag appeared on Twitter and was soon joined by a GitHub repository (*https://github.com/monitoringsucks*) of tools, metrics, blog posts, and complaints to help people vent about, and hopefully solve, the monitoring problem. This is not to knock Nagios, as it does a lot of things very well, but just to provide a warning that setting up a comprehensive monitoring solution is still a surprisingly complicated task.

In this section, I'll discuss the many different aspects of monitoring, including logging, metrics, and alerting.

LOGGING

```
// How real programmers debug
println("************************** here")
```

When there is a problem on your servers, the logfile is usually the first to know. Logging is the most basic, ubiquitous, and well-understood form of monitoring. Just about every programming language has a logging library, such as log4j for Java, and, despite the joke from before, you should always use a real logging library instead of `println`. The important things to know about logging are log names, levels, formats, and aggregation.

Log names

Most logging frameworks give you the flexibility to give names to your loggers and configure each logger separately. For example, when using log4j, you specify the logger name when calling `LogManager.get`:

```
public class CheckoutPage {
  private final Logger logger = LogManager.get(this.getClass());

  public void loggingExample() {
    logger.info("Hello World");
  }
}
```

Notice that I used the class as the name (this.getClass). This is a good practice to follow so that the fully qualified class name appears in every log message, making it easy to figure out where that message came from:

```
2012-11-02 14:34:02,781 INFO [com.mycompany.CheckoutPage] - Hello World
```

You can provide custom configurations for each named logger, such as writing the log output to different files:

```
log4j.appender.com.mycompany.CheckoutPage.file.File=/logs/checkout.log
log4j.appender.com.mycompany.HomePage.file.File=/logs/home.log
```

With this configuration, when debugging an issue on the checkout page, you can look at its log messages in *checkout.log* without being distracted by any log messages from the home page.

Log levels

Most logging libraries support different log levels, such as these ones from log4j: FATAL, ERROR, WARN, INFO, DEBUG, TRACE. These are in order from most to least important. For example, FATAL is used for severe problems that need immediate attention:

```
logger.fatal("The program crashed!");
```

On the other end of the spectrum is TRACE, which is typically only used for low-level diagnostics during development. For example, here is a better way of doing the println("******** here") message:

```
logger.trace("Entering method foo");
```

You can set each logger in your application to a different log level:

```
log4j.logger.com.mycompany.CheckoutPage=ERROR
log4j.logger.com.mycompany.HomePage=TRACE
```

In the preceding configuration, setting the CheckoutPage logger to ERROR means that only messages with that level or above—that is, ERROR and FATAL—will show up in its logs, and all other levels will be omitted. Logfiles can get huge, especially for servers handling hundreds of requests per second (which can translate to thousands of log entries per second). Limiting the log entries to ERROR and above ensures that during normal operation the logfile will only contain information that most likely indicates a problem (e.g., the stack trace for an unexpected exception), which decreases the odds that you miss critical problems because they are drowned out by less important log entries. Once you do identify a specific problem, you can use a more permissive log level for the relevant subsystem (e.g., in this case I set the HomePage logger to TRACE), which will give you more logging information when debugging.

Log formatting

Logfiles have two audiences: developers and tools. That means the logfile format must be both human readable and friendly to tools such as grep. Most logging systems allow you to specify a *pattern* that will be applied to each log message so you don't have to do it manually. For example, here is a pattern for log4j:

```
%d %p [%c] - %m%n
```

This pattern tells the logger to include with each message the date, log level, thread name, logger name, a dash, the log message, and a newline. So the following log message:

```
logger.info("Hello");
```

Will show up as follows in the log:

```
2012-11-02 14:34:02,781 INFO [com.mycompany.CheckoutPage] - Hello
```

Here are some best practices for formatting log messages:

Include a timestamp

> Timestamps are essential to figuring out when things happened (five seconds ago or five days ago?) and the order in which things happened (which is especially useful for debugging concurrency bugs). You should include as much granularity in the timestamp as possible, from the year all the way down to the nanosecond.

Include a unique id

> A unique id, such as a GUID, makes it possible to tie multiple related messages together. For example, in a web server, there is typically a unique id for each request, so if it is in every log message, you can easily filter the log for everything that happened while processing a single request.

Make the text developer friendly

    Use simple, concise English, avoid abbreviations, and provide enough context for each message so you can understand it without looking at the code. For example, compare the following log message:

```
2012-11-02 14:34:02,781 - 12345; 200; chkt;
```

To this one:

```
2012-11-02 14:34:02,781 - userid=12345; status=200; url=/checkout
```

Which one would you rather see while debugging?

Make the text grep friendly

    Most developers use tools like grep to search through logfiles. That means that almost all log messages should be on a single line and make use of delimiters that are easy to parse, such as `key=value` pairs.

Log the full stack trace

    The only exception to the "single line" rule is for stack traces. If some part of your code throws an exception, log the entire stack trace—it will span many lines, but it contains crucial debugging information that's necessary to understand where the problem originated.

Log aggregation

Writing log messages to a file is simple and useful, but it has two limitations. The first limitation is size: if you keep writing to the same file, it will eventually become too large to be useful or you might even run out of disk space and crash your server. Most logging systems allow you to configure *log rotation*, where the logger can create a new file each time the existing one gets past a certain size (e.g., *checkout.log* will be renamed to *checkout-page-09-01-2014.log* once it grows past 10 MB and a new *checkout.log* will be created) and delete logfiles older than a configurable amount of time (e.g., delete logfiles older than two weeks). The second limitation is accessibility. If you have a single server, SSHing to it to read the logfile is not a problem. But when you have dozens or hundreds of servers, it can be very difficult to make sense of the logs on all of them.

    To solve the accessibility problem, there are a number of tools, such as syslog, logstash, and flume, that can help you aggregate your logs from all servers and organize the information in a useful manner, such as loading it into Hadoop or a search index. There are also companies such as Splunk, Sumo Logic, logstash, and Papertrail, which provide log management as a service. For example, Loggly automatically aggregates logs from all your servers and provides a web UI where you can quickly search through all logfiles and create dashboards with logging statistics and graphs.

METRICS

After logging, the next step in monitoring is to gather metrics. There are many different kinds of metrics[10] you can collect and different tools and services for each one, so I'll break it down by level of detail: availability, business, application, process, code, server.[11]

Availability level

Availability is the most basic metric that every company should measure. Can a user access your product or not? This is a "yes" or "no" question. Perhaps a web server is down, a load balancer isn't working, there is a bug in your mobile app, or your site is just too slow because of an overloaded database. From the user's perspective, it doesn't matter because either everything is working or nothing is.

To monitor your product's availability, you need real-world test cases that run against the interface used by your customers, which, depending on the product, could be a website, mobile app, or API endpoint. You can set up your own service to monitor availability, though the same problems that take down your product (e.g., load balancer issues or a data center outage) could also break your availability monitoring. Third-party services such as Keynote and Pingdom might be a better choice, as they specialize in monitoring availability and can monitor uptime from a variety of locations around the world.

Business level

Business metrics are a measure of what your users are doing, such as page views, ad impressions, sales, installs, or any other metrics that are important to your business. These are the metrics that the CEO and the product team look at, so if the numbers suddenly drop, you'll want to know as soon as possible. There are many tools to track business metrics, such as Google Analytics, KissMetrics, MixPanel, and Hummingbird.

---

10 See metrics-catalog on GitHub (*http://bit.ly/metrics-cat*) for a good catalog of metrics broken down by service/protocol type.

11 This level-by-level breakdown is based on "The Virtues of Monitoring" [Meyer 2011].

Application level

Underneath the business metrics is your application code. For client applications, such as a website or a mobile app, you'll want to use real user monitoring (RUM) tools such as Google Analytics, Keynote, New Relic, and boomerang to track payload size, load times, errors, and crashes. For server applications, such as web servers, databases, caches, queues, and load balancers, you can use tools like New Relic and AppDynamics to track QPS, response times, throughput, request and response sizes, URLs hit, response codes, and error counts. This is also the level where you do logging.

Process level

Every application consists of one or more processes that need to be running. Unfortunately, processes crash and servers reboot, so you need to do some extra work to make sure something restarts those processes. There are a number of tools called *supervisors* that you can use to monitor a process and restart it, including Monit, God, Upstart, supervisord, runit, and bluepill.

Code level

Below an application is the code you wrote. There are many useful metrics you can track around your own codebase, such as lines of code, number of bugs, build times, and test coverage. Useful tools in this space include your build system, CI servers (e.g., Jenkins and Travis), and code analysis services such as Code Climate and Codacy.

Server level

You're finally down to the hardware level. Here, you want to measure metrics such as CPU usage, memory usage, hard drive usage, and network traffic. Some of the popular tools in this space are Nagios, Icigna, Munin, Ganglia, collectd, Cacti, and Sensu.

ALERTING

Logs and metrics are only useful when someone is looking at them. Given the amount of log data, the huge variety of metrics, and the number of hours in a day, it's safe to say that no one is looking at the vast majority of your monitoring data. Therefore, to make monitoring truly useful, you need to set up alerting so you are automatically notified when there is something you need to pay attention to, such as a server going down. Many of the previously-mentioned monitoring tools allow you to define rules for when a notification should be sent to someone.

For example, you could define rules like "notify this mailing list if the app server's QPS drops by more than 20% compared to the previous week" or "text message the on-call engineer if this service stops responding." Services like PagerDuty and VictorOps help you manage on-call rotations, notifications (e.g., via email, IM, text message, phone call), and escalation procedures.

A critical aspect of alerting is being able to identify the cause of the issue. Sometimes the metrics or logs will have all the information you need, but when they don't, the first question you ask when something suddenly breaks is "what changed?" To answer this question, it's helpful if you have a *change management dashboard* that shows all changes to the product over time. Many of the configuration management and deployment automation tools mentioned in the deploy section of this chapter come with web UIs that show you all recent deployments and changes. Another option is to connect all of your tools—including deployment, bug tracking, A/B testing, and source control—into a central service, such as Slack or HipChat.

Recap

Agility requires safety.

—[KREPS 2013], JAY KREPS, CO-FOUNDER OF CONFLUENT

Facebook's mantra used to be "move fast and break things."[12] It turns out this is fairly easy to do. So is "move slow and don't break things." The really tricky one is "move fast and don't break things." You're allowed to make mistakes, but breaking things too often will eventually slow you down, as you'll have to spend more time fixing old things instead of building new things. In other words, what actually allows you to make changes quickly is knowing that those changes are safe.

In Chapters 6 and 7, you saw how to write clean code and make changes to it safely, but what happens to the code after you write it is just as important for productivity. This includes integrating your code with other developers through version control and a build process, getting your code to production by setting up hosting, configuration management, and automated deployment, and ensuring your code keeps running in production through logging, metrics, and alerting. In the past, all of these tasks were handled by a separate operations team, but in the

---

12 Facebook's new mantra is "move fast with stable infrastructure" [statt-2014].

last few years, the DevOps movement has emerged to encourage more efficient collaboration between developers and operations. Although DevOps has become a bit of a buzzword, having developers more involved in the build, deployment, and monitoring process has very real benefits.

At LinkedIn, setting up continuous integration, continuous delivery, and comprehensive monitoring allowed the technology organization to move much faster, even in the face of having to handle hundreds of millions of new members and thousands of new employees. We went from a painful, error-prone, bi-weekly release process to one where we could release code many times per hour with fewer bugs. It turns out that to go fast, you need to be confident that your changes cannot do much damage. This is exactly what you get when you invest in automated tests, feature toggles, canary releases, rollback, and other DevOps practices.

The main benefit of the DevOps movement is that it gets developers to realize that software isn't done when it's "code complete" or "QA certified." Software is never done. In the modern world, software is a living, breathing thing that grows and evolves continuously, so you need processes like continuous integration, continuous delivery, and monitoring to constantly check that it's alive and well.

What if software wasn't "made," like we make a paper airplane—finish folding it and fly it away? What if, instead, we treated software more like a valuable, productive plant, to be nurtured, pruned, harvested, fertilized, and watered? Traditional farmers know how to keep plants productive for decades or even centuries. How would software development be different if we treated our programs the same way?

—[FREEMAN AND PRYCE 2009, XV], STEVE FREEMAN AND NAT PRYCE,
GROWING OBJECT-ORIENTED SOFTWARE, GUIDED BY TESTS

PART III

Teams

Startup Culture

Actions, not words

Culture isn't a foosball table or trust falls. It isn't policy. It isn't the Christmas party or the company picnic. Those are objects and events, not culture. And it's not a slogan, either. Culture is action, not words.

—[FRIED AND HANSSON 2010, 249], JASON FRIED AND DAVID HEINEMEIER HANSSON,
REWORK

A startup's culture consists of the beliefs, assumptions, and principles shared by the employees as expressed through their behaviors and actions. Why does culture matter? Because culture beats strategy [Merchant 2011]. To succeed as a startup, it's not enough to have a great idea or a brilliant plan, or even to build a great product, because even the best ideas, plans, and products will fail eventually. Instead, you have to build a great company. And at the core of every great company is a great culture—an environment that allows you to come up with new ideas, new plans, and new products.

Some developers shy away from a "soft" topic like culture but then complain when they don't get recognition for their work, find themselves working on meaningless projects, or are unable to get any work done at all because the office is too loud and the pointy-haired boss keeps interrupting them for useless meetings. Culture isn't a soft topic; it's the very core of what it means to be a company. Remember, startups are about people, and nothing will have a bigger impact on the people at your company than the culture.

In this chapter, I'll discuss how to shape the culture at a startup. First, I'll explain how to define the core ideology, which consists of the company's mission and core values. I will then describe how to put the ideology into practice in every facet of the company. This includes the organizational design, hiring and promotions, motivation, the office, remote work, communication, and process. For each topic, I've included a number of inspiring real-world examples of what a great culture can look like.

Core Ideology

One of the most valuable lessons I've learned in business is that managing a hyper-growth company is like launching a rocket—if your trajectory is off by inches at launch, you can be off by miles out in orbit.

—[WEINER 2012], JEFF WEINER, CEO AT LINKEDIN

If your startup is a rocket, the mission is the destination for that rocket. It tells you *why* the company exists. For any destination, there are many different trajectories that will get you there. This is where the core values come in. They are the principles you use to decide *how* you will accomplish your mission. Taken together, the mission and core values form the company's core ideology—the guiding principles by which you run things.

As a founder, you might want to be involved in every decision in the company, but as the company grows, you'll be involved in exponentially fewer and fewer decisions. If employees start making their own decisions based on different sets of principles, it'll be like trying to move a rocket in several different directions at the same time—you won't get very far. Therefore, you should take the time to define your guiding principles (the core ideology) up front so that everyone can use them to make decisions that move the rocket in the same direction [Collison 2014].

One way to define a company's core ideology is to lock the leadership team in a room for a few days and have them hash it out. Another option is just to ask all the employees. This is the approach used at Zappos, where every year, CEO Tony Hsieh emails the entire company for input:

We will be putting together a mini-book as part of the orientation package for all new hires about the Zappos culture. Our culture is the combination of all of our employees' ideas about the culture, so we would like to include everyone's thoughts in this book.

Please email me 100–500 words about what the Zappos culture means to you. (What is the Zappos culture? What's different about it compared to other company cultures? What do you like about our culture?)

—[HSIEH 2013, 135], TONY HSIEH, *DELIVERING HAPPINESS*

All the responses, which typically include lots of stories and photos, are collected into the "Zappos Culture Book" and distributed to every employee.[1] This approach reinforces the company's mission and values, both by getting them down in writing and by getting employees to participate in the process.

Let's take a closer look at the mission and core values.

MISSION

A mission statement articulates the purpose of the company. It should explain why the company exists, what it does, and who it does it for. Think of it as your company's true north—a dream, a destination, something you, your employees, and your customers can all look up to.

Here are a few great examples:

Google's mission is to organize the world's information and make it universally accessible and useful.

—[ABOUT GOOGLE 2015]

Facebook's mission is to give people the power to share and make the world more open and connected.

—[ABOUT FACEBOOK 2015]

LinkedIn's mission is to connect the world's professionals to make them more productive and successful.

—[ABOUT LINKEDIN 2015]

And here are a few bad examples:

Volvo: By creating value for our customers, we create value for our shareholders. We use our expertise to create transport-related products and services of superior quality, safety and environmental care for demanding

---

1 Zappos also makes its Culture Book available online (*http://www.zapposinsights.com/culture-book*).

customers in selected segments. We work with energy, passion and respect for the individual.

—[VISON, MISSION AND VALUES 2006]

Twitter: Reach the largest daily audience in the world by connecting every-one to their world via our information sharing and distribution platform products and be one of the top revenue-generating Internet companies in the world.[2]

—[FIEGERMAN 2014]

What separates the good mission statement from the bad? A good mission statement should be concise, clear, timeless, and inspiring.

Concise

A mission statement should be no longer than one or two sentences. It should be focused, simple, and easy to remember. Many people could easily recite Google's mission statement from memory, but could you memorize the mission statement for Volvo? Or how about Twitter, whose statement doesn't even fit in a tweet?

Clear

You should be able to understand why the company exists and what it's trying to do from its mission statement without having to ask lots of clarifying questions. Even more importantly, the mission statement should be uniquely identifiable to the company. LinkedIn and Facebook are both social networks, but LinkedIn's mission statement makes it obvious that the company is about professionals, careers, and jobs, and you'd never confuse it with Facebook's mission statement, which is about sharing and connections. By contrast, Volvo's mission statement is full of platitudes that could apply to any company, such as creating value for shareholders and working with energy and passion.

---

2 Twitter released this statement at a 2014 Analyst Day event, caught a lot of flack for it, and then quickly explained that it was actually a "strategy statement" and not a "mission statement" [Fiegerman 2014]. Mission statement or not, it's a useful straw man for this discussion.

Timeless

Don't confuse your mission statement with your current strategy or products. Strategies and products are the *how* and *what*, whereas the mission statement is the *why*. The how and what can and will change in response to a changing world, whereas the why will stay consistent throughout your company's life [Collins Porras 2004, chap. 4]. For example, notice how the Google mission statement says nothing about search. Search is the company's current strategy for making the world's information accessible and useful, but in the future, that strategy may be completely different, perhaps involving mobile phones, wearable devices, or self-driving cars. But no matter what products it builds, the mission of organizing the world's information and making it accessible will remain the same.

Inspiring

Your company's mission has to be something you are passionate about, something that gives you a sense of purpose, and a reason to get up day after day and continue grinding away. If the mission doesn't feel important enough, customers won't buy it, investors won't put money into it, and your team will not be able to maintain the level of focus, energy, and hard work needed to execute a startup. This is because the mission statement answers the most important question of all: *why*.

In the TED talk, "How Great Leaders Inspire Action" [Sinek 2009], Simon Sinek introduces the idea of "The Golden Circle," as shown in Figure 9-1.

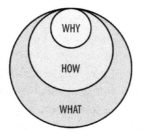

Figure 9-1. The Golden Circle

Sinek explains that most people work from the outside in. For example, when trying to sell a product, you might start with what you do: "We build product X with features Y." Then you might talk about how you do it: "Our competitive advantage is Z." But very few people know why they do it. By why, I don't mean "to make money," but some kind of greater purpose. Most people don't know what that purpose is, so they discuss why in a very fuzzy manner or not at all.

By contrast, great companies and great leaders work in the opposite direction. They start with why and focus on it intensely. The how and what are just supporting details—they are the particular method used to accomplish the why, but it's the why that matters. Sinek gives a great example using Apple:

> If Apple were like everyone else, a marketing message from them might sound like this: "We make great computers. They're beautifully designed, simple to use and user friendly. Want to buy one?"
>
> "Meh."
>
> ...
>
> Here's how Apple actually communicates. "Everything we do, we believe in challenging the status quo. We believe in thinking differently. The way we challenge the status quo is by making our products beautifully designed, simple to use and user friendly. We just happen to make great computers. Want to buy one?"
>
> Totally different right? You're ready to buy a computer from me. All I did was reverse the order of the information. What it proves to us is that people don't buy what you do; people buy why you do it.
>
> **—[SINEK 2009], SIMON SINEK, "HOW GREAT LEADERS INSPIRE ACTION"**

Starting with why—starting with your mission—is one of the most powerful things you can do as a leader. It will make it easier to get customers. It will help you hire. It will help you raise money. Remember, Martin Luther King, Jr. gave the "I have a dream" speech, not the "I have a plan" speech [Sinek 2009]. When your product is struggling and your team has worked an 80-hour week, it's the dream, the why, that will convince you to keep going, and not some plan, and certainly not the prospect of making a profit. This is why a company's mission should not be about money.

Customers don't want to see anything about shareholder value, revenue, or profit in a mission statement, as it just makes the company seem greedy and not trustworthy. And no employee pours their heart and soul into a project to increase the profit margin by 2.3%. Of course, every company has to make money, but the money isn't the purpose of the company, it's just a resource that makes it possible to achieve the real purpose. Money is like oxygen: necessary to sustain life but not the point of life itself. In fact, ignoring money is the best way to come up with a good mission statement:

> If you woke up tomorrow morning with enough money in the bank that you would never need to work again, how could we frame the purpose of this organization such that you would want to continue working anyway? What deeper sense of purpose would motivate you to continue to dedicate your precious creative energies to this company's efforts?

—[COLLINS PORRAS 2004, 228], JIM COLLINS AND JERRY I. PORRAS, *BUILT TO LAST*

One surprising implication from this is that a big, audacious mission can sometimes be no harder to achieve than a much smaller one. Building any kind of startup is hard, but if the payoff from that work is accomplishing a huge and important goal, it can be easier to convince great people to join. And giving great people a magnificent challenge is how you get them to do the best work of their careers [Kawasaki 2011].

Perhaps one of the most audacious mission statements of all time was by President John F. Kennedy: "This nation should commit itself to achieving the goal, before the decade is out, of landing a man on the moon and returning him safely to the earth." Had Kennedy been a CEO, he might instead have said, "Our mission is to become the international leader in the space industry through maximum team-centered innovation and strategically targeted aerospace initiatives" [Heath and Heath 2007, 21]. Fortunately, he chose the former statement when talking to Congress in 1961, and just eight years later, Neil Armstrong and the Apollo 11 crew found themselves on the moon [Kennedy 1961].

CORE VALUES

> It is vital that employees understand that the company is not only concerned with results, but how the results are obtained.

—[COLLINS AND PORRAS 2004, 80], ED HARNESS, FORMER PRESIDENT,
PROCTER & GAMBLE

Your core values are the tenets you use to make every decision in your organization. You don't choose core values so much as you discover them in your team. They are mostly values that you already live by. You believe them deeply, they are important to you, and you'll stick with them no matter what company you join or what product you're building.

Do not confuse core values with cultural norms, management fads, or your current strategy. It's only a core value if you would live by it even if you had enough money to never work again, even 100 years from now, even if you joined a different company, and even if the market punished you for holding this value [Collins and Porras 2004, 223]. For example, imagine you were working in Silicon Valley and were considering "relaxed dress code" as a core value for your company. What happens if, a few years from now, you start competing on Wall Street, where everyone wears suits? Would you stick with the "relaxed dress code" policy? If not, then it's just a cultural norm you're following and it shouldn't be one of your core values. On the other hand, if you strongly believe in "transparent communication," and your company would remain transparent even if you started competing in Wall Street, where secrecy is the norm, then transparency might be a good candidate for a core value.

Ideally, you can get everyone in a room and figure out what core values you all share. If your company already has too many people for that, you can instead try to assemble a "Mars Group" [Collins and Porras 2004, 223]. Here's what you do: imagine that you need to send a team of five to seven people to Mars to create a new branch of your company. Who would you pick? When considering such a mission, you'll naturally choose a broad range of people who have a deep understanding of all parts of the company, which makes them a good choice for articulating the company's core values.

Once you've figured out your core values, write them down and distribute them to all employees. You might even want to share your values publicly, as they can help you find employees, customers, and investors with similar values. For example, Netflix is famous for its culture deck, which has nearly 10 million views on SlideShare as of 2014 [Hastings 2009].

Of course, defining your mission and core values is just the first step. The next step, or really, the next 100 steps, is to deliberately set up your company so that it embodies its ideology in every one of its actions. In the following sections, I'll discuss some of the most important ways to align a company around its mission and values, including organizational design, hiring and promotions, motivation, the office, working remotely, communication, and process.

Organizational design

The first rule of organizational design is that all organizational designs are bad. With any design, you will optimize communication among some parts of the organization at the expense of other parts. For example, if you

*put product management in the engineering organization, you will opti-
mize communication between product management and engineering at
the expense of communication between product management and marketing. As a result, as soon as you roll out the new organization, people will
find fault with it and they will be right.*

—[HOROWITZ 2014, 188], BEN HOROWITZ, *THE HARD THING ABOUT HARD THINGS*

You want to organize the company so that each employee knows exactly what
their job is and can do it efficiently, and that the sum of all of their work moves
the company toward its mission. When the company is small, this tends to happen automatically, so you can ignore organizational design. The founding team
just needs to set a direction and every employee can easily follow along. As the
number of employees grows, this approach becomes less efficient.

The loss of efficiency is due to the fact that complex projects cannot be divided into discrete tasks that can be done completely independently, so there is
always an overhead of communication and coordination. If you do not put any
sort of organizational structure in place, then for a company of n people, each
employee has to coordinate with $n - 1$ other employees. For example, in a company with three people, each employee needs to coordinate with just two other
people, but in a company of 100 people, each employee has to coordinate with
99 others. Therefore, the total communication overhead grows as a factor of n^2
and it doesn't take long before it has a significant impact on productivity [Brooks
1995]. In practice, by the time your company has more than 20–30 employees,
you'll need some kind of organizational design to keep things running smoothly.

At a very high level, there are two types of organizational design you could
put in place: the first is a traditional *management-driven hierarchy*. The second is
to try to build a *distributed organization*.

MANAGEMENT-DRIVEN HIERARCHY

Most people are familiar with the management-driven approach, as it's the one
used at the majority of modern companies. The idea is to break the company into
a number of small teams, each of which reports to a manager and is focused on a
separate task (e.g., an engineering team, a sales team, and a product team). Each
member of a team typically only needs to coordinate with other members of their
team, rather than the whole company. When multiple teams need to work
together, most of the coordination can happen between the managers. Because
each manager only has the bandwidth for a certain number of direct reports, the

company will be arranged into a hierarchy with managers reporting to higher-level managers all the way up to the CEO.

In a hierarchical organization, managers are responsible for most of the coordination and decision making. Of course, managers do much more than that. Peter Drucker, who is considered the founder of modern management, wrote that a manager has five basic operations [Drucker 2008, 8]:

Set objectives
The manager determines the goals, what needs to be done to achieve the goals, and how to communicate the goals to the team.

Organize
The manager divides up the work and selects the people to do it.

Motivate and communicate
Through decisions on pay, placement, and promotion, and through constant communication, the manager "integrates" a group of people into an effective team.

Measure
The manager establishes targets for each person and measures their progress towards those targets as a way to measure performance.

Develop people
The manager helps each person on the team, including himself or herself, to grow their abilities.

There are a number of advantages to a manager-driven, hierarchical organization. The different levels of leadership usually make it clear who has authority and responsibility for any given decision. Employees know who they report to and who evaluates their performance. Teams can become highly specialized and efficient at specific tasks. And finally, it's a time-tested approach that is well understood and has been proven to work even at a huge scale, such as Walmart, which has 2.2 million employees [List of Largest Employers 2014].

There are also a number of disadvantages to hierarchical organizations. Communication across departments tends to be difficult. Multiple layers of organization can lead to lots of bureaucratic overhead that slows everything down. Managers can become bottlenecks for all communication and coordination. Compensation, reputation, and recognition are typically tied to where you are in the hierarchy, which leads many people towards a maniacal focus on climbing the ladder and playing politics rather than doing work. Finally, higher-level managers, who are often trusted with the most important decisions, are often the furthest away from the actual work, and therefore in the worst place to make such decisions.

DISTRIBUTED ORGANIZATION

The alternative to a hierarchical design is a distributed organization (sometimes called a *flat organization*). The idea is for employees to self-organize into the most efficient structure for each task and then reorganize when the task is completed or changes. Depending on the task, different people may assume leadership and coordination roles, but these depend on the requirements of the task as opposed to a fixed title or rigid hierarchy. One of the most famous examples is a video game company called Valve (*http://bit.ly/valve-hndbk*):

> Hierarchy is great for maintaining predictability and repeatability. It simplifies planning and makes it easier to control a large group of people from the top down, which is why military organizations rely on it so heavily. But when you're an entertainment company that's spent the last decade going out of its way to recruit the most intelligent, innovative, talented people on Earth, telling them to sit at a desk and do what they're told obliterates 99 percent of their value. We want innovators, and that means maintaining an environment where they'll flourish.
>
> That's why Valve is flat. It's our shorthand way of saying that we don't have any management, and nobody "reports to" anybody else. We do have a founder/president, but even he isn't your manager. This company is yours to steer—toward opportunities and away from risks. You have the power to green-light projects. You have the power to ship products.

If you've worked in large corporations your whole life and are used to management hierarchies, such an approach may seem chaotic and unlikely to work. Could you really rely on people to self-organize? Wouldn't most employees just slack off without a manager looking over their shoulder? It turns out that both of these concerns are based on assumptions of human behavior in the workplace that have been largely untrue for at least 50 years.

In the 1960 book *The Human Side of Enterprise*, Douglas McGregor discusses the common notion that the average worker dislikes their job and avoids it whenever possible. This may be true of some jobs such as dull, repetitive manual labor, and in those cases, you may need a constant managerial presence to coerce the worker with rewards (salary, bonuses) or threaten them with punishments (firing, humiliation). However, this does not apply to many creative jobs such as programming. Many people love using their creativity and building things, so they actually enjoy their jobs and actively seek out problems to solve. All you have to do is provide them with the right environment, and their internal drive will get them to work hard.

In other words, management is not a fundamental need of a business but an invention. Management, as we know it today, was developed in the early 20th century to meet the needs of businesses in that era. It's a tool, and like all tools, it needs to be updated from time to time to meet new requirements. Most management practices we use today were designed to organize manual labor and assembly line workers to do repetitive, dull tasks. The main goal was to "turn human beings into semi-programmable robots" [Hamel 2011]. The requirements of a modern, high-tech startup are very different, so there is no guarantee the same management practices will work.

At Valve, instead of relying on managers, employees self-organize into "cabals," which are multidisciplinary project teams. People join a cabal if they believe the project is important enough to work on—not because a boss says they have to. All the desks have wheels on them and people move around regularly as they select projects to work on and form new teams. This approach has made Valve incredibly successful. They have made four of the best-selling PC games of all time [List of Best-Selling PC Games 2015], were rated the most desirable game company to work for in 2014 [Tassi 2014], and were worth an estimated $2–$4 billion in 2011, which means the 400-person company made more money per employee than Google or Apple [Chiang 2011].

Other companies are trying distributed organization, too. In 2013, Zappos announced that they were adopting a practice called *Holocracy* and getting rid of all traditional hierarchical structure, managers, and titles [Groth 2013]. Holocracy is also in use at several other companies, including Medium and the David Allen Company [Who is using Holocracy 2014].

> *Research shows that every time the size of a city doubles, innovation or productivity per resident increases by 15 percent. But when companies get bigger, innovation or productivity per employee generally goes down. So we're trying to figure out how to structure Zappos more like a city, and less like a bureaucratic corporation. In a city, people and businesses are self-organizing. We're trying to do the same thing by switching from a normal hierarchical structure to a system called Holacracy, which enables employees to act more like entrepreneurs and self-direct their work instead of reporting to a manager who tells them what to do.*

—[LEINBACH-REYHLE 2014], TONY HSIEH, CEO OF ZAPPOS

Another example of distributed organizations is open source software. Projects such as Linux, Apache, and MySQL show that it's possible to get thousands of developers around the world to work together and produce complicated and successful projects without a central office, in-person meetings, or managers. These projects also prove that the quality and development pace of a distributed project can be higher than can be achieved by any commercial company with a traditional manager-driven hierarchy. I'll discuss open source practices more in "Remote work" on page 423.

The advantage of a flat and distributed organization is that employees have more autonomy and responsibility, which as you'll see later in the chapter, is an essential ingredient in motivation. More autonomy means that the person closest to the problem, who understands it best, gets to make the important decisions while avoiding most of the bureaucratic overhead of a hierarchy. Unfortunately, distributed organizations are relatively rare in the corporate world, so they are not as well understood and documented as management-driven hierarchies. That means that you'll need to find alternative ways to handle Drucker's five management tasks:

Set objectives

Coordinating large changes and new priorities among many distributed teams can be tricky.

Organize

In a distributed organization, it's not always obvious who has the responsibility and authority for any given decision. While management hierarchies have scaled to millions of employees, there are few examples of whether distributed organizations can get that large (though that might not matter for most startups).

Motivate and communicate

Without a manager, you need a different system for reviewing employees, such as peer review. Without a hierarchy, you also need an alternative to promotions, as I'll discuss in "Hiring and promotions" on page 399.

Measure

Each team is now responsible for identifying its own targets and milestones, and tracking progress towards them.

Develop people

It can be tricky to build an effective process for hiring and training people when there are no consistent teams or managers in place.

So, should you go with a hierarchical or flat organization at your startup? There is no right answer. Organizational design, like most interesting problems, is a game of trade-offs. As shown in Figure 9-2, successful companies have been built around almost every type of organizational design, each one with its own strengths and weaknesses.

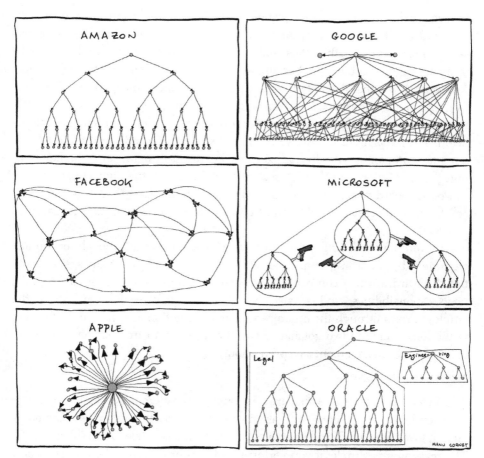

Figure 9-2. Organizational charts of different companies (image courtesy of Manu Cornet [Cornet 2011])

Hiring and promotions

The best way to align your organization around your mission and values is to hire people that are already aligned. This is why an essential part of the hiring process is finding someone who is a great *culture fit*. I'll discuss culture fit, and all other aspects of startup hiring, in Chapter 11.

The only thing I'll add in this chapter is a plea to all tech startups to make diversity a core part of your culture and hiring strategy. Women and minorities are massively underrepresented in the tech industry today. For example, women hold only 25% of all professional IT-related jobs, and 56% of them leave the tech industry halfway through their careers, which is double the quit rate of men [Ashcraft and Blithe 2010, 11]. As a startup, you should explicitly seek out diversity in skills, genders, ethnicities, and backgrounds, not just because it's the right thing to do (it is), but also because it will give you a competitive advantage. Research shows that diversity makes a team more likely to experiment, be creative, and share knowledge [Ashcraft and Blithe 2010, 10] and helps a company reach more customers [Martin and Ferraro 2000], attract more talent [Holmes 2014], and build more innovative products [Nelson 2014, 88]. And the numbers don't lie: companies with diverse executive boards have significantly higher earnings [Barta, Markus and Neumann 2012] and those with the highest percentages of women board directors outperformed those with the least by 53% in return on equity, 42% in return on sales, and 66% in return on invested capital [Carter et al. 2007].

In addition to hiring for culture fit, you need to continuously encourage alignment by rewarding employees who exemplify your core values. The traditional reward in most companies has been the promotion. You get a new title, new responsibilities, and a raise. This leads to a career ladder, where the employee rises through the organization, one promotion at a time, until they get to the top. There are two gotchas to watch out for with career ladders: the Peter Principle and management as a promotion.

THE PETER PRINCIPLE

The Peter Principle states that in a hierarchy, every employee tends to rise to their level of incompetence, so that, in time, "every post tends to be occupied by an employee who is incompetent to carry out its duties" [Peter and Hull 2011, 16]. The reasoning is simple: if you perform well at your current role, you eventually get promoted to a new one. At some point, you might get promoted into a role that exceeds your capabilities, so you won't perform well enough to get another promotion, and you'll get stuck at a role for which you are incompetent.

If you use promotions as rewards, the Peter Principle is the default outcome. Avoiding it requires extra work, such as only promoting employees that are already performing at the level of the new role and implementing training programs to help them get better (see Chapter 12). However, the most common cause of the Peter Principle in engineering organizations comes from promoting developers to managers.

MANAGEMENT AS A PROMOTION

Many software companies believe that the best way to reward a developer is to promote them to management. The problem is that management is not an incremental step up in a technical career but a completely different job with a completely different skill set. Being good at algorithms, architecture, and testing does not automatically mean you're going to be good at prioritization, negotiating complex interpersonal relationships, and developing talent. In most cases, you lose a phenomenal contributor while gaining a mediocre manager, who in all likelihood will just slow down other individual contributors as well [Brown 2014].

But the worst impact of management as a promotion is that you're signaling to your engineering organization that writing code is second-class work. There is no faster way to run a technology company into the ground than by building an organization where only inexperienced and underperforming developers write code while all the talented and accomplished developers manage people instead. You can't manage your way to good code. You need great developers to write it.

To ensure those great developers continue writing code, you need to have a way to reward technical leadership—that is, creating leverage in the company through code contributions rather than by managing people. One way to do this is to have equivalent career ladders for individual contributors (IC) and managers. For example, Table 9-1 shows the career tracks at LinkedIn.

Table 9-1. LinkedIn career ladders

Individual Contributor	Management
Staff Engineer	Manager
Senior Staff Engineer	Senior Manager
Principal Staff Engineer	Director
Distinguished Engineer	Senior Director
Fellow	Vice President

In theory, whichever track you're in, the compensation, level of responsibility, and influence in the company at each level should be roughly the same. In practice, this is difficult to achieve due to a number of systemic biases [McKinley 2014b]. One bias is that management titles carry more prestige in most societies. Being a Director or Vice President is a big deal. Being a senior staff engineer, less so. Another bias stems from the fact that managers typically have powers that individual contributors, even at the same level, don't have, such as knowing the roadmap, people's salaries, and controlling hiring and firing. This creates a power gap. Finally, managers are usually promoted when an existing manager is overwhelmed with too many direct reports, which happens regularly in a growing company. On the other hand, individual contributors are usually promoted only as recognition for great work, which tends to be a less frequent occurrence.

The result is that, at most tech companies, there are vastly more high-level managers (Director and up) than high-level engineers (Principal Staff Engineer and up). At LinkedIn, the ratio of high-level managers to high-level engineers was roughly 5:1. The numbers at Etsy were similar:

> I was the first person at Etsy with the title of "Principal Engineer," which was the technical equivalent to a directorship (i.e., one level below CTO). ... At one point, I was alone at my level. There were five theoretically-equivalent directors at the time. The ratio was at least that bad on the lower rungs. (I have no idea if this is still true at that company, and it might not be.)
>
> For that to make sense, we'd have to believe a few things that don't stand up to scrutiny. First, we'd have to believe in a very high proclivity among engineers to manage, and I think that betrays our expectations. Not very many of us got into this business with the hope of not actually building things.
>
> Second, we'd have to believe that although it took five directors to effectively manage the organization, only one technical leader was required to advise the same group on the details of the work they do every day.

—[MCKINLEY 2014B], DAN MCKINLEY, SOFTWARE ENGINEER AT ETSY AND STRIPE

This sort of disparity sends the message that, even with a dedicated track for individual contributors, management is still a better way to advance your career. There is no easy solution to this problem. If you're going to use career ladders at your company, it's still better to have a separate track for individual contributors than none at all, but you need to pay close attention to the manager/IC ratio. You should also try to even out the power gap by granting individual contributors more powers as they climb the ladder, such as control over product and infrastructure decisions and the freedom to choose their own projects.

An alternative option is to not use career ladders at all. In most flat, distributed organizations, promotions are not used as rewards. You still reward high performers, but instead of focusing on a fancy new title or moving up a ladder, you focus on new responsibilities, compensation, and benefits. It's a bit like rewarding a soldier with a commendation or a medal instead of promoting them up the ranks. For example, you could give senior engineers more influence over the company's direction, more control over which projects they work on, more time to develop their skills, and more salary, equity, and vacation time.

Can a company avoid job titles, career ladders, and promotions forever? It's hard to say. In *The Hard Thing About Hard Things*, Ben Horowitz argues that most startups eventually introduce job titles for two reasons [Horowitz 2014, 159–160]. First, because most other companies use them, your employees may want a title so that they can eventually switch jobs. Second, job titles are a "shorthand for describing roles in the company," which employees, customers, and partners frequently need to navigate the company, especially as it gets larger. Although titles are the norm at most companies, a few companies have made it far without them: CloudFlare has no titles for its 100 employees [Haden 2013], Valve has no titles for its 400 employees [Wagreich 2013], and Zappos is trying to go without titles for its 4,000 employees [Groth 2013].

Motivation

Most companies use promotions and bonuses to motivate employees. In the book *Drive*, Daniel Pink presents research that shows that offering a reward for completing a task only improves performance if that task is dull and repetitive, like manual labor. If the task requires creativity, such as programming, offering a reward can actually hurt performance. The most famous example of this unintuitive result comes from experiments involving the candle problem [Candle Problem 2015]. Participants are presented with a candle, a box of tacks, and a box of matches, as shown in Figure 9-3. The goal is to find a way to attach the candle to the wall so you can light it and not have any of the wax drip onto the table below. Before reading further, take a minute to consider how you would solve this problem.

Would you try to use the tacks to stick the candle directly to the wall? Or maybe you thought you could melt some of the wax and use it as an adhesive? Unfortunately, neither solution works. The correct solution, as shown in Figure 9-4, is to empty out the box of tacks, attach the box to the wall using the tacks, and put the candle in the box.

Figure 9-3. The candle problem [Duncker 1945]

Figure 9-4. The candle problem solution [Duncker 1945]

When this problem was used in experiments, the participants were split into two groups. Group A was told they were being timed in order to collect statistics about the exercise while Group B was told they were being timed because the person who comes up with a solution the fastest would be awarded a monetary prize. Which group performed better? Traditional management and economic theories would predict Group B, but as it turned out, Group B actually took 3.5 minutes longer on average than Group A to solve the puzzle. Offering a monetary incentive hurt performance. That's because solving the candle problem requires creativity. You have to overcome *functional fixedness* and realize that the box is not just for holding the tacks but another component you can use to solve the puzzle.

The reason that offering incentives for a creative task can hurt performance is that you end up focusing your attention on the reward rather than the task. For example, consider the typical annual performance review process. Imagine you're a manager and you sit down with your direct report, Anna, and tell her, "Anna, if you launch the new mobile app by November, you'll get a raise!" This leads to a number of demotivating psychological side effects:

- You are signaling to Anna that building the mobile app quickly must be a painful and undesirable process—otherwise, why would you have to offer a reward for it?

- Anna will feel a lot of pressure to succeed at the task, both because she knows her manager wants it and because she wants a raise. The extra pressure could make her nervous and reduce her creativity and performance.

- You are indicating to Anna that her primary goal is to earn a raise rather than build a high-quality mobile app. The desire for a reward and the pressure to succeed might entice her to ship the app on time no matter the cost even if it means taking shortcuts or gaming the system.

- If Anna isn't able to ship the mobile app on time and doesn't get a raise, it might kill her motivation. She will feel betrayed, as if all her hard work that year had been for nothing.

- Even if Anna gets the app done on time and you do give her a raise, you've now ensured that Anna will never want to work on another mobile app without being promised another raise. In fact, the next raise will have to be bigger than the previous one for it to be really motivating. Rewards, like drugs, are addictive. This is also why many people lose their passion for a hobby once someone pays them for it.

In short, there is extensive research that shows that the most common methods used in the corporate world to try to improve performance—promising a reward like a raise, promotion, or bonus for the completion of a task—are often counterproductive. Of course, not all rewards are bad. Before you can worry about high-level needs like motivation and self-fulfillment, you need to take care of the first few levels on Maslow's hierarchy of needs, such as rent and food. Therefore, you need a baseline salary. Moreover, most people don't actually understand their own motivations, so they will seek out more money even if it won't actually make them happier. Therefore, to hire someone in the first place, you'll still have to offer a competitive compensation package (see "Making an offer" on page 496). However, studies show that beyond a certain level of compensation (approximately $75,000 per year), more money, or more of any other kind of *extrinsic motivator*, does not necessarily produce more motivation [Kahneman and Deaton 2010].

So what does? The answer is *intrinsic motivators*—that is, the internal drive we all have that allows us to enjoy a task for its own benefits. Humans are naturally playful and curious. We regularly invest enormous amounts of time in difficult tasks even though no one is paying us for them. If you're a programmer, you already know this. Have you ever spent a weekend hacking away at a side project? Have you ever learned a new programming language or technology outside of work? Have you ever been unable to sleep because a friend told you a logic puzzle and you just had to solve it? Have you ever contributed to open source? Most of these activities are driven by intrinsic motivation.

How do you encourage intrinsic motivation? Well, by its very nature, you can't drive intrinsic motivation from the outside. All you can do is provide a context that's optimal for bringing out the internal motivation people already have. To do this, you need to create an environment that maximizes autonomy, mastery, and purpose.

AUTONOMY

Autonomy is our natural drive to have control over our lives. We want to decide what we work on, when we work on it, how we work on it, and who we work with. If you want to encourage autonomy, you need to hire people you can trust, set clear goals for them, and then get out of their way. This is why many startups focus on results rather than how you got them. You can work any hours you want, you can come into the office or work from home, and you can implement the project how you want as long as you accomplish your assigned goals. And if you can choose your goals, then the autonomy drive will be even stronger.

A low-cost, low-risk way to experiment with this idea is to have specific days where employees can work on anything they want. LinkedIn holds "hackdays" once a month [Linkedin Hackdays 2015]. Facebook holds "hackathons" every few months [Hackathon 2015]. Atlassian holds "ShipIt Days" once per quarter [ShipIt Days at Atlassian 2015]. The format everywhere is roughly the same: you come up with an idea, you form a team, and you get 24 hours to build a "hack" or quick prototype of the idea. It's a fun event that includes lots of food, coffee, a chance to present what you did to the whole company, and prizes for the best hacks. In 2010, Facebook also introduced the "hackamonth," where any employee who has been at the company for more than a year can join another team of their choosing and work with them for a month [Ferguson 2011].

> I was part of the first hackamonth class. This is a really great program with many benefits to the company. It makes teams fault tolerant. At any point, someone could leave the company, leave the team, they could pass away, whatever. So the hackamonth is a low-risk way to check that your team isn't too reliant on one person. The other thing it does is a cross-cultural exchange. Every team in the company does different things well. One team might be great at code reviewing. One team might be great at testing. One team might be great at UI and UX. So hopefully as you switch teams, you take that with you. You can be an emissary to the other team: "Hey, you guys suck at testing. I'm going to start making us do unit tests." And, of course, it facilitates transferring between teams, and for good talent it's better that they change teams within your company, rather than leaving your company entirely.

—[KIM 2014], DANIEL KIM, SOFTWARE ENGINEER AT FACEBOOK AND INSTAGRAM

A few companies give employees even more autonomy. Back in the 1950s, 3M pioneered *15% time*, a policy that allowed engineers to spend 15% of their time working on projects of their choosing. As of today, many of the inventions that 3M relies on as a business, including Post-it notes and masking tape, were originally developed as 15% time projects. Google offers a similar policy called 20% time, and their employees have used it to create many successful products, including Gmail, Google News, and Google Translate [Pink 2011, 94]. Valve, the video game company I mentioned earlier, takes this idea even further:

> *We've heard that other companies have people allocate a percentage of their time to self-directed projects. At Valve, that percentage is 100.*
>
> *Since Valve is flat, people don't join projects because they're told to. Instead, you'll decide what to work on after asking yourself the right questions (more on that later). Employees vote on projects with their feet (or desk wheels). Strong projects are ones in which people can see demonstrated value; they staff up easily. This means there are any number of internal recruiting efforts constantly under way.*
>
> **—[VALVE HANDBOOK FOR NEW EMPLOYEES 2012, 8] THE VALVE HANDBOOK FOR NEW EMPLOYEES, 2012**

MASTERY

Mastery is the inherent drive to get better at things. Most programmers will jump at the opportunity to learn a new technology or hone their skills. We're naturally attracted to hard problems because we know they will challenge us and force us to get better. We read books, blog posts, and articles to learn best practices. In many ways, programming is a craft, and every programmer wants to be a master craftsman.

Every company tries to hire the best programmers, but the best companies take the programmers they have and invest in them to make them even better. This creates a virtuous cycle. The employee is happy because they are improving their skills and market value. The company is happy because it gets a better, more skilled employee. There are many ways to invest in mastery, such as encouraging employees to regularly join new projects and teams, attend conferences and talks (or better yet, present at conferences at talks), organize reading groups for published papers, blog posts, and books (or better yet, write your own papers, blog posts, and books), and contribute to open source (see Chapter 12 for more information).

Another way to invest in mastery comes from the book *The Alliance* by Reid Hoffman, Ben Casnocha, and Chris Yeh. At most companies, the interview process, the offer letter, and the way managers talk to employees are all based around a shared delusion that the employee will be working at the company forever. In reality, the days of working at the same company for 50 years, climbing the career ladder, and retiring with a gold watch are long gone. The idea behind

The Alliance is that the employer and employee should be more up front about this reality. Instead of treating the offer like a lifelong contract, you should agree to *tours of duty*, which are well-defined missions of a finite length where the employee promises to invest in the company by contributing to specific projects and the company promises to invest in the employee by helping them improve their market value. For example, you might agree to a tour of duty to "ship the new mobile app in 12 months," and in exchange, the company will improve your market value by helping you develop your iOS and mobile design skills. When you finish a tour of duty, you repeat the conversation with the company and agree to a new tour.

This approach replaces the vague and uncertain employee review process with something that is more transparent. And instead of only offering extrinsic rewards (e.g., salary), it makes intrinsic rewards (e.g., the company investing in your mastery) an explicit part of the exchange. A great example of this comes from a blog post by Mike Gamson, SVP of Global Solutions at LinkedIn, called "My Promise to You (Our Employees)":

> Let me start with the bad news. The bad news is that you're going to leave LinkedIn one day. I know you just got here and so it may be strange to think about leaving already, but I want to bring your attention to it so that you and I can partner together on making the most out of the time we spend together in this company. I don't know if you're going to spend two years here, or five, or 10 or more, but I want to make sure that however much time you spend here with us on this journey, that when you look back on your whole career 20, 30, 40 years from now that you will look at the years you spent here as the most transformative years in your career. The years where you learned the most, grew the most quickly, were exposed to the most incredible people and the most innovative thinking. I want these years to be the years that literally change the trajectory of your career. I want you to enjoy more success in your life directly due to the experiences you had here at LinkedIn than you would have enjoyed had you never chosen to work here. My promise to you is that I will dedicate myself to creating and nurturing an environment where career trajectory change happens and to give you every chance to be exposed to the ideas, people, experiences, and opportunities you need to make this happen in your life. When you leave LinkedIn one day, I want you to be truly transformed. What I seek in return is a promise from you that you're going to throw yourself at the opportunity to transform yourself, our company, and

the world. And that you will run after the opportunities here with courage and persistence.

—[GAMSON 2014], MIKE GAMSON, SVP, GLOBAL SOLUTIONS AT LINKEDIN

PURPOSE

If you want to build a ship, don't drum up the men to gather wood, divide the work and give orders. Instead, teach them to yearn for the vast and endless sea.

—ANTOINE DE SAINT EXUPÉRY

Purpose is the inherent drive to work on something with a bigger meaning. We all crave to build something bigger than ourselves. We want to leave our mark on the world. We need to make money to make this possible, but the money isn't really the point—it's just a resource to help us achieve some other purpose.

Early in the chapter, I talked about the importance of a strong company mission. I discussed the fact that people are driven by *why*. This is just another way of saying that people are driven by purpose. The more inspiring your mission and the better you are at communicating it, the easier it will be to motivate employees. For example, recall the discussion of the performance review where you asked Anna to ship a mobile app in 12 months in exchange for a raise. Imagine that you said this instead: "Anna, this mobile app is your chance to touch the lives of the two billion people on the planet who have smartphones. It's a chance for you to learn iOS and mobile development skills. It's a chance for you to take the entire company one step closer to its mission."

Giving Anna a sense of purpose is more likely to motivate her than to offer a reward like a raise. That said, is there still a way to give her a raise without killing her motivation? Yes. The key is to avoid using *contingent rewards*—that is, rewards based on an if-then condition, such as "if you do X, I'll give you Y" [Pink 2011, 36]. Any reward you hang out in front of someone, like a carrot on a stick, is automatically an extrinsic motivator. The employee will be doing the work *in exchange* for a reward, so you'll see all the demotivating side effects we discussed earlier. However, the side effects largely go away if the reward is a surprise.[3]

---

3 Behavioral studies have shown that the most effective way to reward behavior is on a variable schedule—that is, you randomly reward some attempts but not all. Think of a Las Vegas slot machine, where you know that *eventually* you'll win, but not when, which keeps you playing for a long time [Reinforcement 2015].

Instead of promising a reward, you create an environment where Anna is focused on the task itself and is driven by intrinsic motivators (e.g., the company's mission and her desire to learn iOS and mobile development skills). If she does well, you give her a raise as unexpected *recognition* rather than an expected *payment*.

Moreover, instead of an annual performance review, you should do lightweight reviews on a continuous basis, perhaps during weekly one-on-one meetings. This way, you can reward good performance immediately rather than a year later. The reward doesn't always have to be money. In fact, the best rewards are usually more autonomy, mastery, and purpose. Give Anna more freedom to choose her next project. Let her switch teams and learn a new technology. Give her praise and public recognition so that she knows her work is important. Say "thank you" often. Celebrate important milestones. Set aside some budget for regular team outings and offsites, even if it's just to the pizza shop next door.

Of course, raises, bonuses, and re-ups of stock are also important, and as long as they are not contingent rewards, they are a great way to show gratitude. A good way to give out extrinsic rewards like bonuses is to mix them with intrinsic rewards. For example, instead of giving out a bonus in a private one-on-one meeting, you could give it out in a ceremony in front of the whole company. The ceremony taps into the intrinsic drive to work on something important and earn the recognition of your peers. This is how many competitions work, too: the real prize is not just the money but also other people seeing you as the winner.

The office

One of the best ways to get a feel for a company's culture is to walk through its office. For example, consider GitHub's San Francisco headquarters. When you first walk in, you are greeted by several glass trophy cases. One contains a bronze statue of the skeleton of a prehistoric Octocat (the Octocat is GitHub's logo). Another one contains the laptop one of the founders used to implement the first pull request. As you walk past the trophy cases, you find yourself in GitHub's waiting room. Except it's not a waiting room. It's a replica of the oval office (see Figure 9-5). There is a huge wooden desk, an American flag, a giant oval carpet with the GitHub seal (an Octocat holding olive branches and cutlery), plush couches, and shelves lined with old books.

Figure 9-5. The waiting room in GitHub's San Francisco office (photo courtesy of GitHub Office 2015)

Past the waiting room is a massive open area, complete with a full bar, a cafeteria, foosball tables, ping-pong tables, pool tables, and a DJ station. This is where GitHubbers have lunch, hold meetups, and relax. The real work happens on the upper floors. There, you find an open floor plan with lots of employees coding away. Some are sitting, some are using standing desks, and a few of them have dogs relaxing by their feet. In the corner, there is a library stuffed full of technical books. Next to that, you find a conference room. But it's not a conference room. It's The Situation Room. In the center of the room is an octagonal wooden table surrounded by leather chairs, large TVs, an American flag, and several world clocks (see Figure 9-6).

Figure 9-6. GitHub's Situation Room

Bronze statues, a bar, and an oval office may seem extravagant, but consider this: if you work full-time, you will spend more than 2,000 hours per year in an office, or almost half of your waking hours. It's hard to put a price tag on being able to spend that much time in an office environment that you enjoy. Building a great workplace pays for itself by making current employees happy and attracting new employees; and based on a large body of research, it's clear that a good office design can significantly improve productivity [Gifford 2012].

The ideal office for developers needs to have four things:

1. A place where you can work with others.

2. A place where you can do focused work alone.

3. A place where you can get away from work.

4. A way to customize the office for your personal needs.

Note that by their very nature, the first three items should not be in the same place—a principle that most common modern office design completely ignores, as you'll see in the next section.

A PLACE WHERE YOU CAN WORK WITH OTHERS

The workplace needs to make it easy for coworkers to interact with one another. There are two types of interactions: planned meetings and spontaneous discussions. For planned meetings, you need lots of meeting rooms. Each one should have a table, chairs, whiteboards, a TV or projector, and good soundproofing. For spontaneous discussions, about 70% of modern offices have opted to use an open floor plan where a large number of employees sit in huge open areas, either at shared desks or in cubicles [Konnikova 2014]. This arrangement is supposed to improve communication and idea generation, but there is an overwhelming amount of research that proves otherwise.

For example, a 1997 study of a company transitioning from a traditional office arrangement to an open floor plan assessed employees' satisfaction with the physical environment, physical stress, coworker relations, and perceived job performance, and found that the open office was worse across every measure and that "the employees' dissatisfaction did not abate, even after an adjustment period" [Brennan, Chugh, and Kline 2002]. A 2011 study in Denmark showed that open offices can hurt your health. Compared to someone with a private office, occupants in open-plan offices took 62% more sick days [Pejtersen et al. 2011]. Finally, a 2011 review of more than 100 studies about office environments found that though "open offices often fostered a symbolic sense of organizational mission, making employees feel like part of a more laid-back, innovative enterprise," they were, "damaging to the workers' attention spans, productivity, creative thinking, and satisfaction" [Konnikova 2014].

It turns out that "ease of interaction" is a problem for less than 10% of workers [Green 2013], so open floor plans are a solution in search of a problem. This should not be surprising. It's natural for people to strike up a conversation anywhere in the office where two or more coworkers naturally congregate, such as the kitchen, watercooler, a meeting room, or any other common area. In other words, it's easy to design an office that encourages spontaneous conversations. On the other hand, it's harder to design an office where you can avoid spontaneous conversations—and any other type of interruptions—when you need to do focused work.

A PLACE WHERE YOU CAN DO FOCUSED WORK ALONE

Distractions are the enemy of focused work. It only takes a small amount of office noise to impair performance of basic mental tasks such as arithmetic [Perham, Hodgetts, and Banbury 2013]. Programming requires even deeper concentration. You have to load the problem into your head, which is like building a massive house of cards. It takes time, it costs a lot of mental energy, and the slightest interruption can knock the entire house down, forcing you to start over again, as shown in Figure 9-7.

Every loud noise, every coworker dropping by to "touch base," every useless meeting, every email, and every phone call is an interruption, and research shows that it takes a programmer an average of 10–15 minutes to recover from an interruption and start writing code again [Parnin and Rugaber 2011]. Just four interruptions in an hour is enough to drop your productivity to zero.

This is why hackers give you such a baleful stare as they turn from their screen to answer your question. Inside their heads a giant house of cards is tottering.

The mere possibility of being interrupted deters hackers from starting hard projects. This is why they tend to work late at night, and why it's next to impossible to write great software in a cubicle (except late at night).

—[GRAHAM 2004B], PAUL GRAHAM, CO-FOUNDER OF Y COMBINATOR

THIS IS WHY YOU SHOULDN'T INTERRUPT A PROGRAMMER

Figure 9-7. This is why you shouldn't interrupt a programmer (image courtesy of Jason Heeris)

The ideal office for developers is one where they can write code with no distractions. This inherently means that an open office, which is designed to facilitate distractions, is in many ways, the worst possible choice for programmers. A better option is to give developers offices—ideally, private ones—but a shared office for a small team can work, too. Each office should have a door that closes, good soundproofing, and a window. Windows are a must, both for the natural light and to give you something other than your monitor to look at while deep in thought.

The company would love for every one of us to have a window, we hear, but that just isn't realistic. Sure it is. There is a perfect proof that sufficient windows can be built into a space without excessive cost. The existence proof is the hotel, any hotel. You can't even imagine being shown a hotel room with no window. You wouldn't stand for it. (And this is for a space you're only going to sleep in.)

—[DEMARCO AND LISTER 1999, 87-88], TOM DEMARCO AND TIMOTHY LISTER,
PEOPLEWARE

How much does an office cost? More than an open floor plan, sure, but probably not as much as you think. Fog Creek, a software company that builds project management tools, estimates that it costs them about 6% of revenue to provide a private office for every developer (note that Fog Creek is based in New York City, which is one of the most expensive cities in the world for real estate) and that this figure is only a little higher than similar companies they surveyed [Armstrong 2011]. Given the cost of developer salaries, which are on the order of 75% of a startups' expenses [Stump 2011], the productivity and happiness benefits of private offices are well worth the money. This is why a number of software companies give their programmers offices, including Fog Creek Software, CircleCI, SAS, and many divisions in Apple, Microsoft, Oracle, and Google [Ken 2014].

If offices are completely out of the question and you're stuck with an open floor plan, the bare minimum is to reimburse noise-canceling headphones for all employees and to enforce a policy where you can only interrupt someone wearing headphones if it's an emergency. Good noise-canceling headphones cost $100–$200, so for a developer earning $100,000 per year, the headphones need to prevent only two to four hours of time lost to distractions to pay for themselves. Another option for open offices is to set up *coder caves*. These are rooms that are dedicated to quiet, uninterrupted, focused work. A coder cave could be a custom room (see Figure 9-8 for an example at GitHub), a repurposed conference room where talking is prohibited, a chair that is fully enclosed (i.e., a bubble chair), or anywhere else a developer can hide to do some coding or thinking.

A PLACE WHERE YOU CAN GET AWAY FROM WORK

Sometimes you get your best work done away from the keyboard. Ever wake up in the morning and know the solution to a problem from the previous day? Ever have an epiphany in the shower? Ever describe a problem to someone else and realize the solution partway through, even though the other person hasn't said a word?[4] These are not coincidences. Research shows that the brain needs breaks in order to be productive, focused, and creative.

For example, a 2011 study showed that taking regular breaks leads to *goal reactivation*. That is, if you take a brief break from work, when you come back, you are better able to take a step back, re-evaluate your goals, and see the big picture instead of being focused on the nitty-gritty implementation details. The study found that this improves focus and overall task performance [Ariga and Lleras 2011].

Figure 9-8. A coder cave at GitHub (image courtesy of [GitHub HQ], with photography by Eva Kolenko)

---

4 This is known as *rubber duck debugging*, as explained in "Talk to others" on page 44.

For a break to be effective, you need to take it just before you start feeling depleted—distractions that happen at random times, as mentioned earlier, do not work. For example, some people use the Pomodoro technique, where you take a short break every 25 minutes, and a longer break after four repetitions [Pomodoro 2015]. Other people prefer a cycle of working for 90 minutes and resting for 20 minutes, which corresponds to the Ultradian Rhythm [Ciotti 2012]. Try a few different patterns and see what works best for you.

What does all of this have to do with the office? It means that taking breaks should be a regular part of the work culture. Getting a cup of coffee, chatting by the watercooler, getting some exercise, or even just browsing the Web are all reasonable options.[5] The office should be designed so that these interactions can happen away from the desk, such as in a kitchen, cafeteria, lounge, gym, or an outdoor area to take a walk. These are all better ways to encourage serendipitous communication and idea generation than an open floor plan.

In addition to short breaks, longer breaks are essential for maintaining productivity. Every company has an omnipresent worker: someone who is at the office at 9 a.m., chatting on IRC at 9 p.m., and committing code at 3 a.m. [Miller 2014]. This person is always working. Perhaps you've been that person (I know I have). You might even be proud of your long hours and think of yourself as a hero. But longer hours—beyond 50 hours per week—do not increase productivity [Proof That You Should Get a Life]. All they do is increase stress, ruin your health, lead to sloppy mistakes, and eventually make you depressed and disengaged from the work. In other words, the need for heroics is a sign of failure. It means something has been badly misplanned or mismanaged.

It's better to have an environment in which heroes are not needed than a team full of heroes.

—[MILLER 2014], ERNIE MILLER, DIRECTOR OF ENGINEERING AT NVISIUM

Of course, no plan is perfect, and every startup will need a little heroics from time to time, but they should not be a regular part of work. When the occasional hero becomes an omnipresent hero, their work will start to suffer, and so will that of their colleagues, who will feel pressure to keep up and increase their own hours. Avoid this trap by creating a culture where people have not only flexible

---

5 Studies show that taking a break to browse the Web improves performance compared to not taking breaks at all [Silverman 2011].

hours but reasonable hours. Tell people to go home and make sure they take vacations. Force them if you have to. For example, Travis CI enforces a *minimum* vacation policy:

> Everyone now has a required minimum of 25 (paid) vacation days per year, no matter what country they live in. When people want to take time off beyond that, that's good, and the minimum policy still allows for that. But it sets a lower barrier of days that we expect our employees to focus on their own well-being rather than work.
>
> This policy is not just a guideline for our employees, it's mandatory for everyone, including the people who originally founded the company. As leaders, we need to set examples of what constitutes a healthy balance between work and life rather than give an example that life is all about the hustle.

—[MEYER 2014], MATHIAS MEYER, CEO AT TRAVIS CI

Forcing people to not work? And paying them for it? If that sounds extreme, consider the alternative: *burnout.* Burnout goes far beyond fatigue. It is the sense of being emotionally and physically exhausted, all the time. You are constantly worried, everything irritates you, and you can't focus. You'll catch yourself staring off into space, for hours at a time, completely unable to do anything productive. Your decision making suffers, your sleep suffers, and your relationships suffer. Generally, once someone is burned out, they will leave the company, and no pep talk, promotion, or raise will convince them to stay. Remember, vacation is cheaper than severance and training [Newland 2013].

A WAY TO CUSTOMIZE THE OFFICE FOR YOUR PERSONAL NEEDS

A company where every building, every floor, and every department looks exactly the same is sending its employees a message that it thinks of them as little more than replaceable, interchangeable, commodity parts. If you're going to spend thousands of hours per year in an office, you want it to feel like home, and not a dreary maze of identical cubicles. You've already seen a number of studies that show how much the work environment matters, but I'll share one more. Being able to control your work environment matters, too:

> In a 2005 study that looked at organizations ranging from a Midwest auto supplier to a Southwest telecom firm, researchers found that the ability to control the environment had a significant effect on team cohesion and

satisfaction. When workers couldn't change the way that things looked, adjust the lighting and temperature, or choose how to conduct meetings, spirits plummeted.

—[KONNIKOVA 2014], MARIA KONNIKOVA, *THE NEW YORKER*

Give employees as much control over the office as possible. For example, Git-Hub maintains an internal repo where any employee can file a ticket to suggest changes or improvements to the office. If enough interest is generated, the company green-lights the idea and makes it happen. At LinkedIn, we had a "Pimp Your Row" contest every few years, where everyone got a budget to decorate their cubicle row, and the row with the best decorations, based on popular vote, was awarded a prize [Brikman 2011b]. It was fun to walk around the office, vote for your favorites, and see just how unique every part looked. For example, our data infrastructure team built a climbing wall next to their cubes (see Figure 9-9) and the IT team converted their entire office area into a massive *Tron*-themed party (see Figure 9-10).

Figure 9-9. LinkedIn's new horizontally scalable infrastructure

You should also allow developers to get whatever tools they need. If you're a small startup, the easiest option is to allow developers to go buy the hardware and software they want and to reimburse them. If you're a larger company, you probably have an IT department that manages all the software and hardware. In that case, it's a good idea to run a survey every few months to find out what your developers want.

Figure 9-10. The Tron Party thrown by the IT department (photos courtesy of Mike Jennings [Jennings 2011])

What kind of tools do developers typically want? Here's a list to get you started:

- Desk built for programming (flat, large, with an adjustable height)
- Comfortable chair
- Fast laptop or desktop (max out the RAM, CPU, and hard drive)
- One or two large monitors
- Good mouse and keyboard
- Fast Internet connection everywhere in the office
- Plenty of power outlets
- Whiteboard
- Basic office supplies (notebooks, Post-its, pens, markers, printers)

- Storage space (a place for a jacket, bag, and private items)

Remote work

The alternative to a traditional office is to allow employees to work remotely. Many companies allow a developer to work from home on a one-off basis, but an increasing number of *distributed companies* are making remote work the default. Companies where a large percentage of employees work remotely include 37Signals, Automattic, GitHub, StackExchange, Typesafe, Mixcloud, Mozilla, Tree-House, Upworthy, Buffer, and MySQL [Prenzlow 2014]. Most of these companies still have an office, but they are open to hiring people anywhere in the world, so going to the office is optional.

Let's look at the benefits, drawbacks, and best practices of remote work.

BENEFITS

No matter where you are in the world, statistically, the vast majority of programmers are somewhere else. Many companies talk about hiring the best, but if you are only hiring candidates who can work in your local office, then you're only seeing a tiny fraction of the programmers out there. One of the biggest advantages of being a distributed company is that by not having to worry about where a developer happens to live, you are able to hire from a larger and more diverse pool of candidates.

It's liberating to be able to reach out to any developer who looks promising. This is especially useful for companies that participate in the open source community. If a developer starts contributing code to one of your projects, you know they are interested in the things you work on, you can get a sense of their abilities, and you can try to recruit them, no matter where they are in the world.

Remote work is also ideal for focused work. While any office is inherently a one-size-fits-all compromise, when you work remotely, you can choose an environment that perfectly suits you. That might mean working from a couch in your apartment, or a coffee shop, or a co-working space, or sitting outside in a park. You can have a window view, avoid distractions, wear what you want, and control your schedule—which is great for programmers, who are often night owls, and for parents, who may need to take care of their kids during the day. You could even travel the world while you work. For example, there is an engineer at Amazon who lives on a boat:

About four years ago, James and Jennifer Hamilton sold their house and their car and most of their worldly possessions, and they moved onto [their boat] the Dirona. Now, when he's berthed in Seattle, Hamilton bikes to Amazon headquarters, does his shopping via Amazon Prime, and picks up his mail at the local UPS store. But he's untethered. Sometimes, he takes the boat to Hawaii—and works from there.

—[MCMILLAN 2013], ROBERT MCMILLAN, *WIRED*

Remote work can save money, too. The company doesn't have to pay for as much office space or stock up on supplies. The employees don't have to waste time and money commuting to and from work. And employees who stay home with their kids may be able to save money on daycare and babysitters.

DRAWBACKS

Earlier in the chapter, I mentioned that an office needs to have four things:

1. A place where you can work with others.

2. A place where you can do focused work alone.

3. A place where you can get away from work.

4. A way to customize the office for your personal needs.

Working remotely is great for the last three requirements, but for the first, working with others, things are trickier. In a distributed company, most communication has to happen through writing, such as emails, chat, bug discussions, and wikis. This has some advantages, such as the fact that it's asynchronous, so you don't interrupt anyone and you can maintain a record of discussions, but it also has some drawbacks. For example, the feedback loop is slower. In an office, if you have a question, you can get an answer in seconds by tapping someone on the shoulder (though this has downsides, too, as you're distracting that person). With a remote setup, you might send an email or IM today, but not get a response until the following day, especially if you're in different time zones. Also, writing is a lower-bandwidth communication medium than in-person conversations, so for certain types of discussions such as decision making, brainstorming, and feedback, it's less effective.

Meetings are harder, too. You can use video conferencing, but if people are distributed across many time zones, finding a meeting time that works for everyone can be hard. Even if you find a good time, you have to waste 15 minutes at the start of every meeting while you wait for people to connect to the conference, fiddle with their microphone settings, and fight to get screen sharing to work. And even after that, the audio and video are often choppy and people's connections will randomly drop. The experience is just not the same as chatting in person.

But the biggest problem of all is that spontaneous, unplanned interactions are much less frequent. You don't get to eat lunch with your coworkers. You don't play sports together, go for walks, or relax at the local pub after work. It's harder to grab a couple people for a quick brainstorming session, mentor new hires, rally around a common mission, spread common values, build strong relationships with teammates, and celebrate milestones and accomplishments. A "great job everyone!" email is just not the same as cheering, high-fiving, and the sound of a champagne cork popping.

> *The main benefit to working remotely is actually also the main drawback. If you want to just shut up and do work with no distractions, it's really easy, but you also lose a lot of that internal communication because you're not in the same place at the same time. A lot of those ideas that float around when people chat over lunch just don't happen. So you need to encourage that to happen in other ways, like having chat rooms.*
>
> **—[CLAYTON 2014], MAT CLAYTON, CO-FOUNDER OF MIXCLOUD**

Not everyone has the skills needed for working from home. You have to learn how to manage your time, keep your work organized, communicate effectively through writing, handle household distractions (e.g., kids), and remain focused and motivated while alone. Some people thrive in that sort of setting and make for great remote employees, but others need more structure and interpersonal interaction to succeed. You also have to take extra care to ensure that your work remains secure. You don't want your company's private data on a home computer that has no password, is shared by the whole family, is infested with viruses, and communicates with the outside world over an unsecured WiFi connection.

BEST PRACTICES

> *It's a binary property: either the team is fully distributed or fully co-located. I don't believe in remote employees, only in remote (distributed) teams. That means that every single person on the team, even if they live*

on the same street, even if two of them come into the same office every day, even if they sit in the same room, still behaves like a distributed team and makes sure all the information flows in a fully distributed manner. Otherwise you easily get into the problem where two or three people talk at the coffee machine and they forget to take notes and bring the other team members up to speed. There is always someone feeling excluded. That just doesn't work.

—[BONÉR 2014], JONAS BONÉR, CO-FOUNDER OF TRIENTAL AB AND TYPESAFE

What does it mean to be a "distributed team" or to have information flowing in "a fully distributed manner"? The best answer comes from GitHub: your team should work like an open source project [Tomayko 2012]. Open source projects are inherently distributed, so they have developed practices over the last 20 years to make this model work. GitHub has embraced these practices and the constraints that lead to them as a way to run the entire company. Here is an excerpt from GitHub's internal product development documentation:

- *Electronic: Discussion, planning, and operations process should use a high-fidelity form of electronic communication like email, github.com, or chat with transcripts wherever possible. Avoid meatspace discussion and meetings.*

- *Available: Work should be visible and expose process. Work should have a URL. It should be possible to move backward from a piece of product or a system failure and understand how it came to be that way. Prefer git, issues, pull requests, mailing lists, and chat with transcripts over URL-less mediums.*

- *Asynchronous: Almost no part of the product development process requires that one person interrupt another's immediate attention or that people be in the same place at the same time, or even that people be in different places at the same time. Even small meetings or short phone calls can wreck flow so consider laying it out in (a thought out) email or sending a pull request instead.*

- *Lock free: Avoid synchronization/lock points when designing process. This is DVCS writ large. We don't have a development man-*

ager that grants commit bit to repositories before you can do work, or a release manager that approves deploys, or a product manager that approves work on experimental product ideas. Work toward a goal should never be blocked on approval. Push approval/rejection to the review stage or automate it, but surface work early to get feedback.

—[TOMAYKO 2012], RYAN TOMAYKO, SOFTWARE ARCHITECT AT GITHUB

In addition to embracing the open source model, just about every distributed company I talked to, including GitHub, Typesafe, and Mixcloud, pays for all employees to travel to regular, in-person meetings. This is a chance for the company to get everyone unified around the mission, to reinforce the values, to strengthen the culture, and to allow employees to meet face to face and bond with one another.

We fly everyone in three times a year for three to five days. We rotate between office locations like Sweden, Switzerland, and the United States, and once a year where our conference Scala Days happens to take place. One of them is usually mandatory, and then everyone flies in, including sales and marketing and admin people, and the other two are only engineering folks. And people love it. They really appreciate it. We're at 70-plus people now, so it's really costly, but it's worth every penny. We get so much done and we get to know each other. That's probably the most important thing.

Individual teams also meet more regularly. The Akka team meets every other week. They are all in Europe and they fly into somewhere in Europe. And the Play team, they meet every other quarter. They can meet more often, but they have decided not to. So, whatever works for the teams. Of course, we have budgets, but we try to be very flexible when it comes to that because it's so important.

—[BONÉR 2014], JONAS BONÉR, CO-FOUNDER OF TRIENTAL AB AND TYPESAFE

When you look at the distribution of the Mixcloud team, a lot of them are within an hour of London, so a lot of the product team will meet up fairly regularly. If we have something with multiple people working on it, we'll just get everyone into one place for a couple days or so. The guys in Romania, we fly in I'd say once a quarter. They'll come and spend a week on the ground with everyone. And then we started the last couple years of taking the whole product team away for a week on a holiday. It's not really a holiday; it's really more of a work-away. We rent a couple villas, get everyone under the same roof, we work 9–5, and after 5 p.m., we just go out and have fun.

—[CLAYTON 2014], MAT CLAYTON, CO-FOUNDER OF MIXCLOUD

One final piece of advice: most distributed companies start out as local companies. The co-founders usually know each other, live in the same area, and spend the first few months working in the same office (see "Co-founders" on page 468 for more information on finding co-founders). It's helpful to have everyone in the same building in the very early days of a startup when you're still trying to figure out the company culture and find product-market fit. It's only after you know *what* the company is and your focus shifts to figuring out the *how* that you should think about scaling the team by hiring remote workers and becoming a distributed company.

Communication

Every conversation, email, bug report, wiki page, slogan, and press release both reflects and shapes your company's culture. Communication is how you distribute your culture and how you change it. Let's take a closer look at two types of communication: internal communication, which is how employees communicate with one another, and external communication, which is how employees communicate with the outside world.

INTERNAL COMMUNICATION

When it comes to communication, the first thing to determine is what should be said and what shouldn't be said. In other words, how transparent is your company? How much you're willing to share depends on your core values and the type of business you're in, but most startups should default to being as transparent as possible. For example, at HubSpot, one of the core values is to be "radically and remarkably transparent." Internally, they try to share everything they can with employees. On their internal wiki, employees can find the company's financials (cash balance, burn-rate, P&L, etc.), board meeting slide decks, management meeting slide decks, "strategic" topics, and lots of fun HubSpot Lore & Mythology pages [HubSpot 2013].

There are a few things that almost every company should share internally to make sure all employees are aligned and moving the company in the same direction. For example, try this experiment: go around your company and ask each employee, "What are the top three priorities for the company this year?" If you get different answers from everyone, you need to do a better job of internal communication. There should be an easy way for employees to learn about the company's priorities and what projects the company is working on to accomplish those priorities, what projects succeeded or failed in the past, and to see how the company is performing financially.[6] This type of information should be available on an internal wiki or dashboard, and updates should be sent out to all employees on a regular basis (e.g., like a quarterly report). Some types of information, such as the company's mission and values, could even be published publicly, such as the Netflix Culture Deck [Hastings 2009] and the HubSpot Culture Code [HubSpot 2013], which have millions of views on SlideShare.

In addition to wikis and dashboards, an *all-hands meeting* is a great tool for internal communication. You should hold one at least once per quarter. At LinkedIn, we had an all-hands meeting every two weeks. We would get everyone into the same room (and when the company got larger, into the same video conference) and the CEO would discuss the company's priorities, celebrate our successes, and, just as importantly, learn from our failures.

> A healthy company culture encourages people to share bad news. A company that discusses its problems freely and openly can quickly solve them. A company that covers up its problems frustrates everyone involved. The resulting action item for CEOs: Build a culture that rewards —not punishes—people for getting problems into the open where they can be solved.
>
> **—[HOROWITZ 2014, 67], BEN HOROWITZ, *THE HARD THING ABOUT HARD THINGS***

During the all-hands meeting, one or two teams would have a chance to come up and update the company on what they are working on. The CFO might come up and share revenue numbers, or a product manager might tell us about

---

6 One exception is publicly traded companies, where there are strict SEC regulations around revealing financial data.

an upcoming redesign, or an engineer might talk about a technology that we've open sourced. We also had a tradition of having new hires introduce themselves to the company at the start of an all hands meeting. You would have to tell everyone your name, what job you'd be doing at LinkedIn, something about you that isn't on your LinkedIn profile, and then the fun part: you had to demonstrate a special skill or talent, or as a fallback, you could make an animal sound. I saw employees sing, play instruments, perform magic tricks, freestyle rap, perform athletic feats, and imitate cats, dogs, horses, and Donald Duck. There was even a flash mob from a group of interns who interrupted the CEO to do a choreographed dance [LinkedIn 2011].

An alternative form for an all-hands meeting is a periodic company dinner:

> Twilio is an API company, and one of our rituals is the requirement that every employee must build and demo an app built with the Twilio API in order to receive their logo track jacket and Kindle (which is a free company benefit). This goes for all departments: engineering, sales, finance, marketing.
>
> We have a company dinner each Wednesday where new hires demo their apps, and our CEO "knights" them by putting the jacket on them. It's great to see the whole company cheering for the new employee as they show off what they've built, no matter how simple or complex.
>
> For most non-engineering hires, the demo app is the first software development they've ever done. To support them, one of our engineers anchors a weekly code coaching session after hours, where anyone can drop in and get help.

—[CHU 2013], RENEE CHU, SOFTWARE ENGINEER AT TWILIO

Some startups have policies around how employees should communicate with one another. For example, GitHub has published its *15 rules for communicating at GitHub*, although they are more preferences than rules [Balter 2014]. These include a preference for asynchronous communication ("chat is inherently asynchronous; tapping someone on the shoulder is inherently being a jerk"), using the issue tracker as a way to handle most questions, ideas, and bugs, and preferring the issue tracker or chat instead of email for everything other than sensitive conversations ("email is typically reserved only for things like personnel discussions, one-to-one feedback, and external communication"). The payments startup Stripe takes the email idea in a slightly different direction: by convention, every email at Stripe is cc'd to the entire company or a particular team. Although it requires a lot of filtering, it helps the company preserve openness and makes it easy for everyone to stay up to date with what the company is doing [Maccaw 2012].

EXTERNAL COMMUNICATION

Just as with internal communication, the first thing to determine with external communication is what you should and shouldn't say. Some companies hire a PR team to strictly control their image and brand by limiting employee communication with the outside world. Other companies go in the opposite direction and encourage everyone to share as much as possible. Buffer, a startup that builds social media management tools, believes in radical transparency. They publicly share almost everything about the company, including the salary [Gascoigne 2013a] and equity packages [Gascoigne 2014] for every employee, the term sheets from investors [Gascoigne and Widrich 2014], and all the company's metrics, including a detailed breakdown of their financials [Widrich 2013].

The benefit of so much transparency is that it breeds trust. Compensation is no longer a secret that employees carefully guard from one another. Because everyone has access to the same information, there is less room for politics, and no one feels like they might be getting screwed. Moreover, the company is more accountable to its customers, investors, and employees, and any sort of discrimination, inequality, or unethical behavior is more obvious. The month after Buffer opened up their salary information, they got twice as many résumés as normal, and the culture fit among the candidates was much higher [Elmer 2014].

Radical transparency can be found in other startups, such as Moz, SumAll, Semco, and Balanced Payments [Elmer 2014]. You can find it outside of the startup world, too. For example, every publicly traded company is required by law to reveal on a quarterly basis their product metrics, financial performance, and executive compensation. The salary information for many government employees is also a matter of public record.[7] Another famous example is professional sports. For instance, if you're interested in the financial side of Major League

---

7 For example, Transparent California (*http://transparentcalifornia.com/*) lists all the salaries of California state employees.

Baseball, there are websites you can use to look up the salary of each player and a detailed valuation breakdown for each team.[8]

Once you've figured out what level of transparency you're comfortable with, there are three main types of external communication to consider. The first is how you design, market, and distribute your products, which I discuss in "Distribution" on page 159. The second is how you talk about your company through blog posts, open source software, and presentations, which I discuss in "Share" on page 516. The third is how you talk to customers, which I discuss in "Provide great customer service" on page 161.

Process

A company's core ideology is the *why*. The process is the *how*. While the why should be defined early and enforced consistently through the company, the how, for as long as possible, should be left up to each individual. The whole reason you hire talented employees is for their expertise in how to do things. The person closest to the problem is the best one to figure the process for solving it. Imposing a rigid structure from above usually only adds overhead and takes away that person's autonomy. In other words, if you do a good enough job of defining the why, the how will take care of itself.

> Why is culture so important to a business? Here is a simple way to frame it. The stronger the culture, the less corporate process a company needs. When the culture is strong, you can trust everyone to do the right thing. People can be independent and autonomous. ... Ever notice how families or tribes don't require much process? That is because there is such a strong trust and culture that it supersedes any process. In organizations (or even in a society) where culture is weak, you need an abundance of heavy, precise rules and processes.
>
> **—[CHESKY 2014A], BRIAN CHESKY, CO-FOUNDER, CEO OF AIRBNB**

If you get the culture right, your process will reduce down to a single idea: use good judgment.

---

8 See Spotrac (*http://www.spotrac.com/rankings/mlb/*) and Bloomberg Business's MLB Team Valuations (*http://bit.ly/mlb-value*).

USE GOOD JUDGMENT

Hubspot does not have a huge manual of policies and procedures. Instead, there's a three-word policy for just about everything: use good judgment.

- *Social media policy.*

- *Travel policy.*

- *Sick day policy.*

- *Buy a round of drinks at an event policy.*

- *Work from home during a blizzard policy.*

Our policy on all of these (and most other) things: use good judgment.

—[HUBSSPOT 2013], HUBSPOT CULTURE CODE

Nordstrom expresses a similar philosophy in its "employee handbook," which is a single 5"×8" card:

WELCOME TO NORDSTROM

We're glad to have you with our Company.

Our number one goal is to provide outstanding customer service. Set both your personal and professional goals high. We have great confidence in your ability to achieve them.

Nordstrom Rules
Rule #1: Use your good judgment in all situations.

There will be no additional rules.

Please feel free to ask your department manager, store manager, or division general manager any question at any time.

—[COLLINS PORRAS 2004, 117], JIM COLLINS AND JERRY I. PORRAS, *BUILT TO LAST*

This doesn't mean you should have no process at all, but that "use good judgment" should be the default process, and you only enforce additional steps on top of that for special cases where "good judgment" has been proven to not be enough. For example, let's say a developer accidentally introduced a bug while changing a database configuration file. This bug brought down the database in the middle of the night and you had to scramble to fix it. There are three ways to deal with this problem:

1. Discuss and document what went wrong and move on with your life.

2. Build an automated solution to prevent this problem in the future.

3. Introduce a manual process to prevent this problem in the future.

In most cases, option #1 is the right choice. Discussing what went wrong offers an opportunity to learn from your mistakes (or the mistakes of your co-workers) and can improve your "use good judgment" skills enough to ensure that type of bug never happens again. Documenting the issue allows everyone to learn from previous mistakes. It also helps to identify the special cases where "use good judgment" is not enough. For example, if you see in your documentation that the database configuration bug has happened many times before, then you might need a better fix than just discussing and documenting the issue. In that case, your next step should be to look at option #2, automation.

Computers are better at carrying out a rigid, repetitive process than humans, so any time you identify a problem that can't be fixed through judgment alone, you should try to create an automated solution. Automated tests (see "Automated Tests" on page 296), static analysis (see "Static analysis" on page 332), continuous integration (see "Continuous Integration" on page 358), and continuous delivery (see "Continuous Delivery" on page 372) can prevent a huge range of issues. For example, you might be able to catch the database configuration bug before it gets into production by automatically deploying every database configuration change to a staging environment and running automated tests against it. Only if there is no practical way to automate a solution should you consider option #3, a manual process.

Introducing manual process should always be your last resort. For example, you could require that for every database change, the developer has to file a "database ticket" and get it approved by a DBA, and every deployment requires the developer to file a "deployment ticket" and get it approved by a release engineer. The problem is that adding a manual process is expensive. You're adding overhead to every database and deployment change for the rest of your company's history. You're taking autonomy away from your developers, preventing them from learning from their mistakes, and instead treating them like robots that periodically need a few extra mechanical steps to get things right. And you're paying this price with no guarantee that it makes the situation better.

Many manual processes are ineffective because they rely on humans to carry out repetitive tasks, something we're not good at and we tend to resent. It's entirely possible the configuration bug will slip by the DBA or release engineer, just like it slipped by the original developer. Moreover, it's possible that the issue is rare, so the overhead of the manual process will cost your company far more than just fixing the issue when it comes up. In other words, some types of bugs happen so infrequently or are so cheap to fix (see "Feature toggles" on page 363) that reacting to them is more efficient than trying to prevent them.

SOFTWARE METHODOLOGIES

But what about software development methodologies? Do they prevent sloppy errors like the database bug? Should you use a process like Agile, Waterfall, XP, Spiral, Crystal, BDD, FDD, DDD, DSDM, PDD, Lean, Scrum, Kanban, or Scrumban?[9] Some of these processes can be useful for organizing large projects and teams, but don't expect a silver bullet:

> *There is no single development, in either technology or management technique, which by itself promises even one order of magnitude [tenfold] improvement within a decade in productivity, in reliability, in simplicity.*
>
> **—[BROOKS 1995, CHAP. 16], FRED BROOKS, *MYTHICAL MAN MONTH***

When working on a large project, there are two types of complexity: essential complexity and accidental complexity. Essential complexity is an inherent part of the problem you're trying to solve. For example, if you're working on financial trading algorithms, figuring out an algorithm that can outsmart the market is part of the essential complexity of the problem—there is no way to work around it. Accidental complexity is incidental to the problem and arises as a side effect of your particular method of solving it. If you are using C++ to implement your financial trading algorithm, then memory leaks and segmentation faults are incidental complexity that come from having to manually manage memory in the

---

9 Some of these methodologies I made up. See if you can tell which.

language—you could avoid that complexity by choosing a different language with automatic memory management, such as Java.

Essential complexity is a large part of most software projects, and no software methodology can help you avoid that. The best you can hope for from a software methodology is that it minimizes accidental complexity—such as two co-workers wasting time on duplicated effort due to poor communication—though you shouldn't expect much, as the differences between methodologies are usually fairly small. On the other hand, the differences between developers can be huge (see "10x developers" on page 472). The people you hire (the *who*) and the way you get them aligned around a common mission (the *why*) will have a bigger impact on the success of the project than the methodology you select (the *how*).

> The maddening thing about most of our organizations is that they are only as good as the people who staff them. Wouldn't it be nice if we could get around that natural limit, and have good organizations even though they were staffed by mediocre or incompetent people? Nothing could be easier —all we need is (trumpet fanfare, please) a Methodology.
>
> **—[DEMARCO AND LISTER 1999, 114], TOM DEMARCO AND TIMOTHY LISTER,**
> **PEOPLEWARE**

All of this means that introducing a software development methodology is no different than introducing any other type of process at the company: do it only when "use good judgment" has been proven to not be enough. Most of the start-ups I talked to avoided any methodology that came with a fancy name, a book, and a certification, but when they got large enough, just about all of them followed a process that is best described as "roughly Agile."

Why Agile? One of the key themes of this book is that successful companies are the result of evolution, not intelligent design, an idea that meshes nicely with the *Agile Manifesto*, which states that "responding to change" is more valuable than "following a plan" [Beck et al. 2001]. Agile encourages an iterative and incremental development process with regular feedback from customers (see "Speed Wins" on page 51) and, perhaps most importantly, a key aspect of the Agile process is the ability to evolve itself. Most Agile methodologies include regular *retrospective meetings* to evaluate what is and isn't working in the process and adapt it as necessary to fit the organization's needs. For a practical guide on how to set up an Agile process at your own company, check out *Extreme Programming*

Explained: Embrace Change [Beck and Andres 2004] and *The Art of Agile Development* [Shore and Warden 2007].

Why only "roughly" Agile? Because applying any methodology too strictly has drawbacks. One of the goals of most software methodologies is to "bring up the bottom." That is, they impose a process that is intentionally inflexible so as to minimize common errors and maximize the uniformity and predictability of the output. The downside is that programming is an inherently creative task, so any inflexible approach inherently inhibits innovation and creative problem solving. In other words, applying a methodology rigidly to bring up the bottom only does so at the cost of cutting off the top, preventing developers from performing at their best and getting in the way of building a culture that can constantly improve [Petre and Damian 2014].

Recap

The book *Built to Last* [Collins and Porras 2004] outlines the results of a six-year research project into what it takes to build a "visionary company"—that is, a company that is considered to be one of the best in its industry; that has endured through many years, products, and leaders; and has made a lasting impact on the world—such as Disney, IBM, Boeing, and General Electric. One of the key findings in the book is that the leaders of visionary companies focused on creating a great organization rather than a great product—they were "clock builders," not "time tellers." Their greatest creation was not a specific idea or a product but the company itself and what it stands for [Collins Porras 2004].

In other words, great companies start with a great culture. They are built around an inspiring mission. They define their core values and turn to them for every decision. They align the company around the mission and values through organizational design, hiring, promotions, motivation, the office, remote work, communication, and process. And they do all of this not just to create a great product or to make lots of money, but to build a great company.

> *"Company culture" doesn't exist apart from the company itself: no company has a culture; every company is a culture. A startup is a team of people on a mission, and a good culture is just what that looks like on the inside.*
>
> **—[THIEL 2014, 119], PETER THIEL, *ZERO TO ONE***

Tom Preston-Werner, one of the GitHub co-founders, once asked in a talk, "Why do companies exist?" Is it to make money? Or is to make people happy? He argued for the latter using a "subtraction proof":

> *Take a company and subtract the profit. What do you get? A startup. Take a company and subtract the people. What do you get? Nothing. It can't exist.*
>
> **—[PRESTON-WERNER 2012], TOM PRESTON-WERNER, GITHUB CO-FOUNDER**

It's a funny proof, but the talk, called "Optimizing for Happiness" [Preston-Werner 2012], has a serious point: companies should be about making people happy, not about profits. In other words, startups are about people. Startups that optimize for happiness create a virtuous cycle. When employees are happy, they can make the company stronger, and when the company is strong, it can make the employees happier. It is not a coincidence that the most successful startups in the world go out of their way to make employees happy with the zany, quirky, culture hacks you saw in this chapter, such as GitHub's oval office, Google's 20% time, and Twilio's "knighting" ritual. Some of these practices may sound crazy or expensive or wasteful, but they are fun. And be honest, wouldn't you rather work at a company that's fun?

> *There is no reason to believe any longer that only irrelevant* **play** *can be enjoyed, while the serious business of life must be borne as a burdensome cross. Once we realize that the boundaries between work and play are artificial, we can take matters in hand and begin the difficult task of making life more livable.*
>
> **—[PINK 2011, 128], DANIEL PINK, *DRIVE***

Getting a Job at a Startup

You've read Chapter 1 and you know you want to work for a startup. How do you find a good one to join? How do you get the company to be interested in you? What do you do at the interview? How do you evaluate the company and its offer?

The first step to getting a great job is to make yourself great, something I'll discuss in Chapter 12. In this chapter, I will walk you through the process of getting hired at a startup. I'll start by describing how to find startup jobs, then review what it takes to ace the interview, and finally discuss how to evaluate and negotiate job offers.

Finding a startup job

The first step to finding a great startup job is to know what you're looking for. Sit down and try to answer the following questions:

What industries and types of products are you interested in?

Examples: medicine, e-commerce, news, travel, social networking, games, video, finance, communications, security.

What technologies are you passionate about?

Examples: embedded systems, mobile apps, distributed systems, functional programming, robotics, biosensors, machine learning, information retrieval, graphics.

What type of business model are you interested in?

Examples: advertising (display, affiliate, lead gen), commerce (retail, marketplace, auction), subscription (SaaS, membership, paywall), peer to peer (messaging, sharing, buying), transaction processing (merchants, banks), data (business intelligence, market research), open source (consulting, support, hosting, licensing). See [Darville 2014] for a comprehensive list of startup business models.

What role are you looking for?

Examples: entry-level, senior-level, lead, manager, CTO, frontend, backend, tools, devops.

What other factors are you looking for?

Examples: location, commute, company size, travel, free food, work from home.

Not all of these questions will be equally important to you and you might not know the answers to some of them, especially if you're a younger developer. However, write down the ones you do know and care about, as it'll help focus your search.

USE YOUR NETWORK

Opportunities do not float like clouds. They are firmly attached to individuals. If you're looking for an opportunity, you're really looking for people. If you're evaluating an opportunity, you're really evaluating people. If you're trying to marshal resources to go after an opportunity, you're really trying to enlist the support and involvement of other people. A company doesn't offer you a job, people do.

—[HOFFMAN AND CASNOCHA 2012, 153], REID HOFFMAN AND BEN CASNOCHA, *THE START-UP OF YOU*

Now that you have some idea of the job you're looking for, don't rush ahead and start digging through online job boards. As many as 80% of jobs are not publicly advertised [Nishi 2013]. That means that the majority of the time you spend looking for a job should be spent interacting with your network. Get out there and talk with your friends and colleagues and let them know what you're looking for based on your answers from the previous section. They will tell you about hidden job opportunities and give you a more honest look at what the job is like than you'd ever get from a job posting. A referral will also increase your chances of getting the job. Your odds of being hired through a job board are roughly one in 100, while your odds of being hired via a referral are one in seven [Kasper 2012].

So how do you get connected to the right people? How do you build a network? Your network might be larger than you think. LinkedIn is powerful tool to inspect your network, including not just your personal connections (first degree), but their connections (second degree), and the connections of their connections (third degree). If you have just 50 connections, and each of them has 50 connections, and so on down the line, then your third-degree network is 125,000 people (50 * 50 * 50). For example, if you visit the company page of a company you're interested in, you'll be able to see who you're connected to in the upper-right corner, as shown in Figure 10-1.

Figure 10-1. A LinkedIn company page shows how you're connected to the company (image from the [Grishaver 2012])

If you've got a first-degree contact there already, send them a message. If you've got second- or third-degree contacts, click on them to see their profile. On the right side of the profile page, you'll see how you're connected to this person and what you have in common, as shown in Figure 10-2.

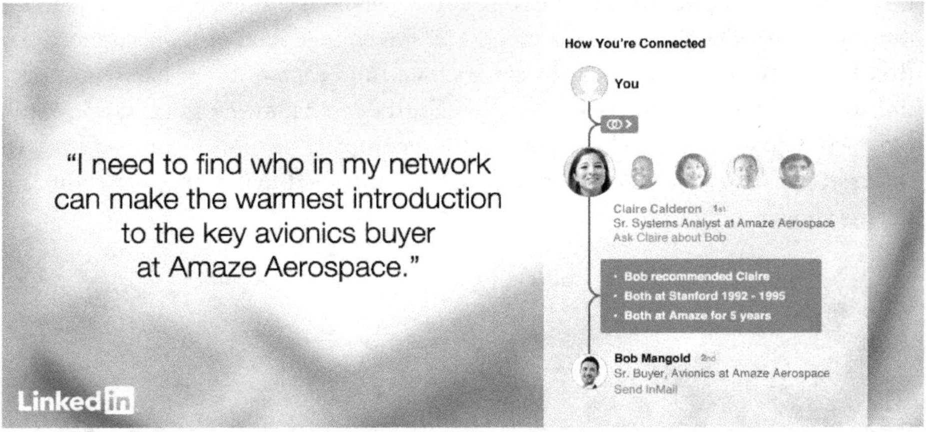

Figure 10-2. A LinkedIn profile shows how you're connected to the person (image from the [Milo 2014])

Browse your contacts on LinkedIn, Facebook, Twitter, and in your email address book. Reach out to them to ask for an introduction or a referral, or just to invite them for a chat over coffee. It doesn't have to be too formal. Most people like to talk about themselves and their work, so just tell them you're interested in learning about what they do. If there are job openings, they will let you know as a natural part of this conversation.

GROW YOUR NETWORK

If you're not already connected to the right opportunities—that is, the right people—then your next priority is to grow your network. If you want to meet new people, you have to go to new places.

Meetup groups and conferences

Are you interested in Java? As of 2014, Meetup.com lists 900 meetup groups in 66 countries for Java, with a total membership of over 280,000 people. Want to hack on Node.js? There are 386 groups, 54 countries, 94,000 members. Excited about big data? You've got 2,156 groups in 72 countries to choose from and more than half a million other data scientists who will join you. If you want something bigger than a meetup, there are also plenty of conferences around the world: for 2013, Lanyrd lists 153 Java conferences, 125 Node.js conferences, and 232 Big Data conferences.

Meetups and conferences are everywhere and they are a great way to learn new skills and meet new people in the community. They also offer plenty of opportunities for companies to advertise their job openings. Many meetups start with hiring announcements and most conference sponsors, organizers, and speakers will advertise jobs.

Can't find any good meetups in your area? Start your own! It doesn't have to be huge. Get the word out and gather 10–20 developers to discuss a topic that interests you. You'll not only get the opportunity to learn something new and meet new people, you'll also build your own brand as a meetup organizer.

Hackathons and competitions

Coding competitions are a great way to improve your skills, meet new people, score free food and swag, and compete for cash prizes. Just about every coding competition is also a recruiting event under the hood: companies (i.e., the sponsors) throw money at these events in exchange for a chance to hire the attendees.

There are many varieties of coding competition, including algorithmic challenges, where everyone gets the exact same problem and constraints and the goal is to figure out the most efficient algorithm to solve the problem; data challenges, where you are given a data set and asked to come up with the most interesting insights or predictions; and hackathons, which are open-ended competitions where you can show off your creativity by producing the best hack, sometimes subject to a specific theme (e.g., best hack to improve education).[1]

> I had a person who emailed me two or three years ago who was a software engineer at a bank—not a JP Morgan or a first-tier bank but a mid-tier, relatively unknown regional bank—and they said, "I want to join a startup, what should I do?" What I said was, go out, do two or three hackathons, and spend a couple weeks building projects. You can change your résumé from being a B or C résumé to being at least B+ or A- in a matter of a couple months. Then get out to Silicon Valley and start applying to companies, because there are so many more opportunities in the Bay Area or any tech center than there are in any other city. They emailed me a year

---

1 In this context, I am using the original definition of "hack:" to write computer programs for enjoyment or to jury-rig or improvise something inelegant but effective, often as a rapid prototype or proof of concept. This is *not* the version used in the news today, which means to illegally break into computer systems and networks.

*later and they were one of the early engineers at Uber, making a lot of
money and doing a lot better now.*

—[MCDOWELL 2015], GAYLE LAAKMANN MCDOWELL, FOUNDER AND CEO OF CAREERCUP

Check out *http://www.hello-startup.net/resources/jobs/* to find coding competitions near you.

Talks, blog posts, open source

If you want a community to notice you, the best way is to contribute to it. Give talks, write blog posts, open source your code, get on the mailing lists, answer questions on Stack Overflow, and chat on IRC. Every time I've attended a conference or meetup, I walked away with 5–10 new connections; every time I've presented at a conference or meetup, I walked away with dozens of new connections. Check out "Share" on page 516 for a full discussion of blogging, talks, and open source.

BUILD AN ONLINE IDENTITY

If you can't find a job through your network, the next next best thing is if a job finds you. Over the last 5 years, I've received approximately 1,300 emails from startup founders, hiring managers, and recruiters. That works out to at least 1 job opportunity in my inbox every single business day. I no longer apply to jobs—they apply to me.

Almost any programmer can accomplish something similar by building an online identity in the right places. If you want companies to find you, your name should show up in the places they go. Your first stop: LinkedIn. As a former LinkedIn employee, I'm certainly biased, so don't take it from me. In *The Recruiter Honeypot*, Elaine Wherry describes how she tried to attract recruiters to a fake online persona for a "JavaScript Ninja" by the name of Pete London:

> *I stewed on the idea of posting my résumé online with a fictitious name for days and then one sleepless night, without telling anyone, I woke up and posted a small three-page website with an about page, résumé, and blog for a supposed Pete London whose interests and engineering persona mirrored my own except he wasn't a founder. I swapped out my post-graduate experience with my husband so it wouldn't be too easy to trace back to me. I returned to bed with a small glimmer of hope—I had been hunting for recruiters for months but now the recruiters would come to me!*

My hopes sank pretty quickly. PeteLondon.com sat alone in Internet ether for weeks with absolutely nada activity. I was about to pull down the entire site when I thought—I'll just post the résumé on LinkedIn as a last resort.

Bam. It was as if I'd finally stumbled upon the door to the party. On December 10, 2009, the first LinkedIn message arrived from Google. Mozilla followed on December 15. Ning and Facebook followed in January. Since then, Pete averaged a recruiter ping every 40 hours and saw 530 emails from 382 recruiters across 172 organizations.

—[WHERRY 2012], ELAINE WHERRY, CO-FOUNDER OF MEEBO

Julia Grace echoes the same ideas about LinkedIn in "Tips for Finding Software Engineering Jobs":

Mistake: "Do people actually use LinkedIn? I don't think so, the last time I updated my profile was two years ago and no one looks at it."

Correction: People use LinkedIn all the time. Really, all the time. It's recruiter crack. ... LinkedIn is also used by anyone who might be interviewing you at a company—they are more likely to read your LinkedIn than your résumé (click a link or open a PDF/Word/text document—which would you do?). Keep it up to date and point people to it—it is much easier to maintain than a PDF/Word/text résumé, easily findable and you don't even have to host it yourself! I have not used a résumé outside of LinkedIn in 4+ years.

Bottom Line: You want to be easily findable for new job opportunities; this is especially true early in your career when no one knows who you are or that you even exist. Let's say a year from now an acquaintance that you met is at a hot new startup and wants to see if you'd be interested in joining. First thing s/he will do is search LinkedIn.

—[GRACE 2014], JULIA GRACE, CO-FOUNDER OF WEDDINGLOVELY, CTO AT TINDIE

If you want to set up a LinkedIn profile that gets a lot of hits, you need to understand how recruiters and hiring managers use LinkedIn. Most of them use a product called LinkedIn Recruiter to run keyword searches and boolean queries along the lines of "Java AND JavaScript AND MySQL." They will also filter the results by years of experience, degree, field of study, previous companies, and location, as shown in Figure 10-3.

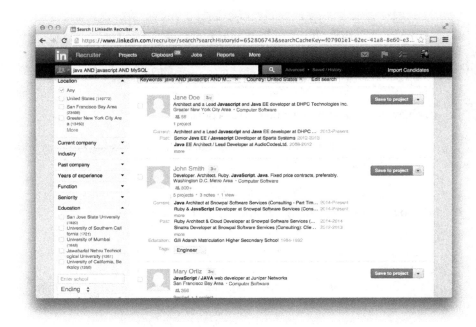

Figure 10-3. LinkedIn Recruiter Search

If you want recruiters to find you, fill out your LinkedIn profile as much as possible. You should put roughly the same things in your profile as you would your résumé.[2] Fill out your work history (job titles and brief descriptions), education (degree, field of study, key projects and classes), key skills (languages, technologies, and techniques you're good at), and list any publications (blog, articles, papers, patents, books, talks), and projects (side projects, open source). Put the most important items at the top and use bullet points instead of paragraphs, as recruiters will only spend around 15 seconds skimming any profile or résumé. Also, make sure to focus on concrete accomplishments and not responsibilities. For example, if you're a programmer, don't list "responsible for product X" (this

---

2 See CareerCup (*http://www.careercup.com/resume*) on more résumé advice.

is obvious from your job title) or "communicated effectively in a collaborative environment" (this is just meaningless filler text) and instead write "designed and developed feature Y from scratch, using technology Z," or even better, quantify your accomplishments, such as, "designed and developed feature Y from scratch in three months, using technology Z, which led to a 50% increase in engagement across the product."

Besides LinkedIn, some other places where you may want to build an online identity include GitHub, Stack Overflow, Twitter, SlideShare, and a personal home page or blog. To check your online identity, just run a search for your name on Google.[3] What results come up? Do they present you in a positive light to a potential employer? Can you be found at all? Most hiring managers and recruiters will perform exactly this sort of search, and if they can't find you on Google or LinkedIn, you don't exist.

ONLINE JOB SEARCH

Although you should spend the vast majority of your time (roughly 80%) building out your network and personal brand, it's also a good idea to spend a little time (roughly 20%) doing some old-fashioned job searches online. Bear in mind that the majority of startup jobs, especially at early-stage startups, won't be found on traditional job boards. Instead, you should focus on startup accelerator portfolios, venture capital firm portfolios, crowdfunding sites, coding competitions, and programmer websites. See *http://www.hello-startup.net/resources/jobs/* for a comprehensive list of startup job resources. Find startups that interest you and reach out to them directly—or better yet, through your network.

Nailing the interview

You might be a fantastic developer and a great fit for the company, but unless you know how to demonstrate that in an interview setting, you still might not get the job. The reason is simple: the interview process is flawed. The typical interviewer has an hour to decide if they want to work with you for the next several years. What can you really find out about a person in an hour? What hiring process can you use that is repeatable across many interviews and many interviewers? While some practices are better than others (see "The interview" on page 487), none will be perfect, and all will demand that you, as a candidate, can

---

3 Preferably in incognito mode, as Google customizes search results for logged in users.

demonstrate interview-specific skills that sometimes fall outside of your normal day-to-day programming activities.

The good news is that interviewing is a skill and you can get better at it with practice. The key things you need to master are coding on a whiteboard, thinking out loud, know thyself, know the company, and short, repetitive Computer Science 101 problems.

CODING ON A WHITEBOARD

Writing code on a whiteboard is a terrible interview practice (see "Interview questions" on page 489), but it's part of the process at most companies. It's an unnatural environment for coding: you write by hand instead of typing, you have no syntax highlighting, no IDE, no compiler, no cut and paste, no Google, no Stack Overflow, and none of the other tools you're accustomed to using. It's painful, but you're going to have to do it. Practice it.

THINKING OUT LOUD

You are probably most comfortable solving problems silently in your head. Unfortunately, if you do this, the interviewer will have no idea how you got to a solution, how to help you if you get stuck, or how to evaluate your performance. Therefore, you need to practice thinking through problems out loud. Also, don't be surprised if you end up struggling. Most interview problems are designed to make you struggle and think a bit, so don't panic if you don't know the answer right away. Keep thinking out loud, proposing ideas, trying examples, and make any progress you can. Thinking through problems out loud can feel unnatural, but it's a generally useful skill (e.g. in-pair coding and design meetings) and an essential one for interviewing. Practice it.

KNOW THYSELF

Besides coding questions, most interviewers will ask you questions about yourself, such as:

- Tell me about yourself.
- What projects have you worked on before?
- Why are you looking for a new job?
- Why do you want to work here?
- What is your ideal job?

- What do you want to be doing in five years? Ten years?
- What are your greatest strengths? Weaknesses?
- What is your greatest accomplishment?
- What was the toughest bug you ever fixed?
- What else should I have asked you?

Some of these sound cheesy, but they come up often. Practice them.

KNOW THE COMPANY

While a company is interviewing you, you should also be interviewing them. A startup job is a serious commitment—it'll easily eat up half of your waking hours for the next several years—so you want to find out as much as possible. Before the interview, research the company and its employees: who are they, what have they done in the past, where are they going in the future? You should also spend time during the interview asking questions about anything you can't find through research. Don't leave the interview without knowing:

- What are the expectations for the role?
- What does success look like in this job?
- Who will be my manager?
- What projects will I work on?
- What is the tech stack?
- What are the hours like? How many of them are spent coding? In meetings?
- How do you build and release code?
- What are the company's mission and values?
- What is the office like?
- What's your favorite and least favorite part of working here?

Almost every interviewer will give you a chance to ask questions. Coming up with questions on the spot isn't always easy and you'll look bad as a candidate if you can't think of anything to ask. Practice it.

SHORT, REPETITIVE CS 101 PROBLEMS

Due to time constraints, most interview questions will be not be large, open-ended, real-world problems but small problems with a limited scope that test basic knowledge, usually from introductory CS courses, of data structures, algorithms, and design thinking. The same small set of topics—big O notation, string manipulation, array manipulation, list traversal, tree traversal, iteration, recursion, and dynamic programming—tend to come up in most interviews, so get yourself a copy of *Cracking the Coding Interview* [McDowell 2011] and *Programming Interviews Exposed* [Mongan, Suojanen and Giguère 2007], which cover 90% or more of what you'll run into in a typical interview, practice the problems in both books, and you'll dramatically improve your chances.

How to evaluate and negotiate a job offer

You found a company you liked, you aced the interview, and now you have an offer. Should you take it? What do you look for? How do you negotiate?

The most important part of a job offer is the people behind it. Are you ready to spend 40+ hours per week with them? Will you be able to learn from them? Will they help you grow your career? Is it fun to be around them? Are they dedicated and talented enough to make this company successful? Are you finding it hard to make such a judgment call from just a few hours of interviewing? Now you know how the interviewer feels.

You don't have much choice but to go with your instinct. Usually, it's right. If something felt off about the people or someone made you feel uncomfortable, there is a chance that it will only get worse. On the other hand, if you had great conversations, found similar passions, and laughed a lot, then it might be a healthy atmosphere. Pay special attention to your direct manager. Try to get an understanding of their management style, what their direct reports think of them, and what sort of role and career path they have lined up for you. This one person will have a disproportionate influence on your success at and enjoyment of a company. The old aphorism is true: people don't leave companies, they leave managers.

If the people are awesome, your next thought should be about the business itself. Is this a product you're passionate about? Do you want to spend thousands of hours on it over the next several years? Do you use it yourself? Would you be proud of showing something like this to your parents? It's possible to work in boring industries or on products you aren't personally interested in, but it will make it harder to do a good job and be happy about your work.

Finally, if you're happy with both the people and the product, you can begin to consider the financial aspects of the offer. There are three key aspects to compensation: salary, equity, and benefits.

SALARY

There are two thresholds when considering a salary:

- Is it enough for my lifestyle?
- Is it a fair rate for the job I'm doing?

The first threshold depends on the person: someone fresh out of college sharing an apartment with roommates will have different salary needs than someone with a house, a mortgage, and kids. If the salary in the offer does not cover your basic living expenses, you either reject the offer or negotiate for a higher salary. Paying rent and eating are not optional.

If the offer passes the first threshold, you should then see how it compares to the competition. Use an online salary calculator to figure out the average salary for a similar position in the area.[4] If the offer covers living expenses, but is below market rate, it's only worth it if the other parts of the offer—the equity and benefits—make up for it.

EQUITY

What is equity? What are stock options? What's an IPO? For most programmers at early-stage startups, equity, and not salary, is the most important part of a job offer. However, coming out of college, I had no idea how equity worked and was often too embarrassed to ask. Searching online didn't help either, as most of the results made heavy use of impenetrable legal and financial jargon. As a result, I didn't pay attention to equity for much of my early career and missed out on a lot of potential earnings. Many of the programmers I interviewed had similar experiences:

> I was deciding between Oracle and Facebook. If Facebook hadn't offered me a higher salary than Oracle, I'm not sure I would have taken the job offer, which is ridiculous, because salary ended up being just a tiny per-

---

4 See http://www.hello-startup.net/resources/salary/.

centage of the overall compensation. But I didn't know what equity was. It meant nothing to me; it was just an afterthought.

—[KIM 2014], DANIEL KIM, SOFTWARE ENGINEER AT FACEBOOK AND INSTAGRAM

This section is a brief introduction to equity and why it matters. I wish I had this information earlier in my career. I hope it helps you!

What is stock?

Imagine two friends start a company. Each one wants to own 50% of the company, but how do they keep track of that? What they need is some sort of convenient mechanism that lets them track ownership of the company and how it changes over time as they sell parts of the company to investors or employees. For modern companies, that mechanism is *stock*, where each share of stock represents the ownership of a small fraction of the company. In the past, companies would print the stock information on paper, called stock certificates, but these days, most stock information is maintained digitally.

For example, the two founders can decide that ownership of the company will be represented by 10 million shares of stock, with each founder getting 5 million shares. The number of shares is arbitrary and the founders could have just as easily decided to represent the company with 1,000 shares or 1 billion shares. However, you need to know the total number of shares (usually called *shares outstanding*) to know what percentage of the company you own. In our example, each founder owns 5 million shares out of 10 million shares outstanding, or 50% of the company.

How do employees get stock?

Now imagine the two founders want to start hiring. One of the incentives they can offer employees is to own a part of the company. This is typically done by issuing new stock to give out as compensation. For example, the founders may create a pool of 1 million shares that they set aside for hiring. They create this stock out of thin air (like printing money!), but note that there are now 11 million shares outstanding, and as each founder still has 5 million shares, they now own 45% of the company instead of 50%. This reduction in ownership is known as *dilution*.

Existing stockholders get diluted every time the company issues new stock for hiring or to give out to investors. This may seem like a bad deal for the founders, but the bet is that hiring new people or taking on more investment will make the company more valuable and more than make up for the dilution. For example, let's say the company was valued at $500,000 before the co-founders start hiring, so each co-founder owned $250,000. After issuing one million shares of stock for hiring, they are able to hire five employees, who help raise the value of the company up to $1 million. Due to dilution, each co-founder now owns a smaller percentage of the company (45% instead of 50%), but the smaller percentage is actually worth more ($450,000 instead of $250,000). In other words, as a stockholder, it's OK to own a smaller slice of the pie as long as the entire pie gets bigger.

If you get an offer from a startup, it may grant you some number of shares—this is your *equity*. For example, you might get an offer that grants you 100,000 shares. By itself, this number means nothing. You need to know how many shares the company has outstanding. Hopefully, this is in your offer. If not, ask what percentage of the company your shares represent on a *fully diluted basis*. This forces the company to tell you not only how many shares it has already given out, but also any stock it's obligated to give out in the future and the option pool set aside for hiring. If the company refuses to give you this number, it's a red flag, and you should not join. If you can, you should also ask about future fundraising and hiring plans to try to get a sense of how much your ownership percentage may be diluted.[5] In our example, you know the company has 11 million shares outstanding, so you would own 100,000 / 11,000,000 = 0.9% of the company.

What is vesting?

You usually don't get all the shares up front; instead, they are distributed to you over a period of time. This is known as *vesting* and a typical vesting schedule lasts four years: you get no shares initially, then 25% of the shares after the first year (the *cliff*), and then the remaining 75% are evenly distributed over the following 36 months. The idea is to grant you the stock incrementally as an incentive to keep you at the company longer. Otherwise, without a vesting schedule, you could quit on your second day and walk away with 100,000 shares. Typically, everyone at the company, including the co-founders, is subject to a vesting schedule.

---

5 There are a number of other questions you should ask the company about its stock options, as described by Andy Rachleff in "14 Crucial Questions about Stock Options".

What are stock options?

Even as you vest, the company doesn't just hand the stock to you. Typically, what you're actually vesting are *stock options*, which give you the right to purchase (AKA *exercise*) the stock at a fixed price called the *strike price*. The strike price represents the *fair market value (FMV)* of the stock at the time you got your offer. Where does the FMV come from? Usually, it is determined by the Board of Directors based on a process known as the 409A valuation.

For example, if the 409A valued the company at $1.1 million, the strike price would be $1,100,000 / 11,000,000 shares = $0.10 per share. After working at the company for four years, you will have vested all of your stock options, but you won't be able to do anything with them until you exercise them. To exercise all of your stock options, you'd have to pay 100,000 * $0.10 = $10,000. Only after exercising your shares can you actually sell them. Your goal, of course, is to sell them for much more than you paid.

How do you sell your stock?

Initially, shares of stock are worth nothing, because you can't sell them to anyone (they are not *liquid*). There are two common types of *liquidity events* (AKA *exits*) by which the stock becomes valuable:

Initial public offering (IPO)
> An IPO is when the company sells its stock to the public. IPOs help companies raise money and allow the shareholders (the co-founders, employees, and investors) to sell their stock to the market.

Acquisition
> When a company is acquired, another company buys the stock from your company's shareholders (i.e., the co-founders, employees, and investors) for cash, its own stock, or some mix of both.

For example, if your company had an IPO and the stock price went to $1/ share, you would be able to sell your shares for 100,000 * $1 = $100,000. Similarly, if your company were to be acquired, the acquirer may agree to pay $1/ share for your stock, in which case you would again get $100,000.[6]

---

6 As with all the calculations in this chapter, this is a simplification. For more information on how acquisitions work, see "14 Crucial Questions About Stock Options."

How is stock taxed?

Any profit you make off of your stock options will be taxed.[7] With the IPO example above, your profit would be $100,000 - $10,000 = $90,000. The laws around how this profit gets taxed are complicated and a full discussion of them is beyond the scope of this book. If you're ever in a position where you're making significant financial decisions regarding stock, make sure to work with a tax specialist. They usually charge just a few hundred dollars, which is only a fraction of the money you'll be dealing with and far cheaper than fixing a tax screw-up later. To help you know what to look for, I'll briefly discuss two main tax issues related to stock options: short-term versus long-term capital gains and the gotchas of exercising options.

Short-term versus long-term capital gains

If you sell your stock options less than one year and one day after exercising them, the profit you make from selling them gets taxed as *short-term capital gains*. That is, it's taxed as normal income, as if it were part of your salary. If you were making $50,000 per year and sold all your stock as described in the preceding IPO example, your taxable income for that year would be $50,000 + $90,000 = $140,000. Using an online tax calculator, the federal tax rate on this income is roughly 24%, or $33,600.

If you exercise the stock, hold it for at least one year and one day, and then sell it, the profit gets taxed as *long-term capital gains*, which are subject to a lower tax rate. The federal taxes on your $50,000 salary would be roughly 12%, or $6,000, and the federal taxes on your $90,000 of stock would be 15%, or $13,500, for a total of $19,500. So by holding the stock for at least one year and one day, you pay $14,100 less in federal taxes.

Gotchas with exercising stock options

Based on the preceding example, it seems clear that exercising your stock options as soon as possible can have huge tax advantages. Every time some stock vests, you might be tempted to exercise it immediately to start the clock ticking on the "one year and one day" long-term capital gains calculation. In fact, some companies even let you *early exercise* your stock, allowing you to exercise it before it has vested. If your company allowed early exercise, you could exercise all of your

---

7 Tax laws are different in every country. The details described in this section only apply to the United States.

stock the day you joined the company, so that 4+ years later, when all of your stock is vested, you'll be able to sell it and immediately get the long-term capital gains tax rate.

However, there are two major gotchas you need to be aware of. The first gotcha is obvious: exercising your stock costs money. In this example, you'd need to spend 100,000 * $0.10 = $10,000. If you joined the company later and the fair market value had gone up, the strike price in your offer might have been higher, such as $3.00/share, so exercising your options would cost 100,000 * $3.00 = $300,000. Not everyone has this type of money lying around. Even if you did, it is a high-risk investment, as you have no guarantee the company won't go out of business a few months later, making all that stock worthless.

The second gotcha is more subtle: if the value of the stock is higher than your strike price when you exercise it, you'll have to pay taxes on the difference between your strike price and the market price—even if you don't sell any of the stock. For example, let's say you joined a startup in January 2014, when the strike price was $0.10. You weren't confident of an IPO, so you didn't exercise the shares. By January 2018, an IPO seems more likely, so you decide to exercise all your shares. Here's the catch: by January 2018, it's possible that the fair market value of the company has gone up. Let's say it's now at $5.00 per share. Your strike price is fixed in your contract, so you would still pay $0.10 per share to exercise your stock options for a total of 100,000 * $0.10 = $10,000. However, your shares are now worth 100,000 * $5.00 = $500,000, so you just "made" $500,000 - $10,000 = $490,000 in profit. The fact that you can't sell the stock and realize any of this profit doesn't matter—you still have to pay taxes on it.

The tax rate on this profit depends on the type of stock. *Incentive stock options* (ISO) will be taxed under the alternative minimum tax rate, whereas *non-qualified stock options* (NSO) are taxed as short-term capital gains. Let's say you had ISOs and your AMT rate worked out to 28%. That means you not only have to pay $10,000 to exercise your shares, but also $490,000 * 0.28 = $137,200 in taxes! And you still have no guarantee that a liquidity event will happen in the future or, even if one does, that the stock will be worth more than $5.00/share.

Do your research

Many people have been burned or even bankrupted by the cost of exercising shares and the associated taxes. This primer barely touches the surface of all the laws and tax implications involved and it does not constitute legal or financial advice. It is your responsibility to thoroughly research equity, work with a tax professional, and make sure you understand how it all works. See [Weekly 2012] and [Payne 2013a] for further reading.

How much are my stock options worth?

Now that you understand the basics of stock, is more equity worth a lower salary? There are three perspectives to consider. The first perspective is to compare the equity in your offer to similar developers and companies in your area. One way to do this is to use Wealthfront's online salary and equity calculator (*http://bit.ly/wealthfront-calc*). Another option is to consult *http://www.hello-startup.net/resources/equity/* for tables that list the typical amount of equity you would get at a startup based on your role, seniority, and employee number.

The second perspective is to think of the lower salary as an investment in the company, your career, and the chance for big returns later. How big could those returns be? There is no way to know. There are too many variables to take into account, so the best you can do is to make a bunch of guesses and assumptions to come up with a rough range of possibilities. You can use the following equation to estimate the risks and rewards (however, bear in mind that it is a simplified calculation, so take it with a grain of salt; in addition, note that this equation assumes that you exercised your stock as soon as it vested, but it does not take taxes into account):[8]

```
A = Difference between the salary in the offer and a fair market salary
B = Number of years you expect to work at the startup
C = Cost to exercise your shares
D = Percentage of the company you own
E = Investor take
F = Value of the company in case of a successful exit

Investment = (A * B) + C
Return = D * (F - E)
```

Let's say a startup offers you a salary of $50,000 per year, whereas the fair market salary for your role is $65,000. That means you're "investing" A = $65,000 - $50,000 = $15,000 per year in exchange for possible future returns from the equity. You expect to be at the company for B = 4 years, which is usually long enough to vest all of your stock. In your offer, you get 100,000 shares of stock at a strike price of $0.10 per share, so to exercise all of your shares, you'd

---

8 See *http://www.hello-startup.net/resources/equity/* for an interactive calculator you can use that implements this formula.

have to spend C = 100,000 * $0.10 = $10,000. This means you are investing the following amount in this startup:

```
A = $65,000 - $50,000 = $15,000
B = 4 years
C = 100,000 shares * $0.10 / share = $10,000

Investment = ($15,000 * 4) + $10,000 = $70,000
```

The total number of shares outstanding when you were granted stock was 11 million, so the 100,000 shares you exercised represent 0.9% of the company. However, it's likely that by the time you reach an exit, your shares will have been diluted because the company has created new option pools to bring in new employees or investors. Let's say the dilution after four years is 50%, so your 100,000 shares end up representing 0.45% of the company, or D = 0.0045.

The investor take can have a large impact on the returns you can expect from your shares. This is because investors usually get *preferred shares*, which means they get to make money off of an exit before anyone else. For example, if the company took $1 million in investment and had a $1 million exit, the investor gets their money back and everyone else gets nothing. This is called a *preference* and it can even be a multiple of the original investment. For example, if a company raised $1 million at a 2x preference and has a $3 million exit, the investor gets $2 million and everyone else splits the remaining $1 million. There are other stipulations that investors can include, such as *participation*, that let them extract even more value from an exit before anyone else. Understanding all the rules and tricks is complicated[9] and you'd need to read through all of your company's term sheets to get an exact figure, so usually the best you can do is a ballpark guess. As a start, you can estimate the investor take as roughly:

```
E = money raised * preference * fudge factor
```

When you get an offer, you need to find out how much money the company has raised from investors in the past and how much it plans to raise in the future and the preference involved (1x is typical these days). It's not always a good sign when a startup has raised a lot of money, as it means it will have to have a bigger exit in order for everyone to be happy with their returns. The fudge factor is up to

---

9 See [feld-2005a] and [feld-2005b] for all the gory details.

you, but be conservative. I generally use a fudge factor of 3x to account for the many tricks investors use to increase their take.

How much will the company be worth if it has a successful exit? There is no way to know for sure, so you should try a range of values to see what your possible outcomes look like. You should look at the company's current valuation and valuations of companies in similar markets as a starting point. For example, if you are building a photo sharing app, perhaps you'd compare yourself to Flickr, which Yahoo! acquired for approximately $22 million in 2005 [Flickr 2015]. No data is available on how much money Flickr raised, so let's assume it was $1 million:

```
D = 0.0045
E = $1,000,000 * 1x preference * 3x fudge factor = $3,000,000
F = $22,000,000

Investment = ($15,000 * 4) + $10,000 = $70,000
Return = 0.0045 * ($22,000,000 - $3,000,000) = $85,500
```

Now let's see what it looks like if your company is more like Photobucket, which raised $15 million in funding and was acquired by News Corp in 2007 for $250 million [Arrington 2007]:

```
D = 0.0045
E = $15,000,000 * 1x preference * 3x fudge factor = $45,000,000
F = $250,000,000

Investment = ($15,000 * 4) + $10,000 = $70,000
Return = 0.0045 * ($250,000,000 - $45,000,000) = $922,500
```

Finally, if you want to use an extreme example, you could look at Instagram, which raised $57 million [Instagram-2015] and was acquired by Facebook for $1 billion in 2012 [Raice and Ante 2012]:

```
D = 0.0045
E = $57,000,000 * 1x preference * 3x fudge factor = $171,000,000
F = $1,000,000,000

Investment = ($15,000 * 4) + $10,000 = $70,000
Return = 0.0045 * ($1,000,000,000 - $171,000,000) = $3,730,500
```

For reference, the average exit for a successful venture-backed startup is roughly $242 million [Lennon 2013].

What are the odds that a startup succeeds? You've probably heard the scary statistic that 90% of startups fail. The real numbers, of course, depend on how you define "startup" and how you define "failure." For example, let's assume this is a VC-backed company, which typically have a failure rate of 75% [Gage 2012]. If your company was acquired for $22 million like Flickr, you are investing $70,000 for a chance to earn $85,500, or one in four odds of a 1.2x return. Ouch. However, if the company has a $250 million exit like Photobucket, then you are investing $70,000 for a chance to earn $922,500, or one in four odds of a 13x return. That's a bit better. And if the company has a $1 billion exit like Instragram, then you're investing $70,000 for a chance to earn $3.7 million, or one in four odds for a 53x return. Now we're talking.[10]

Is it worth it? That depends on the person. For some, a high probability of losing $70,000 is an unacceptable risk. For others, it's worth gambling $70,000 if it buys you startup experience, learning opportunities, career growth, new relationships, and a chance at massive returns. Startups are a gamble and you should only join if you have some tolerance for risk. This brings us to a third perspective on equity: it's a lottery ticket. It probably won't pay out, but if it does, it could change everything.

> It's really comes down to an individual's personal financial situation and goals, but in my opinion, if you're a younger person and you're here in the Valley, you might as well take some bets. Making $10K or $20K more in salary is not going to change your life. Making a million more will.
>
> So, if you're here, you might as well play the game. Roll the dice a couple times. Go work at three different startups over six or seven years. Try them all out, learn a lot, and then settle down and go work at Google, or keep working at startups if you love it. You might get a hit. You might not. If not, bad luck. It's OK: you're still getting paid. Maybe you're getting paid a little less at startups and you're out, say, $50K salary over three years. Who cares? After you pay taxes, it's not going to make a dent in your savings.

—[DELLAMAGGIORE 2014], NICK DELLAMAGGIORE,
SOFTWARE ENGINEER AT LINKEDIN AND COURSERA

---

10 Just a reminder that this calculation is a vast simplification. The odds of a huge exit are lower than the odds of a small exit. Instagram's $1 billion acquisition is exceptionally rare, so the odds there are probably much less than one in four.

Salary versus equity

When it comes to startups, many engineers will tell you that negotiating for salary instead of equity is a newbie mistake:

> When interviewing at Google, I had no idea what I was doing in general. I mean, I was an idiot across the board. I remember I spent all of this time negotiating my salary with my recruiter and I was pushing on totally the wrong things. I was like, "All right, I need $5,000 more a year and we're moving from Germany, so I need help with relocation." In retrospect, and it was quick retrospect after I got there, that was the stupidest negotiating tactic of all time. I should've said you can pay me nothing, just give me stock.

—[SCOTT 2014], KEVIN SCOTT, SVP AT LINKEDIN, VP AT ADMOB, DIRECTOR AT GOOGLE

It would be fair to argue that there is hindsight bias here. If you're the employee of a company as successful as Google, of course you're going to say that more equity is the way to go. But most startups fail, so the equity is usually worthless. Is it still worth taking the chance?

> The way I always advise people to think about it is, if you're going to work for a company where your bet is that the $10,000 of salary is going to be worth more than the upside in your equity package, then you're betting your valuable time and energy on the wrong company. Totally the wrong bet. That is a good framing mechanism for how to think about companies in general.

—[SCOTT 2014], KEVIN SCOTT, SVP AT LINKEDIN, VP AT ADMOB, DIRECTOR AT GOOGLE

Startups aren't all about money, but if you don't believe the equity a company is offering you will amount to anything, it means that you doubt the company will be successful at all, and you're better off turning down the offer entirely.

BENEFITS

So what about benefits? How much are those worth? For some benefits, you can do a little math to estimate their worth. For example, you can estimate how much a health insurance plan costs to see how much it adds to the offer. If the company offers free lunch every day, you can estimate the value of that by multiplying the average cost of a lunch by the average number of days you expect to work.

However, many benefits have value that goes beyond a simple monetary calculation. You can calculate how much a free lunch costs, but not the value of the relationships you may build with your coworkers by eating with them regularly. You can calculate how much you are paid for each vacation day, but it's hard to put a price tag on being able to spend time with your friends and family doing things you love. You can calculate the cost to reimburse part-time classes or host speakers and meetups, but the value of being able to improve your skills and education while on the job is much harder to determine. These are personal decisions and you will have to use your own values to decide how much the perks matter.

NEGOTIATING

You got an offer. You're excited, relieved, happy. Now what? In almost all cases, you should negotiate before accepting the offer. In the job market, you are a merchant selling your skills, and the company is a customer who will offer you the lowest price it can. That's not to say that you will always get a lowball offer, but that the offer is just the first step in a bartering process. Just about every company expects you to negotiate and just about every offer has wiggle room built into the salary, equity, and benefits.

The amount of wiggle room depends on the company and the position. Offers for interns and new college grads, especially at larger companies, are usually standardized. If you're just entering the industry, you have little leverage, so don't expect more than a minor bump in salary or signing bonuses. If you've been around for a few years, there is often 10%–20% wiggle room. If you're a lead developer or senior executive, 30% or more is possible. Note that if you're aiming for a 10% bump in salary, you should ask for 15% instead. You may get the bigger number right away, which is great, or the company may come back with a 10% bump as a counter offer, which is what you wanted in the first place.

Usually, the worst that can happen when you negotiate is that the company says they can't go any higher and you end up with the same offer you started with. In other words, as long as you're professional in the way you do it, it doesn't hurt to ask, as there is only potential upside. It is almost unheard of for an offer to be rescinded just for negotiating, and if that does happen, you wouldn't want to work in such an environment anyway.

Should I tell them my salary?

Early in the interview process, long before you get an offer, many recruiters will ask you for your previous salary. If you tell them, they will use it to minimize the salary in your offer and reduce your negotiating power. You should politely refuse and tell the recruiter that you would prefer not to discuss salary until an offer is on the table.

Recruiters may claim that they need to know your previous salary to make sure they aren't wasting your time with a low offer. It's a good idea to make sure the salary is in the right range early in the interview process, but there is no need for you to reveal your salary to figure this out. Instead, turn the question around and ask the recruiter what salary range is being offered for the job and tell them that you will be happy to indicate if it's in the right ballpark. If the recruiter keeps pushing, politely tell them "I'm really not comfortable answering this question" and remind them that your salary is private, confidential information—there are no laws in the United States that require you to divulge it.

What if they promise a raise later on?

Some recruiters will tell you to accept the current offer as is, because you'll get lots of raises and bonuses in the future. It's not that they are outright lying, but you should assume that anything that isn't written down explicitly in the contract won't happen. A promise of a hypothetical bonus a year from now is not nearly as good as having a guaranteed raise right up front. As a general rule, your ability to improve your compensation is strongest before you join a company. Once you've been there for a year or two, it's a lot harder to get a higher salary or more equity.

Also, you should consider how raises and bonuses are calculated. If you were making $50,000 per year, a $10,000 raise would be a big deal. If you were making $250,000 per year, a $10,000 raise would not make much of a dent. Therefore, most companies calculate raises and bonuses as a percentage of your current salary. So a 20% raise for someone making $50,000 per year is $10,000, but a 20% raise for someone making $250,000 per year is $50,000. Negotiating a higher salary up front gives you a huge advantage, as it will also improve all raises and bonuses in the future.

What can you negotiate for?

Salary is not the only negotiable part of an offer. Negotiating for more equity, especially with startups, may be be more valuable. If the offer comes with stock options, you could ask for a signing bonus that covers the cost of exercising that stock. If you need to move, ask the company to pay for your relocation expenses. If you give talks at conferences, get the company to commit in writing to give you ample time to do it and to pay for the travel expenses. Ask for more vacation time, a bigger 401k match, or any other benefits that matter to you.

The amount of time you have to decide on an offer is also negotiable. The "expiration date" on most offers is fake and only exists to create a sense of urgency. Most software companies aren't hiring for fixed positions. Instead, they are trying to fill a pipeline of good talent throughout the year. Given that there are always positions open, and given that they've already invested weeks or months in finding you, interviewing you, and getting you an offer, they can always afford to give you a few more weeks to think about it. If you need more time, just tell the company you can't make such an important life decision in a hurry.

How to negotiate

Most companies don't make offers based on how much they value your charming personality and wit. They make an offer based on what they think is the going rate for someone of your skill level. If you want a bigger offer, then your goal is to convince them that you're at a higher level than they thought. There are two negotiating strategies you can use.

The first strategy is to try to convince the company you're worth more by discussing the skills you bring to the table and the experience you have, and using market data. Unfortunately, unless you're a big name in the industry, you don't have much leverage with such a negotiating tactic, as it's just your opinion against the employer's. Your only negotiating strength here is that you can refuse the offer. The company has invested a lot of time and money to find you, contact you, phone screen you, bring you on site, interview you, do reference checks, decide to hire you, and put together an offer. You can get most companies to give you a small increase in salary or bonus just so they don't have all this effort go to waste.

The second, more effective strategy is to prove to the company that you're worth more by getting competing offers.

Competing offers

Your biggest negotiating lever as a job candidate is a competing job offer. Instead of pitting your opinion against the employer's, a job offer from another company represents hard data of how much you're worth in the market. If multiple companies are fighting for you, you will seem more valuable, and you may get them into a bidding war. One of my favorite negotiating strategies is to have a conversation along these lines: "Hi, company A, thank you for your offer. I'm trying to decide between you and company B, who is offering me X more salary, and company C, who is offering me Y more equity. I'm more interested in what you're doing and would love to work with you, but it's hard to sacrifice a lot of income to do that. Could you make the decision easy for me?"

When you have multiple options, you'll also find it easier to use the most powerful tool in negotiation: walking away. This is why you should always interview with multiple companies in parallel. It's also why the best time to interview for a job is when you don't need one. If you're desperate to get a job, you are more likely to accept any offer that comes your way. If you already have a job that you can live with, then you can always fall back to it if the negotiations don't work out. Make a habit of exploring the job market every few years, even if you're happily employed. It's a good way to see what opportunities are out there and to make sure you're getting a fair deal at your current job.

Recap

At the beginning of this chapter, I asked you to write down the traits of the job you were looking for:

- What industry and type of product?
- What technologies?
- What business model?
- What type of role?
- What perks and benefits?

Now, at the end of this chapter, you should do the reverse. Put yourself in the shoes of a startup founder and write down the traits of someone you would want to hire. Here are a few examples you might write down:

- Smart.
- Gets things done.
- Good culture fit.

Finally, make one more list: figure out how, as a startup founder, you could assess each of the traits you were looking for. For example, for the three traits above:

- To assess if someone is smart, you need to know how they perform at real-world tasks. This is easy if you've worked with them before or you have a referral from someone you trust. If you have neither, then you do your best to figure it out during the interview, perhaps through technical questions.

- To assess if someone can get things done, you need to know what they have accomplished in the past. This is easy if you've worked with them before or you have a referral from someone you trust. If you have neither, you do your best to figure it out by searching for them online.

- To assess if someone is a good culture fit, you need to know if they share your values. This is easy if you've worked with them before or you have a referral from someone you trust. If you have neither, then you do your best to figure it out during the interview, perhaps through questions about the candidate's actions in the past and their aspirations for the future.

The point of this exercise is to get you to see the hiring process from the perspective of the employer (see Chapter 11 for a deeper look). After going through it, it should be more obvious how to get a job at a startup. You need to use your network. You need to build an online identity. You need to practice interviewing. And most importantly, you need to know what you want in terms of company culture, the opportunity, and the offer.

Hiring for Your Startup

Startups are about people

People are the most important part of a company. Choosing the right people is more important than choosing the right product, marketing strategy, tech stack, or coding methodology. That means that hiring is the most important thing you do. It's also one of the hardest things you'll do. You need to find someone who fits the culture, has the right skill set, is interested in what you do, is available at the right time, and is willing to work for a startup salary. And you need to do it over and over again.

The best piece of advice on hiring for startups is: don't do it. Or at least, don't do it yet. Hiring more people means a higher burn rate, more complexity in running the business, slower decision making, and more time spent searching, interviewing, and training. The best startups do more with less. Be proud of being small and try to accomplish as much as possible with a tiny team. It will teach you to stay focused, make better trade-offs, and develop a passion for high leverage and efficiency. In fact, hiring more people does not necessarily mean you can get more done. As I discussed in "Organizational design" on page 392, communication overhead grows as the square of the team size, which is why larger companies can't move as quickly as smaller ones. Stay small as long as you can.

How do you know it's time to start hiring? The key question to ask is not "what could we do if we hired someone?" but "what couldn't we do unless we hired someone?" If there is something critical to your business that cannot be done without a new hire, no matter how creative you get, then it's time to start hiring. In this chapter, I'll discuss who to hire, how to find great candidates, the interview process, and how to make an offer they can't refuse.

Who to hire

The first step in hiring great people is to know who you're looking for. The key types of hires to think about are co-founders, early hires, later hires, and 10x developers.

CO-FOUNDERS

Having a single founder is #1 on Paul Graham's list of "The 18 Mistakes That Kill Startups." Why? Because starting a company is brutally hard. It involves an enormous amount of stress, risk, and hard work, and most people simply can't handle it unless they have someone else there to share the load. You need other people there to fill in your weaknesses, to give you feedback on ideas, and to cheer you up when things go wrong:

> *The low points in a startup are so low that few could bear them alone. When you have multiple founders, esprit de corps binds them together in a way that seems to violate conservation laws. Each thinks, "I can't let my friends down." This is one of the most powerful forces in human nature, and it's missing when there's just one founder.*

> **—[GRAHAM 2006], PAUL GRAHAM, CO-FOUNDER OF Y COMBINATOR**

When investors see a solo founder, they not only assume that the founder is unlikely to succeed alone, but also that the founder couldn't convince any friends to join. That's a bad sign and it makes fundraising more difficult.

Therefore, two founders is usually the best bet for success. You can divide the work and equity evenly and there is no room for politics. Three founders can work as well: dividing up responsibility is harder, but you can always take a vote to make decisions. Any more than three, and things become more and more unstable. Decision making is harder, dividing up the responsibility and equity is trickier, and politics and in-fighting are more likely.

Do not take finding a co-founder lightly, as you'll be with them for a long time—on the order of 10 years for a successful startup (see "Joining versus founding a startup" on page 22). You should have a long, proven relationship with any potential co-founder before starting a company with them. In some ways, building a startup is like going to war, so it's best if you and the co-founder have survived battles together in the past and you know you can depend on each other in the future.

This is why former co-workers usually make the best co-founders: if you've successfully built something together before, it's more likely you can do it again. Classmates from college are also a good choice if you've worked with them in the past on projects, studied together, and pulled a few all-nighters together. Friends and family are probably the next best bet, but there is more risk involved.[1] If you've never worked with them before, you might not have a good sense of their skills and how you get along under pressure. Moreover, it's harder to be objective and make good business decisions when a personal relationship is on the line. That said, someone you know and trust is almost always better than a complete stranger. Starting a company with a co-founder you met for an hour at a networking or "co-founder dating" event is like starting a family after getting a little too drunk and having a shotgun wedding with a stranger in Vegas. It's not the best foundation for a long-term relationship.

There are four traits to look for in a co-founder. First, you want someone who is "relentlessly resourceful" [Graham 2009]. Look for people who you know will get shit done no matter what obstacles are in the way. Second, you want someone with a complementary skill set. For example, if you're a programmer and good at building products, look for a co-founder who can handle sales and marketing and is good at finding customers. Third, you typically want the co-founders to be similar in age, financial situation, and motivation. It's not going to work if one co-founder is looking to make a quick buck, while the other has a long-term vision of changing the world. And fourth, most importantly, you want someone you can trust. To build trust, you need to have a history with the person, which underscores one more time why colleagues, classmates, and friends make the best co-founders.

Having disagreements is part and parcel of trying to build a startup. You cannot have three co-founders nodding in unison the whole way. However, if your trust in each other breaks, then there's a fundamental split. That's very different than regular disagreements or shouting matches. I suspect that is probably the biggest risk. You can fix bugs, you can pivot, you can change almost anything, but you cannot fix people. If the co-founders

---

1 Studies have shown that each new friendship in a founding team increases the rate of turnover by almost 30% [Grant 2014].

don't trust each other, then at that point you just have to call it quits or one of you has to leave.

—[RANGNEKAR 2014], VIKRAM RANGNEKAR, CO-FOUNDER OF VOICEROUTE AND SOCIALWOK

Having only a single founder may be item #1 of "The 18 Mistakes That Kill Startups," but "fights between founders" is on the list too. To make all the co-founders feel like equals and to make sure they all have some "skin in the game," you should always split the equity evenly (see "Equity" on page 451) and enforce a vesting schedule (see "What is vesting?" on page 453). No matter who had the idea or how much work they did before the company was founded, an even equity split is almost always the right choice.[2] Building a successful startup takes, on average, a decade, so instead of bickering over percentage points and creating resentment on day one, make sure everyone has equal incentive to see this thing through in the long term.

EARLY HIRES

Take your time with finding the first few hires at a startup. You can recover from building the wrong product or using the wrong technology, but a bad hire in the first 5–10 employees can kill a company. The early employees, along with the co-founders, are responsible for defining the company culture, and you can't afford to get it wrong. For example, the founders of Airbnb spent nearly six months interviewing hundreds of candidates to find their first hire. Brian Chesky, the CEO, explained why:

The first engineer was like bringing in DNA into your company. If we were successful, there were going to be a thousand people just like him or her in the company. It wasn't a matter of getting somebody to build the next three features that we needed to ship for users. It was something much more long term and much more enduring, which was, do I want to work with a hundred or a thousand more people like this?

—[CHESKY 2014B], BRIAN CHESKY, CO-FOUNDER, CEO OF AIRBNB

Chesky would also ask candidates, "If you had a year left to live, would you take this job?" and only hire candidates who said "yes." This is an extreme exam-

---

2 Of the top Y Combinator companies, *zero* of them have a significantly uneven equity split [Altman 2014b].

ple and probably not one you should emulate exactly (even Chesky later amended the question to 10 years), but take the underlying lesson to heart: do everything you can to make sure you get the right early employees.

It's also worth remembering that in the early days of a startup, everyone is going to have to work on everything. The product, requirements, team, and technologies are all going to be changing at a very rapid pace. One day you'll be tuning a database query; another day you may be debugging a JavaScript error; the following week, you'll be figuring out how to make backups of your source code; a few days after that, you'll be working on the revenue projections for an investor pitch deck. This means that the early engineers at a startup should mostly be *generalists* or *full-stack engineers*. That is, people who are good at a wide variety of tasks rather than experts at a single task.

> In the beginning, I only hire full-stack people because what you don't want is someone saying, "that's not my job". At an early-stage company, everyone wears many hats. I don't hire specialists until a little bit later in the development of the company.

—[GRACE 2014], JULIA GRACE, CO-FOUNDER OF WEDDINGLOVELY, CTO AT TINDIE

An important note: the opposite of a specialist is not a generalist. Not being an expert at anything doesn't mean you're automatically good at everything. A real generalist is someone who is a tinkerer. You put something new in front of them and they have to take it apart and figure out how it works. They have an insatiable curiosity and have experimented with a little bit of everything. When you look at their résumé, you see a broad range of experience in terms of industry (e.g., travel, medicine, social networking, consumer, enterprise), technologies (e.g., API servers, iOS clients, distributed data stores, deployment automation, programming language design), and roles (e.g., developer, tech lead, product manager, designer).

Perhaps the strongest sign of a generalist is not the experience they already have but the willingness to take on any new experience. If you hear a developer say "Oh, no, I'm not a front end guy" or cringe at the thought of having to learn a new programming language for their next project, they are probably not a generalist. Real generalists love to learn new things regardless of the problem domain and whether they have any experience in it.

This is why it's possible for someone straight out of college (or even college dropouts) to build some of the most successful startups in the world with no experience whatsoever. As Mark Twain said, "They did not know it was impossible, so they did it!" Don't shy away from hiring new college grads or other inexperienced engineers for your startup so long as they demonstrate a passion for learning everything the startup world will throw at them. When it comes to startups, attitude beats aptitude.

LATER HIRES

As the company grows, the problems will become more complex: you'll need to find a way to scale the company to handle more users, customers, traffic, and employees. This is where specialists come in handy. When you need to tune DB queries, set up replication, or shard your tables, it might be time to hire a dedicated DBA; when you need to manage thousands of servers, deploy code to multiple data centers, and set up 24/7 site monitoring, it might be time to hire a dedicated release engineer; and when your site is big enough that it is under constant attack from hackers and spammers, it might be time to hire a dedicated security team. Just be wary of hiring someone who is only good at a single skill and nothing else. Instead, look for T-shaped people, as we discussed in "Knowledge" on page 32.

10X DEVELOPERS

A number of studies show that there is a huge variation in productivity between developers. For example, one of the original studies in this area, "Exploratory Experimental Studies Comparing Online and Offline Programming Performance" [Sackman, Erikson, and Grant 1968], found that "the ratio of initial coding time between the best and worst programmers was about 20 to 1; the ratio of debugging times over 25 to 1; of program size 5 to 1; and of program execution speed about 10 to 1." There were some flaws with this original study, but many studies that came after it have found similar variations in programmer ability: that is, roughly an order of magnitude (or 10x) [McConnell 2011]. Despite the research, the idea of a *10x developer* has received considerable ridicule and many people doubt that such "rock star developers" could possibly exist. And yet, no one seems to doubt the existence of star athletes, artists, writers, and, well, rock stars.

The problem is that when people hear "10x developer," they imagine a mythical programmer who can churn out 10 lines of code for every one line of code written by a normal developer. The flaw with this line of reasoning is that programming productivity is not about typing speed or lines of code. Programming is a creative profession and there are many ways of solving the same problem.

For example, consider how many decisions and how much creativity goes into building a single software product such as a website. What language do you use? What web framework? How do you store data? What do you use for caching? Where do you host the site? How do you monitor it? How do you push new changes? How do you store the code? What kind of automated testing do you set up? If you have 10 average programmers, they will make "average" quality decisions at each step and the costs or benefits of these decisions will multiply. Imagine traffic increases exponentially, and this average team built an average website, with a database that's difficult to scale, hosting that doesn't have enough redundancy, version control without proper backup, and no monitoring. How productive will those 10 coders be if they are spending all their time putting out fires?

A single programmer could outperform this team if the programmer solved the problem in a way where there is an order of magnitude less work to do. By making better decisions and coming up with more creative solutions, a 10x programmer can avoid months of work down the line. In other words, it's not about writing *more* code; it's about writing the *right* code. 10x programmers are really 10x decision makers.

This isn't unique to programming. Would you rather have 10 average scientists or one Isaac Newton? Ten average scientists did not come up with the laws of motion, theory of gravity, or principles of calculus; a single Isaac Newton did. Would you rather let Elon Musk run a company or hand over the keys to 10 average executives? Ten average executives did not come up with PayPal, electric cars, reusable rockets, and the hyperloop; a single Elon Musk did.

All that said, superstar programmers, just like superstar athletes, are exceptionally rare. If you try to build your hiring strategy around only hiring "rock stars," or worse yet, your company struts around as if they are a bunch of "rock stars" already, you'll never grow your team. There may be huge differences in ability between developers, but don't let that obscure three key facts:

1. A developer's performance will vary depending on the task.

2. A developer can get better over time.

3. Most software is developed by teams and not individuals.

The first fact implies that a 10x developer in one company could be a 1x or even a 0.1x developer at another company. Culture, passion, and mission matter (see Chapter 9). The second fact implies that the best way to build a successful company is to hire good developers and give them an environment where they can get even better. Some people find the idea of a 10x developer discouraging because they assume that they could never get that good, as if great developers are born rather than made. But as you will see in Chapter 12, there is a lot of evidence that suggests that it is practice, and not inborn talent, that separates the elite performers from everyone else.

That's why I find the idea of a 10x developer inspiring rather than discouraging. It implies that programmers are not all equivalent, robotic, interchangeable drones; it implies that programming is a craft where you can develop yourself from an apprentice, to a journeyman, and all the way up to a master craftsman; and it implies that what it takes to reach the levels of a master is practice. Elite athletes practice for many hours per day to develop their abilities. If you aspire to be an elite programmer, you should, too. Try to see 10x developers as role models that motivate you to code more, just as a child may see Michael Jordan as a role model who motivates them to shoot hoops more. Similarly, every professional sports team has a "farm system" (e.g., high schools, colleges, minor leagues, talent scouts) to develop talent. If you aspire to build an elite software company, you should, too. Host tech talks, reimburse classes and conferences, encourage blogging and open source, organize hackathons, and build a mentor system. Be the company that creates 10x developers rather than the one that tries to hire them.

Finally, the third fact is a reminder that what really matters is the performance of a team and not a single individual. Team productivity varies as much as individual productivity—by roughly an order of magnitude [Mills 1983]—partly because "good programmers tend to cluster in some organizations and bad programmers in others" and partly due to "organizational factors, such as how good the organization was about defining a clear product vision, defining unambiguous requirements, coordinating efforts of team members, and so on" [Oram and Wilson 2010, 571]. In other words, instead of focusing on hiring a single superstar, focus on developing a sustainable hiring strategy and on developing an organizational structure that lets everyone work together efficiently (see "Organizational design" on page 392).

WHAT TO LOOK FOR

The important traits to look for in any candidate are that they are smart and get things done, that they are a good culture fit, that they have good communication skills, and that you would be OK reporting to them.

Smart/gets things done

Programming, especially in a startup, requires intelligence more than knowledge. That's because the challenges you face at a startup will change frequently, and it's more important that you're smart enough to adapt to the new challenges than knowing every minute detail about the old ones. But smarts alone are not enough. Perhaps you've worked with a smart programmer who could wax eloquent for hours about the theoretical benefits of one technology over another and who spent a lot of time creating design documents, architecture drawings, and UML diagrams, but who never actually shipped any code. Sometimes we call them architects. Other times, professors. Either way, startups need people who are not only smart but who can also get things done [Spolsky 2006]. You want someone who can weigh trade-offs, make decisions with imperfect information, and understand that done is better than perfect.

Note that the kind of "smart" you're looking for is less about IQ or fancy degrees and more about clear thinking and problem solving. You can get a sense of this by asking the candidate questions about a topic you know deeply. You could discuss programming languages (e.g., do a deep dive on functional programming versus object-oriented programming), libraries and frameworks (e.g., ask the candidate to compare Ruby on Rails and SpringMVC), system architecture (e.g., how would you build a URL shortener for Twitter?), specific problem domains (e.g., tell me how to build a machine-learning algorithm to recommend movies), or any other topic where you can ask progressively deeper and deeper questions. Your goal is not to assess the candidate's existing knowledge, but to get them to the point where they don't know the answer ahead of time. The kind of smart person you're looking for is someone who can turn that unknown into a known. They are comfortable dealing with uncertainty, they ask the right questions, and they quickly learn and adapt, no matter what challenge you put in front of them.

You can use a similar line of questions to identify someone who "gets things done," but this time, focus on a domain that the candidate knows deeply. Find something interesting on their résumé, or ask them for the accomplishment they are most proud of, and keep asking deeper and deeper questions until you get to the point where *you* don't know the answer ahead of time. If the candidate can't explain it to you, either they weren't a big contributor to that project (so they don't really "get things done") or they don't understand it well enough (so they aren't "smart").

For the background part, I like to see what someone has done. Not been involved in, or been part of, or watched happen, or was hanging around when it happened.

I look for something you've done, either in a job or (often better yet) outside of a job. The business you started and ran in high school. The non-profit you started and ran in college. If you're a programmer: the open source project to which you've made major contributions. Something.

If you can't find anything—if a candidate has just followed the rules their whole lives, showed up for the right classes and the right tests and the right career opportunities without achieving something distinct and notable, relative to their starting point—then they probably aren't driven. And you're not going to change them.

—[ANDREESSEN 2007], MARC ANDREESSEN, CO-FOUNDER OF NETSCAPE, LOUDCLOUD, OPSWARE, AND NING

Culture fit

Being smart and getting things done are necessary requirements, but not the only ones. You will spend enormous amounts of time with anyone you hire, especially in a small startup. Consider if you'd want to have lunch with this person every day; if you'd want them to review your code; if you'd want to spend time mentoring them or learning from them; if you'd want them calling you at 3 a.m. when the site goes down. You're not necessarily looking to hire someone who will become your friend, but you certainly want to avoid hiring someone who you won't be able to stand. In many companies, this trait has a colorful name: the *no assholes rule*. It's a good rule, but not being an asshole is not enough. What you really want is someone who is a great *culture fit* (see Chapter 9 for an in-depth discussion of startup culture).

Be careful not to confuse culture fit with personal taste. A company's culture is how it acts, and culture fit is about finding people who act like you because they share the same core values (see "Core Values" on page 391). It is not about finding people who look like you or like the same things as you because they share the same background. Many companies get this wrong. For example, here's an excerpt from the blog of a San Francisco startup that I'll leave unnamed:

He was dressed impeccably in a suit... I stole a glance to a few of the people from my team who had looked up when he walked in. I could sense the disappointment. It's not that we're so petty or strict about the dress code that we are going to disqualify him for not following an unwritten rule, but we know empirically that people who come in dressed in suits rarely work out well for our team. He was failing the go-out-for-a-beer test and he didn't even know it.

—[BUENO 2014], FOUNDER OF A SAN FRANCISCO STARTUP

Liking beer is not a core value. Hating suits is not a core value. Believing that dress code doesn't matter might be a core value, but this company clearly doesn't act that way so it's not part of their culture. Instead, they are making hiring decisions based on taste in drinks and clothing, which is not culture fit but prejudice and discrimination [McCorvey 2014].

The right way to determine culture fit is to look for candidates whose core values, as demonstrated by their actions, align with your own. For example, one of Zappos' core values is "deliver WOW through service." Here is how they ensure that every person they hire is passionate about customer service:

Everyone that is hired into our headquarters goes through the same training that our Customer Loyalty Team (call center) reps go through, regardless of department or title. You might be an accountant, or a lawyer, or a software developer—you go through the exact same training program.

It's a four-week training program, in which we go over company history, the importance of customer service, the long-term vision of the company, our philosophy about company culture—and then you're actually on the phone for two weeks, taking calls from customers. Again, this goes back to our belief that customer service shouldn't just be a department, it should be the entire company.

At the end of the first week of training, we make an offer to the entire class. We offer everyone $2,000 to quit (in addition to paying them for the time they've already worked), and it's a standing offer until the end of the fourth week of training.

We want to make sure that employees are here for more than just a paycheck. We want employees that believe in our long-term vision and want to be a part of our culture. As it turns out, on average, less than 1% of people end up taking the offer.

—[HSIEH 2013, 153], TONY HSIEH, *DELIVERING HAPPINESS*

That's a great culture filter. If you aren't passionate about customer service, you shouldn't apply to work at Zappos. However, when it comes to hiring for passion, there's a catch: most people outside of your company won't know anything about your company or its mission, especially when you're a tiny startup. If you're doing something innovative, they might even think you're crazy. Therefore, while it's OK to filter out candidates who don't share your values, you should not filter out candidates just because they lack a *preexisting* passion or interest in your mission [Rabois 2014].

Note the emphasis on the word "preexisting." It's fine to look for candidates that are passionate about a previous company, products they have built before, the technologies they've used, or the industry you're working in. But it is your job to get them passionate about your company and your mission. You have to make the mission clear and visible: it should be obvious in the product, visible in all marketing materials, on your company page, and in every job description. Every interviewer should know it and discuss it. You should make sure every candidate understands it and only then make any sort of judgment call.

A lot of people throw around the word "passion," but how can you never have worked at a company and be passionate about working at that company? I find that really bizarre. Unless it's your own company, it's hard to be super passionate about something unless you're in the trenches.

I want a person to have passion for themselves. *They want to be a better version of who they are and they want to improve their quality of life. If I need them to get passionate about LinkedIn, I know how get them passionate about LinkedIn. But they need to be passionate about* their *lives and* want *to contribute, or it won't last.*

—[GROSSKURTH 2014], FLORINA XHABIJA GROSSKURTH, WEB DEVELOPER AND MANAGER AT LINKEDIN, DIRECTOR OF PEOPLE OPERATIONS AT WEALTHFRONT

Good communication skills

Communication skills are more important than technical skills. In fact, most technical skills are just communication skills in disguise. For example, writing clean code is mostly about writing code in a way that other programmers can understand (see Chapter 6)—that is, clearly communicating your intent. Therefore, all else being equal, always prefer a programmer who has better communication skills.

When you're considering a candidate, are you able to have a pleasant conversation with them? If they owned some subsystem in your company, would they be able to explain to a new hire how it works? Do they maintain a blog, and if so, can you follow their writing? Could they give a talk at a conference? Can you understand their code? If your roles were switched and the candidate were interviewing you, would they be a good representative of your company?

I would be OK reporting to them

This final item is a quick sanity check on all the previous ones. If you would never want this person as your boss, it usually means that you think they aren't smart, they don't know how to get things done, they don't fit into your company's culture, or you can't understand them. Even if it's a junior candidate, it's a good idea to consider what would happen if they were in charge some day, and if that thought makes you uncomfortable, you might not want to hire them.

Finding great candidates

Now that you know what kind of developers to look for, let's talk about how to find them. Most startups underestimate just how long it takes to find great talent. Imagine you're a team of two co-founders and you want to hire 12 engineers. How much of your time do you think that will take? The answer: roughly 990 hours, or about 20 hours of recruiting per week for an entire year [Recruit Engineers in Less Time 2015].

So how can you speed this up? What's the best way to find new people for your startup? Recruiters? Agencies? Job boards? While all of these can be useful, the best starting point is referrals.

REFERRALS

The best hiring strategy for your company can be summarized in four words: everyone is a recruiter. If you want to find the best candidates, start with the people you already know. The co-founders should hire the best people they know;

those new hires come in with their own networks and they should try to hire the best people they know; and so on, down the line. Referrals produce the highest quality hires, help you fill jobs faster (29 days for referrals versus 45 days for career sites), and have the highest retention rate (referrals have a 45% retention after two years, compared to 20% from job boards) [Sullivan 2012].

Referrals won't happen on their own, so you have to actively seek them out. For example, spend time manually going through your contacts on LinkedIn, Facebook, Twitter, and your phone, and contact everyone that could be a reasonable fit. Similarly, when you're at a conference, meetup, chatting with investors, or even relaxing with friends or family, don't be afraid to talk about your company and your mission (see "Mission" on page 387). Don't be obnoxious or pushy, but realize that most founders spend about 25%–50% of their time sitting in coffee shops talking about their vision to their friends. Also, make sure to get everyone at the company involved with referrals by offering incentives such as cash, fun prizes, or recognition for each referral hire. In the early days, almost all of your hires should come in through referrals. Over time, this percentage will drop, but try to never let it dip below 40%–50%. If it does, it means you're either not doing enough to encourage referrals or, even worse, your employees can't recommend your company to their friends [Recruit Engineers in Less Time 2015].

EMPLOYER BRANDING

The next best thing to finding a great candidate via referrals is if a great candidate can find you. Manually searching for candidates and convincing them it's worth applying takes a lot of hard work, so if you can create a company image that makes candidates want to work at your company, you'll be ahead of the game. To do this, you need to build a *brand* as an awesome employer (see "Branding" on page 176).

Here's the catch: 74% of workers are *passive* candidates [Hollon 2011]. They are open to opportunities but they are not actively looking for a job, so they'll never take the time to look at a job posting or visit your career site. Therefore, the best way to build an employer brand that attracts engineers is to create valuable content that they will look at for its own sake and not because they are looking for a job (see "Inbound marketing" on page 173). You want the kind of content that engineers click on when it pops up on Hacker News, Reddit, in their Twitter feed, or during a Google search. For example, you could create an engineering blog where you describe the types of problems your company is solving and the technologies you've built to solve them. You could talk about these technologies at conferences and you could open source the technologies on GitHub. You can also host hackathons, meetups, and drinkups and create a company Twitter account, Facebook page, LinkedIn company page, and corporate home page to cultivate a community around your technologies and products.

Even better than a single corporate brand is if each person at the company has a strong personal brand. Encourage personal blogs, personal Twitter accounts, side projects on GitHub, giving talks, and writing papers on any topic, even if it's unrelated to your company. This will not only make them better and happier employees, as we'll discuss in Chapter 12, but if your employees have a strong following, they will attract people to your company.

> One thing that has been surprisingly effective in my personal experience has been writing Quora answers: I've written answers to questions about what it's like to work at Pinterest, what it's like to be a frontend engineer at Pinterest, how to decide amongst Google/Facebook/Pinterest for a job offer, etc. Turns out that people who are considering places to apply or to join tend to go online to do research, and a lot of people come across my writing that way. A good number of new hires at Pinterest have told me that they joined because they liked what they read in my Quora posts.
>
> —[CHOU 2014], TRACY CHOU, SOFTWARE ENGINEER AT QUORA AND PINTEREST

Note that most of the content you create should not overtly try to hire people. For example, don't bother with recruiting videos. You know the kind I mean: quick panning shots of people standing around a whiteboard or playing ping-pong, light background music with a quick beat, an interview scene with an executive sitting off center looking at someone to the side of the camera and telling them about the profound work they do, and then a fade to the company logo. No one outside of your company actually watches these.

Instead, create content that is valuable for its own sake—content your audience can learn from and tools they can use. A candidate that's already using your company's open source software, learning new skills from your blog posts and tech talks, and following some of your employees online will be more receptive to hiring. It's also more likely that this candidate will be a great fit for your company. The developer that submits a pull request to one of your repos or asks interesting questions at one of your tech talks is clearly passionate about the same technologies that you are. Perhaps they'll be interested in working at your company, too.

At Typesafe, we've been spoiled. As most companies built around open source software, we've been able to hire people through the open source community—and that's essentially the longest and most thorough interview process you can think of. For example, I've been able to hire people for the Akka team that have been committing to our projects for years and that the team already knows and feel comfortable working with.

Open source also helps because if people are engaged and passionate and working on open source, you can start by just looking into their GitHub repos. It's almost too easy. You can immediately start filtering people that are decent, but perhaps not the type you're looking for.

—[BONÉR 2014], JONAS BONÉR, CO-FOUNDER OF TRIENTAL AB AND TYPESAFE

SEARCHING ONLINE

Even if you've set up a good referral program and built an online brand, you're still going to have to do some manual searching for candidates. See *http://www.hello-startup.net/resources/jobs/* for a comprehensive list of websites you can use, including startup accelerator portfolios, venture capital firm portfolios, crowdfunding sites, programmer websites, coding competitions, and finally, job boards. I list job boards last because they are typically the least effective channel for finding candidates. If all you do is post a job on a job board (known as *post and pray*), then you are only reaching active job seekers, or at best, about one out of every four candidates. With programmers, that percentage is even worse. All the best programmers I know have only applied to a job once in their entire lives, just when they were coming out of college. After that, they got hired almost exclusively through referrals or because someone reached out to them. For most programmers, job postings are obsolete.

In fact, no one likes job postings. Consider the following sample:

We are looking for candidates who strive in a fast-paced startup-like environment. Open communications, empowerment, innovation, teamwork and customer success are the foundations of the team.

Job Responsibilities

- *Translate customer problem descriptions into concrete requirements.*
- *Propose, design, develop, and implement new features and enhancements.*

- *Produce high-quality requirement, functional, and design documents.*
- *Collaborate with developers and development managers across the organization.*

Qualifications

- *Strong C programming skills.*
- *Results-oriented.*
- *Work well both as part of a group and independently.*
- *Detail oriented with excellent written and verbal communication skills.*

Let's start with the obvious: most of the content is meaningless. Consider phrases such as "results oriented," "works well both as part of a group and independently," and "detail oriented with excellent written and verbal communication skills." Now ask yourself a question: has anyone ever looked at one of these phrases and thought to themselves, "Results oriented? Nah, guess I can't apply." These are all vacuous phrases that have no impact whatsoever. I bet you skipped over them entirely on the first read-through. The job posting also does nothing to distinguish your company from the competition. The job posting for a "Software Engineer" at one company is indistinguishable from another. Considering that companies spend millions of dollars on marketing and branding to make themselves stand out from the competition, their job postings are remarkably uniform. Finally, the biggest problem of all is that most job postings are selfish. They are focused entirely on what the company wants and are full of long lists of requirements and qualifications. The candidate's needs are almost totally forgotten. In particular, the job posting doesn't help a potential candidate answer the most important question of all: why would I ever want to apply to this job in the first place?

If you are going to use job boards, then to create a good job posting, you'll need to think of it as an ad. You need to explain not only what the job is, but more importantly, why a candidate would want to apply. Avoid standard HR-speak and boring lists of requirements, channel your inner Don Draper, and get creative![3] Also, you need to post your job ads in the places where programmers

---

3 See my blog post "Your Job Posting Sucks" (*http://bit.ly/yb-job-posting*) for inspiration.

actually go, such as Reddit, Hacker News, and Stack Overflow.[4] Better yet, use the job board in reverse: instead of hoping a candidate finds your job post, take the time to find the candidate and reach out to them directly. Passive candidates aren't spending time looking for a job, but they are open to new opportunities that find them.

RECRUITERS

In the early days of a startup, the majority of your candidates should come from referrals. The founders and early employees should be personally reaching out to their connections and bringing them in for interviews. Although this is time consuming, the need for everyone to be personally involved probably means a recruiter won't be of much help.

As a company grows larger, the hiring process will take more and more time. If you've already asked everyone in your personal networks to join, all you're left with is lots of searching online. With more open jobs to fill, you have to spend more time filtering candidates, contacting them, walking them through the process, scheduling interviews, putting together offers, checking references, and keeping all of this organized in an applicant tracking system. This is where hiring a full-time recruiter can begin to pay off, leaving engineers free to focus on the interview (which I'll discuss in the next section).

Generally, hiring an in-house recruiter, though more expensive, is a better bet. An in-house recruiter will be living and breathing your startup, and in turn will be a better advocate for your company. Moreover, you can work closely with an in-house recruiter to define the exact requirements for the job and the types of candidates you are looking for. For example, at LinkedIn, I regularly sat down with the recruiters and walked them through the technologies we used, the kind of people we were looking for (existing employees are always a good model), the company culture, and some of the strategies that worked well in the past for closing candidates. I also discussed how to scan a résumé, a LinkedIn profile, a GitHub profile, and a Stack Overflow profile. Don't skip this step, as there is a big difference between how someone in HR and someone in engineering reads your résumé (this is especially well-illustrated by Steve Hanov on his blog (*http://steve hanov.ca/blog/index.php?id=56*)).

---

4 See *http://www.hello-startup.net/resources/jobs/* for the full list.

PREMATURE OPTIMIZATION

You've probably heard this classic joke about hiring:

> *The boss took half of the résumés we received today and threw them in the trash. He said, "I don't hire unlucky people."*

It's a funny anecdote, but not a practice anyone actually follows, right? Well, not deliberately. The following subsections list a few "industry-standard" hiring practices that are barely different from randomly throwing away half the résumés. They are a form of premature optimization that eliminates candidates for the wrong reasons [Braithwaite 2014].

Typos

If you're hiring copyeditors, throwing away a résumé because of a spelling or grammatical mistake might make sense. If you're hiring programmers, it's a poor heuristic. And that's not because programmers shouldn't know grammar or spelling (they should), but because minor typos are a random occurrence. Everyone makes typos and no matter how much you try, you can't always spot them in your own writing (just ask my editor).

Poor targeting

The way you represent your company in blog posts and tweets, on your career page, and the titles you advertise in job ads will determine what kind of candidates you attract. The quickest way to eliminate all diversity from your job applicant pool is to advertise yourself as a company for brogrammers, ninjas, and Unix beards where you spend all your time crushing code[5] and chugging beer.[6]

> *Another thing I did was start advertising in plain English. We tried placing ads for ninjas, rock stars, and so on, but I discovered this was the cultural equivalent of advertising for white males who drink dry martinis. Not that white males who drink dry martinis can't do the job, but there's no real difference between advertising for a ninja and throwing half your resumés*

---

5 Actual job ad: "Want to bro down and crush some code? <redacted> is hiring" [Gross 2012].

6 Actual ad for a hackathon: "Need another beer? Let one of our friendly (female) event staff get that for you" [Gross 2012].

away because you don't like unlucky people. Either way, you end up with fewer résumés.

—[BRAITHWAITE 2014], REGINALD BRAITHWAITE, DEVELOPER AT GITHUB

College degrees

Many companies throw away résumés from anyone who doesn't have a college degree (some require that to be a degree in computer science; some look for specific GPAs; some will only look at a select few universities and ignore all others). While this may seem like an effective heuristic, it's still premature optimization. For example, Google looked at data of the thousands of people they have interviewed and hired and found that GPAs and test scores are worthless as a criteria for hiring or predicting job performance except for brand-new college grads, where there was a slight correlation [Bryant 2013]. A computer science degree from a top university might help someone write better code, but the way to check that is to actually check their coding abilities and not just the presence of a degree.

Some of the most famous programmers and startup founders, such as Mark Zuckerberg, Steve Wozniak, Paul Allen, Bill Gates, Larry Ellison, and Michael Dell, never got their college degrees [Burnham 2012]. That doesn't mean a college degree isn't valuable, but throwing away résumés just because they don't list the "right" university degree is not a whole lot better than throwing away résumés at random.

Avoiding premature optimization

The best technique I've found for not prematurely eliminating good candidates comes from my interview with Gayle McDowell:

> One of the mistakes people make is they look for a list of attributes on a résumés, find one is missing—maybe there are no outside projects listed, so you think, "this person must not be very passionate about software"— and they cross that person off. The problem is the person might have lots of outside projects, but they didn't know to put it on their résumé. My view point comes from working with **many** engineers and realizing how terrible engineers are with résumés.
>
> So what I advise instead is to take the approach of **looking for some-thing that shines.** That can be a great GPA from a great school. That can be a cool project outside of work or even just a lot of little projects outside

of work. That can be an award that someone got at their current employer. Just look for something that shines.

—[MCDOWELL 2015], GAYLE LAAKMANN MCDOWELL, FOUNDER AND CEO OF CAREERCUP

Look for something that shines, and if you find it, that's usually enough to start the interview process.

The interview

Years ago, we did a study to determine whether anyone at Google is particularly good at hiring. We looked at tens of thousands of interviews, and everyone who had done the interviews and what they scored the candidate, and how that person ultimately performed in their job. We found zero relationship. It's a complete random mess.

—[BRYANT 2013], LASZLO BOCK, SVP OF PEOPLE OPERATIONS AT GOOGLE

Interviews are imperfect. Typically, interviwers have roughly an hour to decide if they want to work with this person for the next several years. It's nearly impossible to get enough signal from such a short and artificial process. The ideal interview might not be an interview at all: you would just hire the person for a few weeks, see how they perform, and then decide. This is usually impractical, so the interview process is a compromise that is, at best, a compressed and lossy process.

Interviewers are even more imperfect. A famous example comes from orchestra auditions. In the 1970s, fewer than 5% of orchestra members were female, and it was generally believed that women just couldn't perform as well as men. In the early 1980s, orchestras began using blind auditions, where the musician performs behind a screen so that the jury can hear the music but not see who is playing. As a result, by the late 1990s, the number of female orchestra members had grown to 35%, a sevenfold increase [Goldin and Rouse 1997]. Another example comes from a 2010 study of parole judges that found that a prisoner's odds of being granted parole were significantly affected by the time of day of their parole hearing. The odds start at around 65% in the morning, gradually drop to nearly 0% just before noon, and then jump back to 65% after lunch. The judges' stomachs were more important in parole decisions than any of the evidence presented [Danziger, Levav, and Avnaim-Pesso 2011].

There are two takeaways from this. First, you might want to avoid interviewing candidates just before lunch. Second, and more importantly, you have to recognize that your interview process will result in incorrect decisions from time to time. Occasionally, you will reject a good candidate or accept a bad candidate. Good companies recognize the weaknesses in interviewing and err on the side of caution. If you hire the wrong person, you're going to spend time ramping them up, wondering why they aren't pulling their weight, cleaning up after them when they leave a mess, putting them on a performance plan, and eventually firing them. And after all that, you have to spend a bunch more time hiring their replacement. Trying to fix the result of hiring a bad candidate is much more painful than occasionally missing out on a good candidate, so say no unless you're absolutely sure.

With all that in mind, let's walk through the basic parts of an interview.

THE INTERVIEW PROCESS

Step 1: Connect

Earlier in this chapter, I discussed how to find good candidates. The next step is to connect with them. You can do this in person or via an email, a message on LinkedIn, or even a tweet. Many will not respond. Of those that do, most will not be interested. Of the few that remain, your goal is to get them excited about opportunities at your company and to schedule them for a phone screen.

Step 2: Phone screens

I don't like talking on the phone, but phone screens are a necessary evil. On-site interviews are expensive, both in terms of money (flight, hotel, car, food) and time (your company loses at least 1–2 person-days of productivity for each on-site interview). Therefore, the goal of a phone screen is to filter the list of candidates down to those who are likely to pass your on-site interview. That means that the phone screen should be nearly identical to the on-site interview in terms of questions and difficulty, but shorter.

Two or three phone screens is standard at most companies. The first call is typically with a recruiter or hiring manager who describes the company, the role, and tries to get a sense of what the candidate is looking for. Assuming the candidate's and company's interests align, you can schedule a second and third call, which will be normal technical interviews with founders, hiring managers, and peers. To be able to work on code during the phone screen, you can use collaborative online editors such as Google Docs, CollabEdit, or Stypi.

Step 3: On-site interview

If the candidate does well in a phone screen, the next step is to bring them on-site. They should meet with 4–8 people in the company, which is usually enough to reduce the effects of bias but not so many as to overwhelm the candidate and make the process take too long. Each interviewer can have a different focus: communication skills, culture fit, coding, system design, and closer.

In the early days of a startup, the founders should be involved in interviewing every candidate, as the early hires have a huge influence on the success or failure of a company. Later on, as the company gets bigger, the interviewers should primarily come from whatever team the candidate is interviewing for.

Every interviewer should come out of the interview with either a "yes" or a "no." "Maybe" is not allowed. A "yes, but for someone else's team," is not allowed. Only hire candidates that get a "yes" from all interviewers. Hiring a bad candidate is worse than passing over a good candidate, so even a single "no" is usually enough to reject someone. The only exception is if someone who has worked closely with the candidate in the past strongly vouches for them. Real-world work experience beats a single "no" from an artificial interview.

INTERVIEW QUESTIONS

Interviewing is more of an art than a science, but there are some basic principles you can follow in both phone screens and on-site interviews to try to make the best use of the interviewer's and the candidate's time. A great interview gives the candidate a chance to teach, learn, and demonstrate their technical skills.

Ask the candidate to teach you something

Don't confuse interviews with interrogations. Many interviewers jump straight into technical questions, unleashing a barrage of brain teasers and coding puzzles without so much as a hello. You are not there to grill the candidate for information; you will not get a candidate to confess that they are a bad coder; they are not your enemy. Interviews are stressful enough as it is, so be kind.

Treat an interview like you would any other polite conversation between two human beings. Introduce yourself. Briefly talk about what you do and the type of role you're trying to fill. Ask the candidate how they are doing, if they need water, or a break. Then, like in any good conversation, move the topic to the candidate and try to learn about them. Ask them to tell you a little about themselves, talk about the projects they have worked on in the past, describe what kind of projects they hope to work on in the future, and find out why they are interested in your company.

Most people like to talk about themselves, so this can be a great way to ease the candidate into the interview. It's also a good way to learn about their experience, their passions, and what they are looking for. At least one interviewer—preferably the hiring manager—should spend most of the interview time discussing these topics and should come out of the interview with a good sense of whether the candidate is a good fit for the role and vice versa.

This part of the interview is also a great way to see the depth of the candidate's knowledge, their passion for their previous work, and their ability to communicate. Dive deep and ask lots of questions. Do you understand what work they have done in the past? Was it clear what they built, what technologies they used, and how it worked? Ideally, you want the candidate to teach you something new. This was Sergey Brin's tactic at Google interviews:

> *"I'm going to give you five minutes," he [Sergey] told me. "When I come back, I want you to explain to me something complicated that I don't already know." He then rolled out of the room toward the snack area. I looked at Cindy. "He's very curious about everything," she told me. "You can talk about a hobby, something technical, whatever you want. Just make sure it's something you really understand well."*

—[EDWARDS 2011], DOUGLAS EDWARDS, GOOGLE

You can even make this more formal and ask the candidate to do a presentation. Instead of just trying to teach one interviewer something, you can have them teach your entire team:

> *The business we're in is more sociological than technological, more dependent of worker's abilities to communicate with each other than their abilities to communicate with machines. So the hiring process needs to focus on at least some sociological and human communication traits. The best way we've discovered to do this is through the use of auditions for job candidates.*
>
> *The idea is simple enough. You ask a candidate to prepare a ten- or fifteen-minute presentation on some aspect of their past work of interest to your group. It could be about a new technology and the experience with first trying it out, or about a management lesson learned the hard way or*

about a particularly interesting project. The candidate chooses the subject, possibly with your approval. The date is set and you assemble a small audience made up of those who will be the new hire's coworkers.

Of course the candidate will be nervous, perhaps even reluctant to undertake such an experience. You'll have to explain that all candidates are nervous about the audition and give your reasons for holding one: to see the various candidates' communication skills, and to give the future co-workers a part in the hiring process.

**—[DEMARCO AND LISTER 1999, 103], TOM DEMARCO AND TIMOTHY LISTER,
*PEOPLEWARE***

Give the candidate a chance to learn something

While you are interviewing a candidate, they are also interviewing you. They are trying to figure out what the company does, what role they could play, what technologies you use, and who they will be working with. Every interviewer should give the candidate plenty of time for questions so they can learn about your company. Also, at least one interviewer, preferably the hiring manager, should give the candidate a tour of the office and an overview of what you do at the company. Walk them through the technologies you use, what products you are building, who the users are, and where the company is going. Live demos, code walkthroughs, architecture diagrams, slide decks, and videos are all fair game. Talk about the culture and the mission (see Chapter 9). Show your passion and see if you can infect them with it.

I was a compiler guy and I noticed that many of my compiler buddies were going to work at Google. I had no idea why a compiler person would go work at this silly little search engine company, but I sent my résumé in and I did my interview and it was still the best interview I've ever had. It was just awesome. It was like doing engineering improv with insanely smart people. It was one of the most energizing things I'd done since I had taken my qualifying exams. I'm a weirdo for being energized by qualifying exams. But those sort of mental challenges are really fun.

Google was super thoughtful about who they were interviewing. They knew that I was a compiler guy by looking at my résumé, so they stacked the deck with my interviewers: all six of them were compiler people. All of them. So I immediately had an expertise connection with them. We could talk about my research, we could talk about people we knew in common, and then after that little ice-breaker bit, by the time you dove into a problem, you were completely loose. We were all systems people, so we thought about things approximately the same way. It was just really thoughtful stuff like that.

—[SCOTT 2014], KEVIN SCOTT, SVP AT LINKEDIN, VP AT ADMOB, DIRECTOR AT GOOGLE

Every interviewer is an ambassador for the company, so choose wisely. In the early days of a startup, you don't have enough people to be picky, so everyone will have to participate in all interviews. But as a company grows, hiring roles can be more specialized. Some developers are great at technical interviews and identifying strong coders; some are great closers, able to convince a candidate looking at multiple job offers to choose yours; and some developers are better at getting candidates to apply for a job in the first place through branding tasks like blog posts, conference talks, and open source projects. All of these are equally important hiring tasks and all of them require different skill sets that take time to develop.

If you don't carve out explicit time for hiring tasks and reward employees for doing them, then hiring will always be seen as second-class work. Employees will never have time for blogging or open source, candidates will have uninspiring interviews, and you will struggle to build a strong team. Instead of treating hiring tasks as a distraction that takes time away from the "real work," you should build them into the schedule just like any other task. Each developer should have specific goals (e.g., close three candidates or write two blog posts per month) that are included in time estimates when planning projects and discussed as part of the employee review process.

To avoid being overwhelmed by hiring tasks, it can be a good idea to have each developer focus on one at a time. For example, you could have a team of technical interview specialists who dedicate five hours per week for coding interviews, a team of closers who dedicate five hours per week to convincing candidates to join, and a team of branding specialists who dedicate five hours per week to blogging, maintaining open source projects, and giving talks. You can periodically rotate engineers between the hiring teams to help them develop new skill sets (see Chapter 12 for more information on dedicating time to learning).

Have the candidate demonstrate their technical skills

The industry standard for a technical interview is to ask the candidate to work on a Computer Science 101 data structures and algorithms problem, come up with the whole solution up front (instead of iteratively) while thinking out loud, and then to write it by hand on a whiteboard with no syntax highlighting, no auto-complete, no Google, no Stack Overflow, no compiler, no open source libraries, no documentation, no tests, and no easy way to refactor. Premature optimization is the root of all evil, but not in interviews, where we force the candidate to optimize the hell out of individual code paths with no profiling and usually at the cost of clarity and simplicity. If someone wrote code like this in the real world, you would probably fire them. So why do we interview this way?

Brainteasers are even worse. Consulting companies and some software companies—most famously Google—used them for years, but there is no evidence that they have any correlation with performance at real job tasks:

> On the hiring side, we found that brainteasers are a complete waste of time. How many golf balls can you fit into an airplane? How many gas stations in Manhattan? A complete waste of time. They don't predict anything. They serve primarily to make the interviewer feel smart.

—[BRYANT 2013], LASZLO BOCK, SVP OF PEOPLE OPERATIONS AT GOOGLE

There are more effective ways to assess technical ability that give both the candidate and the interviewer a better experience. Here are some real-world examples:

Bring your own laptop (BYOL)

Ask the candidate to bring their own laptop, already configured with whatever coding environment they like. Alternatively, ask them what OS and coding tools they use and set up a laptop for them ahead of time. If you want to see real-world coding in action, let them use Google, Stack Overflow, and any other tools and techniques they typically use during normal coding.

> At Coursera, we do a live-coding exercise: you bring your own computer and you solve a problem using your own laptop. I think is a lot better than a coding on a whiteboard. We have a rubric for grading

*it, and we keep track of exactly how people are performing, so we
know which candidates are outliers.*

**—[DELLAMAGGIORE 2014], NICK DELLAMAGGIORE, SOFTWARE ENGINEER AT
LINKEDIN AND COURSERA**

Take-home challenge

Give the candidate some problems to work on from the comfort of their
own home. When they come on-site for an interview, review the code with
them. The take-home challenge shouldn't be a required part of the interview, as not all candidates have time for it, and it shouldn't be the only
technical interview you do, as some candidates will cheat by asking their
friends for help, but it is a nice option to offer candidates who get nervous
at in-person interviews because it gives them a chance to demonstrate their
skills in a more natural coding environment.

*We've experimented at Pinterest with having a coding challenge
that goes first, before interviews. That was primarily early on when
we didn't have enough engineers to be doing all the interviews that
we needed to. So we would give people coding challenges, which
worked well both to vet their interest in the company—if they
weren't willing to sit down for three hours to do a code challenge,
they probably weren't that interested—and to assess their technical
ability in a way that was time-efficient for our team. We could review
the challenges asynchronously at a time convenient for us. If the
code looked terrible, we could quickly send a rejection email and not
spend any more time on the candidate.*

—[CHOU 2014], TRACY CHOU, SOFTWARE ENGINEER AT QUORA AND PINTEREST

Real-world problems

Instead of artificial Computer Science 101 questions, have the candidate
work on something you're actually doing at your company. This will give
you a better idea of how the candidate would perform in the real world and
it will give the candidate a better idea of what the company does.

*At Jawbone, VP of Data Monica Rogati hands candidates a dataset
and gives them three hours to explore it and present their findings.*

"This tests four key qualities I look for in data scientists: technical skills, creativity with data, communication skills, and being results-driven," she says, while also giving candidates a glimpse into daily life at the company.

—[COLE 2014], SAMANTHA COLE, *FAST COMPANY*

If I'm interviewing you, it's almost always, "This is what I've been working on this week, I have this thing coming up next, I don't really know how to deal with it yet, how would you do it?" And then along-side that, if you're a technical hire, we'll have you pair code on actual github.com code with somebody who is going to be on the team with you.

—[HOLMAN 2014], ZACH HOLMAN, SOFTWARE ENGINEER AT GITHUB

Pair coding

Pretend you've already hired the candidate and work with them as if it's their first week and you're helping them ramp up. Sit with them at the computer and pair code on a real project, trading off who is writing the code and who is navigating/observing. You'll get to see how quickly they learn and the kind of code they would write if you hired them. The candidate will get to see the product up close, the technologies involved, and what a typical day at work would look like.

I hired one young guy where he showed up in the morning to inter-view and at the time, the company was just me. So I said, "Hey, great to meet you. Sit down and let's just pair program for the day." Before he left for the day, I told him that he was hired. It was one of the best hires I ever made. I think that was a good process.

—[THOMPSON 2014], DEAN THOMPSON, CTO OF NOWAIT

Bring a candidate to work day

You can take the pair-coding concept even further and replace the interview with a normal day at work. Give the candidate a computer and a mentor, let them check out the code, get things running, make some changes, have lunch with the team, and join a meeting. It takes some logistical work to set up, but it may be the best way for you to see what the candidate would be like on the job and for the candidate to see what it would be like to work at your company.

> We usually fly people in, sometimes for a few days, and work with them. We actually ask them to sit down and work through a few issues and to be part of meetings and brainstorm sessions and we see how much they engage. Sometimes that can be intimidating the first day, but if it's a couple of days, they start relaxing, and you can see what kind of person they are, if they engage, and if they are passionate.
>
> I don't really believe in quizzes, but I do believe in coding with the candidate. I don't use made-up coding exercises—they are usually too contrived. We work on real code, usually the project's core code base.

—[BONÉR 2014], JONAS BONÉR, CO-FOUNDER OF TRIENTAL AB AND TYPESAFE

Making an offer

If you have a candidate who got a "yes" from every interviewer, you have to move quickly. The first step is to check references. The candidate will provide their own references, and you should use them, but don't be afraid to also search your own network for anyone who has worked with the candidate before (see "Use your network" on page 440). Your main goals are to verify the candidate's résumé, and more importantly, get a sense of what they are like to work with. Let's say you are thinking of making an offer to Anna. Here are some questions you might ask Anna's references:

- How do you know Anna? Did you work together? For how long?
- Tell me about Anna's career. What are her greatest accomplishments?
- What are Anna's greatest strengths? What is she working on improving?
- What is Anna's experience with *<some relevant skill for the job>*?
- What was it like working with Anna? Would you work with her again?
- Why is Anna leaving her current job? What is she looking for?
- Is Anna in the top 1% of people you've worked with? The top 10%?

If the reference checks go well, try to get the candidate an offer as quickly as possible. Don't let more than a day or two go by so that the candidate knows that you're interested and they'll still have your company fresh on their mind. Wait too long and they are likely to take an offer from somewhere else, as almost all good candidates interview with multiple companies simultaneously. Remember, speed wins.

> So, Chris [Wanstrath], one of the founders, sent out a tweet asking, "Does anybody know Ruby?" And I'm like, "Yea, I know Ruby!" And then Chris asked, "Does anybody know Java?" I'm like, "I did Java in school, I sort of know Java." So Chris says, "Email me your résumé." So I emailed my résumé and a little later, he asks "Do you want to go grab some coffee?" And I'm like, "Sure."
>
> About 10 minutes before the meeting, they were like, "Do you just want to go to the bar and start drinking instead?" And I'm like, "OK, bar interview. Yea."
>
> We talked for about half an hour and then I went to the bathroom. I came back, and they were like, "All right, here's your offer, give us your yes or no in five minutes." I think they were being facetious, but I was like, "OK, yes." And that was it.
>
> **—[HOLMAN 2014], ZACH HOLMAN, SOFTWARE ENGINEER AT GITHUB**

You might want to copy GitHub's spirit, if not its exact practice. The point is not to do all of your interviews at a bar—Zach's story was an exception and not the normal way GitHub hires people—but to find a way to get the candidate to be excited about the interview and the company, and to get them an offer before the excitement fades. You should make the offer in person or by phone, as it gives you a chance to congratulate the candidate, show your enthusiasm for having them join your team, and remind them once more of the impact they can have on the company's mission. After that, follow up with the written offer via email.

WHAT SHOULD YOU OFFER?

How do you make an offer the candidate can't refuse? One word: listen.

> The first conversation that I have with somebody is, "What are you looking for and what do you want?" It's not me pitching Tindie. I just listen to what they say. The person who talks more in the conversation generally feels

the conversation went better. So I listen—I really listen. I ask, "What do you want?" before I try to do the sell, because if you try to sell first and then you ask, people will often just tell you what you want to hear.

I found that there are just some people who don't understand what it's like to be at an early-stage company. What they describe is maybe a Google or a Facebook. And so at that point it just becomes clear: no hard feelings, but this isn't right for us. And then I describe Tindie and at the end of that conversation, I say, "You should take some time after this conversation to think about if you want to continue in the interview process."

It's not the most scalable approach, but it has been very helpful for us. I've never had somebody not accept an offer when we finally got to the point of giving an offer. I try to really get an idea of what they want and what they're looking for.

I always ask people, "If you have three job offers in front of you, how do you decide which offer to take?" And that's often very revealing. The answer I've gotten the most is, "I don't know". So then I push on them, and most of the time it yields interesting insight into what is important to them, what they value, and if working at Tindie and what Tindie offers aligns with what they want (not just in terms of salary, but experience, direct involvement with the business, etc.).

One person I interviewed said, "Well, I'll have to talk about it with my wife because it is a family decision where I'm going to work." So I said, "Do you want me to speak with your wife?" And he said, "Yes!" So then I spoke with his wife about it. It wasn't that I was interviewing her, but it was just very clear that this man had two kids—he had a family—and he wasn't the only person making this decision and there were other factors at play. I think that that was the reason he later accepted the job.

—[GRACE 2014], JULIA GRACE, CO-FOUNDER OF WEDDINGLOVELY, CTO AT TINDIE

Many companies focus on salary above all else, but it is only one of the bargaining chips you have available when trying to convince a candidate to join. A good offer should describe the opportunity, compensation, and benefits.

The opportunity

The opportunity is the most important part of the offer. The job offer is a chance to be part of a larger mission, work with amazing people, grow your career, have a huge impact, and build something from the ground up (see Chapter 9 for more information on mission and culture). You should be reminding the candidate of these at every step of the way: in the job description, in the initial email, during the phone screen, and during the interview. You should include these in the offer letter, too. Instead of a boring legal document, it should be a personalized and inspiring letter. For example, the Apple offer letter, like most Apple products, comes in a beautifully designed white package with elegant typography. It includes the following text:

> There's work and there's your life's work.
>
> The kind of work that has your fingerprints all over it. The kind of work that you'd never compromise on. That you'd sacrifice a weekend for. You can do that kind of work at Apple. People don't come here to play it safe. They come here to swim in the deep end.
>
> They want their work to add up to something.
>
> Something big. Something that couldn't happen anywhere else.
>
> Welcome to Apple.
>
> **—[HOROWITZ 2012], PAUL HOROWITZ, OS X DAILY**

Now be honest, would you rather see an offer letter like that or a bunch of legal jargon about "at will employment" and how you could be fired at any time?

Compensation

Your goal is to offer a compensation package that removes compensation from the conversation. To do that, the compensation needs to be fair and transparent. Fair means that the compensation is enough for the candidate to live a comfortable life and is competitive with the market. Fair also means that the offer is competitive with other employees at your company. That's where transparency comes in. Transparency breeds trust. If every employee knows how you determine compensation, they don't have to worry that the coworker sitting next to them might be making twice as much for the same job.

The easiest way to be fair and transparent is to use a formula for calculating compensation. You discuss the formula with the candidate before showing them the compensation numbers, so they know exactly how you came up with the numbers and that the formula applies to everyone at the company. It doesn't guarantee the candidate will be happy with the numbers, but at least they will feel like they are being treated fairly. Your company will have to come up with its own formula depending on your values and the type of business you're in. For example, the simplest formula for calculating salary is a list of predefined salaries based on seniority, such as the one shown in Table 11-1.

Table 11-1. Predefined list of salaries based on seniority

Seniority	Salary
Junior	$100,000
Senior	$150,000
Executive	$200,000

You can use one of the online salary calculators to find numbers that are competitive for each level of seniority in your location. A more complicated option is to take into account other factors, such as job type, location, and experience. Here is the formula used at a startup called Buffer [Gascoigne 2013a]:

```
Salary = job type * seniority * experience + location
         (+ $10K if salary choice)
```

Buffer has different base salaries for different job types (e.g., $60,000 for engineer, $75,000 for an executive officer), a multiplier for seniority (e.g., 1.1x for VP, 1.2x for CEO), a multiplier for experience (e.g., 1x for junior, 1.2x for senior), an adjustment for living expenses (e.g., $12,000 for Austin, $24,000 for San Francisco), and a choice to get $10k more salary or 30% more equity. So, if you were using this formula to make an offer to a junior engineer living in San Francisco who opted for more salary, you would get:

```
Salary = $60,000 * 1.0 * 1.0 + $24,000 + $10,000 = $94,000
```

The formulas for equity are all built around when you join a company (see "Equity" on page 451 for a primer on equity). Later employees take on less risk, so they get less equity. The easiest option is a table of predefined values. Consult *http://www.hello-startup.net/resources/equity/* for tables that list the typical amount of equity to give to a startup employee based their role, seniority, and employee number. Alternatively, you can come up with a formula.[7]

---

7 There are several formulas listed in "How I Negotiated My Startup Compensation" by Michelle Wetzler.

One well-known formula is called *The Equity Equation* [Graham 2007]. The idea is that you should be willing to give away n% of your company to someone (an employee or an investor) if you believe they can increase the average outcome for your company so that the (100 - n%) you have left is worth more than the full 100% was before. This idea can be represented with the following equation:

$$n = \frac{i-1}{i}$$

Here, i is the average outcome of the company after you hire the new person. For example, if you could hire a new programmer who you believe will increase the value of the company by 20%, then i = 1.2, and n = (1.2 - 1)/1.2 = .167. In other words, you could give this programmer up to 16.7% of the company and still break even. Of course, you're also going to pay the programmer salary and benefits. If those add up to, say, $100,000, and the company is worth $1 million, then the $100,000 represents 10%, and you're left with 16.7% - 10% = 6.7%. Factoring in that the candidate is likely to negotiate and that you want to make some profit and not just break even, you might fudge this number a bit and end up with something like 3% in the actual offer.

As a rule of thumb, be more generous with equity for employees than investors. While investors usually only add value to a company at the very beginning and sometimes hurt the company in the long run by pushing for an early exit, employees usually add more and more value to a company over time. Offering an employee more equity aligns your interests because the more value the employee creates for the company, the more value the employee is creating for themselves.

Moreover, when it comes to hiring, most startups cannot compete with larger companies on salary, so you have to offer more equity to make up for it. You can present it as an investment opportunity. For example, if the candidate has to forfeit $10,000 salary per year to join your startup instead of a big, established company, then after four years, they have invested $40,000 (actually, less than that due to taxes) in return for, say, 3% of the company (plus many intangibles, such as startup experience, learning opportunities, and new relationships). If the company ends up being worth $10 million, then that $40,000 investment will be worth roughly $300,000 (this is a vast simplification; see "Equity" on page 451 for more information). Of course, the vast majority of startups fail, so be honest with the candidate and tell them that this is a high-risk investment. At a startup, especially in the early days, you want to hire people who are comfortable with taking risks.

Benefits

Be creative with benefits: you can sometimes offer something that's relatively cheap for the company but extremely valuable to an employee. For example, offering an extra week of vacation costs the company roughly 1/50th of the candidate's compensation, a bit like a 2% raise, but the ability to spend more time with loved ones may be worth much more than 2% to the candidate. The only way to know is to listen.

Some ideas for benefits you could offer:

- Insurance (health, dental, vision, life)
- Time off (vacation days, holidays, sick days)
- Food (free breakfast, lunch, dinner, snacks, and drinks)
- Compensation (relocation reimbursement, 401k match, bonuses)
- On-site benefits (day care, dry cleaning, massages, car repair)
- Health (reimburse gym memberships, exercise classes, sports teams)
- Schedule (support flexible work hours and working from home)
- Activities (money for team outings, reading groups, and volunteer groups)
- Learning (money for books, classes, hosting talks, attending conferences)
- Commute (train pass, metro pass, parking pass, shuttle system)
- Autonomy (hackathons, 20% time, incubator)
- Hardware (powerful laptops and desktops, big screens, tablets)
- Work environment (private offices, nice chairs, pet-friendly)

FOLLOW-UP AND NEGOTIATION

Most candidates will need some time to make a decision, but don't let the process drag out too long. Time kills deals. Schedule regular follow-ups, such as having the hiring manager give the candidate a call to see how they are doing and ask if they have any questions. Offer the candidate a lunch with an employee, the CEO, the CTO, or anyone else who could help them make up their mind. Or, consider sending a care package. When I was thinking about my offer from TripAdvisor, they sent me a fleece and a nice card. It probably didn't cost much, but it made a big difference in how it made me feel about the company, and I still remember it to this day.

If the candidate is interested, they might negotiate the offer. Don't be offended: it's a normal part of the process. You should know all of your limits ahead of time: how much the salary can budge, how much more equity you could offer, and what benefits you could toss in to sweeten the deal. If you're using a formula to calculate salary and equity, then tell the candidate up front that you use the same formula for everyone at the company, and that in the interest of transparency and fairness, those numbers are not negotiable (however, you can still be flexible on the benefits). You might lose some candidates to another company that outbids you, but you might gain many more by creating a more fair and transparent workplace, especially for women, who are less likely than men to negotiate a job offer [Small et al. 2007].

Recap

In November 2014, Apple became the first company in history to be valued at over $700 billion dollars [Fletcher 2014]. Apple is renowned for elegant design, clever marketing, cutting-edge hardware, integrated software, efficient supply chains, and an obsession with secrecy. But what did Steve Jobs, Apple's late co-founder, describe as the company's most important task and greatest talent? The answer: hiring.

> The key observation is that, in most things in life, the dynamic range between average quality and the best quality is, at most, two-to-one. For example, if you were in New York and compared the best taxi to an average taxi, you might get there 20% faster. In terms of computers, the best PC is perhaps 30% better than the average PC. There is not that much difference in magnitude. Rarely do you find a difference of two-to-one. Pick anything.
>
> But, in the field that I was interested in—originally, hardware design—I noticed that the dynamic range between what an average person could accomplish and what the best person could accomplish was 50 or 100 to 1. Given that, you're well advised to go after the cream of the cream. That's what we've done. You can then build a team that pursues the A+

players. A small team of A+ players can run circles around a giant team of B and C players. That's what I've tried to do.

—[JAGER AND ORTIZ 1998, 12], STEVE JOBS

In this chapter, I discussed some of the ways to identify A players. I talked about who to look for (relentlessly resourceful co-founders, endlessly curious generalists, T-shaped specialists) and what to look for (smart, gets things done, good culture fit, good communication skills), but the most important thing is how to look for them. You've probably heard this platitude from every single company out there: "we only hire the top 1% of programmers." Pause for a second, and consider what that really means. Every company wants to hire the top 1%. Every single one. But mathematically, you know they can't all get what they want, no matter how good they are at interviewing. Joel Spolsky has a great example of this [Spolsky 2005a]: imagine a hypothetical scenario where you got 100 applications for a job opening and your interview process was so good that you managed to select the best candidate out of the 100 and reject the rest. Does that mean you are hiring the top 1%? Nope. Consider what happens to the 99 programmers you rejected.

They go look for another job.

The next time you or anyone else posts a job, it's possible that you get applications from the same 99 rejects, plus a single new application from one of the roughly 18 million other programmers around the world. Even if your interview process was again good enough to select that 100th candidate, you're not hiring the top 1%, but just a random candidate out of 18 million, or roughly the top 99.99999% [Spolsky 2005a].

Spolsky's insight, while obviously exaggerated, is probably not that far from the truth for most companies. The top 1% of programmers rarely, if ever, apply for jobs, so if your hiring strategy consists of posting a job online and waiting for applications, then no matter how good of a hiring process you have, you are almost certainly not hiring the best programmers available.

The best programmers won't come to you. You have to go out there and find them. You have to cast a line out into your network, open source, and conferences. To get a bite, you have to attract good developers by building and engineering a brand through blogging, open source software, and talks. And you have to reel them in by showing them an interview process and making them an offer that makes you stand out from all the other companies. That's how you get A players and that's how you become the most valuable company in the world.

I think it [recruiting] is the most important job. Assume you're by yourself in a startup and you want a partner. You'd take a lot of time finding the partner, right? He would be half of your company. Why should you take any less time finding a third of your company or a fourth of your company or a fifth of your company? When you're in a startup, the first ten people will determine whether the company succeeds or not. Each is 10% of the company. So why wouldn't you take as much time as necessary to find all the A players? If three were not so great, why would you want a company where 30% of your people are not so great? A small company depends on great people much more than a big company does.

—[JAGER AND ORTIZ 1998, 13], STEVE JOBS

Learning

In a time of drastic change, it is the learners who inherit the future. The learned usually find themselves equipped to live in a world that no longer exists.

—[HOFFER 2006, SECT. 32], ERIC HOFFER, *REFLECTIONS ON THE HUMAN CONDITION*

The software industry may be one of the fastest-changing industries in history. Since the year 2000, we've seen dozens of major new programming languages (e.g., C#, D, F#, Scala, Go, Clojure, Groovy, Rust); huge updates to older programming languages (e.g., C++ 03, 07, 11, and 14, Python 2.0 and 3.0, Java 1.3, 1.4, 5.0, 6.0, 7.0, and 8.0); the development of hundreds of frameworks, libraries, and tools that accompany these languages (e.g., Ruby on Rails, .NET, Spring, IntelliJ IDE, Jenkins); dozens of new databases (e.g., MongoDB, Couchbase, Riak, Redis, CouchDB, Cassandra, HBase); the rise of new hardware platforms (e.g., commodity hardware, multicore CPUs, smartphones, tablets, wearables, drones); the rise of new software platforms (e.g., Windows XP, 7, 8, 10, OS X 10.0–10.10, Firefox, Chrome, iOS, Android); the rise of Agile methodologies (e.g., XP, Scrum, Lean, TDD, pair programming, continuous integration); the explosion of open source software (e.g., GitHub, Linux, MySQL, Hadoop, Node.js); the ubiquity of cloud computing (e.g., Amazon EC2, Heroku, Rackspace, Microsoft Azure); and much more. If you work in the software industry, a huge percentage of your knowledge becomes obsolete every year.

This is why all the best software developers and software companies in the world have one thing in common: they are all obsessed with learning. Joe Armstrong, the creator of the Erlang programming language, said that the best way to become a better programmer is to "spend 20% of your time learning stuff—because it's compounded" [Seibel 2009, 234]. Eric Ries, the author of *The Lean*

Startup, defined learning as the "essential unit of progress for startups" [Ries 2011a, 49]. And in this final chapter of the book, I'm going to discuss how and why every programmer and every startup should incorporate dedicated time for learning into their schedule. I'll start by describing the principles of learning and then move on to the three most common learning techniques: study, build, and share.

Principles of learning

In professional sports, grueling workouts and intense training sessions are a standard part of the job. Similarly, professional musicians, dancers, and chess players spend hours honing their craft every day. And yet with most office jobs, once you graduate from college and complete a ramp-up program at your new company, dedicated time for learning comes to an end. In other words, if you walk around the typical office, almost everyone you see is stuck at a plateau—they are not learning and they are not improving their skills [Newport 2012, 85]. Everyone, that is, except the elite performers.

In the book *Outliers*, Malcom Gladwell argues that in most disciplines, what separates the elite achievers from everyone else has less to do with innate talent and more to do with spending an enormous amount of time practicing. Studies across many different fields indicate that it takes on the order of 10,000 hours of practice to achieve mastery. This is known as the *10,000-hour rule*. For example, the Beatles performed over 1,000 all-night concerts (8+ hours) in the early 1960s at bars in Hamburg, amassing over 10,000 hours of practice before returning to the UK and becoming one of the most successful bands of all time. Similarly, Bill Gates was lucky enough to go to a high school where he had unrestricted access to a computer, a rarity in the late 1960s, and was able to amass over 10,000 hours of practice on the computer before he went on to create Microsoft [Gladwell 2011, Part 1].

Of course, 10,000 hours by itself does not guarantee success. Other factors, such as luck, genetics, and the type of practice you do also play a critical role. In *So Good They Can't Ignore You*, Cal Newport argues that elite performance not only requires a lot of practice but specifically *deliberate practice*. Deliberate practice means you have a feedback mechanism that lets you track your level of performance, and in each practice session, you intentionally choose activities that push you just beyond your capabilities. A classic example of deliberate practice is weight lifting. Elite lifters don't work out—they train. They use the weight on the bar as a feedback mechanism, they track their performance in each workout in a workout journal, and every training session, they try to lift a few more pounds than in the previous session (a concept called *progressive overload*). It's possible to apply the training mentality to creative tasks as well, although your feedback mechanism may be harder to measure. For example, the feedback mechanism for the Beatles was the audience's reaction, night after night. The feedback mechanism for a programmer might have aspects that are easy to measure, such as whether the code passes all the automated tests (see "Automated Tests" on page 296), and aspects that are more subjective, such as the feedback from another programmer in a code review (see "Code reviews" on page 329).

Either way, deliberate practice will stretch your abilities, and stretching usually involves a fair amount of discomfort. Deliberate practice is "often the opposite of enjoyable" [Newport 2012, 97]. Just as a weightlifter gets used to the sensation of physical exertion and seeks out activities that make their muscles burn, you need to become accustomed to the sensation of mental exertion and seek out tasks that strain your mind.

Accumulating thousands of hours of deliberate, uncomfortable practice is not easy. To get to 10,000 hours, you'd need to practice roughly 20 hours per week, every week, for 10 years. That's a serious time commitment. To make it work, you need to:

- Choose your skills wisely.

- Dedicate time to learning.

- Make learning a part of your job.

CHOOSE YOUR SKILLS WISELY

Some skills are more valuable in the market than others. In 2015, learning COBOL is not as valuable as learning JavaScript or Swift. In *The Pragmatic Programmer*, Andy Hunt and Dave Thomas recommend that you think of your learning as building a *knowledge portfolio* that you manage, similar to a financial portfolio [Hunt and Thomas 1999, 13]. You can only spend 10,000 hours a handful of times in your life, so you need to invest regularly (make learning a regular habit) and choose your investments wisely. To keep your portfolio diversified and balanced between conservative and high-risk investments, you need to keep up with industry trends to see what skills and techniques are valuable today, and what is just appearing on the horizon and likely to be valuable tomorrow.

Ideally, you're always experimenting with new stuff. I enjoy downloading and trying out new technologies. I'll regularly check out a new WebSocket library, a new server-side framework, or a new swipe gesture technology even if I don't have a real use case for them at the moment. It's really easy for me to learn about new technologies because I have a strong technical network and I can just watch what other people, who I have a lot of respect for, have discovered and think are worth sharing on Twitter and LinkedIn.

—[SHOUP 2015], MATTHEW SHOUP, PRINCIPAL NERD AT NERDWALLET

Of course, you don't have to become a master of every skill. As I've mentioned several times in this book, it's a good idea to work at being a *T-shaped person*, where you not only develop deep knowledge and mastery in a single discipline but also broad knowledge and familiarity across other disciplines (see "Knowledge" on page 32). In fact, this book is all about building knowledge across multiple disciplines, including business, design, marketing, software engineering, operations, culture, and hiring. If you've made it this far, you're well on your way to a nicely shaped "T."

A human being should be able to change a diaper, plan an invasion, butcher a hog, conn a ship, design a building, write a sonnet, balance accounts, build a wall, set a bone, comfort the dying, take orders, give orders, cooperate, act alone, solve equations, analyze a new problem, pitch manure, program a computer, cook a tasty meal, fight efficiently, die gallantly. Specialization is for insects.

—[HEINLEIN 1988, 248], ROBERT A. HEINLEIN, *TIME ENOUGH FOR LOVE*

It may take 10,000 hours to develop mastery, but you can develop familiarity with a new skill much faster. In *The First 20 Hours*, Josh Kaufman shows how you can learn the basics of a new skill—such as a new sport, a new musical instrument, or a new programming language—in just 20 hours, or roughly two 20-minute sessions, every day, for a month. To make this work, you have to dedicate time to learning.

DEDICATE TIME TO LEARNING

People come up with all sorts of excuses for why they aren't learning new things. The most common is that they're too busy. But the reality is that busy is a decision—you don't *find* the time to do things, you *make* the time. Every time you hear yourself saying "I don't have the time for learning," realize that what you're actually saying is "I'd rather prioritize something else over learning." Passing up too many learning opportunities is a short-sighted approach, especially in the rapidly changing software industry, in which the only way to build a successful career or company is to continuously make yourself better.

Every night, at 11 p.m., I sit down for 20–40 minutes to learn something new. Depending on my mood, I may watch a video, read a book, write a blog post, or play around with a new technology. This routine completely transformed my career. In 2006, I spent my 11 p.m. learning hour figuring out how to use Ajax to update parts of my homepage in response to a click instead of reloading the entire page. In 2007, this side project helped me land a job at TripAdvisor, where Ajax became one of the major tools I used every day. In 2008, I became fascinated with web page performance, and during my 11 p.m. learning hour, I created a script to automate a web performance optimization known as image spriting. In 2009, this script helped me land a job at LinkedIn, where they were struggling to manage image spriting by hand. In 2010, I used my 11 p.m. learning hour to explore many different web frameworks. In 2011, thanks to this experience, I ended up leading a project to rebuild LinkedIn's web framework infrastructure (see "Evolving the tech stack" on page 186).

Make learning a regular part of your schedule. Find a time that works for you—perhaps just before work, during lunch, or before bed—and commit to it for 20–40 minutes every day. This might not seem like much time, but it adds up remarkably quickly after just a few months. Of course, this is even easier to do if you can make learning a part of your job.

MAKE LEARNING PART OF YOUR JOB

The best companies in the world allow, or rather, encourage, employees to spend a part of their work time learning new skills. In other words, they are paying their employees to learn so that they walk out better engineers than when they came in. For example, HubSpot reimburses book purchases, Google reimburses university classes, and LinkedIn offers training courses for how to build mobile apps on iOS and Android. Andy Grove, former CEO of Intel, described job training programs as "one of the highest-leverage activities a manger can perform":

> Consider for a moment the possibility of your putting on a series of four lectures for members of your department. Let's count on three hours preparation for each hour of course time—12 hours of work in total. Say that you have 10 students in your class. Next year they will work a total of

about 20,000 hours for your organization. If your training efforts result in a 1% improvement in your subordinates' performance, your company will gain the equivalent of 200 hours of work as the result of the expenditure of your 12 hours.

—[GROVE 1995, 223], ANDY GROVE, *HIGH OUTPUT MANAGEMENT*

Supporting learning on the job has many benefits beyond productivity. In Chapter 9, you saw that tapping into mastery, the inherent drive to get better, is one of the most powerful ways to motivate employees (see "Motivation" on page 403). In Chapter 11, you saw that while there are 10x engineers, the odds of finding them are low, and a better hiring strategy is to find good people and give them the opportunity to get better (see "10x developers" on page 472). And in the book *So Good They Can't Ignore You*, Cal Newport argues that the secret to a successful career is not obsessing over your "true calling" or "passion" but mastering "rare and valuable skills" [Newport 2012, 229]. By offering dedicated time for learning at your company, you simultaneously make it a more attractive place to work for potential hires and improve the performance of everyone already working there.

Learning techniques

Let's now turn our attention to the three most common learning techniques used by the best software developers and software companies:

- Study.
- Build.
- Share.

STUDY

According to the book *Peopleware*, the average software developer does not own a single book on the subject of his or her work [Demarco and Lister 1999, 12]. As a programmer and an author, I find that terrifying. But in a sense, that also means there is a massive opportunity. If you are a programmer, you can get ahead of all your peers by taking the time to read and study on a regular basis:

- Read articles, blog posts, and books (reading *Hello, Startup* is a good start!). See "Recommended reading" on page 529.

- Read academic papers. Papers We Love (*http://paperswelove.org/*) is a wonderful repository of academic computer science papers.

- Take a class. Coursera and Khan Academy provide many free, online courses across a variety of topics, including programming and startups.

- Attend a talk, meetup group, or conference. See Meetup.com (*http://www.meetup.com/*) and Lanyrd (*http://lanyrd.com/*).

- Read code, especially from open source projects. *The Architecture of Open Source Applications* offers a guided walkthrough of the code of many popular projects, including Berkeley DB, Eclipse, Git, and nginx.

I've found three things that make my study time more effective. First, set concrete, measurable goals. For example, for 2015, I set a goal of reading 30 books (I track my progress using Goodreads). That's a little more than one book every other week, so if two weeks go by and I haven't finished a book, I know I'm behind. I also have a goal of learning at least one major new technology every year, such as a new programming language or database. I've found the *Seven in Seven* series of books, such as *Seven Programming Languages in Seven Weeks*, *Seven Databases in Seven Weeks*, and *Seven Concurrency Models in Seven Weeks*, to be a great great way to tackle this goal—they really stretch your mind by introducing you to a variety of technologies specifically chosen to highlight different programming paradigms, such as object-oriented programming in Ruby versus declarative programming in Prolog or document-oriented storage with MongoDB versus column-oriented storage with HBase.

Second, take notes. For example, I try to summarize every book I read and save my favorite quotes from it on Goodreads. I jot down new ideas, questions, and thoughts I get while reading in my idea journal (see "Keep an idea journal" on page 37). And occasionally, I publish some of these new thoughts on my blog. But even if I wrote down these thoughts on a piece of paper and threw it away immediately after, the mere act of taking notes makes my studying a more active process and helps me better remember and understand these new ideas.

Finally, third, involve your friends and coworkers in the learning process. At LinkedIn, we had a reading group that selected a new computer science paper every few weeks and got together to discuss it. When we were beginning to use Scala, we also had a study group of people who took the "Functional Programming in Scala" course on Coursera. It's easier to stick with something when you have someone else to push you and to discuss questions and ideas.

In fact, public commitments are a great way to make sure you follow through with your learning. When I was struggling to get myself to write, I took on a 30-day blog fitness challenge (*http://bit.ly/30-day-fit*) with several coworkers, in which we each had to write one blog post every day for a month. When a non-technical friend asked me how Bitcoin worked and I realized I couldn't explain it without using a lot of programming jargon, I promised him that I'd write a blog post (*http://bit.ly/bitcoin-analogy*) that explained it in a way that was accessible to both technical and non-technical audiences. And when my team at LinkedIn was struggling with how to do stream processing in Scala, I promised to learn it and blog about it (*http://bit.ly/play-node*).

Struggling with my writing skills in front of everyone, digging through the math in Bitcoin papers, and fighting with obscure functional programming concepts was not always fun, but it had a huge payoff. After the 30-day blog fitness challenge, I was a better writer and traffic to my blog had increased by ten times. After I wrote the blog post on Bitcoin, I had improved my ability to discuss technical topics with a non-technical audience and my post hit the front page of Hacker News, which increased traffic to my blog even more. And after I wrote the post on stream processing, my blog hit the front page of Hacker News again, the Play and Scala community saw my feedback and improved some of the APIs, and I had learned enough about functional stream processing to kick off a project that helped reduce the load time of the LinkedIn home page.[1]

BUILD

As a kid, I hated reading. My parents desperately tried everything to get me to read, even offering to pay me a few dollars for each book I read, but I continued to prefer TV, video games, hanging out with friends, and just about anything else to reading. What finally got me to read was becoming a person who needed reading. What kind of person is that?

A maker.

As soon as you try to create something, you find out that you have no idea what you're doing. You discover huge gaps in your knowledge. You realize that

---

1 *https://github.com/brikis98/ping-play*

you're missing crucial skills. Eventually, the solution becomes obvious: reading. It dawns on you that reading gives you superpowers. You spend a few hours with a book, and when you're done, you're able to do new things, think new thoughts, and see new worlds.

But until you start making things, most of your learning, whether from books or from school, will feel largely useless. This is why you often hear kids complaining, "When will I ever need calculus?" or "What's the point of learning ancient history?" And they're right. When your life consists of TV, video games, and hanging out with friends, you really don't need calculus or history. It's only when you need to build something that these skills become useful, which for me didn't really happen until after college. Sure, I had plenty of projects and home-work assignments from classes, but they were always of the "connect the dots" variety. Someone else decided what I'd do, the tools I could use, the starting point, and the ending point, and all I had to do was walk from one to the other. And then the year would end, I'd throw the project away, and never see it again. Nothing I did mattered, so nothing I learned mattered.

Once I got a job, I had to choose my own projects. I had to figure out what was important and what wasn't. I had to select the tools I'd use. I had to figure out my own timelines and scheduling. And I had to maintain some of my projects for years. I started programming professionally, but I realized I didn't really know how to build software. I started a blog, but I realized I didn't really know how to write. I started trying to get in shape, but I realized I didn't really know how to exercise. I started to try to make something of myself and I realized that I needed help.

That's when I started reading on a regular basis. And I haven't stopped since. If you're having trouble motivating yourself to read, the best thing you can do is to find a project where you have to build something you don't know how to build. Do that, and the reading will take care of itself.

In the spirit of deliberate practice, find projects that will stretch your abilities. If you don't know how to build websites, create a home page or blog for yourself. If you've never used Ruby, build your home page or blog with Ruby on Rails. If you've never implemented an inverted index, build a search feature for your homepage from scratch (as explained in "Technologies you should never build yourself" on page 196, it's OK to reinvent the wheel for the sake of learning). Follow online trends and find reasons to try out new libraries, languages, and techniques. You can do this by taking on new challenges at work, and, if your company offers it, using hackathons and 20%-time as a chance to build and learn something new (see "Autonomy" on page 406).

If you don't have the opportunity to do this at work, then you'll have to do it in your spare time. The best engineers typically have a few side projects that they tinker on late at night or on the weekends. These are a fantastic way to learn and a great addition to your résumé. You can also contribute to open source projects, solve coding challenges, and participate in coding competitions.[2]

SHARE

The final stage of learning is sharing. To understand why, let's do a thought experiment. I'm going to ask you two questions. Take a minute to think of the answers before reading further:

- Who are the best software engineers in the world?
- What are the best software companies in the world?

Did you come up with a list of names? If so, the most interesting thing about this list is how short it is. There are thousands of software engineers and software companies doing incredible things, but when I ask you for the best, only a few names pop into your head. Why these names and not others? It's because these engineers and companies not only do great work but also spend time *telling* you that they do great work. I'd bet that for every programmer and company on your list, you've read their writing (e.g., blogs, papers, books), seen their presentations (e.g., talks, conferences, meetups), and/or used their code (e.g., open source).

The best companies and programmers tend to share almost everything they do. For example, Linus Torvalds created Linux (the most popular server operating system) and Git (the most popular version control system), and released both as free, open source projects. Google published papers that freely gave away the details of how it built two of the core infrastructure technologies that power search indexing, MapReduce, and the Google File System, which were later implemented as free, open source projects (Hadoop and the Hadoop File System). Facebook started the Open Compute Project, where it freely gave away details of how its highly efficient and scalable data centers were built. And there

---

2 See *http://codekata.com/* and *http://www.hello-startup.net/resources/jobs/#coding-competitions*.

are entire companies built around open source that give away almost everything they do, such as Mozilla, Red Hat, and Typesafe. The question is, why?

Why you should share

Why do software developers and software companies give away so much of their work? Why would they invest thousands of hours and millions of dollars into a project and then release it for free? The reason is that sharing gives back more than you put in, in the form of mastery, quality, labor, marketing, and ownership.

Mastery

> The best way to learn is to teach. To explain a topic to someone else, you have to understand it more deeply yourself. Every time I've prepared a talk, written a blog post, or as in this case, written a book, I've walked away knowing much more than I knew going in. Taking the time to share your knowledge is one of the easiest and most effective ways to level-up. In fact, the hallmark of a "senior" engineer is that they make everyone around them better, and the only way to do that is to teach.

Quality

> When is your home cleanest? Just before guests arrive. The same is true of anything that you share with others. One of the unexpected benefits of open sourcing your code is that the mere act of preparing the code for open source often leads to higher-quality code because you know that "guests" will be looking at it. You'll probably take the time to clean up the code, add tests, write documentation, and generally make the project more presentable to the rest of the world. The same is true if you write a blog post or give a talk about your work. The act of sharing a project makes that project better.

Labor

> Every time someone uses your open source code and files a bug, they are doing QA, for free. Every time someone submits a patch to your open source project, they are developing software for you, for free. Every time someone writes a blog post about your open source project, they are writing documentation for you, for free. And if that blog post is a scathing negative review, well, even then they are giving you a design review, for free. Sharing your work with others allows the entire software community to contribute, which makes it possible for projects to become larger and

higher quality than anything you could do on your own (especially as a small startup).

Marketing

If you're a developer, the best way to make yourself look good in front of an employer is to share you work. Think of it like inbound marketing for your career (see "Inbound marketing" on page 173). Instead of blindly spamming your message to the world (e.g., through job applications) and hoping someone takes notice, you attract the employer by sharing valuable content. If developers at a company are reading your blog posts and watching your talks, they will see you as an expert and want to hire you. The work you share becomes a permanent part of your résumé. In fact, it's even better: as John Resig, creator of jQuery said, "When it comes to hiring, I'll take a Github commit log over a résumé any day" [Resig 2011].

If you're an employer, it works the other way, too. The best way to make yourself look good in front of developers is to share your work. If a developer has been using your company's open source code for years, they are more likely to want to join your company and continue using that code. An open source project is a better job advertisement than any job posting.

Ownership

As a developer, if I put thousands of hours of effort into a project, I tend to get attached to it. It's my baby. If it's a proprietary project, leaving the company is a bit like getting a divorce and losing custody of the kids. It's painful, and after you've done it a few times, it's hard to be as passionate about investing in something that isn't really yours. However, if you get to give talks about the work, publish blog posts and papers, and best of all, open source your project, then it's yours for life. It becomes a permanent part of your toolbelt, something you can take with you anywhere you go, something you can show to others, and something you'll be proud to work on.

The culture of sharing is one of the reasons the software industry has been so successful. Compared to something like Wall Street, where a competitor won't tell you the time of day, the tech industry is remarkably open. And when we all share, we all win. Or, to paraphrase Isaac Newton, in a culture of sharing, we can all see further by standing on the shoulders of giants.

So now that you know why you should share, let's discuss what you should share (and what you shouldn't).

What you should and shouldn't share

There are three common objections to sharing your work:

1. I don't have time.
2. No one will look at my work.
3. Everyone will steal my work.

We discussed objection #1, lack of time, earlier: if you want to be successful, you make time for sharing activities such as writing, speaking, and contributing to open source. Objection #2, that no one will look at your work, is not a problem even if it happens. Writing, speaking, and open source, first and foremost, are learning tools for *you*. Writing is just thinking on paper [Zinsser 2006, 147], and the primary goal of a blog is to improve your own thinking, so it's worth doing even if no one reads it. Speaking is very similar to writing in that putting together a presentation and articulating your ideas to others can help clarify your own thoughts. And the work you do to open source your code makes that project better.

That said, if you practice your writing, speaking, and coding, you'd be surprised how your audience can grow. It starts with your friends and colleagues, but slowly, especially if you share your work on sites like Twitter, Facebook, LinkedIn, Reddit, and Hacker News, strangers will find your work, share it, and sometimes offer gratitude or feedback. Moreover, on the Internet, no one can meet you in person, so your identity *is* writing, speaking, and open source. Whatever turns up when I Google your name is who you are, so in the modern world, you are what you share. And if you're worried that no one will be interested in what you have to say, just remember that everyone is at a different stage in their learning:

You'd be amazed at how many things you take for granted as "common knowledge" are actually brand new to other smart people. There's simply too much to know in this world, and we're all continually learning. (I hope). Often I'll get discouraged because I feel like I'm writing about things that have already been discussed into the ground by others. The thing I have to remember is that there's a "right time" to learn something, and it's different for everyone. ... No matter where you are in your education, some people will be interested in hearing your struggles. This is an important thing to keep in mind when you're blogging. Each person in your audience is on a different clock, and all of them are ahead of you in some ways and behind you in others. The point of blogging is that we all agree to share where we're at and not poke fun at people who seem to be behind us, because they may know other things that we won't truly understand for years, if ever.

—[YEGGE 2005], STEVE YEGGE, SOFTWARE ENGINEER AT AMAZON AND GOOGLE

Objection #3, that competitors may steal your work, only matters if that work gives the competitor an advantage. In other words, do not share your "secret sauce." For example, Google's search ranking algorithm is one of its biggest competitive advantages, so the company will probably never reveal the exact formula. But for everything else, especially generic infrastructure projects, you benefit more from giving them away and getting the community involved than from keeping them hidden. This is why Google has published papers on technologies such as MapReduce and BigTable, and why many of its complicated infrastructure projects, such as Android, Go, and V8 are developed as open source projects.

Lessons learned

Now that you understand the importance of sharing, I'd like to share with you some lessons from the programmers I interviewed (see "Interviews" on page 20). One of the questions I asked was, "If you could go back to yourself in college, what advice would you give to your younger self?" These are the lessons they found valuable in their careers—I hope you'll find them valuable in yours:

Brian Larson, Software Engineer at Google and Twitter
> One piece of advice I would give to anyone is try to always be thinking about the team and what you can do to make everyone around you more productive. It's surprising how many people are unwilling to fix the thing that has been annoying everyone at the company for years and they are just used to it now. You show up fresh and you say "that thing is totally screwed up and I'm going to fix that!" You could build a whole career out of fixing those things and people will be like, "Wow, that guy is a superstar. He fixes all the things that have been annoying us for years."

Daniel Kim, Software Engineer at Facebook and Instagram
> If I could go back in time and tell myself one thing, I would try to drill into my 18-year-old, grade-obsessed, aimless, and reactive self that learning to

program is perhaps one of the greatest skills you can learn today. At its heart, programming is problem solving, and it literally enables you to change the world, at scale. The abstract theory of computer science is great, but beyond that there is a nearly limitless world of practical applications of it; so get started.

Dean Thompson, CTO of NoWait

First of all, work for the best people you possibly can. Best in the human sense and best in the sense of most capable in their work. Focus less on the money, the geography, and the product, and more on working for the best people. That's really rules 1 through 10. Second, learn to maintain connections. Reid Hoffman has this very much right: make a habit of being generous to people and giving them small gifts in terms of your time and help. And third, don't jump into the first problem that catches your fancy and solve it no matter how hard it is to solve. Look for cases where you can apply a little bit of your own effort and swing something that wanted to happen anyway. Instead of "I'd like a lake, I'd like it there, I'm going to start digging," a better approach is, "I'd like a river, let me go find a place where there is a pretty good gully and redirect it a little bit."

Florina Xhabija Grosskurth, Web Developer and Manager at LinkedIn, Director of People Operations at Wealthfront

I would tell myself to keep being hungry even when I thought I had achieved something great. Because it was in the moments where I was the hungriest and hustling the hardest that I actually learned and contributed the most. And it was the times I thought I knew my stuff that I became passive and less resilient.

There were times when I would come to work and think "Maybe today they will fire me. They will discover that I'm just not good enough." And the day would go by and I would do some magical beautiful thing and I'd think "Wow, this was a great day. They didn't fire me, and I did this awesome thing. Go me!"

So that's what I would tell myself. Keep the hunger high. Don't feel satiated, ever.

Gayle Laakmann McDowell, Founder and CEO of CareerCup

One of the biggest things I learned in my career is to try to say "yes" a lot more. One story is I had a company contact me wanting my help. They were preparing for acquisition interviews, which I had never done before. I was about five months pregnant and it was not something that I really wanted to do. I had done all-day interviews before at Google, and it was not fun. But I had that idea in the back of my mind: I need to not say "no" to stuff. So I said, OK, I'll do this.

It turned out to be a lot more fun that I thought it would be—when you don't have to write up interview feedback, interviews aren't so bad—and it also turned out to be a very big business opportunity. The company that I worked with ended up getting acquired by Yahoo! and they brought me in to help Yahoo! work on their interview process. It was this thing I was going to say "no" to, and now I have this new consulting business, two dozen clients, and a lot of successes because I said "yes."

Jonas Bonér, Co-founder of Triental AB and Typesafe

One thing that was really clear for me is that you can't prepare for a startup. It just happens. Just go with it. And try to fix things along the way. It's still important to read books like this one and learn from experiences, but at the end of the day, you just have to react to whatever comes in your way.

Jorge Ortiz, Software Engineer at LinkedIn, Foursquare, and Stripe

Put yourself in situations where you are slightly out of your depth. If you are too comfortable, you are not learning enough. If you are totally overwhelmed, you are just going to flail and fail. But if you're in a situation where you're struggling, but just barely keeping it together, I think that's when you're doing your best work.

Julia Grace, Co-Founder of WeddingLovely, CTO at Tindie

First, luck plays a bigger role than I thought. Hard work, extreme dedication, and perseverance are all very important, but my mental framework about starting and evaluating companies dramatically changed after seeing what actually succeeds and what doesn't. You might have a great product, but if your timing is off or if you're in a nascent market that isn't large enough—those are factors you can't overcome.

Second, don't believe everything that you read. A lot of the startup stories you see in the tech press are the heavily edited marketing narratives. It's not necessarily that the stories are wrong, but they don't paint the whole picture. Think of them as the tip of a very large, complex iceberg.

And third, you should never go work at a startup or start a company because you think you'll become rich. If anyone ever says this, or that it's a glamorous lifestyle, they have no idea what they are talking about. It's often a long slog of many, many years of hard work where the odds are never in your favor.

Kevin Scott, SVP at LinkedIn, VP at AdMob, Director at Google

What I think I would tell the earlier version of myself is that it's OK to be impatient and get frustrated. I've always been impatient. I used to beat myself up about it and I'd say to myself, "you should be more patient, you should be more patient." Bullshit. I think my impatience has served me reasonably well. And it's a particular flavor of impatience that is typical of engineers. You walk around, and you see the world in terms of all of the things that are wrong or that could be better. Impatience is your desire to act on that impulse, and that's a good thing. It's not a stupid quirk of youth. As long as you're not so impatient that your health is impacted, the desire to move fast and drive change is OK. It really is.

None of what we do is easy. You will get frustrated. You're trying to bring brand-new things that have never existed into existence. You're trying to build things that are so complex that it takes hundreds, or thousands, or tens of thousands of people's collective effort to bring them into existence. It can be frustrating, stressful, and at times, depressing. But that's OK. If you're not experiencing those things, you're probably not going to make a difference. I used to have this myth in my head that someday I would've accomplished a bunch of stuff and then I won't have to be impatient anymore or I won't have to be stressed or I won't have to be aggravated or disappointed. Nah. As soon as all of those things are resolved is when you're no longer making progress.

Martin Kleppmann, Co-founder of Go Test It and Rapportive

A key idea I came across while in college was this quote from Paul Graham:

> *College is where the line ends. Superficially, going to work for a company may feel like just the next in a series of institutions, but underneath, everything is different. The end of school is the fulcrum of your life, the point where you go from net consumer to net producer.*

—[GRAHAM 2005], PAUL GRAHAM, CO-FOUNDER OF Y COMBINATOR

This was basically the thing that got me into startups.

Mat Clayton, Co-founder of Mixcloud

Don't worry so much and just release stuff faster. It took us a long time to figure that one out. We waited a lot at the start before launching and we should have launched four to five months earlier. It's not a mistake we really make anymore. Our launch schedule now is about six or seven times per day, and every quarter, we try to speed that up. Just keep releasing stuff really quickly. Now is better than later. There is a very good quote by General Patton: "A good plan violently executed now is better than a perfect plan next week."

Matthew Shoup, Principal Nerd at NerdWallet

Don't underestimate the power of creativity. Creativity is more powerful than technical knowledge. Everyone talks about technical chops being important, but just because you understand the technologies doesn't necessarily mean that you can put them to good use. You can always learn technology, but it's only when you have creativity that you can create anything. And creativity is a muscle that needs to be flexed. Practice, practice, practice.

Nick Dellamaggiore, Software Engineer at LinkedIn and Coursera

I was pretty reserved in college and this limited my opportunities in kicking off my career. I was fortunate to navigate my way into the LinkedIn opportunity, but I feel this was partly by luck. My advice to my college self is to fully leverage the college environment by maximizing networking opportunities, joining CS clubs, doing internships and picking up side projects to learn what they don't teach you in class. Focus on establishing your personal brand early on and continue to build on this as you enter the workforce. Oh, and stop playing so much *Quake III*.

Steven Conine, Founder of Wayfair

Trust your gut and make decisions on people fast. When you're building a team, sometimes you hire someone and you just know this person doesn't fit in. Fix those mistakes as soon as possible. It will cause more stress in the short term, but in the long term, you will do better and your life will be easier.

Tracy Chou, Software Engineer at Quora and Pinterest

Engineers need to think strategically about how their work aligns with the company's goals. At a startup, there are so few people that what each person does becomes much more important. Some engineers just want to nerd out on the technology, but if it's not relevant to the product or business, they just can't afford to spend time on it. There's another critical point: time estimation. In the strategic alignment calculus, engineers need to be constantly evaluating trade-offs—should I refactor this or ship some shitty code?—and one of the key inputs to that decision is how long different alternatives take. Accurate time estimation and project forecasting for software is hard, but it's necessary.

Vikram Rangnekar, Co-founder of Voiceroute and Socialwok

I'd tell myself two things. First, while following your gut and instincts is good, test often and be humble enough to evolve your idea with what you've learned. Second, understand marketing and distribution. Telling a great story is hard but it can define your product and help it stand above in the increasingly crowded world of software. And a well thought-out distribution strategy can help you get that story out to the right audience.

Zach Holman, Software Engineer at GitHub

There are no emergencies. I mean, obviously there are emergencies, like the server is down and you have to fix it, but I think a lot of what happens in tech is that everybody feels that something is an emergency even though it's actually benign. I talk about us being very asynchronous as a company —I can submit a pull request and you can get back to me the next day— and a lot of people ask, "But what happens if something needs to happen *right now*?" Well, if I submit a pull request that's an "emergency," then everyone gets stressed and jumps in with snippy responses and sarcasm, like, "Let me show you exactly why you're wrong" or "No, you're an asshole, and this is the dumbest thing in the world."

We're typing words on a piece of digital paper—it's not something that needs to be this crazy. When this stuff happens, I try to force myself to step out for a while. Usually, half an hour goes by, and you realize it's not something that you have to be personally passionate and angry about, and that it's not an emergency. It doesn't have to happen *right now* and you don't have to steal someone's attention to make it happen today.

Recap

In the *Game of Thrones* series, one of the characters, who I will leave unnamed to avoid spoilers, ends up joining a guild. Every day, the master of the guild assigns this character a number of tasks, including one that repeats over and over again: learning. Every night, when the character returns to the guild after completing the day's tasks, the master of the guild asks, "What three new things do you know, that you did not know before?"

I believe this is a great practice to follow in your own life. Find a friend or loved one and every night, ask each other what three new things you've learned during the day. As long as you learn something new, no matter how small, every day, your knowledge will compound, and you'll be amazed at how much better you are after just a year. Is it enough to turn you into the best programmer in the world? Probably not.

But your goal in learning isn't to be the best programmer in the world. It's to be a better programmer than you were yesterday. One of the most inspiring things I saw while interviewing programmers for this book, as well as from reading books like *Founders at Work* and *Coders at Work*, is that everyone, including the best programmers in the world, starts at zero. Everyone has self-doubt and everyone who is successful got there by making just a little bit of progress day after day after day.

> *The one common denominator [that great thinkers and creators] have shared with me over the years is that they all feel like they have to get up every day and do it again. They all feel like they may very well be discovered as phonies, they very well may never, ever achieve what they had hoped.*

—[FIELDS 2014], DEBBIE MILLMAN, HOST OF *DESIGN MATTERS*

The difference between good programmers and bad programmers, between the elite and the average, has less to do with innate genius and more to do with perseverance. Good programmers never stop learning. They incorporate deliberate practice every day, even though it's uncomfortable and even though they are busy. And that's the secret to building a great career: you have to be good at something before you can expect a great job [Newport 2012, xix]. And the way to be good at something is to spend a lot of time studying, building, and sharing.

Read something new every day. Build something new every month. And every time you learn something new, share it with the world through writing, talks, and open source. This is why I wrote this book: to share what I know with all of you and to learn new things myself, both from the process of writing and from your feedback. I'd love to hear your thoughts, your startup experiences, and whether you found this book valuable, so feel free to email me at *feedback@hello-startup.net*. Even better, pay it forward and share what you learned from this book with others in the form of blog posts, talks, and open source. Thank you for reading!

Recommended Reading and References

Recommended reading

For a list of recommended reading for each chapter in this book, as well as some topics not covered in this book, see *http://www.hello-startup.net/resources/recommended-reading/*.

Reference list

1. [a-cambrian-moment] "A Cambrian Moment." The Economist, January 18, 2014. *http://www.economist.com/news/special-report/21593580-cheap-and-ubiquitous-building-blocks-digital-products-and-services-have-caused.*

2. [about-facebook-2015] "About Facebook." Facebook. Accessed January 8, 2015. *https://www.facebook.com/facebook?sk=info.*

3. [about-google-2015] "About Google." Accessed January 8, 2015. *http://www.google.com/about/.*

4. [about-post-it-brand-2015] "About Post-It® Brand." Accessed February 24, 2015. *http://www.post-it.com/wps/portal/3M/en_US/PostItNA/Home/Support/About/.*

5. [about-us-2015] "About Us." LinkedIn. Accessed January 8, 2015. *https://www.linkedin.com/about-us.*

6. [adams-2001] Adams, James L. *Conceptual Blockbusting: A Guide to Better Ideas.* Fourth Edition. Cambridge, Mass: Basic Books, 2001.

7. [advertising-spending-in-the-us-2014] "Advertising Spending in the U.S. 2014." Statista. Accessed March 14, 2015. *http://www.statista.com/statistics/272314/advertising-spending-in-the-us/.*

8. [al-qudsi-2011] Al-Qudsi, Mahmoud. "Everyday Inspiration". TEDxDeadSea, 2011. *https://www.youtube.com/watch?v=bPwgkf1aZ9I.*

9. [alfred-2009] Alfred, Randy. "Oct. 21, 1879: Edison Gets the Bright Light Right." Wired, October 21, 2009. *http://www.wired.com/2009/10/1021edison-light-bulb/*.

10. [altman-2014a] Altman, Sam. "Lecture 1: How to Start a Startup." How to Start a Startup, September 23, 2014. *https://clip.mn/embed/yt-CBYhVcO4WgI*.

11. [altman-2014b] Altman, Sam. "Lecture 18: Legal and Accounting Basics for Startups." How to Start a Startup, November 20, 2014. *http://startupclass.samaltman.com/courses/lec18/*.

12. [andreessen-2007] Andreessen, Marc. "How to Hire the Best People You've Ever Worked with," June 6, 2007. *http://pmarchive.com/how_to_hire_the_best_people.html*.

13. [andreessen-2011] Andreessen, Marc. "Why Software Is Eating The World." Wall Street Journal, August 20, 2011, sec. Life and Style. *http://www.wsj.com/articles/ SB10001424053111903480904576512250915629460*.

14. [ariga-lleras-2011] Ariga, Atsunori, and Alejandro Lleras. "Brief and Rare Mental *Breaks* Keep You Focused: Deactivation and Reactivation of Task Goals Preempt Vigilance Decrements." Cognition 118, no. 3 (March 2011): 439–43. doi:10.1016/j.cognition.2010.12.007.

15. [armstrong-2011] Armstrong, Rich. "The Price of (Dev) Happiness: Part Two." Fog Creek Blog, September 1, 2011. *http://blog.fogcreek.com/the-price-of-dev-happiness-part-two/*.

16. [arrington-2007] Arrington, Mike. "Confirmed: MySpace To Acquire Photobucket For $250 Million." TechCrunch, May 7, 2007. *http://techcrunch.com/2007/05/07/myspace-to-acquire-photobucket-for-250-million/*

17. [ashcraft-blithe-2010] Ashcraft, Catherine and Sarah Blithe. "Women in IT: The Facts." National Center for Women & Information Technology, April, 2010. *http://www.ncwit.org/sites/default/files/ legacy/pdf/NCWIT_TheFacts_rev2010.pdf*

18. [asimov-2014] Asimov, Isaac. "Isaac Asimov Asks, How Do People Get New Ideas?" MIT Technology Review, October 20, 2014. *http://www.technologyreview.com/view/531911/isaac-asimov-asks-how-do-people-get-new-ideas/*.

19. [atwood-2006b] Atwood, Jeff. "Object-Relational Mapping Is the Vietnam of Computer Science." Coding Horror, June 26, 2006. *http://blog.codinghorror.com/object-relational-mapping-is-the-vietnam-of-computer-science/*.

20. [balter-2014] Balter, Ben. "15 Rules for Communicating at GitHub." Ben Balter, November 6, 2014. *http://ben.balter.com/2014/11/06/rules-of-communicating-at-github/*.

21. [barta-markus-neumann-2012] Barta, Thomas, Kleiner Markus, and Tilo Neumann. "Is There a Payoff from Top-Team Diversity?" McKinsey & Company, April 2012. *http://www.mckinsey.com/ insights/organization/is_there_a_payoff_from_top-team_diversity*.

22. [beck-andres-2004] Beck, Kent, and Cynthia Andres. *Extreme Programming Explained: Embrace Change.* 2nd edition. Boston, MA: Addison-Wesley, 2004.

23. [beck-et-al-2001] Beck, Kent, et al. "Manifesto for Agile Software Development." 2001. *http:// www.agilemanifesto.org/*

24. [bentley-1988] Bentley, Jon. *More Programming Pearls: Confessions of a Coder*. 1st edition. Reading, MA: Addison-Wesley Professional, 1988.

25. [berkun-2010] Berkun, Scott. *The Myths of Innovation*. 1st edition. Sebastopol, CA: O'Reilly Media, 2010.

26. [bianchi-2013] Bianchi, Nicole. "4 Reasons to Keep An Idea Journal." Inkwell Scholars, March 13, 2013. *http://inkwellscholars.org/4-reasons-to-keep-an-idea-journal/*.

27. [biello-2006] Biello, David. "Fact or Fiction?: Archimedes Coined the Term *Eureka!* In the Bath." Scientific American, December 8, 2006. *http://www.scientificamerican.com/article/fact-or-fiction-archimede/*.

28. [blank-2013] Blank, Steve. *The Four Steps to the Epiphany*. 2nd edition. K&S Ranch, 2013.

29. [blank-dorf-2012] Blank, Steve, and Bob Dorf. *The Startup Owner's Manual: The Step-By-Step Guide for Building a Great Company*. 1st edition. Pescadero, CA: K & S Ranch, 2012.

30. [bls-2012] BLS. "Number Of Jobs Held, Labor Market Activity, And Earnings Growth Among The Youngest Baby Boomers: Results From A Longitudinal Survey." Bureau of Labor Statistics, US Department of Labor, July 25, 2012. *http://www.bls.gov/news.release/pdf/nlsoy.pdf*.

31. [bls-2014] BLS. "America's Young Adults At 27: Labor Market Activity, Education, And Household Composition: Results From A Longitudinal Survey." Bureau of Labor Statistics, US Department of Labor, March 26, 2014. *http://www.bls.gov/news.release/pdf/nlsyth.pdf*.

32. [booch-1991] Booch, Grady. Object-Oriented Design: With Applications. Benjamin/Cummings Pub., 1991.

33. [box-draper-1987] Box, George E. P., and Norman R. Draper. *Empirical Model-Building and Response Surfaces*. 1 edition. New York: Wiley, 1987.

34. [braithwaite-2014] Braithwaite, Reginald. "I Don't Hire Unlucky People," October 4, 2014. *http://braythwayt.com/posterous/2014/10/04/i-dont-hire-unlucky-people.html*.

35. [branson-2014] Branson, Rick. "Facebook's Instagram: Making the Switch to Cassandra from Redis, a 75% *Insta* Savings." Planet Cassandra, October 15, 2014. *http://planetcassandra.org/blog/interview/facebooks-instagram-making-the-switch-to-cassandra-from-redis-a-75-insta-savings/*.

36. [brennan-chugh-kline-2002] Brennan, Aoife, Jasdeep S. Chugh, and Theresa Kline. "Traditional versus Open Office Design A Longitudinal Field Study." Environment and Behavior 34, no. 3 (May 1, 2002): 279–99. doi:10.1177/0013916502034003001.

37. [brikman-2011] Brikman, Yevgeniy. "This Is Where I Work. Remix." April 30, 2011. *http://www.ybrikman.com/writing/2011/04/30/this-is-where-i-work-remix/*.

38. [brikman-2013a] Brikman, Yevgeniy. "Play Framework: Async I/O without the Thread Pool and Callback Hell." LinkedIn Engineering Blog, March 27, 2013. *http://engineering.linkedin.com/play/play-framework-async-io-without-thread-pool-and-callback-hell*.

39. [brikman-2014a] Brikman, Yevgeniy. "So Long, and Thanks for All the T-Shirts." April 2, 2014. *http://www.ybrikman.com/writing/2014/04/02/so-long-and-thanks-for-all-t-shirts/*.

40. [brikman-2014b] Brikman, Yevgeniy. "You Are What You Document." May 5, 2014. *http://www.ybrikman.com/writing/2014/05/05/you-are-what-you-document/*.

41. [brooks-1995] Brooks, Frederick P. Jr. *The Mythical Man-Month: Essays on Software Engineering.* Anniversary edition. Reading, MA: Addison-Wesley Professional, 1995.

42. [brown-2014] Brown, Derek. "Management Is Not a Promotion," October 8, 2014. *https://www.linkedin.com/pulse/20141008201310-9454814-management-is-not-a-promotion*.

43. [bryan-2012] Bryant, Adam. "The Phones Are Out, but the Robot Is In." New York Times, April 7, 2012, sec. Business. *http://www.nytimes.com/2012/04/08/business/phil-libin-of-evernote-on-its-unusual-corporate-culture.html*.

44. [bryant-2013] Bryant, Adam. "In Head-Hunting, Big Data May Not Be Such a Big Deal." New York Times, June 19, 2013, sec. Business. *http://www.nytimes.com/2013/06/20/business/in-head-hunting-big-data-may-not-be-such-a-big-deal.html*.

45. [buchheit-2010] Buchheit, Paul. "If Your Product Is Great, It Doesn't Need to Be Good." February 9, 2010. *http://paulbuchheit.blogspot.com/2010/02/if-your-product-is-great-it-doesnt-need.html*.

46. [bueno-2014] Bueno, Carlos. "Inside the Mirrortocracy," June 2014. *http://carlos.bueno.org/2014/06/mirrortocracy.html*.

47. [burnham-2010] Burnham, Bo. *Bo Burnham: Words, Words, Words.* Directed by Shannon Hartman. Comedy Central, 2010.

48. [burnham-2012] Burnham, Kristin. "Tech's 10 Most Famous College Dropouts." ITworld, May 9, 2012. *http://www.itworld.com/article/2827248/it-management/tech-s-10-most-famous-college-dropouts.html*.

49. [bushey-2014] Bushey, Ryan. "WhatsApp Delivered a Mind-Melting 64 Billion Messages in One Day." Business Insider, April 2, 2014. *http://www.businessinsider.com/whatsapp-64-billion-messages-24-hours-2014-4*.

50. [butterick-2015] Butterick, Matthew. "Butterick's Practical Typography." Accessed June 21, 2015. *http://practicaltypography.com/*

51. [calacanis-2013] Calacanis, Jason. "Pitching Sequoia? Here's the Big Question You'll Need to Answer." PandoDaily, February 20, 2013. *http://pando.com/2013/02/20/sequoias-why-now/*.

52. [candle-problem-2015] "Candle Problem." Wikipedia, the Free Encyclopedia, January 3, 2015. *http://en.wikipedia.org/w/index.php?title=Candle_problem&oldid=625263317*.

53. [cap-theorem-2014] "CAP Theorem." Wikipedia, The Free Encyclopedia, December 17, 2014. *http://en.wikipedia.org/wiki/CAP_theorem*.

54. [carlson-2014] Carlson, Nicholas. "Larry Page Tried To Sell Google For $1.6 Million — $358 Billion Less Than It's Worth Today." Business Insider, April 24, 2014. *http://bit.ly/sells-google*.

55. [carter-et-al-2007] Carter, Nancy M., Lois Joy, Harvey M. Wagner, and Sriram Narayanan. "The Bottom Line: Corporate Performance and Women's Representation on Boards." Catalyst, October

15, 2007. *http://catalyst.org/system/files/The_Bottom_Line_Corporate_Perfor-mance_and_Womens_Representation_on_Boards.pdf.*

56. [chan-2012] Chan, Joel. "Do Creative People Have More Bad Ideas than Average?" Quora, July 8, 2012. *http://www.quora.com/Do-creative-people-have-more-bad-ideas-than-average/answer/Joel-Chan.*

57. [chan-et-al-2011] Chan, Joel, Katherine Fu, Christian Schunn, Jonathan Cagan, Kristin Wood, and Kenneth Kotovsky. "On the Benefits and Pitfalls of Analogies for Innovative Design: Ideation Performance Based on Analogical Distance, Commonness, and Modality of Examples." Journal of Mechanical Design 133, no. 8 (2011): 081004. doi:10.1115/1.4004396.

58. [chang-2013] Chang, Emily. "Reid Hoffman Discusses Founding LinkedIn." Bloomberg.com, May 9, 2013. *http://www.bloomberg.com/news/videos/b/3faa53d4-73d0-41a4-90a9-c459ed23de64.*

59. [chang-et-al-2006] Chang, Fay, Jeffrey Dean, Sanjay Ghemawat, Wilson C. Hsieh, Deborah A. Wallach, Mike Burrows, Tushar Chandra, Andrew Fikes, and Robert E. Gruber. "Bigtable: A Distributed Storage System for Structured Data." OSDI'06: Seventh Symposium on Operating System Design and Implementation, November 2006. *http://research.google.com/archive/bigtable.html.*

60. [chen-2013] Chen, Andrew. "Andrew Chen's answer to Growth Hacking: How Do You Find Insights like Facebook's *7 Friends in 10 Days* to Grow Your Product Faster?" Quora, March 19, 2013. *http://www.quora.com/Growth-Hacking/How-do-you-find-insights-like-Facebooks-7-friends-in-10-days-to-grow-your-product-faster/answer/Andrew-Chen?srid=XPv&share=1.*

61. [chesky-2014a] Chesky, Brian. "Don't Fuck Up the Culture." Medium, April 20, 2014. *https://medium.com/@bchesky/dont-fuck-up-the-culture-597cde9ee9d4.*

62. [chesky-2014b] Chesky, Brian. "Lecture 10 - Culture." How to Start a Startup, October 24, 2014. *http://startupclass.samaltman.com/courses/lec10/*

63. [cheung-adora-2014] Cheung, Adora. "Lecture 4 - Building Product, Talking to Users, and Growing." How to Start a Startup. October 2, 2014. *http://startupclass.samaltman.com/courses/lec04/.*

64. [chiang-2011] Chiang, Oliver. "Valve And Steam Worth Billions." Forbes, February 15, 2011. *http://www.forbes.com/sites/oliverchiang/2011/02/15/valve-and-steam-worth-billions/.*

65. [chomsky-2002] Chomsky, Noam. *Syntactic Structures.* 2nd edition. Berlin; New York: De Gruyter Mouton, 2002. *http://www.amazon.com/Syntactic-Structures-Edition-Noam-Chomsky/dp/3110172798.*

66. [christensen-cook-hall-2006] Christensen, Clayton M., Scott Cook, and Taddy Hall. "What Customers Want from Your Products." HBS Working Knowledge, January 16, 2006. *http://hbswk.hbs.edu/item/5170.html.*

67. [chromostereopsis-2014] "Chromostereopsis." Wikipedia, the Free Encyclopedia, December 2, 2014. *http://en.wikipedia.org/w/index.php?title=Chromostereopsis&oldid=636323294.*

68. [chu-2013] Chu, Renee. "What Are the Coolest Startup Culture Hacks You've Heard Of?" Quora, April 16, 2013. *http://www.quora.com/What-are-the-coolest-startup-culture-hacks-youve-heard-of/answer/Renee-Chu?srid=XPv&share=1.*

69. [church-2012] Church, Michael O. "Don't Waste Your Time in Crappy Startup Jobs." Michael O. Church | Rants, Essays, and Diatribes., July 8, 2012. *http://michaelochurch.wordpress.com/2012/07/08/dont-waste-your-time-in-crappy-startup-jobs/*.

70. [ciotti-2012] Ciotti, Gregory. "The Science of Why Energy Management Is the Key to Peak Productivity." iDoneThis Blog, October 19, 2012. *http://blog.idonethis.com/science-of-better-energy-management/*.

71. [cleese-1991] Cleese, John. "Lecture on Creativity." 1991. *http://genius.com/John-cleese-lecture-on-creativity-annotated*

72. [cockburn-williams-2001] Cockburn, Alistair, and Laurie Williams. "The Costs and Benefits of Pair Programming," 2001. *http://collaboration.csc.ncsu.edu/laurie/Papers/XPSardinia.PDF*.

73. [cohen-2010] Cohen, Jason. "Why Getting 10 Customers Is All That Matters." Venture Beat, August 18, 2010. *http://venturebeat.com/2010/08/18/why-getting-10-customers-is-all-that-matters/*.

74. [cole-2014] Cole, Samantha. "6 Tech Leaders On What It Takes To Get Hired At Their Companies." Fast Company, August 20, 2014. *http://www.fastcompany.com/3034552/hit-the-ground-running/5-tech-leaders-on-what-it-takes-to-get-hired-at-their-companies*.

75. [collins-porras-2004] Collins, Jim, and Jerry I. Porras. *Built to Last: Successful Habits of Visionary Companies.* 3rd edition. Concordville, PA.; Norwood, MA: HarperBusiness, 2004. *http://www.amazon.com/Built-Last-Successful-Visionary-Essentials/dp/0060516402*.

76. [collison-2014] Collison, Patrick. "Lecture 11 - Hiring and Culture, Part II". How to Start a Startup, October 28, 2014. *http://startupclass.samaltman.com/courses/lec11/*.

77. [cook-2011] Cook, John D. "Norris' Number," November 22, 2011. *http://www.johndcook.com/blog/2011/11/22/norris-number/*.

78. [cook-2013] Cook, David. "David Cook's Answer to Growth Hacking: How Do You Find Insights like Facebook's *7 Friends in 10 Days* to Grow Your Product Faster?" Quora, March 14, 2013. *http://www.quora.com/Growth-Hacking/How-do-you-find-insights-like-Facebooks-7-friends-in-10-days-to-grow-your-product-faster/answer/David-Cook-6?srid=XPv&share=1*.

79. [cook-2014] Cook, John D. "Time Exchange Rate." August 17, 2014. *http://www.johndcook.com/blog/2014/08/17/time-exchange-rate/*.

80. [cooper-2004] Cooper, Alan. *The Inmates Are Running the Asylum: Why High Tech Products Drive Us Crazy and How to Restore the Sanity.* 1st edition. Indianapolis, IN: Sams - Pearson Education, 2004.

81. [coppola-2014] Coppola, Davide. "C++ Benchmarks: Vector vs List vs Deque." Bits of Bytes, May 20, 2014. *http://blog.davidecoppola.com/2014/05/cpp-benchmarks-vector-vs-list-vs-deque/*.

82. [cornet-2011] Cornet, Manu. "Organizational Charts." Bonkers World, June 27, 2011. *http://www.bonkersworld.net/organizational-charts/*.

83. [coverity-inc-2013] Coverity, Inc. "Coverity Scan Report Finds Open Source Software Quality Outpaces Proprietary Code for the First Time," May 7, 2013. *http://www.coverity.com/press-releases/ coverity-scan-report-finds-open-source-software-quality-outpaces-proprietary-code-for-the-first-time/*.

84. [danziger-levav-avnaim-pesso-2011] Danziger, Shai, Jonathan Levav, and Liora Avnaim-Pesso. "Extraneous Factors in Judicial Decisions." Proceedings of the National Academy of Sciences 108, no. 17 (April 26, 2011): 6889–92. doi:10.1073/pnas.1018033108.

85. [darville-2014] Darville, Niclas. "Business Models." GitHub Gists, August 1, 2014. *https:// gist.github.com/ndarville/4295324*.

86. [dean-barroso-2013] Dean, Jeffrey, and Luiz André Barroso. "The Tail at Scale." Communications of the ACM 56, no. 2 (February 1, 2013): 74. doi:10.1145/2408776.2408794.

87. [decandia-et-al-2007] DeCandia, Giuseppe, et al. "Dynamo: Amazon's Highly Available Key-Value Store." SOSP '07 Proceedings of Twenty-First ACM SIGOPS Symposium on Operating Systems Principles, 2007, 205–20.

88. [demarco-lister-1999] DeMarco, Tom, and Timothy Lister. *Peopleware: Productive Projects and Teams.* 2nd edition. New York, NY: Dorset House Publishing Company, Incorporated, 1999.

89. [denning-2011] Denning, Steve. "The Lost Interview: Steve Jobs Tells Us What Really Matters." Forbes, November 17, 2011. *http://www.forbes.com/sites/stevedenning/2011/11/17/the-lost-interview-steve-jobs-tells-us-what-really-matters/*.

90. [diffusion-of-ideas-2012] "Diffusion of Ideas." Wikipedia, the Free Encyclopedia, February 28, 2012. *http://en.wikipedia.org/wiki/File:Diffusion_of_ideas.svg*.

91. [doll-2013] Doll, Brian. "10 Million Repositories." GitHub, December 23, 2013. Accessed December 24, 2014. *https://github.com/blog/1724-10-million-repositories*.

92. [doug-2012] Doug, Tim. "From MongoDB to Riak." Bump Dev Bog, May 14, 2012. *http:// devblog.bu.mp/post/40786226011/from-mongodb-to-riak-7138*.

93. [drell-2011] Drell, Lauren. "6 Companies With Awesome Employee Perks." Mashable, August 7, 2011. *http://mashable.com/2011/08/07/startup-employee-perks/*.

94. [drucker-2008] Drucker, Peter F. *Management.* Revised edition. New York, NY: HarperBusiness, 2008.

95. [duncker-1945] Duncker, Karl. *On Problem Solving.* Psychological Monographs, 58, American Psychological Association, 1945. OCLC: 968793.

96. [edwards-2011] Edwards, Douglas. "The Beginning." Wall Street Journal, July 16, 2011, sec. Life and Style. *http://www.wsj.com/news/articles/SB10001424052702304911045764443636685127 64*.

97. [elman-2011] Elman, Josh. "Thoughts on Growth." A talk for Greylock Discovery fund companies, December 12, 2011. *http://www.slideshare.net/joshelman/thoughts-on-growth*.

98. [elmer-2014] Elmer, Vickie. "After Disclosing Employee Salaries, Buffer Was Inundated with Resumes." Quartz, January 24, 2014. *http://qz.com/169147/applications-have-doubled-to-the-company-that-discloses-its-salaries/*.

99. [entity–attribute–value-model-2014] "Entity–attribute–value Model." Wikipedia, the Free Encyclopedia, December 20, 2014. *http://en.wikipedia.org/w/index.php?title=Entity%E2%80%93attribute%E2%80%93value_model&amoldid=637792851.*

100. [etherington-2013] Etherington, Rose. "Apple Unveils iOS 7 Software by Jonathan Ive at WWDC." Dezeen, June 10, 2013. *http://www.dezeen.com/2013/06/10/new-apple-ios-software-flat-design-jonathan-ive-wwdc/.*

101. [evans-2014] Evans, Benedict. "Mobile Is Eating the World." October 28, 2014. *http://a16z.com/2014/10/28/mobile-is-eating-the-world/.*

102. [facebook-2014] "Facebook." Wikipedia, The Free Encyclopedia, December 24, 2014. *http://en.wikipedia.org/wiki/Facebook.*

103. [feld-2005a] Feld, Brad. "Term Sheet: Liquidation Preference." Feld Thoughts, January 4, 2005. *http://www.feld.com/archives/2005/01/term-sheet-liquidation-preference.html.*

104. [feld-2005b] Feld, Brad. "Term Sheet: Protective Provisions." Feld Thoughts, January 18, 2005. *http://www.feld.com/archives/2005/01/term-sheet-protective-provisions.html.*

105. [feld-2014] Feld, Brad. "Founder Suicides," October 2, 2014. *http://www.feld.com/archives/2014/10/founder-suicides.html.*

106. [ferguson-2010] Ferguson, Kirby. "Everything Is a Remix." Everything Is a Remix, 2010. *http://everythingisaremix.info/.*

107. [ferguson-2011] Ferguson, Dave. "Hackamonth: Mixing Things Up." Facebook Engineering Notes, April 27, 2011. *https://www.facebook.com/notes/facebook-engineering/hackamonth-mixing-things-up/10150161285048920.*

108. [fershleiser-smith-2008] Fershleiser, Rachel, and Larry Smith, eds. *Not Quite What I Was Planning: Six-Word Memoirs by Writers Famous and Obscure.* New York: Harper Perennial, 2008.

109. [fiegerman-2014] Fiegerman, Seth. "Twitter Users to Twitter: Here's What Your *Mission Statement* Should Be." Mashable, November 13, 2014. *http://mashable.com/2014/11/12/twitter-mission-statement/.*

110. [fields-2014] Fields, Jonathan. "Is It Really Possible To Design Your Life?", 2014. *https://www.youtube.com/watch?v=zwGLx7l1Ybc.*

111. [first-round-review-2015] First Round Review. "From 0 to $1B - Slack's Founder Shares Their Epic Launch Strategy," January 27, 2015. *http://firstround.com/review/From-0-to-1B-Slacks-Founder-Shares-Their-Epic-Launch-Strategy/.*

112. [fletcher-2014] Fletcher, Nick. "Apple Becomes First Company Worth $700bn." The Guardian, November 25, 2014, sec. Tech. *http://www.theguardian.com/technology/2014/nov/25/apple-first-company-worth-700bn-iphone.*

113. [flickr-2015] "Flickr." Wikipedia, the Free Encyclopedia, January 4, 2015. *http://en.wikipedia.org/w/index.php?title=Flickr&oldid=639212185.*

114. [florence-2014] Florence, Ryan. "You Can't Not Have a Framework," May 19, 2014. *http://blog.ryan-florence.com/you-cant-not-have-a-framework.html*.

115. [fowler-2005] Fowler, Martin. "InversionOfControl," June 26, 2005. *http://martinfowler.com/bliki/InversionOfControl.html*.

116. [fowler-2010] Fowler, Martin. "FeatureToggle." Martinfowler.com, October 29, 2010. *http://martinfowler.com/bliki/FeatureToggle.html*.

117. [fowler-2011] Fowler, Martin. "FrequencyReducesDifficulty." Martinfowler.com, July 28, 2011. *http://martinfowler.com/bliki/FrequencyReducesDifficulty.html*.

118. [sadalage-fowler-2012] Sadalage, Pramod J., and Martin Fowler. *NoSQL Distilled: A Brief Guide to the Emerging World of Polyglot Persistence*. 1st edition. Upper Saddle River, NJ: Addison-Wesley Professional, 2012.

119. [fowler-et-al-1999] Fowler, Martin, Kent Beck, John Brant, William Opdyke, and Don Roberts. *Refactoring: Improving the Design of Existing Code*. 1st edition. Reading, MA: Addison-Wesley Professional, 1999.

120. [fralic-2012] Fralic, Chris. "How Many Months to 1 Million Users?" Nothing to Say, April 13, 2012. *http://nothingtosay.com/2012/04/monthsto1musers/*.

121. [franusic-2013] Franusic, Joël. "Chart of Y Combinator Companies' Hosting Decisions, 2011 Edition," January 2, 2013. *http://jpf.github.io/domain-profiler/ycombinator.html*.

122. [freedman-weinberg-1990] Freedman, Daniel P., and Gerald M. Weinberg. *Handbook of Walkthroughs, Inspections, and Technical Reviews: Evaluating Programs, Projects, and Products*. 3rd edition. New York, NY: Dorset House, 1990.

123. [freeman-pryce-2009] Freeman, Steve, and Nat Pryce. *Growing Object-Oriented Software, Guided by Tests*. 1st edition. Upper Saddle River, NJ: Addison-Wesley Professional, 2009.

124. [fried-hansson-linderman-2006] Fried, Jason, David Heinemeier Hansson, and Matthew Linderman. *Getting Real: The Smarter, Faster, Easier Way to Build a Successful Web Application*. Chicago, IL: 37signals, 2006.

125. [fried-hansson-2010] Fried, Jason, and David Heinemeier Hansson. *Rework*. 1st edition. New York: Crown Business, 2010.

126. [gage-2012] Gage, Deborah. "The Venture Capital Secret: 3 Out of 4 Start-Ups Fail." The Wall Street Journal, September 20, 2012, sec. Small Business. *http://www.wsj.com/articles/SB10000872396390443720204578004980476429190*.

127. [gallo-2011] Gallo, Carmine. "Steve Jobs: Get Rid of the Crappy Stuff." Forbes, May 16, 2011. *http://www.forbes.com/sites/carminegallo/2011/05/16/steve-jobs-get-rid-of-the-crappy-stuff/*.

128. [gamson-2014] Gamson, Mike. "My Promise to You (Our Employees)," July 21, 2014. *https://www.linkedin.com/pulse/20140721140018-8377769-my-promise-to-you-our-employees*.

129. [gara-2014] Gara, Tom. "Skype's Incredible Rise, in One Image." Wall Street Journal, January 15, 2014, sec. Internet. *http://blogs.wsj.com/corporate-intelligence/2014/01/15/skypes-incredible-rise-in-one-image/*.

130. [gascoigne-2011] Gascoigne, Joel. "Idea to Paying Customers in 7 Weeks: How We Did It." Social, February 16, 2011. *https://blog.bufferapp.com/idea-to-paying-customers-in-7-weeks-how-we-did-it*.

131. [gascoigne-2013a] Gascoigne, Joel. "Open Salaries at Buffer: Our Transparent Formula and All Our Salaries." Open, December 19, 2013. *https://open.bufferapp.com/introducing-open-salaries-at-buffer-including-our-transparent-formula-and-all-individual-salaries/*.

132. [gascoigne-2014] Gascoigne, Joel. "Open Equity: Buffer's Equity Formula And Full Individual Breakdown." Open, April 14, 2014. *https://open.bufferapp.com/buffer-open-equity-formula/*.

133. [gascoigne-widrich-2014] Gascoigne, Joel, and Leo Widrich. "We're Raising $3.5m in Funding: Here Is the Valuation, Term Sheet and Why We're Doing It." Open, October 27, 2014. *https://open.bufferapp.com/raising-3-5m-funding-valuation-term-sheet/*.

134. [gertner-2014] Gertner, Jon. "The Truth About Google X: An Exclusive Look Behind The Secretive Lab's Closed Doors." Fast Company, May 2014. *http://www.fastcompany.com/3028156/united-states-of-innovation/the-google-x-factor*.

135. [gifford-2012] Gifford, Julia. "Can an Office Environment Really Affect Productivity?" DeskTime Insights, August 20, 2012. *http://blog.desktime.com/2012/08/20/can-an-office-environment-really-affect-productivity/*.

136. [girotra-terwiesch-ulrich-2009] Girotra, Karan, Christian Terwiesch, and Karl T. Ulrich. "Idea Generation and the Quality of the Best Idea." SSRN Scholarly Paper. Rochester, NY: Social Science Research Network, December 8, 2009. *http://papers.ssrn.com/abstract=1082392*.

137. [github-hq-3-2015] "GitHub HQ 3.0." studio hatch. Accessed January 12, 2015. *http://www.weare-hatch.com/github-hq-3.0/*

138. [github-office-2015] "GitHub Office." Custom Spaces. Accessed January 13, 2015. *http://customspaces.com/office/DhXb6EKlE9/github-office-san-francisco/*.

139. [gladwell-2004] Gladwell, Malcom. "Choice, Happiness and Spaghetti Sauce." TED, 2004. *http://www.ted.com/talks/malcolm_gladwell_on_spaghetti_sauce*.

140. [gladwell-2011] Gladwell, Malcolm. *Outliers: The Story of Success*. Reprint edition. New York: Back Bay Books, 2011.

141. [glass-2009] Glass, Ira. "Ira Glass on Storytelling, part 3 of 4" PRI Public Radio International, 2009. *https://www.youtube.com/watch?v=BI23U7U2aUY&feature=youtube_gdata_player*.

142. [godin-2003] Godin, Seth. "How to Get Your Ideas to Spread." TED, 2003. *http://www.ted.com/talks/seth_godin_on_sliced_bread*.

143. [godin-2009] Godin, Seth. "Fear of Bad Ideas." Seth's Blog, December 21, 2009. *http://sethgodin.typepad.com/seths_blog/2009/12/fear-of-bad-ideas.html*.

144. [goldin-rouse-1997] Goldin, Claudia, and Cecilia Rouse. "Orchestrating Impartiality: The Impact of. *Blind* Auditions on Female Musicians." National Bureau of Economic Research, January 1997. *http://www.nber.org/papers/w5903.*

145. [goldman-papson-1999] Goldman, Robert, and Stephen Papson. *Nike Culture: The Sign of the Swoosh.* 1st edition. Thousand Oaks, CA: SAGE Publications Ltd, 1999.

146. [google-2014] "Google." Wikipedia, The Free Encyclopedia, December 25, 2014. *http://en.wikipedia.org/wiki/Google.*

147. [google-zeitgeist-2012] "Google Zeitgeist 2012." Accessed March 14, 2015. *http://www.google.com/zeitgeist/2012/#the-world.*

148. [gorman-2013] Gorman, Michael. "Eric Migicovsky on Pebble's Origin, Smartwatch Philosophy and What's Wrong with the Competition." Engadget, September 11, 2013. *http://www.engadget.com/2013/09/11/eric-migicovsky-pebble-ceo/.*

149. [gowers-2000] Gowers, Timothy. "The Importance of Mathematics (Part 1)." The Millenium Meeting of the Clay Mathematics Institute, May 24, 2000. *https://www.youtube.com/watch?v=BsIJN4YMZZo&feature=youtube_gdata_player.*

150. [grace-2014] Grace, Julia. "Tips for Finding Software Engineering Jobs," April 9, 2015. *http://www.juliahgrace.com/blog/2015/4/9/an-unconventional-guide-for-getting-a-software-engineering-job.*

151. [graham-2004a] Graham, Paul. *Hackers and Painters: Big Ideas from the Computer Age.* 1st edition. Sebastopol, CA: O'Reilly Media, 2004.

152. [graham-2004b] Graham, Paul. "How to Make Wealth," May 2004. *http://www.paulgraham.com/wealth.html.*

153. [graham-2005] Graham, Paul. "Hiring is Obsolete," May 2005. *http://paulgraham.com/hiring.html.*

154. [graham-2006] Graham, Paul. "The 18 Mistakes That Kill Startups," October 2006. *http://www.paulgraham.com/startupmistakes.html.*

155. [graham-2007] Graham, Paul. "The Equity Equation," July 2007. *http://paulgraham.com/equity.html.*

156. [graham-2008] Graham, Paul. "Be Good," April 2008. *http://paulgraham.com/good.html*

157. [graham-2009] Graham, Paul. "Relentlessly Resourceful," March 2009. *http://www.paulgraham.com/relres.html.*

158. [graham-2012a] Graham, Paul. "Schlep Blindness," January 2012. Accessed February 23, 2015. *http://paulgraham.com/schlep.html.*

159. [graham-2012b] Graham, Paul. "Startup = Growth," September 2012. Accessed December 23, 2014. *http://www.paulgraham.com/growth.html.*

160. [graham-2012c] Graham, Paul. "How to Get Startup Ideas," November 2012. *http://paulgraham.com/startupideas.html.*

161. [graham-2013] Graham, Paul. "Do Things That Don't Scale," July 2013. *http://paulgraham.com/ds.html*.

162. [graham-2014] Graham, Paul. "Before the Startup," October 2014. *http://www.paulgraham.com/before.html*.

163. [graham-essays] Graham, Paul. "Essays". *http://paulgraham.com/articles.html*

164. [grant-2014] Grant, Adam. "Don't Start a Company with Your Friends." Adam Grant's Blog, October 16, 2014. *http://adammgrant.tumblr.com/post/100159814037/dont-start-a-company-with-your-friends*.

165. [green-2013] Green, Sarah. "Research: Cubicles Are the Absolute Worst." Harvard Business Review, November 13, 2013. *https://hbr.org/2013/11/research-cubicles-are-the-absolute-worst*.

166. [grishaver-2012] Grishaver, Mike. "Introducing a New Look for Company Pages." LinkedIn Official Blog, September 6, 2012. *http://blog.linkedin.com/2012/09/06/new-look-for-company-pages/*.

167. [griswold-2014] Griswold, Alison. "Airbnb's Latest Milestone: 1 Million Homes, and Hardly Anyone Who Noticed." Slate, December 8, 2014. *http://www.slate.com/blogs/moneybox/2014/12/08/airbnb_has_1_million_homes_brian_chesky_announces_milestone_and_almost_no.html*.

168. [gross-2012] Gross, Doug. "In Tech, Some Bemoan the Rise of *Brogrammer* Culture." CNN, May 7, 2012. *http://www.cnn.com/2012/05/07/tech/web/brogrammers/index.html*.

169. [groth-2013] Groth, Aimee. "Zappos Is Going Holacratic: No Job Titles, No Managers, No Hierarchy." Quartz, December 30, 2013. *http://qz.com/161210/zappos-is-going-holacratic-no-job-titles-no-managers-no-hierarchy/*.

170. [grove-1995] Grove, Andrew S. *High Output Management.* 2nd edition. New York: Vintage, 1995.

171. [google-java-style-2014] "Google Java Style," March 21, 2014. *https://google-styleguide.googlecode.com/svn/trunk/javaguide.html*.

172. [gun-sirer-2013] Gün Sirer, Emin. "Broken by Design: MongoDB Fault Tolerance." Hacking, Distributed, January 29, 2013. *http://hackingdistributed.com/2013/01/29/mongo-ft/*.

173. [hackathon-2015] "Hackathon." Facebook. Accessed January 9, 2015. *https://www.facebook.com/hackathon*.

174. [hadamard-2007] Hadamard, Jacques. *An Essay on the Psychology of Invention in the Mathematical Field.* Hadamard Press, 2007.

175. [haden-2013] Haden, Jeff. "Why There Are No Job Titles at My Company." Inc.com, October 2013. *http://www.inc.com/magazine/201310/jeff-haden/why-there-are-no-job-titles-at-my-company.html*.

176. [hale-2010] Hale, Coda. "You Can't Sacrifice Partition Tolerance." Coda Hale Writes Things, October 7, 2010. *http://codahale.com/you-cant-sacrifice-partition-tolerance/*.

177. [hale-2014] Hale, Kevin. "Lecture 7 -How to Build Products Users Love." How to Start a Startup, October 14, 2014. *http://startupclass.samaltman.com/courses/lec07/*

178. [hall-2011] Hall, Nicole. "Are There REALLY More Mobile Phones Than Toothbrushes?" @AskJamieTurner Blog, October 2011. Accessed December 23, 2014. *http://60secondmarketer.com/blog/2011/10/18/more-mobile-phones-than-toothbrushes/*.

179. [hamel-2011] Hamel, Gary. "Reinventing the Technology of Human Accomplishment." University of Phoenix Distinguished Guest Video Lecture Series, 2011. *http://www.managementexchange.com/video/gary-hamel-reinventing-technology-human-accomplishment*.

180. [hammant-2007] Hammant, Paul. "Introducing Branch By Abstraction." Paul Hammant's Blog, April 26, 2007. *http://paulhammant.com/blog/branch_by_abstraction.html*.

181. [hammant-2013] Hammant, Paul. "Google's Scaled Trunk Based Development." Paul Hammant's Blog, May 6, 2013. *http://paulhammant.com/2013/05/06/googles-scaled-trunk-based-development/*

182. [hamming-1995] Hamming, Richard. "You and Your Research." June 6, 1995. *https://www.youtube.com/watch?v=a1zDuOPkMSw&feature=youtube_gdata_player*.

183. [hanov-2010] Hanov, Steve. "How a Programmer Reads Your Résumé." Steve Hanov's Blog, 2010. *http://stevehanov.ca/blog/index.php?id=56*.

184. [harford-2011] Harford, Tim. "Trial, Error and the God Complex." TED, 2011. *http://www.ted.com/talks/tim_harford?language=en*.

185. [harris-2011] Harris, Derrick. "Facebook shares some secrets on making MySQL scale." Gigaom, December 6, 2011. *https://gigaom.com/2011/12/06/facebook-shares-some-secrets-on-making-mysql-scale/*.

186. [hastings-2009] Hastings, Reed. "Netflix Culture: Freedom & Responsibility." August 1, 2009. *http://www.slideshare.net/reed2001/culture-1798664*.

187. [hathaway-2013] Hathaway, Ian. "Tech Starts: High-Technology Business Formation and Job Creation in the United States." Kauffman Foundation Research Series: Firm Formation and Economic Growth, August 2013. *http://www.kauffman.org/~/media/kauffman_org/research%20reports%20and%20covers/2013/08/bdstechstartsreport.pdf*

188. [hickey-2009] Hickey, Rich. "Are We There Yet?" InfoQ, November 12, 2009. *http://www.infoq.com/presentations/Are-We-There-Yet-Rich-Hickey*.

189. [history-of-mcdonalds-2015] "History of McDonald's." Wikipedia, the Free Encyclopedia, February 16, 2015. *http://en.wikipedia.org/w/index.php?title=History_of_McDonald%27s&oldid=647462227*.

190. [heath-heath-2007] Heath, Chip, and Dan Heath. *Made to Stick: Why Some Ideas Survive and Others Die*. 1st edition. New York: Random House, 2007.

191. [heeris-2013] Heeris, Jason. "This Is Why You Shouldn't Interrupt a Programmer." The Slightly Disgruntled Scientist, October 17, 2013. *http://heeris.id.au/2013/this-is-why-you-shouldnt-interrupt-a-programmer/*.

192. [heinlein-1988] Heinlein, Robert A. *Time Enough for Love*. Reissue edition. New York: Ace, 1988.

193. [henney-2010] Henney, Kevlin. *97 Things Every Programmer Should Know: Collective Wisdom from the Experts*. Sebastopol, CA: O'Reilly Media, 2010. *http://www.amazon.com/Things-Every-Programmer-Should-Know/dp/0596809484*.

194. [hoff-2013] Hoff, Todd. "Scaling Pinterest - From 0 To 10s Of Billions Of Page Views A Month In Two Years." High Scalability, April 15, 2013. *http://highscalability.com/blog/2013/4/15/scaling-pinterest-from-0-to-10s-of-billions-of-page-views-a.html*.

195. [hoff-2014] Hoff, Todd. "The WhatsApp Architecture Facebook Bought For $19 Billion." High Scalability, February 26, 2014. *http://highscalability.com/blog/2014/2/26/the-whatsapp-architecture-facebook-bought-for-19-billion.html*.

196. [hoffer-2006] Hoffer, Eric. *Reflections on the Human Condition*. Titusville, NJ: Hopewell Publications, 2006.

197. [hoffman-2014] Hoffman, Reid. "Reid Hoffman at Startup School SV 2014." Y Combinator Startup School 2014, October 2014. *https://www.youtube.com/watch?v=nef6uTa2a5w&feature=youtube_gdata_player*.

198. [hoffman-casnocha-2012] Hoffman, Reid, and Ben Casnocha. *The Start-up of You: Adapt to the Future, Invest in Yourself, and Transform Your Career*. Crown Business, 2012.

199. [hofstadter-1999] Hofstadter, Douglas R. *Gödel, Escher, Bach: An Eternal Golden Braid*. 20 Anv edition. New York: Basic Books, 1999.

200. [hollas-2011] Hollas, Judd. "A Comparison of Angel Investors and Venture Capitalists." EquityNet Blog, September 12, 2011. Accessed December 25, 2014. *https://www.equitynet.com/blog/angel-investors-vcs/*.

201. [hollon-2011] Hollon, John. "Survey: 74% of Workers Are Passive Job Seekers Ready to Consider a Move." TLNT, March 8, 2011. *http://www.tlnt.com/2011/03/08/survey-74-of-workers-are-passive-job-seekers-ready-to-consider-a-move/*.

202. [holman-2011] Holman, Zach. "Open Source Doesn't Just Market Itself," April 18, 2011. *http://zachholman.com/posts/open-source-marketing/*.

203. [holmes-2014] Holmes, David. "In Case You Needed Another Reason to Promote Diversity in Tech..." PandoDaily, November 17, 2014. *http://pando.com/2014/11/17/in-case-you-needed-another-reason-to-promote-diversity-in-tech/*.

204. [horowitz-2012] Horowitz, Paul. "Apple's Inspirational Note to New Hires." OS X Daily, May 7, 2012. *http://osxdaily.com/2012/05/07/apple-inspirational-note-to-new-hires/*.

205. [horowitz-2014] Horowitz, Ben. *The Hard Thing About Hard Things: Building a Business When There Are No Easy Answers*. HarperBusiness, 2014.

206. [how-to-start-a-startup-2014] "How to Start a Startup". CS183B at Stanford University, Fall 2014. *http://startupclass.samaltman.com/*

207. [hsieh-2013] Hsieh, Tony. *Delivering Happiness: A Path to Profits, Passion, and Purpose*. Reprint edition. New York: Grand Central Publishing, 2013.

208. [hubbard-2010] Hubbard, Douglas W. *How to Measure Anything: Finding the Value of Intangibles in Business.* 2nd edition. Hoboken, N.J: Wiley, 2010.

209. [hubspot-2013] HubSpot. "Culture Code: Creating a Lovable Company." March 20, 2013. *http://www.slideshare.net/HubSpot/the-hubspot-culture-code-creating-a-company-we-love.*

210. [humble-2011] Humble, Charles. "Twitter Shifting More Code to JVM, Citing Performance and Encapsulation As Primary Drivers." InfoQ, July 4, 2011. *http://www.infoq.com/articles/twitter-java-use.*

211. [humble-farley-2010] Humble, Jez, and David Farley. *Continuous Delivery: Reliable Software Releases through Build, Test, and Deployment Automation.* 1st edition. Upper Saddle River, NJ: Addison-Wesley Professional, 2010.

212. [hunt-thomas-1999] Hunt, Andrew, and David Thomas. *The Pragmatic Programmer: From Journeyman to Master.* 1st edition. Reading, MA: Addison-Wesley Professional, 1999.

213. [innosight-2012] Innosight. "Creative Destruction Whips through Corporate America," Winter 2012. *http://www.innosight.com/innovation-resources/strategy-innovation/upload/creative-destruction-whips-through-corporate-america_final2012.pdf.*

214. [instagram-2015] "Instagram." CrunchBase. Accessed January 9, 2015. *http://www.crunchbase.com/organization/instagram*

215. [ish-shalom-2014] Ish-Shalom, Amir. "Viber Replaces MongoDB with Couchbase," February 2014. *http://www.couchbase.com/viber.*

216. [iss-configuration-2011] "ISS Configuration." Wikipedia, The Free Encyclopedia, May 21, 2011. *http://en.wikipedia.org/wiki/International_Space_Station#mediaviewer/File:ISS_configuration_2011-05_en.svg*

217. [jack-suri-2010] Jack, William, and Tavneet Suri. "Mobile Money: The Economics of M-PESA." National Bureau of Economic Research Working Paper Series No. 16721 (2011). doi:10.3386/w16721.

218. [jager-ortiz-1998] Jager, Rama Dev, and Rafael Ortiz. *In the Company of Giants: Candid Conversations With the Visionaries of the Digital World.* Reprint edition. McGraw-Hill, 1998.

219. [jennings-2011] Jennings, Mike. "Tron Remix party by LinkedIn's IT Team." July 5, 2011. *https://plus.google.com/photos/103556494439052499738/albums/5701742938738736385*

220. [jetbrains-appcode-2014] JetBrains AppCode. Twitter post, 24 Feb 2014, 2:28AM. *https://twitter.com/appcode/status/437896886649757696.*

221. [jiang-2010] Jiang, Changhao. "BigPipe: Pipelining Web Pages for High Performance." Facebook Engineering Notes, June 4, 2010. *https://www.facebook.com/notes/facebook-engineering/bigpipe-pipelining-web-pages-for-high-performance/389414033919.*

222. [jobs-2007] Jobs, Steve. "Apple Confidential - Steve Jobs on Think Different." Sept. 23, 1997. *https://www.youtube.com/watch?v=9GMQhOm-Dqo.*

223. [jobs-2011] Jobs, Steve. Steve Jobs' Vision of the World, November 19, 2011. Accessed December 30, 2014. *https://www.youtube.com/watch?v=UvEiSa6_EPA*.

224. [johnson-2011] Johnson, Steven. *Where Good Ideas Come From*. Reprint edition. New York: Riverhead Books, 2011.

225. [johnson-2014] Johnson, Eric. "A Long Tail of Whales: Half of Mobile Games Money Comes From 0.15 Percent of Players." Re/code, February 26, 2014. *http://recode.net/2014/02/26/a-long-tail-of-whales-half-of-mobile-games-money-comes-from-0-15-percent-of-players/*.

226. [jones-1996] Jones, Capers. "Software Defect-Removal Efficiency." IEEE Computer, April 1996.

227. [json-types] "JSON Types." PostgreSQL: Documentation. Accessed January 5, 2015. *http://www.postgresql.org/docs/9.4/static/datatype-json.html*.

228. [kahneman-deaton-2010] Kahneman, Daniel, and Angus Deaton. "High Income Improves Evaluation of Life but Not Emotional Well-Being." Proceedings of the National Academy of Sciences 107, no. 38 (September 21, 2010): 16489–93. doi:10.1073/pnas.1011492107.

229. [kasper-2012] Kasper, Kimberley. "Jobvite Declares May National Employee Referral Month." Jobvite, May 2, 2012. *http://www.jobvite.com/press-releases/2012/jobvite-declares-may-national-employee-referral-month/*.

230. [kauffman-2014] "Kauffman Index of Entrepreneurial Activity Interactive." Kauffman.org, April 9, 2014. *http://www.kauffman*. Accessed December 21, 2014 *http://www.kauffman.org/multimedia/infographics/2013/kiea-interactive*.

231. [kawasaki-2011] Kawasaki, Guy. "12 Lessons Steve Jobs Taught Guy Kawasaki." Silicon Valley Bank CEO Summit, October 6, 2011. *https://www.youtube.com/watch?v=DR_wXoEwOMM*.

232. [kay-1997] Kay, Alan. "The Computer Revolution Hasn't Happened Yet," 1997. *https://www.youtube.com/watch?v=oKg1hTOQXoY&feature=youtube_gdata_player*.

233. [kay-2012] "The Future Doesn't Have to Be Incremental." Founder School, 2014. *https://www.youtube.com/watch?v=gTAghAJcO10*.

234. [ken-2014] ken. "Ask HN: What Companies Have Private Offices for Programmers?" Hacker News, May 1, 2014. *https://news.ycombinator.com/item?id=7676377*.

235. [kennedy-1961] Kennedy, John F. "Special Message to the Congress on Urgent National Needs." John F. Kennedy Presidential Library and Museum, May 25, 1961. *http://www.jfklibrary.org/JFK/JFK-Legacy/NASA-Moon-Landing.aspx*.

236. [kennedy-2014] Kennedy, Erik D. "7 Rules for Creating Gorgeous UI (Part 1)." Medium, November 13, 2014. *https://medium.com/@erikdkennedy/7-rules-for-creating-gorgeous-ui-part-1-559d4e805cda*.

237. [kernighan-plauger-1978] Kernighan, Brian W., and P. J. Plauger. *The Elements of Programming Style*. 2nd edition. New York: McGraw-Hill, 1978. *http://www.amazon.com/The-Elements-Programming-Style-Edition/dp/0070342075*.

238. [kesteloot-2014] Kesteloot, Lawrence. "Norris Numbers," June 1, 2014. *http://www.teamten.com/lawrence/writings/norris-numbers.html*.

239. [kleon-2012] Kleon, Austin. *Steal Like an Artist: 10 Things Nobody Told You About Being Creative.* First Edition. New York: Workman Publishing Company, 2012.

240. [kleppmann-2015] Kleppmann, Martin. *Designing Data-Intensive Applications.* Sebastopol, CA: O'Reilly Media, 2015. *http://shop.oreilly.com/product/0636920032175.do?cmp=af-strata-books-videos-product_cj_9781491903094_%25zp.*

241. [kniberg-2013] Kniberg, Henrik. "Spotify – the unproject culture." Passion for Projects keyote, May 21, 2013. *http://blog.crisp.se/wp-content/uploads/2014/03/unproject.pdf*

242. [knoblauch-2014] Knoblauch, Max. "Internet Users Send 204 Million Emails Per Minute." Mashable, April 23, 2014. *http://mashable.com/2014/04/23/data-online-every-minute/.*

243. [konnikova-2014] Konnikova, Maria. "The Open-Office Trap." The New Yorker, January 7, 2014. *http://www.newyorker.com/business/currency/the-open-office-trap.*

244. [kreps-2013] Kreps, Jay. "Lessons from Building and Scaling LinkedIn." InfoQ, June 30, 2013. *http://www.infoq.com/presentations/linkedin-architecture-stack.*

245. [kreps-2014] Kreps, Jay. E-mail message, November 23, 2014.

246. [krieger-2011] Krieger, Mike. "Sharding & IDs at Instagram." Instagram Engineering Blog, September 30, 2011. *http://instagram-engineering.tumblr.com/post/10853187575/sharding-ids-at-instagram.*

247. [krug-2014] Krug, Steve. *Don't Make Me Think, Revisited: A Common Sense Approach to Web Usability.* 3rd edition. Berkeley, CA: New Riders, 2014.

248. [kumar-2015] Kumar, Manu. "Frequency, Density, Pain, Friction." K9 Ventures, February 10, 2015. *http://www.k9ventures.com/blog/2015/02/10/finding-problem-worth-solving/.*

249. [lalonde-2012] Lalonde, Olivier. "YC W12 Startups' Hosting Decisions." Olivier Lalonde's Blog, August 23, 2012. *http://syskall.com/yc-w12-startups-hosting-decisions/index.html/.*

250. [langley-2014] Langley, Adam. "Apple's SSL/TLS Bug." ImperialViolet, February 22, 2014. *https://www.imperialviolet.org/2014/02/22/applebug.html.*

251. [leblanc-2014] LeBlanc, Martin. Twitter post, May 14, 2014, 10:56AM. *https://twitter.com/leblanc-startup/status/466638260195041280.*

252. [lee-2014] Lee, Stephanie M. "Controversial DNA Startup Wants to Let Customers Create Creatures." SFGate. Accessed January 4, 2015. *http://www.sfgate.com/business/article/Controversial-DNA-startup-wants-to-let-customers-5992426.php.*

253. [leichtman-2014] Leichtman Research Group. "49% Of US Households Have A TV Connected To The Internet." Leichtman Research Group, June 6, 2014. *http://www.leichtmanresearch.com/press/060614release.html.*

254. [leinbach-reyhle-2014] Leinbach-Reyhle, Nicole. "Shedding Hierarchy: Could Zappos Be Setting An Innovative Trend?" Forbes, July 15, 2014. *http://www.forbes.com/sites/nicoleleinbachreyhle/2014/07/15/shedding-hierarchy-could-zappos-be-setting-an-innvoative-trend/.*

255. [lennon-2013] Lennon, Mark. "CrunchBase Reveals: The Average Successful Startup Raises $41M, Exits at $242.9M." TechCrunch, December 14, 2013. *http://techcrunch.com/2013/12/14/crunchbase-reveals-the-average-successful-startup-raises-41m-exits-at-242-9m/.*

256. [leonard-2014] Leonard, John. "Viber Explains Why It Ditched MongoDB and Redis in Favour of Couchbase." Computing News, February 21, 2014. *http://www.computing.co.uk/ctg/news/2330148/viber-explains-why-it-ditched-mongodb-and-redis-in-favour-of-couchbase.*

257. [letrent-2014] LeTrent, Sarah. "Twist and Shout: NASA Prints 3-D Wrench in Space." CNN, Fri December 19, 2014. Accessed December 22, 2014. *http://www.cnn.com/2014/12/19/tech/feat-3d-wrench-nasa/index.html.*

258. [levie-2014a] Levie, Aaron. Twitter post. August 7, 2014. *https://twitter.com/levie/status/497171727781462016.*

259. [levie-2014b] Levie, Aaron. "Lecture 12 - Building for the Enterprise." How to Start a Startup, October 30, 2014. *https://www.youtube.com/watch?v=tFVDjrvQJdw&feature=youtube_gdata_player.*

260. [libin-2012] Libin, Phil. "Keynote Phil Libin at TNW2012." April 27, 2012. *https://www.youtube.com/watch?v=_-8xAUx5Y6s.*

261. [lieberman-montgomery-1988] Lieberman, Marvin B., and David B. Montgomery. "First-Mover Advantages." Strategic Management Journal 9, no. S1 (June 1, 1988): 41–58. doi:10.1002/smj.4250090706.

262. [lieberman-montgomery-1998] Lieberman, Marvin B., and David B. Montgomery. "First-Mover (Dis)advantages: Retrospective and Link with the Resource-Based View." Strategic Management Journal 19, no. 12 (December 1, 1998): 1111–25.

263. [lilly-2015] Lilly, John. "Design Like You're Right. Listen Like You're Wrong." Medium, February 23, 2015. *https://medium.com/@johnolilly/design-like-you-re-right-listen-like-you-re-wrong-308e3930fdbf.*

264. [linkedin-2011] LinkedIn. Mob-In: Flash Mob at LinkedIn All-Hands Meeting!, 2011. *https://www.youtube.com/watch?v=kZrMa_lw2bo&feature=youtube_gdata_player.*

265. [linkedin-2014] "LinkedIn." Wikipedia, The Free Encyclopedia, December 28, 2014. *http://en.wikipedia.org/wiki/LinkedIn.*

266. [linkedin-hackdays-2015] "LinkedIn Hackdays." Accessed June 21, 2015. *https://engineering.linkedin.com/tags/hackday.*

267. [linster-2014] Linster, Marc. "Postgres Outperforms MongoDB and Ushers in New Developer Reality." Enterprise DB, September 24, 2014. *http://blogs.enterprisedb.com/2014/09/24/postgres-outperforms-mongodb-and-ushers-in-new-developer-reality/.*

268. [list-of-apple-inc-slogans-2015] "List of Apple Inc. Slogans." Wikipedia, the Free Encyclopedia, March 9, 2015. *http://en.wikipedia.org/w/index.php?title=List_of_Apple_Inc._slogans&oldid=650660136.*

269. [list-of-best-selling-pc-games-2015] "List of Best-Selling PC Games." Wikipedia, the Free Encyclopedia, January 7, 2015. *http://en.wikipedia.org/w/index.php?title=List_of_best-selling_PC_games&oldid=641497258.*

270. [list-of-largest-employers-2014] "List of Largest Employers." Wikipedia, the Free Encyclopedia, December 18, 2014. *http://en.wikipedia.org/w/index.php?title=List_of_largest_employers&oldid=637245078.*

271. [list-of-multiple-discoveries-2015] "List of Multiple Discoveries." Wikipedia, the Free Encyclopedia, February 8, 2015. *http://en.wikipedia.org/w/index.php?title=List_of_multiple_discoveries&oldid=646209829.*

272. [liu-et-al-2012] Liu, Siyuan, Ho Ming Chow, Yisheng Xu, Michael G. Erkkinen, Katherine E. Swett, Michael W. Eagle, Daniel A. Rizik-Baer, and Allen R. Braun. "Neural Correlates of Lyrical Improvisation: An fMRI Study of Freestyle Rap." Scientific Reports 2 (November 15, 2012). doi:10.1038/srep00834.

273. [livingston-2009] Livingston, Jessica. *Founders at Work: Stories of Startups' Early Days.* 1st edition. Berkeley, CA: Apress, 2009.

274. [lord-2011] Lord, Timothy. "Canonical Drops CouchDB From Ubuntu One." Slashdot, 2011. *http://linux-beta.slashdot.org/story/11/11/22/171228/canonical-drops-couchdb-from-ubuntu-one.*

275. [luu-2014] Luu, Dan. "How Do Types Affect Productivity and Correctness? A Review." November 7, 2014. *http://danluu.com/empirical-pl/.*

276. [maccaw-2012] Maccaw, Alex. "What It's like to Work for Stripe." Alex MacCaw on Svbtle, August 28, 2012. *http://blog.alexmaccaw.com/stripes-culture.*

277. [machefsky-2008] Machefsky, Ira. "TiVo Market Share." Thenumbersguru.com, August 27, 2008. *http://thenumbersguru.blogspot.ca/2008/08/tivo-market-share.html.*

278. [macmillan-levy-2013] MacMillan, Douglas, and Jared Ari Levy. "Twitter Investors Williams to Branson Await IPO Windfall." Bloomberg.com, September 25, 2013. *http://www.bloomberg.com/news/articles/2013-09-26/twitter-investors-williams-to-branson-await-ipo-windfall.*

279. [markowitz-2015] Markowitz, Eric. "How Instagram Grew From Foursquare Knock-Off to $1 Billion Photo Empire." Inc.com. Accessed February 24, 2015. *http://www.inc.com/eric-markowitz/life-and-times-of-instagram-the-complete-original-story.html.*

280. [marshall-2006] Marshall, Matt. "Aggregate Knowledge Raises $5M from Kleiner, on a Roll." Venture Beat, December 10, 2006. *http://venturebeat.com/2006/12/10/aggregate-knowledge-raises-5m-from-kleiner-on-a-roll/.*

281. [martin-1996] Martin, Robert C. "The Dependency Inversion Principle," May 1996. *http://www.objectmentor.com/resources/articles/dip.pdf.*

282. [martin-2005] Martin, Robert C. "The Principles of OOD," May 11, 2005. *http://www.butunclebob.com/ArticleS.UncleBob.PrinciplesOfOod.*

283. [martin-2008] Martin, Robert C. *Clean Code: A Handbook of Agile Software Craftsmanship*. 1st edition. Upper Saddle River, NJ: Prentice Hall, 2008.

284. [martin-ferraro-2000] Martin, Lynn, and Geraldine Ferraro. "Reaping the Bottom Line Benefits of Diversity." ASAE, July 2000. *http://www.asaecenter.org/Resources/articledetail.cfm?ItemNumber=13096*.

285. [maslow-1966] Maslow, Abraham H. *Psychology of Science*. First Edition. S.l.: Joanna Cotler Books, 1966.

286. [mason-2010] Mason, Andrew. "The Story Of Groupon: From Failure To An Industry-Changing, Profit Machine - with Andrew Mason." Mixergy, July 5, 2010. *http://mixergy.com/interviews/andrew-mason-groupon-interview/*.

287. [masters-2012] Masters, Blake. "Peter Thiel's CS183: Startup - Class 2 Notes Essay," April 6, 2012. *http://blakemasters.com/post/20582845717/peter-thiels-cs183-startup-class-2-notes-essay*.

288. [mcclure-2007] McClure, Dave. "Startup Metrics for Pirates: AARRR!" August 8, 2007. *http://www.slideshare.net/dmc500hats/startup-metrics-for-pirates-long-version*.

289. [mcdowell-2011] McDowell, Gayle Laakmann. *Cracking the Coding Interview: 150 Programming Questions and Solutions*. 5th Revised & enlarged edition. CareerCup, 2011.

290. [mcmillan-2013] McMillan, Robert. "Why Amazon Hired a Car Mechanic to Run Its Cloud Empire." Wired, February 19, 2013. *http://www.wired.com/2013/02/james-hamilton-amazon/*.

291. [mcconnell-2004] McConnell, Steve. *Code Complete: A Practical Handbook of Software Construction, Second Edition*. 2nd edition. Redmond, Wash: Microsoft Press, 2004.

292. [mcconnell-2011] McConnell, Steve. "Origins of 10X – How Valid Is the Underlying Research?" Construx, January 9, 2011. *http://www.construx.com/10x_Software_Development/Origins_of_10X_%E2%80%93_How_Valid_is_the_Underlying_Research_/*.

293. [mccorvey-2014] McCorvey, J.J. "Just Being Who We Are Is Extremely Risky: An Honest Discussion On Race In Silicon Valley." Fast Company, December 2014. *http://www.fastcompany.com/3037940/a-different-kind-of-valley-life*.

294. [mckinley-2012] McKinley, Dan. "Why MongoDB Never Worked Out at Etsy." Dan McKinley: Math, Programming, and Minority Reports, December 26, 2012. *http://mcfunley.com/why-mongodb-never-worked-out-at-etsy*.

295. [mckinley-2014a] McKinley, Dan. "Data Driven Products Now!," September 18, 2014. *http://mcfunley.com/data-driven-products-now*.

296. [mckinley-2014b] McKinley, Dan. "Thoughts on the Technical Track," December 9, 2014. *http://mcfunley.com/thoughts-on-the-technical-track*.

297. [merchant-2011] Merchant, Nilofer. "Culture Trumps Strategy, Every Time." Harvard Business Review, March 22, 2011. *https://hbr.org/2011/03/culture-trumps-strategy-every*.

298. [meyer-2011] Meyer, Mathias. "The Virtues of Monitoring." Paperplanes, January 5, 2011. *http://www.paperplanes.de/2011/1/5/the_virtues_of_monitoring.html*.

299. [meyer-2014] Meyer, Mathias. "From Open (Unlimited) to Minimum Vacation Policy." Paperplanes, December 10, 2014. *http://www.paperplanes.de/2014/12/10/from-open-to-minimum-vacation-policy.html.*

300. [meszaros-2007] Meszaros, Gerard. *xUnit Test Patterns: Refactoring Test Code.* Upper Saddle River, NJ: Addison-Wesley, 2007. *http://www.amazon.com/xUnit-Test-Patterns-Refactoring-Code/dp/0131495054.*

301. [micco-2012] Micco, John. "Tools for Continuous Integration at Google Scale." Google Tech Talk, 2012. *https://www.youtube.com/watch?v=KH2_sB1A6lA&feature=youtube_gdata_player.*

302. [milewski-2014] Milewski, Bartosz. "Category: The Essence of Composition." Bartosz Milewski's Programming Cafe, November 4, 2014. *http://bartoszmilewski.com/2014/11/04/category-the-essence-of-composition/.*

303. [miller-2007] Miller, Kerry. "The Restaurant-Failure Myth." BusinessWeek, April 16, 2007. Access December 24, 2014. *http://www.businessweek.com/stories/2007-04-16/the-restaurant-failure-mythbusinessweek-business-news-stock-market-and-financial-advice.*

304. [miller-2014] Miller, Ernie. "Human-Driven Development," December 17, 2014. *http://erniemiller.org/2014/12/17/humane-development/.*

305. [milliot-2014] Milliot, Jim. "BEA 2014: Can Anyone Compete with Amazon?" PublishersWeekly.com, May 28, 2014. *http://www.publishersweekly.com/pw/by-topic/industry-news/bea/article/62520-bea-2014-can-anyone-compete-with-amazon.html.*

306. [mills-1983] Mills, Harlan D. *Software Productivity.* Boston: Little, Brown. 1983.

307. [milo-2014] Milo, Udi. "Seeing Who You Know and How You Know Them Just Got Easier With LinkedIn," January 29, 2014. *http://blog.linkedin.com/2014/01/29/seeing-who-you-know-and-how-you-know-them-just-got-easier-with-linkedin/.*

308. [milstein-2013] Milstein, Dan. "How To Survive a Ground-Up Rewrite Without Losing Your Sanity." OnStartups.com, April 8, 2013. *http://onstartups.com/tabid/3339/bid/97052/How-To-Survive-a-Ground-Up-Rewrite-Without-Losing-Your-Sanity.aspx.*

309. [mirani-2013] Mirani, Leo. "A Snapshot of One Minute on the Internet, Today and in 2012." Quartz, November 26, 2013. *http://qz.com/150861/a-snapshot-of-one-minute-on-the-internet-today-and-in-2012/.*

310. [monaghan-2014] Monaghan, Angela. "Self-Employment in UK at Highest Level since Records Began." The Guardian, August 20, 2014, sec. Business. *http://www.theguardian.com/uk-news/2014/aug/20/self-employment-uk-highest-level.*

311. [mongan-suojanen-giguere-2007] Mongan, John, Noah Suojanen, and Eric Giguère. *Programming Interviews Exposed: Secrets to Landing Your Next Job.* 2nd edition. Indianapolis, IN: Wrox, 2007.

312. [moore-mckenna-2006] Moore, Geoffrey A., and Regis McKenna. *Crossing the Chasm: Marketing and Selling High-Tech Products to Mainstream Customers.* Revised edition. New York, NY: HarperBusiness, 2006.

313. [moskovitz-2013] Moskovitz, Dustin. "Good and Bad Reasons to Become an Entrepreneur," August 14, 2013. *https://medium.com/i-m-h-o/good-and-bad-reasons-to-become-an-entrepreneur-decf0766de8d*.

314. [moskovitz-2014] Moskovitz, Dustin. "Lecture 1 - How to Start a Startup." How to Start a Startup, September 23, 2014. *http://startupclass.samaltman.com/courses/lec01/*.

315. [nash-2010] Nash, Adam. "Why T-Shirts Matter." Psychohistory: The Personal Blog of Adam Nash, November 29, 2010. *http://blog.adamnash.com/2010/11/29/why-t-shirts-matter/*.

316. [nash-2011] Nash, Adam. "Be a Great Product Leader." Psychohistory, December 16, 2011. *http://blog.adamnash.com/2011/12/16/be-a-great-product-leader/*.

317. [nash-2012] Nash, Adam. "User Acquisition: Viral Factor Basics." Psychohistory, April 4, 2012. *http://blog.adamnash.com/2012/04/04/user-acquisition-viral-factor-basics/*.

318. [nelson-2014] Nelson, Beryl. "The Data on Diversity." Communications of the ACM 57, no. 11 (October 27, 2014): 86–95. doi:10.1145/2597886.

319. [newland-2013] Newland, Jesse. "Optimizing Ops for Happiness." Speaker Deck, March 28, 2013. *https://speakerdeck.com/jnewland/optimizing-ops-for-happiness*.

320. [newsql-2015] "NewSQL." Wikipedia, the Free Encyclopedia, January 1, 2015. *http://en.wikipedia.org/w/index.php?title=NewSQL&oldid=640568144*.

321. [nerney-2012] Nerney, Chris. "Apple's App Store Nears 25 Billion Downloads. That's a Lot of Downloads." ITworld, February 20, 2012. *http://www.itworld.com/article/2729773/mobile/apple-s-app-store-nears-25-billion-downloads—that-s-a-lot-of-downloads-.html*.

322. [newport-2012] Newport, Cal. *So Good They Can't Ignore You: Why Skills Trump Passion in the Quest for Work You Love*. New York: Business Plus, 2012. *http://www.amazon.com/Good-They-Cant-Ignore-You/dp/1455509124*.

323. [nishi-2013] Nishi, Dennis. "Take Your Search for a Job Offline." Wall Street Journal, March 24, 2013, sec. Personal Finance. *http://www.wsj.com/news/articles/SB10001424127887323869604578368733437346820*.

324. [norman-2013] Norman, Don. *The Design of Everyday Things: Revised and Expanded Edition*. Revised Edition. New York, New York: Basic Books, 2013.

325. [norretranders-1999] Norretranders, Tor. *The User Illusion: Cutting Consciousness Down to Size*. New York, N.Y.: Penguin Books, 1999.

326. [north-2011] North, Ken. "NoSQL Speed Bumps." Dr. Dobb's, April 1, 2011. *http://www.drdobbs.com/database/nosql-speed-bumps/229400759*.

327. [novich-2013] Novich, Jeff. "Why Patient Communicator Failed." Planet Jeffro, January 12, 2013. *http://planetjeffro.com/post/40340494649/why-patient-communicator-failed*.

328. [oh-2014] Oh, Robert. "CrossFit Injuries Part 1: Injury Research." CrossFit Ero Blog, November 25, 2014. *http://crossfitero.com/2014/11/25/tuesday-11-25-14-crossfit-injuries-part-1-injury-research/*.

329. [online-analytical-processing-2014] "Online Analytical Processing." Wikipedia, the Free Encyclopedia, December 30, 2014. *http://en.wikipedia.org/w/index.php?title=Online_analytical_processing&oldid=640262759*.

330. [oppezzo-schwartz-2014] Oppezzo, Marily, and Daniel L. Schwartz. "Give Your Ideas Some Legs: The Positive Effect of Walking on Creative Thinking." Journal of Experimental Psychology. Learning, Memory, and Cognition 40, no. 4 (July 2014): 1142–52. doi:10.1037/a0036577.

331. [oram-wilson-2010] Oram, Andy, and Greg Wilson. *Making Software: What Really Works, and Why We Believe It.* 1st edition. Sebastopol, CA: O'Reilly Media, 2010.

332. [oreilly-2009] O'Reilly, Tim. "Work on Stuff That Matters: First Principles." O'Reilly Radar, January 11, 2009. *http://radar.oreilly.com/2009/01/work-on-stuff-that-matters-fir.html*.

333. [orsini-2013] Orsini, Lauren. "How Software Developers Really Spend Their Time." ReadWrite, April 25, 2013. *http://readwrite.com/2013/04/25/how-software-developers-really-spend-their-time*.

334. [palihapitiya-2013] Palihapitiya, Chamath. "How we put Facebook on the path to 1 billion users." From the udemy course "Growth Hacking: an Introduction", 2013. *https://www.youtube.com/watch?v=raIUQP71SBU*

335. [palladino-2012] Palladino, Patricio. "Brainfuck Beware: JavaScript Is after You!," August 9, 2012. *http://patriciopalladino.com/blog/2012/08/09/non-alphanumeric-javascript.html*.

336. [parnin-rugaber-2011] Parnin, Chris, and Spencer Rugaber. "Resumption Strategies for Interrupted Programming Tasks." Software Quality Control 19, no. 1 (March 2011): 5–34. doi:10.1007/s11219-010-9104-9.

337. [payne-2013a] Payne, Andy. "Startup Equity For Employees," January 4, 2013. *http://www.payne.org/index.php/Startup_Equity_For_Employees*.

338. [payne-2013b] Payne, Alex. "Letter to a Young Programmer Considering a Startup." Alex Payne — Online Writing, May 23, 2013. *https://al3x.net/2013/05/23/letter-to-a-young-programmer.html*.

339. [pejtersen-et-al-2011] Pejtersen, Jan H., Helene Feveile, Karl B. Christensen, and Hermann Burr. "Sickness Absence Associated with Shared and Open-Plan Offices—a National Cross Sectional Questionnaire Survey." Scandinavian Journal of Work, Environment & Health 37, no. 5 (September 2011): 376–82. doi:10.5271/sjweh.3167.

340. [penenberg-2009] Penenberg, Adam L. *Viral Loop: From Facebook to Twitter, How Today's Smartest Businesses Grow Themselves.* First Edition. New York: Hachette Books, 2009.

341. [penenberg-2012] Penenberg, Adam L. "Groupon and Its Pivots: A Mega, Meta Mash-Up of the News." Fast Company, August 2, 2012. *http://www.fastcompany.com/1844311/groupon-and-its-pivots-mega-meta-mash-news*.

342. [perham-hodgetts-banbury-2013] Perham, Nick, Helen Hodgetts, and Simon Banbury. "Mental Arithmetic and Non-Speech Office Noise: An Exploration of Interference-by-Content." Noise & Health 15, no. 62 (February 2013): 73–78. doi:10.4103/1463-1741.107160.

343. [peter-hull-2011] Peter, Laurence J., and Raymond Hull. *The Peter Principle: Why Things Always Go Wrong.* Reprint edition. New York: HarperBusiness, 2011.

344. [petre-damian-2014] Petre, Marian, and Daniela Damian. "Methodology and Culture: Drivers of Mediocrity in Software Engineering?" In Proceedings of the 22Nd ACM SIGSOFT International Symposium on Foundations of Software Engineering, 829–32. FSE 2014. New York, NY, USA: ACM, 2014. doi:10.1145/2635868.2666607.

345. [phillips-2014b] Phillips, Andrew Garcia. "The Billion-Dollar Startup Club." The Wall Street Journal. Accessed December 23, 2014. *http://graphics.wsj.com/billion-dollar-club/.*

346. [pink-2011] Pink, Daniel H. *Drive: The Surprising Truth About What Motivates Us.* Riverhead Books, 2011.

347. [plato-2008] Plato. *The Republic.* Translated by Benjamin Jowett. Digireads.com, 2008.

348. [pomodoro-2015] "Pomodoro Technique." Wikipedia, the Free Encyclopedia, January 8, 2015. *http://en.wikipedia.org/w/index.php?title=Pomodoro_Technique&oldid=630392339.*

349. [powell-2003] Powell, Corey. *God in the Equation: How Einstein Transformed Religion.* New York: Free Press, 2003.

350. [prenzlow-2014] Prenzlow, Shawn. "How Many Companies Are 100% Distributed? (Research Summary)." Scott Berkun, December 28, 2014. *http://scottberkun.com/2013/how-many-companies-are-100-distributed/.*

351. [preston-werner-2010] Preston-Werner, Tom. "Readme Driven Development," August 23, 2010. *http://tom.preston-werner.com/2010/08/23/readme-driven-development.html.*

352. [preston-werner-2012] Preston-Werner, Tom. "Optimizing for Happiness," 2012. *http://vimeo.com/39016099.*

353. [proof-that-you-should-get-a-life] "Proof That You Should Get a Life." The Economist, December 9, 2014. *http://www.economist.com/blogs/freeexchange/2014/12/working-hours.*

354. [rabois-2014] Rabois, Keith. Twitter post, September 17, 2014, 9:30AM. *https://twitter.com/rabois/status/512277439116881920.*

355. [rachleff-2014a] Rachleff, Andy. "14 Crucial Questions about Stock Options." Wealthfront Knowledge Center, January 16, 2014. *https://blog.wealthfront.com/stock-options-14-crucial-questions/.*

356. [raice-ante-2012] Raice, Shaydi, and Spencer E. Ante. "Insta-Rich: $1 Billion for Instagram." Wall Street Journal, April 10, 2012, sec. Tech. *http://www.wsj.com/news/articles/SB10001424052702303815404577333840377381670.*

357. [raskin-2000] Raskin, Jef. *The Humane Interface: New Directions for Designing Interactive Systems.* Reading, MA: Addison-Wesley Professional, 2000.

358. [raymond-2001] Raymond, Eric S. *The Cathedral & the Bazaar: Musings on Linux and Open Source by an Accidental Revolutionary.* 1st edition. Sebastopol, CA. O'Reilly Media, 2001.

359. [recruit-engineers-in-less-time-2015] "Recruit Engineers in Less Time." Grove by Sequoia Capital. Accessed January 10, 2015. *http://www.sequoiacap.com/grove/posts/6bja/recruit-engineers-in-less-time.*

360. [red-bull-2015] "Red Bull." Wikipedia, the Free Encyclopedia, March 13, 2015. *http://en.wikipedia.org/w/index.php?title=Red_Bull&oldid=651250884.*

361. [reeves-nass-2003] Reeves, Byron, and Clifford Nass. *The Media Equation: How People Treat Computers, Television, and New Media Like Real People and Places.* Stanford, CA; New York: Center for the Study of Language and Inf, 2003.

362. [reinforcement-2015] "Reinforcement." Wikipedia, the Free Encyclopedia, January 5, 2015. *http://en.wikipedia.org/w/index.php?title=Reinforcement&oldid=636110760.*

363. [renolds-wyat-2011] Reynolds, Carl J, and Jeremy C Wyatt. "Open Source, Open Standards, and Health Care Information Systems." Journal of Medical Internet Research 13, no. 1 (February 17, 2011): e24. doi:10.2196/jmir.1521.

364. [resig-2011] Resig, John. Twitter post, 5 Feb 2011, 11:22AM. *https://twitter.com/jeresig/status/33968704983138304.*

365. [rheem-2010] Rheem, Carroll. "Consumer Response to Travel Site Performance." A PhoCus Wright Whitepaper, April 2010. *http://www.phocuswright.com/Free-Travel-Research/Consumer-Response-to-Travel-Site-Performance#.VQnBZ2TF-iY.*

366. [richmond-2012] Richmond, Shane. "Jonathan Ive Interview: Simplicity Isn't Simple," May 23, 2012, sec. Technology. *http://www.telegraph.co.uk/technology/apple/9283706/Jonathan-Ive-interview-simplicity-isnt-simple.html.*

367. [ries-2011a] Ries, Eric. *The Lean Startup: How Today's Entrepreneurs Use Continuous Innovation to Create Radically Successful Businesses.* First Edition. New York: Crown Business, 2011.

368. [ries-2011b] Ries, Eric. "How DropBox Started as a Minimal Viable Product." TechCrunch, October 19, 2011. *http://social.techcrunch.com/2011/10/19/dropbox-minimal-viable-product/.*

369. [robertson-2014] Robertson, Tim. "Ruby Garbage Collection: Still Not Ready for Production." Omniref Blog, March 27, 2014. *https://www.omniref.com/blog/blog/2014/03/27/ruby-garbage-collection-still-not-ready-for-production/.*

370. [rogers-2003] Rogers, Everett M. *Diffusion of Innovations.* 5th edition. New York: Free Press, 2003.

371. [rossi-2011] Rossi, Chuck. Push: Tech Talk, 2011. *https://www.facebook.com/video/video.php?v=10100259101684977&oid=9445547199&comments.*

372. [roth-2006] Roth, Mark. "Some Women May See 100 Million Colors, Thanks to Their Genes." Pittsburgh Post-Gazette, September 13, 2006. *http://www.post-gazette.com/news/health/2006/09/13/Some-women-may-see-100-million-colors-thanks-to-their-genes/stories/200609130255.*

373. [sackman-erikson-grant-1968] Sackman, H., W. J. Erikson, and E. E. Grant. "Exploratory Experimental Studies Comparing Online and Offline Programming Performance." Commun. ACM 11, no. 1 (January 1968): 3–11. doi:10.1145/362851.362858.

374. [saeta-2014] Saeta, Brennan. "Why We Love Scala at Coursera." Coursera Technology, February 18, 2014. *https://tech.coursera.org/blog/2014/02/18/why-we-love-scala-at-coursera/*.

375. [saffron-2014] Saffron, Sam. "Ruby 2.1 Garbage Collection: Ready for Production," April 8, 2014. *http://samsaffron.com/archive/2014/04/08/ruby-2-1-garbage-collection-ready-for-production*.

376. [sales-and-related-occupations-2013] "Sales and Related Occupations." Bureau of Labor Statistics, May 2013. *http://www.bls.gov/oes/current/oes410000.htm*.

377. [schaal-2015] Schaal, Dennis, and Skift. "TripAdvisor Is Tracking Whether Its TV Advertisements Really Work." Skift, March 4, 2015. *http://skift.com/2015/03/04/tripadvisor-is-tracking-whether-its-tv-advertisements-really-work/*.

378. [schneeman-2013] Schneeman, Richard. "Anatomy of an Exploit: An In-Depth Look at the Rails YAML Vulnerability." SitePoint, February 4, 2013. *http://www.sitepoint.com/anatomy-of-an-exploit-an-in-depth-look-at-the-rails-yaml-vulnerability/*.

379. [schurter-2011] Schurter, Michael. "Failing with MongoDB," Schmichael's Blog, November 5, 2011. *http://blog.schmichael.com/2011/11/05/failing-with-mongodb/*.

380. [sciacca-2013] Sciacca, Annie. "SpoonRocket Brings Healthy Fast Food Right to Your Doorstep." San Francisco Business Times, October 11, 2013. *http://www.bizjournals.com/sanfrancisco/print-edition/2013/10/11/spoonrocket-brings-healthy-fast-food.html*.

381. [seibel-2009] Seibel, Peter. *Coders at Work: Reflections on the Craft of Programming*. 2009 edition. New York: Apress, 2009.

382. [sellers-2011] Sellers, Mike. "Mike Sellers' Answer to As First Time Entrepreneurs, What Part of the Process Are People Often Completely Blind To?" Quora, June 10, 2011. *http://www.quora.com/As-first-time-entrepreneurs-what-part-of-the-process-are-people-often-completely-blind-to/answer/Mike-Sellers*.

383. [sen-2012] Sen, Paul. *Steve Jobs: The Lost Interview*. Directed by Paul Sen. May 11, 2012. Magnolia Home Entertainment.

384. [sessions-2006] Sessions, Roger. "A Better Path to Enterprise Architectures." MSDN, April 2006. *https://msdn.microsoft.com/en-us/library/aa479371.aspx*.

385. [sharma-2012] Sharma, Chetan. "State of the Global Mobile Industry." 2012. *http://www.slide-share.net/chetansharma/annual-state-ofglobalmobileindustry2012chetansharmaconsulting*.

386. [shipit-days-at-atlassian-2015] "ShipIt Days at Atlassian." Accessed January 8, 2015. *https://www.atlassian.com/company/about/shipit*.

387. [shore-warden-2007] Shore, James, and Shane Warden. *The Art of Agile Development*. 1st edition. Sebastopol, CA: O'Reilly Media, 2007.

388. [silverman-2011] Silverman, Rachel Emma. "Web Surfing Helps at Work, Study Says." Wall Street Journal, August 22, 2011, sec. Management. *http://www.wsj.com/news/articles/SB10001424053111904070604576518261775512294*.

389. [simonton-2003] Simonton, Dean Keith. "Scientific Creativity as Constrained Stochastic Behavior: The Integration of Product, Person, and Process Perspectives." Psychological Bulletin 129, no. 4 (July 2003): 475–94.

390. [sinek-2009] Sinek, Simon. "How Great Leaders Inspire Action." TEDx, 2009. *http://www.ted.com/talks/simon_sinek_how_great_leaders_inspire_action.*

391. [singapore-startups] "Singapore Startups - Government Funding and Assistance Schemes." Accessed December 31, 2014. *http://www.guidemesingapore.com/doing-business/finances/singapore-government-schemes-for-startups.*

392. [six-degrees-patent-2013] "Six Degrees Patent." Wikipedia, the Free Encyclopedia, November 9, 2013. *http://en.wikipedia.org/w/index.php?title=Six_Degrees_patent&oldid=580926972.*

393. [small-business-2014] "Small Business Trends." The US Small Business Administration. Accessed December 21, 2014. *https://www.sba.gov/offices/headquarters/ocpl/resources/13493.*

394. [small-et-al-2007] Small, Deborah A., Michele Gelfand, Linda Babcock, and Hilary Gettman. "Who Goes to the Bargaining Table? The Influence of Gender and Framing on the Initiation of Negotiation." Journal of Personality and Social Psychology 93, no. 4 (2007): 600–613. doi:10.1037/0022-3514.93.4.600.

395. [smith-2003] Smith, Adam. *The Wealth of Nations.* Bantam Classics, 2003. *http://www.amazon.com/The-Wealth-Nations-Bantam-Classics/dp/0553585975.*

396. [solomon-2012] Solomon, Mike. "Scalability at YouTube." PyCon US, 2012. *https://www.youtube.com/watch?v=G-lGCC4KKok*

397. [spolsky-2000] Spolsky, Joel. "Things You Should Never Do, Part I." Joel on Software, April 6, 2000. *http://www.joelonsoftware.com/articles/fog0000000069.html.*

398. [spolsky-2001] Spolsky, Joel. "Good Software Takes Ten Years. Get Used To It." Joel on Software, July 21, 2001. *http://www.joelonsoftware.com/articles/fog0000000017.html.*

399. [spolsky-2002] Spolsky, Joel. "The Iceberg Secret, Revealed." Joel on Software, February 13, 2002. *http://www.joelonsoftware.com/articles/fog0000000356.html.*

400. [spolsky-2005a] Spolsky, Joel. "News." Joel on Software, January 27, 2005. *http://www.joelonsoftware.com/items/2005/01/27.html.*

401. [spolsky-2005b] Spolsky, Joel. "Making Wrong Code Look Wrong." Joel on Software, May 11, 2005. *http://www.joelonsoftware.com/articles/Wrong.html.*

402. [spolsky-2006] Spolsky, Joel. "The Guerrilla Guide to Interviewing (version 3.0)." Joel on Software, October 25, 2006. *http://www.joelonsoftware.com/articles/GuerrillaInterviewing3.html.*

403. [srinivasan-2013] Srinivasan, Balaji S. "Market Research, Wireframing, and Design." Stanford Startup Engineering Class, 2013. *https://spark-public.s3.amazonaws.com/startup/lecture_slides/lecture5-market-wireframing-design.pdf.*

404. [start-up-ny-2014] "Start-up NY." Accessed December 31, 2014. *http://startup.ny.gov/.*

405. [statt-2014] Statt, Nick. "Zuckerberg: *Move Fast and Break Things* Isn't How Facebook Operates Anymore." CNET, April 30, 2014. *http://www.cnet.com/news/zuckerberg-move-fast-and-break-things-isnt-how-we-operate-anymore/.*

406. [stroustrup-2012] Stroustrup, Bjarne. "Why you should avoid Linked Lists." GoingNative, 2012. *https://www.youtube.com/watch?v=YQs6IC-vgmo*

407. [stump-2011] Stump, Joe. Starting Your Startup, 2011. *http://vimeo.com/26134764.*

408. [subramaniam-hunt-2006] Subramaniam, Venkat, and Andy Hunt. *Practices of an Agile Developer: Working in the Real World.* 1st edition. Raleigh, N.C: Pragmatic Bookshelf, 2006.

409. [sullivan-2012] Sullivan, John. "10 Compelling Numbers That Reveal the Power of Employee Referrals." ERE.net, May 7, 2012. *http://www.ere.net/2012/05/07/10-compelling-numbers-that-reveal-the-power-of-employee-referrals/.*

410. [suzuki-suzuki-1993] Suzuki, Shinichi, and Waltraud Suzuki. *Nurtured by Love: The Classic Approach to Talent Education.* 2nd edition. Princeton, N.J. Alfred Music, 1993.

411. [tassi-2014] Tassi, Paul. "The Ten Most Desirable Video Game Companies to Work For." Forbes, August 21, 2014. *http://www.forbes.com/sites/insertcoin/2014/08/21/the-ten-most-desirable-video-game-companies-to-work-for/.*

412. [tattersall-2014] Tattersall, Steven. Twitter post, November 28, 2014, 5:08AM. *https://twitter.com/tattlemuss/status/538318484539998209*

413. [tellis-golder-1993] Tellis, Gerard J., and Peter N. Golder. "Pioneer Advantage: Marketing Logic or Marketing Legend?." SSRN Scholarly Paper. Rochester, NY: Social Science Research Network, May 1993. *http://papers.ssrn.com/abstract=906046.*

414. [tepper-2012] Tepper, Allegra. "How Much Data Is Created Every Minute? [INFOGRAPHIC]." Mashable, June 22, 2012. *http://mashable.com/2012/06/22/data-created-every-minute/.*

415. [the-standish-group-2013] The Standish Group. "CHAOS Manifesto 2013: Think Big, Act Small." 2013. *http://www.versionone.com/assets/img/files/CHAOSManifesto2013.pdf*

416. [the-top-20-reasons-startups-fail-2014] "The Top 20 Reasons Startups Fail." CB Insights - Blog, October 7, 2014. *https://www.cbinsights.com/blog/startup-failure-reasons-top/.*

417. [thiel-2014] Thiel, Peter, and Blake Masters. *Zero to One: Notes on Startups, or How to Build the Future.* 1st edition. New York: Crown Business, 2014.

418. [thompson-2013] Thompson, Caleb. "5 Useful Tips For A Better Commit Message." Giant Robots Smashing into Other Giant Robots, April 26, 2013. *http://robots.thoughtbot.com/5-useful-tips-for-a-better-commit-message.*

419. [tolentino-2014] Tolentino, Melissa. "Bloodiest Job Cuts in Tech History." SiliconANGLE, July 18, 2014. *http://siliconangle.com/blog/2014/07/18/bloodiest-job-cuts-in-tech-history/.*

420. [tomayko-2012] Tomayko, Ryan. "Your Team Should Work like an Open Source Project," November 9, 2012. *http://tomayko.com/writings/adopt-an-open-source-process-constraints.*

421. [topol-2015] Topol, Eric. *The Patient Will See You Now: The Future of Medicine Is in Your Hands.* Basic Books, 2015. *http://www.amazon.com/The-Patient-Will-See-You/dp/0465054749.*

422. [traynor-2014] Traynor, Des. "Price Is What You Pay, Value Is What You Get." Inside Intercom, November 24, 2014. *http://blog.intercom.io/price-is-what-you-pay-value-is-what-you-get/.*

423. [turner-2014] Turner, Vernon. "The Digital Universe of Opportunities." EMC Digital Universe, April 2014. *http://www.emc.com/leadership/digital-universe/2014iview/digital-universe-of-opportunities-vernon-turner.htm.*

424. [twitter-2014] "Twitter." Wikipedia, The Free Encyclopedia, December 20, 2014. *http://en.wikipedia.org/wiki/Twitter.*

425. [vanderburg-2011] Vanderburg, Glenn. "Cohesion." Glenn Vanderburg: Blog, January 31, 2011. *http://www.vanderburg.org/Blog/Software/Development/cohesion.rdoc.*

426. [van-grove-2014] Van Grove, Jenn. "Tech Startups Are Becoming Worth $1 Billion Faster Than Ever." TheStreet, November 13, 2014. *http://www.thestreet.com/story/12952381/1/tech-startups-are-becoming-worth-1-billion-faster-than-ever.html.*

427. [van-hoven-2014] Van Hoven, Matt. "The Growth of the Visual Web in 5 Charts." Digiday, May 7, 2014. *http://digiday.com/platforms/5-charts-growth-visual-web/.*

428. [vella-2013] Vella, Roy. "The Mobile Wave." September 3, 2013. *https://www.youtube.com/watch?v=SHydE6poE8.*

429. [victor-2014] Victor, Bret. *The Humane Representation of Thought.* Vimeo, 2014. *http://vimeo.com/115154289.*

430. [vison-mission-values-2006] "Vision, Mission and Values." Volvo, 2006. *http://www3.volvo.com/investors/finrep/ar06/eng/fundamentalvalues/pops/printable/6_vision_mission.pdf.*

431. [vohra-2012] Vohra, Rahul. "How to Model Viral Growth: The Hybrid Model." LinkedIn Pulse, October 11, 2012. *https://www.linkedin.com/pulse/20121002124206-18876785-how-to-model-viral-growth-the-hybrid-model.*

432. [wagreich-2013] Wagreich, Samuel. "A Billion Dollar Company With No Bosses? Yes, It Exists." Inc.com, March 4, 2013. *http://www.inc.com/samuel-wagreich/the-4-billion-company-with-no-bosses.html.*

433. [walker-2003] Walker, Rob. "The Guts of a New Machine." The New York Times, November 30, 2003, sec. Magazine. *http://www.nytimes.com/2003/11/30/magazine/the-guts-of-a-new-machine.html.*

434. [webb-2012] Webb, Dan. "Improving Performance on Twitter.com." Twitter Engineering Blog, May 29, 2012. *https://blog.twitter.com/2012/improving-performance-on-twittercom.*

435. [weekly-2012] Weekly, David. *An Introduction to Stock and Options.* 2012.

436. [weiner-2012] Weiner, Jeff. "From Vision to Values: The Importance of Defining Your Core," October 29, 2012. *https://www.linkedin.com/pulse/20121029044359-22330283-to-manage-hyper-growth-get-your-launch-trajectory-right.*

437. [wendel-2013] Wendel, Ulf. "MySQL 5.7: SQL Functions for JSON." Ulf Wendel, October 9, 2013. *http://blog.ulf-wendel.de/2013/mysql-5-7-sql-functions-for-json-udf/*.

438. [wetzler-2012] Wetzler, Michelle. "How I Negotiated My Startup Compensation." Keen IO, August 21, 2012. *https://keen.io/blog/29904565692/how-i-negotiated-my-startup-compensation*.

439. [wexler-2012] Wexler, Daniel. Google Plus Post, May 18, 2012. *https://plus.google.com/u/0/107919048662113456495/posts/AyGGqF9mLdB*

440. [wherry-2012] Wherry, Elaine. "The Recruiter Honeypot." Elaine Wherry's Blog, June 26, 2012. *http://www.ewherry.com/2012/06/the-recruiter-honeypot/*.

441. [who-is-using-holocracy-2014] "Who Is Using Holacracy?" Structure & Process: Collaboration Consulting, November 13, 2014. *http://structureprocess.com/holacracy-cases/*.

442. [widdicombe-2014] Widdicombe, Lizzie. "The Programmer's Price." The New Yorker, November 24, 2014, sec. American Chronicles. *http://www.newyorker.com/magazine/2014/11/24/programmers-price*.

443. [widrich-2013] Widrich, Leo. "How Much Revenue Did Buffer for Business Generate in November?" Open, December 8, 2013. *https://open.bufferapp.com/how-much-revenue-did-buffer-for-business-generate-in-november/*.

444. [williams-2005] Williams, Evan. "Ten Rules for Web Startups," November 2005. *http://evhead.com/2005/11/ten-rules-for-web-startups.asp*.

445. [williams-2014] Williams, Robin. *The Non-Designer's Design Book*. 4th edition. Peachpit Press, 2014.

446. [wilson-2013] Wilson, Fred. "When Things Don't Work Out." AVC, March 2013. *http://avc.com/2013/03/when-things-dont-work-out/*.

447. [wolf-1996] Wolf, Gary. "Steve Jobs: The Next Insanely Great Thing." Wired, February 1996, Issue 4.02. *http://archive.wired.com/wired/archive/4.02/jobs_pr.html*.

448. [wood-2012] Wood, John. "Getting off the Couch(DB)." Signal Engage, January 24, 2012. *http://www.signalengage.com/2012/01/24/getting-off-the-couchdb/*.

449. [work-2011] Work, Sean. "How Loading Time Affects Your Bottom Line." KISSmetrics Blog, April 2011. *https://blog.kissmetrics.com/loading-time/*.

450. [yegge-2005] Yegge, Steve. "You Should Write Blogs," January 23, 2005. *https://sites.google.com/site/steveyegge2/you-should-write-blogs*.

451. [yegge-2007] Yegge, Steve. "Code's Worst Enemy." Stevey's Blog Rants, December 19, 2007. *http://steve-yegge.blogspot.com.au/2007/12/codes-worst-enemy.html*.

452. [yarow-2012] Yarow, Jay. "How Apple Really Lost Its Lead In the '80s." Business Insider, December 9, 2012. *http://www.businessinsider.com/how-apple-really-lost-its-lead-in-the-80s-2012-12*.

453. [youtube-stats-2014] "YouTube Statistics." YouTube. Accessed December 27, 2014. *https://www.youtube.com/yt/press/statistics.html*.

454. [zappos-2014] "Zappos." Wikipedia, The Free Encyclopedia, December 10, 2014. *http://en.wikipedia.org/wiki/Zappos.*

455. [zinsser-2006] Zinsser, William. *On Writing Well, 30th Anniversary Edition: The Classic Guide to Writing Nonfiction.* 30 Anniversary edition. New York: Harper Perennial, 2006.

Index

Numbers

A

B

T

About the Author

Yevgeniy (Jim) Brikman loves programming, writing, speaking, traveling, and lifting heavy things. He does not love talking about himself in the third person. He is the founder of Atomic Squirrel, a company that helps startups get off the ground. Previously, he worked as a software engineer at LinkedIn, TripAdvisor, Cisco Systems, and Thomson Financial. He completed his BS and master's at Cornell University. See *ybrikman.com* for more information.

Colophon

The cover fonts are Benton Sans, Benton Sans Condensed, Guardian Sans, Helvetica Bold Condensed, The Sans Mono Condensed, and IDAutomationOCRb. The text font is Scala Pro; the heading font is Benton Sans; and the code font is Dalton Maag's Ubuntu Mono.

Get even more for your money.

Join the O'Reilly Community, and register the O'Reilly books you own. It's free, and you'll get:

- $4.99 ebook upgrade offer
- 40% upgrade offer on O'Reilly print books
- Membership discounts on books and events
- Free lifetime updates to ebooks and videos
- Multiple ebook formats, DRM FREE
- Participation in the O'Reilly community
- Newsletters
- Account management
- 100% Satisfaction Guarantee

Signing up is easy:

1. Go to: oreilly.com/go/register
2. Create an O'Reilly login.
3. Provide your address.
4. Register your books.

Note: English-language books only

To order books online:
oreilly.com/store

For questions about products or an order:
orders@oreilly.com

To sign up to get topic-specific email announcements and/or news about upcoming books, conferences, special offers, and new technologies:
elists@oreilly.com

For technical questions about book content:
booktech@oreilly.com

To submit new book proposals to our editors:
proposals@oreilly.com

O'Reilly books are available in multiple DRM-free ebook formats. For more information:
oreilly.com/ebooks

Have it your way.

CPSIA information can be obtained
at www.ICGtesting.com
Printed in the USA
JSHW021130040121
10696JS00007B/302